The Aviation Consumer

Used Aircraft Guide

Sixth Edition

Andrew B. Douglas, Editor

Volume One

Belvoir Publications, Inc.

ISBN: 1-879620-18-9

To order copies of Used Aircraft Guides not included in this collection, contact the Back Issues Department, The Aviation Consumer, 75 Holly Hill Lane, Greenwich, Connecticut 06830, (203) 661-6111, or fax (203) 661-4802.

Cover photography by Stephan Wilkinson

Cover design by Lynn Dowling

Contents - Volume I

Introduction

Welcome to the sixth edition of *The Aviation Consumer Used Aircraft Guide*. This two-volume set represents our most ambitious project to date, with more aircraft covered than ever before. Here you'll find a wealth of information on almost every type of production airplane in the marketplace. We've included updated price histories, accident data, service difficulties, and perhaps most important, the observations of the owners, themselves. This new edition represents a substantial expansion of our previous work, with almost 200 more pages and many new airplanes.

Since the publication of the fifth edition in 1991, little has changed in the light aircraft industry. Piper continues to have financial trouble, Cessna chairman Russ Meyer continues to say his company will begin manufacturing piston airplanes the moment tort reform is passed, and other than a few small glimmers here and there there's still an overall lack of activity. Production remains at a virtual standstill.

That's both good and bad news for those in the used aircraft marketplace. While updating the price data for this book, we were pleased to find that small airplanes as a class are appreciating in value at a healthy rate: in some cases far exceeding the current rate of inflation. Almost all of the aircraft in this book are at least holding their value from year to year. That means that—at the moment, anyway—buying an airplane could actually provide a better return on your investment than leaving your money in the bank. It would appear that the combination of low interest rates and economic recovery is having a strong effect on some used-plane prices.

That's good news if you're an airplane owner, but tough if you're looking to buy. There's no telling how long the current situation will continue; this "boom" may turn out exactly like the real estate debacle of the 1980s.

We owe thanks to all those who contributed to this book, but in particular to *The Aviation Consumer* Editor Dick Weeghman, who recently proved himself brighter than the rest of us by shifting his home base from the cold, crowded Northeast to balmy Sarasota, Florida.

Andrew Douglas
Editor, Belvoir Books

Aerospatiale Tampico TB-9

As the dowagers of the aircraft training fleet yield to the ravages of time, a new Gallic star with nice credentials and good looks has arrived and is winning hearts, fleet contracts and even a few used-plane customers.

Granted, squadrons are not available on the used market yet, but this bird is worth looking closely at since it's in production and has the backing of a giant corporate entity and is bound to become more numerous. And, frankly, it makes the Cherokee/C-152/Skyhawk crowd look dowdy.

The only catch is price: Since the Tampico Club has been available only since 1990, the average equipped price of one of that vintage has not had time to sag very much, and according to the *Aircraft Bluebook Price Digest* comes in at a hefty $84,000. However, we found some for $75,000 VFR equipped with about 1,000 hours total time.

History

Except for its smaller, 160-hp engine, the Tampico TB-9 actually is pretty much a clone of the 180-hp Tobago and 250-hp Trinidad, These others were introduced earlier, in 1986 and '85, respectively. Reversing the usual process in the States of starting small and working upscale, Aerospatiale backed into the U.S. trainer market with the Tampico, not until 1990, even though U.S. certification came along in 1989. Aerospatiale presumably held off until 1990 to tackle the U.S. market because Piper in 1988 was talking about bargain-basement prices of $46,000 for its Cadet trainer, a Warrior with a new name. And that was not something Aerospatiale could compete with.

But with flight schools in the United States now becoming ever more desperate for new trainers, the Tampicos are starting to flow across the Atlantic in greater numbers. And schools like Embry-Riddle in Florida, Parks College in Ohio and the University of North Dakota are incorporating them in their flight departments. Also, one long-established east-coast FBO, Westair, at White Plains, N.Y., operates a fleet of Tampicos, Tobagos and Trinidads.

The new look in trainers: a slick package with nice styling and gentle flying manners, to boot.

Only small changes have occurred in the Tampicos in the few years they've been here. The electrical system went from 12-volt to 24-volt, and a spin-on oil filter replaced the oil screen. Also, at one point they went to a high-speed starter to get the engine cranking more easily, but encountered durability problems and went back to the old one.

Performance

Thanks mainly to their climb-pitch

props, Tampicos climb like rockets and cruise like turtles. The takeoff angle and climb rate with two aboard is dramatic, and you're looking at around 900-1,000 fpm, with a deck angle that obscures everything out front. (For what it's worth, book max climb is 738 at gross.) The rationale for the climb prop goes back to conditions in France, where students often learn on grass strips, at high elevations. To use the Cessna Skyhawk (the common homesick-angel benchmark) for comparison to check short-field performance, we can report the Tampico comes within 81 feet of the obstacle takeoff distance of a Cessna Skyhawk with a 160-hp engine and within 98 feet of its obstacle landing distance. (And for nit-pickers, the Cessna is 63 pounds heavier at gross.)

Cruise speeds with the Tampico climb prop is not a thrilling prospect for cross-country trips, with the book calling for a vapid 105 knots/120 mph true pulling 73% power. The Skyhawk, by comparison, has a big 15-knot edge on the Tampico, with a 75% book cruise of 120 knots at 8,000 feet. And it still climbs slightly better.

Handling

With control rods instead of cables, the Tampico bends to the pilot's touch with a kind of smooth majesty. The ailerons are not what you'd call sprightly, or as light as, say, a Grumman (or now American General) Tiger's. But control response in general is quite pleasant.

And our stability checks disclosed no unusual characteristics or quirkiness.

Stalls are boringly benign and reassuring. It's hard to imagine a pilot ever getting bitten by a nasty stall or wing drop in this aircraft, power on or off, flaps up or down, straight or turning.

Takeoff stall demos seem even more spectacular than in most trainers thanks to the extreme nose-up angle and the resulting casual nod as airspeed bleeds down to nothing.

The flaps produce healthy gobs of drag. Even using the generous 80-knot final approach suggested by some instructors (which is well over the commonly recommended 1.3 Vso of 65 knots for something closer to short-field landing length), newcomers will be surprised how altitude disappears in big gulps on the turn from base to final. And if that's not enough, the bird slips nicely, with no book warnings about doing so. Also, incidentally, lowering or retracting flaps produces no untoward pitch reactions.

The Tampico further pleases transitioning pilots with its Bonanza-like willingness to yield smooth, easily judged landing touchdowns. But we understand that at one school they've experienced a few scrapes on the fiberglass tailcone bottom as students pulled the nose up on flare a bit too enthusiastically. Apparently the tail tiedown hook is positioned a bit too far forward to offer protection.

And in crosswind challenges, the Tampico pilot will be reassured to know that the aircraft passed its certification with a 25-knot crosswind component.

Cabin Comfort & Load Carrying

The Tampico's width and airiness will captivate pilots, especially students used to the cramped quarters in the Cessna 152s. Headroom is not always so great. But we understand a new front seat has just been introduced that gives another inch and a half of headroom for heads and coifs. To get specific, cabin width is a luxurious four feet, two inches.

Pilots sit up high instead of down deep in a typical cockpit enclosure and, thanks to grand side windows that curve into the roof, have a great view of the outside world, not to mention other traffic. Open the gull-wing door, and you can rest your elbow on the sill and let the breeze flow through. The folks at Embry-Riddle caution not to taxi around with the doors full open, however, lest they get blasted with a gust of wind or prop wash on the ramp. The ventilation solution they've devised in sunny Florida is a short standoff rod (maybe eight inches long) that holds the door open.

The full-size seat in the rear allows space not only for two, but three, believe it or not. So a couple have to be tiny. But at flight schools a student can ride in the rear seat and watch the fellow at the controls cope with instrument flight.

Maximum useful load is 911 pounds, so subtract maybe 70 pounds for a decent batch of equipment, and you're looking at 841 pounds for people, baggage and fuel. Top off the tanks, and that leaves a pretty decent 600 pounds of payload, or three 170-pounders and a healthy 90 pounds for kids or baggage. Depending on balance, of course, don't expect to get any more than 142 pounds (the modest structural limit) in the baggage compartment. The compartment itself is quite roomy, but the roughly triangular shape of the door makes for less than ideal loading.

Naturally, with a gull-wing door on both sides, getting in and out of the Tampico is a ball. Climbing in the rear seat is, though, different, because you have to tip up the entire front seat. It's a rigid one-piece bucket-seat shell fastened hinged at the floor in front. The gull-wing doors loft upward and stay there obligingly without sagging or biting. A plastic lip on the front of each door permits front-seaters to grab on and pull them down. A single lever locks the door with utter sublime simplicity and security, compared to the awkward double side and top latches on many U.S. aircraft.

Cockpit Design

The instrument panel is marvelously styled in three prominent, distinct segments: left, center and right. In lots of the Tampicos, the entire right section is simply cut away, leaving a curved blank concavity for the instructor to stare at, or a convenient place to dump charts (or maybe play solitaire on cross-countries). But at the same time it gives a bit more visibility out the right front portion of the windshield. We understand progressively larger panel sections can be added: half sized and full sized, for those who desire to add more instruments, or redundant ones.

Cost/Performance/Specifications

Model	Year Built	Average Retail Price	Cruise Speed (kts)	Useful Load (lbs)	Fuel Std/Opt (gals)	Engine	TBO (hrs)	Overhaul Cost
TB-9	1990	$84,055	105	911	40	160-hp Lyc. O-320-D2A	2,000	$9,500
TB-9	1991	$88,935	105	911	40	160-hp Lyc. O-320-D2A	2,000	$9,500
TB-9	1992	$125,795	105	911	40	160-hp Lyc. O-320-D2A	2,000	$9,500
TB-9	1993	$120,887	105	911	40	160-hp Lyc. O-320-D2A	2,000	$9,500

American pilots also will have to learn to interpret certain vertical instruments, stowed like half a dozen tiny book ends on top of the radio stack, for engine temps, fuel and oil pressure, etc. And instead of the familiar rocker switches for the fuel pump, landing lights and strobes, etc., the Tampico has pushbuttons. They're located handily at the base of the radio stack.

The throttle quadrant resides perfectly under the pilot's hand in a delightful ergonomic arrangement. The trim wheel has a nice solid feel, is positioned perfectly under the pilot's palm and doesn't take forever to crank to a proper position. Flaps are activated by a little lever above the mixture control. And the fuel selector is positioned at the base of the center console where both front-seat occupants can keep an eye on it.

Maintenance Considerations

Schools and FBOs like Embry-Riddle and Westair that expose the Tampicos to endless brutal punishment as trainers tell us the aircraft stand up well and are easy to maintain.

Jack Haun, maintenance chief at Embry-Riddle, told us also that the Aerospatiale people are among the most eager to work with and help out his crew that he's encountered. He said the school had experienced a few problems with high-speed starters and chewed-up ring gears. So now Aerospatiale has gone back to the slower starters that may not launch a start as well, but seem to stand up longer. He said mechanics liked the easy access behind the instrument panel, thanks to the unusual eyebrow cowlings.

John Pfeiffer, Westair's maintenance chief, told *The Aviation Consumer* that his fleet had stood up well to their rigorous training regimen, as well. There were only three Service Difficulty Reports on the Tampicos, not enough to show any trends as yet. They called out the following problems: cracked fuel transmitter, leaking brake fluid reservoir and worn trim outboard hinge.

We also noted a General Aviation Airworthiness Alert noting that right and left stabilator trim tab hinges exhibited abnormal wear after a relatively short time in service.

Safety Record

With so few aircraft in the U.S. fleet so far, the Tampicos have not had time, or inclination, to build an accident record, good or bad. We found only three accidents, and no injuries. They involved a hard landing, an overshoot and a taxi accident. The overshoot occurred when a student pilot landed in a crosswind and touched down well to the right of the centerline and departed the runway to avoid the runway lights.

Expensive Choice?

Owners scouting for a used Tampico may at first be put off by the high price in comparison with comparable small-engine "economy" four-placers. But most of the others of similar engine size and passenger capability, such as the Skyhawks and Warriors are not really much cheaper—maybe $10,000 or so.

And a 1990 Cadet is actually more costly, according to the *Aircraft Bluebook Price Digest*. Biggest price bargain in this class is the by-now slightly ancient (14-year-old) American General Cheetah, at around $27,000.

Aerospatiale Trinidad TB-20, -21TC

Used-plane hunters can take some comfort from the fact that the Trinidad is one of the few late-model, high-performance singles supported by continuing production. On the other hand, prices of new Trinidads are soaring, and the resale value of used ones has not sagged greatly. The aircraft has been marketed in the United States for the past ten years. Since this was handled somewhat indifferently during the early stages, and the design still is not widely known, a bit of background might help.

History

The Trinidad is the top of the line of a small family (four) of single-engine aircraft developed and built by Socata of Tarbes, France. Socata is the general aviation division of government-owned aerospace conglomerate Aerospatiale. The family includes the TB-9 Tampico and -10 Tobago, fixed-gear singles of 160 and 180 hp, and the 250-hp, retractable-gear TB-20 Trinidad and -21TC Trinidad. The models share a common fuselage, wing and empennage. Commonality aids production scheduling. For instance, a batch of fuselages and flying surfaces can be built. What model a particular ship set becomes can be adjusted according to what is ordered from the field.

For a 260-hp aircraft, the 159-knot cruise speed is nothing to rave about. Aileron controls are stodgy and heavy. But slow-speed handling is quite good.

The TB design, which also is called the Caribbean series, was introduced at the Paris Air Show in 1977. The TB-20 was awarded French approval in December 1981. The first Trinidad in the United States arrived in the late summer of 1983. FAA certification came the next year. The TB-21 gained FAA certification in March 1986.

Because of the company's poor experience trying to sell the almost-STOL Rallye here in the 1970s, it approached the North American market very cautiously. After a couple of failed efforts to introduce the TB line, Socata established its own operation just outside of Dallas, Tex. Aerospatiale General Aviation (AGA) shares facilities with Aerospatiale Helicopter Corp. in Grand Prarie.

Weight Evolution

The first TB-20s had a maximum takeoff weight of 2,943 pounds. This was increased to 3,086 pounds in 1984, along with a maximum ramp weight of 3,097 pounds, but the maximum landing weight remained 2,943. This has been a concern to some pilots, even though it is a typical condition for many piston aircraft, particularly twins.

In 1990, starting with serial number 950, maximum landing weight was increased to 3,086 pounds. Unfortunately, structural modifications were made to the landing gear attach points and they are not retrofittable to earlier models. At the same time, the electrical system was changed from 14 to 28 volts. A change to a higher-speed starter motor is in the works. This change has already been accomplished on the TB-9 and -10 models.

Though tall fliers will find the headroom confining, the 50-inch-wide cabin width of the Trinidad puts most comparable U.S. aircraft to shame. The generous full-fuel payload also makes other aircraft's load-carrying seem anemic.

To its credit, the detail and systems changes Aerospatiale/Socata has made to the design are almost completely the result of customer experience. Also to its credit, according to reader feedback, the company has been responsive to customer requests for assistance.

Construction

The relatively simple, monocoque fuselage has a comparatively low parts count. According to the company, it takes about 600 man hours to construct a Trinidad. This is far lower than, for instance, the man hours required to build a Mooney or Bonanza airframe. Most of the cabin is fabricated from reinforced glass fiber. This sits on top of the load-bearing structure, the fuselage tub. The cabin doors (yes, there are two) are cut out of the cabin structure. The door sill is the top of the tub, so there is a minimum number of holes in the load-bearing structure. The largest is the relatively small, triangular baggage bay access door on the port side of the fuselage.

The wing, too, is a relatively simple, straightforward structure. Dihedral is fairly pronounced. The spar is milled rather than built-up. The constant-chord wing has a relatively small area of 128.1 square feet (compared to 181 for the F33A, 174.7 on the Mooneys, and 170 on the Arrow). At the low end of the speed range, this is made up for by large, long-span, slotted flaps. Stall speed clean and in landing configuration are comparatively high at 70 and 50 KIAS, compared to 64 and 52 for the Bonanza and 61 and 56 for the Mooney.

Flight controls are actuated by push rods rather than the more typical cables. Since much of the wing trailing edge is occupied by the flaps, the ailerons are relatively short span.

It is a simple, yet sleek design. A prominent distinction is the vertical stabilizer, which is located forward of the horizontal, all-flying tail or stabilator. Both control surfaces have trim tabs. Pitch trim is an anti-servo tab. The rudder trim tab is an additional surface appended to the rudder that looks like an afterthought. The main landing gear is trailing link.

Powerplant

The Lycoming IO-540 powerplant, which is in widespread use in a number of variants and airframes, continues in production. The C4D5D version used in the TB-20 is rated at a conservative 250 hp. The turbocharged TB-21TC combines the AB1AD version of the same powerplant, also rated at 250 hp, with a variable wastegate-controller Garrett AiResearch turbocharger. Recommended TBO for both is 2,000 hours. The 2,000-hour TBO is a plus. But as with any large engine, overhaul costs are high.

If your heart is set on the TB-21, be prepared for a shock at overhaul time. The average cost of $30,000 looked like a misprint, but in the words of one facility manager we talked to, ". . . it is a very expensive engine to overhaul, and we don't see many of them."

Cabin Comfort, Loading

Another feature that distinguishes the TB series is the top-hinged, gull-wing cabin doors. These make access to any seat quite simple, with a minimum of fumbling and clambering. The cockpit/cabin is very modern looking and is well organized. It is 50 inches wide, the most expansive in its class. In fact, it is one inch wider than the commodious Piper PA-32 family of wide singles.

The Trinidad can accommodate up to five people. There are individual bucket seats up front. Up to three (small) passengers can be carried on the rear bench seat when the optional center lap belts are installed. The airplane is quite comfortable for four. The seats include an adjustable lumbar support.

To go with its notable spaciousness and comfort, the Trinidad can carry a comparatively hefty payload. It is almost a full-tanks and full-seats airplane, which is unusual for singles and light twins. It also has a generous c.g. range to permit loading flexibility. At an average equipped weight of 1,990 pounds, payload with full fuel (86.2 gallons usable/517.2 pounds) is 589.8 pounds. That equals 3.5 170-pounders. To put things in perspective, its full-fuel payload exceeds that of any other four-place single. It is close to the Lance/Saratoga SP and even beats the A36 and B36TC Bonanzas. Only the Cessna 210 surpasses its payload capability, but with less comfort.

Cockpit Design

Visibility from all seats is excellent. The windshield and side windows wrap up into the roof line. Ergonomically, the cockpit is well organized.

Models built before 1987 have the fuel selector mounted to the left of and just below the pilot's yoke. This arrangement was the subject of an AD (more about this later). The three panel modules can be released quickly and tilted back for maintenance access. Additional access panels are provided in the glare shield. There are a lot of pockets and crannies for manuals, charts and odd pieces of gear.

The interior is well thought out. The biggest drawback is the relatively small, odd-shaped baggage door. It is hinged at the bottom and when fully opened projects. Care must be taken when loading the baggage bay. Access to the baggage bay for bulkier items than can fit through the door can be gained from inside the cabin. The rear seat back can be folded down or removed.

Operations

There is nothing peculiar about operations. From pre- to post-flight, the airplane is quite straightforward.

Inspection of the engine compartment is difficult because a number of fasteners must be unscrewed. Then, the one piece cowl has to be put in a safe place while the inspection is performed so that a wind gust or prop or jet blast from other aircraft doesn't send it sailing down the ramp. Too many operators probably just won't bother frequently enough to catch the deteriorating hose or loose connection or nesting bird before they create a problem.

Once a pilot gets accustomed to some of the different information presentations, such as the vertical temp and pressure gauges and the two-part electrical switches (one of which actuates the electric turn and bank — a trap for the unwary), it is an easy airplane to operate.

Normal takeoffs call for 10 degrees of flap. Standard flap control is an electric switch that permits settings anywhere from up to full-down (40 degrees). It must be monitored during operation to get the right setting. An increasing number are fitted with the optional pre-select switch (up, 10 and 40 degrees). In maximum performance takeoffs, and climbing at best angle, the forward view is filled with cowling. Rate of climb at Vy of 95 KIAS is 1,250 fpm. Critical speeds are Vne, 187 KIAS; Va (maneuvering) 129 KIAS; Vlo (gear operating) 129 KIAS; and Vfe (maximum flap extended) 103 KIAS. So descent management takes some thought (and possible negotiation with ATC). One concern with both models should be shock cooling the engine in descent, unless you decide to extend the gear at the top of descent, when indicated airspeed probably will be below Vlo.

Modular instrument panel looks jazzy, and sections are hinged at the bottom so they can be tilted back for maintenance access.

Control response is good. Highest effort is in roll. The stubby ailerons and the push rod control mean you have to work a bit harder to get large displacement. It probably is most noticeable to someone used to flying a Bonanza, a Bellanca or a later-model 210. But it isn't a drawback. Pitch and yaw control effort is lower. So it is more an issue of balance, or control harmony, than hard work.

The good trade-off is that the airplane, thanks also in part to its comparatively high wing loading, handles turbulence well. It also displays good manners during instrument flight.

Performance

The spaciousness and comfort of the Trinidad comes at the cost of cruise performance, but it still is respectable. According to factory figures, 75 percent power at 8,000 feet nets a true airspeed of 159 knots. Endurance, with 45-minute reserve, is 5.65 hours. At the same altitude, 65 percent generates 149 knots and a bladder-busting 6.4 hours endurance.

The turbocharged version does not perform quite as well at lower altitudes, like most turbo models. The crossover point comes at about 12,000 feet. At its maximum operating altitude of 25,000 feet, 75 percent power generates a true of 187 knots and endurance of 4.5 hours; 65 percent power produces 169 knots and 6.2 hours.

Handling

Slow-flight manners are good. While the stall speeds are marginally higher than with other singles, the stall is very mild. The typical result is more a high rate of sink rather than a pronounced break. The flight controls are fully functional right through the stall. Intentionally cross-controlling near the stall or even in it (hardly recommended practice) produces sink rather than a snap.

Pitch change with initial flap extension is minimal. It is more pronounced when full flaps are selected, particularly at the higher end of the allowable speed range. Saving full flaps until the landing is assured means adjusting trim or accepting high pitch forces down to the flare, at which point the up trim has to be put back in. Full flaps generate a lot of drag, which means either accepting a steeper approach (good for obstacle clearance) or a partial power approach.

Low-speed technique is rewarded with a bit of practice and establishing a procedure that works best for you. The low-speed performance is exceptional, once you are fully transitioned to the airplane. In this respect, it shows a bit of the Rallye heritage.

Landings, except for the most highly botched and abusive, can be done repeatedly with grace. Lightly loaded, with just the pilot aboard it takes a bit more attention, because c.g. is forward. But its manners (and willingness to forgive) are very good.

Airworthiness Directives

Most of the other changes made to the TBs are reflected by service bulletins and Airworthiness Directives. A word of caution is in order to pilots considering this and other used aircraft and who will research the products before buying. Just buying relevant ADs will not give you the full story. Traditionally, ADs detailed any inspections and modifications. Most now refer to a manufacturer's related service bulletin for details. Fifteen ADs were issued on the TB-20 and -21 by early 1991. Five of these are almost standard in the general aviation fleet: paper induction air filters, Bendix ignition switches, Bendix magneto impulse couplings, Hartzell propellers and Airborne vacuum pumps. Another, on engine rocker arm assemblies, also is widespread. It affects most 320, 340, 360 and 540 series Lycoming engines. An AD issued in 1990 requires a one-time inspection of oil coolers on all TB series airplanes for cracks and what the text merely calls "distortions." If anything is amiss, the oil cooler must be replaced.

The AD on the fuel system that was mentioned earlier was issued to deal with a condition that resulted in fuel starvation in a few instances. In the original design, fuel lines run from the tanks forward and up to the panel-mounted fuel selector. Two conditions could occur: Fuel could drain to the low point, causing the fuel pump to cavitate. The original Dukes fuel boost pump is lubricated by fuel. Dry lines resulted in its failure. Or, vapor lock could occur, blocking normal fuel flow. The fix for the original system is to replace the boost pump with a wet-or-dry Weldon pump and to install a check valve in the line to preclude draining. In 1987 and later models, the fuel selector has been relocated to the center console. Also, it has been modified so that it is not necessary to pass through the "off" position when changing tanks.

Three accidents have been attributed to fuel starvation. One example why a thorough inspection and records search is essential when buying an aircraft is the

Trinidad that crashed on short final due to engine stoppage. The fuel system AD had not been complied with.

Three ADs have been issued on the horizontal tail; two of them require repetitive inspections. One requires replacement of the elevator trim tab control attachment. The second requires repetitive (every 100 hours) inspection of the stabilator actuator rod end assembly and attach fittings. It also is necessary to replace the rod ends if play or loose fittings are found. Replacing the original assembly with a modified one eliminates the requirement for repetitive inspection.

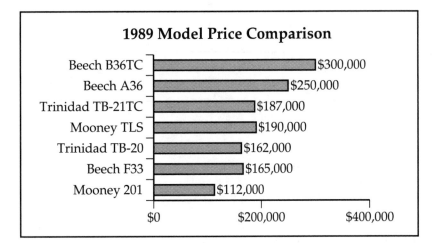

1989 Model Price Comparison

Beech B36TC	$300,000
Beech A36	$250,000
Trinidad TB-21TC	$187,000
Mooney TLS	$190,000
Trinidad TB-20	$162,000
Beech F33	$165,000
Mooney 201	$112,000

The third AD requires 100-hour inspections of the fuselage frame at the horizontal stabilizer hinge and attach fittings. If cracks are found, the fuselage frame must be replaced. The airplane then can be flown without the inspection for another 700 hours. Or, instead, a modified frame can be installed to preclude any further inspections.

Another repetitive AD affects the ailerons. The skin and balance weight attach rivets must be inspected every 100 hours. Substantial cracking requires aileron replacement. An improved part eliminates the inspection requirement.

For aircraft through serial number 1052, the fuselage frame at the nose landing gear and aft engine mount location must be inspected for cracks after 1,500 hours and every 500 hours thereafter. Socata has developed a kit to fix the potential problem. If it is installed, the periodic inspection is not required.

Possible interference between the main landing gear and supporting structure must be inspected for under another AD. If no signs of interference are found, modification must still be made within 100 flight hours.

Gear Abuse?

The two ADs above suggest that the landing gear has been subject to a great deal more abuse than the designers anticipated.

Another AD requires inspection of the battery tray and surrounding structure for electrolyte leakage and subsequent corrosion. It also requires modification of the battery box to eliminate leaks.

Service Difficulty Reports

There is an obvious link between Service Difficulty Reports (SDRs) and ADs: If there is even the appearance of a pattern among SDRs, an AD frequently is not far behind.

There were 47 SDRs submitted on the TB-20 and -21 between January 1985 and May 1991. Many of the airframe SDRs dealt with empennage and wing attach fittings that were dealt with by subsequent ADs. To a lesser extent, the same can be said of the SDRs on landing gear problems. Most of the others are random and deal with manufacturing or installation error and do not suggest any patterns.

Safety Record

Between January 1986 and May 1991, 12 incidents and accidents involving TB-20 and -21s have been reported by FAA. Two of these were fatal, claiming a total of five lives. In one of the fatal accidents, a wind shear encounter is suspected. While on short final, the airplane rolled inverted and crashed. In the other, in which the pilot and three passengers were killed, fuel contamination caused a loss of power. During the ensuing emergency landing, the pilot stalled the aircraft in an attempt to avoid wires. The brief of the latter accidents states: "Unaware of low point fuel drain; failed to sump for months." In two other accidents, pilot unfamiliarity with the airplane and its systems was mentioned. One was a classic gear-up attributed to failure to use the check list. In the other, the pilot landed gear-up after an electrical failure; he did not use the emergency check list and emergency gear extension procedures.

There is not much to be drawn from the records. Most can be attributed to pilot knowledge, error or decisions. The electrical system failures show no pattern, for instance. One was the result of a shorted, internally damaged battery (but there is no information to indicate whether the event was caused by manufacturing, installation or maintenance error).

The design is maturing, with the factory responding well to weaknesses that have been made apparent through operating experience. Support appears to be good, and better than many other designs on the market. Aerospatiale appears to be settling into the North American marketplace, and concern about being "or-phaned" is minimal.

The only trouble is finding a variety of used ones to pick among.

Cost/Performance/Specifications

Model	Year Built	Average Retail Price	Cruise Speed (kts)	Useful Load (lbs)	Fuel Std/Opt (gals)	Engine	TBO (hrs)	Overhaul Cost
TB-20	1984	$92,000	164	1,212	86	250-hp Lyc. IO-540-C4D5D	2,000	$15,500
TB-20	1985	$103,000	164	1,212	86	250-hp Lyc. IO-540-C4D5D	2,000	$15,500
TB-20	1986	$117,000	164	1,212	86	250-hp Lyc. IO-540-C4D5D	2,000	$15,500
TB-21TC	1986	$134,000	187	1,288	86	250-hp Lyc. TIO-540-AB1AD	2,000	$30,000
TB-20	1987	$132,000	164	1,212	86	250-hp Lyc. IO-540-C4D5D	2,000	$15,500
TB-21TC	1987	$152,000	187	1,288	86	250-hp Lyc. TIO-540-AB1AD	2,000	$30,000
TB-20	1988	$149,000	164	1,212	86	250-hp Lyc. IO-540-C4D5D	2,000	$15,500
TB-21TC	1988	$172,000	187	1,288	86	250-hp Lyc. TIO-540-AB1AD	2,000	$30,000
TB-20	1989	$162,000	164	1,212	86	250-hp Lyc. IO-540-C4D5D	2,000	$15,500
TB-21TC	1989	$187,000	187	1,288	86	250-hp Lyc. TIO-540-AB1AD	2,000	$30,000
TB-20	1990	$172,000	164	1,212	86	250-hp Lyc. IO-540-C4D5D	2,000	$15,500
TB-21TC	1990	$202,000	187	1,288	86	250-hp Lyc. TIO-540-AB1AD	2,000	$30,000
TB-20	1991	$185,000	164	1,212	86	250-hp Lyc. IO-540-C4D5D	2,000	$15,500
TB-21TC	1991	$220,000	187	1,288	86	250-hp Lyc. TIO-540-AB1AD	2,000	$30,000
TB-20	1992	$230,000	164	1,212	86	250-hp Lyc. IO-540-C4D5D	2,000	$15,500
TB-21TC	1992	$265,000	187	1,288	86	250-hp Lyc. TIO-540-AB1AD	2,000	$30,000
TB-20	1993	$242,000	164	1,212	86	250-hp Lyc. IO-540-C4D5D	2,000	$15,500
TB-21TC	1993	$280,000	187	1,288	86	250-hp Lyc. TIO-540-AB1AD	2,000	$30,000

Owner Comments

I am a military pilot, but I also run an aerospace R&D firm that uses a TB2I Turbo-Trinidad for business transportation and as a technology demonstrator. It is well suited to both tasks.

Cockpit Design: The most striking feature of the Trinidad is its accommodation. The cabin is as wide as a Navajo's, doesn't taper at the rear seats, and has some of the largest windows you'll find on a general aviation aircraft. The only compromise is the low headroom, which might be a problem for the six-footers among you, but doesn't affect my 5' 7" frame too much. I like the gull-wing doors, as I find they really ease access to all the seats. For flight-safety purposes they are supplemented by two kick-out rear windows, giving a one-to-one passenger-to-exit ratio.

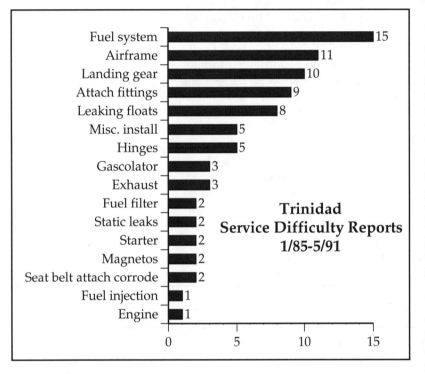

**Trinidad
Service Difficulty Reports
1/85-5/91**

The modular instrument panel is logical and shows good attention to detail, with such features as the canted right-side instrument sub-panels. The central console is excellent, with the trim wheel falling under your palm when your hand rests on the throttle. The combination switch-breakers elegantly save space while putting most of the important functions within fingertip reach. In fact, the entire electrical system shows the Trinidad's Airbus heritage, by incorporating multiple busses with several different kinds of circuit-breaker, each optimized for its role.

There is enough panel space for just about any avionics equipment, if the room is used a little creatively. The only real criticism I have of the panel is the awkward location and labeling of the cabin heating and ventilation system.

Flying Qualities: The handling qualities of the Trinidad, while safe and stable, do give away its Tobago ancestry. The ailerons are heavy at high speed, and the very short-coupled directional axis (note the fin location) makes this higher-powered variant quite demanding in yaw. As if to compensate, Aerospatiale has installed an over-geared rudder trim that has to be experienced to be believed: One turn at cruise speed will peg the slip ball at the end of its race! I can understand why the company didn't mess with a successful design, but I think that the ailerons and rudder could be better harmonized for this aircraft's performance envelope.

On the plus side, the aircraft is very good for instrument work, handles crosswinds with aplomb, and has excellent preselectable flaps that seem as powerful as the early Cessna singles'. Very nice. To top it all, the trailing-link main landing gear translates even my carrier landings into "squeakers."

I find that the aircraft's performance matches the book figures quite well, although I need to apply corrections for all the extra antennas. On the subject of the

flight manual, I think the format is reasonable, but some of the contents need to be cleaned up. In particular, the electrical emergency procedures section is over complicated, and there are several parenthetic mystery airspeeds throughout the manual. I wrote Aerospatiale a detailed review of the entire document and I am awaiting their response.

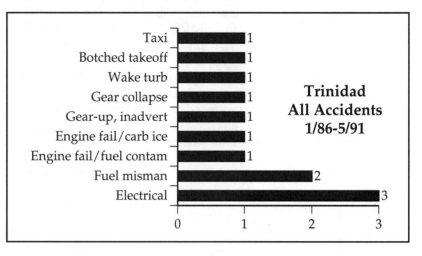

Loading: The Trinidad has a generous loading envelope and useful load, even when fully equipped. The only constraint is the small triangular baggage door, which forces larger items to be heaved through three zippered accesses behind the rear seats. I can't decide if Aerospatiale decided on the small baggage door to preclude loading abuses or for structural reasons. My guess would be the former. In either case, I don't think safety would suffer much if the opening were to be enlarged.

Company backup: I had a few problems with the company at the outset, but just as I was beginning to get really frustrated, they came through for me. I think my early support difficulties are behind me.

Conclusion: The Trinidad is a refreshing change among a sea of Pipers and Cessna's. It is excellently engineered, caters very well to the needs of its inhabitants, performs well, if not blindingly, and looks good, too. I'm sure that the design will continue to mature, and I hope to see a Twinidad in the future.

Captain John Maris
Engineering Test Pilot
Cold Lake. Medley,
Alberta, Canada

I purchased my first Trinidad (TB-2O) in August of 1985. After four years and 600 hours plus a move from the flatlands (Texas) to the mountains (Oregon), I traded it for a new TB-21TC. The trade-in I received was exactly what I had paid for the TB-20 four years prior. In the last two years I have put 300 hours on the 'TB-21C. I could not be happier with my purchase decisions.

The Trinidad really shines when it comes to reliability, and cost of maintenance. The majority of the service my Trinidads have received were by small FBOs with great mechanics—none of whom were "Factory Authorized Service Centers." With both aircraft I purchased maintenance manuals and parts catalogs. With these, the mechanics have had no problems correcting squawks, ordering parts, or performing required inspections and maintenance. Virtually all parts have been available and in hand within 48 hours of order.

The support provided by Richard Bridgeman (Aerospatiale's Product Support Manager for the U.S.) has been outstanding. Warranty claims have been handled promptly, with no hassle, and I received Aerospatiale's check usually within 30 days after my request for reimbursement. The cost of annual inspections has been low, even when you consider that I have been flying new aircraft. The four annuals for the TB-20 averaged 21.25 hours, including necessary repairs. Parts were limited to filters, brake linings, etc. Nothing major needed to be changed.

The two annuals for the TB-21TC averaged 17.45 hours, including necessary repairs. Using average parts and labor prices I have paid, annuals for the TB-20 averaged less than $750 and for the TB-21TC less than $650. Fifty-hour inspections on both aircraft usually average less than four hours or $175 parts and labor. Both Trinidads have performed up to book figures.

Weight and balance is a real strong suit. In the TB-21TC I routinely carry four adults, luggage and fuel for three hours at 75% power, plus IFR reserves. The Trinidad is spacious, comfortable, easy to get in and out of, and looks and feels great. Visibility is exceptional.

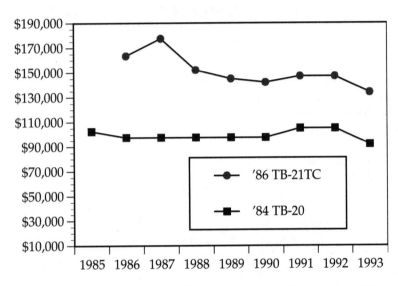

I usually fly between 11,500 and 20,000 feet. If it's just me or me and my wife, we usually fly as high and fast as possible. With passengers we stay below the oxygen levels, weather permitting. Our cruise speeds average between 170 and 185 knots.

I was intrigued by the speeds turned in by the Mooney TLS with essentially the same engine with 20 more horsepower. To get the blazing speed at 12,500 feet, Mooney recommends a power setting of over 90%. This is justified by the fact the T1O-540 is substantially derated from its 350-hp installations in aircraft such as the Malibu Mirage.

Since the Trinidad TC installation is even more derated, I set up my plane at 12,500, 30 in. mp, 2400 rpm, 18.9 gph (about 90%), and I see 185-knot true airspeeds. This leads me to believe that the performance difference between the two aircraft when comparing apples to apples is far less than the marketing hype might have you believe.

The engine in the Trinidad TC runs very cool. CHTs in climb rarely exceed 375 degrees, in cruise 320 is the norm. Pulling back power slowly (two inches every two minutes) results in 500-1,000 fpm descents with no shock cooling problems. At first I was concerned about the accuracy of the gauges, so I had an Insight GEM installed. The GEM indicates slightly lower temperatures than the factory gauge. In the Pacific Northwest, IFR is the rule rather than the exception. The Trinidad TC with its 1,100 fpm climb and 25,000-foot service ceiling can usually climb through and top most of the bad winter weather. The plane is very stable in the turbulence found around our mountain ranges.

Michael P. Kelley,
Sunriver, Ore.

American Champion Scout

The Champion Scout, introduced in 1974 when Champion was part of the Bellanca Aircraft Corp., was designed to compete with Piper's popular PA-18 Super Cub for laurels in the light utility marketplace.

The Scout and the Cub, joined later by the Christen (now Aviat) A-1 Husky (see the Aug. 15, 1992 issue), exist primarily to serve as aerial jeeps or compact pickup trucks. But they also appeal to a number of sporting pilots for use on the back forty or to transport fishing or hunting gear to remote islands in the North.

History

The 8GCBC Scout was introduced as the newest member of the Bellanca Champion line in 1974. Initially a dirt-simple airplane aimed at the bush and light aerial application (in less prissy times, crop dusting) segments of the market, it sprouted a fixed-pitch propeller and not much else. Options were few.

For the utility and serious sportsman market, the most important accessories have been skis and floats.

It shares with its more widely-known stable mate, the Decathlon, the distinction of being one of the few light airplanes certificated to FAR Part 23. At the same time, it reflects a heritage that extends back to the Great Depression year of 1929. That's when Aeronca was formed. It spawned the Champ of post-World War II fame.

The 65-hp Aeronca 7AC Champion of 1945 was transmogrified—along with changes in ownership—into the 150 hp 7KCA Citabria (yes, true: it is airbatic—a corruption of aerobatic, which in itself first was just acrobatic—spelled backwards) first offered by the Champion Aircraft Co. in 1965.

Aerobatic Eye-Opener

Champion struggled mightily, but prospered mildly, at best, and was absorbed into the also-struggling Bellanca Aircraft Corp. in 1970. In its brief almost-heyday, Champion developed and produced in the Citabria and Decathlon airplanes that made aerobatic training and practice, and even air show performances and precision flying competition, available to a fair greater number of people.

The Scout was the first long-wing Champion variant. It also was offered with a 180-hp powerplant. In the late 1950s and through the 1960s, versions powered by 140-

Sitting tall on a stiff landing gear, the Scout weathervanes more than some taildraggers. Fixed-pitch and constant-speed props are alternatives.

and 150-hp engines were offered with flaps and are mistakenly called Scouts by some people. The determinant is the greater wingspan. It is 36 feet compared to 32 feet for the Decathlon (the "clipped wing" version) and 33 feet, five inches for the Citabria.

In 1978, a constant-speed propeller was offered as an option. A 70-gallon usable fuel capacity was offered to augment the standard Scout usable fuel load of 35 gallons. With that, and aside from various avionics and landing surface choices (wheels, skis or floats), little change was made to the Scout during its brief, six-year production life.

Rebirth

Until, that is, it was reborn this year as the third product offered by American Champion Aircraft Corp. (ACA) of Rochester, Wisconsin, (800) 223-9381 or (414) 534-6315.

First, another digression. Champion collapsed in the bankruptcy of its parent, Bellanca, in 1980. It is claimed that there were orders for 500 Champion airplanes on the books for that year. But the company went south and, eventually, the type certificates and tooling did so, literally, going through several owners while the physical remains moldered in Texas, far away from their most recent Wisconsin home.

Decked out in an ag spray system, the Scout had optional wire cutters on windshield and gear struts. Another optional side benefit was corrosion proofing for ag or seaplane versions, including stainless steel cables.

A series of plans was announced about a return to production. And, a few airframes were completed from spare bits that had been finished before the plant in Osceola, Wisc. closed. There was strong interest in returning the line to production, especially the aerobatic airplanes, but many schemes failed until the latest rebirth of the company.

Biggest Change

The return to production of the Scout (which originally was planned for 1991) includes a significant physical change: the wood-spar wing has been redesigned and the airplane re-certified with a metal spar. The Decathlon and Citabria had received the transplant earlier.

According to Jerry K. Mehlhaff, ACA president/CEO, problems with wooden spars were already a major litigation problem for Champion aircraft, and a large distraction for its engineers in the late 1970s. Mehlhaff would like to see all Citabria, Decathlons and Scouts converted to metal spars.

Up until this year, 359 Scouts had been built. Mehlhaff told *The Aviation Consumer* that the seventh unit of the reborn Scout was scheduled to fly during the first week of September. Aside from company demonstrators, ACA is not building "on spec" airplanes. All are built to order.

In addition to the wing spar, ACA has developed other changes. These include metal flaps, balanced ailerons, aileron spades and newly designed front struts that are fabricated from an extruded metal. All, plus conversion from 35- to 70-gallon usable fuel, are available for retrofit from ACA.

The Competition

As already noted, the core competition for the Scout are the PA-18 Super Cub and A-1 Husky. A number of other competing designs have come and gone (and some have come back and gone again, such as the Interstate), and others, such as the ebbing and flowing Taylorcraft have tried to muscle into the narrow turf holding of two-place utility airplanes.

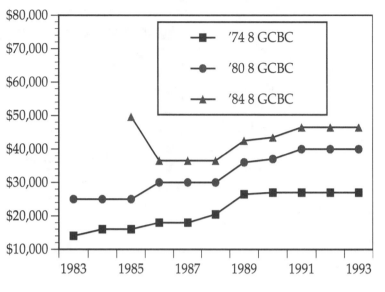

In some applications, such as power, pipeline and natural-resource patrol, airplanes such as the Cessna 172 and 182 (and 180 and 185) also are competition.

However, for off-airport, bush-type operations, tail draggers still are the airplanes of choice (again, including the Cessna 180 and 185 and such relatively esoteric airplanes as the Lockheed/LASA 60 and the Helio Courier).

If the qualification of continued support by some level of production is important to potential buyers, the Scout and Husky are without competition.

Performance

There are interesting equipment-related tradeoffs in Scout performance. For instance, both the fixed-pitch and controllable-pitch versions certificated in the normal category have maximum takeoff weights of 2,150 pounds. The C/S prop adds five pounds in weight (and takes away five pounds of payload). Or is it 15 pounds? The factory figures are in conflict. Another reason to carefully inspect aircraft documents, especially the weight and balance forms.

The fixed-pitch version can be operated in the restricted category—for instance, for crop dusting—at a 2,600-pound gross weight.

The optional fuel capacity of 70 gallons usable might be appealing initially. But, un-

---

Champion 8GCBC Scout Service Difficulty Reports: 1/88 - 7/93

Wing Spars (Cracks)	7
Flight Controls	
Trim Tab	7
Aileron Hinge	1
Flap Actuating	1
Pitot/Static System	2
Engine	
Valve Train	1
Camshaft	1
Ignition System	1
Throttle	1
Oil Line	1
Propeller (Corrosion)	1
Fuel System—Tank	1
Main Gear (Mounting)	1
Tailwheel (Mounting)	1
Brake System	1

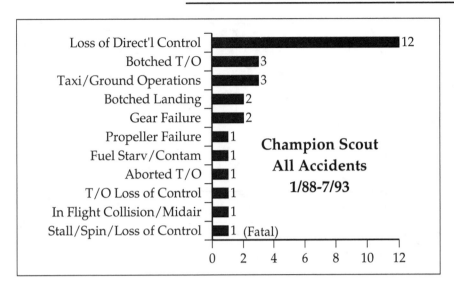

Loss of Direct'l Control ▇▇▇▇▇▇ 12
Botched T/O ▇ 3
Taxi/Ground Operations ▇ 3
Botched Landing ▇ 2
Gear Failure ▇ 2
Propeller Failure ▇ 1
Fuel Starv/Contam ▇ 1
Aborted T/O ▇ 1
T/O Loss of Control ▇ 1
In Flight Collision/Midair ▇ 1
Stall/Spin/Loss of Control ▇ 1 (Fatal)

**Champion Scout
All Accidents
1/88-7/93**

0 2 4 6 8 10 12

less you are involved in patrol work, the standard tanks may help avoid a number of problems, especially operating over gross. There also are some basic considerations related to mass and inertia. The Scout is not approved for any aerobatic maneuvers, including spins. The dynamics of a stall/spin encounter with 420 rather than 210 pounds of weight in the wings—and farther from the center of rotation—are quite different from those of the standard airplane.

Equipped empty weight varies greatly with installed equipment, too. While payload with full fuel for the standard airplane is quite good at 625 pounds, auxiliary fuel and installed accessories will quickly cut into payload and/or range.

The aft baggage bay—which is not very accessible—has a fairly generous allowance for the type of 100 pounds. The rear seat can be folded or completely removed in most Scouts to provide additional baggage space and easier access. According to factory figures, rate of climb is slightly better for a fixed-pitch-propeller-equipped Scout, but cruise speed and range are slightly lower than the numbers for a C/S- equipped version. However, the numbers are close enough together to be essentially unmeasurable in the hands of the average pilot, so the big differential becomes payload reduced by the weight of installed options.

Handling

A big difference between the Scout and its siblings is that it sits higher on the main gear. Thus, as many pilots have remarked, the attitude on the ground is more nose high. This, together with the stiff yet resilient spring steel main gear (smite the ground with too much of a sink rate, and it'll spring you back into the air at an alarming rate) and large tires requires more precision and finesse from the pilot during ground handling, takeoff and landing, particularly when there is wind about.

The good aspect of Scout behavior on the ground and in ground effect (it floats a lot more than the Decathlon or Citabria) is that it is over fairly rapidly in the hands of an adequately competent pilot.

Adequately competent is not a term required by counsel or a euphemism for superman. Any conventional-gear airplane requires better speed control, directional control and control coordination than the average tricycle-gear airplane. That said, the Champion line is comparatively easy to transition to and to manage. Speed and attitude control are key. And recognizing when wind speed and direction are beyond one's competence is an essential element of safe operation.

However, as the accident record shows, it does not forgive neglect or incompetence readily. Most accidents and incidents occur on or close to the ground, and involve directional control problems from the wind and because of poor judgment or flying ability.

Decathlons are noted for their heavy aileron forces. The Scout, with its longer wing, is even more taxing. Long spells in unstable conditions or flights in which a lot of maneuvering is required can lead to serious fatigue (unless you are a weight training fitness buff).

Pitch forces are quite light. In the hands of some pilots, even too light: there have been a number of instances/incidents/accidents caused by pilot-induced oscillations (PIOs) a/k/a porpoising. Rudder forces lie between the two. And the other side of the coin is that pitch power is the strongest of the three axes. In certain conditions, such as crosswind landing, roll and yaw control can be inadequate or too difficult to apply.

Aileron spades, which are aerodynamic aids to increase roll control and reduce the level of effort, have been offered for several Champion models in the aftermarket. ACA now offers them for the Scout, even as kits for retrofit to used airplanes.

Cabin Design

One of the greatest attributes of all Champions is visibility to the outside. Both front and rear seat occupants benefit. Seats are not luxurious, but they are adequate for pilots of most sizes for all but the longest-duration missions.

Placement of instruments, gauges, controls and switches, including (or especially) electrical accessories may take some getting used to for pilots new to this category of airplane.

Keep it Simple

Perhaps the greatest appeal of the Scout is its relative simplicity. This includes the powerplant and attendant systems. About as bullet proof as airplane pieces go, they are easy to support in relatively remote spots. Most components and systems are fairly easy to get at, too. For instance, the belly pan is a continuous piece that is easily removed to check lower fuselage members for corrosion and to inspect control cables, pulleys and fairleads.

Maintenance History

The service record of the Scout is as straightforward as the airplane itself. But there are a few tricks. For instance, most problems are the result of neglect, harsh operation or operating environment and wear and tear.

Cost/Performance/Specifications

Model	Year	Average Retail Price	Cruise Speed* (kts)	Useful Load (lbs)	Fuel Std/Opt (gals)	Engine	TBO (hrs)	Overhaul Cost ea.
8GCBC	1974	$27,000	106	835	35/70	Lyc. O-360-C2E	2,000	$10,500
8GCBC	1975	$28,000	106	835	35/70	Lyc. O-360-C2E	2,000	$10,500
8GCBC	1976	$29,000	106	835	35/70	Lyc. O-360-C2E	2,000	$10,500
8GCBC	1977	$30,000	106	835	35/70	Lyc. O-360-C2E	2,000	$10,500
8GCBC	1978	$31,500	106	835	35/70	Lyc. O-360-C2E	2,000	$10,500
8GCBC	1979	$35,000	106	835	35/70	Lyc. O-360-C2E	2,000	$10,500
8GCBC	1980	$40,000	106	835	35/70	Lyc. O-360-C2E	2,000	$10,500
8GCBC	1984	$46,500	106	835	35/70	Lyc. O-360-C2E	2,000	$10,500

*With fixed-pitch prop. Prices from *Aircraft Bluebook Price Digest*

Vibration-related problems are relatively frequent, suggesting propeller balancing and regular inspection of engine mounts will pay off in reduced accessory problems.

Wing spar cracks are the most frequent of all service problems. While they have occurred in less than two percent of the fleet, concern about them resulted in airworthiness directives. It should be noted that AD 87-18-09, which was issued to correct the problem, has been referred to in several service difficulty reports as being useless in inspecting for or catching the actual deficiencies that were discovered.

There have been no Scout accidents attributed to spar failure, but cracks have been found in seven aircraft that were reported in the SDR system.

The other repetitive problem both in the SDR system and in more informal reports is weakness in main and tailwheel mounting systems and materials.

Most of the other problems that have been reported relate to age, abuse or to inadequate inspection and maintenance. Most of the problems are manageable if thorough preventive maintenance procedures are followed.

Accident Record

The majority of Scout accidents are, as mentioned above, related to handling on or near the ground. There is no pattern that singles out the Scout. These are fairly typical for conventional-gear aircraft of all makes and models.

However, it is worth noting that half of the Scout's landing accidents occurred "in the bush," or away from airports. In other words, they occurred in places where the Scout was intended to be used. These can be inhospitable places full of traps for wind spurts or for momentary mental lapses.

The single fatal accident recorded in the past five-and-a-half years was the result of loss of control during low flight.

On the whole, the record of the Scout is benign. Probably the two most important elements of safe Scout operation are good initial training and use of a good restraint system (some Scouts feature a five-point harness—a definite safety plus).

Summary

The Scout is now a unique product. It is one of the few general aviation airplanes in production. For pilots who want to visit more primitive locations or who want the flexibility of being able to operate from land, sea or snow, the Husky is one of the few viable alternatives, particularly now that it is being supported by a new manufacturer.

Societies

As with many other makes, societies have come and gone with the waxing and waning of enthusiasm on the part of a few individuals. There is now an active Bellanca Champion Club. The Brookfield, Wisc.-based association, which claims no direct relationship with the Rochester, Wisc.-based ACA, claims 1,300 active members and a bimonthly newsletter that includes maintenance, retrofit and parts tips, (414) 783-6558.

Owner Comments

The 8GCBC Scout is a good honest plane, and in my opinion, used Scouts are the best value in the high-power two-place utility market at this time. When asked what it is, I sometimes tell strangers that it's a Citabria that's been on steroids, although this isn't really fair to either the Scout or Citabria.

I am Chief Tow Pilot for the Colorado Soaring Assn. We operate a low serial number '74 Scout at Owl Canyon Gliderport, north of Fort Collins, at 5,500 msl. The Scout allows us to tow gliders with gross weights from 600 to 1,400 pounds, and get off the ground in 1,200 to 1,500 feet most of the time, even with density altitudes over 9,000 feet. Glider towing is severe service, with five to seven landing cycles per hour beating up the airframe, and the same maximum climb/maximum descent cycles working on the powerplant. The Scout tolerates this well.

As for handling, in the air, the Scout is heavy in roll, light in pitch, and medium in rudder pressures. The flaps are moderately effective, and can be supplemented by slips to increase drag, although these are limited by rudder travel. Stalls are straightforward, with a pronounced break and some tendency to fall off on a wing. Crosswind component is somewhat limited by rudder and aileron effectiveness, but is still more than most people will want to try. The "spade" ailerons now available from American Champion may improve response (I haven't flown them), but watch your head on the ground! I carry scars from a Husky.

Ground handling is more demanding than in Cubs and Citabrias, despite the nearly identical cockpit (to the latter). The Scout sits quite tall on a stiff gear, and tends to weathervane a bit more than some taildraggers. Transitions to takeoff and to landing require close attention and prompt application of controls to keep things straight. The brakes/tires (8.50 x 6.00 on double-puck Clevelands, similar to a Cessna 185's) are extremely effective, and can put the prop in the dirt very easily. These props are hard to find and expensive.

Over-the-nose visibility is fairly good for a tall taildragger, but pilots transitioning from Citabrias have to work at getting the nose up for three-point landings.

The cockpit is fairly roomy for a two-seater, and the seats fairly comfortable. If the seat-back AD needs compliance (it should have been taken care of by now), consider the adjustable front seat: The mechanism is quite awkward, but will accommodate a wider range of pilot sizes. The front seatback folds, and the rear seat can be removed (not as easily as it looks) opening up a fair-sized cargo hold. Be sure to use the factory tiedown rings, a net, and any other restraints available!

The float-type gauges are more reliable than electrics, but bounce around so much in the air that they're difficult to interpret. Use known fuel fill against time at a known fuel flow rate. The fuel is on or off only; some operators prefer to run one tank quite low, then switch to the other as a "reserve." This is not possible on the Scout.

Most towplane operators opt for the fixed-pitch prop of the flattest pitch possible, and the Scout prop can be quite efficient. A variable-itch Hartzell prop is optional, and is definitely faster, although not as efficient in acceleration and climb. Mixed use operations might benefit from it. The variable pitch prop is subject to more maintenance, as well as an onerous A.D.

The wooden-spar wings have a notorious A.D. for cracks in the spars. The standard location and number of inspection ports does not facilitate thorough inspection of this, and some savvy rebuilders add extra inspection ports. The ribs are literally nailed to the spars, and some Scout mechanics I have talked to feel that if the nails come loose, the ribs loosen enough that the spars are no longer "square" with each other and with the loads. These should be thoroughly checked and re-nailed if required. Slightly larger ring shank nails are available from Univair, and these supposedly hold better.

I have seen similar spar cracks recently in an Aeronca 15AC and a Champion 7FC which use substantially the same wing construction as the Scout. American Champion has metal spar wings available to retrofit the wooden spar wings on most Scouts, and all their new production Scouts are of the metal spar variety. The metal spar wings are quite expensive, however. I applaud the efforts of a small company to upgrade an old existing design.

The other major airframe squawk is the undercarriage. The spring steel main gear is itself quite robust—quite stiff in fact, even at full gross weight. The problem is with original main gear attaching "U" bolts. The original is little more than a bent rod, threaded on the ends for a nut. This is prone to cracking on the bends, especially on Scouts with lots of landing cycles, or operated from rough fields.

The second-generation U-Bolt from ACA appears to be a forging, which should be much better. I have heard rumors of cracks on some of these. Univair has an STC'd solution that uses flat bar stock clamping the gear leg to the fuselage with MS bolts, thus eliminating the stress of bent metal. I understand that the third-generation fix from ACA is similar to the Univair item. Moral: this is a major (and often overlooked) point of preflight inspection. If you have not done so, plan on replacing these. (MS hardware is sometimes in short supply: If ACA doesn't have them in stock, try Univair, and vice versa.)

A similar condition exists with the tailspring and its U-bolt. The Scout tail is fairly heavy, and can really beat up these parts. Again, preflight the tailspring carefully and keep the U-bolt snug. We keep a complete assembly on hand, and replace the tailspring U-bolt every 1,200 to 1,500 landing cycles.

To sum up maintenance considerations, although I have pointed out some problem areas to watch for, the amount of maintenance required is not unreasonable for this type of airplane, and is certainly more easily accomplished than on many competing types. As I have pointed out, a glider towplane really experiences severe service, and we tend to see things that the normal operator would not.

Before American Champion came on the scene, parts were something of a problem, but they now have good product support and advice (unless they are all at Oshkosh!). Here in Denver, Univair has developed quite a bit of expertise on the Scout, and offers a fairly large line of PMA'd parts of very good quality. Their phone and counter sales staff are generally knowledgeable on correct parts selection and application. Many of us appreciate Univair's long-term commitment to older and out-of-production airplanes.

Curt Cole
Denver, Colo.

American Champion Citabria/Decathlon

For the budget-conscious aviator who wants to dabble in aerobatics, the choices are few. Among the best are the Bellanca/Champion Citabria and Decathlon.

These airplanes, while not exactly high-tech, are of more modern design than most other two-seat tail-draggers. Best of all, they're back in production, complete with a brand-new all-metal wing structure.

Lineage

The Champion line is second only to Mooney in confusion when it comes to figuring out which model is which. (Mooney takes the trophy for having a single model—the M20J—that has gone by no less than five different names.)

Here we'll be discussing in detail only the aerobatic versions of the Champion aircraft. That leaves out the Champ, and the late-'70s vintage Scout bushplane. The general comments should apply to those aircraft, however, provided they're of the same vintage.

The first 7ECA Citabria (That's "AIRBATIC" spelled backwards—get it?) was built in 1964, equipped with a 100-hp Continental O-200. It was a direct descendant of the old Champ, but was aerobatic and had a larger engine. Some 440 were built before the larger Lycoming O-235 engine was bolted on in 1966. It remained in production in pretty much the same configuration until Bellanca went under in 1980. A total of 1,350 or so were built.

In 1967 a bigger engine was hung on the same basic airframe to produce the 7GCAA, 7GCBC and 7KCAB—all still called Citabrias. The basic difference was that the 7KCAB variant had an injected engine with inverted fuel and oil systems, the 7CGAA had no flaps, and the 7GCBC had a long wing and flaps for better short-field performance. The 7GCAA and 7GCBC ran until 1980, the 7KCAB until 1977.

The Decathlon is a favorite at airshows—it's a perfect choice for stunts like this.

Though production of the three variants was pretty much equal for the first few years, the 7GCBC (long wing, flaps) soon began to outstrip its two siblings in popularity. Undoubtedly, the Decathlon also stole some buyers away from the 7KCAB, leading to its early demise. At the end of production, the tallies were as follows: 396 GCAAs, 1,214 GCBCs, and 618 KCABs.

Still confused? Wait—there's more. In 1971, the 8KCAB-150 Decathlon was introduced. Aerobatic, with inverted fuel and oil sys-

The Citabria is an excellent trainer, but a modest aerobatic ship.

tems and a 150-horsepower injected engine, it would at first glance seem pretty much the same airplane as the 7KCAB Citabria. However, it offered a shorter, semi-symmetrical airfoil wing that gave it vastly improved aerobatic handling (including double the roll rate). There were also other structural and aerodynamic differences (though outwardly the two are quite similar) and a constant-speed prop option.

In 1977 the Super Decathlon was brought on line, sporting a 180-horsepower engine. This last one is the preferred model for aerobatics, and fetches premium prices on the used market.

A total of 638 Decathlons and Super Decathlons were built, of which 487 remain. (As a side note, production of non-aerobatic 8GCBC Scout totaled 359.)

Companies

The Champion line is most associated with Bellanca, also makers of the wooden-winged Viking retractable. That company folded in 1980 and sold the rights to the Champion line. A couple of airplanes (a few Scouts, Decathlons, GCBC and ECA Citabrias) were built in the mid-'80s in an attempt to get the line going again.

In the past couple of years, however, new owners have been trying to breathe life into the line once again. Under the name of American Champion Aircraft, Jerry and Charlene Mehlhaff have begun small-scale production (on order only) of Decathlons.

More importantly, however, American Champion has made two significant enhancements to the design. One was in response to a string of fatal airframe failures that led to an emergency airworthiness directive (more on this later). The other was to re-engineer the wing structure, replacing the wooden spars with aluminum ones.

This last move is a shrewd one. Not only does it remove a potential source of liability (wood tends to rot, sooner or later, if not impeccably maintained), it gives American Champion a nice side business in modifying the existing fleet. The company is so interested in getting the wooden wings out of circulation that it offers a core refund for every returned set, regardless of condition.

Handling

It's easy for the "old-timers" and ex-military pilots out there to forget that nearly all GA pilots who've gotten their training in the last 30 years or so have never had the experience of flying a taildragger or, for that matter, an airplane with a stick.

Speaking as one of those "youngsters," this editor can heartily recommend it. It's a real eye-opener, a humbling experience, and a whole lot of fun, as my brief hands-on experience in a 7ECA Citabria showed me. (Ironically, that same airplane showed up in our accident survey. It was groundlooped in August, 1991.)

Taildraggers, of course, are negatively stable when rolling down the runway—that is, the c.g. is behind the geometric center of the landing gear, and it really wants to be in *front* of the pivot point. Therefore, it's up to the pilot to keep it back there where it belongs. The gyrations of a novice usually wind up looking like a fair imitation of the venerable "drunken farmer" airshow routine.

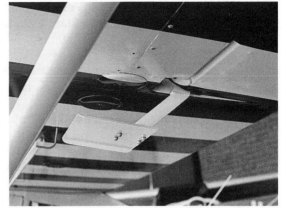

Aileron "spades" go a long way towards reducing the heavy aileron stick forces.

It's not as squirrely as a more short-coupled airplane like the Pitts, but, to drag out an old cliche, "it ain't no Cessna." (Nosedragger, that is. All you 120 and 140 pilots out there have an airplane that's as demanding as the best [or worst] of 'em.)

Once in the air, the Citabria is delightful. It is definitely a "rudder" airplane. Ignoring the ball results in a horrible, mushy ride: staying coordinated is far more pleasant.

Overall, the handling is quite docile, with plenty of aerodynamic warning before the stall (there's no warning system, by the way, which may partly explain some of the stall/spin accidents our survey turned up). One problem area is aileron forces at high speeds. It takes a lot of muscle to get the airplane to roll, and many Decathlon owners have added "spades" to reduce the stick forces.

Another potential handling trouble spot is PIO (pilot-induced oscillation) during landings. Though certainly not unique to Champion aircraft, the spring-steel main gear can bounce the airplane back up into the air if the pilot dumps it too hard. If he or she fails to go around, another bounce, groundloop and/or nose-over and/or prop strike can result.

Aerobatics (Airbatics?)

The Decathlon, in particular, is quite a capable aerobatic performer. While it'll never win the World Aerobatic Championship, it can hold its own in lower-level competitions. It also is a favorite at airshows: it's larger and slower than a Pitts, so it's easier for the crowd to follow.

The Decathlon can do almost any aerobatic maneuver (there are a few exceptions). Its wing has more ribs and bracing than that of the Citabria, and is stressed to +6, -5 g loading. The fact that it has less dihedral and a semi-symmetric airfoil makes inverted flight much easier than in the Citabria. The shorter wing gives it a 120-degree/sec. roll rate, compared with 60 deg./sec. for the Citabria. A beefed-up fuselage helps give the Decathlon a 20-mph increase in redline airspeed.

The Citabria does have its place, though. It's lighter, takes off in less distance (though the Decathlon is certainly no slouch), can climb faster, and is generally less expensive to operate and maintain. And it's perfectly adequate for casual aerobatics, at lease as long as it's not asked to stay upside down very long.

Comfort

Speaking of controls, an hour in the cockpit of a Citabria may well convince you that control yokes are for the birds. Using a stick is easy and intuitive and, more importantly, it stays out of the way. There's actually room to fiddle with charts and flight logs without having a yoke blocking your lap.

The throttle quadrant is where it should be for a right-handed person, under the left hand. Same for carb heat.

The rudder pedals and brakes, however, are another matter. The rudder pedals are at the front corners of the cockpit, so the pilot's feet are splayed far apart. Earlier models of the airplane have heel brakes, which (while they do work well) are tough to get used to.

On top of that, seat adjustability is limited, so those who are short find that their legs are straight out, spread wide apart, and the stick is too close to the crotch. Pilots who are very tall might have trouble, too.

The seats are comfortable, though, and there's sufficient head and shoulder room for most. Visibility is reasonably good, considering all the struts and so forth that are in the way.

The noise level is about on par with the proverbial boiler factory. Headsets are mandatory if you wish to maintain your sanity or understand a single word said on the radio.

Systems—or Lack Thereof

As one would expect, there's nothing fancy here. The fuel system is utter simplicity, with three sump drains, one direct-reading mechanical gauge in each wing root, and a simple fuel selector. Fuel supply is by gravity feed, of course, but there's also a boost pump.

The inverted fuel system in the Decathlon consists of a fuselage tank above the pilot's feet (not the greatest in terms of crashworthiness).

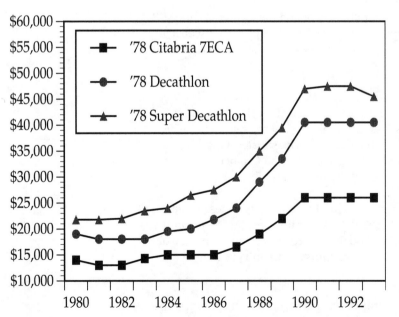

Avionics and instruments are usually fairly Spartan. There's not much room for anything unusual, anyway. The panel is so small that some of the switches are found on the wing root. Rarely is there more than a transponder and single navcom. The layout is non-standard—it has to be, since there isn't room to arrange the instruments in the normal "sacred six" pattern. There isn't much space for gyros in any case.

Maintenance

Lack of amenities, however, has its advantages. After all, if it's not there, it can't break, and that really helps when it comes time to pay the maintenance bill. Though maintenance is simple and low-cost, it pays to seek out a mechanic who's familiar with tube-and-fabric airplanes and who has experience with wood.

The covering is Dacron, which is quite durable. Owners suggest keeping the airplane out of the sun if possible, though, since a re-cover job can be costly and time consuming.

Points of particular interest are corrosion in the tubing, particularly in the vicinity of the tailwheel and aft of the baggage compartment. Also watch for cracked seat backs (there have been accidents in which the pilot's seat back failed, planting his torso on the aft stick with disastrous results).

The landing gear U-bolts can become cracked after a while, especially in airplanes subjected to rough-field or training operations.

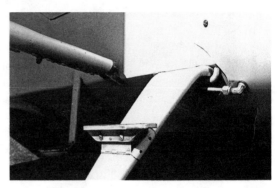

A maintenance item to watch for is the gear attach U-bolt, seen here above the fuel line fitting.

Beware of any airplane that's had any sort of wing damage. The wooden spars may be cracked, and any suspect wing should be dealt with as outlined in FAA AC43-16. Speaking of wings, there's also a service bulletin covering the wing rib nails. A full set of service bulletins should be a part of any owner's (or prospective owner's) library, since they can point out areas of weakness.

Design Improvements

Just in the last few years there have been two significant developments regarding the Decathlon: redesign of the lift strut attach fitting and the development and certification of an all-aluminum wing structure to replace the older wooden spar/metal rib skeleton.

The lift strut attach fitting was the culprit in an accident in April, 1990. It had cracked and failed in flight, allowing the wing to fold. It turned out that the part had been improperly heat-treated. This resulted in a factory service bulletin call-

Cost/Performance/Specifications

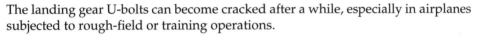

Model	Year	Average Retail Price	Cruise Speed (kt)	Useful Load (lb)	Std/Opt Fuel (gal)	Engines	Remarks	TBO (hr)	Overhaul Cost
7ECA	1964-65	$11,500	95	590	36	100-hp Cont. O-200-A	No flaps	1,800	$10,000
7ECA	1966-69	$14,750	104	590	36	115-hp Lyc. O-235-C1	No flaps	2,000	$9,500
7ECA	1970-73	$17,750	104	590	36	115-hp Lyc. O-235-C1	No flaps	2,000	$9,500
7ECA	1974-77	$23,000	104	590	36	115-hp Lyc. O-235-C1	No flaps	2,000	$9,500
7ECA	1978-84	$28,500	104	590	36	115-hp Lyc. O-235-K2C	No flaps	2,000	$9,000
7GCAA	1968-71	$18,000	112	510	36	150-hp Lyc. O-320-A2D	No flaps	2,000	$9,500
7GCAA	1972-75	$22,300	112	510	36	150-hp Lyc. O-320-A2D	No flaps	2,000	$9,500
7GCAA	1976-78	$27,500	112	510	36	150-hp Lyc. O-320-A2D	No flaps	2,000	$9,500
7GCAA	1979-80	$31,000	112	510	36	150-hp Lyc. O-320-A2D	No flaps	2,000	$9,500
7KCAB	1967-70	$19,400	112	510	36	150-hp Lyc. IO-320-E2A	Inverted	2,000	$11,500
7KCAB	1971-74	$22,000	112	510	36	150-hp Lyc. IO-320-E2A	Inverted	2,000	$11,500
7KCAB	1975	$26,000	112	510	36	150-hp Lyc. IO-320-E2A	Inverted	2,000	$11,500
7KCAB	1976-77	$27,500	112	510	36	150-hp Lyc. AEIO-320-E2B	Inverted	2,000	$12,000
7GCBC	1967-70	$18,300	110	500	36	150-hp Lyc. O-320-A2B	Flaps	2,000	$9,500
7GCBC	1971-74	$22,000	110	500	36	150-hp Lyc. O-320-A2B	Flaps	2,000	$9,500
8KCAB-150	1971-75	$27,000	121	530	40	150-hp Lyc. IO-320-E1A	Inverted	2,000	$11,500
8KCAB-150	1976-78	$37,000	121	530	40	150-hp Lyc. AEIO-320-E1,2B	Inverted	1,600	$12,000
8KCAB-150	1979-80	$44,300	121	530	40	150-hp Lyc. AEIO-320-E2B	Inverted	1,600	$12,000
8KCAB-180	1977-79	$49,500	131	530	40	180-hp Lyc. AEIO-360-H1A	Inverted	1,400	$13,000
8KCAB-180	1980-84	$58,800	131	530	40	180-hp Lyc. AEIO-360-H1A	Inverted	1,400	$13,000

Prices from Aircraft Bluebook Price Digest

ing for repetitive inspection and an NTSB safety recommendation which asked the FAA to issue an AD. The recommendation also cited five other examples of cracked fittings, none of which resulted in an accident, and stated that the entire fleet of Decathlons might have the bad fittings. A rare Emergency Airworthiness Directive was issued later that year, making the inspections mandatory until a new fitting was designed and produced. That has since been done.

The other major development, the metal wing, has been certified and is presently being retrofitted to existing Decathlons. Reportedly a version for the Citabria is in the works.

Accidents

These airplanes are great for low-and-slow, "fun" flying. As a result, there are a lot of the kinds of accidents one would expect from this sort of activity. In an accident survey covering 1986 to late 1991 and the entire Bellanca 7 and 8 series, the types of accidents that stand out are those stemming from low flying (including aerobatics performed at altitudes too low to recover) and, naturally, the groundloop.

Groundloops are relatively rare in tricycle-gear airplanes, but extremely common in taildraggers. Even the Champions, which are docile by taildragger standards, are squirrely on the ground: 49 (or 27.5 percent) of the 178 accidents on our survey were either takeoff or landing ground-loops. Landing accidents were more common: only seven of the 49 were takeoff groundloops.

The good news about groundloops is that they're fairly benign accidents. The airplane is moving slowly, so injuries are uncommon. None of the groundloops was fatal, and only nine involved injuries.

Right behind groundloops were stalls, mostly stall/spins. There were 24, or 13.5 percent of the total. Half were fatal. The stall behavior of the airplane isn't that bad: rather, these accidents occurred more as a result of the kind of flying performed. Five of these accidents directly involved aerobatics flown at altitudes that didn't leave enough room for spin recovery. Another five involved low flying or buzzing Another five came during banner-tow operations.

Speaking of low flying, in addition to the five stall/spins noted above, low flying was implicated in another 21 accidents, seven of which involved aerobatics. Some 11 of the low-flying accidents resulted in fatalities.

Thus, better than half of the accidents—94 in all—fell in only three categories:

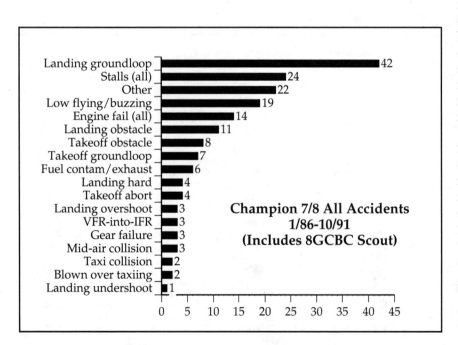

Champion 7/8 All Accidents
1/86-10/91
(Includes 8GCBC Scout)

groundloops, stalls, and low flying, including aerobatics.

There was a fair number of accidents (19) that involved collisions with obstacles on the ground. Many of these were as a result of bushplane-type operations.

Notably lacking is the usual number-one killer for small airplane pilots, the VFR into IFR accident—there were only three. There also were very few engine-failure accidents: only 14, (7.9 percent) while some other singles have engine-failure accident rates up in the 20-25 percent range. There wasn't a single fuel-mismanagement accident, were only five fuel exhaustion accidents and one fuel contamination accident.

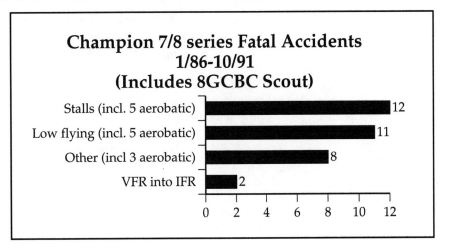

These statistics speak volumes about the airplane. First, docile as it is among taildraggers, it's still quite a handful. Second, many of the accidents come as a direct result of the airplane being used for the things it does best—low, slow flying and aerobatics. Last, its simplicity and durability is attested to by the relative lack of mechanical failure or system mismanagement accidents.

Sources

Unlike many airplanes, there is a variety of sources for parts. First and foremost, of course, is American Champion. They're located in Rochester, Wisc., (414) 534-6315.

Another place to go for parts and service is Santa Paula, Calif., home of Air Repair, (805) 525-5553, and Screaming Eagles, (805) 525 7121, a pair of shops that specialize in the line. Air Repair can sell you copies of all the factory service bulletins, a worthwhile investment.

Conclusion

At the very least, pilots owe themselves some time in one of the Champion line. They're special-purpose airplanes, to be sure, but pleasantly different from the run-of-the-mill "modern" airplane. Some stick time in one will show many pilots a side of aviation they've never seen before.

If the mission (low, slow, and entertaining) meets the pilot's needs, the Citabria is a worthy choice.

Owner Comments

I've flown my 1975 7GCBC Citabria about 600 hours in the last eight years. It's currently got about 1,700 hours total. I burn leaded mogas with a Petersen STC. I use it mostly for fun flying and recreational aerobatics, with one or two long trips each year.

Cruise performance is about the same as a C-172, and climb is much better due to the lower weight. A problem related to weight is that the airplane is at gross with two adults and half tanks. My wife complains about the view of the back of my neck, but it's handy to have her in the back seat to hold the wings level while I fold a chart (stability in cruise flight is more-or-less neutral).

Aerobatic performance is fine for basic loops and aileron rolls. I avoid negative-g maneuvers because it bothers me to see the oil pressure drop to zero with the prop windmilling.

A Citabria is about as simple and reliable as any airplane flying. Annuals run about $200, with me doing most of the work. I'd estimate my total operating costs, including reserves, at about $50/hr (this would be lower if I flew it more). The battery seems to have been the biggest maintenance item. It needs to be cleaned and checked monthly if the airplane is doing aerobatics. It's a pain to work on because it's located in the aft fuselage inside a sealed plastic box.

The plane has been down for quite a while for a recover due to hail damage. While the wings were open, we discovered that some of the nails that fasten the ribs to the spars were unserviceable. They were replaced with improved nails (there's a service bulletins covering this). Other than the nails, the wings were in good shape. I'll reserve judgment for a few years on whether the new aluminum spars are superior to spruce.

Univair has about all the airframe parts one could want for a Citabria. I've tried a couple of times to deal with American Champion, but they weren't positive experiences. If I were advising someone who was looking for a used Citabria or Decathlon, I'd tell them to buy the whole set of service bulletins and use them as a guide for a pre-purchase inspection. I'd further advise them to find a mechanic who genuinely likes tube-and-fabric airplanes. Finally, I'd tell them to plan to store the airplane, at least in the shade. (A recover job costs $2,000 for materials and takes 250-300 man-hours.)

Paul Maseman
Tucson, Ariz.

I own a 1975 7KCAB Citabria with a total time of 1,850 hours. The aircraft was rebuilt in 1985 and recovered using the Stits process. I've put about 400 hours on it since then.

While I use the airplane mostly for pleasure and limited aerobatics, I do take it on a cross-country now and then. Because the POH does not give information on startup/taxi/climb fuel burn, time or distance I simply plan for eight gph. This turns out to be fairly accurate when cruising at 9,000-12,000 feet and 2,450 rpm. These altitudes and rpm settings usually produce a ground speed of 100 to 105 knots.

With two adults and full fuel the airplane is usually right at its gross weight of 1,650 lbs, so there isn't much left over for carrying baggage. The takeoff performance at gross weight, however, is surprisingly good even during the summer months at high elevation airports in the mountains of northern Arizona and New Mexico.

One major source of problems has been the Bendix fuel injector servo used on the airplane's Lycoming AEIO-320-E2B engine. My particular servo has been pulled for repair four times—twice while I have owned the airplane. The last time it was pulled in response to a failure of an internal seal in the servo which caused it to deliver too much fuel to the engine. This "flooded" the engine, which rendered it incapable of delivering more than about 1,500 rpm without running very roughly. This occurred in flight, and fortunately I was able to make it to an airport. I've since learned that Bendix issued several service bulletins dealing with product improvements to this servo.

During the summer months the engine tends to run hot, with oil temperatures reaching 230 degrees after long climbs. With the engine running this hot, there's some problem with vapor locking in the fuel lines; however, use of the boost pump has eliminated any fluctuating fuel pressure problems. Once the oil temperature cools off to about 180 degrees the fuel pressure remains steady without use of the boost pump.

Ultra-simple, direct-reading mechanical fuel gauges are located in the wing roots.

With an oil consumption rate of about a quart every eight hours and annual costs which run about $300, the airplane is relatively inexpensive to operate. If I need parts, they can usually be obtained through American Champion Aircraft.

The Citabria is a lot of fun to fly and is a stable taildragger to handle on the ground. All in all, it's a wonderful little airplane.

Peter Baker
Phoenix. Ariz.

I owned a 1970 Champion Citabria 7ECA for about one year. My previous airplane was a 1974 Cessna Skylane. With all of my training in a C150, then the Skylane, I was slightly apprehensive about the transition to a Citabria, particularly after reading previous comments about it in your publication. Much to my surprise, I found the little taildragger about as tame as you could imagine. My insurance carrier required me to get 10 hours of dual, of which half was spent shooting landings, the rest being an introduction to basic aerobatics. I found the airplane simple to land, either three-point or wheel landings (I prefer the latter). The only thing that took getting used to were the heel brakes—once you had your heels on them, however, they worked fine.

For a simple, fun-to-fly airplane, the Citabria would be hard to beat. Preflight is a five-minute affair. Entry and exit are only slightly tricky, but once inside I found ample room for my 6'1", 200-lb. frame. The overhead switches for the magnetos and other necessities again are different, but seem quite normal after a few times. The Citabria is a bit on the loud side, but then, what isn't? Headsets are a must.

Ground handling is very good. The heel brakes don't seem to get in the way at all. Occasional taps are all you need to spin the airplane around like a top. Takeoff distances are short, even with two aboard and full fuel. The tail comes up quickly, and the rudder is more than adequate for staying lined up with the runway. Once in the air, the controls are nice, with slightly more effort required for the ailerons. Fuel burn is around five gph.

Landings, even in moderate crosswinds, never seemed to present any problems.

The rudder provided positive control throughout the landing rollout.

The cost of ownership was reasonable, as far as I was concerned. Insurance for a non-instrument-rated pilot of 150 hours with no previous taildragger experience was $1,200 a year. Nonscheduled repairs for my year of ownership included a new set of brakes ($25) [presumably pads—Ed.] and a new cowl door ($75 plus paint).

All in all, I regret my decision to sell the Citabria. It provided me with all I really needed, but I saw the new Super Decathlon at Oshkosh this year, and perhaps....

John Knuth
Beecher, Ill.

I own a 1974 Citabria with the 115 hp, O-235-C engine. It's a fun, fun airplane. Inexpensive to fly and maintain, and you can fly it straight and level or turn it upside down if you like. It has no complex systems, so there's not much that can go wrong. Other than the known Lycoming cam problems, the engine is fairly bulletproof.

My only real concern with the airplane is the aging wooden spar. With the reports I've read about spar failures in Scouts and strut bracket failures in Decathlons, I've made it a practice to always wear a parachute when doing aerobatics. When the metal spar becomes available for the Citabria, it will probably be at the top of my priority list.

I don't consider it a good cross-country aircraft because of its slow cruise speed. But for sightseeing and simple aerobatics it can't be beat.

Here are some specific comments:

• Performance and loading—The 7ECA with the 115-hp engine is an excellent performer. This is almost double the horsepower of the old 7AC Champ which, of course, had a lower empty weight. At gross, the aircraft will climb about 700 fpm. Getting into or out of any field (even small ones) is never a problem. When doing aerobatics, the airplane must be put in a dive to reach the entry speed—but then, so does the 150-hp version. Full tanks and two people will bring the airplane to maximum gross.

• Handling—As taildraggers go, the Citabria is a very docile, easy-to-fly airplane. But to a pilot with no taildragger experience, it's all he or she can do to keep it on the runway (at least until the pilot's used to it). The controls are very responsive, and with the proper technique crosswinds are handled easily. The heel brakes are no problem once you get used to them.

• Cockpit—The front seat in my airplane does not move and since I am 6' tall, if I stretch my legs out, I can touch the firewall. This can be a little uncomfortable on a long flight. Actually, I feel more comfortable in the rear seat. Getting in and out of the Citabria is not a problem once you get a routine down. Lifting something heavy into the rear baggage compartment can be a little awkward.

Barry Palmer
East Hanover, N.J.

Aviat Husky

Even to the initiated, from a distance a Husky looks like a Super Cub. Though traditional-looking, the Husky is one of very few light airplanes certified to FAA Part 23 as opposed to the older CAR 3.

It is a very carefully thought-out airplane and has a number of features that distinguish it from other two-seat tail-draggers, as will be detailed later. Essentially, it was designed to satisfy what its originator, Frank L. Christensen, saw as a limited market for a light utility aircraft.

History

Christen Industries is now Aviat, Inc. Christensen, who was sole owner, sold his interests to Malcolm White, a businessman and aviation enthusiast from England. Apparently, only the name has changed. The principal officials and functionaries at the Afton, Wyo. plant and, more important, the products, remain the same.

Christen Industries started in the early 1970s as a supplier of specialized accessories for sport-aviation enthusiasts. These ranged from inverted oil systems (which became standard Lycoming factory issue) and fuel pumps to pilot restraint systems. Then the Eagle aerobatic biplane was introduced. This is broadly credited with teaching the homebuilt industry how to package a kit (although dear old Jim Bede deserves some of the credit for that, too). In 1982, Christensen purchased the type certificates for the Pitts family of aerobatic biplanes. These continue in production at the Afton facility.

Fifty Years of Experience

The design had to complement the experience and techniques used by the Afton workforce and facility that Christensen had acquired in the early 1980s. That facility, where aircraft have been manufactured for more than 50 years, produces two certified versions of the Pitts Special (a third is available on special-special order) as well as the Christen Eagle kit-built biplane. Tube and fabric, with a bit of metal bending thrown in, essentially describes the technology of the facility (which should in no way demean the considerable skills represented there).

At the time Christensen began the Husky project, no light utility aircraft were being manufactured. He tried to buy the rights to the Super Cub, the Champion line and the Interstate/Arctic Tern, but considered the asking prices (including the assumption of product lia-

The Husky's climb performance is impressive. Steep climb angles, high climb rates and short takeoff ground rolls permit operation from extremely short fields.

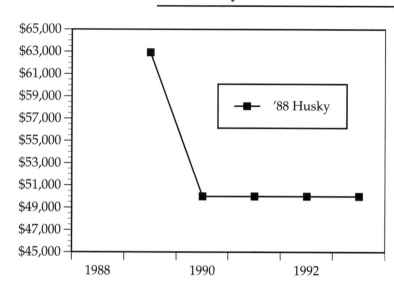

bility for previously produced airplanes) unrealistic.

He and E. H. "Herb" Andersen, Jr. determined that they could develop and certify their own design at lower cost and in less time than would be required in taking on an existing product.

The A-1 Husky was designed and proved in 18 months from initial design work to certification, which was obtained in July, 1987. The prototype was completed and flying in just seven months.

Airplane Description

Principal design objectives were good short- and rough-field performance; ruggedness, accessibility and serviceability to simplify support in primitive conditions; outstanding slow-speed handling coupled with docile stall characteristics; good endurance and reasonable cruise capability.

As mentioned above, the end product is a quite conventional-looking two-seat, tandem tail dragger. In terms of materials and structure also, the Husky is very straightforward. The fuselage is welded 4130 chrome/moly tubular steel with a full-depth aft fuselage for greater strength. The aircraft is powered by a Lycoming O-360-C1G rated at 180 hp mated to a TRW/Hartzell constant-speed propeller.

The engine cowl and forward fuselage are skinned with aluminum. The aft fuselage and flying surfaces are covered with a polyester fabric; the seams are taped with cotton and fastened to the structure by oversized pop rivets.

The wings are fabricated with dual aluminum spars and aluminum ribs. They are supported by fore and aft struts. These were designed of fixed length to eliminate corrosion and other problems that have been encountered in a large number of strut-braced airplanes.

Much of the airplane can be "field stripped" quickly. For instance, the nose bowl is split to permit fast removal without touching the propeller assembly; the cowl has large doors on either side for easy engine compartment access; the fuselage is metal-clad to the aft end of the cabin and is made up of several removable panels. The aft fuselage, which includes the battery bay, is accessible through a large panel on the port side.
Provisions for Skis, Too
The Husky is approved for both retractable and wheel replacement skis. The latter are available in widths of from eight to 16 inches. It also is approved for banner or glider tow hook installation and on EDO 89-2000 floats. Large, 24-inch-diameter tundra tires for serious bush work are available.

To simplify manufacturing and provide inventory control, all A-1s are built with float attach fittings installed. The only additions required for float operations are lifting rings and ventral fin. For the same reason, dual-puck brakes—required for the tundra tires—are standard on all aircraft.

The Fowler-type, slotted flaps are hinged to move aft as they are deployed for high lift. Even at full—30 degree—deflection, they provide lift rather than drag.

Design Attention

A great deal of aerodynamic attention has been paid to the ailerons, as well, to compensate for the real estate taken for the flaps. They are symmetrical in section, and the leading edge has a larger radius than the wing trailing edge it abuts to maintain attached air flow during low-speed and high angle of attack flight.

The cockpit seats are fixed structures, with modest comfort adjustments made by changing cushions. The back of the rear seat folds forwa6rd to allow access to the baggage compartment.

Counterbalanced aerodynamic spades hang from the bottom of the aileron leading edge. The spades act to boost aerodynamic authority of the ailerons and to reduce pilot input forces. These devices were borrowed directly from the four-aileron Pitts. The design permits full roll authority well into the stall.

Best and Worst

The Husky has been in production for seven years. Production has been fairly leisurely: a total of 233 A-1s had been sold through 1992.

All changes have been incremental improvements, largely as a result of real-life service experience. To its credit, the company has designed all improvements to be field-retrofittable to existing airplanes. Since early units can be updated by later improvements, there is no better or worse model year. The key for any prospective buyer is to ensure that all modifications and any mandated changes have been performed.

Not so Golden Oldies

In terms of used aircraft, of course, there are many competitors. But most of them are not old just in calendar years; they are long in the tooth and have been sore used. Many strut-braced airplanes, especially the Piper and Champion lines, have

Cost/Performance/Specifications

Model	Year	Average Retail Price	Cruise Speed (kt)	Useful Load (lb)	Std/Opt Fuel (gal)	Engines	TBO (hr)	Overhaul Cost
Husky	1988	$50,000	122	610	50	180-hp Lyc. O-360-C1G	2,000	$10,500
Husky	1989	$56,000	122	610	50	180-hp Lyc. O-360-C1G	2,000	$10,500
Husky A-1	1990	$63,000	122	610	50	180-hp Lyc. O-360-C1G	2,000	$10,500
Husky A-1	1991	$71,600	122	610	50	180-hp Lyc. O-360-C1G	2,000	$10,500
Husky A-1	1992	$78,900	122	610	50	180-hp Lyc. O-360-C1G	2,000	$10,500
Husky A-1	1993	$80,000	122	610	50	180-hp Lyc. O-360-C1G	2,000	$10,500

Prices from *Aircraft Bluebook Price Digest*

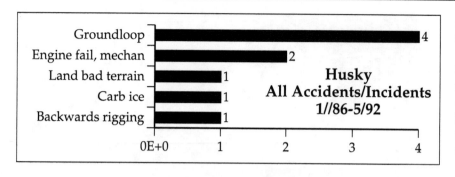

Husky
All Accidents/Incidents
1//86-5/92

suffered from corrosion of strut attach fittings.

Quite a few PA-18s have been used for crop dusting and other abusive applications that have exposed the airframes to additional strain and corrosion.

A number of Husky A-1s were put to work in demanding environments, such as spotting and patrol. Some of these have been operated in excess of 100 hours per month. The comparative newness of the design doesn't mean a given Husky has not had time to be exposed to abuse. So with any airplane in the light utility category, a thorough evaluation of the airplane and supporting records is very important.

In many respects, including fit and finish, performance, good flying qualities and maintainability, the Husky is the class of the category. The fact that it is the only one that has remained in continuous production is an advantage in terms of product support and the likelihood of continuing product improvement.

Flight Handling

Pilots not qualified in conventional gear airplanes (taildraggers) find they need a lot of very basic, old-fashioned flight instruction to adequately fly the Husky and its kin. Foremost among these is coordinated control input. Many of us largely forget, or never learned in the first place, that rudder pedals serve more important functions than foot rests.

Precise control of airspeed and vertical speed also are important. The correct combination of alignment, sink, airspeed and attitude is elusive at first, or if you're rusty. But, my, is it satisfying when achieved.

Tailwheel steering authority on the Husky is good, which makes ground handling simple except in high winds. A touch of differential brake swings the aircraft around briskly. The brakes are powerful. Even at low taxi speeds, over enthusiastic application will bring the tail off the ground (and too much can mean damage to that very expensive constant-speed propeller). It is a very different kind of flying from what most pilots are used to. And pilots of all varieties can benefit from it.

The Husky is a forgiving, straightforward airplane to fly. As such, it would be a good trainer or recurrent reminder for experienced pilots. Forgiving, yet demanding, is perhaps a better description. Bad handling or bad speed control will be rewarded with loss of control. At least recovery can be made quickly.

Properly managed, takeoff ground runs are over in a hurry. The aircraft wants to fly. Power-on stall speed with flaps extended is 38 KIAS. Even at high density altitude, that speed is quickly gained. In a properly managed approach and touchdown, flying is over in a hurry, too. The best technique for assuring the airplane will stay on the ground is to retract the flaps during the brief ground run.

Even maximum performance takeoffs result in continuous climb. There is no sagging-off even while flaps are retracted. It is a credit to the airplane that, once a pilot is familiar with it, such performance does not require superior technique.

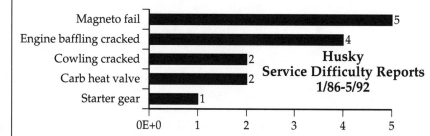

Husky
Service Difficulty Reports
1/86-5/92

Bungee Pull

Aside from managing speed and sink rate control, the biggest trick to landing the Husky is to ensure that the trim is full aft. This requires a high effort if the proper speed is not achieved first, because of the nature of the bungee trim system. This is most difficult in solo flight, because of the forward c.g. bias of the airplane.

With the trim full back, there is still an inch or so of elevator travel in the stick, and it takes some effort to get the tailwheel-low attitude that makes for a satisfactory landing.

The best recovery technique for bounced, poorly aligned or otherwise botched approaches, at least initially, is to add power and go around. The Husky will bounce mightily and can easily get sideways—not a good way to recontact the ground.

With full power, the airplane leaps back into the air; with just a touch, it still flies.

No-flap takeoffs require more ground run, naturally, but taking off in the three-point attitude produces a short run and healthy climbout (1,500 fpm at sea level at the best rate of climb speed of 63 KIAS).

Control harmony is fair. Rudder and aileron forces are pretty linear in relation to airspeed. Because of the bungee trim system, elevator deflection forces are fairly high, even at low speed. In fact, it trims like a heavy airplane—a little bit at a time, and almost always in response to any power or attitude change. Rudder authority is good right down through low-speed flight.

Stability

For a lightly wing-loaded and responsive airplane, the Husky is quite well-mannered in cruise. Properly trimmed, it does not require a lot of attention to maintain course. The different cues in instrument flight and at night—when reflections from the lights on the panel occur in the side windows, workload increases, but it still is better to fly in that environment than many of the other light utility aircraft.

It Can Snap

While the Husky is nearly spin-proof with full flaps, it will reward uncoordinated control input with a snap over the top in power-on stalls in the clean configuration. It will not spin, but the resultant spiral or corkscrew maneuver is more alarming.

Speed builds very quickly during this exercise, and must be attended to immediately. However, almost any reaction leads to recovery. Also, during cruise in turbulent air, speed control is important at most altitudes since indicated airspeed is fairly close to the Vno of 103 KIAS (Vne is 132 KIAS).

Flat-out Virtuous

The big virtue of the Husky is that even during slow flight, properly configured, the attitude of the aircraft is flat; it is flying on the wing rather than hanging on the prop. This is a big safety advantage for spotting, patrol and other low-altitude, low-speed operations, since at these speeds the Husky is not flying on the edge of a stall, and the airplane very largely takes care of itself so that the pilot can safely look elsewhere.

In this configuration, even at altitude, stalls are very mild and recovery almost instantaneous. Even with ham-handed and -footed control inputs, the Husky would not enter a spin.

Great visibility to the side, rear and down is the treat of the operation, next to the docile flying qualities. The thick-chord wing obstructs much visibility above the pilot's eye level, although the skylight helps.

In the hands of a qualified pilot, the Husky can be a good neighbor even at busy airports with a mix of traffic. At the recommended approach speed of 52 KIAS any approach will seem to take all day. But it can be flown at an indicated 100 knots right to the threshold and slowed to proper touchdown speed without Bob Hoover at the controls.

Cockpit/Cabin Comfort

One does not enter the Husky. It is mounted. It takes a nimble person to do it with some grace. The preferred technique is to sit on the door sill, slide aft as far as possible, place the left leg over the stick, grab the overhead structure and slide the right foot and all else into place.

For a conventional-gear airplane, forward visibility is very good for pilots of average to tall height despite the large, high wing (shorter pilots can adjust the view by using thicker seat cushions). There is a transom light overhead which helps spotting traffic in turns.

Long missions in other light utility aircraft can be fatiguing, both because of the constant need to keep the airplane right side up during low-speed operation, and also because control forces—especially roll control—are high and therefore fatiguing. The Husky ranks very favorably in this category, especially after pilots learn to adjust pitch forces by anticipating trim input.

The passenger enjoys the best seat in the house. Visibility and comfort is best in the rear seat. The seat is wider, the angle of the back rest is better, and there is more leg room fore and aft compared to the captain's chair (front seat).

However, solo flight is approved only from the front seat, since only Plastic Man could reach critical controls such as propeller, mixture, mags, carburetor heat and flaps from the rear. Taller pilots with large feet will find that the greatest difficulty flying the Husky is staying off the brake pedals (this is not a problem in the rear seat, because there is more leg room).

Front-Seat Discomfort

One of the biggest shortcomings of the Husky, at least for tall pilots, is the front seat. It is a fixed part of the structure. All adjustments are made by changing cushions. But after an hour or two, discomfort becomes the most noticeable element of flight, overwhelming the good performance, fine visibility and relatively low control effort. This is compounded by the fact that an inertia reel shoulder harness is not currently available in the Husky.

Performance

As already mentioned, slow flight is the Husky's strong suit. It was not designed as a cross-country hauler. But the airplane also has a reasonable cruise speed, quite competitive with modern light aircraft such as the Cherokee, Skyhawk, Skylane and Tobago.

The single door is split top and bottom. There is no speed restriction on flying with both halves or the top half open. The upper element is secured by a hefty clip when open. There are sliding window panels on the port side.

Cruise at 55 percent power is 113 knots; at 75 percent, 121; top speed at sea level is 126. Listed fuel consumption at 55 percent is 7.7 gph; at 75 percent it is 9.3 gph. Still-air range at 55 percent is 695 nm. With power set for an airspeed of 96 KIAS, endurance is seven hours.

After some practice, you can operate the Husky from a football field. Factory numbers for ground runs at sea level are: maximum performance takeoff, 150 feet; landing 250 feet. Even in high density altitude conditions (for instance, at seven to eight thousand feet) and at full gross weight, the Husky's performance is impressive.

It performs very well on floats. Part of this is attributed to close attention to the relative angle of incidence between the floats and the wing. Cruise at 5,000 feet is a quite respectable 106 knots. It will get off the water in eight seconds (approximately 500 feet) in zero wind conditions.

Load Carrying

When loading a Husky, center of gravity is not an issue, since the bias is toward the front end of the range with just one aboard. Standard useful load is 610 pounds. A full load of fuel—300 pounds—leaves 310 pounds of payload available. The baggage compartment behind the rear seat is rated at 50 pounds.

Maintenance Record

Service Difficulty Reports and Airworthiness Directives are fairly slim for the Husky. Three ADs have been issued. They are 90-20-5, 91-14-22 and 91-23-2. The first addressed a problem with the lower elevator lift brace; the second dealt with cracking pilot seat welds; the third replaced the carburetor air intake box.

From January 1, 1986 to May 15, 1992 a total of 23 SDRs have been filed on the Husky. The greatest number (five) concerned faulty magnetos. Four targeted baffles and two lower cowling/inlet air filters and have been attributed to excessive vibration. The others are fairly random.

A number of maintenance complaints that have not resulted in SDRs have been attributed to vibration caused by the direct, relatively rigid engine installation.

Also, there have been cases of high wear in the stainless steel control cables, particularly at pulleys where large turns are made. At one point, the factory considered changing to galvanized control cables. This was not confirmed at press time.

Accident Record

Despite the uses for which the Husky was designed, the wrecking rate in civil service has been fairly benign. Accident records from the beginning of 1986 to May 15, 1992 show no fatal accidents, and only one involving injury (to two people) in a total of nine accidents or incidents.

If you want to play with statistics, an extraordinary 33 percent occurred during cruise. All of these were related to carburetor ice. Another 56 percent occurred during the landing phase, which might be expected with a tail dragger. And two of these five accidents were the result of excessive braking (we said those brakes were powerful).

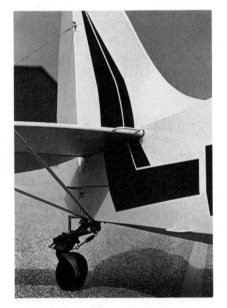

The large eight-inch Scott tailwheel is steerable. Lift/ ground handling points are provided on the aft fuselage and elevator leading edge.

The other accident occurred during takeoff. It was the result of the forward control stick being installed backwards. Public use operations do not report accidents and are not investigated by FAA or NTSB. The U.S. Border Patrol, which purchased a fleet of 14 Huskies, has had a number of accidents.

Two of these reconfirmed that wake turbulence is not peculiar to heavy transport aircraft.

The Border Patrol lost two aircraft as a result of what has been determined by the FAA to be an extreme case of aircraft flying through their own wake, which stalled the elevator and created a nose-down pitching moment from which recovery was not possible at the low altitudes being flown (50 feet AGL or lower).

According to FAA, this phenomenon would be encountered by any aircraft flown in the same configuration and conditions. FAA, based on its and Christen factory test flights, has recommended changed procedures that would enable aircraft to avoid encounters with their own wake.

Safety Analysis

Several Husky accidents suggest the airplane is built stoutly, at least as far as the occupants are concerned. Pilots familiar with this category of airplane have commented that the arrangement of controls, and the handling of the airplane, is better in the Husky than other aircraft.

The biggest shortcoming is the anti-ergonomic front seat design. Another is the lack of inertia reel harness. Increasingly in general aviation, one has to ask: Compared to what? Compared to everything else out there, the Husky is a winner.

Owner Comments

I purchased a Husky in July 1991 to replace a Super Cub that had been destroyed in a tornado/microburst. In my view the only items that would make this a better airplane are a map pocket somewhere around the front seat and thicker windows and windshield to combat noise.

Low-speed handling is excellent, with none of the sloppiness, stop-to-stop control movements necessary in the Cub at either low-speed or high-crosswind situations. The aileron spades on the Husky, similar to those on the Pitts, provide excellent low-speed handling assistance.

Ground stability is excellent, and I believe better than the Cub and other taildraggers in the critical 30-40-mph range where rudder effectiveness is diminished. The bungeed elevator trim is excellent, and unlike the Cub, total trim wheel travel is only a couple of turns. I like the "heavier" feel of the bungee trim.

The construction throughout is very similar to the Pitts, and control linkages are heavy-duty and well balanced. I have flown the aircraft extensively IFR, and it is very stable. The flap system is, in my view, principally useful during heavy takeoffs on short fields. For landing, the flaps seem to produce more lift than drag, and slowing the aircraft down can be a problem.

It seems that smoother landings are made without using flaps. With flaps partially deployed in the pattern, the aircraft still floats extensively. (This may be my landing technique since I have only 75 hours in the aircraft.)

Marshall N. Carter
Boston, Mass.

The Husky is very easy to fly, is a stable instrument platform and meets or exceeds the manufacturer's performance specifications. Problems have been minor. Bushings on rudder hinges have been replaced and polished to ease friction in rudder travel. The same will be done for elevator bushings at the next inspection. The oil pressure/temp gauge was replaced because the factory installation had the capillary tube tight from engine to firewall, and all extra "slack" coiled behind the panel. A new gauge was installed with the full loop between the engine and firewall so it does not have to be over-flexed to remove the oil screen for examination.

The front half of the left side window seems happiest open about an inch and will not stay closed. Elevator trim could use a bit more "up" authority, as the last inch of back stick travel is too stiff.

The cabin heater cooks the pilot's right foot, and nothing else. A heated pitot is not available. Cabin noise is high. Bungees on the landing gear seem a tad stiff. Factory and dealer response has been outstanding. You can always reach one of the Heiner brothers by phone. They are the engineering and factory test pilots, and can answer virtually any question. They are very interested in user experiences.

Based on my experience with the oil pressure/temp gauge problem, the factory installation method has been modified. A new cabin heater plenum will soon to be available based on a user design, and aircraft newer than mine have different trim springs, which will soon be available for retrofit.

Parts availability from the factory has been near instantaneous at reasonable prices. The airplane opens easily for inspection and repair; 100-hour inspections average about $150 inclusive, so far.

Fuel burn is about 10.5 gph at 75% power and about 7.5-8 gph at 55%. Handling qualities are excellent. Short-field ability is truly "less than a football field." Stalls are straightforward, and recovery quick and easy. I do not think it is possible to spin the airplane with full flaps. I am unable to get much of an accelerated stall. It is easier to fly than many taildraggers, tracking very well on the ground, and has ample power to go around from almost any situation.

I could not be happier with the airplane. It is fun to fly, either slowly with the door open, or as fast as a PA-28-181 for cross-country. The finish and workmanship were excellent on delivery, and have held up in more than a year and 400 hours of use. Count me as a very satisfied customer.

I had full IFR avionics installed by Mike Hiett of Specialized Aircraft Services at 4A7. His experience fabricating installations in other Huskies was of great help, because of the limited panel space.

Robert L. Coley
Atlanta, Ga.

I have the first Husky to be put on EDO 2000 floats (after the prototype used for certification). I ordered it in October 1987, and it was finally delivered on June 1, 1989. There was a lot of foot-dragging by EDO Corporation, plus some engineering which had to be remedied by our local Alaskan mechanics who had years of experience installing floats.

The dealer, Bob Hoff, and his wife Jane, of Aero-Mark in Idaho Falls, flew the Husky up on wheels to Island Lake Seaplane Service in North Kenai, where I had the floats waiting. It has been a pleasure doing business with Aero-Mark, as they take excellent care of their customers.

Wide open, I can only hit 110 mph. Bob Hoff blames this slow speed on the fact I didn't put the four streamlined covers on the float attachment fittings. I left these off at my mechanic's suggestion, as he has had firsthand experience with corrosion of the fittings under these covers, especially if operating on salt-water—which I do on my clam digging expeditions.

The Husky is nose heavy, with the big 180-hp Lycoming up front, which means you can really pile stuff in the baggage compartment and the back seat without too much worry about any aft c.g.

All in all, we are pleased with this airplane. We have about 200 hours on it. Our mechanic does the annuals on it in less than a day with my help. So far no major problems have shown up.

Walt Pedersen
Sterling, Alaska

Beech 77 Skipper

The Beech Skipper was barely out of the starting blocks when the Great Aviation Depression set in. Beechcraft built only 312 of these two-place trainers, starting in 1979, and it abruptly halted production in 1981. Most Skippers are now in private hands, though a few still find duty on flight school lines and at Beech Aero Centers across the country. How has the airplane fared, and what can a prospective owner expect from the two-placer? *The Aviation Consumer* takes a look.

History

As a competitor with the Cessna 152, the Skipper actually stood a chance at creating a similar market niche for Beech. Though the design never reached maturation, the Model 77 (its numeric designation) represented a good training airplane. Despite its pleasant flying qualities (and barring a dramatic upswing in the training market), the Skipper has taken its spot on the endangered species list of general aviation, to dwindle through the years from the forces of attrition.

We first flew the Skipper in 1979, reporting on it in our January 1, 1980 issue. At that time we were mostly interested in comparing this newcomer with the Cessna 152 (the all-time training leader) and the Piper Tomahawk (another new design). Startlingly similar in outward appearance to the Tomahawk, the Skipper flew quite differently. It also represented a "major commitment" by Beechcraft to the bottom end of their product line.

Beech started up Beech Aero Centers (more on these later), producing Jeppesen-Sanderson-style textbooks and course materials for flight training. It looked as though Beech was really getting its act together to compete with Cessna Pilot Centers, all the while furthering the brand-loyalty theory of future aircraft sales, their real motive. Then the bottom dropped out.

Light-aircraft deliveries entered the graveyard spiral from which they still have not recovered, and the Skipper was an early casualty. While the Beech Aero Center concept worked at some FBOs, only a few survive to this day. However,

The little two-placer has a nice combination of good looks, pleasant handling and a roomy cockpit.

Beech still publishes a newsletter for Aero Centers, and active clubs have regular fly-ins around the country. We found just such an Aero Center at Hammonton Aviation in Hammonton, N. J.

Takes a Licking and Keeps On Ticking

We even found old serial number 39, the same Skipper we flew back in 1979, on their line. We were very interested to see how it had held up, after nearly 2,000 hours of training and rental time had been put on the tachometer.

Well, the engine had already been overhauled once, after a student taxied into a ditch and caught the prop, causing sudden stoppage. And the tail skid had once been rammed up into the empennage after over-rotation on a soft-field takeoff. This required moderate repair, and the new lines of rivets sit in evidence. Other than that, the airframe had held up pretty well. Oh, there are places where fairings or inspection panels look a little ratty, but this is akin to the cracked plastic fairings one finds on Cessna landing gear and struts. Incidentally, the second Skipper on the line also hit its tail skid, but it didn't take as long to fix. As George Arslanian of Hammonton Aviation said, "We got pretty good at doing tail skid repairs, the second time around."

The tail on the Skipper is reasonably powerful, aerodynamically. But the cause of dinging the skid isn't the T-tail configuration, as many might surmise. No, Beech did its homework with the tail aerodynamics on the Skipper. It delivers good control feel and response right down to taxi speeds, unlike the Tomahawk (and other Pipers with T-tails), which demonstrates an on-again-off-again behavior around rotation speed.

The Skipper's elevator control forces are light, but not so much so that overcontrol is a problem. Cessna 152s bang their tails on the ground from time to time, too, requiring sheet-metal repairs in the area of the tie-down ring. Minor accidents just come with the territory, when airplanes are relegated to the training environs.

Handling Qualities

Our evaluation pilot in 1979 characterized the Skipper "a delight to fly." Today we really can't argue with that appraisal. And our more recent flight was on a hot and gusty day with a strong crosswind—conditions that put not inconsiderable demands on the Model 77. Control forces in the airplane are well harmonized. Control response makes it easy for a student pilot to perceive the effects of his inputs. The Skipper is an "honest" airplane in that it is easy to see what the airplane is doing, versus what the pilot is doing.

Adverse yaw, for instance, is rather pronounced in the Skipper. There is no question about the rudder pressure and movement that the pilot has to employ to coordinate with aileron. However, there is a lack of good directional cues over the engine cowling, so instructors in Skippers have to guide their students' eyes to point out yaw. Pitch attitude is difficult for the beginning student to discern, as well, thanks to the sloping nose as viewed from the pilot's seat (kind of like a Porsche). But no trainer is perfect.

The ailerons on the Skipper are pleasantly light, and the roll rate is perhaps even a bit too high. (But after all, Wolfgang Langeweische does say in *Stick and Rudder*, that aileron design is the most difficult control for airplane builders to work out.) The odd thing about the Skipper's ailerons is that they rather rapidly lose effectiveness as the stall is approached—much more than other trainers. If the pilot continues into a full stall in the airplane, it is very easy to allow some yaw-induced roll to develop. Attempting to pick up the falling wing with aileron yields little result. As soon as the stall is broken, however, the ailerons are ample to right the little ship again.

To Spin or Not?

Adverse aileron at the stall is what will spin a Skipper, however. In fact, it won't spin *without* aggravated aileron at the entry. With no aileron input, you will get a steep spiral, which must be recognized for what it is and recovered from before overstressing the airplane. This leads to the classic dilemma about the use of ailerons in stalls. Should an airplane bite you when you use adverse aileron? Or should the ailerons keep flying right through the stall? Should trainers be spin-resistant, or spin-capable?

It's only our opinion, but we like a wing that gives up flying more definitively, without need for opposite aileron to induce a spin (if indeed a spin is what you wanted in the first place). The bottom line is that the Skipper is different than the Tomahawk or Cessna 152 in this regard. It is actually more like some of the pre-World War II trainers. So instructors in Skippers ought to be sure to discuss stalls and spins in depth with their students.

As a two-seat airplane for the private pilot, the Skipper is very easy to trim. It holds trim speed tenaciously, in fact, regardless of power and flap extension. As a trainer, though, it might have been better to require the student to cope with trim a bit more. Skipper CFIs will have to be careful to make sure their students learn proper trimming. Elevator forces are light enough to allow pilots to just about ignore trim in the landing pattern—a bad habit. Incidentally, the trim indicator is an inaccurate and difficult-to-see affair below the throttle quadrant, so maybe it's good there isn't much need for it—except to make sure it is properly set for takeoff.

Landings and takeoffs in the Skipper are quite easy, even in a gusty crosswind. The airplane has sufficient controllability to do what you want it to do, despite its feeling kite-like (one pilot called it skittery), a trait it shares with the Cessna 152. It is rudder-limited in crosswind authority— more so than a lot of airplanes. The nose is easy to hold off at flare, and there is no tendency toward PIO. The elevator, as we said, is powerful, even at slow speeds.

Skipper interior is wide and roomy. Professional-looking panel is head-and-shoulders above competitive two-placers.

Performance

The Skipper is no homesick angel, that's for sure. Despite the fact that it is equipped with a Sensenich propeller that develops well over 2500 rpm, the airplane takes forever to climb. And we flew it from a strip basically at sea level. We also had only one-third fuel on board. On one touch-and-go we didn't get organized and off again until nearly the end of the

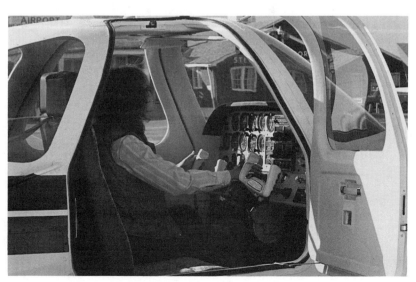

paved runway at Hammonton. We rose to about 50 feet and flew nearly level with the trees for another couple thousand feet. Consciously removing any sideslip remaining from our crosswind takeoff, we got the airplane to climb.

We'd like to fly the Skipper some more, but our impressions in the pattern, and on extended climbs, is that the Skipper is unusually sensitive to sideslip. We did lean the mixture to best power and got well over a hundred rpm more. (Referring to a Lycoming service bulletin about the O-235 engine led to the conclusion that the carburetor is definitely over-rich, and probably should be overhauled.) One thing is for sure—Beech's book figure for rate of climb is exaggerated at 720 feet per minute. The best-climbing trainer around is the Cessna 152, with its advanced-design gull-wing propeller. Operating a Skipper from a high-density-altitude strip with obstacles is something to be considered with caution.

Load Carrying

The load-carrying ability of the Skipper falls right in line with other two-place trainers. Full fuel (29 gallons) and two normal-sized adults puts you at gross weight, or even a tad over. The gross weight is 1,675 pounds, and our test plane had an empty weight of 1,177 pounds, owing to a dual-navcom full-IFR panel; thus, our useful load was just 498 pounds. The cavernous area behind the seats of the Skipper usually goes for naught, since you can't really use it unless you're solo.

The day we flew the Skipper was hot, humid and turbulent. A speed check barely got us up to 85 knots indicated, and this was at 2600 rpm. At 2,500 feet and full throttle we should have been showing upwards of 95 knots, according to the book. Our flight in 1979 came out closer to book figures, so we really couldn't get down to specifics from the later flight. From our previous flight with the Skipper and the similarly configured Piper Tomahawk we know that the Skipper is the slower. The Cessna handily beats both the T-tails.

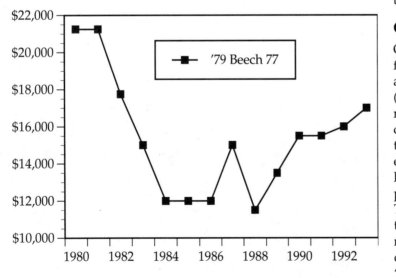

Creature Comfort

One of the Skipper's main claims to fame is its instrument panel, a wide and substantial affair crafted of metal (there is no plastic in sight). Instruments, controls and gauges are logically and clearly laid out, except for the trim indicator we mentioned earlier, and the carb heat lever, which is located and configured like the propeller pitch control on a larger plane. The engine gauges are nicely positioned above the throttle quadrant, and normal scan includes them much more often than in a lot of presumably more "sophisticated" birds.

The other thing nice about the Skipper is its cabin width—fully five inches wider than the Cessna 152's. It may be even a bit *too* wide, in our opinion. We got the impression of being surrounded by the airplane, rather than a part of it. Of course, it takes a shoehorn to get some people into the Cessna, so that's the other end of the spectrum. Cabin noise is quite high, again indicative of an unrefined design. Sitting farther away from your cabinmate means you have to speak up that much more.

Switches and circuit breakers are the typical beefy Beechcraft variety. We overheard a Skipper student say that she felt the metal panel and the kind of no-nonsense presentation were an indication of Beechcraft airplanes overall—solid and reliable. There's no doubt about it. The Skipper may fly differently than other Beechcraft, but it carries a Beechcraft motif throughout. That's okay—the Cessna 152 doesn't exactly fly like its big brother the 210 either, but it certainly *is* a Cessna in shape and form. Thus starts the brand-loyalty scheme of things.

Maintainability

The Skipper seems to be an easy airplane to maintain. We foresee two possible considerations, however, which could cause it to cost more than the ubiquitous Cessna 150/152 series. First, there aren't many Skippers out there. We called several Beech dealers who clearly stated that they had sold Skippers in their day, but that there weren't any around anymore—and certainly none on their flight lines. One dealer said he was a full-line Beech dealer, but when queried about the Skipper said, "Oh, no. We haven't trained or rented those for years; we use the Cessna 152."

NASA-developed GAW wing with its curling trailing edge was supposed to deliver high tech to general aviation airfoils. It delivers lots of lift, but isn't really an improvement over the Cessna 152's wing.

The small number in the Skipper fleet could make finding a mechanic who even recognizes one, much less has a maintenance manual, difficult. We'd recommend a new Skipper owner take his plane to a Beech dealer or Aero Center for his first inspection. The goal in this would be to learn as much as possible about the airplane, as well as to make sure everything is up to snuff (Beech service bulletins, etc.). This tactic would certainly cost a little more the first time around, but you would then be better equipped to direct a non-Skipper A&P at a future inspection.

Cost/Performance/Specifications

Model	Year Built	Average Retail Price	Cruise Speed (kts)	Useful Load (lbs)	Fuel Std/Opt (gals)	Engine	TBO (hrs)	Overhaul Cost
77	1979	$17,000	97	575	29	115-hp Lyc. O-235-L2C	2,000	$10,000
77	1980	$17,500	97	575	29	115-hp Lyc. O-235-L2C	2,000	$10,000
77	1981	$18,000	97	575	29	115-hp Lyc. O-235-L2C	2,000	$10,000

The other problem is a source of parts, the only such being Beechcraft, of course. Beech's parts prices have historically been higher than the rest of the industry, so we'd expect the same for the Skipper. But the Skipper is such a simple airplane that, barring major airframe damage or the need for airframe parts, contributions to the Wichita economy should be minimized.

Powerplant

The engine in the Skipper is the Lycoming O-235-L2C, the same one in the Cessna 152 and Piper Tomahawk. This engine has had its problems with spark plug fouling, stuck valves and hard starting (among others), particularly in the Cessna, though its performance should be airframe-independent. Overhaul cost for the little Lycoming is listed as $10,000 in the *Aircraft Bluebook Price Digest*, about $500 less than the O-320 series. Experience has showed that the O-235 can actually cost more to overhaul, since the likelihood of cylinder and/or valve problems is greater.

The most important maintenance item on the Skipper is the integrity of the exhaust system. When we first opened the door of our '79 test ship, we immediately noticed the presence of a carbon monoxide test strip, an indication that leaky exhaust can spell trouble in this airplane. There was a rash of muffler problems with early Skippers, and the cabin design lends itself to sucking in stray exhaust and promptly turning a test strip black—perhaps because of the control cable channel on the underbelly of the plane. The muffler and stack design were changed early on, and all Skippers should have the newer system, but it would make sense always to pay particular attention to the exhaust on this bird.

A minor but annoying item has to do with the fuel tank vents, located near the wing root and leading edge of each wing. It is easy to bump one of the vents (a short piece of aluminum tubing facing into the airstream), and inadvertently cause an imbalance of fuel flow from the tanks. Apparently, if the vents aren't exactly symmetrical between the left and the right, a slight pressure differential results between fuel tanks. The Skipper's fuel system has positions for both or off, so in the both position the fuel can flow preferentially from one wing. Though the flow will proceed normally with quite divergent readings on the gauges, Skipper instructors tell us it's difficult to convince a student that things are okay when one tank reads empty and the other one is still quite full.

SDRs

A search of FAA Service Difficulty Reports filed by mechanics revealed no statistically significant trends concerning the Model 77. There *were* quite a number of reports filed on the shoulder harness attach brackets, but these were back in 1981. The bracket was promptly covered by an Airworthiness Directive late in that year, correcting the problem. It was the same situation with door hinges, save for the AD. Check the door alignment and hinges on any Skipper you're eyeing, for (as with the Tomahawk) latching the doors can be a pain. And since it is common practice to leave the doors open on the ground to improve ventilation, fumbling around with the overhead latch comes at just the wrong time—right as you're cleared onto the active runway. Also, check the nose gear fork, since Beech issued a "mandatory" service bulletin calling for inspections and noting the wheel could break off if cracks progressed sufficiently.

Accident History

We found four fatal accidents involving Skippers. One resulted from a student

The Skipper and the Tomahawk, two "modern" competitors for the throne of the Cessna 152. The Beechcraft has generally better workmanship than the Piper, and less dramatic stall behavior.

pilot taking a friend on an "unauthorized" night flight and losing control of the plane. He had no night experience. Another pilot had been known to skip his wheels on the surface of a lake. Nothing was found but a wheel floating in the water. The third Skipper struck trees on a VOR approach after the plane stalled due to excessive ice on the wings. And the last was a stall/spin after the engine failed because of a loose nut on an exhaust valve adjusting screw. The plane was on its test flight after top overhaul—the mechanic was in the left seat.

 The other Skipper accidents were almost exclusively training-related: propeller strikes, smashed nose gears, veering off runways, landing short—that sort of thing. With the Skippers finding themselves in private hands in increasing ratio, these accidents should decline in frequency in the future.

Summing Up

We still like the Skipper, though our editor on this assignment would have to disagree with the earlier assessment that the Skipper has more retail appeal than the 152. The Skipper flies as well as the Cessna, but it's a "fifty-footer" in comparison. Sure, it looks pert, cute and friendly from a distance. But closer than 50 feet and you notice the bluntness of the cowl, the rivet heads along the whole fuselage (Beech uses such big rivets), the unsculptured sheet metal construction of the whole plane. The Cessna, on the other hand, benefits from years of evolution, so its lines are about as cleaned-up as can be cost-effectively accomplished on a two-seater.

The Skipper can be had for a little less money than a 152. The Cessnas are growing in value as flight schools snap up the good ones for their fleets. But the Beech might cost a little more to maintain in the long run, owing to its different-ness (there weren't enough made) and the unknowns of parts prices. The Skipper is noisier and slower than the 152. Its lethargic rate of climb should be of concern where it matters, but otherwise could be lived with.

The good visibility, roomy cabin and flighty controls make it fun to fly for both pilot and passenger. It would be nice to see a turnaround in general aviation include the resumption of Skipper production, but don't hold your breath.

Beech Musketeers 19, 23

As the parade of aircraft cancelled for lack of interest—or overwhelming price shock—grows longer, the Beech Sundowner and Sport vie for attention as affordable, if unexciting basic transportation with wings.

In a world where performance and looks have always been boasting points, prosaic matters like cabin room and ease of access, instead, are the most often quoted selling points for these two models. "You may get there faster, in another airplane" their owners frequently concede, "but we'll arrive in greater comfort."

Alas, they won't arrive with the elegance of the rest of the Beech models, since the Sundowners and Sports were the curious legacy of a Musketeer line that sacrificed panache for utilitarianism. They used sensible construction materials like sandwich foam, and employed assembly line economies like constant-chord wings and skin bonding. Though they were designed with admirable qualities like fine, massive one-piece windshields, mile-wide landing gear and tough-enough construction to permit a utility category rating at full gross, they've rarely dazzled the beholder with good looks.

A Sundowner flares for the landing, the scenario for trouble if good speed control is not used. A bungled, bounced landing can wipe out the nosegear and prop. Stiff rubber shock mounts in the landing gear contribute to the bounce problem.

History

The Musketeers come in two basic models: the 19 and the 23. The Model 19 is powered by a 150-hp Lycoming and normally seats two. The Model 23 will seat four and most often comes with a 180-hp Lycoming. (We won't consider the retractable-gear Sierra Model 24 in this report.)

As with the Piper Cherokee, the Musketeer went through a series of engine changes before settling down. The first Musketeer in 1963 appeared with a 160-hp Lycoming. (The first 160-hp Cherokee had led the way two years earlier.) In 1964 Beech switched engines, putting in an oddball 165-hp Continental IO-346-A. Basically an IO-520 with two cylinders lopped off, it tended to run hot in the Musketeer.

This A23 model lasted until 1968, when it was succeeded by the 180-hp B23. Meanwhile, in 1966, Beech had brought out its Model 19 Sport, a 150-hp trainer that seated two and weighed in at a gross 150 pounds less than that of the A23. In 1970, the two models became the B19 and C23, respectively.

The Sport went through some strange weight machinations as the FAA discovered that the 2,250-pound-gross B19 could not meet minimum certification standards for climb performance at that weight. So AD 73-25-4 was issued, limiting the gross weight of all B19s built up to then to 2,000 pounds. That included serial numbers MB-481 through -616. When a special Beech kit was installed, the gross could be raised back up to 2,150 pounds. All the Sports built after 1973 incorporated the mods and had gross weights of 2,150 pounds.

The B19 continued in production until 1979, when the two-place Beech Skipper made its bow (and itself experienced an ephemeral existence; production was halted in 1981). The Beech 23 Sundowner held on until 1983, when it also bit the dust.

Performance

Lackluster is perhaps a flattering description for both models. Owners talk about getting a TAS of from 91 to 100 knots in the Sport, and 100 to 117 knots in the Sundowner. These speeds are easily eclipsed by all their competitors.

The Sport has a cavernous cabin, but fill it to gross on a warm day, and expect a dismal climb rate and service ceiling.

Climb performance, especially in the Sport, can be downright dismal, especially on a hot day. Said one owner, "On a hot day at full gross count on 300-400 fpm climb *max*." Another wrote, "I have noticed at or near gross weight, my Musketeer falls off in performance in hot weather much more than the book shows." To be fair, however, several owners claimed the handbook figures claimed by Beech were quite realistic. One said he was able to climb to 9,500 feet at an average of 500 fpm with a cruise climb of 81 knots. Said another, "The speed, rate-of-climb, etc. figures published by Beechcraft are reasonable and not exaggerated."

Indeed, for the Sundowner, Beech listed the 75-percent cruise at 8,500 feet at only 136 mph, and claimed only a 792-fpm rate of climb at sea level with full throttle, loaded to gross weight.

Payload and Range

Except for earlier models of the Sport, both the 19 and 23 carry 57 gallons of usable fuel. With the Sport, that translates to a range with reserve at high cruise of about 620 nm. With the Sundowner, the figure is about 530 nm. Competitors of the Sundowner with the same 180 hp—like the Piper Cherokee, Gulfstream American Tiger and Cessna Cardinal—all carry about seven gallons less fuel. But their greater speed allows them to cover about the same distance on less fuel.

Naturally, if you load the cabins of any of these airplanes with people and baggage, to stay within the weight limits, you normally have to take off with a lot less fuel than the tanks will hold. Since the Sundowners can be expected to have an equipped useful load of about 900 pounds, that means hauling three people and a bit less than 50 pounds of baggage with full fuel. With the Sport, figure on two people and full fuel—but watch the climb.

In summary, the useful load of the Musketeers compares quite closely with the others in their class.

Cabin Comfort

Here is where all the Musketeers shine. The cabins are big and roomy, with space to spare. And all but some of the earlier models have entry doors on both sides of the cabin—a nice feature—though some owners complained of leaking doors.

Handling Qualities

Owners talk in flattering terms about Musketeer handling characteristics—*in the air*. They report smooth and responsive controls, and stability in rough air. But one owner complained of a "severe" pitchup when flaps were lowered anywhere in the white arc.

The great handling shortcoming of the Musketeers is generally acknowledged to be wicked landing habits—corroborated by accident tallies on the birds. They have a distinctly unpleasant porpoising tendency, and many a student—and even quite a few fully rated pilots—have put on a memorable display of kangaroo leaps down the runway—often ending in calamity with a collapsed nose gear and damaged prop—and therefore an engine that is a candidate for a teardown.

The trailing beam landing gear has rather stiff rubber shock absorbers instead of air-oil oleos, as on most lightplanes. And pilots ruefully note how an inadvertent three-point touchdown on this gear can result in a series of jolting crow hops down the runway before the pilot is aware of what's happening.

Musketeer owners who responded to our call for comments reported awareness of this unhappy reputation. But they figured they had mastered the idiosyncrasy and were happy with their machines. Observed one matter-of-factly: "Precise speed control is important because there is a tendency to porpoise." As with the Mooney, you carry a higher-than-needed airspeed into the flare at your own risk.

Once safely slowed down on the ground, the landing gear is praised, at least for its turning alacrity. Using just nosewheel steering alone without brakes, the Musketeers will pivot in their own wing length—great for maneuvering around the ramp, and parking.

Aerobatic Bonus

Both aircraft, incidentally, are certified for aerobatics (with only two aboard, of course) when equipped with features like quick-release doors, G-meters and inertial reel shoulder harnesses. Pilots may be reassured to know the aircraft is strong enough to handle this rating without extra strengthening measures.

Strength notwithstanding, with hard landings a fact of life for many Musketeers, it pays to check landing gear, engine mounts and wing attach fittings with special care.

Safety Record

As we mentioned earlier, Musketeer owners who commented to us for this report wrote that they were aware of the reputation of their aircraft for landing problems but were able to compensate. Unfortunately, the safety statistics suggest that a frightening number of other Musketeer pilots were not able to do so. A search of the accident records for Model 19s and 23s for 1980 through 1985 discloses by far the greatest proportion of accidents stems from botched landings—ballooning, porpoising, bouncing, loss of directional control, hard landings—you name it.

Though seldom fatal, these accidents exacted a high toll in machinery, with a sizable number of nosegears being lopped off and props (and presumably engines) damaged. On one occasion the pilot actually bashed off the nosegear but took the aircraft around, only to come around to the inevitable crunch on a final landing with only two main landing wheels.

Has the metal carnage diminished over the years? Hardly at all, as far as we could tell. For the five years overall, we estimated that about 46 percent of all Musketeer accidents involved landing mishaps. For the Model 19 Sport, 55 percent of the accidents were botched landings of one kind or another. For the Model 23 the figure was slightly lower—41 percent.

Student Calamities?

Are students perpetrating most of the damage on the landing accidents? Our tally suggests that about 64 percent of the landing problems on the Sports involved student pilots—which would seem appropriate for a trainer. And on the Sundowner, 39 percent of the landing prangs were perpetrated by students.

In a special study of accident patterns among 33 aircraft over the five-year span from 1972 through 1976, the NTSB ranked the Model 23 Sundowner worst in the hard landing category—and nearly five times as bad as both the Cherokee and Skyhawk.

In terms of overall safety rating, the Model 23 came out in the same study with a rather mediocre record—once again, not as good as aircraft like the Cherokee and Skyhawk. The Sundowner came up with a fatal accident rate of 2.5 per 100,000 flying hours, vs. 1.97 for the Cherokee PA-28 series and 1.47 for the Cessna 172. It bested the Gulfstream Traveler, however, at 2.94.

Another accident category in which the Model 23 fared poorly was overshoots. The Sundowner was third worst among the 33 compared, following only the Grumman Traveler and the Cessna 195.

Our study of accidents over the five years from 1981-1985 showed no other particular pattern, though in three instances carburetor ice was suspected of

Double cabin doors on all but early model Sundowners and Sports make for easy access.

Owners report door and windshield leaking in rain can cause instrument damage.

causing engine failure accidents, and in 16 instances Musketeer pilots either exhausted their fuel totally or ran a tank dry.

Landing Strategies

Some experienced Musketeer flight instructors we talked with said they felt the aircraft was unjustly maligned for its landing characteristics. They stressed that the key element behind most of the landing (and takeoff) problems is proper speed control. The villain in almost every instance, they said, is too much speed on final and in the flare. If the pilot tries to plant the aircraft on the runway too soon, it will bite. The greater springback reaction from the rubber shock on the nosegear (than from a conventional oleo strut) can be expected to generate a healthy bounce, and the chain of awkward events has begun, unless the pilot knows how to make a recovery.

One instructor said he told students to aim for an approach speed of 1.3 Vso (flaps-down stall speed), subtracting a knot or so for each hundred pounds under gross. He said that actually the wide landing gear stance on the Musketeers allowed them to handle greater crosswind components than many other aircraft. But the brakes seem more effective than normal, and an inadvertent over-strenuous stab on the rollout could lock a brake, rip a tire and cause bedlam.

One paradoxical aspect to the disadvantage of carrying too much speed, on the Sport at least, is the hazard of coming in too slow and running out of stabilator for the flare, dropping the nose for the inevitable bounce. Pilots report the aircraft is nose heavy, especially with flaps down, and a better strategy is to keep on a bit of power right through the flare.

At one Beech dealership they reported they were surprised by better landing characteristics that resulted from putting on the optional spin kit, which added strakes to the nose and stabilator along with a ventral fin to the rear fuselage. Other Musketeer instructors said they did not see any benefit from this strategy.

Maintenance

Owners who responded to our survey reported they were for the most part happy with the low maintenance demands of the Musketeers. Said one, "It is by far the best mechanical device I have owned." The reliability of the 180-hp Lycoming in the Sundowners received high marks as well. What few complaints there were centered around leaky windshields and doors, and water getting into the vacuum pump or air filter, shutting down the gyros.

Service Difficulty Reports show some evidence of gear stress from landing problems. There were a half dozen instances of gear housing cracks and breaks on the Model 23 and several cases of broken engine mounts, and severe shimmy on landing from broken nosegear components.

Though both aircraft are followed by a cloud of suspicion because of their horrible landing accident record, a careful checkout by a knowledgeable Musketeer instructor may remove much of the onus for aficionados of (1) low prices, (2) abundantly roomy cabins, (3) low maintenance and (4) easy two-door access.

On the Model 19 there were 11 cases of aileron push-pull tubes and rod ends that failed. Identical reports were made out on 11 cases where fuel cells had delaminated at the top skin between the skin and ribs near the filler opening. Another 11 reports told of cracks in the right inboard side of the keel assembly under the rudder pedal support. And 19 identical reports were filed on heavy corrosion at station 68 where the firewall pad contacts the aluminum structure. Beech issued mandatory service instructions (No. 1245) calling for inspection of this area.

There were 14 cases of cracked elevator spars during inspections made according to Beech Service Instructions No. 1167. Another AD on the Musketeer stabilators (78-16-06) called for inspection of the trim tab actuator rod. Among the key ADs affecting the Musketeers is the repetitive one (73-20-07) calling for inspection of the forward wing attach frames and brackets for possible cracks. A 1985 AD on these aircraft (85-05-02) ordered a fuel selector stop to be installed (along with a decal) on the fuel selector valve guard to reduce the chance of accidentally turning the fuel selector valve to the off position.

In 1988 FAA issued an AD requiring that electric fuel boost pumps in certain Super Musketeers and Sierras be replaced with units having nylon-graphite vanes. The old carbon-graphite vanes were reported breaking and causing engine stoppages. And the NTSB said fuel caps of Musketeers over 10 years old should be pressure checked yearly because of the threat of leakage causing water contamination in the fuel and engine stoppages.

Modifications

There is a paucity of mods for the Musketeer series, except for the usual autopilot and strobe and carb ice detector accessories. There is, however, an STC for an adjustable trim tab on the left aileron, by Aero-Trim, Inc. in Bay Harbor, Fla.

Recapitulation

As the great shakeout of the 80s continues, the chief virtue of the Musketeers is their low price. They have to be considered the bargain buys of their respective classes. And here we are talking about the Sundowner in particular. We believe the Sport is, frankly, too doggy to consider even in these dog days.

Cost/Performance/Specifications

Model	Year Built	Average Retail Price	Cruise Speed (kts)	Useful Load (lbs)	Fuel Std/Opt (gals)	Engine	TBO (hrs)	Overhaul Cost
19	1966-67	$14,125	108	875	57	150-hp Lyc. O-320-E2C	2,000	$9,500
19A	1968-69	$14,625	108	875	57	150-hp Lyc. O-320-E2C	2,000	$9,500
B19	1970-73	$15,875	108	875	57	150-hp Lyc. O-320-E2C	2,000	$9,500
B19	1974-77	$16,935	108	875	57	150-hp Lyc. O-320-E2C	2,000	$9,500
B19	1978	$18,000	108	875	57	150-hp Lyc. O-320-E2C	2,000	$9,500
23	1963	$13,000	111	1,000	57	160-hp Lyc. O-320-D2B	2,000	$9,500
A23	1964-66	$14,825	119	1,025	57	165-hp Cont. IO-346-A	1,500	$13,500
A23	1967-68	$15,750	119	1,025	57	165-hp Cont. IO-346-A	1,500	$13,500
B23	1968-69	$18,125	119	975	57	180-hp Lyc. O-360-A2G	2,000	$10,500
C23	1970-73	$19,900	119	975	57	180-hp Lyc. O-360-A4G	2,000	$10,000
C23	1974-76	$23,500	119	975	57	180-hp Lyc. O-360-A4J	2,000	$10,000
C23	1977-79	$28,000	119	975	57	180-hp Lyc. O-360-A4K	2,000	$10,000
C23	1980-81	$34,750	119	975	57	180-hp Lyc. O-360-A4K	2,000	$10,000
C23	1982-83	$44,500	119	975	57	180-hp Lyc. O-360-A4K	2,000	$10,000

Buyers willing to sacrifice five to 10 knots of cruise speed and who-knows-how-much climb rate will find the Sundowner a surprising bargain.

Owner Comments

Maintenance costs have varied with the number of ADs and where the annual was performed. Expensive ADs have included main gear remounting and one-half valves in the cylinders. Anyone considering purchasing an older Musketeer should verify that the engine has the one-half-inch valve stems instead of the original three-eighth- inch stems.

A potentially costly AD requires removal of the wing tips to check for corrosion inside the wings. Also, a recurring AD requires checking wing attach bolts and spars annually for cracking, etc. Older Musketeers had a free swivel on the nose gear, and braking was required while taxiing. On an icy ramp, braking just doesn't cut it. The Beech nose wheel steering kit is a necessity for winter flying "up north."

Another kit, no longer available, I wish I had installed is the split nosebowl. This allows removal of the bottom engine cowling without having to pull the prop spinner and prop off first. A simple adjustment such as tightening the generator belt requires removing both the top and bottom cowlings with the nosebowl attached to the bottom cowling. The split nosebowl kit should result in much cheaper annual labor costs.

Maintenance headaches include multiple problems with the Goodyear brakes. There is a series of brake system improvements available, primarily to fix air lock problems with a shuttle valve which controls the four master cylinders.

Musketeers have a greater fuel capacity than most competitors, but slower cruise speeds eliminate the potential advantage in range.

Going to a firewall-mounted master reservoir and Cleveland brakes (originally certified in 1963 but not factory installed until the early 70s) should solve all brake problems.

The early Musketeers did not utilize a battery box, but instead used a special vented 25-amp/hr battery with two small plastic tubes going through grommets in the fuselage bottom. The problem is that no battery manufacturer currently produces this size of vented manifold battery. Beech has a kit available with a new mounting bracket, battery box, large vent hoses, etc., for $600 or so.

I found a used battery bracket and box with hoses in a salvage yard and had it installed in accordance with the service instruction for under $150 with a 35 amp/hr standard aircraft battery, which really helped starter cranking on cold days.

Douglas E. Mulloy
Seattle, Wash.

As for performance, our 1980 Sundowner isn't fast, but it's solid, docile, forgiving and as friendly as an old glove.

We cruise at 9,500 feet at about 2250 rpm indicating 113 knots and burning 9.8

gph. Our average climb rate from sea level to altitude with a full load is about 500 fpm at a cruise climb of 81 knots. It takes us about 18 to 20 minutes to get up there.

There are no handling problems or idiosyncrasies that I know of. The plane handles turbulence very nicely, and control pressures are always very light and responsive. It's not likely that a power-on stall would come without the plane talking to the pilot for several seconds before it tipped. Stalls under slow flight or approach to landing are more subtle, but still with considerable warning, both from the buzzer and from buffeting. It's as if the plane really doesn't want to stall.

As for maintenance, since new, the plane has had only one airworthiness directive (the oil cooler). The maintenance on this plane has been very minor. It has required no major work at all yet, at 1,400 hours TT. The vacuum pump has been replaced, and the starter gear shaft went through a bearing.

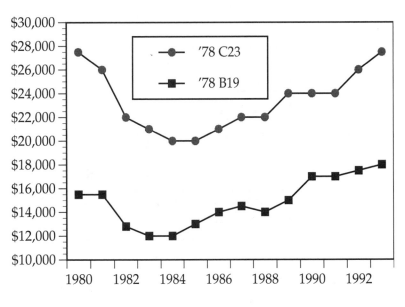

Annual inspections have cost from $250 to $750, with me participating as much as I'm allowed. The higher-cost annual occurred when we had to fix the starter and vacuum pump. My total maintenance cost for 1985 was $1,380, with close to 100 hours flown. The two years before that the Sundowner required significantly less maintenance for the same amount of flying. My average maintenance cost since new has been very close to $9 per tach hour.

In terms of comfort, the Sundowner is very roomy and comfortable. We have taken some five-hour non-stop flights with no discomfort. The noise level seems very tolerable; we can carry on an almost normal conversation in flight. Heating, ventilation, defrost and control layout are quite adequate and well done. The seats are comfortable, and the large windows and high seating position make for very good visibility. The two doors are commonplace to us, but much appreciated when we see other folks crawling across their planes to get to the pilot's seat. Weakness: when it rains, it leaks—getting the floor carpeting wet. The paint job is of questionable quality. It has developed lots of pimples or very small bumps on the top surfaces.

Overall, the important thing to us is reliability, comfort, friendliness and trouble-free operation. We are not enamored by great speed or high performance or the added maintenance that comes with retractable gear or variable pitch props. The Sundowner has probably hit our specs as close to anything we know.

Ray Bell
Los Gatos, Calif.

I have owned my 1975 Sundowner over nine and a half years, and have many good things to say about it. It is by far the best mechanical device I have owned. It has been very reliable and is consistently available whenever I need it. It is very good on maintenance. The Lycoming 180 is a very reliable workhorse and goes extremely well on 100LL. The aircraft is solid, well built and stable in rough air.

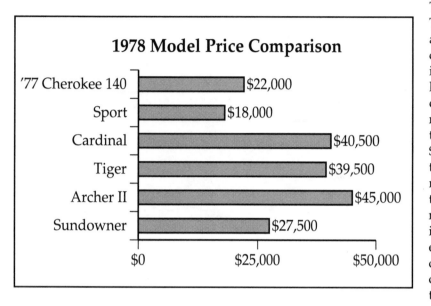

1978 Model Price Comparison

'77 Cherokee 140 — $22,000
Sport — $18,000
Cardinal — $40,500
Tiger — $39,500
Archer II — $45,000
Sundowner — $27,500

There are some drawbacks, however. The plane is now out of production, and parts are getting hard to come by; consequently, the price of an annual inspection has gone up more than a little. During the first seven years of ownership the average price of an annual ranged from $600 to $1,000. For the last two years, however, it was $1,400 and $1,800 respectively. Although I did use the Beechcraft East maintenance facility the last two years, this year I'm going back to the original, a former Aero Center dealer versed in dealing with the smaller aircraft. The established Beechcraft maintenance facilities are fine for the larger Beechcraft, but I don't recommend them for the Aero Club line.

Secondly, I did get hit with that infamous surprise of which all Sundowner owners must be aware. I keep my aircraft outside in harsh New England weather, and for nine years the plane weathered well until the seals on the instrument vacuum pump filter eventually deteriorated. All Sundowners leak around the doors and windshield and must be dried out after a heavy rain.

One fine August day after one such rain, I innocently flipped on my master switch only to have an aging, tired vacuum pump proceed to dump about a cup and a half of pure rain water directly into the innards of my directional gyro and artificial horizon. It was (expensive) overhaul time for these!

Beechcraft East subsequently relocated the filter mount in accordance with a previously issued service bulletin, but why wasn't this done ahead of time? Even at the factory? My insurance company disowned me.

However, in spite of these conditions, I still love my Sundowner. I know I could not afford to replace it with any comparable still-in-production model. It is indeed unfortunate that the Aero Club line never sold very well. Often this line was shadowed by the stigma that they were slow, and expensive to buy, and the fact is that they are roomy and very comfortable. Any slowness is noticed only on paper next to the competitors' figures. The speed, rate of climb, etc. figures published by Beech are reasonable and not exaggerated. After arriving from a long cross-country, one feels comfortable and relaxed.

The Sundowner is a very good value for the money. I would suggest to those looking for a used model to first check that all service bulletins have been complied with (especially the one described above). The Beech factory often pro-rates the parts and labor for compliance, and in some cases have paid for the entire job.

Once this is done, any owner can expect to get very good enjoyment and practical transportation for his investment.

Lowell G. Powers, Jr.
Newport, R. I.

We have a '74 Sundowner. Performance is excellent. Usually flown 200 pounds under max gross, it will climb at 78 knots at 800 fpm at density altitudes over 3,000 feet. At cruise, the numbers are close to the POH. Handling is excellent— smooth and very responsive. There is a moderate pitch-up, pitch-down with power changes, and a severe pitch-up when lowering flaps at any speed in the white arc.

Maintenance has not been a problem. In 200 hours, one set of brake pads, my request; one leaky spark plug wire, replaced complete set, my request. Added oil filter and adapter. Replaced battery. Comfort is fantastic. You get out without being tired because you are not fighting the airplane. Noise level with the air vents open measured 73 dBA at 2500 rpm. Parts availability: Stock at the parts houses in the Los Angeles area or at Beech FBOs locally. Cost: Fuel consumption the last 200 hours has averaged 8.2 gph; oil consumption, one quart every seven to eight hours; annual inspection, $350. The Sundowner, I believe, is a much neglected aircraft. Flying one will make you a believer.

David Lipsky
La Mirada, Calif.

Until recently I owned a 1968 Beech Musketeer B23 with the 180-hp engine. Performance: Cruise 117 knots at 5,000 feet with 75 percent power at 10.5 gph. Handling: Cruise aileron response much like a Cherokee 140, not particularly crisp. Landing: Precise speed control is important because there is a tendency to porpoise.

Maintenance: Typical Beechcraft with good documentation and adequate accessibility. Very high quality support from Beech with continuing service letters and high-level support. The Lycoming 180-hp is obviously reliable and Beech even has the larger plugs, harness and high-altitude mags fitted. I fixed the brakes, DG, voltage regulator, and our Musketeer did evidence cylinder cracks, requiring a top overhaul at 1,100 hours. This was likely due to a previous owner flying the aircraft in unapproved aerobatics with sudden engine cooling.

Comfort: There is excellent front and rear seat room. Parts availability: Very good. Cost of operation: maintenance $1,000 (due to top overhaul), $20 hourly in gas. Average annual is $400.

In summary, this is a much maligned plane which actually is a real bargain to fly and own, if not very exciting in airwork or appearance. It is very well built and quite strong, but slightly slow and can tend to porpoise if not landed properly. It really would be an excellent first plane for a careful pilot and can be bought for next to nothing with careful shopping.

Dr. Andrew Reiland
Leominster, Mass.

Beech Sierra 24R

Has history smiled upon the Beech Sierra after more than 20 years of life in the slow lane? Perhaps, in a sly Mona Lisa way. Has it qualities that commend it over a quartet of rivals? Some, indeed; but it also has a few faults—some rather nasty.

A glance at the facts suggests that the Model 24R merits rating, once again, as a very average airplane in the 200-hp retractable class. Sort of an equal among equals. It ranks along with the Cessna Cardinal RG and Rockwell 112 as one of the least costly (to buy) used economy retractables around and has held its value well over the years. The Mooney 201 far exceeds it in price. Even the Piper Arrow costs a few thousand dollars more, year for year, on the average. And you have to go back another decade or more earlier to find a 225-horse Beech Debonair that costs as little. Presumably these price differences can be equated with pilot esteem, because all these airplanes cost about the same when new.

History

A 200-hp fixed-gear Model 24 called the Super III came out back in 1966. Then, the Model 24R with retractable gear came on the scene in 1970. The A24R in 1970 came without two features everyone praises on later models: a second cockpit door and a third, left-side baggage door. These features were added in 1971. With the B24R in 1973 came a new instrument panel and quadrant-style (multi) power-plant controls instead of push-pull controls. Also, the baggage door was enlarged and a Hartzell prop replaced the McCauley.

One of the aircraft's most attractive qualities is its price on the used market. It's one of the cheapest retractables in its class.

In 1977 the C24R came out with aileron gap seals and nicer bearings for smoother aileron control, plus a bit of extra usable fuel, a new cabin vent system along with a two-inch longer prop giving more thrust. Finally, wheel-well fairings were added under the wing.

Cabin Comfort

This has always been the big selling point among owners, as with the Rockwell 112. "The superb visibility, spacious and comfortable interior and door configuration are the plane's greatest virtues," echoed one pilot. Along with right and left doors for the front seat, there is a largish door for the baggage compartment that can handle kids nicely. There is even an optional small jump seat. The rear compartment is structurally capable of holding 270 pounds—about the heaviest in this class of aircraft. But can you actually throw kids in the jump seat and stay within the Sierra's weight and balance limits? Our calculations show you probably can. We figured that with a modestly equipped airplane, you could get two 170-pounders in the front seat, a couple of 115-pounders in the middle and still toss a couple of 70-pound kids in the rear while carrying 50 gallons of fuel.

Can you ever load a full 270 pounds in the rear compartment, realistically? Once again, our calculations say you can and still stay within the weight-and-balance envelope, though it probably wouldn't make much sense because you probably would end up with empty middle seats. One pilot said the first thing he did was throw out the jump seat to avoid temptation.

Comparing the Sierra's useful load with that of its competitors in the 200-hp retractable class, it appears the Beech comes out slightly short—on the order of 50 pounds or so for IFR-equipped birds. Figure on an IFR useful of about 925-950 pounds. If you use 925 pounds, that allows you full fuel, three 170-pound adults and 60 pounds of baggage. With four adults, count on about 25 gallons of fuel.

Performance

This is the area where pilots typically say they trade off for the large, comfortable, beamy cabin. The Sierra isn't fast. In its class, it brings up the rear in cruise speed with the equally sluggish, beamy, comfortable Rockwell 112. Owners say to count on about 135 knots/155 mph TAS with 75 percent power and 132 knots or so at 65 percent. The Piper Arrow with the same engine should go about seven knots faster; the Cardinal RG some 11 knots faster, and the Mooney 201 a crazy 20 to 30 knots faster. The addition of wheel well fairings in 1977 is reported to have reduced the drag of the main gear dangling out in the breeze, and added a few knots. The fairings smoothed the turbulent airflow. But the nose gear still dangles rather low.

With the '77 Sierras fairings were added to the main gear wheel wells to reduce drag caused by the dangling wheels. Rubber donut shock absorbers (like the Mooney's) contribute to less than feather-smooth touchdowns.

However, even the fixed-gear Gulfstream Tiger can be expected to go sailing by the Sierra at full bore with only 180 horses.

In a perverse sense, the Sierra is slower where you want it to be fast, and faster where you want it to be slow—on final approach and in the stall payout. Figure on a power-off stall speed, dirty, in the Sierra of 60 knots/69 mph. That's 11 knots higher than the Arrow, nine higher than the 112B and five higher than the supposedly "hot" Mooney 201.

Handling

Everybody agrees the Sierra is a delight in the air, but something less when landing. The ailerons are marvelously light, and the airplane is fun to maneuver in the air. Though the stall speed is relatively high for this class of aircraft, it's tough to get a stall break because of limited stabilator travel. And the stalls you can induce are mild and give good warning.

The landing gear acts as a good speed brake because, as with many other Beechcraft, the gear can be lowered at a fairly high airspeed—135 knots/155 mph, in fact—or darn close to cruise speed.

Landing Problems

Through the years, the Sierra's landing qualities have stirred the most excitement among pilots—just like the other fixed-gear Musketeers, Sundowners, etc. Collectively, they have a rotten record of botched landings and collapsed gear and bent props to their credit. The Sierra is no exception. Instructors and chauvinistic owners may rant and rave that the airplane does not deserve its poor reputation because it was perpetrated by ill-trained pilots. And that may be so, but the record is a miserable one, to say the least.

If the airspeed is not just right, the Sierra can float, and the stabilator can tend to oscillate and contribute to over-controlling. Also, the aircraft tends to run out of nose-up pitch authority during landing (without a load in the rear), and this can result in a nosewheel-first wheelbarrow landing. Naturally, confronted with a history like this, any wary buyer should have a mechanic pay the utmost attention to the integrity of the landing gear. Also, check for evidence of gear-up landings. They happen with disturbing frequency in this aircraft.

There are doors all over the place, for great ingress and egress. The rear compartment can take a jump seat for kids, or hold a great quantity of baggage (up to 270 pounds structurally).

Maintenance

Owners report they are fairly happy with upkeep of their Sierras—with a modest cost burden. Annuals reported to us ranged well below $1,000. There was some grumbling by owners about the high cost of Beech parts, but these days we'd be surprised if they weren't all high. At least the parts appear to be available. Also, one owner positively raved about how supportive Beech was when he needed help and information.

The Service Difficulty Reports point the finger of blame primarily at the landing gear. A study of SDRs from the beginning of 1980 to the end of November 1986 showed landing gear problems outnumbering most other mechanical problems by a factor of seven or so. Checking the records to see how consistent a problem this has been, we noted most of the SDRs showed up in the first two years of our study, in 1980-1981, with 10 the first year and 14 the second. From then on, the rate dropped sharply, to where an average of only 4.4 landing gear SDRs were reported each year. So presumably the problem has been diminished greatly.

Problems leading to gear collapse or failure to retract included: failure of torque shaft arm; plunger on limit switch was hanging, not letting retract arms lock; downlock spring broken; gear actuator shaft broken; downlock switch failed; nose gear yoke broken, etc.

Fuel Pump Problems

We noted seven instances of failure of the Dukes fuel pump in Sierras through the last six years. Naturally, the unpleasant result was that the engine quit. Also we noted half a dozen reports of broken or worn aileron rod ends. These sometimes resulted in ailerons failing to respond or jamming (once on takeoff).

There were only a half dozen cases reported of engine mechanical problems, and these showed no particular trend—i.e., dowel pin sheared, crankcase cracked, crankshaft broken, piston cracked, valve stretched and cylinder cracked. The Model 24Rs appear to have had a rather mild history of Airworthiness Directive concerns. The only AD to appear in the 80s mandated a fuel selector stop and decal designed to prevent inadvertently shutting off the fuel. Seven ADs appeared in the '90s, but none specific to the Sierra; all are "blanket" ADs affecting several different airplanes.

Safety

Accident reports for the six years up to 1987 echo the gear problems disclosed in the SDRs. The preponderance of accidents in the Sierra stem from (1) inadvertent gear-up landings, (2) gear mechanical problems, (3) hard landings. Obviously, most are pilot-related since dummy fliers forget to put the gear down for landing or retract it after landing or before getting completely airborne on takeoff. Sometimes the gear-up crunch results from poor coordination with a flight instructor. And hard landings and groundloop/swerves (there were quite a few of the latter) can be classified either as pilot error or design-induced error, depending on your inclination. Most likely, both are to blame.

In a study we conducted in 1984 comparing accident rates of 17 single-engine retractables, the Beech Sierra showed up poorly in fatal rate—14th best out of the 17 (or fourth worst) and even worse in total accident rate—16th. These are determined by accidents per 100,000 hours. Far better, incidentally, were the Beech 33 Debonair and Cardinal RG. The Piper Arrow and Commander 112/114 also were ranked better. Our most recent figures showed only nine fatal accidents since 1980, from a variety of causes and no trends: one from weather, another from an engine problem, one from fuel mismanagement, another from a stall/mush problem and five from miscellaneous causes.

Safety Features

The Sierra has some nice features that might help in a crash. All four seats have shoulder harnesses as standard equipment, and the ability to scram in case of a problem on the ground through the three doors is a major asset. But the "horned" control wheels mostly have no padding or protection against pilot impact. Also, in terms of fuel management, the location of the fuel gauges in a hard-to-see place at the bottom left of the control panel hardly can be considered ideal. But we counted only half a dozen cases of fuel exhaustion over the last six years and just three of fuel mismanagement. As mentioned above, an AD called for installation of a stop to prevent inadvertent selection of the "off" position. The fuel selector is located below the throttle quadrant where both pilots can see it.

Cost/Performance/Specifications

Model	Year Built	Average Retail Price	Cruise Speed (kts)	Useful Load (lbs)	Fuel Std/Opt (gals)	Engine	TBO (hrs)	Overhaul Cost
A24R	1970	$22,500	131	1,140	52	200-hp Lyc. IO-360-A1B	1,800	$13,500
A24R	1971	$23,000	131	1,140	52	200-hp Lyc. IO-360-A1B	1,800	$13,500
A24R	1972	$24,000	131	1,140	52	200-hp Lyc. IO-360-A1B	1,800	$13,500
B24R	1973	$25,500	131	1,140	52	200-hp Lyc. IO-360-A1B6	1,800	$13,500
B24R	1974	$26,500	131	1,140	52	200-hp Lyc. IO-360-A1B6	1,800	$13,500
B24R	1975	$28,000	131	1,140	52	200-hp Lyc. IO-360-A1B6	1,800	$13,500
B24R	1976	$30,500	131	1,140	52	200-hp Lyc. IO-360-A1B6	1,800	$13,500
C24R	1977	$32,500	137	1,065	57	200-hp Lyc. IO-360-A1B6	1,800	$13,500
C24R	1978	$35,000	137	1,065	57	200-hp Lyc. IO-360-A1B6	1,800	$13,500
C24R	1979	$37,500	137	1,065	57	200-hp Lyc. IO-360-A1B6	1,800	$13,500
C24R	1980	$40,000	137	1,065	57	200-hp Lyc. IO-360-A1B6	1,800	$13,500
C24R	1981	$44,000	137	1,056	57	200-hp Lyc. IO-360-A1B6	1,800	$13,500
C24R	1982	$49,000	137	1,065	57	200-hp Lyc. IO-360-A1B6	1,800	$13,500
C24R	1983	$57,000	137	1,065	57	200-hp Lyc. IO-360-A1B6	1,800	$13,500

Owner Comments

I bought my '78 Sierra in '82 (on my wife's insistence) while looking for a "neater" ship. She liked the ease of entry, comfort and roominess. If a non-pilot wife, knowing nothing about planes, agrees we ought to *buy* a plane and points to *that* retractable, I am smart enough to keep my mouth shut. We got the plane with 1,000 hours on it as a bank repo for $22 grand—hard to pass up.

Sure, for a retractable, it does only 137 knots at 75 percent power; and at 65 percent it offers a sedate 132 knots. But it does it in such a stable and predictable manner, and with remarkable visibility, including almost straight down by the wing root. The 135-knot gear-drop speed has come in very handy entering major airport areas where I keep speed up until the 45-degree entry, plop the gear and watch the speed drop to approach numbers slick as silk. Flaps at 100 knots and I'm at 75 knots on final.

Sure, it looks like a tank, but flies easily with only moderate pressures on the yoke. Added a remote-controlled aileron trim tab this year, and the resulting lateral balance made this a hands-and-foot-free straight-tracking machine.

Owners rave about air handling on the Sierras, but concede they're almost the slowest in their class. Presumably a drag cleanup of items like the dangling nosegear would help.

I find the wide wheel-track a comfort in crosswind landings. And landings are easy. When I first read that 61 to 65 knots was touchdown, I understood why people had difficulty making smooth landings in this plane. They hadn't trained in the Grumman TR-2, "the rock!" Like the TR-2, it takes a bit of power to paint on. The plane is, incidentally, placarded against slips of more than 30 seconds. I avoid slips as my Lycoming tends to go into an immediate coughing spasm in three seconds.

Insurance has run between $1,400 and $1,500 each year. Over four years, annuals ranged between $60 and $375 for an average of $240. At 1,300 hours I replaced a starter ($300). Overhauled the prop for $720. Redid the interior for $950. My numbers show about a $44/hour total cost for the first 100 hours per year.

Sure, it takes longer to fly there than in other retracts. But we've traveled 850-mile clips in a one-stop day (5.5 hours plus pit stop) and have enjoyed a roomy, comfortable, broad-visibility environment. My fuel burns are around 9.6-10 gph at 75 percent and 8.5-9 gph at 65 percent.

Rudy Leeman
Antioch, Calif.

I have owned my '78 Sierra for five years. I bought it from a flight school with 900 hours on it, and it is now at TBO. I added a Precise Flight vacuum backup system and had an avionics shop put a connection in the number one nav antenna line for my Terra handheld radio.

The plane has a door on the pilot's side, and has a cargo door that is unexcelled in single-engine aircraft. The superb visibility, spacious and comfortable interior and door configuration are the plane's greatest virtues. The large and easily accessible cargo area allow me a great deal of flexibility in loading.

Although the door seals were replaced, all the doors still leak during heavy rains while tied down, and I have never accustomed myself to the smell of wet carpets. The no-nonsense flat metal instrument panel is the best overall design I have seen in a plane in this class. It makes no difference that the fuel gauges are hidden by the yoke, since they are terribly inaccurate. The plane has manual flaps and trim.

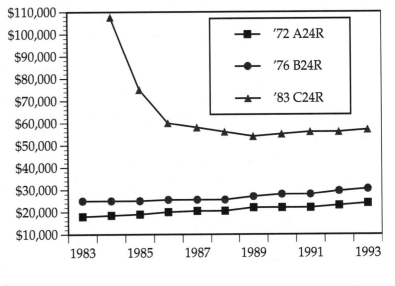

The worst aspects of the plane are the noise level and cruise speed. I know all planes are noisy, but I have never found any comfort in that fact. Ear plugs by EAR and headsets have been the solution. At 65 percent I get close to book figures: 125 KTAS @ nine gph. It's an airslug. I wonder what a flap gap seal kit would do for the plane. Handling is very good and the plane makes a good IFR platform .

Maintenance, not including annuals, never runs less than $10 per hour. Annuals average around $1,500. Part of that high cost has been Beechcraft's pricing policy for parts. One piston, the door seals, landing gear actuator seals, a door window and a starter motor are some items requiring replacement since I have had the plane. If the plane were faster and the parts less expensive, I would think this Beechcraft is one of the greatest singles around. It is just too slow to stir up any excitement.

Raymond Ritter
Oakland, Calif.

Performance: POH is accurate for cruise. I operate at 75 percent on trips and flight plan for 135 knots and 11 gph. Endurance with full tanks is five hours at 75 percent power. The Sierra is not a particularly fast airplane, compared to the Arrow or Mooney 201, but there are other advantages.

Handling: Ground handling is very good. Visibility is terrific. In the air, the Sierra is very stable. Landing is different from most aircraft in its class. The plane is so high off the ground, and the pilot sits so upright that he is much higher when he lands than in an Arrow or 201. Also, the rubber biscuit shock absorbers will not absorb an ugly landing like an oleo. Plan on a firm arrival every time in a Sierra, and once in a while the rubber biscuits will bounce you back off the runway. I can count my real greasers on one hand in 400 hours. The Sierra is a paved-runway aircraft. I've never flown it in and out of small grass strips, but was never thrilled with the ground acceleration and climb performance.

Maintenance: The IO-360 engine is wonderful. Starts terrific, hot or cold and never misses a beat. I installed a factory reman engine and prop three months after purchase. The work was done at the Textron-Lycoming service center in Williamsport, Pa.

Incredible as it sounds, they (and I'm sure other facilities as well) will hang a $10,000 engine and $2,000 prop on your aircraft and never do a vibration analysis at running speeds. After the installation in early '83, I brought the aircraft to Summit Aviation in Delaware and found that the engine/prop assembly exceeded tolerances by four times. The vibration was so high that the people at Summit couldn't believe it. They thought the prop must have been bent. Anyway, weights were added to the spinner, and the aircraft is now incredibly smooth.

The Sierra panel is very well set up and easy to use. But I don't care for the positioning of the engine gauge and fuel tank gauge. Noise is high, as in any single. The heating and ventilating system is adequate.

Cost of operating works out to about $55 an hour. This includes all routing maintenance, annual, insurance, fuel, oil and T-Hangar. Reserves for engine and prop would add about $5 an hour to this figure. Normal annuals, without any major projects included, are $400.

Idiosyncrasies: Usable fuel—tanks hold 60 gallons total, but usable fuel is only 52 gallons. That is eight gallons or nearly a full hour of cruise that cannot be used. I believe this problem was straightened out in later models, but it sure is annoying to make an intermediate fuel stop when you know there are plenty of reserves sloshing around in the tanks that you can't get at.

Oil filter: There isn't one. The engine is so close to the firewall that it cannot be installed. This is ridiculous on a $38,000 airplane ('74 new cost) and a 10-grand engine. I change oil every 25 hours to compensate for the lack of the oil filter.

Landing gear: Strange is the best word I can think of. The mains fold outward and hang in what could be the cleanest part of the wing. The nosewheel pivots 90 degrees and more or less stows behind the bottom engine cowl opening. Unfortunately, the nosewheel still hangs down in the slipstream quite a bit. This must account for some of the drag on the aircraft and its slow speed.

In defense of the gear system, it is very sturdy looking (massive magnesium castings) and has the simplest emergency extension system going. Also, there is a very nice pressure switch in the pitot system that prevents retraction at low airspeed (approx. 60 mph). This prevents accidental retraction on rollout or while taxiing.

Engine cowling: The only thing that can be checked without removing the top half of the cowling is the engine oil and brake fluid. The top cowl should have been a hinged affair, like a Bonanza's.

Michael E. Capocefalo
Auburn, N.Y.

Beech 33 Debonair, Bonanza

The handsome straight-tail Debonairs and Bonanzas have an excellent safety record, satisfying speed, marvelous handling and comfortable cabins. They're expensive, though, and have a few nettlesome quirks.

The Model 33 has been a sleeper. It used to be considered less desirable than its exotic looking and even sweeter handling stablemate, the Model 35 "butterfly" Bonanza. Of late, however, a wait-and-see attitude concerning the V-tail's "fix" has used-plane buyers voting for the straight-tail version with their checkbooks. The role reversal has prices for 35s lagging $3,000-12,000 behind those for contemporary 33s. Still, both models are perennial blue-chippers, commanding and holding substantially higher prices than their competitors.

A slick aerodynamic package, the top-of-the-line 285-hp F33A can be identified by trapezoidal rear window. It's been in production since 1970.

Owners are ecstatic about the handling, performance, comfort and quality of their Debonairs and Bonanzas. But they aren't too thrilled about the tendency of their steeds to fish-tail in light turbulence. Their enthusiasm also is blunted a bit by tight c.g. limits, poorly arranged controls and the stupendous cost of Beech parts.

Genealogy

Historians say the Model 33 was Beech Aircraft's answer to a challenge by Piper's Comanche 250, which performed almost as well as the venerable V-tail Bonanza but cost much less ($19,800 versus $25,300 in 1960). The first 33 was merely a stripped-down version of an M35 Bonanza and was priced at $19,995, which did not include such typically standard fare as exterior paint, sun visors, a VSI or a turn and bank indicator. To further preclude any class confusion, the threadbare 33 was given a conventional tail, a smaller engine (a 225-hp Continental IO-470) and a name of its own: Debonair.

Beech cranked out 233 of the original Debonairs in 1960. The next year, a third side window, a hat rack and more equipment were added, and gross weight was boosted from 2,900 to 3,000 pounds. Beech built 154 A33s in 1961. The B33 Debonair debuted in 1962 with a reorganized panel and the N35 Bonanza's 74-gallon fuel system as an option. This model stayed in production three years, and 426 were built.

The C33, introduced in 1965, had a flock of minor refinements, including a sleeker dorsal fin, individual rear seats (replacing a bench), a better heater, a larger hat shelf and a 50-pound nudge in gross weight. A larger rear window and a fifth seat were options. A 285-hp version of the Debonair, dubbed the C33A, came out in 1966. Its more powerful IO-520 engine (same as the one used in the V35 Bonanza) accommodated a gross weight of 3,300 pounds. Beech built 304 C33s and 179 C33As.

The "C" models were the last of the Debonair line (there are no "D" models, by the way). Beech stopped the charade and changed the name to Bonanza in 1968. But that was just about the only change. E33 and E33A Bonanzas differ only slightly from their predecessors, save for their elevated title and sloped, one-piece windshields. Perhaps the most remarkable event that year was the introduction of a third model, the E33C. This one has a stronger tail, a jettisonable cabin door and a positive-pressure fuel pump, and is certified for aerobatics. (All other Model 33s are certified in the Utility category.) Beech built 116 E33s, 85 E33As and 25 E33Cs in 1968 and '69.

The 225-hp version was renamed the F33 in 1970. It has larger rear windows and more baggage area. The F33 was the last of the 225-hp models and is the rarest: only 20 were built. In 1972, Beech returned a "small-engine" Bonanza to production; however, it built only 50 of the 250-hp G33 models that year and in 1973.

The 285-hp F33A Bonanza has been in continuous production since 1970, with more than 1,400 built by 1993. Other than avionics improvements, the model has remained virtually untouched over the years. Since 1985, Beech has been offering a package deal on the airplane, equipped with King avionics and popular options such as a large cargo door, extra soundproofing and a three-blade McCauley propeller. 1993 list price, equipped, was just under $264,000

The 33 Bonanzas have latched, instead of Dzus-fastened, lift-up cowls for easy preflight inspection.

About 105 F33Cs were built from 1970 through '79, but since then Beech has been building aerobatic Bonanzas only on special order, with a minimum order of 10 required. The last batch, of 21, was cranked out for the Mexican air force in 1985. To date, some 130 F33Cs have been built, but many of them are being used as military trainers outside the U.S.

Design Quirks

Owners say their Model 33s are veritable baby carriages when flown by the book. "The ease with which it handles, takes off and lands is just great," said one owner. "Nail your MP and rpm, and you'll fly down the ILS on rails," said another. A 33 may be relatively easy to fly, but there are some traps that can (and do, according to accident records) bring good pilots to grief.

Nonstandard location of the gear and flap controls is one trap. The yoke, thick as a branch of an oak tree, is another. It blocks the pilot's view of some very important items near the bottom of the panel, including the gear position indicator lights and power controls. Transitioning pilots also find the arrangement of the power controls a bit different. Rather than lined up next to the prop control, the mixture knob is located below the throttle. The fuel selector also is in an awkward location: on the sidewall, next to the pilot's left knee. The optional fuel system in 33 and A33 Debonairs is a labyrinth. When using the aux tanks (separate bladders that boost usable capacity from 44 to 63 gallons), excess fuel is returned from the engine to the left main bladder only. So, the drill is to run this tank half empty before switching to the auxiliaries. Another quirk is the gauges, which show fuel quantity in one tank at a time. Relief came with the B33 model. After 1961, Beech offered the Model 35 Bonanza's system (two leading-edge bladders holding a total of 74 gallons, usable) as the optional setup for the 33s and changed the gauges to total quantity indicators. In 1980, the 74-gallon tanks became standard equipment.

Another potential trap—the propensity of old-style, unbaffled fuel bladders to unport—has been addressed by two airworthiness directives. The ADs require at least 13 gallons in each main tank for takeoff and prohibit slips and turning-type takeoffs if the mains are less than half full.

Performance

A Model 33 can outperform just about any other four-seat, retractable single (though Mooneys come close and burn less fuel). Figure 135 to 155 knots on 9-12 gph for a 225-hp model. The more powerful 33s are faster, of course, and use more fuel. Figure 165-172 knots on 13-15 gph for a 285-hp model. Climb performance also is relatively good. Max rates of climb for 225-hp models are between 900 and 1,000 fpm; for 285-hp models, 1,100 to 1,200 fpm. Several owners have reported that climb performance tends to taper off a bit after 5,000 to 8,000 feet, however. Still, the airplanes soldier on at 500-600 fpm in the thin air. Service ceilings vary from a rather optimistic 19,800 feet for the original 33 to 17,850 feet for the F33A.

The airplanes are rather slippery; lower the nose, and they'll pick up speed quite readily. Early Debonairs have a relatively low max gear speed: 122 knots. However, the 154-knot limit on B33 and later models helps a bit during descents and pattern work. Maximum flap speed is a low 104 knots on early Debs, but it was raised to 113 knots on the C33 and to 123 knots on the F33A. Flap levers in airplanes built in 1979 and later have a detent for an "approach" setting (15 degrees) that can be selected up to 154 knots.

Handling

The controls are delightfully crisp and nicely harmonized. They can truly be caressed, rather than bullied about (as in a Mooney). But nimbleness has its price. "It takes only a few seconds' inattention for the Bonanza to fall off into a dive," wrote one owner. "The F33A is not unstable—far from it—but it can be a slippery handful in turbulent IMC if the autopilot goes out," wrote another. Stalls also are relatively sharp but easily recovered with proper technique.

Under normal conditions, though, the airplanes are sweethearts. "Landings are all squeakers," said an owner. "All one has to do is set up the recommended approach airspeeds." An interconnect allows coordinated, shallow turns to be made with ailerons or rudder, only. However, owners say the interconnect makes gusting crosswind takeoffs and landings extra challenging. Some also complain about the taxing of their right leg muscles during takeoff and climb. The ground-adjustable rudder trim tab apparently leaves much to be desired. (An electric rudder trim mod is available; more on that later.)

Comfort and Loading

The cabin is spacious and comfortable, and it provides excellent visibility. "You can fly for hours and still show up for a business meeting without that wrung-out feeling," said an owner. "It's a flying limousine." Like most short-coupled airplanes, though, a 33 will tend to do Dutch rolls if the air isn't absolutely calm. "Back-seaters can find Sik-Saks useful on hot, bumpy days," one owner advised. A yaw damper is one of the more useful options that has been available.

A fifth seat is among the least useful options. "This is emphatically not a five-seat airplane," an owner said. Even if a child (forget an adult) could be persuaded to sit in the baggage compartment, the narrow c.g. limits would be seriously jeoardized. Accommodating adults in the third and fourth seats is problematic. "In most cases, it's simply not legally possible to put two adults in the rear seats and a bunch of bags in back," one owner reported. Another said he has to put 50 pounds of shot in the nose when he flies with his wife and two children.

The problem isn't loading; 33s can haul a respectable load, at least on paper. It's balance. The aft c.g. limit is fairly easy to bust before departure; and a pilot has to grapple with the fact that along the way, the c.g. is going to move even farther aft as fuel is consumed. The c.g. problem is even worse in the V-tail Bonanza. If you often fly with a full cabin, a better bet might be an A36 Bonanza or a Cessna 182RG.

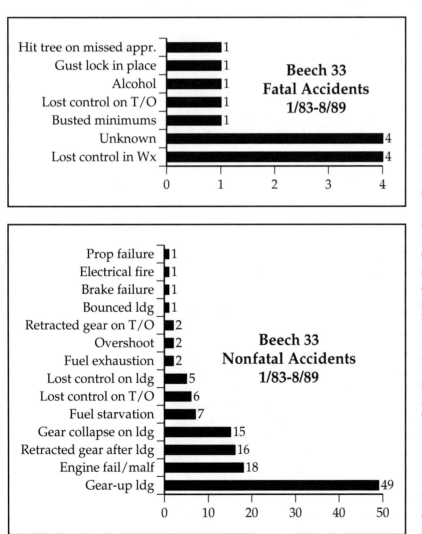

Safety Record

A while back, we found Model 33s to have the lowest accident rate among single-engine retractables for the years 1972 through 1981. However, as mentioned earlier, a 33 can be a handful in IMC. Records of fatal accidents from 1983 through August 1989 include four airplanes that crashed out of control in bad weather. Two of the pilots didn't have instrument ratings; one wasn't current on instruments; another had reported icing. Three airplanes hit trees during improperly flown approaches.

Considering the nonstandard location of the gear and flap controls, and their concealment by the heavy yoke, it isn't surprising that quite a few 33s have been sliding around on their bellies, which is harmful mostly to the pilots' pride and pocketbooks. It is curious that although an automatic gear-extension system, called the "Magic Hand," has been on the options lists since the C33 Debonair was introduced, very few airplanes have it.

Maintenance

It would be reasonable to expect that with so few changes over the years, a 33 could be maintained by just about any A&P. Curiously, owners' feedback,

Service Difficulty Reports and even a few nonfatal accidents indicate that 33s quite often suffer from poorly performed maintenance, which underscores the need for experienced and capable service. For example, among engine problems cited in recent SDRs were two oil leaks caused by improperly mounted alternators, two alternate air doors that were rendered useless by improperly installed springs, and an air filter clogged with paint. One engine-failure accident was traced to installation of a wrong oil line in an IO-470 engine. These are just a few examples.

Recent experience also suggests that prospective buyers pay special attention to rudder spars and hinges. There were four reports of failures and a recent Airworthiness Alert on cracked spars found in five of 15 airplanes inspected. Beech Aircraft issued "mandatory" service bulletins affecting Debonairs and Bonanzas calling for inspections for cracked forward rudder spars. The company issued the service bulletin after a fleet operator reported discovering a broken hinge bracket and finding cracks on inspecting other airplanes. Cracks in the spar could cause a loss of aircraft control. Beech estimated an inspection would take one mechanic 25 hours to perform. A cracked rudder must be replaced.

The cabin is spacious and comfortable even on the old B33 Debonairs.

Beech said that inspections should be made within the next 50 flight hours if the airplane has 1,000 or more hours. Then, inspections must be made every 500 hours or during an annual, whichever comes first. Airplanes with fewer than 1,000 hours were exempt from these requirements.

Another problem seems to be landing gear position switches. Seven SDRs noted malfunctions due to the switches' exposure to dirt and moisture. Wing attachments also should be checked. Eight reports cited cracked and corroded bolts and fittings. Beech Aircraft recommends that wing bolts be checked every five years, but no AD requires this. Leaking fuel bladders are a constant problem; look for replacement of Goodyear cells with Uniroyals.

A prospective buyer also should ensure that an earlier model has had its Goodyear brakes replaced with Clevelands and that a 285-hp engine has been updated with a heavier "permold" crankcase. The older cases are prone to cracking, and an AD requires they be checked every 100 hours until replaced. Other ADs require repetitive inspections and work on items such as Hartzell props, landing gear uplock rollers and elevator control fittings.

Owner feedback provided no consensus on maintenance requirements. Some said their planes need constant attention; others contended they're no different from any other complex single (which may be saying the same thing). However, there is nearly unanimous lament about the cost of parts. One owner said Beech told him that the CHT probe he needed for his E33A was no longer in stock, but a $3,000 "instrument cluster kit" could be substituted. Another owner joined the chorus of outrage over prices but added that Beech parts "do seem to be of a higher quality and last longer than I've experienced with other airplanes." In any case, buying and refurbishing an older 33 can be an expensive proposition. "The Bonanza is a dream for the pilot-at-heart but a nightmare for the pauper-at-pocketbook," said an owner who bought a 20-year-old model for $42,000 and then spent another $68,000 upgrading the panel, interior and paint.

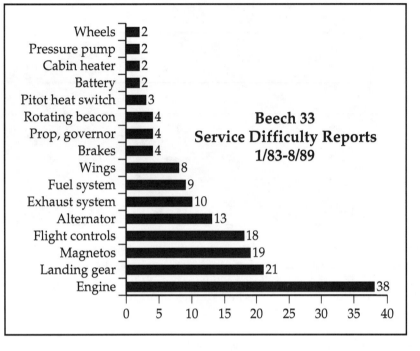

Beech 33
Service Difficulty Reports
1/83-8/89

Owners' Group

The American Bonanza Society is one of the best groups around. Members receive an informative newsletter and can attend service and proficiency clinics offered at about a dozen locations each year. The address is Mid-Continent Airport, 1922 Midfield Road, P.O. Box 12888, Wichita, Kans. 67209; (316) 945-6913.

Class Comparison

The toughest choice for a prospective buyer might be between a 33- and 35-model Bonanza. Among the other four-seaters, the speed and economy of the Mooney M20, especially the newer 201s, are something to consider. A Mooney will set you back about $40,000 less, which might make living with its Pee Wee Herman cabin and Schwartzenegger controls a bit easier. Cessna 182RGs also are relative bargains, but they're about 14 knots slower on about the same fuel and suffer from chronic landing gear problems. On the plus side, a Skylane RG can carry four adults, bags and enough fuel to fly for four hours, with no c.g. problems. And, like the 33s, they have a good safety record.

Then there's the Bellanca Viking, which has nice handling and a big engine, which somehow provides great climb performance but a lugubrious cruise. A Viking won't carry as much as a 33, and the cabin is tight and noisy. But you can get one of the wood and fabric jobs for about half the price. Don't expect to get away cheap on maintenance, though.

If you really need speed and the ability to carry four people and gear, a six-seat A36 or even a Cessna 210 might be a better choice. The stretched Bonanza doesn't have the tricky c.g. range, but its controls aren't quite as nice, either.

The 210 is downright truck-like, but it has good performance and can haul the Boston Pops. Prices of older A36s are reasonable, compared to the 33s, but late models are out of sight. The Cessnas generally can be had for $20-30,000 less than contemporary 33s, but the last 210s built seem to have become collectors' items with bloated prices.

Owner Comments

I own a 1961 Debonair with 4,600 hours TTAF and 1,500 hours on a reman IO-470K engine. With regard to engine maintenance, I have had no expensive mechanical breakdowns, no stuck valves, no cylinder cracks or oil leaks. I burn autogas mixed with Marvel Mystery Oil. The compression test after 1,500 hours was 72-74/80 on all cylinders. I also use AeroShell 15W50 mixed with two pints of STP at every 50-hour oil change. My annuals cost me $800.

The A33 is a stable platform in rough air. Trim control is adequate, and turn control is satisfactory. I average about 12 gph and cruise at 130-135 knots. Noise level could be improved with air seals on the doors and, perhaps, exhaust silencers; but I have been impressed with the economy and flight performance. I'm very happy with my Debonair.

John P. Miller, M.D.
Albertville, Ala.

I've owned a Debonair for the past five years. The plane is an absolute joy. The ease with which it handles, takes off and lands is just great. En route it trims out just fine. During climb-out, she does well up to about 8,000 feet and then slows down for the next 6,000 or so.

Annual inspection costs have varied. The first one cost $3,700, but this was mostly for catch-up work from the previous owner and included Cleveland brakes. The second was a surprising $680, with only $2.80 in parts. The third was a disaster. The elevators had to be reskinned, the exhaust system replaced and fuel-sending units redone, to the tune of $7,500. The next two annuals cost less than $800 each. One big problem that keeps popping up is the nuts and bolts on the exhaust stacks that become loose and require replacement.

Lawrence Haber
West Bloomfield, Mich.

The 1969 E33A I own is a fine aircraft; but parts are out-of-sight, and Beech couldn't care less. For example, a CHT probe is "no longer available" because the vendor (AC/Delco) quit. Beech's solution: a $3,002 "instrument cluster kit" (which, as of this writing, is no longer available). A new uplock cable was $63.25. A friend's A36 was grounded three weeks because the local Beech dealer doesn't stock a cowl latch. Beech advertises heavily to convince owners to buy Beech parts. I'd rather they'd spent the ad money on service and availability.

Richard Van Hoomissen
Portland, Ore.

I owned two Debs, the most recent a '65 C33 model, and have had a '72 A36 Bonanza for the past six years. The 33 is stable, very positive in its control characteristics—a smooth and forgiving instrument platform. Over about five years of flying the 33s, I had three problems. The major one was finding 80 octane fuel. I used 100 and worried about it, changed plugs about every 50 hours, but had no trouble.

The second problem was a hole about the size of a tuna fish that blew out of the manifold just below

If the standard throw-over wheel obscures part of the lower panel, the massive dual control bar doubles the obscuration. However, the dual controls have been high on the list of preferred items for thieves.

the "Y" of the exhaust system on a takeoff in crummy weather. The third was a cylinder that blew, again on takeoff. I thought about replacing the 225-hp engine with a 250 or 285. Though it can be done, it's not worth the trouble and cost.

Annuals for the 33s ran from $400 to $900, not counting such items as tires, paint, upholstery touch-up, etc. I got good service from Clark Aircraft Service in Opa Locka, Fla.; Blue Ridge Aviation, Gainesville, Ga.; and Epps in Atlanta.

A potential buyer should check the tanks, because if the originals are still in the plane, they'll leak sooner or later. Check the fuel tank change valves, too; they get sticky with age. Make sure mixture and prop controls are firm, as they have a tendency to creep off settings when worn.

Sylvan Meyer
Miami Beach, Fla.

At last, my chance to extol the virtues of my 1968 E33A. Its background included 18 years of high and dry living in Oklahoma and Texas. Compared with several contemporary models I inspected, it was free of corrosion, even in the gear mechanisms and under inspection plates. It also was one of the few Bonanzas I tried that didn't have the door pop open in flight. Before I bought the airplane, its engine had been reassembled with the first "heavy case" (-BA) after the crankcase cracked at roughly 150 SMOH. I'd only purchase a Continental-powered plane with a well-seasoned, heavy-case crankcase, one with a service history devoid of cracks.

My six hungry cylinders burn 13 gph at 8,000 feet, where true airspeed is as high as 173 knots. With 74 gallons of usable fuel, she'll easily outlast my personal range, with IFR reserves. The plane has plenty of get-up-and-go. On a recent trip to Colorado, we easily operated at 14,000 feet with a climb reserve of 500 fpm at 3,250 lbs. This plane is loaded with all the panel toys and still has a 1,200-lbs. useful load. Note that the E33A has the highest combination of airspeed and payload of all Beech 33s.

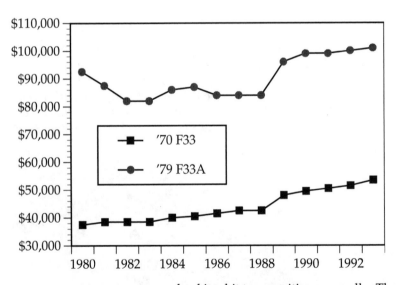

The Bonanza combines ample cabin space and good performance. It is very stable in pitch and roll, and flies well hands-off when trimmed. The 33 is a sweetheart on IFR procedures. Electric trim really helped; the elevator trim wheel is a bit too sensitive manually. The Dutch roll in turbulence really surprised me. Back-seaters can find Sik-Saks useful on hot, bumpy days below the top of the haze.

The Bonanza is a dream for the pilot-at-heart but a nightmare for the pauper-at-pocketbook. Substantial cash investment and realistic reserves must be allotted. I chose to invest in a '68 because of the performance premium and moderate initial price ($42K). For that, I also received my own panel-full of '60s vacuum-tube nostalgia. For safety's sake, I now fly behind a modern electronic wonder-panel. The King wizards at Joliet Avionics installed a total panel retrofit, all pre-wired and bench-tested with new switches and breaker panel. Of course, the interior had to go, and the paint needed a spectacular new look (Aircraft Mods, Mattoon, Ill.). So, for a $110K investment, I have a near-ultimate, four-place, factory-built, non-turbo, non-pressurized transportation machine.

At 200 to 300 hours per year, my operating cost is about $100/hour, which includes all expenses, an obsessive-compulsive approach to maintenance, engine and avionics reserve, etc. Remember, also, to save $2,000 to $4,000 for a top overhaul and $6,000 for crankcase cracks. I have had excellent service not only from Joliet Avionics, but from Slaybough Aviation in Decatur, as well.

Ralph Glasser, M.D.
Springfield, Ill.

I purchased my F33A new in 1987 and have flown it 750 hours. It is a great IFR platform and solid as a truck. Parts availability is fine; the prices, of course, are ridiculous. I have had to replace the starter, pressure pump, voltage regulator, mufflers and the alternator (twice). For some reason, the side glass has crazed, even though the aircraft has been hangared. Beech is very good about warranty claims; Teledyne Continental, horrible. TCM takes about four months to issue a credit. I've found Ronson Aviation in Trenton to do great work on a timely basis. Their maintenance department is superb. The airplane has dual wheels, which means you can't see the landing gear indicator lights without leaning way forward. Ronson added a set of duplicate indicators at the bottom edge of the floating panel. I would recommend this change to anyone with the antiquated steering assembly.

The F33A has a very noisy engine. Under no circumstances should long flights or single-pilot IFR be attempted without an intercom and noise-canceling headset. While the aircraft is a joy to fly, it needs to be handled by the numbers. Nail your MP and rpm, and you'll fly down the ILS on rails. The only criticism I have is the need to maintain major right rudder when taking off. Other than that, it is very docile in all flight regimes. With a gear operating speed of 154 knots, you can be high and fast, and drop like a stone without shock-cooling the engine.

My only problem with the airplane is that it is an antique. Other than the avionics, there is nothing in an '87 model that isn't in a '70 model. It is built in a factory out of the '50s with a design out of the '40s. I look forward to buying a modern airplane someday, and I am sure it won't be a Beech. It may be from Piper, the only one doing anything new.

Richard Tems
Doylestown, Pa.

I have owned an E33A for more than 10 years, an Arrow and a Comanche 250 and 260B before that. The Beech is the most stable, dependable plane I have ever owned. Although, perhaps, not as much fun to fly as the 260B Comanche, it is a superb instrument airplane. It dies a bit after 5,000-6,000 feet but manages to cruise at 150-160 knots.

Maintenance has not been too bad. I have updated the radios and autopilot (the old Brittain was a joke). Parts are available, but if you must buy them through Beech, they are VERY expensive. It is fortunate that I don't need major parts frequently. All in all, the E33A is the best plane I have ever owned, and it has never let me down. I have flown it over 1,400 hours and plan to keep it as long as they let me fly.

Arthur M. Vash
Boston, Mass.

Located below the pilot's left knee, the Debonair's fuel selector is in a less than desirable position.

I replaced a '66 Mooney M20E with a '74 F33A three years ago. The cabin is more comfortable, with airline-type seats, foot room, etc. One wears the Mooney, and it seemed to handle telepathically. That I find I must fly the 33 does not denigrate its handling qualities, which are crisp and responsive. There's a lot of panel space, but the c.g. limits are poor. With wife and infant child in back, myself and daughter in front, the baggage area is restricted to 125 pounds with other bags underfoot and 50 pounds of shot placed in the nose at the wheel arm. That puts c.g. within the envelope, but it may move too far aft with fuel burn. So, I weigh and calculate, in spite of advice that "it can handle it."

Annuals have cost about $1,000, but there are always extras: $1,400 for propeller overhaul; $2,500 for a backup vacuum pump; new windshield, $1,500. Now, the bladders are starting to leak. If it's not one thing, it's another. The IO-520 requires a soap bath every 50 hours to check for leaks and cracks. There's nothing wrong with the crankshaft, but should you open the case it's got to come out and be dyed and electrocuted. Makes one feel good.

I flight plan for 160 knots at 22/2300 and burn 14.5 gph. It's great for short family trips; however, in going N.Y. to Fla., I wish that the wings would slide back a foot. It's stable hands-off when trimmed, if the tanks are balanced; otherwise, an easy spiral. There's no rudder trim, so you need a heavy right foot on takeoff. Descents must be planned so as not to climb over the 150s in the pattern.

Marvin Levine, D.D.S.
Bronx, N.Y.

Cost/Performance/Specifications

Model	Year	Average Retail Price	Cruise Speed (kt)	Useful Load (lb)	Std/Opt Fuel (gal)	Engines	TBO (hr)	Overhaul Cost @
33 Debonair	1960	$32,500	156	1,170	44/63	225-hp Cont. IO-470J	1,500	$13,500
A33 Debonair	1961	$34,500	160	1,250	44/63	225-hp Cont. IO-470J	1,500	$13,500
B33 Debonair	1962-64	$38,500	160	1,250	44/74	225-hp Cont. IO-470J	1,500	$13,500
C33 Debonair	1965-67	$44,000	160	1,200	44/74	225-hp Cont. IO-470J	1,500	$13,500
C33A Debonair	1966-67	$52,000	174	1,525	44/74	285-hp Cont. IO-520B	1,700	$13,500
E33 Bonanza	1968-69	$47,500	160	1,200	44/74	225-hp Cont. IO-470K	1,500	$13,500
E33A Bonanza	1968-69	$52,500	174	1,385	44/74	285-hp Cont. IO-520B	1,700	$13,500
E33C Bonanza	1968-69	$55,000	174	1,380	44/74	285-hp Cont. IO-520B	1,700	$13,500
F33 Bonanza	1970	$49,500	160	1,200	44/74	225-hp Cont. IO-470K	1,500	$13,500
G33 Bonanza	1972-73	$56,000	174	1,365	44/74	250-hp Cont. IO-470N	1,700	$13,500
F33C Bonanza	1970-90	$61-139K	174	1,525	44/74	285-hp Cont. IO-520BA	1,700	$13,500
F33A Bonanza	1970-75	$67,000	172	1,280	44/74	285-hp Cont. IO-520BA	1,700	$14,500
F33A Bonanza	1975-80	$91,000	172	1,280	44/74	285-hp Cont. IO-520BB	1,700	$14,500
F33A Bonanza	1980-85	$119,000	172	1,280	44/74	285-hp Cont. IO-520BB	1,700	$14,500
F33A Bonanza	1985-89	$154,000	172	1,280	44/74	285-hp Cont. IO-520BB	1,700	$14,500

Beech Bonanza 35

The big question for a lot of prospective V-tail Bonanza buyers has to be: Is the world's most coveted and controversial aircraft out of the woods? The answer appears to be: "Yes." The program of tail strengthening, combined with a concerted campaign to flush out all the latent empennage afflictions that could contribute to catastrophe seem to have produced sterling results. The number of inflight airframe breakups has dropped to heartening, low levels after years of unpleasant statistics.

With production halted over a decade ago, in 1982, there are no new replacements to the line, so now a big consideration for buyers involves checking out ever-older birds for hidden flaws.

History

The first V-tail Bonanzas were so ingeniously conceived it appears they sprang from the mind of designer Ralph Harmon and others full-blown in the dim past of 1945. They were fast and slick, and the basic format was retained for decades through myriad fine-tuning and strengthening and bigger-engine iterations.

But by no means were the aircraft's design features hastily concocted. Instead they received the benefit of wind tunnel testing and considerable study to find ways to boost speed and increase safety. As a result, they received fully retractable tricycle gear, with no projecting bumps or humps as on some other aircraft. Extensive use of flush-riveting was also used.

A unique fuselage design incorporated a sled-like keel arrangement and box structure to increase crashworthiness. Big side windows were hinged at the top with quick release openings at the bottom to allow easy escape in an emergency. A side benefit that was blessed forever afterward by rear-seat passengers was access to cooling breezes during taxi in hot weather.

Avoid Straight 35s

The first so-called "straight 35" model Bonanza had a 165-hp Continental engine that produced an amazing 175 mph at cruise speed. Inexpensive though these oldies may now be, we would counsel potential buyers to avoid this model like the plague. That's because it has the highest percentage of inflight breakups of any of the V-tail Bonanzas. By 1984 a total of 75 of the 1,500 "straight 35s" had experienced fatal breakups. That adds up to five percent or one out of every 20.

Unlike later models, the "straight 35" lacks a shear web in the main wing spar—a design strategy undertaken to save weight. And though Beech offered a "35R" wing-strengthening conversion program in 1951, there were not many takers for the expensive mod (then $6,000, compared to the cost of a new C35 of only $12,990). We understand only 13 of the 1,500 aircraft were converted. We estimate some 600 unmodified straight 35s are still flying without any major structural modification. Stay away, folks, is our advice.

With the succeeding A35, Beech made important strengthening improvements, added a new wing carrythrough structure and thicker wing skins and fuselage

stringers, while beefing up the fuselage bulkhead at the tail attachment. On the B35, a slight power boost during takeoff of 11 hp was engineered by allowing a slightly higher rpm.

With the C35 major changes were made to the stabilizer. The chord was increased by 14.4% and the dihedral increased slightly in an attempt to reduce yawing. The chord increase was made by simply extending the leading edge, but leaving the front spar where it was. This created a greater "overhang"

The "straight 35" got an astounding 172 mph on 165 hp on its maiden flight in 1945. To save weight, the airplane had no shear web in the wing spar. This proved to be a bad mistake: the straight 35 has the worst in-flight breakup record of all V-tails.

forward of the spar that would figure in tail-twisting during inflight breakups, and would later be secured by a bracket after a big FAA/Beech investigation into the breakup problem.

With the E35, buyers had the option of a 225-hp Continental engine. Also, aileron trim was added for the first time, and back-seat passengers got a couple inches more leg room. The magnesium flaps were replaced with aluminum ones.

In the G35 the wing was beefed up once again. And gear extension speed went up from 125 to 140 mph, the first in a series of speed boosts that would make the landing gear an effective speed brake.

Second Generation

The H model represents what Larry Ball in his book, "The Incomparable Bonanzas," calls the beginning of a second generation of Bonanzas. It got a bigger, new 240-hp powerplant which for the first time in the line offered identical takeoff and max. continuous horsepower. This was the first wet sump design for the Bonanzas, allowing oil to be carried internally rather than in a separate oil tank. Additional strengthening was also added to tail, fuselage and wings.

The big change on the J35 was a bigger, new 250-hp fuel-injected power-plant. Earlier engines had carburetors. Emergency gear-extension speed went to a whopping 200 mph. Right-hand rudder pedals could be collapsed completely flat for more leg room when not in use.

On the K35 the standard fuel capacity was boosted from 40 to 50 gallons, which with the 20-gallon aux tanks gave a finally decent 70 gallons. Also, an optional fifth jump seat was offered, allowing more chances to load aft of the weight-and-balance envelope. Throw it away is our advice.

Improved Fuel Management

Elongated, curved rear side windows were added to the N35. Horsepower went up to 260, and fuel capacity rose to 80 gallons, while the number of fuel tanks was reduced to two. This was done by offering optional 40-gallon tanks in place of the standard 25-gallon tanks. This, along with first-time "full time" fuel quantity gauges provided to both tanks naturally simplified fuel management, and should be regarded as a good safety feature.

The addition of new, long leading edge fuel tanks displaced wing landing lights, which in turn were moved to the nose and nose gear strut. A new utility shelf increased baggage space by almost six cubic feet. And irony of irony, shoulder harnesses became optional equipment because, according to Larry Ball's book, "of low utilization." Pilots concerned with tracking troublesome magnesium components might also note the ailerons were switched to aluminum.

Big change on the P35 was a completely redesigned instrument panel, with the famous "piano keyboard" switch arrangement abandoned. Also, normal landing gear extension speed went up from 140 to 165 mph.

The S35 Bonanza went big-time in more ways than one with a 285-hp powerplant and a longer cabin with a new aft window shape like the Baron's. The aft bulkhead was moved back 19 inches. But the extra cabin length didn't come free: a 25-pound lead weight was added to the nose for balance. Now the Bonanza had room for six seats—two more in back. Again, we'd counsel they be abandoned. But a nice optional rear cargo door allowed easier access to the back of the cabin.

Visibility out front took a nice jump with the V35 model as a one-piece windshield was made standard. And on the V35A that followed, a bigger, swept windshield was added that allowed more space behind the instrument panel for maintenance. A V35TC turbocharged model was added to the line for the first time, also. Normal gear-down speed went from 165 to 175 mph. The big safety improvement on the V35Bs was addition of anti-slosh fuel cells to prevent inadvertent unporting of fuel during slips, skids and turning takeoffs.

Performance

Bonanzas are justifiably famous for their speed, and owners report cruise figures of from 150 to 175 knots, depending on engine power. Said Frank Andrews, "Easily the most speed available under $30,000. My 35G (with 225 hp) trues out just over 156 knots on 12 gph." Naturally, the big 285-hp birds do even better. Mooney pilots love to boast, with some justification, of their power/speed ratios, but the Bonanzas zip right along, and allow lots more elbow room, in the bargain.

The flip side of the Bonanza's clean design, of course, is that in an upset or spiral dive the aircraft will pick up speed in a flash.

Handling

Everybody waxes ecstatic. A flier can easily develop a love-hate relationship with the aircraft. The controls are silky smooth, light and facile like almost nothing else. Aileron and pitch pressures are near perfect (very light stick forc-

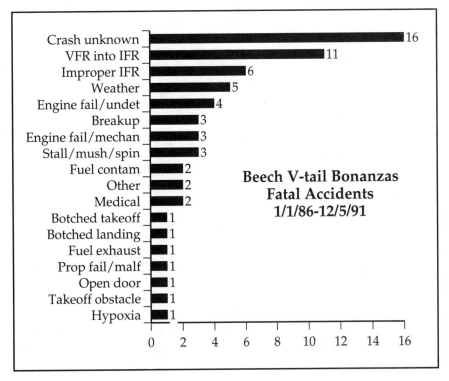

Beech V-tail Bonanzas
Fatal Accidents
1/1/86-12/5/91

Crash unknown	16
VFR into IFR	11
Improper IFR	6
Weather	5
Engine fail/undet	4
Breakup	3
Engine fail/mechan	3
Stall/mush/spin	3
Fuel contam	2
Other	2
Medical	2
Botched takeoff	1
Botched landing	1
Fuel exhaust	1
Prop fail/malf	1
Open door	1
Takeoff obstacle	1
Hypoxia	1

Bonanza KFC 200 Autopilot

Because the avionics and autopilot make up an important part of the used-airplane buying decision, a discussion of the flight control typical of Bonanzas is worthwhile. Due to the sheer longevity and popularity of the Bonanza line, almost any autopilot system ever made has at one time or another been installed. That includes everything from a Brittain vacuum system to a state-of-the-art Bendix/King KFC 150 or S-Tec System 65.

The controversy surrounding the King KFC 200 in the wake of some media reports has raised questions about the value of the KFC 200 in a used Bonanza. As a former KFC 200 product specialist with Bendix/King, this reporter came to know the system and the difficulties that are frequently encountered. Forewarned is fore armed, and with the knowledge of what to look for, you might be able to snatch up a good deal.

The Beech Bonanza was one of the first airplanes to get the KFC 200 from the factory. Consequently, King Radio and Beechcraft learned a great deal about the system on Bonanzas (and Barons). Perhaps the biggest problem encountered in the early going was a groundloop in the attitude gyro (KI 256) and flight computer (KC 295). These mis-groundings induce noise in the attitude pick-offs, and while the airplane can't respond quickly to this noise, it really warms up the servos, which spend their life trying to go both ways at once.

To make matters worse, a misunderstanding of the electrical interconnect led to a "daisy-chain" in the power supply. Where the best interconnect will provide a separate wire from the avionics bus to each servo, Beechcraft (and more than a few field installations in Bonanzas, and other airplanes) ran a single wire from the bus to the roll servo, then to the pitch servo, etc. If you think of the wire as an electron hose, you can imagine that the last one on the line was not getting all the juice it needed, having to share with the equipment upstream.

Servo Failures

In addition, the servo grounds were often less than adequate. The sum total of these deficiencies is autopilot servos which are trying to react quickly to noise signals, but lack the current necessary to function efficiently. The consequences were frequently servo failures. Typically, one or both directions would fail because the power transistors would fry. Occasionally, we see servo motors get clogged with brush material and fail, or change their speed and drive characteristics. Fortunately, because of the fail-passive design of the KFC 200 servos, they would cease to drive in one direction. But it is possible that the servo would drive, uncommanded, in one direction, and we've seen it happen on a few cases.

The autopilot flight manual always has as the first limitation, "During autopilot operation, a pilot with a seat belt fastened must be seated at the left pilot position." It would be good if this guy was awake, too, because he should be alert for any deviation from the prescribed flight path, either as a result of the autopilot driving unintentionally, or not controlling the airplane due to a servo or even a vacuum failure.

Key Check Points

What should a Bonanza buyer look for? Naturally, the later Bonanzas, particularly the post 1983 models, are best with regard to the factory installations. All the lessons were learned, including installation of ruggedized KS 27X "A" servos, available since 1984. These servos are direct replacements for original equipment and should always be installed whenever an older servo is changed.

Ships built before about 1978 are suspect, as are all field installations. Sadly, very few avionics shops are competent to make a complicated autopilot installation, and many will take the steps that Beech took unintentionally, in our opinion. After all, it often takes 100 hours for the problems to turn up, and many more before the owner realizes that these are chronic failures, related to the installation.

Besides checking for wiring problems, a Bonanza buyer should be conscious of the roll servo location.

On early Model 35 airplanes (s/n D-9961 and below), the roll servo is located in the wheel well on the pilot's side. In that area, the servo is exposed to the weather, mud and slop kicked up into the well. Sure, the servo is covered, but experience tells us that a servo installed inside the fuselage will live a healthier life. Besides, a wing-mounted servo is a dead give-away that the STC is an early one, and prone to the foibles we covered above.

Three Generations

The V-tailed Bonanzas have three distinct generations of KFC 200—naturally the later the better, although modifications are not always retrofittable. A quick way to tell which system iteration you are dealing with is to glance through the little window on top of the KC 295 flight computer. If the number is -01 or -03, look out. This indicates the earliest certification. A dash-thirty something is mod-term, and will perform adequately, while a number in the seventies indicates the best combination of servo and computer.

In 1987, Bendix/King changed the roll servo to one with higher RPM. This also necessitated a change in the computer. Anytime the roll servo is changed, make sure the same part number goes back in. Many shops "know" that the roll servo in a Bonanza is a -00, and fail to check that the bird has been modified until the plane comes back.

A peek at the control wheel also will offer a clue to the relative epoch of the KFC 200. The first systems had a one-piece Manual Electric Trim switch. This is a dead giveaway for a slow trim speed, and an early certification. Other things being equal, we'd put any airplane with a split switch ahead of single button switch.

When considering the purchase of a KFC 200-equipped Bonanza, a review of the autopilot system is in order. A good KFC 200 service center will be able to tell with a few hours of inspection time if the KFC 200 is properly installed. Most of the Beechcraft stores will be very familiar with each of the deficiencies we've described.

es per G—don't yank back at high speeds, or the airframe can be overstressed), and landings are, time and again, a dream.

But the tail-waggle is there, and it's real, and except for diehards it's a nuisance in turbulence, especially in the back seat. Lots of people have methods for reducing the annoyance factor, perhaps by trying to anticipate the waggle with the rudders, or just holding pressure to keep them steady. But probably the best, if most expensive solution, is to hook up a yaw damper.

Load and Cabin Comfort

A ride in a Bonanza cabin is pure joy. Not only is there shoulder and head room to squander, but the giant windows give an unmatched airiness and visibility. The aircraft's loading Achilles' heel is its relatively narrow weight-and-balance envelope. It's all too easy to get out of the envelope to the rear—a potentially nasty situation in any airplane. And on later models, as fuel burns out of the leading edge wing tanks, the center of gravity shifts farther to the rear, aggravating the situation. In fact, the V-tail Bonanzas have generally stricter rear cg limits than the straight-tail models, which means that the same load will put you a lot closer to the aft limit in a V-tail.

Flying with an aft cg markedly reduces an aircraft's longitudinal stability. This means that turbulence will cause greater airspeed excursions. It also means that control wheel forces will become much lighter, making it easier for the pilot to pull too hard and overstress the airplane.

Maintenance Record

Our inspection of a six-year run of Service Difficulty Reports suggests that buyers should be alert to three main problem areas: damaged control cables, rods, fittings, etc.; malfunctioning, out-of-order landing gear components; and corrosion.

We noted numerous instances of broken, rusty, twisted and frayed cables (what else can happen to them?); cracked ruddervator control horns and torque fittings and bent or worn push rods.

There were also quite a few reports of corrosion in the aft fuselage section—many uncovered during the thorough inspection required by Beech Aircraft Corp. as part of the tail-brace installation. (AD 87-20-02 and Beech Service Bulletin 2188 apply here. The Beech kit part is P/N 35-4016-3.) Uncovering these discrepancies can only have saved much grief later on. Corrosion was found under stringers and on ruddervator skins and ribs.

Proper ruddervator balance has always been a critical matter on the V-tail Bonanzas, to prevent flutter, which can contribute to severe structural damage and even inflight breakups. The balance margin is so narrow that unbalance could result from repainting the ruddervators without rebalancing afterwards.

During the course of one inspection to comply with the Beech Service Bulletin mechanics found they could not balance the left ruddervator per Beech specs. It was decided to strip and repaint to correct the balance. During the stripping a two-oz. weight came loose from the trailing edge. It had broken loose from the screw for who knows how long a period. Another SDR noted that under a repainted section of the ruddervator of a V35B there was body filler covering up holes in the skin caused by corrosion and missing rivets.

Unbalanced ruddervators can result in this kind of serious empennage twisting. Luckily, this aircraft landed intact.

Corrosion is often encountered with magnesium components like the ruddervators, and on some Bonanzas the flaps and ailerons. But check other components as well, as the Bonanza fleet ages. Some corrosion may have been well hidden. One report on a P35 Bonanza noted heavy corrosion on the top flanges of the aft keel assemblies caused by moisture in the fiberglass quilt laminated between the floor panel and keel flange. This was discovered after the rear floor panel was removed during the annual inspection. Corrosion also has been found on wing spar caps and wing bolts and wing attach fittings, as the bolts were removed for a five-year inspection recommended by Beech.

Spar Cracking

While on the subject of damage control, we should note that the FAA issued AD 91-14-13 calling for inspection of Bonanza wing spar carry-through webs for cracks. These were to be accomplished on aircraft with 1,500 hours or more and repeated every 500 hours. AOPA petitioned the FAA to rescind the AD, and the agency dropped the 500-hour repetitive inspection, but retained the initial inspection requirement, asking that reports of cracks be relayed to them.

Beech Service Bulletin 2360, which details the inspection, was issued before the AD came out, noting there had been reports of web cracking. Beech estimated four man-hours would be required for visual and dye-penetrant inspection during a routine inspection. The company can supply structural reinforcement kits if cracks are found. In some cases cracks can simply be stop drilled. (Incidentally, despite the FAA dropping the 500-hour repetitive inspection, Beech recommended it in its "mandatory" Service Bulletin.)

Gear Watch

Judging from both SDRs and accident reports, the landing gear should be a subject for close scrutiny by prospective buyers. Aside from the absolutely horrendous number of inadvertent gear retractions, there are numerous reports of gear system malfunctions and gear collapsing episodes. It's hard to isolate any special weak area in malfunctioning gear parts since there were reports on everything from corroded braces to broken plunger assemblies, broken rod end bearings, frayed uplock cables, inoperative down limit switches, broken idler arms, brace

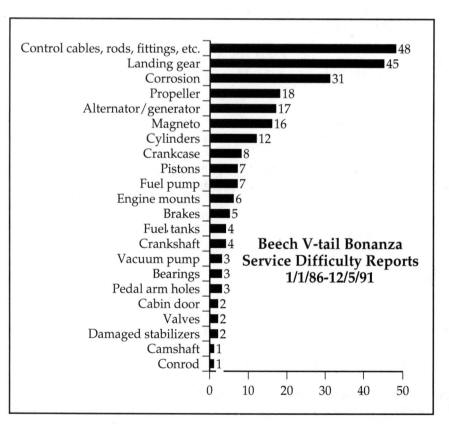

Control cables, rods, fittings, etc.	48
Landing gear	45
Corrosion	31
Propeller	18
Alternator/generator	17
Magneto	16
Cylinders	12
Crankcase	8
Pistons	7
Fuel pump	7
Engine mounts	6
Brakes	5
Fuel tanks	4
Crankshaft	4
Vacuum pump	3
Bearings	3
Pedal arm holes	3
Cabin door	2
Valves	2
Damaged stabilizers	2
Camshaft	1
Conrod	1

Beech V-tail Bonanza Service Difficulty Reports 1/1/86-12/5/91

0   10   20   30   40   50

castings, retract arms, etc., ad nauseum.

Crankcase Bugaboo

We were interested to note only a handful of reports on cracking crankcases in our six-year rundown, but the FAA warned that some engine reports may not have been included in the run they made for us. In the past, the Continental IO- and TSIO-520 series engines have been prey to the curse of cracking crankcases, so it pays to check closely. The cracks are not a safety hazard, of course, but a possible economic one.

Bonanza buyers also should be aware of research by *The Aviation Consumer* (May 1, 1991 issue) tracking a relatively high incidence

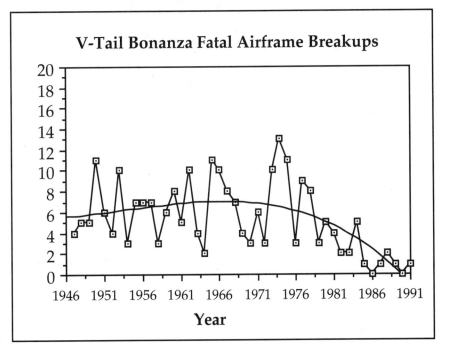

of cylinder cracking in Continental -520 series engines. Although we tracked this as occurring less often in Bonanzas than in Barons and Cessna 402s, Continental has issued a "mandatory" service bulletin (M91-6) calling for inspections every 35 hours of -520-series cylinders with certain part numbers that that were manufactured after 1980. The engine builder, however, is offering new cylinders that eliminate the need for inspections. For what it's worth, we noted a dozen cases of cylinder problems on Bonanzas in our SDR run.

Safety Record

As we mentioned earlier, V-tail Bonanza pilots forget to lower the gear or yank it up unintentionally in astounding numbers. We counted no fewer than 188 instances in our six-year run of 668 accidents. That's 28 percent of all accidents during that period. Once again, the harm is mostly to the pocketbook (and everybody's insurance rates).

Since the gear/flap switch arrangement is the reverse of many other retractable aircraft, quite possibly this contributes to the apparently common tendency to raise gear instead of flaps after landing or during a touch-and-go. The best counsel a new Bonanza pilot can heed is to leave the flaps down until the aircraft is back at the tiedown area, and the correct lever has been calmly sorted out. Don't expect the squat switch to prevent a collapse; all too often it doesn't, the statistics show.

Ghastly Gear Glitches

As we noted above, even without the pilot contributing to the problem, the gear often enough will collapse of its own accord, thanks to mechanical problems. We tallied 79 gear collapses and 16 gear mechanical failures of other types—gear wouldn't come down, wouldn't go up, etc.

We also tallied a number of gear collapses occurring after the aircraft encountered an electrical failure. Every new Bonanza trainee should be instructed in how to crank the gear down manually. It appears that all too often the pilot will stop turning the little crank when it becomes stiff and before the mechanism is fully extended. Keep turning it until it stops. A typical SDR comment: "Total electric failure. Manually put gear down. Gear collapsed on rollout." (Incidentally, we listed these as electrical failure accidents, since that was the primary or original problem, so the gear-collapse tally is higher than our chart reflects.)

Although engine failures luckily don't often result in fatal accidents, they happen often enough to be a major concern. We counted 74 of them all together, or 11 percent of the total accidents. Half were attributed to mechanical breakdowns of some type or other; the others were a mystery. There were only seven fatal engine failures in the six-year study period.

Fatals

The biggest category of fatal Bonanza accidents is the scary one of "crash unknown." The biggest Bonanza killer that can be identified involves VFR pilots blundering into weather they can't handle and IFR pilots doing the same.

A cabin door opening is blamed for a fatal crash, while in six other instances the pilots made it back to terra firma alive. But they didn't always get off scot-free since all too often the aircraft went off the end of the runway. One airplane was destroyed by fire after it hit some trees. In another case the flustered pilot landed with the gear up.

Beech issued a "mandatory" service bulletin in 1990 (No. 2190) that should be heeded, since it outlines inspection procedures to prevent inadvertent door openings, says that unpleasant aerodynamic effects will not occur, and even provides a red sticker warning everybody to properly latch the door before takeoff.

Cost/Performance/Specifications

Model	Year	Average Retail Price	Cruise Speed (kts)	Useful Load (lbs)	Fuel Std/Opt (gals)	Engine	TBO (hrs)	Overhaul Cost
35	1947-48	$19,000	152	992	40/60	165-hp Cont. E-165	1,500	$13,000
A35	1949	$19,500	150	1,070	40/60	185-hp Cont. E-185-1	1,500	$13,000
B35	1950	$20,500	150	1,075	40/60	196-hp Cont. E-185-8	1,500	$13,000
C/D35	1951-53	$24,500	155	1,053	40/60	205-hp Cont. E-185-11	1,500	$13,000
E35	1954	$27,250	157	1,050	40/60	225-hp Cont. E-225-8	1,500	$13,000
F35	1955	$28,000	157	1,053	40/60	225-hp Cont. E-225-8	1,500	$13,000
G35	1956	$29,000	165	1,053	40/60	225-hp Cont. E-225-8	1,500	$13,000
H35	1957	$32,250	170	1,067	40/60	240-hp Cont. O-470-G	1,700	$14,000
J35	1958	$35,000	174	1,080	40/60	250-hp Cont. IO-470-C	1,500	$14,500
K35	1959	$36,000	174	1,118	50/70	250-hp Cont. IO-470-C	1,500	$14,500
M35	1960	$37,000	174	1,118	50/70	250-hp Cont. IO-470-C	1,500	$14,500
N35	1961	$38,500	170	1,270	50/80	260-hp Cont. IO-470-N	1,500	$14,500
P35	1962-63	$40,500	170	1,270	50/80	260-hp Cont. IO-470-N	1,500	$14,500
S35	1964-65	$47,000	178	1,415	50/80	285-hp Cont. IO-520-BA	1,700	$15,000
V35	1966-67	$49,500	177	1,459	50/80	285-hp Cont. IO-520-BA	1,700	$15,000
V35TC	1966-67	$55,000	200	1,400	50/80	285-hp Cont. IO-520-BA	1,700	$18,000
V35A	1968-69	$53,000	177	1,442	50/80	285-hp Cont. IO-520-BA	1,700	$15,000
V35A-TC	1968-69	$58,500	200	1,379	50/80	285-hp Cont. TSIO-520-D	1,400	$18,000
V35B	1970-72	$66,000	177	1,428	50/80	285-hp Cont. IO-520-BA	1,700	$15,000
V35B-TC	1970	$66,500	200	1,365	50/80	285-hp Cont. IO-520-BA	1,400	$18,000
V35B	1973-75	$75,500	177	1,415	50/80	285-hp Cont. IO-520-BA	1,700	$15,000
V35B	1976-78	$87,500	177	1,415	50/80	285-hp Cont. IO-520-BA	1,700	$15,000
V35B	1979-81	$108,500	177	1,415	50/80	285-hp Cont. IO-520-BB	1,700	$15,000
V35B	1982	$130,000	177	1,415	50/80	285-hp Cont. IO-520-BB	1,700	$15,000

Price from Aircraft Bluebook Price Digest

History of Tail Repair

Despite the V-tail's long history of inflight breakups, Beech Aircraft year after year ardently defended the aircraft's strength and flying qualities and blamed the problem on pilot incompetence. Typically, the explanation went, pilots would get caught in bad weather beyond their skill level and lose control of the aircraft. In the ensuing dive the aircraft would exceed redline limits, and in attempting to pull out, the pilot would rip off the wings and/or tail. Stay within the envelope, the message was, and all would be fine.

Strangely, however, a minuscule fraction of Beech 33s, identical to the V-tails except for the tails, were experiencing inflight airframe failures.

At any rate, after the resale value of the V-tails had plummeted alarmingly, members of the American Bonanza Society asked the FAA to check out the airplane and once and for all come up with an assessment as to whether the aircraft was flawed. Beech Aircraft agreed to cooperate fully in the investigation, according to then-president Linden Blue. The FAA thereupon commissioned the Department of Transportation to study the matter, and a blue-ribbon panel of engineering experts did so.

Beech Tizzy

Their findings, in a nutshell, were that although the V-tail Bonanzas evidently met the certification regulations, those engineering requirements failed to encompass the idiosyncrasies of the V-tail configuration. The DoT report therefore recommended further testing of the tail. Beech Aircraft, which had pledged its support, flew into a tizzy and fired a legal salvo aimed at blocking release of the report to the public. The company sued the FAA, the DoT, etc. A judge ruled Beech was out of line, however, and that the public interest overbalanced their private interest. The report was made public.

With some alacrity—interesting considering decades of refusal to publicly retest the aircraft to corroborate its strength—Beech launched a series of wind tunnel and flight tests, with the FAA looking on. And surprise! Beech and the FAA discovered the tail didn't meet the FAA's strength requirements. It turned out there was a corner of the "legal" envelope in which the tail could be overstressed.

Slow-down Order

Result: The FAA issued a slow-down order (AD 86-21-07) to remain in effect until a fix was provided. And Beech came out with a tail-bracing kit almost identical to one offered by B&N on the aftermarket as a safety measure (so similar, in fact, that Beech purchased the rights). On some aircraft, skin doublers were added as well. Another interesting aspect to this development was that while Mike Smith, B&N and Knots 2U all were offering similar kits to strengthen the tail, Beech Aircraft, echoed by the American Bonanza Society, was counseling Bonanza owners to steer away from them because they might insidiously transfer dangerous loads elsewhere.

The Beech leading edge tail cuff goes on the C35 through V35B models, thanks to AD 87-20-02, but an extra wrap-around reinforcement goes on C35 through G35 models. As it turns out, certain V-tail models are deemed sufficiently safe to require no tail beefups. These are the original model 35, the A35 and the B35. We would caution potential buyers of these models that their record is not exactly lily-white, however. The DoT report showed that no fewer than 75 model 35s have gone down in pieces from in-flight structural failure through the years, along with 19 A35s and nine B35s.

A Good Buy?

An *Aviation Consumer* study in 1989 was launched to determine if the V-tail Bonanzas represented a good buy, in light of the tumble that resale prices took while its reputation suffered from breakup fears. Indeed, resale prices appeared to plunge sharply in comparison with the model 33, starting in 1983. In fact, in 1989 V-tail model 35s, almost across the board, could be bought on the average for $3,000 to $12,000 less than straight-tail 33s built in the same year. However, a quick look at the curve of the resale prices on the nearby chart for 1979 models suggests the gap appears to have begun disappearing in 1990.

We should also note that the V-tail still takes considerable attention from owners and mechanics to ensure proper ruddervator balance, particularly after painting. Failure to do so could cause metal-bending vibration or flutter. Perhaps triggered by a severe case of empennage twisting in a 1949 V-tail in 1990 that drew widespread attention, the FAA issued a special airworthiness alert to V-tail Bonanza owners with procedures to guard against imbalance. The FAA noted that since 1947 there have been 11 reported cases of V-tail flutter problems, resulting in varying degrees of airframe damage, though in each case the pilots landed safely.

Longtime pilots of Bonanzas and Barons will tell you that sooner or later almost everyone will experience the thrill of a door popping open, often during the takeoff roll. It makes a horrendous noise, sucks out half the charts on your lap and is nearly impossible to close while airborne. But keep your cool (and before takeoff counsel your passengers to do the same), and remember it's no sweat. Just return and land.

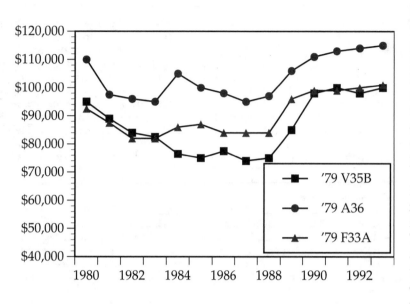

Legend:
- ■ '79 V35B
- ● '79 A36
- ▲ '79 F33A

Breakups

The six years of accident records suggest that the V-tail Bonanza's penchant for inflight airframe failures has been largely tamed. Although we hesitate to announce final breakup figures since there were so many unexplained fatal crashes (16), we were able to identify only five fatal breakups in the study period.

In two of the six years we could find no fatal breakups at all recorded, and in three of those years, only one each. This represents a big improvement in a daunting record of past breakups totaling 240 V-tails since 1947. It's difficult to tell whether the tail brace kits, or the mass empennage inspection and upgrade have improved the situation most. We'd guess both together did the job.

Incidentally, in some of the recent breakups the tail-strengthening kit had been installed, we are told, so that alone appears not to be infallible protection. And we spotted two cases where serious structural damage had occurred in flight, attributed to tail flutter, but the pilots landed safely.

Fuel (Mis)management

In this safety study, as in past ones, we noticed a fairly high incidence of fuel mismanagement accidents in Bonanzas. Time and again pilots ran one tank dry while they still had fuel in another. Typical comment: "Engine quit on final. Landed short of runway. Fuel selector on empty tank. Other tanks full." As we noted earlier, it wasn't until the N35 model that a pilot could see how much fuel was in each tank all the time without switching.

In a number of cases the engine quit when the pilot switched fuel tanks. The report occasionally noted that the pilot had failed to use the auxiliary boost pump. But if an engine does quit from fuel starvation, the Bonanza pilot faces a dilemma: turn on the boost pump or not? If he doesn't, according to a CAB study, the engine may take as long as 35 seconds to restart. If he does, he may flood the engine if the pump is left on too long. The owner's manual of one model Bonanza instructs the pilot to turn on the boost pump "momentarily" when switching from a dry tank.

So the pilot must tread a narrow line between a fuel-starved engine on the one hand and a flooded-out engine on the other hand. Not a happy choice.

In other instances the pilot failed to get the fuel selector in the correct detent. Since the selector detents are poorly defined in some models, it's possible to hang up the selector between tanks, shutting off the fuel. Also, the location of the fuel selector under the pilot's left leg doesn't make for great viewing.

Among other safety items worth mentioning, we noticed an SDR reporting that fuel selector screen assemblies continue to be installed upside down, "due to a lack of understanding as to how this important screen works." And we see that

Beech with Service Bulletin No. 2305 has issued instructions on inspection and installation of the fuel strainer screen, along with a warning placard. If installed upside down, Beech warns, unfiltered fuel could enter the engine, which could cause power interruption.

Comparative Standing

Our most recent comparative study of accident rates (for the years 1984-1986) placed the V-tail Bonanza second best in total accident rate among 11 other four-place retractables (after the Beech 33—wouldn't you know it?) and fifth best in fatal rate (after the Beech 33, Mooney M20, Cessna 172RG and Arrow).

Owner Organization

The American Bonanza Society provides a good-looking four-color newsletter, plus lots of technical advice, and it sponsors pilot training and maintenance clinics around the country. Their address is Box 12888, Wichita, Kans. 67209, (316) 945-6913.

Owner Comments

Of the three V-tails I've flown (S35, V35A, V35B), the V35A is more stable and has less of the characteristic "fishtail" than the other two, although it does show up in gusty winds. Moderate (10-14 kt) crosswinds are handled well, but above that the aileron/ruddervator interconnect makes cross-controlling limited. Thus, a crab approach, judicious use of power, and good timing are necessary to avoid side-stressing the gear. Even though the main gear is very strong, I wouldn't subject it to a side load.

We added flap and aileron gap seals two years ago and noted the most pronounced change was low-speed controllability, particularly from the ailerons during landing. There has been some noted increase in the climb rate at higher altitudes, particularly on the rare occasion when we go above 13,000. It makes it to 17,000 with greater ease now. We also removed the metal passenger step at the same time, but I cannot honestly say I've noticed any speed increases.

Of the problems I've noticed, one is the longevity of the nose-mounted landing light. This light burns out often (18 hours), even though we've vertically mounted the element.

Another problem we've been unable to trace is a once-a-year "popping" of the landing gear circuit breaker during gear transit. It seems random and unrelated to anything we can identify, but results in a gear neither up nor down. The instrument panel lights are the primary indication of a mid-transit stoppage. Reset the breaker, everything's okay.

One other comment I'd like to make concerns the retrofit of shoulder harnesses. Beech sells a pair of the belts for $1,500+, or over $3,000 for front and rear. Installation is extra. I encourage Beech to support a near-cost installation program for these belts. It should help to avoid the human costs of injury, promote a better corporate image, and result in a better legal atmosphere from which to make a defense.

Ken Peppard
Dumfries, Va.

Last of the line was the V35B, which was introduced in 1970. A one-piece windshield that was more swept than earlier models improved access to the rear of the instrument panel.

The Bonanza's complex systems (at least compared to a C-172) require that the pilot *know* the flight manual. For example, the 20-gal. aux tanks run dry in just over one hour with 12 gph consumed and 4 gph returned to the left main.

Old avionics from the 1950s are incredibly heavy—like 28 pounds for an ADF. Consider upgrading to improve useful load and cg. Note that the old ADF had a six-pound antenna in the tailcone, of all places.

The airplane is fast and enjoyable for pilots who spend the time and effort to learn its systems and can afford to maintain it properly.

Frank Andrews
Everett, Wash.

Over the last three years we have replaced both fuel sending units ($198 each) and spent approximately $2,000 on the KFC 200 autopilot/flight director. The last problem was encountered by my partner in IMC when the trim deflected full down upon manipulation of the rocker switch on the autopilot panel with the autopilot (including altitude hold) engaged. King was very responsive to this problem, diagnosing it over the phone, and by fax giving a written explanation to assist the electronics shop in repairing.

The V-tail is a joy to fly. Its responsiveness is unequalled by any airplane I have ever flown. The A36 I also fly is more stable, but much heavier on the controls.

The V35B is a good instrument platform. Because of the high gear-operating speeds, it is an easy task to remain at cruise speed until the outer marker, reduce to 17 inches of mp, drop the gear, enter 15 degrees of flaps, and track the ILS. I see no need for speed brakes on this airplane.

The front seats of the V35B are the place to be. There is a definite tail waggle in turbulence that affects the rear-seat ride. However, anyone who has flown much in the 5th and 6th seats of an A36 will tell you that the "waggle" way back there is not much less than that of the V-tail in the same air conditions, and the 3rd and 4th seats of the V-tail are much more comfortable than the rear seats on the A36.

Since the CG moves to the rear as fuel is burned off, it is mandatory that cg be figured for takeoff and landing.

Gary B. Blasingame
Athens, Ga.

I owned an H model Bonanza for 16 years. It was fast, comfortable, economical (10.8 gph at 185 mph) and a smooth delight to fly in turbulence. Maintenance was very reasonable. Beech dealers either had parts or flew them in overnight, though I seldom needed. Excellent company support by Beech. Tail wagging is exaggerated by non-owners.

Richard Kays
Dublin, Calif.

My 1958 J35 is easier to land than my old Cherokee. It also is much more complex, as you have prop, gear, cowl flaps, and a more complex fuel system to monitor. My plane has two mains and two aux tanks, and you must burn one hour out of the left main prior to switching to the aux tanks. The left main will gradually become more full with time, as the extra fuel that the fuel pump puts out is returned to that tank.

The price of parts from Beech is somewhat staggering. My electric boost pump went west, so I looked into the price of a new one from Beech. It was $1,924. I had better luck having a shop in Dallas rebuild the original for $600.

Steve Fremgen
Carrollton, Tex.

I have owned and operated a 1952 Model 35 Bonanza since February 1989. The airplane is a MARVEL! To say that the Bonanza set the standard in the '40s and '50s is an understatement. In many ways the competition has never caught up.

On a 100F day at sea level at full gross weight (2,700 lbs.) the aircraft is in the air before 1,500 feet of runway and climbing at 850-900 fpm with gear retracted. On that same day, 12 minutes later at 8,500 feet, the true airspeed is 165 mph, burning 9.6 to 9.8 gal/hour of auto gas. If you are in no hurry, you can cruise at 150 mph burning eight gph.

What about "Tail-wag" with the V-tail? I will say that it is quite noticeable in moderate to severe turbulence. However, a light touch on the rudder will dampen most of it out, and although it is noticeable in the front seats, I have not found it unpleasant.

There is no problem maintaining an early Bonanza. Parts are readily available either new or used. New parts from Beech are readily available but very expensive. A good reconditioned used part is a much better value.

How about cost? Due to the bad publicity generated by *The Aviation Consumer* (probably justified) and the "V-tail scare" of the late 1980s (that resulted in the V-tail cuff modification) the prices of early 35 model Bonanzas are a bargain.

William B. Roberts,
Fremont, Calif.

Beech A36TC/ B36TC Bonanzas

The Beech Bonanza has always been considered the very top of the line in single-engine aircraft, and the top of the Bonanza line for the last decade have been the A36TC and B36TC turbocharged long-fuselage straight-tail models. (The normally-aspirated 36 is really in a different class; we won't cover it here.)

The 36 turbos offer a sizeable cabin, good high-altitude cruise numbers and the security of the straight-tail design. They have held their value extremely well. But the A model had serious range shortcomings, and both aircraft tend to run hot and fall short of rated engine TBO times.

Genealogy

Among the many improvements of the B36TC over the A model are longer wings, higher gross weight and greater fuel capacity.

The history of the turbo Bonanza is a truncated one. Back in 1966, Beech brought out a turbocharged version of the standard butterfly Bonanza called the V35TC. Those were the early days of turbocharging, and apparently neither Continental nor Bonanza pilots were up to the task; the V35TC had terrible turbo reliability problems. The V35TC lasted five years, and only 132 were built.

But as turbocharging grew more popular, Beech reintroduced the idea of the turbo Bonanza in 1979. The company wisely chose to turbo the more stable straight-tailed A36 model Bonanza, and the result, powered by a 300-hp Continental TSIO-520-UB, was the A36TC. It had a sophisticated variable absolute pressure controller that automatically maintained manifold pressure during altitude and temperature changes.

The A36TC was a modest success, selling a total of 272 aircraft in three years, but pilots, with some justification, beefed about the limited fuel capacity of 74 gallons. So in 1982, Beech finally made the airplane what it should have been all along: the B36TC, with a longer wing for better high-altitude performance, and 40 gallons more fuel capacity. The two big changes improved the book range by nearly 50 %.

Significant Improvements

The B36TC had many other improvements, as well. Gross weight went up by 200 pounds to 3,850. In addition to getting the four-foot tip extension, the wing also got a whole new carry-through structure. In effect, Beech put a Baron 58 wing on the B36TC. A new propeller and hub improved ground clearance. The B36TC had anti-siphon fuel caps, flush fuel drains, a new boost pump system that eliminated some complex fiddling required during takeoff in the A36TC, and larger fuel lines for better resistance to vapor lock. The B36TC also had a couple of weird-looking vortex generators on the wing leading edge out near the tips. The extended wing tips apparently played havoc with the airplane's spin recovery, and after trying all sorts of other things (like limiting rudder travel and increasing down elevator travel) Beech finally came up with the vortex generators, which allowed the B36TC to meet the minimum FAA spin-recovery requirements. Nobody's quite sure how they work, but they seem to do the job.

Resale Market

The A36TC and B36TC are real blue-chippers on the resale market. They were fearsomely expensive to buy new, and they're fearsomely expensive to buy used. In 1979, a new A36TC cost $137,000 and is worth $133,000 today (we're using Bluebook retail figures, which tend to run a bit higher than actual selling prices.) That's an impressive 97 percent after 14 years.

By comparison, the same numbers for a 1979 T210 are $99,000 new and $92,000 used for a 93 percent resale value. The Mooney 231's numbers are $85,000 new, $61,500 used and 72 percent.

Later-model 36TCs took a huge jump in new sticker price, so percentage value retained is only a bit higher than the T210 and 231. But the fact remains that, for any given model year, you'll have to pay about double the price of a Mooney 231, which has similar performance through the middle altitudes. Obviously, people put a lot of stock in the Bonanza TC's comfort, quality and extra high-altitude capabilities—not to mention the perception of quality and status.

Performance

The 36TCs are good performers in terms of cruise speed. The 36TC can generally keep up with the likes of the Mooney 231 and Cessna T210N, but newer planes like the Mooney 252, Turbo 210R and Piper Malibu are faster. Owners report typical cruise speeds in the 180-knot range at middle altitudes.

Conventional tail is one of the blessings of the 36 line.

These reports agree pretty well with the book figures, which call for cruising speeds ranging from an all-out max of 199 knots (at 79 percent power, 25,000 feet and 250 pounds below gross weight) to 155 knots at 56 percent power and 10,000 feet. The book number for 75 percent/20,000 feet is 190 knots; at 69 percent/15,000 feet, the figure is 174 knots.

There's very little speed difference between the A and the B models. At very high altitudes, where the B's bigger wing comes into play, the B has an edge of a couple of knots.

Owners report fuel flows of 17-18 gph at cruise power. That assumes a middling power setting and a mixture rich enough to keep the valves from cooking.

Pilots praise the airplane's climb performance. They consistently report climb rates between 1,000 and 1,500 fpm, and have no trouble getting on up to 20,000 feet. Much higher than that, and the turbo wastegate is fully closed in the "bootstrap" mode, and manifold pressure begins to fall off. But cruising at the max certified ceiling of 25,000 feet is a reasonable thing to do, say TC pilots, unless the day is hot and the load heavy.

A36TC can carry four and baggage, but range is limited on 74 gallons of fuel capacity. Six riders and luggage would leave practically no weight for fuel.

Payload/Range

The A model has a gross weight of 3,650 and a typical IFR empty weight of around 2,400 to 2,500 pounds. Typical useful load is around 1,150 pounds. With only 74 gallons (444 pounds) of fuel available, a hefty 700-800 pounds is available for the cabin even with full tanks. That's the equivalent of four people and some baggage.

The bad news, of course, is you can't fly very far on 74 gallons. Factory specs list ranges from 609 to 730 nm, depending on altitude and power setting, but these are a bit optimistic. Taking into account full-rich climbs to altitude (necessary for engine cooling), richer-than-peak cruising (also a good idea for engine longevity) and IFR reserves, you wouldn't want to fly one more than three hours. Five or six hundred nm is more like it.

If you want to take advantage of the big cabin and put six adults inside, range will be limited indeed. Six 170-pounders each carrying 20 pounds of luggage leaves zero—yep, *absolutamente nada*—for fuel. (You could hold a nice conference on the ramp, though.) The A36TC is a six-place airplane only if some of the six are kids.

The B model does a bit better. Empty weight is about 60 pounds higher, but gross weight is up by 200 pounds, for a net useful load boost of 140 pounds. If you take the bonus in fuel, the B36TC will carry three adults up to 1,000 nm, or even a bit more if you throttle way back. If you want to settle for the short range of the A36TC and only pour in 74 gallons, the B will carry one more passenger than the A model.

However, even the B36TC looks bad next to a Cessna T210R in terms of payload. The big Cessna will haul 250 pounds more weight, comparably equipped, which translates into an extra passenger and a half, or an extra 40 gallons of fuel— enough to fly 500 miles farther.

Creature Comforts

Unlike the T210R, however, it's actually possible to fit six people in the cabin. (The back two seats of a 210 are suitable only for midgets.) Virtually every 36TC has the optional "club car" seating, which puts the four rear-seaters facing each other, Orient Express-style. Owners seem to like the bizjet-style separation of crew and passengers, but tall folks in the back will require some sort of intricate leg-interlock system. Weight limitations almost assure that at least a couple of the club section passengers will be kids. The big right-side cargo door is also a boon to the rear-seaters.

Cabin noise level is fairly low. "It's quieter than the S35 and the Skylane I used to own," commented one B36TC owner.

Handling

The stretched 36 model Bonanzas handle much differently than the shorter V-tail 35s and straight-tail 33s. The 36s were stretched several inches forward of the wing, which lengthened the cabin and improved the limited c.g. envelope of the short-body Bonanzas. The result is a much heavier-feeling airplane. Lateral response is also slower. "It's not as much fun to fly as the V-tails," commented one owner. "You fly it by the numbers instead of by feel." With two people up front and the rear cabin empty, the 36TCs tend to be nose-heavy on landing and takeoff. While the heavier pitch forces may not feel as sporty, they certainly contribute to better stability and make the 36 a safer airplane to fly IFR.

Engine

All the 36TCs have the same engine: a 300-hp Continental TSIO-520-UB. TBO is 1,600 hours, but reports suggest that not many make it that far. Few 36TCs have been around long enough to go to 1,600 hours (many are flown by private individuals who put 200 hours or less a year on them), but the pattern seems to indicate a top overhaul somewhere in the 800-1,200 hour range. We queried one overhauler about the engine, and he replied, "It has no major problems I'm aware of, but the last major we did came at about two-thirds the TBO time. It needed a top overhaul, and the guy decided since he was spending that much money anyway, he might as well do the major."

Part of the problem may be hot running due to a lack of cowl flaps—an odd choice by Beech for such a sophisticated temperature-sensitive aircraft.

Watch for Cracks

The engine is subject to the notorious cylinder-cracking AD, number 86-13-4, which calls for inspection of the cylinders for cracks every 50 hours. (The -UB

Cost/Performance/Specifications

Model	Year	Average Retail Price	Cruise Speed (kt)	Useful Load (lb)	Std/Opt Fuel (gal)	Engines	TBO (hrs)	Overhaul Cost
A36TC	1979	$133,000	199	1,388	40/74	300-hp Cont. TSIO-520-UB	1,600	$21,500
A36TC	1980	$142,000	199	1,388	40/74	300-hp Cont. TSIO-520-UB	1,600	$21,500
A36TC	1981	$147,000	199	1,388	40/74	300-hp Cont. TSIO-520-UB	1,600	$21,500
B36TC	1982	$173,000	200	1,468	102	300-hp Cont. TSIO-520-UB	1,600	$21,500
B36TC	1983	$181,500	200	1,468	102	300-hp Cont. TSIO-520-UB	1,600	$21,500
B36TC	1984	$207,000	200	1,468	102	300-hp Cont. TSIO-520-UB	1,600	$21,500
B36TC	1985	$220,000	200	1,468	102	300-hp Cont. TSIO-520-UB	1,600	$21,500
B36TC	1986	$240,000	200	1,468	102	300-hp Cont. TSIO-520-UB	1,600	$21,500
B36TC	1987	$260,000	200	1,468	102	300-hp Cont. TSIO-520-UB	1,600	$21,500
B36TC	1988	$280,000	200	1,468	102	300-hp Cont. TSIO-520-UB	1,600	$21,500
B36TC	1989	$300,000	200	1,468	102	300-hp Cont. TSIO-520-UB	1,600	$21,500
B36TC	1990	$320,000	200	1,468	102	300-hp Cont. TSIO-520-UB	1,600	$21,500
B36TC	1991	$350,000	200	1,468	102	300-hp Cont. TSIO-520-UB	1,600	$21,500
B36TC	1992	$434,446	200	1,468	102	300-hp Cont. TSIO-520-UB	1,600	$21,500
B36TC	1993	$459,270	200	1,468	102	300-hp Cont. TSIO-520-UB	1,600	$21,500

engine is not alone; virtually all 520s are subject to it.) The engine is also prone to crankcase cracks, as are virtually all other front-alternator Continental 520 engines. Check carefully for cracks on any 36TC considered for purchase—a bad crack will cost a minimum of $5,000 to replace or repair, mostly because of the teardown costs.

The engine/boost-pump combination on the A36TC is an odd one that requires some extra fiddling by the pilot on takeoff. The A36TC book calls for a full-rich fuel flow of 32.5 to 34.0 gph on takeoff. If this is not achieved, the pilot must turn on the fuel pump to "Low" or "Auto" (the book doesn't say how you decide which one), and then lean the mixture back to the correct fuel flow. The same complex rigmarole must be continued throughout the climb in warm weather.

The B36TC book warns the pilot not to use the boost pump in the "Hi" position because of excessive fuel flow. Beech, in a masterpiece of understatement, says that this "may cause engine combustion to cease on the takeoff roll."

Safety Record

We have not computed precise accident rates for the A36TC and B36TC per se. However, the 36 series of Bonanza as a whole has an excellent safety record. For the period 1972-1981, the 36 series had the fourth-best fatality rate out of 17 single-engine retractables evaluated by *The Aviation Consumer.* Fatal accident rate was 1.5 per 100,000 flight hours. (The range of the other 16 retractables was from 0.8 to 3.3.)

A36TC engines tend to run hot and have an awkward fuel boost pump arrangement.

In total accidents, the 36 series did even better—second best. Total rate was 4.5 per 100,000 in a range of 4.6 to 15.0. FAA records show a total of 14 fatal 36TC accidents since 1980, 12 for the A model and two for the B. Part of the reason for this discrepancy is the larger number of A models built and their longer exposure to accident risk. But even adjusting for exposure factors (figuring aircraft-years), the B model seems to have a fatal rate half that of the A. We have no explanation for this and suspect it may be a statistical aberration. (The number of B accidents is, after all, very small, which makes it statistically less significant.)

Of the 12 A36TC fatal crashes, five were weather-related. In one case, a VFR pilot wandered into IMC and lost control. In the ensuing spiral dive, the airplane broke up in flight—one of the very few instances of a straight-tail Bonanza coming apart in the air. Two fatal crashes came after engine failures, another during a landing overrun.

One gruesome accident occurred after an in-flight fire. A leaking idle mixture adjustment screw fed raw fuel onto the turbocharger, and the engine erupted in flames shortly after takeoff. The pilot, blinded by the fire, managed to get the plane on the ground and survived (barely), but the front-seat passenger burned to death. The two rear-seat passengers escaped through the big rear door—a good argument for a rear exit if there ever was one. (This accident is described in detail in the December 1, 1984 issue of *The Aviation Consumer*.)

The two B36TC fatal accidents were both weather-related: a spiral dive into the ground by a disoriented pilot and an ILS approach that went awry.

We noticed a familiar Bonanza pattern in the non-fatal accidents: inadvertent gear retractions on the ground. The 36TCs, like most other Bonanzas, have the flap lever on the left and the gear lever on the right—the reverse of the common arrangement. As a result, hundreds of pilots have inadvertently retracted the landing gear after touchdown when they meant to retract the flaps. Five A36TC pilots suffered this embarrassing fate.

Two's company in club-car seating, though a third would be okay. High roof line, big windows give the cabin a sense of spaciousness.

There was confusion of another sort involving the flap lever; one hapless pilot, meaning to raise the flaps after takeoff, mistakenly turned on the boost pump instead. The A36TC has an unfortunate (in our opinion) boost pump arrangement that can flood the engine and stop it stone-dead. The plane crash-landed in a field. Fortunately, no one was hurt.

Service Difficulty Reports

FAA records of service problems highlight several areas to watch out for when inspecting an A36TC or B36TC for possible purchase. Here's a list of the main A36TC problems from a decade of SDR files:

• Cracked boarding steps. Beech service instruction 972 refers to this problem, but A36TCs aren't listed as having it. Check it anyway.

• Cracked oil cooler baffles (10 reports).

• Cracked crankcases (10 reports).

• Cracked cylinders (four reports).

• Cracked turbocharger inlet, part number 642668 (15 reports).

The B36TC models, with benefit of 20/20 hindsight, did not reflect these problems. However, two B model trouble spots were the fuel return line, which tended to chafe against the wastegate drain (four reports) and cracked cooling baffles at the air pressure pump inlet above the oil cooler (four cases).

Airworthiness Directives

The 36TC models have only a couple of ADs that are unique to the type. One, for older A models, requires modification of the fuel drain hose. Both A and B models are subject to 84-8-4, which requires modification of the oil line check

Merlyn intercooler mod adds a scoop to lower left cowl.

valves. But 36TC owners don't get off easy; the airplane is subject to many of the "shotgun" ADs on engines and accessories that cover numerous aircraft types. Examples: Hartzell props, Airborne pumps, ELT batteries, air filters, Bendix mags, and cracked cylinders. The biggest potential problem is the repetitive inspections for cylinder cracks, AD 86-13-4.

Modifications

A36TC buyers should look for the 30-gallon tiptank STC offered by Beryl D'Shannon (P.O.Box 840, Lakeville, Minn. 55044; (800) 328-4629), one of the best-known purveyors of Bonanza mods. Fuel in the tip tanks must be transferred with a pump into the main tanks. Speed will probably suffer a few knots. Installation time is estimated at two or three man-days.

Two companies now offer intercooler mods for the A and B models. Both mods allow power to be produced at lower manifold pressures, thereby reducing stress and heat in the engine. Considering the 36TC's reputation for running hot and failing to make TBO, we think an intercooler is a superb idea.

Merlyn Products (W. 7510 Hall Ave., Spokane, Wash. 99204; (509) 838-1141) intercooler system is $5,995 (kit only) or $6,495 installed. Weight is 21 pounds.

Turboplus, Inc. (1520 26th Ave., NW, Gig Harbor, Wash. 98335; (800) 742-4202) offers a similar intercooler system for similar prices.

Another desirable mod to look for on a used 36TC (or to consider adding after you buy it) is a set of speed brakes for descending rapidly from high altitudes without overcooling the engine. Precise Flight (P.O. Box 7168, Bend, Ore. 97708, Bend Ore.; 800-547-2558) offers wing-mounted speed brakes at a cost of $3,695. Installation time is estimated at 48 man-hours, which should bring total cost into the $5,000 range.

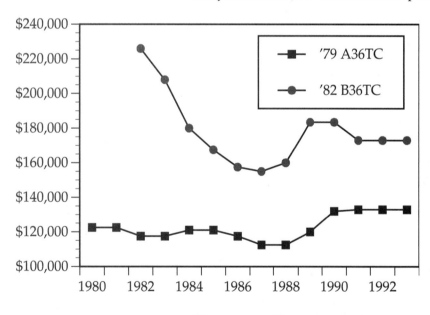

Owner Comments

I purchased my 1983 B36TC in January, 1985 as a demonstrator with about 100 hours on it. Since then I have flown it another 300 hours or so. I moved up from an F33A primarily to gain more cabin room for a growing family. My wife and two young children have flown several long trips, including one coast-to-coast, with a great degree of comfort. The plane flies well, although it tends to be a bit nose-heavy on landing with only the front seats occupied. On takeoff, the engine has a slight tendency to overboost a couple of inches, especially when cold. This amount of overboost, however, is approved for up to five minutes and has never caused a problem.

Engine cooling is good, although there are no cowl flaps. Forward speed plus extra-rich fuel mixture keeps it cool. Only once have I had to reduce climb angle for engine cooling, and that was on a 90-degree-plus day.

Climb fuel flows are about 30-32 gph, but fortunately you don't have to spend that much time climbing, since the plane will get to FL 200 in about 18 minutes.

I flight plan for 160 knots at sea level, increasing two knots per 1,000 feet of altitude. Fuel burn is 17 gph at 65 percent power, which the plane will maintain up to its certified ceiling of 25,000 feet. By comparison, the F33A burned 14 gph at the same power setting. Endurance is five hours with a reasonable reserve.

Common to all Bonanzas is a lift-up cowling that allows easy access for inspection. Silver battery box is conveniently located, has a short run to the engine.

As far as maintenance goes, I've had some problems, although nothing overwhelming. A turbo controller was replaced under warranty, and the plane had to be repainted, apparently due to factory quality control problems. (I battled with Beech over this.) Landing gear uplocks have to be adjusted every inspection, but that's no big deal.

Our annual/100-hour inspections run about $1,300 at Beechcraft East on Long Island, N.Y. Oil is changed every 33 hours. The oil filter lives behind a maze of hoses and brackets, and I always make sure I'm not around to hear the mechanic's comments as he struggles to change it.

Parts availability is excellent, with most parts available the next day by Federal Express if not in stock. Parts prices are high. (If you're not building planes, you've got to make money somehow.) Total operating costs seem to run in the $145/hour range. That includes hangar and insurance, but not engine reserves.

In short, Beech set out with the B36TC to rectify the problems they had with the A36TC, and they did their homework. There are no tricks to perform in the middle of the takeoff roll, range is excellent, and the plane is a delight to fly.

Lorne Sheren
Watchung, N. J.

I purchased a 1982 B36TC in October 1986. I am the third owner of the aircraft, which has 670 hours total time and 400 hours on a Continental factory reman "zero-time" engine. I was told the original engine failed because of loss of oil at

An improved boost pump system on the B36TC eliminated some complex fiddling during takeoff in the A36TC. Vapor lock resistance was improved by larger fuel lines.

the turbo oil feed line. I can't verify the cause of the failure, but the plane was landed safely with no airframe damage. I have flown the plane about 100 hours and have had failures of the pressure pump and the starter vibrator. The airplane just had a $1,200 annual at PT Aero in Providence, and there were no discrepancies. I think the price is quite reasonable for such a complex aircraft.

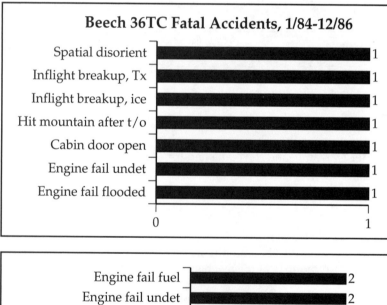

Beech 36TC Fatal Accidents, 1/84-12/86

Spatial disorient	1
Inflight breakup, Tx	1
Inflight breakup, ice	1
Hit mountain after t/o	1
Cabin door open	1
Engine fail undet	1
Engine fail flooded	1

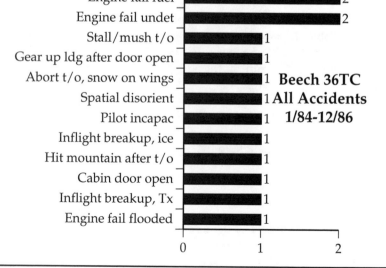

Beech 36TC All Accidents 1/84-12/86

Engine fail fuel	2
Engine fail undet	2
Stall/mush t/o	1
Gear up ldg after door open	1
Abort t/o, snow on wings	1
Spatial disorient	1
Pilot incapac	1
Inflight breakup, ice	1
Hit mountain after t/o	1
Cabin door open	1
Inflight breakup, Tx	1
Engine fail flooded	1

This is my fourth straight-tail Bonanza, and I think it's the best one. My basis for this statement is speed, low noise level, excellent c.g. envelope, 102 gallons of usable fuel, built-in oxygen for all seats, better wing loading (with the extended wing, it carries ice very well, as opposed to the A36), and it offers superb passenger comfort and loading.

My only complaint is the lack of cowl flaps and the resulting high cylinder head temperatures during long climbs. I am installing a Merlyn intercooler, and will let you know how that works out. With the extra fuel, the range is fabulous. I have made non-stop flights from St. Louis and Tampa to Providence.

Speed buildup on descents is very moderate, and when I take my eyes off the gauges, the wing does not drop and the red line isn't the first thing I see when I look back. (That should be a fix for the in-flight breakup problems suffered by the V-tail models.) I believe the wingtip extension has a great deal to do with this improved stability, along with the extended fuselage and wing placement.

Justin Strauss
Cranston, R.I.

I bought a 1981 A36TC with 500 hours on it in 1983. I paid $125,000. It now has about 1,300 hours on it, which works out to about 200 hours a year.

I generally plan on getting about 170 knots block-to-block, usually at about 12,000 feet, although sometimes I have to go higher to get over the mountains out here. That's at 75 percent power. I lean it about 50 degrees rich of peak TIT, and this results in a fuel burn of about 17 gph. It has very good climb performance; I typically see 1,400 or 1,500 fpm after takeoff, although that's usually below gross weight. For the cruise altitudes I usually fly at, it takes less than a minute per thousand feet to get there.

I do have to watch the cylinder head temps on climbout. On a warm day, I may have to climb as fast as 130-135 knots to keep the CHT 50 degrees below the red line, which is where I like to see it. I've had no major problems with the machine. The airframe has been pretty much maintenance-free, and the annual inspection usually runs around $1,200 to $1,300. I have had avionics problems, however. And the engine required a premature top overhaul at 1,200 hours because of low compression and excessive oil consumption. TBO is supposedly 1,600 hours, but I think it's pretty standard among A36TC owners to need a top overhaul at half or two-thirds of the TBO.

The standard tanks hold only 74 gallons usable, but I have tip tanks that give me an extra 40 gallons, so I have good range. Comfort is good, and the noise level is lower than the Skylane and the S35 Bonanza that I owned before. The V-tail was more fun to fly, though. It was lighter on the controls and more responsive. The A36TC feels like a bigger, heavier airplane, and you tend to fly it more by the numbers than by feel.

Wedge-shaped vortex generators on the wing leading edge were added to aid in spin recovery after the wings were extended.

The TC is the only plane I've ever bought that hasn't depreciated. I had its value checked recently when I renewed my insurance policy, and it was the same I paid for it four years ago. If I had bought a Baron or something like that, I'd be looking at about half the value.

Robert Day
Steamboat Springs, Colo.

We bought our 1980 A36TC about four years ago and paid $122,000. It had only about 300 hours when we bought it, and now has 850. It has been a very trouble-free airplane. Our engine has been excellent, with the compression never registering less than 74. There have never been any oil leaks.

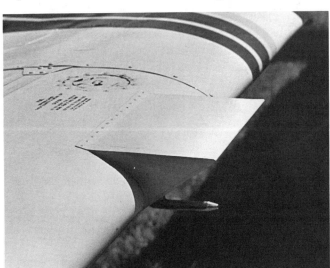

When you look in *Trade-A-Plane*, you see lots of ads with total times of 800 or 1,000 hours and 300 hours on a factory reman engine, but I don't think those people used common sense when they operated the engine. If you run it according to the fuel flows in the book, you'll burn it right up. You have to run on the lean side of peak to match the Beech fuel-flow numbers.

We have recently installed a Merlyn intercooler. We haven't had a chance to run it during the summer or at real high altitudes yet, but so far we are pleased with it. If we run the same mp settings as before, we get about a four-five-knot speed increase with a very slight increase in fuel flow—maybe 0.2 or 0.3 gph more. (On a recent trip, we got 196 knots at 19,000 feet at 29 inches and 2,400 rpm.)

Ability to climb handily up to 20,000 feet or more affords passengers the comfort of a better ride over the weather.

Running the same fuel flow, we definitely go faster. Or, we have the option of running the same speed as before, but we use 26 inches of mp instead of 29 and use about one gph less.

Cylinder head temperatures seem to be running about the same as before. The TIT seems a little lower, but we find we're still mixture-limited by the TIT redline (1650 degrees) at the higher power settings.

The intercooler has to be removed to change the plugs or inspect the turbo-charger, but it can easily be done in about five minutes. Merlyn product support seems to be good—they've made some improvements since ours was installed, and they just called to say they'd be retrofitting the improvements to our airplane for free. Overall, I'm happy with it.

In terms of performance, our airplane seems to indicate 155 knots almost all the time. At our typical cruise altitude of 11,500 or 12,500, that usually works out to 183-187 knots true. That's at 29 inches and 2400 rpm, which is about 67 percent power. We burn 18 gph, so both our speeds and fuel flows are higher than the book.

Rate of climb is good, about 1,100 fpm at gross on a cool day. Recently we went to 16,500 feet in about 15 minutes. In normal weather, we can climb at 110-120 knots and keep the CHT needle at 200 degrees or below, but out in the desert, we have to increase climb speed to 120-130 knots. CHTs in cruise are no problem It's a little short on fuel, so we installed the Beryl D'Shannon tip tanks, which bring capacity up to 104 gallons. There's supposedly a 200-pound gross weight increase that goes along with the tiptank STC, but I've never seen it on paper.

We've had almost no maintenance problems. The only defect I can recall is a cracked fairing that cost about $10. There was a vapor-lock service bulletin a while ago, which required replacement of the fuel lines (with half-inch ones, like the B36TC has), fuel selector and modification of the fuel pump. The bill was something like $2,600, but Beech paid for everything. That was pretty amazing for a five-year old airplane on its second owner.

It's a very quiet airplane, much quieter than the Baron 58 I used to have. It flies nicely, very similar to the Baron. My partner used to have a V35B, and at first he thought the A36TC felt trucky by comparison. But it's much better on the dials. The V35B is like a Porsche 911, the A36TC is more like a Lincoln Town Car.

Dave Zalibra
Los Angeles, Calif.

Beech 17 Staggerwing

With warbird prices out of sight, and even some more modern designs overpriced on the used market, the Beech Staggerwing may be the best-kept secret of the classic-antique-warbird crowd. Even if the design weren't more than 50 years old, the Staggerwing would still be one of the raciest, most stylish production aircraft around. And when one considers the age of the design and its performance, it really starts making modern production aircraft look sickly.

Long on History

The Staggerwing was the first design produced by Walter Beech's fledgling company. After Beech left Curtiss-Wright in 1931, he and a handful of engineers, production workers and support staff started the Beech Aircraft Co. Designed by engineer Ted Wells, the prototype Staggerwing first flew in November, 1932. With fixed gear and seating for up to five people, it managed to notch a top speed of 201 mph behind a 420-hp Wright R-975 radial engine. Cruise speed was a comfortable 180 mph. Only four of these fixed-gear models were built.

Production really got started with the B17L model in 1934. Featuring retractable landing gear and drag-producing under-wing flaps (later to be called dive brakes or speed brakes when used on Lockheed's P-38 Lightning fighter), the B17L also had a smaller engine—the Jacobs 225-hp L-4. This dropped the top speed to 174 mph, and cruise to 162.

The G17S model, sporting a 450-hp P&W Wasp Junior engine, was the last of the Staggerwing line.

Some 46 of these Staggerwings were built during 1935 and 1936. The B17L shared production with the B17E model for a short time. The latter had a 285-hp Wright Whirlwind and some airframe changes (drag flaps on the upper wings, ailerons on the lower, and 70 gallons of fuel tankage). However, only four of these were built.

The more popular model that year was the B17R, which featured a Wright R-975 radial up front. With that much power, gross weight went from about 3,200 pounds to 3,600 pounds. Cruise speed increased to 202 mph at 9,000 feet. In all, 15 of these were built. By 1936, the C17B models started rolling out.

Powered by a Jacobs L-5 radial of 285 hp, with a fixed-pitch prop, this model tipped the scales fully loaded at 3,150 pounds and could cruise at 177 mph on 17.5 gallons per hour. Production amounted to 39 copies. The C17R, produced at the same time, was a higher-powered version. The Wright Whirlwind continued to provide the motive power, and cruise speed was a nominal 202 mph. Only 19 of these were built.

Despite its age, the Staggerwing offers performance comparable to many modern production aircraft, along with a certain incomparable style.

The Golden Years

By far, the Staggerwing models you're most likely to come across are the D17, E17 and F17. These rolled out the Beech factory doors from mid-1937 until World War II began and the military's requirements took precedence.

The D17R saw power jump to 450 hp with a new version of the Wright Whirlwind up front. Cruise speed stayed the same—202 mph—but gross weight went up to 4,250 pounds. Fuel consumption was a reasonable 23 gph, which produced a still-air range of almost 1,500 miles with the optional 174-gallon fuel system.

The drag flaps were replaced by a set of plain flaps on the lower wing. Combined with the D17S, which differed in having toe brakes, a new windshield and reinforced wingtips, some 94 of these were built. Another eight D17A models, with the smaller Wright R-760 of 350 hp, were also built.

The E17B also rolled out in 1937. A 285-hp Jacobs L-5 radial gave this model a cruise speed of 177 mph on 16.8 gph. With the optional fuel tanks, the E17B could cover more than 1,300 air miles. Its gross weight was lower than that of the D17 models at only 3,390 pounds. A total of 54 E17Bs rolled out the factory doors.

The 1938 model year saw the debut of the F17D Staggerwing. With a 3,590-pound gross weight being pulled by a 330-hp Jacobs, the F17D could cruise at 182 mph while burning 17 gph. The optional 125-gallon fuel system gave this model a bladder-busting endurance of more than seven hours and a range of more than 1,300 miles.

Japan Attacks

With the opening of World War II, Beech continued to crank out Staggerwings, only now they were leaving the factory in military livery. Both the Army Air Corps (forerunner of the U.S. Air Force) and the Navy bought Staggerwings, as did the governments of several foreign countries. All told, Beech built some 412 military D17S Staggerwings. In addition, another 118 Staggerwings were "impressed" by the Air Corps, which meant that they were appropriated from their owners and put into military duties. The Air Corps designation of these aircraft was UC-43BH, while the Navy designated theirs as GB-2s.

In service, the Staggerwing did not attain the glamour of some other civilian designs. For example, while the Piper Cub was credited with becoming an impromptu tank buster and close air support aircraft, and the Douglas DC-3 won fame and even managed to score a "kill" against a Japanese Zero while flying cargo missions "Over The Hump" in the China-Burma-India theater of the war, the Staggerwings did yeoman's duty hauling freight and VIPs around the country and around the world. After the war, the survivors were sold as surplus and joined the civilian fleet.

The Final Few

The Staggerwing continued in production for a short time after the war. Some 20 G17s models were built before the line ended. The G17S mounted a 450-hp Pratt and Whitney R-985 Wasp Junior up front. Burning nearly 25 gph, this sturdy radial gave the G17 a top speed of 212 mph and a cruise speed of 201. The optional 170-gallon fuel system allowed a 1,300-mile cruising range.

Meanwhile, Walter Beech's engineers were busy revolutionizing general aviation. Design and testing paid off in the introduction of the soon-to-be classic model 35 Bonanza. With its first flight in December 1945, the Bonanza announced the end of Staggerwing production. By 1949, Beech had delivered the last model G17S. Its $29,000 price tag and "old-fashioned" styling couldn't compete with the $8,000 Bonanza and its more modern lines. By the time the last Staggerwing rolled out the factory doors, Beech had built 782 of the speedy biplanes. Today, according to the most recent FAA census, 259 Staggerwings are registered in the U.S., but not all are active. Another 20-odd aircraft are believed to be flying overseas.

With the large, well-rounded nose precluding visibility straight ahead, the value of S-turns while taxiing cannot be underestimated.

Features

As a reminder of an earlier era, when flying was more than just a way of getting from here to there, the Staggerwing has something more than mere cachet. In its features we can see both the precursors of what would become industry standards and the stone-age attributes which, thankfully, have been left by the wayside in aviation's progress.

Examples of things ahead of their time abound in the Staggerwing. The aforementioned drag flaps are one. Retractable landing gear are another. It should be recalled that, during the 1930s, even some front-line military fighters, like the Boeing P-36 Peashooter, had fixed landing gear. Beech's gear system for the Staggerwing was the progenitor of that found in Barons and Bonanzas today—electrically driven with manual emergency extension.

Another harbinger of the future was the throw-over yoke. Although Staggerwings could be purchased with dual controls, many were delivered with a single throw-over control. In either case, the yokes sprout from a central column mounted on the floor. Later Beeches, like the Baron, would have the same arrangement, albeit with the central column coming out of the instrument panel instead of the floor.

Overly complicated fuel management also appeared with the Staggerwing, to be carried down the Beech line even unto recent times. Fuel tanks spread like tumors throughout the airframe, giving pilots as many as six tanks to cope with. Despite this profusion of tanks, there was only one fuel gauge to serve them all. With a separate selector switch, the pilot would first switch the fuel gauge to whatever tank he was interested in burning fuel from. If the gauge showed sufficient fuel in that tank, he could then switch the fuel tank selector. Unfortunately for many pilots, such an arrangement was an open invitation to fuel mismanagement. Under the stress of a windmilling engine, it becomes a challenge to figure out which tank actually has gas in it and then get the engine operating off that tank.

Manually operated brakes were also a feature of the early models. The brakes were operated by a large handle sticking straight up from the floor on the right side of the central yoke column. Differential braking was accomplished by pulling back on the handle and then gently applying a little rudder in the desired direction. This could be more than a handful in a gusty crosswind.

Handling

In the air, the Staggerwing is described by most as being fairly docile, considering her size. However, the design is old, and a big radial engine imposes some handling quirks all by itself. Although the rudder looks adequate to the task at hand, it's not the most powerful control surface in the world. Groundlooping during takeoff is a real and present danger, especially in a left crosswind. Between torque, P-factor and weathervaning, an unplanned trip into the weeds off the side of the runway can be all too easy. Compounding the problem is the blanking effect of the rather wide fuselage, which drastically cuts down on the prop wash over the rudder with the tail down.

Likewise, go-arounds can be a real handful. With the flaps down, and maybe the left wing lowered into a crosswind, simply jamming on the power is an invitation to disaster. The airplane will try to roll to the left, and if the pilot simply rolls the yoke to the right, it only gets worse due to the comparatively powerful adverse yaw of those big ailerons.

Landings can be a real bear in this ancient taildragger. Note the plain flaps on the lower wings, and the retractable tailwheel.

A simple tail-dragger checkout will not do for handling the Staggerwing. Recovery from an incipient groundloop is more a matter of converting the airplane's control weaknesses into strengths than it is a question of finessing the controls.

For example, the heavy adverse yaw the ailerons produce can provide just the right assist to the rudder. If the airplane is veering to the right (thus forcing the left wingtip down) and you've already run out of left rudder, rolling the yoke to the right (in the direction of the veer) can save the day. You'll get no help from the tailwheel (it's either locked for landing or fixed permanently in position, depending on the model).

In the air, the Staggerwing is not the most stable airplane. In all but the smoothest air it requires constant attention. The pilot is flying all the time. And those big ailerons with their adverse yaw mean none of this feet-on-the-floor sort of flying. Pilots really learn to use the rudder as a primary fight control. Stalls are reasonably gentle, and in some loadings the aircraft will not actually stall. Instead, it behaves more like a Piper Cherokee, with the nose hunting up and down as the aircraft alternately burbles into the stall and mushes back out. In the pattern, be prepared to carry power almost up to the moment of touchdown. Power-off sink rate can make your head spin, and power-off spot landings from the key position will be largely a matter of luck. Most likely, the aircraft will run out of altitude before rolling out aligned with the runway.

Actual landing technique is enough to keep Staggerwing owners talking for days on end. Two schools of thought prevail: Those who favor wheel landings and those who favor full-stall landings. A very few try for three-point landings, since these are more likely to produce prolonged bouncing, crow hopping and/or a good groundloop.

Those who favor wheel landings argue that, by touching down in a level attitude and holding the tail up, they have much more directional control during the groundroll. And don't forget that locked tailwheel. Those who prefer full-stall landings point to the reduced touchdown speed, which in turn reduces the possibility that the ship will float back into the air when it encounters a bump or hump in the runway. Some favor a combination of both. One pilot, who instructs in a Staggerwing, tells us he prefers to try for the full-stall landing, and if the thing is the least bit squirrelly on touchdown, he'll raise the tail to improve directional control.

Maintenance Matters

On the whole, the Staggerwing is a rugged airplane. Things are simple enough that outright failures are pretty rare. Indeed, a six-year printout of FAA service difficulty reports only turned up one reported malfunction (and that of a group of broken nose ribs on the upper wing of a C17L). But as with any airplane of this size and age, be prepared for some hefty maintenance bills.

However, two trouble spots do exist: The electrical system and the landing gear system. The electrical system came from the factory with a generator. These were in vogue at the time (indeed, they were state of the art back then). But nowadays, generators are recognized as generating far more problems than they do electricity. Fortunately, the generator can be replaced by an alternator. The 50-amp alternator is not only more reliable, it also has enough power to allow operation of the landing gear with the landing lights on.

The landing gear is another potential trouble spot. The old limit switches can get balky, causing the gear motor to run too long, or not long enough. Either way, it spells trouble. Getting the landing gear properly rigged (including a retraction test at each annual) and having the limit switches rebuilt or replaced can save both money and trouble over the long run.

The brakes also deserve special attention. Most aircraft have been converted to hydraulic brakes, according to Mike Parrish of the Staggerwing Museum Foundation. But even so, the brakes should be considered a critical item during any inspection.

Mods

Unlike so many other aircraft, there's not a welter of mods out there for the Staggerwing. However, most that do exist are fairly well thought out and straightforward. Many are eminently worthwhile. One potentially money-saving mod is

The classic lines of the Staggerwing will turn heads wherever it goes. A prerequisite for ownership is finding a mechanic who's knowledgeable and experienced with aircraft of this era.

getting an EGT/CHT unit installed. Admittedly, nine-cylinder units are hard to come by, but K.S. Avionics of Hayward, Calif. will sell you one.

A mod that will definitely save money is an autogas STC. Petersen Aviation of Minden, Neb. holds the STC for the D17S (one of the more common models). Petersen Aviation, Route 1, P.O. Box 18, Minden, Neb. 68959.

Fabric replacement options available under STC are far too numerous to list here. Suffice it to say that, whatever is desired in the way of recovering jobs—from straight replacement to Razorback—is available. We suggest you consult your A&P for his advice.

Organizational Chart

Staggerwing ownership brings with it exclusive membership. And in the case of this grizzled biplane veteran, membership has its privileges. Probably the first organization to contact, even before you start shopping for a Staggerwing, is The Staggerwing Club. A repository of knowledge and experience with the Staggerwing, the club publishes a newsletter for members and networks for parts. The club has the engineering drawings as well as a wealth of technical data. Its address is Box 126, Mansfield, Ohio 44901.

And when it comes to parts, The Staggerwing Museum Foundation in Tullahoma, Tenn. is another organization owners simply must join (and support). The Museum Foundation, working hand in hand with The Staggerwing Club, can help prospective owners find a decent airplane, a mechanic to inspect and maintain it and a CFI to check him out in it.

The Museum Foundation can also help with parts and mods. Under the direction of Olive Ann Beech (Walter's wife), Beech Aircraft donated all the engineering and detail drawings of the Staggerwing line to the Museum. This includes the customer-ordered paint scheme drawings, with colors specified, so an owner seeking a truly authentic restoration can do it down to the smallest detail. The wealth of technical data allows some parts fabrication and greatly eases getting some of the more popular mods (like hydraulic brake conversion).

You don't have to own a Staggerwing to join. Indeed, the Museum has taken other aircraft under its wing, and now provides support for owners of Twin Beech Bugsmashers, Twin Bonanzas (T-Bones), Spartans, Travel Airs, and Howards. The Staggerwing Museum Foundation, P.O. Box 550, Tullahoma, Tenn. 37388, (615) 455-0691.

Owner Comments

This airplane requires a great deal of maintenance, but that goes with the territory. Fortunately, my father is an A&P and we do our own maintenance. Oil consumption and leakage are somewhat heavy, which I understand is normal for the Jacobs engine. One thing in particular I don't like is that one of the five fuel tanks is located in the bottom of the fuselage just behind the wheel wells. I understand that a gear-up landing on a runway can end with a fire due to this.

Overall, though, I think this is a fine antique airplane, if you are willing to put up with a few minor quirks. I forget all about the drawbacks of the airplane when I see the crowd gathering as I'm taxiing to the ramp. The Staggerwing is truly a lot of fun to fly.

Michael Allen
Star, N.C.

There aren't many Staggerwings around, relatively speaking, although there are almost always several for sale at any given time. The trouble is that they are scattered all over the U.S., and looking at even a few could involve a lot of travelling. The best way to see as many as possible in one place is to attend the annual Staggerwing Club Convention at Tullahoma, Tenn. each October.

In addition to the five or six airplane in the Staggerwing Museum, there could be 30 or 40 fly-in attendees—a substantial proportion of the entire Model 17 population. There is no better way to learn a lot about Staggerwings very quickly.

The Staggerwing Club is superb—very friendly people and an impressive reserve of parts, manuals, technical expertise, etc. The club newsletter is the best source of aircraft for sale. Joining the club is an essential first step for an aspiring Staggerwing owner. A second essential step is to read *Staggerwing* by Robert Smith.

Prices for Staggerwings vary considerably. It is possible to buy one for under $100,000 or more than $200,000. These are complex airplanes, and a ground-up rebuild will be a major expense. As the population of basket cases diminishes, full restorations must necessarily commence from flyable, and therefore costly, raw material. Good advice can be obtained from a number of rebuilders who specialize in Staggerwings (see the club newsletter).

The aircraft is magnificent to fly. There is lots of room inside, and many are equipped with up-to-date avionics and instruments because they remain such practical travelling machines. You can obtain a TAS of 165-170 mph at a reasonable cruise setting, and yes, it actually will reach 200 mph. The controls are light, well harmonized and responsive, and the negative stagger allows the pilot good visibility into turns, which is a rare experience in a cabin biplane.

With the 450-hp Pratt & Whitney R985, you can plan on 20- 24-gph fuel flows. Tank arrangements vary, but it will generally be necessary to limit fuel loadings only to the extent that you are carrying three passengers and a lot of luggage, or five people total (which is a cozy fit). A D17 with five tanks holds 121 U.S. gallons.

Even experienced pilots are best advised to get a full checkout on a Staggerwing. All the traditional taildragger quirks are there in spades. Care is always required on takeoff and landing. It is noteworthy that the manual lists a 90-degree crosswind limit of only 10 mph. That said, the airplane is a delight to fly, and rewards a careful pilot with an experience not to be matched in a modern aircraft. The Staggerwing is an aviation ultimate.

Paul McConnel
London, U.K.

We have owned a Navy GB-2 (D17S) Staggerwing for more than five years. We bought it with new coverings, but in pieces and still needing much work. Since then, we have flown it for about 500 hours day, night, IFR and off grass strips and hard runways. She is comfortable on 1,500-foot strips, if you are. At the present time, we give dual instruction (yes, we have a dual yoke), and have considerable experience working with students, private pilots on up to ATPs. Our bird has a P&W R985 with chrome cylinders, put together by Covington Engines in Oklahoma. We keep 60-weight oil in it and run neither too cold nor too hot. The oil cooler door (which is between No. 1 and 2 cylinders) and the valve allow very precise temperature control, but must be watched like a hawk until you are stabilized in cruise. This is something that's not common to most single-engine aircraft.

You can forget making multiple takeoffs and landings on hot days, since the engine will overheat. This engine uses about a quart of oil per hour, so after 20 or 25 hours we just drain and refill. Rarely do we ever add oil, although we do buy it by the 55-gallon drum. (Our engine also has the optional 9.5 gallon oil tank.) We recommend anyone running this engine to install a nine-probe EGT. The peace of mind when leaning is worth it. Also, we use platinum spark plugs.

We average 20 gph in cruise and about 15 gph in the training environment. We burn autogas (major brand, when possible). Be careful not to actually fill the tanks, because it runs back in the wing and dries out the wood. Before starting the engine, be sure to pull the prop through to check for hydraulic lock. If you find one cylinder locked, it will probably be one of the two bottom cylinders. They're at eye level and easy to get to. But don't forget to back the piston off on that cylinder before you remove the spark plug to let the oil out.

The Staggerwing is fun to fly, but seems to have no positive stability at all. A summer day under the cumulus is going to be tough. Add to this the yawing from those long ailerons and you had better make a choice between learning to keep the ball centered or cleaning up after your sick passengers.

Whatever trouble the Staggerwing may be, she's worth it. I have, in the last five years, experienced almost every human emotion there is from just watching people visually take in her lines, or glide their fingertips through the dust on her wings. Perhaps I am different, but I like the fingerprints they leave. They are evidence that I have provided pleasure to someone I don't know yet. I say yet because they always come back to talk about her.

Richard Fuchs
St. Louis, Mo.

Cost/Performance/Specifications

Model	Year	Price*	Cruise Speed (kts)	Useful Load (lb)	Std/Opt Fuel (gal)	Engine	Avg. Fuel Flow (gph)	Maximum Range*
C17R	1936	$96,000	144	1,515	74/166	225-hp Jacobs L-4	14	1,900
F17D	1939	$90,000	158	1,510	77/125	330-hp Jacobs L-6	17	1,300
F17D	1939	$99,750	158	1,510	77/125	330-hp Jacobs L-6	17	1,300
D17A	1939	$165,000	156	1,510	98/170	350-hp Wright R-760	17.5	1,700
D17S	1942	$149,000	176	1,450	102/174	450-hp Pratt&Whitney R-985	23	1,495
D17S	1943	$100,000	176	1,450	102/174	450-hp Pratt&Whitney R-985	23	1,495
D17S	1943	$150,000	176	1,450	102/174	450-hp Pratt&Whitney R-985	23	1,495
D17S	1944	$100,000	176	1,450	102/174	450-hp Pratt&Whitney R-985	23	1,495
G17S	1946	$185,000	175	1,450	124/170	450-hp Pratt&Whitney R-985	24.9	1,370
G17S	1947	$225,000	175	1,450	124/170	450-hp Pratt&Whitney R-985	24.9	1,370

*Notes: Typical prices of models offered for sale in *Trade-A-Plane* over the past few years. Due to the rarity of the model, no trends can be established. Range is absolute maximum with no reserve.

Beech 76 Duchess

In 1974, Beech's designers—beset with the task of creating a step-up plane for the Beech Aero Centers—started laying the groundwork for a simple, yet advanced light twin based on the Beech Sierra design. The prototype sported a T-tail, two doors (a la Musketeer), and a pair of conventional-rotating 160-hp Lycomings (which were later replaced by counterrotating 180-hp engines). Forty-four months after its inception, the Model 76 Duchess attained FAA type certification and began rolling off the Liberal, Kans. assembly lines.

No sooner had the Duchess hit the market, of course, than the light-twin arena suddenly became quite crowded, what with the Grumman Cougar's debut in 1978 and the arrival of Piper's Seminole in 1979. (Cessna's T303 Crusader—née Clipper—was to have been an entrant in the light-light-twin derby, but Cessna thought better of the move at the last minute and reconfigured the T303 as a Seneca-class medium hauler.)

Nonetheless, Beech's Aero Centers quickly placed orders for over 200 of the bonded-construction T-twins; and in the first few years of sales Beech's lightest light twin held its own with the competition—slightly outpacing the Seminole and Turbo Seminole in combined sales. A total of 437 were built.

Novel Construction

Although the Duchess's lines clearly reflect its Musketeer ancestry, the Model 76 is anything but a double-breasted Sierra in actual construction. The Sierra's outward-retracting gear design was abandoned in the Duchess, for example, along with the Mooney-style rubber shock biscuits. (The Duchess displays a pair of megalithic oleo shocks on the main gear, while the nose strut is taken *in toto* from the A36 Bonanza.) Like the Sierra, the Duchess has bonded wet wings; but unlike the other Aero Center airplanes, the Model 76's main tanks extend to the wingtips, carrying 50 gallons usable (each). Also, the Duchess's ailerons are bigger (and travel farther) than the Sierra's.

In the fuselage, extensive use was made of honeycomb-sandwich construction

High-flying T-tail pays off in both stylistic and aerodynamic ways.

techniques to produce a light, crashworthy, and at the same time vibration/noise-resistant cabin. A feature unique among twins is the Duchess's cabin door configuration (borrowed from the Sierra): there are doors and walkways for both pilot *and* copilot, plus a large baggage door on the left aft fuselage behind the wing.

T-tail Trade-offs

The Duchess's most distinctive design hallmark, however, is its T-tail. Although considered by many to be merely a stylistic (i.e., marketing) device, the T-tail actually contributes in meaningful ways to the airplane's performance. Because the horizontal surfaces are out of the propellers' slipstreams and sit far to the rear atop a *swept* tail fin, their effectiveness is enhanced; and as a result, the horizontal tail area can be reduced—with a commensurate reduction in drag—at no penalty in pitch control. (In fact, the pitch authority of the Duchess tail is so great that the original prototype experienced problems with excessively high nose angles in stalls. This problem was ameliorated, however, with the switch to heavier, 180-hp engines from the earlier 160-hp Lycomings.) As a side benefit, propwash buffet is also eliminated.

The real-world payoff of the T-tail for the Duchess can be measured in terms of pitch control in the flare (excellent), allowable c.g. range (10.9 inches total, versus 8.3 for the Sierra), and the amount of trim change needed after gear or flap deployment (little, if any). The T-tail's end-plate effect also contributes to rudder effectiveness, providing a low single-engine minimum control speed (Vmc) of 67 knots CAS, which is one knot below the airplane's clean stall speed (Vs) of 68 KCAS. (In a twin-engine plane, it is desirable from a safety/controllability standpoint to encounter the stall at an airspeed higher than Vmc.) Of course, these benefits do not come without a modest weight penalty for the added structure needed to carry the lofty horizontal stabilizer—estimated by Beech, in this case, at 15 pounds.

Following the Model 76's introduction, few substantive design changes were made (although myriad minor adjustments have been incorporated in later models and published as service bulletins; see below). In early 1979, improved door locks became standard, and cowl flap hinges were changed from aluminum to steel; in mid-1980, an improved engine mount was introduced; in 1981, a landing gear horn muting system (to keep the horn from sounding prematurely during high-speed power-off letdowns) was introduced. For 1982, Beech increased the number of static wicks from five to 12. Overall, the design of the Model 76 remained virtually unchanged during its five-year run—a testament to the airplane's basic soundness.

Bonded wet wings hold 50 gallons of fuel each. Wingtips are made of flexible plastic, to reduce "dings."

Performance

Owners praise the Duchess as a capable medium-range cross-country machine, with 75-percent power cruise speeds typically in the 160-knot/184-mph region at fuel flows of just under 10 gallons per hour per engine. To underscore the plane's obvious economy-of-operation appeal, Beech in 1982 appended a "super economy" cruise performance page to the Duchess handbook, claiming a 142-knot/163-mph speed at 14,000 feet, with props at 2100 rpm and manifold pressures at 18.0 inches (fuel consumption: 6.8 gph/engine). We doubt, frankly, that anyone would choose to operate the plane in this fashion, but the point is well taken: this *is* a bonafide economy twin. With a maximum takeoff weight of 3,900 pounds (100 pounds more than the normally aspirated Piper Seminole—25 pounds *less* than the Turbo Seminole), the Duchess turns in rather mediocre takeoff numbers; to wit, a sea level ground roll of 1,017 feet and a 50-foot obstacle clearance distance of 2,119 feet—no better than the Travel Air (Beech's original 180-hp twin) and actually quite a bit worse than the competition. (Piper's Seminole gets off and over in 880 feet and 1,400 feet, respectively.)

On landing, the comparisons with Brand 'P' are even more striking: the Duchess rolls a full 1,000 feet after touchdown at gross weight, versus the Seminole's 590 feet. With heavy-duty brakes, the Seminole will—according to Piper—roll a mere *383 feet* after a no-wind touchdown. One wonders whether Piper's tape measures are made in the U.S.

Rotation speed in the Duchess comes at 71 knots (81 mph), which corresponds with Beech's "intentional one-engine inoperative speed" (Vsse) as well as with the two-engine best angle of climb speed (Vx). Upon attaining 85 knots (the best rate of climb speed for single- *or* all-engine operation), a full-throttle climbout yields a 1,248-fpm rate of ascent initially, decaying to 1,000 fpm at 4,000 feet.

In both looks and flying qualities, the Duchess is a quantum leap better than its single-engine progenitor, the Sierra.

The Duchess's single-engine performance specs are nothing to write home about—although, of course, the same is true for other twins in this category. On one engine, the Duchess turns in an anemic 235-fpm sea-level climb rate at gross (vs. a complexion-whitening 217 fpm for the Seminole and 180 fpm for the Turbo Seminole). The climb dwindles to 50 fpm at the service ceiling of 6,170 feet (vs. 4,100 feet for the lighter-gross-weight Seminole—again, a question of whose numbers you believe).

The usable fuel capacity of 100 gallons gives the Duchess an endurance, at 75-percent cruise, of around four hours with IFR reserves. The published range (with reserves) varies from 623 nautical/717 statute miles to upwards of 800 nautical and 900 statute, depending on whether 75-percent cruise or "super economy" power settings are used.

All in all, the Duchess's performance is on a par with—and in most cases no better than—that of the 1958 Travel Air's. Which raises the obvious question: Why would Beech go to the trouble and expense of certifying a *new* 180-hp light twin when it could just as easily have revived the Travel Air, a proven (and much-loved by some) design?

When we put this question to a Beech spokesman in 1979, he answered by saying that the Travel Air was and is a complicated design, expensive to produce (as are the Barons that derive from that same type certificate); the Duchess employed state-of-the-art materials and construction techniques, affording a lighter airframe (by about 200 pounds, compared to the Model 95); and in designing the Duchess, Beech had the opportunity to create a twin with truly superior slow-speed handling characteristics.

Counter-rotating 180-hp Lycomings yield a cruise speed of 158 knots and a range of about 700 nm with reserve.

All of which is true. In 1982, one could only lament the fact that Beech's efforts did not result in a twin with a lower price tag. The 1982 Duchess sold for a whopping $171,875 (average-equipped) —two and a half times more than a comparably equipped Travel Air sold for in 1968.

Handling and Comfort

The Duchess is nothing if not comfortable. Although the cockpit tapers noticeably just forward of the pilots' thighs, the Bonanza-like head room and 44-inch cabin width (the cabin is wider, amazingly, than that of the Baron) contribute to the feeling that one is actually flying a much larger airplane. The accommodations are strictly first-class.

Pilots transitioning to the Duchess from single-engine aircraft will appreciate the fact that the plane's panel layout (with the exception of the vertically displaced tachometers) is both logical and eyepleasing. Gear and flap switches are where they should be—gear on the left, flaps on the right—as are the power levers (mercifully, Beech abandoned the irksome center-panel "prop/throttle/mixture" grouping found on the Barons and placed these controls in the standard TPM arrangement in the Duchess).

Starting the Duchess's carbureted O-360s is easy enough if you remember to press *in* on the ignition switch while cranking, to engage the primer (a solenoid-operated system which, mysteriously, feeds fuel only to cylinders one, two and four of each engine).

On the ground, the Duchess handles a bit differently from its Piper counterpart. The slow damping action of the main gear oleos—combined with the plane's large spanwise mass distribution—gives the Duchess a curiously ponderous feel while taxiing, even setting up a Dutch-roll-like oscillation as one goes around corners. Likewise, the slightest touch of the brake pedals tends to collapse the nose oleo. These idiosyncrasies are basically harmless, however.

On takeoff, the Duchess requires a positive tug on the yoke to break ground (not too much, though, or you'll overrotate). In the air, visibility is excellent. In fact, the nose slopes away so precipitously that it is difficult, at first, to judge the plane's angle of attack.

Unlike the Aero Center singles upon which the Model 76 design is based, the Duchess has no rudder-aileron interconnect—nor is one needed. The controls are light (as twins go) and well-harmonized, inviting comparisons with such single-engine aircraft as the Bonanza and Saratoga. Stability is excellent in the pitch and roll modes; yaw is less good, with some tendency toward short-period waggle in turbulence. Overall, however, the plane is decidedly well-behaved.

Slow-Speed Traits

True to the designers' original intentions, the Duchess excels at low-speed controllability—with or without both fans turning. Pitch, roll, and yaw control remain crisp at speeds near blue-line (85 KIAS), and—thanks to the presence on the center pedestal of trim knobs for ailerons, rudder, *and* elevator—the plane trims up quickly for hands-off flight after shutting down either engine. (Handling is the same with either engine out, of course; there is no "critical" engine.)

Stalls are conventional in all respects, except that the controls remain surprisingly effective at vanishingly low airspeeds. With both engines developing power, the airplane can be flown well below 50 knots IAS, dirty, without stalling.

One of the nice aspects of the T-tail is that, since it sits high above the wing's wake, it doesn't "feel" disturbances caused by lowering/raising the gear or flaps. On deploying the landing gear (at up to 140 knots) or flaps (up to 110 knots), there is no noticeable change in pitch attitude.

An interesting quirk of the airplane is its maximum gear-*raise* speed of 113 knots, occasioned by the design of the forward-retracting nose strut. Once the gear has been lowered (as a speed brake, say), it cannot be raised again until airspeed has been allowed to bleed off to under 113 knots.

Safety

According to NTSB records, there were only six accidents involving Duchesses in the first few years after the aircraft was introduced in 1978, two of them fatal. (Interestingly, only one of the six pilots involved was over the age of 33.)

• One Duchess was destroyed (and the two persons aboard killed) on a VFR flight from Long Beach to Ramona, Calif. when the aircraft encountered zero-visibility weather and collided with the ground in a controlled descent.

• A Duchess sustained heavy damage on a training flight from Little Rock, Arkansas when the flight instructor allowed his student to land gear-up.

• Confusion in the cockpit resulted in another gear-up landing (again with substantial damage)—this time in Sioux City, Iowa—when an instructor told his student to cancel a practice single-engine go-around. The CFI landed the plane wheels-up.

• Inclement weather claimed a non-instrument-rated Duchess pilot with 20 hours in type. The aircraft crashed out of control at night, in icing conditions.

Cost/Performance/Specifications

Model	Year Built	Average Retail Price	Cruise Speed (kts)	Useful Load (lbs)	Fuel Std/Opt (gals)	Engine	TBO (hrs)	Overhaul Cost @
76	1978	$70,000	158	1,456	100	180-hp Lyc. O-360-A1G6D	2,000	$11,500
76	1979	$74,000	158	1,456	100	180-hp Lyc. O-360-A1G6D	2,000	$11,500
76	1980	$80,000	158	1,456	100	180-hp Lyc. O-360-A1G6D	2,000	$11,500
76	1981	$86,000	158	1,456	100	180-hp Lyc. O-360-A1G6D	2,000	$11,500
76	1982	$93,000	158	1,456	100	180-hp Lyc. O-360-A1G6D	2,000	$11,500

• A hard landing in icing conditions caused major damage to a Duchess on its nighttime arrival in South Bend, Ind. Four people escaped serious injury.

• Fuel exhaustion and fuel mismanagement were mentioned in the description of "probable cause" for a double-engine-stoppage accident. The 24-year-old pilot had departed Monmouth, N.J. for West Chicago, Ill., nonstop, against undetermined headwinds; substantial damage occurred when the plane, out of fuel, made an off-airport landing near its intended destination.

Note: Perhaps it's worth mentioning that none of the 12 persons involved in the four non-fatal accidents cited above suffered serious injuries. (Perhaps it's worth observing, too, that although weather radar is available as an option on the Duchess, anti-icing equipment of the type that might have prevented two of these accidents is not.)

A review by our sister publication, *Aviation Safety*, showed the Duchess to have a fatal accident rate much better (lower) than its peers in the "new" light twin class, the Gulfstream American Cougar and the Piper Seminole and, in fact, a much better rate than the general aviation fleet as a whole.

Economics of Operation

Beech in 1982 estimated the direct hourly operating cost of the Duchess at $63.79—including $37.05/hr for gasoline ($1.95/gal at 19 gph), $1.59/hr for oil, $15.57/hr for "inspection, maintenance, and propeller overhaul" (assuming shop rates of $27/hr), and an engine exchange allowance—including FWF accessories and installation labor—of $9.58/hr (total, for both engines together). One owner claimed a direct operating cost of $53.24/hr *minus* engine reserves, so it appears Beech's numbers are pretty much on target.

Twin doors make coming and going a breeze. A large third door in the rear cabin serves bags and kids.

Piper, for what it's worth, estimated a direct hourly operating cost of $60.57 for the normally aspirated Seminole, based on 17.7 gph fuel consumption (at $1.95/gal). The Turbo Seminole's higher fuel flows and greater overhaul costs brings its direct operating expense to $70.49 per hour.

Maintenance Considerations

From a reliability standpoint, the Duchess has one thing going for it that the Seminole does not: namely, the A-series Lycoming O-360 engine. Unlike the E-series O-360s installed in the Seminole, the Model 76's O-360-A1G6D engines are among Lycoming's oldest and most proven O-360 variants, utterly worthy of the 2,000-hr TBO bestowed upon them. The Seminole's O-360-E1A6D engines, on the other hand, are a more recent design with valve train components common to the O-320-H "Blue Streak" engine of Skyhawk fame.

As almost everyone knows by now, the O-320-H has had a history of severe tappet-spalling problems. (The spalling—which seems cold-weather related—is partially preventable by the use of Lycoming's special LW-16702 oil additive.) What you may *not* have known is that the O-360-E (and TO-360-E) engines on the Seminole also have the potential for tappet-destruction problems. In fact, that

Lycoming requires regular use of the LW-16702 "mystery oil" as a prerequisite to warranty coverage for O-360-E engines. (The oil additive is *not* required for the Duchess's engines.)

This is not to say, of course, that the Duchess does not have its share of maintenance problems; seven AD notes and 45 service bulletins in the first four years of operation say otherwise. For the most part, however, the Duchess's maintenance glitches are minor. Most of the ADs, for example, involve one-time inspections or fixes applicable to early-serial-number aircraft. The only important repetitive AD affecting the aircraft (other than the one targeting the plane's Southwind combustion heater) is a 1980 AD (80-19-12) requiring 50-hr checks of the engine mounts for cracks. Unfor-tunately, the AD names all Duchesses from S/N -1 on up, and even though an improved engine mount is available, it is not clear from the wording of the AD whether installation of the heavy-duty mount eliminates the repetitive inspection re-quirement.

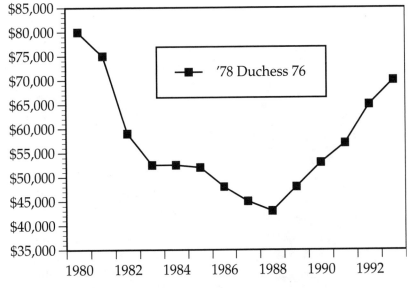

Space prohibits an exhaustive listing of Duchess-related Service Instructions here. Most of these bulletins involve minor product improvements or non-mandatory inspections. Some, however-er, are of major importance (such as S.I. 1147 pertaining to engine mount replacement; and S.I. 1166, regarding improved main gear doors). Prospective Duchess buyers would be well-advised to crosscheck aircraft logbooks against the Beech S.I. Master Index available through any Beech dealer) to see whether applicable service bulletins have been complied with.

Owner Comments

Our company operates two Duchess aircraft. They have both exceeded our expec-tations in all aspects. The handling characteristics are very good, although the elevator seems to be a bit light. True airspeeds vary between 155 and 160 knots at 65 percent power with a fuel flow of 19 gallons per hour.

Our direct operating cost averaged $53.24 per hour with no engine reserves. These figures were for a seven-month period during which the aircraft flew 506 hours. Their normal load is one and occasionally two passengers, and we average about 150-mile stage lengths.

Our only major unscheduled problem was one engine overhaul at 1,400 hours, due to a lifter that disintegrated. As far as the airframe is concerned, our problems have been the gear doors, which tend to develop cracks, and an engine mount inspection at 50-hour intervals. We had one cracked mount. Beech has provided a fix for the gear doors and has given us very good product support.

Single-engine performance is a little better than average for this class of aircraft, and handling characteristics on one engine are very good. From a pilot's point of view, these aircraft are a delight to fly, and from an accountant's standpoint, easy to feed.

Marvin Pippen
Wharton, Tex.

Duchess has the luxury of trim controls not only for pitch, but rudder and ailerons as well. Note carb heat knobs above mike. Engines are not fuel injected. Crossfeed control levers are at bottom.

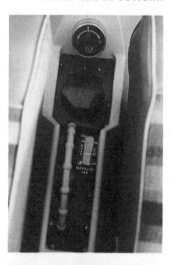

I selected the Duchess as a moderate-range business machine and feel that it will handle that task well. The visibility is good, and the handling predictable. It is a little noisier than the Seminole, but the visibility gain makes up for it. Also, the two entry doors are a decided convenience. Handbook figures on fuel consumption and speed appear to be accurate. The prospective purchaser will want to get the beefed-up engine mounts (standard on later models), or else a repetitive AD inspection will have to be made every 50 hours. There apparently is some cracking of mounts on some of the earlier models; hence the AD.

The Duchess pilot will want to take special care when securing after a flight. The rudder trim should be rolled full down and the rudder locks installed. They're hard to figure out, but do it anyway. The elevator surface droops naturally at rest and will damage the rudder if the rudder is allowed to swing in the wind.

Last, but not least: have a set of "starter engaged" indicator lights installed on the panel if the airplane doesn't already have them. As I learned, extended cranking will cause the starter relay to hang up, keeping the relay engaged. The result of all of this is that the starter will be damaged (probably destroyed) and the battery run down. The trouble is that you don't know it. A voltmeter would be handy at times like this. (The lesson here is to get familiar with the electrical system.) Incidentally, I have to give high marks for the position of the circuit breakers and engine instruments in the Duchess. All are handy and well laid out.

Garwood Burwell
Madison, N.J.

Mine is a 1980 aircraft which has proved to be fairly satisfactory. There were considerable problems with the gear actuators, which required replacement six times. They continually leaked and blew seals. Also, the passenger windows are now showing stress cracks where they are riveted. Beech was supposed to be looking into this. Handling qualities are very satisfactory, and landings and take-offs are to the book. Speed on the average is 165 knots at 75 percent power. Fuel burn is seven gph/side. The carbureted system is easy to start. The interior is very roomy and comfortable, with easy access through the twin doors and rear door.

The annuals run around $1,200, with about $125 per month for general maintenance. The avionics panel is small, limiting equipment choice, and the yoke doesn't accommodate sufficient space for wiring push-to-talk buttons or remote ident switches, etc. Sound in the cabin could be better, and a prop synch would be nice. Visibility is excellent and loading adequate. In summary, I would like to see more horsepower to obtain a cruise of 185 to 190 knots. Range is good, but with larger engines or turbocharging, this could be increased. In all, it is a good economical twin with fine handling characteristics—a high-quality aircraft.

Nathan Goldenthal
Peoria, Ariz.

Beech
95 Travel Air

Pilots dipping into the great bargain warehouse of used twins will quickly find the elderly Travel Airs to be diamonds in the rough.

How rough depends on the nonchalance with which the aircraft have been cared for through the decades. The tough decision for a buyer, then, is whether the modest price savings—maybe $5,000 to $10,000—offered by the Model 95, should swing a choice away from one of the sweet-flying newer light twins like the Beech Duchess or Piper Seminole. Mechanics in

Blunt engine nacelles and squared-off tail are the hallmarks of the Travel Airs.

the field tell us there are lots of really doggy Travel Airs out there moldering in tiedown slots around the country, so it pays to be especially careful with this class of aircraft. That's not to take anything away from the basic design, though, because it's solid stuff, built to last—in fact, it's really an economy Beech Baron forerunner with 180-hp engines.

There's no problem identifying the Travel Airs. They're the ones with the homely, old-fashioned squared-off vertical tails. (If they look the same as T-34 Mentor trainer tails, it's for good reason: they're the same.) The other main identifying feature: blunt little engine nacelles—shark-shape they are not.

History

The Travel Air started out in 1958 with four seats and carbureted engines. It had a shortish six-foot-11-inch-long cabin with a small rear window. The Model B95 in 1960 came with another 100 pounds of gross weight and an optional fifth seat. The Model B95A a year later had a longer cabin, up to six seats and yet another 100 pounds of gross weight. Its biggest improvement, however, came in the form of fuel injected engines instead of carburetion. Next, in 1966, came the D95A, with new one-half-inch valves, raising engine TBOs from 1,200 to 2,000 hours. And finally, in 1968, the E95 introduced a bigger, more steeply slanted one-piece windshield.

Paralleling changes for the Beech Bonanza line—since, after all, the Travel Air has essentially a Bonanza fuselage—the Travel Airs received bigger rear windows, starting with the B95A in '61.

Performance

No speed demons, the Travel Airs can be expected to motor along at no better than about 150 to 160 knots in cruise—quite a bit slower than any of the Barons. But the flip side is a relatively miserly fuel burn of only 16 to 19 gph from the 180-hp Lycomings. Now and then, an owner actually reports urging a hustling 170 knots TAS out of the bird—as called for in the book at 75% power. Modest though they may be, these speeds put the Travel Air at the head of the pack of comparable light twins.

Figure on a range with reserve (at 65% power) of about 900 nm—again a figure that decently eclipses that of comparable twins in our group.

Alas, the Travel Air does not shine in the area of engine-out service ceiling. Figure on no more than 4,100 feet when the chips are down and loading is heavy—worst in its class except, interestingly, for the much newer Piper Seminole (whose S/E ceiling is pegged at 4,100 feet).

Load Carrying

With an equipped useful load of about 1,400 pounds, the pilot can count on carrying full fuel along with four adults and a little baggage—this time, best in our comparison group, except for the Cessna Skymaster. The monster baggage compartment behind the rear seats, and its placarded hefty 270-pound structural limit, might be a temptation to overload, so watch out. A smaller nose baggage compartment has the same weight capacity, c.g. envelope permitting. One pilot told us he liked to load small high-density items there like extra oil.

Creature Comfort

There's only one cabin door for crew and passengers, but the interior layout is standard Bonanza/Baron; i.e., beautiful and beamy with high, handsome windows. Flip open the center windows on a hot day and enjoy the breeze. "The Travel Air exudes typical Beech comfort and quality," said one owner. "There is plenty of shoulder and leg room for everyone. All four seats have seat rail and back adjustments and individual overhead air outlets." Said another: "This is the quietest lightplane cabin I have flown in. The seat height makes long flights less tiring than sitting with legs straight out in front of you."

Cabin is big, roomy and comfortable, with good visibility.

Handling Qualities

Again, typical Bonanza/Baron control responsiveness—the kind that makes owners feel, well, sporty, rather than like bus drivers. In the same vein, landings are a breeze. "Properly trimmed," glowed one owner, "the aircraft will all but land itself."

Safety Record

No particularly wicked accident trends related to aircraft deficiencies were detected in a scan of mishaps in FAA accidents/incidents for a five-year period. Four weather mishaps, a pair of fuel mismanagement/exhaustion accidents and a like number of engine failures claimed the greatest proportion of fatal accidents among Travel Air pilots during the period.

As with most other aircraft whose mechanical shortcomings we've traced in these Used Aircraft Guides, landing gear problems of one type or another exacted the greatest toll in nonfatal accidents.

We'd probably be most concerned about the possibility of engine failure in this model aircraft, since power losses ranked fourth highest in 14 different root accident causes we isolated in the five-year run.

But that's not to say the Travel Air represents any greater risk in this category than most other aircraft. It's perennially a big one for most aircraft categories. At any rate, no particular pattern was evident in the five engine stoppages we counted—at least those

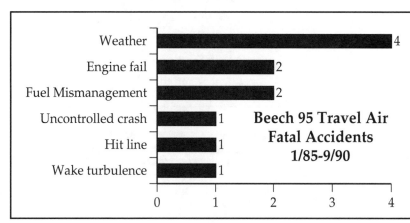

Beech 95 Travel Air Fatal Accidents 1/85-9/90

that were unrelated to fuel mismanagement. Indeed, in many cases, the investigators could not even determine the causes of the engine stoppage. In one, a dislodged oil quick drain plug caused oil pressure fluctuation. A handful of valve and cylinder cracking occurrences reported as service difficulties to the FAA would lead us to suspect that other engine stoppages were not reported as accidents after pilots made their way successfully back to an airport.

Fuel Mismanagement

At least one apparent fuel mismanagement fatality would lead us to regard with wariness the fuel gauge arrangement on the Travel Air. There are only two gauges for the four tanks: two mains and two aux tanks. A toggle switch allows the pilot to shunt readings back and forth between tanks.

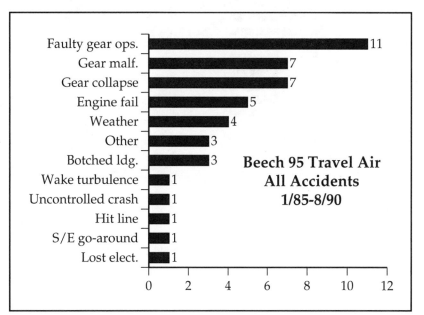

Beech 95 Travel Air All Accidents 1/85-8/90

On one fatal accident where an engine failed, the fuel selectors were on the aux tanks, but the fuel gauges were set on the mains. It turned out that the aux tanks were empty, while the mains had 10 gallons each. To add to the problem, the pilot feathered the prop on the right engine, although the left one had stopped for lack of fuel. In another nonfatal accident the left fuel selector was not positioned properly in the detent, resulting in a power stoppage on takeoff.

Gear Embarrassment

The biggest Travel Air gear bugaboo was the familiar one of pilots either failing to lower the gear for landing or inadvertently retracting it instead of the flaps on the rollout. Naturally, there's good reason to suspect the unconventional gear/flap lever arrangement on the aircraft (with flaps left, gear right) contributed to the problem for transitioning pilots. This doesn't usually cost lives, just lots of dollars from engine sudden stoppages and belly and prop crunching.

Although sometimes used as a multiengine trainer, we were interested to note a complete absence of stall/spin accidents stemming from engine-out work reported on this particular model Beech twin.

Maintenance Considerations

Owners for the most part told us they regarded the Beech twin as posing no special maintenance burden, though some railed about the familiar theme that Beech parts were so expensive. Despite the fact that the aircraft are decades old, most also reported they had no problem getting parts. Commonality with the Baron/Bonanza line in many components made the supply quite reasonable, many said. But we did hear some laments that parts peculiar to the Travel Air were not in abundant supply by a long shot, and sometimes they had to be scrounged from salvage yards.

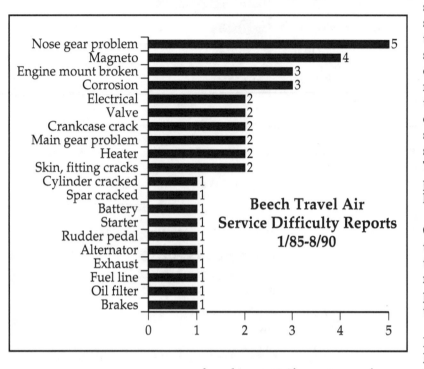

Beech Travel Air
Service Difficulty Reports
1/85-8/90

One owner related a long search to find tail skin metal after a hovering helicopter ripped his to pieces. He said the magnesium control surfaces are best replaced by a specialist in the art, rather than training your local mechanic.

Incidentally, there's a Beech service bulletin calling for "mandatory" inspection and replacement if necessary of magnesium elevator control fittings after one report of a broken one. It was caused by an apparent overload, perhaps caused by a prop or jet blast.

Glen Foulk, service manager for Cutter Aviation in Phoenix, Ariz., who gives service clinics for the American Bonanza Society on Travel Airs, said he had encountered no big parts problem, except perhaps for cowl flap motors. The general maintenance situation for the aircraft, he said, was very straightforward. Prices are high, but not more than for any other aircraft. He did note that the cowlings were hard to get off, though, fastened with "lots of screws" with nuts rather than nut plates.

Incidentally, concerning cowl flap motors, one irate owner complained bitterly of having to pay Beech $2,700 for an entire cowl flap motor assembly when all he needed was a microswitch.

Corrosion and Cracking

Since these are not spring-fresh aircraft, we were surprised to note the paucity of reports on corrosion and cracking, but buyers should have a close check made for these problems. We also counted several instances where the engine mounts were broken.

Judging from the relatively large number (if you can call "five" a large number) of reports calling out nosegear mechanical problems, special attention should be given by potential buyers to this area.

The bladder fuel tanks should also be given scrutiny by shoppers. "Don't expect to get 10 years out of those bladders," one owner told us. "Keeping the airplane outside and filled with fuel, we figure on five years for each."

ADs, SBs

Carrying the saga of inadvertent door openings of Bonanzas, Barons and Travel Airs through yet another chapter, Beech issued a "mandatory" service bulletin in September 1990 providing a warning placard to make sure the cabin door is properly latched before takeoff.

The SB observed there have been reports of accidents following a cabin door opening because the pilot did not make sure the door was properly latched prior to takeoff. "In each accident the pilot failed to continue to fly the airplane and either lost control or allowed the airplane to stall at low altitude." For what it's worth, we noted no such accidents in the the latest five-year run we scrutinized on the Travel Airs.

Smallish rear baggage door opens onto a grandiose compartment that will hold 270 pounds structurally. A nose compartment helps W&B efforts.

An Airworthiness Directive issued in 1989 (89-5-2) requires inspection of the magnesium elevator and replacement if cracks are found.

Wing Spar Check

As with the Barons, Travel Airs should (by Beech SB) be checked for cracks in the forward wing spar carry-through structure. Reinforcement kits are available from Beech. Also, buyers should carefully check the aircraft logs for prop age on Hartzells, since the five-year mandatory overhaul can cost a pretty penny.

One owner told us how through the years the various prop nicks on his aircraft had been filed down and dressed out. So when they went in for AD compliance, it was found that all four blades were "under spec." "When I got them back, I was amazed at the size of the big paddles. They gave us another genuine five knots," he marveled.

Like Model Comparison

When analyzed for performance and load carrying, the Travel Airs stand up quite favorably with other light twins powered by smaller mills of 180-hp or so. A check of prices reveals the Travel Air to be the cheapest, as well, by anywhere from $500 to $6,000.

All things considered, our preference would be for one of the newer line of twins, just to shave off a decade of wear and tear, or just sitting idle. For its roominess and triple-door access, frankly the Beech Duchess would be our choice of a light twin below the Baron/Cessna 310 class.

We'd consider the extra $6,000 or so over the Travel Air probably worth the investment against the silent ravages of time, corrosion and cracking. But an older Travel Air with a good bill of health could sway us strongly.

Both gear and flap levers, along with prop and throttle levers, are in the reverse position from many other twins. Note the fuel gauge toggle switch just below and to the left of the black gear wheel lever. It must be switched between main and aux tanks to show fuel available from two gauges to the top left of the throttle quadrant.

Belonging

Hitch up with the American Bonanza Society for support on all the Bonanza/Baron class aircraft. P.O. Box 12888, Wichita, Kans. 67277, (316) 945-6990.

Owner Comments

I have been very pleased with my 1958 B95. At 10,000 feet it trues between 190 and 200 mph and burns 17 gph. The only problem I've had is corrosion on the magnesium control surfaces. I stripped and repainted them, but the corrosion returned in a few months. My advice is to buy new magnesium skins—aluminum, if available.

The 95 is a nice-flying airplane with solid yet responsive handling. Beech quality is quite evident, even on this 30-year-old plane. The 180-hp Lycomings make for excellent fuel economy and low maintenance. I think the Travel Air is a very under-rated light twin.

Bryan Huber
Jonesboro, Ark.

My 1958 Travel Air has treated me well during one year of ownership. It is simple (for a twin) and has reasonable single-engine performance. It carries a lot for a long distance in comfort. The airplane is very easy to fly. Cruise performance is fair: 145 knots @ 16 gph.

In short, it is a good compromise between performance and cost for a twin. My most bitter experience has been in dealings with Beechcraft. Their prices for parts are abusive. For example, a microswitch on a cowl flap motor failed. Could they sell me the part? No, only a complete cowl flap motor assembly. Could I contact the switch manufacturer directly? No, they only sell to us. How much for this assembly? $2,700. For a microswitch? I will never own another Beechcraft product.

William Norfleet
League City, Tex.

Show me another twin-engine flying machine that offers anywhere near the same in terms of comfort, speed, economy, simplicity, safety and peace of mind, for double the money as my Travel Air, and I'll buy it.

Bob Asadoorian
Methuen, Mass.

Our 1959 Model 95 is a delightful airplane. I get 150-160 knots TAS on about 15 to 16 gph. It handles beautifully. It also carries a good load. It pays to be very patient in searching for a Travel Air which has been properly taken care of by its prior owners. I looked at one which turned out to be assembled from three different airplanes. Parts are available, which is pretty unusual for a 1959 airplane.

I am happy I have one of the early models; it's lighter and doesn't have fuel injection. Beginning in 1961, Beech used two fuel injection systems, and I have heard that one of them is very expensive to overhaul.

Joseph N. Hosteny
Chicago, Ill.

I have operated a 1964 D95A Rayjay-equipped Travel Air since 1979. For the last eight years the plane has been based at an elevation of 5,300 feet with a 4,200-foot runway at Boulder, Colo. The turbos are, of course, a great advantage here in the west.

The advantage of this aircraft is the Beechcraft quality throughout, the Lycoming powerplants (hard to find on Beechcraft products), and in my case a wonderful radio package with a Century III autopilot. All of this adds up to excellent economy and great comfort. This is a much better aircraft than a Twin Comanche. I like to call it the "poor man's Baron."

In the years of operating this aircraft, there have been no maintenance surprises. The biggest problems I have experienced are turbo exhaust leaks, induction leaks and an under-designed wastegate. Century Aviation, the parts supplier for Rayjay, charges $300 to $500 to overhaul each wastegate.

I feel this is a high expense, but all-in-all I have had great luck with the performance and suffered little maintenance. It has been 2,000 hours since the last engine overhaul on both engines, and I have not had a jug off as yet. The lowest cylinder compression is 74 pounds, which in my opinion is very good.

On a recent trip east, I used one quart of oil per engine over a period of 14 hours (turbos operating eastbound). The speed and fuel burn is somewhat involved with the turbo option, but I figure at 8,000 feet 160 knots costs me 18 gph. This summer I departed from the Aspen, Colo. airport, which has a density altitude readout on the taxiway which gives continuous information to pilots. The reading that day was 11,400 feet. I had no problem on takeoff, and climbout with four adults and two hours of fuel.

The downside of this aircraft is that it has a tendency to do the Beech "rock" in heavy turbulence. The engine cowling has never looked graceful to me. Also, the

Cost/Performance/Specifications

Model	Year	Average Retail Price	Cruise Speed (kt)	Useful Load (lb)	Std/Opt Fuel (gal)	Engines	TBO (hr)	Overhaul Cost @
95	1958	$31,000	170	1,365	106	180-hp Lyc. O-360-A1A	2,000	$9,500
95	1959	$32,500	170	1,365	106	180-hp Lyc. O-360-A1A	2,000	$9,500
B95	1960	$33,500	170	1,465	106	180-hp Lyc. O-360-A1A	2,000	$9,500
B95A	1961	$36,500	170	1,565	106	180-hp Lyc. IO-360-B1A	2,000	$12,500
B95A	1962	$37,500	170	1,565	106	180-hp Lyc. IO-360-B1B	2,000	$11,500
D95	1963	$40,500	170	1,565	106	180-hp Lyc. IO-360-B1B	2,000	$11,500
D95A	1964	$41,500	170	1,565	106	180-hp Lyc. IO-360-B1B	2,000	$11,500
D95A	1965	$43,000	170	1,565	106	180-hp Lyc. IO-360-B1B	2,000	$11,500
D95A	1966	$44,500	170	1,565	106	180-hp Lyc. IO-360-B1B	2,000	$11,500
D95A	1967	$46,500	170	1,565	106	180-hp Lyc. IO-360-B1B	2,000	$11,500
E95	1968	$49,000	170	1,550	106	180-hp Lyc. IO-360-B1B	2,000	$11,500

Various landing and taxi light configurations are found, some with lights in the nose and nose strut, but not here. Wing lights are standard.

old-fashioned non-swept tail is handy for fitting in a shallow hangar, but looks dated on the ramp next to aircraft with swept vertical stabilizers.

Now for the best part—flying the airplane. The ailerons are a delight, with fast, smooth and positive roll response. Most light and medium twins handle heavily, including Barons. This is not the case with the Travel Air. Another positive feature is that the cabin is extremely quiet. The aircraft "blue book" lists comparable Bonanzas for only $1,000 less. This sounds like two for the price of one to me, and how can you beat the Lycoming IO-360s?

Barry M. Barnow
Boulder, Colo.

If it looks like a T-34 Mentor tail, there's a good reason. They're identical.

I am chief pilot for the West Houston Aero Club, which has leased a 1959 Travel Air for the past nine months. We have flown the plane 143 hours, mostly in training. Our maintenance has averaged $34.33 per hour including an annual and 100-hour inspections.

Fuel has averaged 14.5 gph, mostly with one engine caged. Speed at 75% power is 155 knots with both mills turning. One notable maintenance item involved the retractable boarding step, which is retracted by a bungee cord in the aft fuselage and extended by a cable in the aft fuselage which runs to the nose gear assembly. The step failed to retract, and the loose cable wrapped around the nose gear assembly.

Extending the gear caused the cable to bend the mechanism which engages and closes the nose gear door. Fortunately, no other damage occurred, and we noticed the damage before the next flight. The step is now permanently extended, and the offensive cable has been removed. The plane is an excellent trainer, especially for those who plan to transition to the larger Baron B55 or B58 series.

The aircraft systems, control feel and single-engine performance are similar to the heavier Barons. The Lycoming 180s are superb, having required no significant engine maintenance right up to TBO. Compression is still in the 70s on both engines. We have Baron drivers who come for recurrent training in our Travel Air because they fear the potential damage full power engine cuts might do to their big Continentals.

Stall characteristics are gentler than with the heavier Barons. If sufficiently provoked, however, the Travel Air can demonstrate a dramatic wing-drop characteristic of the Bonanza wing all these Beechcraft share.

Single-engine flight is possible up to 6,000 feet with a student, instructor and 80 gallons of fuel (max is 112 gallons). Single-engine control is excellent—as it is in the larger Barons. Vyse is comfortably above Vmca (100 mph and 84 mph). We are careful, however, to avoid single-engine stalls.

With the ability of the wing to stall completely and unload suddenly, we halt the Vmca demo at the first sign of buffet or stall warning light, as the Beech manual recommends. To give the student a feel for Vmca loss of directional control, I will restrict the rudder travel with my feet.

The strange position of the flaps, gear, throttle and prop controls are not a problem. Our heavy single is an A-36 Bonanza, and several of our students go on to fly Barons. Of course, the student touches not one switch until the plane has cleared the runway and come to a complete stop. "Flat switch is the Flap switch."

The American Bonanza Society's Baron/Travel Air Pilot Proficiency Program is excellent, and at $650 is a true bargain. Both the ground school and flight training are top notch, and the aircraft walk-around offers straight answers by maintenance people who know about the systems and their upkeep.

Jack Hirsch
Houston, Tex.

Light Twin Comparison

Model	Price	75% Cruise (kts)	Range at 65% w/res. (nm)	S/E Ceiling (ft)	Max Useful Load (lbs)	Usable Fuel (gals)	TBO (hrs)
'68 Travel Air E95	$49,000	174	900	4,400	1,615	106	2,000
'78 Duchess	$55,000	162	711	6,170	1,459	100	2,000
'79 Seminole	$54,500	166	725	4,100	1,462	108	2,000
'72 Twin Comanche	$50,500	157	748	5,800	1,393	84	2,000
'78 Cessna Skymaster	$49,500	169	590	7,100	1,861	88	1,500

My 1967 D95A was manufactured with most of the available options: long-range tanks, prop and windshield and anti-ice, fifth seat and soundproofing. The original owner added Rayjay turbos, a Skyox oxygen system, Hoskins strobes, a Brittain B4 autopilot and the Smith speed kit. The engines had one top overhaul at about 700 hours, but no other major repairs.

Two partners and I bought the plane 15 months ago at a distress sale for $13,500. It had 2,100 hours total time and had not flown in two years.

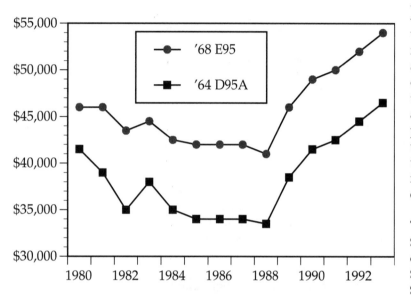

An AD required replacement of all 43 engine hoses with fire retardant versions. These had to be custom manufactured, which cost us $1,763 at Hoses Unlimited in Oakland. Another $2,800 in parts and labor put the airplane back in service. Insurance for the first year cost $3,000 for pilots with 170, 20 and zero multi time. In May of this year, after putting 150 hours on the plane, we took it to LyCon in Visalia to have the engines rebuilt.

The Cermichrome rebuilds cost $24,600, including all new gears and cams. Prop reconditioning added $2,443, and the annual was $500, plus $120 to comply with the spar inspection (no cracks) and stabilizer AD. One of our electric boost pumps went south just before the annual. Beech wants $650 for this little item, but LyCon found one for $400.

The Travel Air exudes typical Beech comfort and quality. There is plenty of shoulder and leg room for everyone. All four seats have seat rail and back adjustments and individual overhead air outlets. The panel is large and accommodates lots of equipment.

The nonstandard layout of prop/throttle and gear/flaps has not been a noticeable problem since they are quite clearly distinguished by size and shape. And with the dual yoke, the gear lever is difficult to get your hand on, anyway.

The real drawback is load capability. With the long-range tanks full, you can only carry three 170-pound people, no baggage. If you fill the seats and add 100 pounds of baggage, you have to leave 45 gallons at home, somehow. There is no easy way of measuring partially full tanks. However, one partner accidentally overloaded the plane by 200 pounds and took off from a 6,000-foot airport at 80 degrees. This turboed version didn't even work up a sweat.

The Travel Air is a real diamond in the rough. Hidden behind the straight tail and four-banger powerplants is a fast, comfortable, reliable and inexpensive twin. If you never carry more than one or two passengers, you'd be hard pressed to find a sweeter personal or small business airplane. And no, ours is not for sale.

William Schmidt
Santa Clara, Calif.

Beech
55 Baron

The large and small of it: the E55 in the foreground and B55 in right echelon. Despite the extra 50 horsepower of the E55, performance and load carrying are surprisingly similar.

With delightful control feel, relatively simple systems and perceived quality of design and construction, the "short-cabin" Barons are among the most desired light twins. Barons always have been considered the class-acts among twins, and some pilots who have flown the big-cabin 58 models actually prefer the "little" ones for their wonderful control response and harmony.

But, like any other airplane, the 55 Baron embodies some important compromises. For instance, the dreamy controls apparently are fair-weather friends. According to some owners, they're a bit too sensitive in rough weather, and an autopilot is considered a necessity for forays into IMC. And though they are touted as veritable baby carriages to fly, 55 Barons have recently been involved in several fuel-mismanagement, loss-of-control and hard-landing accidents. Also, recent records show that pilots are still being tripped up by the 55's nonconforming gear and flap switch layout. Despite its reputation as easy to fly, the airplane does require good initial and recurrent training.

In the rather voluminous feedback owners provided for this report, there seems to be no consensus concerning the costs of caring for and feeding the airplanes. Most owners assert that they enjoy relatively low operating and maintenance costs, but some characterize the Baron as a budget-buster. One owner presents an hourly expenditure of $200 for his airplane as evidence the airplane isn't for the financially "faint-hearted." In chorus, though, owners sing of Beech's continued strong product support and wail about its high parts prices.

History

The Model 55 was Beech Aircraft's first Baron. The airplane was unleashed in 1961 to do battle with Cessna's 310 and Piper's Aztec. Like the Model 95 Travel Air, which it replaced, the 55 comprised a Bonanza's fuselage fitted with a conventional tail. But, instead of the Travel Air's rather anemic 180-hp Lycomings, the original Baron packed 260-hp Continental IO-470L engines. After building 190 Barons that first year, Beech came out with the A55, which has a 10-inch longer fuselage and could be ordered with a second fold-down rear seat, bringing potential seating capacity to six (more on that later). A total of 309 A55s were built in 1962 and '63. The airplane's nose then was extended seven inches to provide more room for baggage and avionics equipment, and gross weight was bumped from 4,880 to 5,000 pounds.

Beech built 1,954 of the "long-nose" B55s from 1964 through 1982 (not including about 70 T-42A versions for the U.S. Army). Among a number of minor refinements during this time was an increase in gross weight to 5,100 pounds, starting with S/N TC-955 in mid-1965. (Earlier B55s were eligible for the higher gross through a Beech STC kit.)

The C55 Baron appeared in 1966 with a 12-inch longer fuselage and 285-hp Continental IO-520C engines. The "little Baron with the big engines" also was certified with a gross weight of 5,300 pounds. The airplane was redesignated the D55 in 1968 and the E55 in 1970. It, too, was dropped from production in 1983, after 1,201 were built (451 Cs, 316 Ds and 434 Es).

Singular Systems

Quite a ruckus has been raised over the years about the nonstandard control layout in the 55 Baron. Unlike most other light twins (and later versions of its big brother, the 58 model), the 55 has its gear lever on the right side of the power quadrant, the flap lever on the left. Positioning of the throttle and propeller control levers also defies conventional wisdom: The props are on the left; the throttles in the middle.

A whopping 400 pounds of baggage can be loaded into the rear compartment through the wide loading door with the fifth and sixth seats removed. A nose locker helps balance the load.

Though the unusual power control arrangement doesn't seem to be causing anything but, perhaps, apprehension for transitioning pilots (location of the large tachometer, manifold-pressure and fuel-flow gauges above their respective controls seems to help newcomers sort things out), the swapped gear and flap switches continue to contribute to bent metal and big repair bills.

In the first half of the '80s, for instancd, no fewer than eight pilots inadvertently retracted the gear, rather than the flaps, while rolling out after landing. (All but one pilot had more than 100 hours in type, and the low-timer was an FAA flight-test engineer.)

Early models can draw fuel into their engines either from the main tanks (37 usable gallons, each side) or the auxiliaries (31 gal/side). The fuel system was simplified in 1974 with interconnected tanks and three-position (on, off, crossfeed) selectors. Also that year, extra aux tanks became available for the E55 model, boosting max fuel capacity to 166 gallons.

Accommodations

The cabin is spacious, plush and comfortable. The tapered fuselage, however, tends to put a cramp on any normal-sized adults banished to the rear fold-down seats, though it does provide a couple of big windows to ease their exile. Since the rear seats can be gained only by clambering over the middle seats or through the baggage hatch, they're more appropriate for Missy and Junior than Aunt Maude and Uncle Gimpy. (Even with little folks in back, though, the pilot will need to check weight and balance carefully.)

The right front seat of a 55 Baron has to qualify as one of the world's greatest places to be, with comfort enhanced by a retractable center armrest, adjustable rudder pedals, lots of headroom and good visibility. Minor spoilers are a lack of room to stow charts and a massive control bar that hides various switches and circuit breakers. Also, some owners complain that the cabin is noisier than they would like, even with extra soundproofing installed.

Useful loads in the accompanying specifications are maximums. A typically equipped 260-hp Baron can carry about 1,800 pounds of people, bags and fuel; a 285-hp model, about 1,950 pounds. There is no zero-fuel-weight restriction, but care is needed to avoid busting the aft c.g. when the rear seats or aft baggage compartment is used. Balancing the load is facilitated by a nose compartment that can hold up to 300 pounds (270 in early models with gross weights below 5,100 pounds). With the fifth and sixth seats removed, 400 pounds can be loaded in the rear cabin; and many Barons have an extended aft baggage compartment approved to hold up to 120 pounds.

Nice touches like fuel sight gauges in the wing should help pilots avoid fuel mismanagement problems.

Performance

True airspeed of a small-engined Baron cruising at 75 percent power is about 190 knots on 27 gallons of fuel per hour. That's faster than the naturally aspirated Aztec and Cessna 310, but a good bit off the Aerostar's pace. The big-engined Baron is about five knots faster and five gph thirstier than its stablemate.

Takeoff and landing performance is average. A B55, for instance, can take off or land over a 50-foot obstacle within 2,160 feet. The E55 needs only about 2,050 feet to clear the obstacle on takeoff but a bit more than 2,200 feet to get back over it on landing. Short-field technique can cut these figures roughly in half, but it is rather hairy (involving lift-off below Vmc, for example). Two-engine climb rates of 1,630 to 1,700 fpm for the small-engined Barons and 1,670 to 1,680 fpm for the more powerful models outpace the Aztec by a wide margin but lag behind the Aerostar and 310. The B55's single-engine ROC is a paltry 318 fpm—again, better only than the Aztec. At 388 fpm, the E55's single-engine performance is about par with the 310 and Aerostar.

Handling

The 55 Baron is proof that a light twin doesn't have to handle like a truck. Responsive and well-harmonized, the airplane's controls are one of its biggest selling-points. As one owner put it, "Once you've flown an E55...everything else feels like a tin can." As mentioned earlier, however, hand-flying may be delightful in nice weather, but when it gets bumpy, an autopilot comes in handy.

There are trim controls for elevator, rudder and ailerons. Early models have relatively low gear- and flap-extension speeds (143 and 113 knots, respectively). Gear speed was raised to 152 knots, beginning with airplanes built in 1969. The

B55 came with approval to lower flaps 15 degrees at 153 knots, and full-flap speed was raised to 122 knots, beginning with TC-955 in 1965.

Safety Record

NTSB and FAA records show a total of 108 accidents during the period we examined. Thirty accidents involved fatalities and/or serious injuries. Nearly one-third of these involved loss of control: two during missed approaches; seven on takeoff. Two pilots had their fuel selectors improperly positioned on aux tanks and lost power from one engine on takeoff. Another lost control when a "safety pilot" intentionally pulled an engine. The others involved a propeller separation, a downwind takeoff, a sharp turn during a night departure over water, and one that occurred under unknown circumstances in IMC.

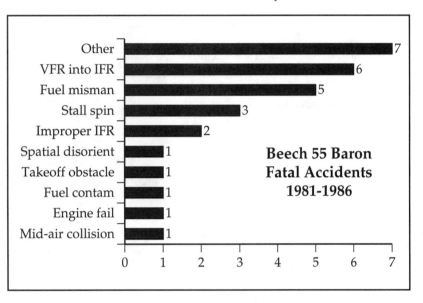

Beech 55 Baron
Fatal Accidents
1981-1986

Eight fatal accidents occurred in bad weather. Four airplanes hit cloud-covered mountains during VFR flights. Another was unable to maintain altitude in ice and severe turbulence. One struck a tree while making a visual approach in fog; another hit a guy wire while scud-running in fog below a 500-foot overcast. One pilot, who wasn't instrument-rated, managed to shoot an ILS approach in 300-and-2 conditions only to crash while circling to land. Three other crashes occurred when pilots apparently busted minimums. Fuel mismanagement played a role in four accidents, including two Barons that were taken aloft with nearly empty tanks.

Almost half (36, to be precise) of the 78 nonfatal accidents from 1983 through June 1988 were gear-up landings. Mechanical problems were behind 11 of them. In several, pilots either simply forgot to lower the gear, didn't notice it hadn't extended or didn't use emergency extension procedures. As mentioned earlier, eight pilots found themselves bellying onto the runway after mistaking the gear switch for the flap switch. Eleven accidents involved fuel mismanagement; five, loss of control. Though the landing gear on the Baron has a reputation for toughness (touted by Beech as withstanding drop-tests at 600 fpm at gross weight), six of the airplanes were landed hard enough to inflict substantial damage.

Maintenance

The IO-470L generally is considered a bulletproof engine, though a few owners, as well as several recent Service Difficulty Reports, mentioned occasional cylinder problems. The IO-520's reputation is not so good; operators have been beset by cracking crankcases. Continental's switch to so-called "heavy" cases in the late '70s helped somewhat, but case cracks (and broken camshafts) appeared rather frequently in a stack of recent SDRs.

Other potential problem areas indicated in recent reports include: cracked Janitrol cabin heaters; alternator failures; cracked and broken elevator horns and torque tubes; inoperative fuel-boost pumps; cracked and corroded landing gear braces;

broken gear-uplock cables and springs; broken gear motors; prop hubs and governors; and cracked magneto housings. A few SDRs mentioned broken throttle and mixture cables.

Among the notable Airworthiness Directives are: 87-18-06 Rev. 1, requiring replacement of recline-actuator handles on copilot and center passenger seats to prevent inadvertent unlocking; 84-26-02, replacement of paper air filters; and 84-09-01, requiring various inspections and modifications to ensure that the emergency window will open.

Owners of Beech 55, 56TC, 58 and 95 Barons are looking (or should be looking) for cracks in the wing forward spar carry-through. The cracking, according to Airworthiness Directive 90-8-14, could lead to "loss of the airplane." Beech first apprised owners through a 'mandatory' service bulletin. The bulletin—No. 2269—was originally issued in August of 1989. In March 1990, Beech revised the bulletin, saying "Recent engineering investigation has shown that increased allowable crack lengths as described in this service bulletin will not compromise the integrity of the forward spar carry-thru [sic] structure."

The AD specifies that the carry-through must be inspected at 1,500 hours total airframe time, and repeated every 500 hours if no cracks are found. To get at the carry-through, the mechanic must remove the front seats and the carry-through cover (floor). From there, it's a standard crack inspection. The carry-through and webs are cleaned, then checked using visible dye-penetrant. If no cracks are visible, he can button it up and come back in 500 hours. But if cracks are visible, it's time to get out the rulers. The cracks must be measured, and depending on where they are and how long they are and how many there are, repaired. For example, cracks in the bend radius of the spar carry-through can be up to 2.25 inches long. If they're that long or less, they can be stop drilled. However, only one such crack per side is permitted, and it's discovery means the inspection must be repeated in 200 hours to see if it has gotten any bigger.

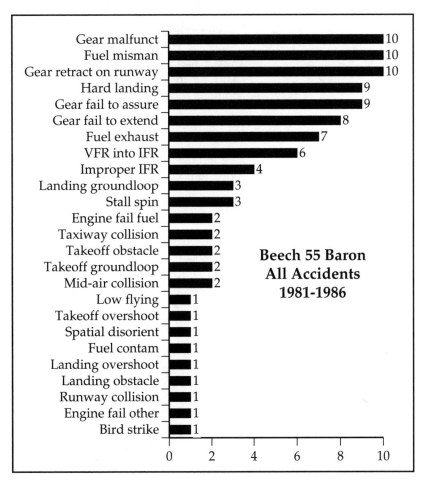

**Beech 55 Baron
All Accidents
1981-1986**

If the crack is between 2.25 and four inches long, it can still be stop-drilled, but it must be repaired within 100 hours using a Beech-supplied kit. Any longer than that (or more than one crack in a single radius), and the Beech kit must be used prior to further flight.

The other area of concern is the spar web face, in the area of the huck fasteners. Here, cracks are limited to one inch length. Only one crack is allowed per side, and Beech specifies that it can't be stop drilled. Instead, the mechanic must look at it again in 200 hours to see if it's grown. If it has grown, or if it was more than an inch long to begin with, another Beech kit is needed for the proper repair. The repair must be made within the next 25 hours, or immediately if it is between two fasteners and extends more than a half inch beyond the fasteners.

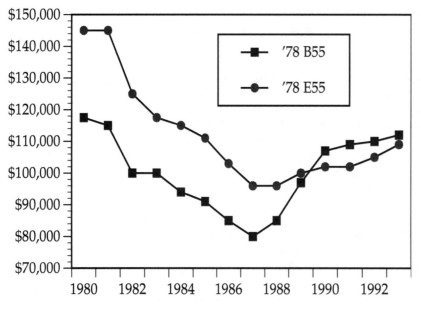

Beech figures one man should be able to complete the inspection in four hours, provided the airplane is already apart for an annual or similar inspection. Like EPA mileage estimates, your labor charge may vary. However, even with a top-notch mechanic, owners are looking at about $175 just for the inspection. If cracks are found, there's the added cost of stop drilling. And then there's the price of the kits if the cracks need repairs. The kits cost several hundred dollars each. Installation time depends on the shop's sheet metal proficiency. The average shop should be able to install one kit in about 55 to 60 hours. Given a $50/hour shop rate, that's about $3,000.

Thus, a Baron owner with one oversized crack on one side might be looking at somthing in the neighborhood of $4,000 to comply with the AD. He can add another $4,000 for each additional crack needing a kit.

For the record, our own examination of NTSB accident records does not disclose any Baron accidents that were attributed to this problem. Indeed, we found no mention of it at all, so it isn't a real safety problem yet. However, Beech is wisely trying to head it off before it becomes one.

Modifications

Among the major aftermarket upgrades available for 55-series Barons is Friday International's V/G System, which uses vortex generators on the wing leading edges and the left side of the vertical stabilizer to improve the airplane's low-speed handling and stall characteristics. (See the July 15, 1987 issue of *The Aviation Consumer.*) The company claims its system reduces stall speed in landing configuration 10 knots, Vmc by 12 knots (to 75 knots) and accelerate-stop distance by 1,070 feet (to 2,100 feet) for the big-engined models.

Improvements to the 55, A and B models "are even more dramatic," a company spokesman said. A kit, including a new airspeed indicator with revised markings, costs $3,450 and requires about seven hours to install. Friday International Corp., 600 Franklin Drive, Friday Harbor, Wash. 98250; (800) 992-3435.

Bigger engines are available from Colemill. Factory-rebuilt 300-hp IO-520E engines and three-blade Hartzell props turn 55, A and B models into "President 600s" for $52,500. Rebuilt 300-hp IO-550Cs and four-blade Hartzells turn C, D and

E models into "Foxstars" for $68,500. (Brand-new engines tack about $7,000 onto the bill.) Colemill Enterprises, P.O. Box 60627, Cornelia Fort Airpark, Nashville, Tenn. 37206, (615) 226-4256.

Petersen Aviation has STC'd an alcohol/water-injection system that allows Barons with IO-520 engines to run on 91-octane auto gas. The system costs $5,900 and takes about 35 man-hours to install, or another $1,000 at Petersen. (The company is planning to go after approval of the system on IO-470-powered Barons, as well.) Petersen Aviation, Route 1, Box 18, Minden, Neb. 68959, (800) 352-3232.

Another mod worthy of mention is baffled fuel tanks. Barons built before 1971 didn't have them, and a few have experienced power losses due to unporting during slips and turning takeoffs. The tanks costs $1,400, each, and take about eight hours to install. They're available from Floats and Fuel Cells, 4010 Pilot Drive, Suite No. 3, Memphis, Tenn. 38118, (800) 647-6148.

Owners' Group

Baron owners don't have an association of their own, but the Wichita-based American Bonanza Society, (316) 945-6913, counts 400 Baron owners among its 8,200 members. The ABS publishes an informative newsletter and conducts service and proficiency clinics at about a dozen locations each year.

Owner Comments

When I bought my Model 55 Baron (one of the first produced) in 1973, it was not in very good condition. I upgraded the airplane with Cleveland brakes, a new one-piece windshield, new avionics and a new interior and paint job. The Baron has been a joy to fly. It's similar to the Travel Air I owned previously but is more stable and powerful. Generally, it is very comfortable; but the cockpit is a bit noisy and crowded. There's little room for pilot supplies in the front seats.

Reliability over the years has been outstanding. Operating costs are at a minimum for a twin. I recommend a 55 Baron to anyone who enjoys flying a multiengine airplane. At today's prices, it is a genuine bargain.

Like the Bonanzas, the Barons have a throw-over control wheel as standard. Inadvertent cabin door openings have dogged these aircraft, and care must be taken to get a secure door latch.

George C. Burnett, Sr.
La Jolla, Calif.

The B55 Baron's IO-470L engines are strong and seem to be a great match with the airframe. No turbos and no pressurization make this a low-maintenance airplane. "Beechcraft-only" parts, however, are expensive; but Beech has a strong support network, which is a big advantage. The American Bonanza Society has been a big help, too.

Over the last five years, owner-assisted annual inspections of my 1978 B55 have averaged about $900 each, and have taken about 35 man-hours. The original engines went to TBO easily. The remans now have 400 hours with no problems. Among major items that had to be replaced were a windshield (covered by Beech warranty), a fuel cell ($1,800) and a Bendix radar magnetron ($1,500). The airplane has excellent speed: 186 knots on 23 gph at 65 percent power and 8,000 feet. Single-engine performance is typical of light twins. Don't do full stalls!

Jim Morris
Melbourne Beach, Fla.

I have owned a B55 Baron for seven years. I plan on 190 knots at 7,000 to 12,000 feet and a block-to-block fuel burn of 25 gph. I have the 142-gallon system, so range and endurance are excellent. I have flown all Baron models; the B seems to be an excellent airframe and engine combination. It is almost as fast, burns five gph less fuel and is much quieter than the IO-520-powered Barons. It is fun to fly and has a harmonious control feeling that is remarkable.

It's very easy to land and doesn't pitch up when you use flaps. The landing characteristics make the transition from IFR to VFR on a tight approach in a crosswind a lot easier; you don't have to worry about fighting to get it on the ground. Engine-out characteristics seem to be above average for a light twin. For IFR trips, I recommend an autopilot. If the plane is properly trimmed and rigged, it is not too bad to hand-fly, but if you drop a wing and don't make a correction, it will keep dropping. My Baron has a good yaw damper, which really smooths the ride for passengers in rough air.

With full deicing equipment, the Baron does as well as any other twin in icing conditions. However, it has been my observation that with no boots, it doesn't do as well in ice as some other twins without boots. The fifth and sixth seats are good either for small people or for short trips, though the large windows don't give people back there a closed-in feeling. I would recommend the extended rear baggage bay, which was an option, for anyone looking for a used Baron. Also, Cleveland brakes are a must; they were well worth the $800 it cost to put them on the plane. I could complain about the high cost of Beech parts, but at least you can always get them. Also, the plane is well-designed and built like a Swiss watch, so you don't need airframe parts that often. For parts that are common to other makes, like engines and brakes, you can go to another supplier, such as Van

Cost/Performance/Specifications

Model	Year	Average Retail Price	Cruise Speed (kt)	Useful Load (lb)	Std/Opt Fuel (gal)	Engines	TBO (hr)	Overhaul Cost @
55	1961	$37,000	188	1,630	100/136	260-hp Cont. IO-470L	1,500	$13,500
A55	1962	$40,000	188	1,700	100/136	260-hp Cont. IO-470L	1,500	$13,500
A55	1963	$41,000	188	1,700	100/136	260-hp Cont. IO-470L	1,500	$13,500
B55	1964-66	$48,500	190	1,670	100/136	260-hp Cont. IO-470L	1,500	$13,500
B55	1967-69	$57,000	190	1,670	100/136	260-hp Cont. IO-470L	1,500	$13,500
B55	1970-72	$63,000	190	1,670	100/136	260-hp Cont. IO-470L	1,500	$13,500
B55	1973-75	$78,500	190	1,670	100/136	260-hp Cont. IO-470L	1,500	$13,500
B55	1976-78	$100,000	190	1,693	100/136	260-hp Cont. IO-470L	1,500	$13,500
B55	1979-81	$125,000	190	1,693	100/136	260-hp Cont. IO-470L	1,500	$13,500
B55	1982	$147,500	190	1,693	100/136	260-hp Cont. IO-470L	1,500	$13,500
C55	1966-67	$49,500	200	1,670	100/136	285-hp Cont. IO-520C	1,700	$14,500
D55	1968-69	$55,000	200	1,670	100/136	285-hp Cont. IO-520C	1,700	$14,500
E55	1970-72	$64,000	200	1,682	100/136	285-hp Cont. IO-520C	1,700	$14,500
E55	1973-75	$76,000	200	1,682	100/136	285-hp Cont. IO-520C	1,700	$14,500
E55	1976-78	$94,000	200	1,682	100/166	285-hp Cont. IO-520C	1,700	$14,500
E55	1979-81	$133,000	200	1,682	100/166	285-hp Cont. IO-520CB	1,700	$14,500
E55	1982	$167,000	200	1,682	100/166	285-hp Cont. IO-520CB	1,700	$14,500

Dusen. It's nice to know, though, that Beech stands ready to support the plane. I don't think I've ever owned anything that has brought me as much satisfaction as my Baron. It's extremely well designed and built—a class act.

Bill Packer
Flint, Mich.

My B55 has been a delight to own and fly. I purchased it new in 1974 and have put on 1,450 hours since. The Baron is easy to fly and just doesn't have any bad or idiosyncratic qualities. It is consistently faster than book. At 65 percent power, with a full load, it will true at 193 knots; lightly loaded, it will push 200 knots. I find the aircraft very comfortable for four people and, with the fifth and sixth seats removed, enough room (if not payload) for all their luggage. Cockpit and cabin visibility are definite strong points. Overall, the Baron has been a very reliable aircraft, with the majority of downtime attributable to avionics squawks.

A quality six-channel EGT is a must with the Continental IO-470L installation in the Baron. Without one, premature cylinder overhaul is altogether too common. My engine logs bear this out. After several cylinders were overhauled, due to low compression, the engines were pulled for major overhaul at 1,375 hours. Why all these problems in a carefully flown, single-pilot, new airplane? My theory is that the factory EGT installation is inadequate, with its temperature probes located in the right-hand exhaust collector of each engine, just aft of the No. 1 cylinder. Unfortunately, the critical cylinder in the left engine was outboard, on the left side, and goes unmeasured.

Note reverse position of prop controls, at the left, and throttles in the center. Also, the flap and gear switches are reversed from the conventional, inviting inadvertent gear retraction on landing rollout among the uninitiated. Aircraft has the luxury of trim in all three axes, however.

The Janitrol heater had been problematic until recently. The problem was finally traced to an improperly set pressure switch. Also, keeping the nose and inboard main gear doors properly rigged is a constant chore. They seem to come out of rig easily and are time-consuming to re-rig. Despite the B55 being considered an "economy" twin, it is not for the faint-hearted when it comes to operating expense. Figure block fuel flows in the 24.5 to 27.5 gph range at 65 percent power. Annual inspections cost $3,000 to $5,000. If you fly 100 to 150 hours a year, as I do, better figure it'll cost in the $200/hour range to operate, considering both direct and indirect expenses.

Roy Larson, M.D.
Thousand Oaks, Calif.

Having owned both a B55 and a C55, I feel that the C (and, I assume, also the D and E models) have several advantages over the B. I prefer the IO-520 engine; the larger nose compartment is very convenient; and the weight and balance allows for better load distribution.

The Baron handles beautifully. It is easy on the controls but not overly sensitive. If flown by the book, it shows excellent takeoff and climb performance. You really have to goof up the approach and flare to make a bad landing. The plane is stable in IFR conditions and, if properly trimmed, only slight pressure on the rudder pedals will maintain heading. On short flights, I use 55 percent power and true out at around 170 knots; 65 percent power adds about 10 knots; and 75 percent almost 10 more, but fuel consumption goes up substantially (34 gph versus 25 gph at 55 percent power). The airplane's only bad trait seems to be its single-engine stall characteristics.

The penalty of bigger engines in the E55 is greater likelihood of crankcase cracking.

I first read about the vortex generators developed by Friday International in the July 15, 1987 issue of *The Aviation Consumer* and subsequently had them installed. They really changed the handling characteristics at slow and near-stall speeds, but there is no speed penalty. Although not claimed by Friday International, I feel the system also improved rate of climb. Accelerate-stop distance on my model was reduced a bit over 1,000 feet and Vmc by 12 knots.

Since installing the V/G System, I have tried single-engine stalls with full power on the good engine, and found the airplane manageable with average technique. I would strongly urge every Baron owner to install this modification. With this mod, the Baron is the finest plane in its class.

My biggest complaint is the cost of Beech parts. But the plane is so well built, you don't need parts too often (but when you do, the bill is staggering).

Sandy Craig
Nantucket Island, Mass.

Since I bought my 1981 Model B55 last year, I have flown 320 hours in all types of weather. I thought my Piper Arrow was a solid platform, but this B55 is like the Rock of Gibraltar. I normally fly at 9,000 to 12,000 feet at 2,200 rpm with a true airspeed of 178 knots and a fuel burn of 10.5 to 11 gph per side. I am now installing two factory-remanufactured engines, because one engine started to show very fine bronze particles in the oil screen. With a total of 1,670 hours on 1,500-hour TBO engines, I think these engines did more than their share. On a scale of 1 to 10, I rate this airplane a 10 in all categories.

G.L. Vandelogt
Camden, S.C.

I recently sold my 1964 B55 for almost exactly what I paid for it 10 years ago and, then, bought a 1976 B55. It seems even better than the older one. I like the fuel system (no switching tanks), but I do miss the large flaps on the early model. I flight plan for 190 knots at 26 to 28 gph. With full fuel, 142 gallons, and a decent load, I climb at 1,500 to 1,700 fpm. Costs of annuals have been minimal. I just can't say enough about those IO-470L engines. It seems they are indestructible, if you treat them right. The thing I like best about my Baron is that, when I give another plane owner a ride, he can't believe how quiet, smooth and fast it is. I thought the same thing on my first ride.

Art Danchuk
Santa Ana, Calif.

Beech 58 Baron

The airplanes are nice-looking, have good performance, competitive payload/range numbers and good handling. They are very appealing airplanes for those fortunate few who can pay the tab, which can be a prime consideration—especially for upkeep.

The Model 58 Baron was introduced late in 1969 (as a 1970 model). Essentially, it was a 10-inch fuselage stretch of the 55 series, with a list price of $89,850, just about $6,000 more than the shorter E-55 Baron. It quickly became one of the all-time favorite Barons. A big, double aft cargo door and three-bladed propellers were the hot options. The aft doors became standard.

The 58 is approved as an amendment to the same CAR (or CAM) 3 certificate that covers the 55s.

History of the Line

The 58TC and 58P were introduced in 1976. Unlike the rest of the Barons, these share a new FAR 23 certificate. Empty and maximum takeoff weights are quite a bit higher than those of the normally aspirated 58. Empty weight of the TC is roughly 430 pounds higher than the 58; the P is nearly 650 pounds heavier. Maximum takeoff weights of the two turbocharged models are 700 to 800 pounds higher than that of the 58, depending upon the year of manufacture.

The most obvious visible difference among the three is that the aft door is on the port, or left, side of the 58P fuselage and is a single door. The now-standard double doors (originally identified as cargo doors) are on the right side of the 58 and 58TC. The interior configuration is the same in all three 58s, except that the center fuselage windows in the 58P are not openable for ventilation on the ground.

The 58 Barons stretch the cabin living space along with the pocketbook of the owner. Of the three: the 58TC, top, the normally aspirated 58, center, and the 58P, bottom, only the middle one is still in production.

One thing all three shared initially is the lightweight Continental crankcase as well as the cracking that plagues them (heavy cases, too, in many instances). The 58 situation was improved somewhat with a change to the IO-520-CB; the 58TC and P to the TSIO-520-LB. In 1979, the TC and P were upgraded to the TSIO-520-WB rated at 325 hp. Maximum takeoff weight was increased from 6,100 to 6,200 pounds. Pressure differential of the P was slightly increased from 3.7 to 3.9 psi.

Recommended TBO on the L/LB is 1,400 hours. The WB is 1,600. The 58's C/CB now is 1,700 hours.

The next significant change to the series was a whopper. Along with the substantial (a veritable revolution at staid Beech Aircraft Corp.) changes made to the series for the 1984 model year, the 58 got an engine and power upgrade to the Continental IO-550-C rated at 300 hp. Maximum takeoff weight was increased 100 pounds, to 5,500.

The big news that year was that Beech bit the bullet on the stretched Bonanzas and Barons (but not on the short fuselage models, of which only the F-33A remains in production): it reconfigured the arrangement of the gear and flap switches to the accepted industry standard of gear selector on the left, flap selector on the right.

Beech had been criticized for adhering to the old U.S. Army/airline configuration that was featured on the Beech 18 and all subsequent Beech twins until Dukes and King Airs were reconfigured. It has been a damned-if-you-do, damned-if-you-don't situation. Beech twin operators are used to the non-standard arrangement. Introducing similar airplanes with critical controls relocated invites trouble, just as the pilot new to the brand stands in danger of selecting the wrong lever.

And, of course, the predictable happened. One of the first new 58P customers, a long-time Baron operator, retracted the landing gear of his spanking-new, very expensive twin shortly after taking delivery.

One reader has had Barons configured both ways. He reports: "Different models, and even different years of the same model, will have these handles reversed. My 58TC had the gear on the left and the flaps on the right. My 58 has the gear on the right and the flaps on the left. You can imagine how much I enjoyed the four months that I was flying both airplanes!!! Talk about being careful."

Redesigned Cockpit

Beech did not change the gear and flap handles and rest there. The cockpit was completely redesigned. The center control column, with the throw-over yoke (or large bar for dual control airplanes), was replaced with individual control columns.

Most Barons are equipped with dual controls. The large control bar obscures many key switches, gauges and controls. Larger pilots find the yoke sits low enough so that legs can interfere with control inputs. This is especially a problem if two large people are in the cockpit, particularly if the person in the right seat is not a pilot. Interference with control input has happened at critical times.

The new control arrangement mounts the yoke a bit higher, which helps eliminate the problem for most pilots. It also makes more of the panel visible and accessible. Older, less-bold pilots are used to accommodating themselves to less-than-ideal configurations and conditions. Some claim the need to work around the large control bar makes them more careful pilots, visually confirming every action. Smaller "turbine-type" engine instruments are used. This and the rearrangement of many subsystem elements frees up a lot of the panel for avionics (28 percent more space, the ads say). Even with radar installed, there is plenty of space for extensive avionics installation.

Known (?) Icing Approval

One of the most important changes came late in the 58 series life cycle. Known-icing approval was not obtained until 1984 or '85 for the 58 (the 58P was approved a bit earlier).

Many Barons are equipped with boots, electric or alcohol props and alcohol windshield anti/deice equipment. Even with placards in the cockpit and notices in the operating manual, many pilots assume that the presence of the equipment equals approval. This is a false assumption that can lead to a host of problems, from physical danger in the clag to dismaying (and expensive) enforcement action from those friendly and helpful folks at FAA.

Another important variation in configuration to watch for is fuel capacity. Most 58 series have at least 166 gallons usable fuel capacity, although a few normally aspirated 58s have the standard 136-gallon capacity. An increase in optional fuel capacity was introduced in 1976. The addition of wing tip tanks increases usable fuel to 190 gallons.

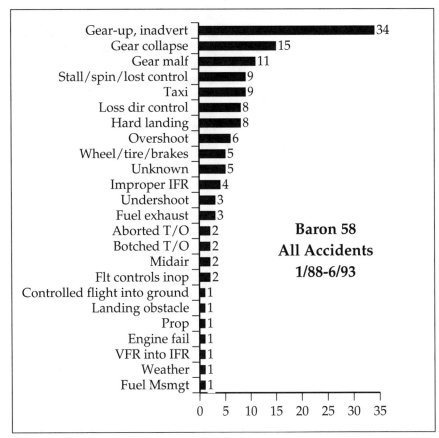

Baron 58
All Accidents
1/88-6/93

Pilots flying a mixed fleet of Barons have something else to watch for besides cockpit configuration. Four hours into a flight is rather late to recall that the 58 you are flying today has 136-gallon capacity, not 166 or 190. It is easy to get confused, especially since we all tend to assume rather than confirm at times.

The Fleet

The original Model 58, as mentioned above, has outlived its turbocharged kin. The 58 (serial number prefix TH), as mentioned earlier, continues in production. More than 1,677 have been built to date; nine were delivered in the first half of this year despite an equipped list price that approaches three-quarters of a million dollars.

Of the 14 Beech models still in production, only the 1900D was produced in higher numbers. (Of course, the numbers are dismal. Model 58 production represents 22 percent of all Beech production for the first half of 1993: a total of 41 aircraft were built.) The 58TC (prefix is TK) was produced from 1976 to 1984 (only one was delivered in its last year). Only 151 total were built.

The 58P (prefix TJ) outlasted its FAR 23 brother by a year. It also outsold it by a big margin: 497 were built.

The Competition

In the used-aircraft market, there is a lot of competition for the 58 series, from the Aero Commander 500 and 600 series piston twins, Piper Aztec, Seneca, Navajo

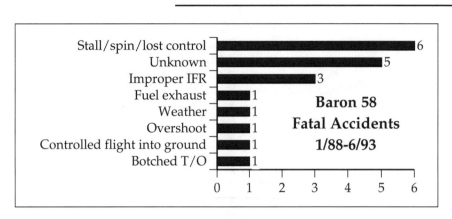

and Aerostar through the Cessna 300 series (exclude the 336/337) and 402 and 414.

Want to quickly narrow the field? How about still in production? If you squint hard at the claims and make generous allowances, that leaves you with the Seneca. The closest competition to the 58 series, setting aside for the moment issues of age, since the 58 is now 23, consists of the Cessna 310 and turbo 310/320, Piper Navajo, the Aerostar series and the Cessna 340. The Cessna models win in the elbow-room category. The Barons take the visibility prize. In terms of operational considerations, most pilots would give the nod to the Barons for their combination of handling characteristics, fairly high structural load capabilities, including maneuvering and gear and flap speeds, and fuel management simplicity.

As close as one can get to apples and apples in the used market, the Cessnas generally win the price competition; Barons tend to remain pricey on the aftermarket. As a fast example, a 1970 310 has a *Blue Book* average retail price of $53,500 compared to $80,000 for a 58; a 1979 340 at $150,000 compares to $171,000 for a 1979 58P.

Some 58 owners report that their hull values have appreciated recently, despite the fact that there are quite a few being offered for sale. The 58TC has to be considered a specialty airplane because so few were built, but there are enough 58 and 58P models to represent a healthy market and a wide selection.

One owner has concluded: "On balance, it is probably the best twin in its class; I've looked at several alternatives and find that I can spend a great deal more, but I'd get something similar or inferior for a big price."

Another says of his 58P: "With modifications I've made, the Baron is the best owner-flown piston twin in the sky. It is right up there with most turboprops that burn more fuel and cost more to own and operate."

Performance

As light twins go, all of the 58s have comparatively good payload with full fuel. A typically equipped older 58, with auxiliary fuel giving a total of 166 gallons usable, can lift 724.5 pounds and fly for approximately 5.5 hours at an intermediate power setting—a still-air range of just over 1,000 nm—with IFR reserves.

Beech ads say the new 58 can carry six people (that's FAA 170 pounders) and luggage 600 nautical with reserves. A typically equipped 58P has a full-fuel pay-

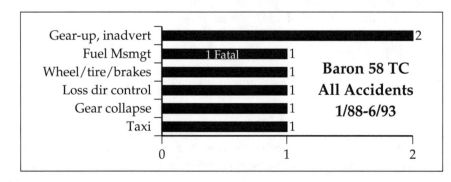

load of just over 700 pounds and a range at roughly 60 percent power of more than 1,100 nm at either 15,000 or FL 250 (TAS is 201 at the lower altitude and 218 at the maximum of FL 250).

All three versions have loading flexibility. With baggage space in the nose and aft cabin as well as smaller space between the cockpit and middle seats with the club seating arrangement, there are a lot of options for maintaining loading within the allowable cg range.

The 58TC and 58P are biased toward the forward cg limit. In fact, with many airplanes, full fuel and two people up front (only one in some) can put weight and balance out beyond the front limit.

The 58P Baron and the later 58s have conventional double control wheels without the massive linking bar common in older Barons. Also gear and flaps and throttle quadrant order are "conventional."

One 58P owner says: "This forward CG was so notorious that the Beechcraft pressurized Baron school I attended told us to put a 50-pound bag of sand in the aft baggage compartment." Another writes: "The CG on my 58TC was right at the forward limit with just the front seats occupied. Any luggage had to go in the back. This was inconvenient with golf clubs." The owner of the 58TC also says the oxygen bottle took up too much space in the nose baggage bay to fit in golf clubs, but there is plenty of room for them in the nose of his 58.

Handling

There are very few pilots who do not like the handling characteristics of Beech Bonanzas and Barons. Generally speaking, they have light control pressures and are highly responsive. This extracts a price in turbulence, especially in IMC.

While Barons are generally considered good instrument platforms, and the 58s the best of the group, workload is relatively high because of the responsiveness.

Yaw sensitivity (one hesitates to call it instability, because the airplanes aren't going to depart and turn upside-down or fly sideways) is a characteristic of Beech designs right through the Duke and 90 series King Air. A good, well-adjusted yaw damper is a welcome aid and a barf-saver for many passengers.
Comparatively high gear and flap operating speeds help the design fit in easily in high-density areas. The basic good handling extends into the lower end of the envelope for the pilot properly trained and familiar with its characteristics. Many operators praise the short-field capabilities of the 58.

However, this is where the weight and weight distribution differences between the 58 and TC/P are clearly displayed. A couple of owners confess to operating out of marginal fields in areas of the country where high-density calculations are a must.

One 58P owner writes that the normal 100-knot approach speed was a problem for him, "Since I fly from a 3,000-foot strip in Louisiana. After I overshot one landing, I investigated it carefully." His solutions involved reconfiguring the airplane to put more weight aft, including relocating the battery and installing an air conditioning unit in the tail cone to replace the nacelle-mounted factory design. The changes "moved the CG about 4-1/2 inches aft and reduced approach speed to 90 knots.

Another owner reports that 80 knots is a comfortable speed over the fence in a vortex generator-equipped 58, and the airplane still floats a bit at that airspeed (the book says stall in landing configuration is 74 knots; 1.3 times Vso is 96.2, or about 100 indicated on the ASI for most of us). His 58TC at 90 knots was on the margin: "As slow an airspeed that I was at all comfortable with crossing the fence. When you pulled off the power, it landed right now, to the accompaniment of a stall horn and often a buffet."

The 58TC and P Vso is 78 KIAS; 1.3 times that is 101.4. The owner had vortex generators installed on his TC, which made it feel better. These devices are credited with reducing stall speeds seven knots on 58s and six on the TC; 1.3 Vso ends up at 87.1 and 93.6, respectively. These, of course, are gross weight numbers. They would be lower at typical landing weight. But add the affects of temperature and humidity, and you are pushing the envelope at these speeds. Another factor is the forward cg bias of the TC and P. This makes landing main gear first difficult, especially using full flaps. This, in turn, makes squeezing into fields of marginal length for ambient conditions a bit dicey. The forward cg bias added to the tendency of so many pilots to land three-point or nose-gear first puts a lot of strain on the gear. This is true even of the 58 (and almost any other tricycle gear airplane).

Cost/Performance/Specifications

Model	Year	Average Retail Price	Cruise Speed (kts)	Useful Load (lbs)	Fuel Std/Opt (gals)	Engine	TBO (hrs)	Overhaul Cost ea.
58	1970-73	$88,500	195	2,185	136/166	285-hp Cont. IO-520-C/CB	1,700	$15,000
58	1974-76	$116,000	195	2,132	136/166	285-hp Cont. IO-520-C/CB	1,700	$15,000
58	1977-79	$166,000	195	2,068	136/190	285-hp Cont. IO-520-C/CB	1,700	$15,000
58	1980-81	$200,000	195	2,063	136/190	285-hp Cont. IO-520-CB	1,700	$15,000
58	1982-83	$233,000	195	2,057	136/190	300-hp Cont. IO-550-C	1,700	$17,000
58	1984-86	$337,000	195	2,057	136/190	300-hp Cont. IO-550-C	1,700	$17,000
58	1987-89	$417,000	195	2,057	136/190	300-hp Cont. IO-550-C	1,700	$17,000
58	1990-92	$542,000	195	2,057	136/190	300-hp Cont. IO-550-C	1,700	$17,000
58TC	1976-77	$106,000	214	2,320	166/190	310-hp Cont. TSIO-520-L/LB	1,400	$22,500
58TC	1978	$125,000	214	2,320	166/190	310-hp Cont. TSIO-520-L/LB	1,400	$22,500
58TC	1979	$144000	232	2,412	166/190	325-hp Cont. TSIO-520-WB	1,600	$27,500
58TC	1980-81	$175,000	232	2,412	166/190	325-hp Cont. TSIO-520-WB	1,600	$27,500
58TC	1982	$211,000	232	2,412	166/190	325-hp Cont. TSIO-520-WB	1,600	$27,500
58P	1976-77	$128,500	223	2,155	166/190	310-hp Cont. TSIO-520-L/LB	1,400	$22,500
58P	1978	$136,000	223	2,155	166/190	310-hp Cont. TSIO-520-L/LB	1,400	$22,500
58P	1979	$173,000	241	2,220	166/190	325-hp Cont. TSIO-520-WB	1,600	$27,500
58P	1980-81	$198,000	241	2,220	166/190	325-hp Cont. TSIO-520-WB	1,600	$27,500
58P	1982-83	$255,000	241	2,220	166/190	325-hp Cont. TSIO-520-WB	1,600	$27,500
58P	1984-85	$376,000	241	2,220	166/190	325-hp Cont. TSIO-520-WB	1,600	$27,500
58P	1984-85	$480,000	241	2,220	166/190	325-hp Cont. TSIO-520-WB	1,600	$27,500

Prices from Aircraft Bluebook Price Digest

Too many pilots approach and land with too much speed and too little pitch. This is aggravated in airplanes with a forward cg bias. Not only do structures and systems suffer, but it is easier to lose directional control.

One characteristic of Barons is a function of angle of incidence. When it is ready to fly, it wants to do so. Pilots who try to hold it on the runway encourage wheelbarrowing on the nose gear. No airplane handles too well on the runway during either takeoff or landing on the nosegear alone. All that said, the 58 is a good-flying airplane throughout its intended speed range. It can handle fairly rough and relatively short strips better than some other twins when properly operated. The relatively fast gear-operating speed also reduces the time of maximum exposure (from lift off to positive climb after gear retraction).

Comfort

People sit high in Barons. The chairs are fairly high, which encourages a good position and relative comfort for fairly long flights. The biggest shortcoming is cabin width, which is most notable for the pilot manipulating the controls.

Visibility is good from all seats. From a passenger standpoint, the middle seats, particularly with club seating, are the most comfortable. The big aft door and separate over-wing door to the cockpit make loading more graceful than many other light twins.

Noise level is about standard for the class: noisy, despite all the claims about super soundproofing, etc.

The two best aids for noise and vibration are cruise climb and cruise power settings with lower rpms and good dynamic balancing of rotating components.

Maintenance

The good part about parts supply for the 58 is that the normally aspirated version is still in production. One owner writes: "Maintenance costs are about average for a high-speed normally aspirated twin. Beech parts remain very expensive items, but fortunately we rarely have to buy from Beech." All 58 series owners who have responded to our request for input refer to the high cost of maintenance. One says: "Proper preventive maintenance eats a big chunk of change every year, and that's with minimal or no labor cost. Just the same, I know of nothing in its class that does as well."

To enjoy "dependable and comfortable transportation," one 58P owner says has required "detailed knowledge of systems and a relatively high maintenance cost because of these many systems annuals run about $10,000." The owner of a

Beech Baron 58 Series Service Difficulty Reports: 1/88-6/93

Model	58	58TC	58P
Engine			
Engine Mounts	46	0	0
Cylinders	33	2	21
Engine Controls	21	0	1
Mags	14	1	9
Pistons	8	0	0
Crankcase	8	1	4
Exhaust Syst.	8	2	8
Oil Syst.	7	1	3
Oil Cap/Dipstick	7	0	0
Conn Rod	3	0	1
Valve Train	4	0	14
Bearings	3	0	1
Starter	3	0	2
Accessory Pads	1	0	1
Turbocharger Sys.	N/A	0	13
Metal Contam.	3	0	1
Pedestal	4	0	0
Engine Instruments	4	0	1
Fuel System			
Pumps	16	0	6
Injection/Induction	15	1	9
Tanks	4	1	1
Caps	3	0	1
Vents	0	0	1
Lines	2	0	1
Gauges	2	0	1
Propeller			
Hubs, blades, gov	42	1	7
Spinner	9	0	2
Alternator	15	1	13
Electrical	1	0	1
Landing Gear			
Main	28	0	13
Nose	11	1	5
Emergency Ext Sys	8	0	1
Wheels/Brakes	7	1	1
Airframe			
Spars	8	2	0
Skin - cracks	0	0	1
Firewall	1	0	1
Doors	0	1	3
Windows	0	0	10
Pressure Bulkhead	0	0	1
Wing Attach	1	0	0
Corrosion-Water	2	0	0
Controls			
Flaps	8	1	2
Cockpit/yoke	3	0	0
Horiz. Stab	0	0	1
Elevator	2	0	3
Elev. Trim/Tab	2	0	6
Rudder	2	0	0
Cables	2	1	0
Autopilot Servos	2	0	4
Rudder Pedal	2	0	0
Systems			
Pressure/Gyro	9	2	6
Heater	8	0	3
Air Conditioning	0	0	3
Deice	2	0	1
Windshield	3	0	0
Prop	3	0	4

1975 58 says, after four years of operation, that it is the least expensive airplane he has owned. The owners who have written seem very realistic or at least resigned to the cost of operating sophisticated airplanes.

According to Service Difficulty Reports, the propulsion system has been the most troublesome. Several owners mention fuel tanks as a constant headache—a 58P owner says he anticipates a fuel cell overhaul with every overhaul at a cost close to $2,000—but there have been surprisingly few SDRs on tanks in the past five years.

There has been a plague of engine-mount problems on the 58. Whether this can be attributed to age or design (although the first "fix" redesign had some interference problems) is difficult to tell from the reports. However, the design has been in the field for 23 years and has flown in a variety of roles, from owner-flown use at less than 100 hours a year to commercial use, including flight training, at several thousand hours per year.

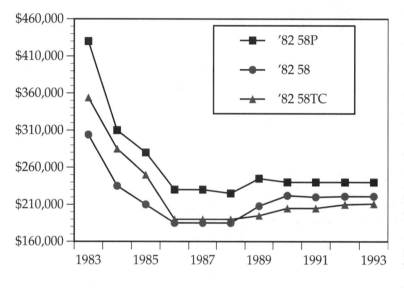

Some service technicians suspect that many engine and accessory problems with the later powerplants are the function of vibration (many recommendations for dynamic balancing show up in the SDRs) and thermal shock. Both can be controlled by the owner/operator to a large extent.

Another system with recurring problems is the landing gear. Beech used to emphasize the fact that the Baron gear—the same as on the former Air Force and Navy T-34 trainers —had been dropped tested to a rate of 600 fpm. However, in the real world of poor directional control/side loads and three-point landings and wheelbarrow takeoffs, the gear and surrounding structure suffer. Knowledgeable operators spend a fair amount on preventive maintenance of the gear system, ensuring that elements are kept clean and properly lubricated in addition to thorough, regular inspection.

In addition to minimizing vibration and carefully managing engine temperatures, many of the SDRs suggest careful inspection, especially with older airplanes. Many developing problems in the gear, flight controls and other systems are difficult to spot in "good enough" inspections by technicians who are not familiar with the 58.

Modifications

Numerous mods are available for the 58 series. In addition to the usual variations in autopilots and other avionics systems, there are a number of propulsion and operational mods. Colemill Enterprises (Nashville, Tenn., 615-226-4256) and RAM Aircraft Corp. (Waco, Tex., 817-752-8381) offer a number of reengining and related modifications.

Micro Aerodynamics, Inc. (Anacortes, Wash., 206-293-8082) and VG Systems (St. Paul, Minn., 800-992-3435), along with Boundary Layer Research (Someplace, Wash., 800-257-4847) have developed aerodynamic modifications to reduce critical airspeeds and improve low speed handling.

Safety Record

Most of the accidents covered by FAA briefs for the past five years suggest that pilot action and maintenance factors rather than design considerations played the major role. The three largest categories of fatal accidents are "unknown" (although interpreting the briefs suggest loss of control and/or weather as the major elements), in-flight loss of control and improper IFR procedures. Somewhat surprising is that—according to the skimpy FAA data—eight of the 19 fatal accidents in normally aspirated 58s involved student pilots.

Overall, the largest category of accidents is landing-gear-related. The largest single category here is gear-up landing and retraction of gear during the landing roll ("selected gear rather than flaps up"). Gear collapse and gear malfunctions are the next largest categories. There also was a number of incidents in which pilots recovered from a gear-up landing, successfully making a go-around with damage below the dollar level that would make them accidents. The two actions suggested by the gear-related accidents are confirm, confirm, confirm, and maintain and inspect.

Overall, the wrecking record reinforces the value of getting good training and staying current in both operational and preventive maintenance practices. It does not suggest any peculiar design characteristic that could be considered design-induced pilot error accident-causing except for the issue of cockpit configuration, especially non-standard gear and flap selector location.

This characteristic is well known (or notorious, depending upon your point of view) and should be able to be overcome through good training and rigorous use of the checklist and touch-speak-see verification.

On the plus side, the low incidence of fuel mismanagement accidents suggest that the simple on/off/crossfeed management system is pilot friendly.

Summary

The Baron 58 series is generally considered to be stout as light twin airplanes go, despite the tender nose gear. Aside from urgings to better training and better pilot and maintenance technique, there are one or two other caveats that apply to the 58 and other airplanes.

While it is the pilot's regulatory responsibility to oversee refueling, most leave it to line people to handle. Especially if the wing tip tanks are installed, refueling should be supervised to ensure that the refueler does not damage the tank

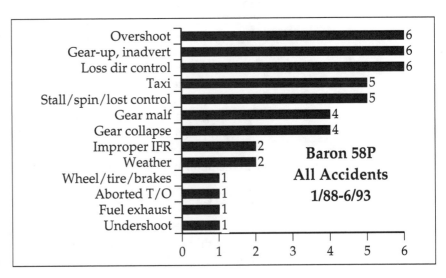

Baron 58P
All Accidents
1/88-6/93

Overshoot	6
Gear-up, inadvert	6
Loss dir control	6
Taxi	5
Stall/spin/lost control	5
Gear malf	4
Gear collapse	4
Improper IFR	2
Weather	2
Wheel/tire/brakes	1
Aborted T/O	1
Fuel exhaust	1
Undershoot	1

with the nozzle. And if the airplane is not going to be flown for a couple of days, especially in warm weather, the tanks should not be filled until it is time to depart. Expansion can cause damage.

Also, while the Baron is fairly sturdy, the doors don't accept abuse or carelessness any better than those on any other airplane. This is particularly critical on the 58P, but it applies to all.

On the 58P, the rear door pressure seal can be damaged by careless loading of cargo and passengers. Using the door as a handle can distort it, again ruining the pressure seal. But in any of the Barons, careless operation of the doors, putting weight on the doors and damaging the seals will result in air leaks or even doors that are prone to pop open.

The pilot should not trust loading or door operation to anyone else. Doors, especially the cockpit door, tend to open just as lift is generated. While this usually does not create an overwhelming aerodynamic or flight handling problem, if any, pilots have lost control of their aircraft because of surprise or distraction.

The airplane is good-looking, has good performance, competitive payload/range numbers and good handling characteristics. The 58 is a very appealing airplane for those fortunate few who can pay the tab. In that respect, one operator suggested that the relatively large number of 58s currently on the market is a reflection of the fact that more people are being forced to quit flying because of the economics.

Another operator hopes this is true. The 58 is a very attractive airplane for his charter operation. But the older models do not have known icing approval, the upgrade is too expensive and the later models have held their value too well to make them commercially viable in terms of the rates he would have to charge.

The 58 appears to be one of those twins a lot of pilots would like to own, if only they could afford it.

For More Information

There are as many tales of pilots buying 58s only to find hidden problems that were not uncovered before the purchase. Information saturation is the only answer. Aside from current owners and operators, probably the best source of information and guidance is the American Bonanza Society, Wichita, Kans., (316) 945-6913. As one owner quipped, they accept Baron owners. He continued: "The ABS is probably the best airplane owners association in the world."

Another source of information is the "Baron Newsletter," published quarterly by: Dave Neumeister, Lansing, Mich., (517) 882-8433.

This is largely a compilation of Baron-owner input, SDRs and other information, including plugs for modifiers, insurers and other interested vendors. There is a directory of services, but it seems limited to those who have had some contact with the publisher, who also puts out newsletters on other makes.

Owner Comments

I have owned a 58P Baron since 1978. It replaced a C55 Baron I had for 4-1/2 years. With modifications I made, the Baron is best owner-flown piston twin in the sky. In the 2,000 hours I put on it, including two trips to Europe, it has provided dependable and comfortable transportation. Doing this has involved detailed knowledge of its systems and a relatively high maintenance cost because of these many systems.

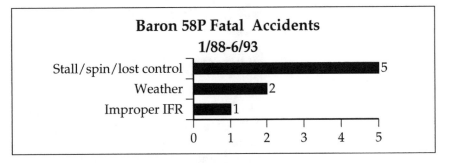

The only adverse characteristic of the plane—which I corrected— was its original landing approach speed about 100 knots. Since I fly from a 3,000-foot strip in Louisiana (ISA+20 in the summer), this was a problem. After I overshot one landing, I investigated it carefully.

To provide room for a turbocharger behind the engine crankcase and to clear the spar, the engine had to be moved 12 inches forward of the original location on the wing for nonturbocharged Barons. Placing 1,000 pounds 12 inches further forward moved the CG 5 inches forward of where it was on the C Baron (which came in at 80 knots). Beech reduced the chord of the flaps from 15 inches on the D-55 and earlier Barons to 10 inches on the E55 Barons and the 58s. This moved the center of lift one inch forward, leaving the CG 4 inches farther forward of the center of lift on the turbocharged 58 than on the nonturbocharged 55. When the plane came from the factory, with full fuel, pilot, and copilot, the CG was outside the forward limit.

This forward CG was so notorious that the Beechcraft pressurized Baron school I attended in 1978, told us to put a 50-pound bag of sand in the aft baggage compartment to fly better. That went out with the DC-2.

After I studied this, I moved 65 pound of batteries from the nose to the tail. I also changed the nacelle mounted air conditioner to a JB air conditioner in the tail. This moved the CG about 4 1/2 inches aft and reduced my approach speed to 90 knots. It still enabled me to fill all six seats and be in the aft CG limits.

To further shorten the landing distance, I installed reversing props. The STC for these is held by the George Bailey Company of Orlando, Fla. They save brakes as well as eliminating dangers of skidding on wet runways.

As with all airplanes 18 years old, maintenance costs are high. My annuals run about $10,000 and usually require a fuel cell overhaul. This runs close to $2,000 including labor. Beech backup is excellent with Dave Peterson and J.D. Crandall at the factory available to provide information. Continental Engine is also helpful in keeping the airplane going, although I must say the two original sets of engines had cracked crankcases. I am now using -B engines with larger crankshafts which have gone 1,100 and 1,400 hours respectively with no cracks.

Dr. Louis J. Capozzoli
Baton Rouge, La.

I owned a 58TC for 18 months and a straight 58 for the last seven months. The straight 58 is an entirely different airplane from the 58TC/58P. They may look identical, but they are very different, and they fly differently. The 58 flies pretty much like all the old 55 series Barons. The 58TC and 58P fly like a much heavier airplane. In my 58TC I used an approach speed of about 90 KIAS, depending on the landing weight, to get into Santa Paula. That was as slow an airspeed that I was at all comfortable with crossing the fence. When you pulled off the power, it landed right now, to the accompaniment of a stall horn and a buffet.

I put Vortex generators on the 58TC, and I could detect no measurable change in stall speeds in the landing configuration. The airplane felt better at a 90-knot approach speed with the V/Gs, but that's all. I have been told by other Baron owners, and by V/G Systems, that there is much less benefit to be gained by the 58TC/58P series, compared to the rest of the fleet. Maintenance: I figure that it cost me about $2,000 more per year to operate the 58TC over the 58, and a 58P would cost more than that. In addition to the turbochargers, there are lots of little things that add up.

The landing gear on the 58TC is different and much heftier than the 58, and this difference, coupled with the forward CG, may make it harder to get the usual Baron squeaker landings. (At least that was always the excuse that I used!)

Jeffrey D. Cannon
Toluca Lake, Calif.

I have had a 1971 model 58 Baron since 1973. Maintenance cost are about average for a high-speed normally aspirated twin. The early model 58s like mine cruise an honest 225 to 230, depending on loading. Beech parts remain very expensive items, but fortunately we rarely have to buy from Beech. ADs have been moderate, but my expenses probably aren't meaningful for others as I do much of my own work with help of a licensed mechanic.

We've had to replace the fuel tanks a couple of times because of leaks, and the AD on the back-end of the fuselage was time consuming and difficult. The IO-520 engines are intermediate in the range of problems that engines cause, and upgrade to the 550 is a serious but expensive consideration at major overhaul time.

The electric cowl flap has failed once, a very expensive replacement. The engines run on the hot side, and require monitoring, apparently a design defect as I've talked to other owners who have similar problems.

On balance, it is probably the best twin in its class; I've looked at several alternatives for replacement, and find that I can spend a great deal more money for a newer airplane, but I'd get something similar or inferior for a big price. Proper preventive maintenance eats a big chunk of change every year, and that's with minimal or no labor cost. I know of nothing in its class that does as well.

Michael S. Greenwald, M.D.
Joliet, Ill.

Comfort is lacking for long flights. Six people, luggage and fuel are impossible. Maintenance costs are high, but not any more than other airplanes this sophisticated. Fuel economy is poor—it turns 36-38 gph at 21,000 feet. Very few mechanics know any of a P58's systems.

Thomas A. Martin
Wichita, Kans.

Beech
60 Duke

The Beech Duke has a visceral appeal among some owners and prospective buyers, who become dreamy eyed over its shark-nosed profile and solid, corporate looks. Beech used to nurture this image, pitching the Duke in advertisements as an integral part of the lifestyle of attractive, successful people who are on the move. The price tag reinforced this stylish image—the last Duke was built in 1982 and went for about $600,000 equipped. It's little wonder, then, that some owners fondly refer to their airplanes as the Mercedes Benz of pressurized, piston twins.

The stylish Duke has endeared itself to many pilots with its pleasant handling qualities and good performance and load-carrying abilities. The airplane can, however, be a maintenance headache.

But prospective Duke buyers should be forewarned: A few who thought they were getting a great deal on a used Duke (some are going for less than $100,000) ended up with hangar queens that emptied their checking accounts. Others, perhaps with bigger checking accounts, freely admit as much but still dote on the Duke as if it were a favorite child. Such divergent opinions underscore the need to carefully consider whether a Duke, given its virtues and peccadillos, fits your budget and personal needs.

History

The Duke underwent steady refinement following its introduction in 1968 as the Model 60, but its configuration remained basically unchanged. In 1971, the Model A60 was introduced with a modest increase in gross weight (up 50 pounds from 6,725 to 6,775), but useful load and performance dropped a bit. According to book figures, the straight 60 is a much better short-field performer than the A60. However, Duke owners tell us those early figures were extremely optimistic, and that the A60 is only slightly inferior in takeoff and landing performance to its predecessor.

In 1974, the B60 was introduced. It offered a slightly larger cabin and more fuel capacity but suffered small degradations in speed and useful load. Thereafter, there were no major configuration changes.

All Dukes are powered by 380-hp Lycoming TIO-541 engines. Early models were maintenance headaches and had 1,200-hour TBOs. But the engines have been upgraded over the years and now have a 1,600-hour TBO. Several Duke owners, in fact, tell us they've gone well past that figure by operating the engines properly and, in particular, ensuring that they are properly warmed up and cooled down to avoid shock cooling. It's advice worth taking, given the number of cylinder problems we noticed in Service Difficulty Reports. (We'll go into detail later about various engine modifications and what to consider in Duke powerplants. Some Duke engines are now employing intercoolers, apparently with mixed results.)

Performance

The Duke travels at a good clip but guzzles fuel. At 24,000 feet, max cruise is about 220 knots (250 mph) at 65-70 percent power. Fuel consumption is about 40 gallons per hour. (One Duke owner told us he flight plans 52 gallons the first hour, 43 gallons for every hour thereafter and uses 68 percent power.) In contrast, at 55 percent power, fuel consumption drops to about 30 gph, but speed falls to about 185 knots. (You might as well be flying a Cessna 310.) The Duke edges out other pressurized twins in performance, with one exception, the pressurized Aerostars, which fly 10-15 knots faster on about 25 percent less fuel.

Climb performance is important for a pressurized airplane designed to cruise above 20,000 feet. Here, the Duke turns in respectable performance. A climb to 24,000 feet, at full gross on a warm day, takes just 28 minutes, reports one corporate owner. Others say the airplane climbs 7,000 to 1,000 fpm, depending on weight. The addition of intercoolers improves climb performance and offers other benefits, according to some owners; others say they think the benefits of intercoolers are dubious. At any rate, the Duke's climb performance is generally considered superior to any other owner-flown pressurized twin—except, again, for the pressurized Aerostars.

Beech's ads sold the airplane as integral to the lifestyles of affluent, successful people. The Duke has but one baggage compartment, in the nose, but it can hold up to 500 pounds.

Although the Duke's range is rather limited—its standard fuel tanks hold just 142 gallons—most have optional long-range fuel tanks that hold from 202 to 232 gallons, depending on the model. Top off the optional tanks, and you can turn up the manifold pressure and make a four-hour, 900-nm trip with IFR reserves. At reduced power and full fuel, you can fly the Duke 1,000 nm—average for its class.

The Duke wasn't designed for short runways. Most owners say they won't even think about using anything with less than 3,000 feet. One owner, though, says he regularly flies his Duke out of a 2,650-foot runway in Pennsylvania. This compels us to repeat the story we mentioned in our last Duke evaluation about how motorcycle daredevil Evel Knievel once ordered the pilot of his Duke to land on a drag strip. The Duke ended up with its snout through a truck trailer Knievel used as a dressing room. Another limitation of the Duke is that its initial climb on takeoff is rather poor, until it reaches about 500 feet, according to some owners.

Single-engine performance is about average for this class of airplane. In other words, you'll be mumbling curses and prayers when an engine quits, even under ideal conditions. Expect a climb, at full gross weight and sea level, of 307 fpm (this assumes a perfectly running airplane flown with flawless technique). Service ceiling with one dead engine is 15,100 feet. Some pilots say that intercoolers improve single-engine performance.

Weight and Loading

The Duke is not a six-person airplane with full fuel, but it still beats anything in its class in terms of useful load and range. Late model Dukes generally have a useful load of better than 2,000 pounds, even when carrying full equipment. Earlier models, which tend to have less equipment and weigh several hundred pounds less, do even better: Some straight 60 and A60 models have useful loads approaching 2,300 pounds. Such figures compare favorably with the cabin-class Cessna 421, which has seven seats to fill compared to the Duke's six.

Again, one drawback is the Duke's healthy rate of fuel consumption, which translates into a smaller payload. Compared to other pressurized twins, the Duke uses a few hundred more pounds of fuel on a long trip. Still, the Duke shines in one respect: It can carry full fuel and two to four people. But there are variations in load-carrying capabilities. One corporate owner of a lavishly equipped Duke reports that he makes three-hour, 600-mile trips with six people and 136 gallons of fuel. In contrast, a private owner, whose Duke has optional fuel tanks, says he's at gross with full fuel, 100 pounds of baggage and two people.

The Duke's single baggage compartment is located in the nose and can carry up to 500 pounds. According to one owner, this makes it easy to get the Duke out of its forward c.g. limits but difficult to get out of its aft limits. Another owner says he finds the airplane's weight and balance characteristics benign—that is, hard to get out of c.g. in any manner.

Passenger Comfort

Owners and users give the Duke decent marks for overall passenger comfort. Its cabin pressure differential is 4.7, so at 24,000 the Duke has a cabin altitude of 10,000 feet, which is superior to most six-seat pressurized twins. On the downside, the Duke is similar to Bonanzas and Barons in that it has a tapering cabin, so that two adults in the back seats will travel elbow to elbow. In 1974, though, the B60 model's side panels and ducting were reworked to offer a bit more lateral cabin room. More recent models come with redesigned seats that supposedly increase the amount of aisle space by a few inches.

As for noise levels and cabin heat, one owner reports the rear cabin seats are about as quiet as a King Air's, but that the heater is inadequate in wintertime or at high altitudes, unless the cabin is filled with warm bodies.

Flight Characteristics

Pilots compliment the Duke's handling characteristics. Its controls have a solid (some say heavy) yet responsive feel, which is not surprising, since the Duke is the heaviest of all six-passenger airplanes. One owner, praising the Duke as a rock-solid IFR platform, said, "ILS approaches are like a railroad track." Predictable and docile, the Duke trims up well and holds its airspeed, and pitch changes are minimal when the flaps or gear are extended. One pilot, though, said the Duke's controls were too heavy for him, and that he prefers lighter and more responsive inputs. In turbulence, one pilot says the Duke is a "bear to fly" without a yaw damper, while another says adroit foot work can be substituted for a yaw damper.

Cockpit Engineering

If you're on the hefty side, it may be a tight squeeze entering the Duke's cockpit. But once inside, owners report the ride will be comfortable and fairly quiet, except during climbs or power settings above 2,500 rpm. As for the cockpit layout, it's user friendly: All the necessary controls, switches and avionics are within easy reach and view of the pilot.

Better yet, the power controls and gear and flap levers have been placed in the standard order (they're reversed in the Baron, except for the 58P). The flap system also is straightforward, with just three lever positions: up, approach and land. Maximum gear-extension speed is a phenomenal 175 knots. Also, dual control wheels are standard equipment, and the cowl flaps are electrically operated. A glance out the window will confirm whether they're working.

Cockpit visibility, though, is barely adequate. To see over the glare shield, a pilot of average height might be tempted to pull his seat forward; however, the seat will also automatically move up, which may put the pilot's head next to the headliner.

Beech Duke Fatal Accidents
1/83-5/89

Safety

The Duke in recent years has established a remarkably good safety record. FAA records show only four fatal crashes between 1983 and mid-1989. These accidents reveal no pattern. There was a crash on an IFR approach; a collision with trees while turning final; a power loss in which airspeed was allowed to drop below VMC; and a crash for reasons not specified in the FAA data.

The list of nonfatal accidents is another story. Gear collapses—a total of 15—headed the list. Although nobody was reported to have suffered serious injuries, we'd hate to have been around when the owner was presented with the repair bill. Generally, these collapses were traced to some sort of mechanical failure.

However, those failures were, to some extent, probably triggered by the Duke's high touchdown speeds, heaviness (it weighs nearly 7,000 pounds) and its tendency to wheelbarrow during braking, which can over stress the gear and result in blown tires. A few owners also have speculated that some gear collapses may have resulted from either skimping on maintenance or the inability to find knowledgeable mechanics to work on the gear. Whatever the case, if you're thinking of buying a Duke, make sure you scrutinize its logs for evidence of past gear damage.

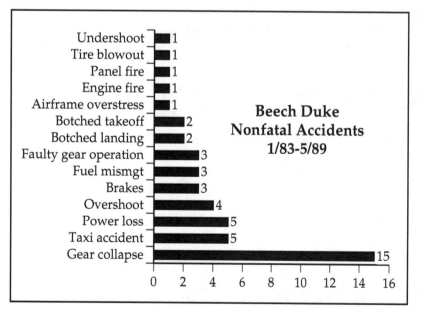

Beech Duke
Nonfatal Accidents
1/83-5/89

The record also included five instances of power failures attributed to mechanical problems. There were two engine stoppages because of turbocharger failures; another after an intake valve failure; and a broken exhaust clamp was blamed for a third. The cause of a fifth engine failure was not mentioned in the FAA's data. Another power outage was thought to have been caused by water contamination. Only one engine fire occurred, and it was blamed on an improperly routed fuel line that had become chafed.

The accident data didn't reveal any instances of fuel unporting, which has caused several Baron and Bonanza crashes.

Operating Costs

Pressurized twins with amenities such as air conditioning typically cost a small fortune to maintain, but the Duke seems to be in a class of its own. It's not uncommon to hear Duke owners complain about mechanics automatically jacking up their prices for a Duke. Most satisfied owners correctly point out that the key to keeping bills down, and ensuring that the Duke's engines reach TBO, is to properly operate and maintain the airplane. And woe to those who got a "good buy" on a used Duke that was not properly operated or maintained. It can be an expensive mistake.

Owners praise the organization of the Duke's cockpit. This one is in a lavishly equipped B60, complete with stereo system and copilot's flight instruments.

What, exactly, do we mean by expensive? One former Duke owner told how he paid a wholesale price for a beautiful 1977 airplane that had just received a "squawk-free annual." A great deal, he thought.

Here is a list of repairs he started to incur almost immediately: a new right engine starter, $1,000; radio work that included fixing a bad radio antenna, a burned-out radar antenna and eliminating paint dust in everything, $8,000; replacement of camshafts in both engines, $20,000; repair of both turbos, which were scraping their housings, $6,000; "piston slap" problems in both engines, $3,000; deice boot repairs, $1,200; windshield heat power supply problems, $2,400; prop sync controller repairs, $1,000; new Cleveland brakes necessitated by bad master cylinders and badly warped and pitted rotors, $2,800; minor fuel leak that caused a blue stain on the left wing, $400; replacing a lead-acid battery (which was an unauthorized installation) with nicad batteries, $400. Once the airplane was sold, the new owner soon encountered other problems, including a badly heated windshield, $8,000, and other assorted squawks, $3,000. If none of these expenses would put a dent in your pocketbook, though, you might be content with a later-model Duke.

One pilot/manager, for example, related that his boss paid $89,000 for an A-60 and then put in $70,000 worth of maintenance during the next two years. "The airplane has been an almost continuous problem, but I still like it," he wrote, adding that his boss still likes it, too. To help reduce such costs, though, many owners stress that it's important to find a shop that is familiar with the Duke, rather than letting a mechanic who has never worked on the airplane learn at your expense. The Duke Flyers Association, which was formed in 1988 and has some 125 members, can help in this area. On a brighter side, prospective buyers will be glad to know that parts availability has not been a problem.

Engine Troubles

Don't even consider a pre-1976 Duke unless you're sure its trouble-plagued 380-hp Lycoming TIO-541 engines have received the appropriate fixes. A pair costs some $64,000 to overhaul, which underscores the need for prudence in this area. As for other engine problems, here are four major ones that we've identified through owner complaints and Service Difficulty Reports:

• Cylinders and pistons. Until 1974, the TBO of the TIO-541 was only 1,200 hours, primarily because of cylinder woes, with cracking around the exhaust ports the major problem. Since then, engines built or overhauled with improved pistons and cylinders have had a TBO of 1,600 hours. One factor in cylinder failures was improper pilot technique in warming up and cooling down the engines; if temperature changes were too abrupt, cylinder stress would result. (Incidentally, a check of SDRs revealed numerous cylinder problems.) Still, Dukes built in 1976 and later (serial number 804 and up) have the upgraded engines. They have a 1,600-hour TBO, and owners report operating them for 1,600 and even 2,000 hours.

• Turbochargers. The 60, A60 and 1974 B60 models had cast-iron turbo housings that tended to crack from the heat. This was no small problem in flight, since a turbocharger failure in a pressurized airplane can lead to partial or total cabin depressurization. However, the cracking problems stopped in 1974, when stainless steel blowers were fitted. By now, almost all cast-iron turbo housings have been replaced with the stainless steel ones; however, a few old ones remain, so be sure you're not getting one of them. If you are, make sure you get a price reduction.

• Crankcases. Through 1977, Dukes had a high incidence of crankcase cracks (which goes to show, at least, that Continental isn't the only company to have crankcase cracking problems). The Duke's crankcases were beefed up in 1988, starting with engine serial number 781.

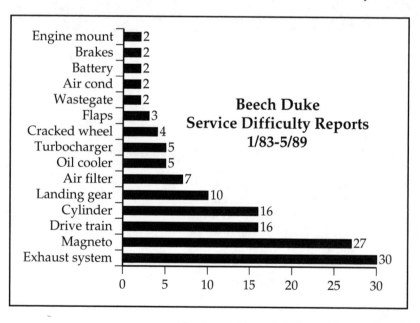

Beech Duke
Service Difficulty Reports
1/83-5/89

Other Service Problems

To maintain its stylish, high-priced image, Dukes came equipped with a jet-style nickel cadmium (nicad) battery. You'd think that this would give a high degree of dependability and wear. But the battery is improperly cooled, and it can be destroyed by a slight improper adjustment of the voltage regulator. Average life is just two years or less. That may seem like a decent enough battery life, but not when the battery costs thousands! Fortunately, later model Dukes have lead-acid batteries. Beech has stopped offering lead acid conversion kits, but you could probably have a Beech dealer install one with a field approval. Our suggestion is that you try and buy a Duke with lead-acid batteries.

Turbocharger problems also have popped up in Service Difficulty Reports. One involves the turbocharger controllers, which are notoriously unreliable. During a demonstration ride, be sure to check for manifold pressure drift. Mixture control cables also have had their share of problems. Be sure to see that you're getting the upgraded versions, since replacing mixture control cables costs several thousand dollars.

The Duke's heated windshield drew various complaints: delamination, static discharges that pitted the plastic, and St. Elmo's fire that caused havoc with the airplane's electrical system. Jim Gorman, president of the Duke Flyers Assn., says he's heard of delamination problems on earlier Dukes but not later models. He speculated that St. Elmo's fire might be caused by not having the static discharge lines attached to the ailerons. (Incidentally, we didn't find any SDRs pertaining to windshields.)

Other reports point to various problems with the exhaust. The Model 60, in particular, had short exhaust stacks that lead to flap corrosion. The condition of the exhaust pipes also should be checked at the rear by the slip joints; they came off and triggered a fire in one case.

Muscular 380-hp engines give the Duke hot speeds, but with high fuel burn. Figure on laying out almost $60,000 to overhaul a pair.

Various magneto, landing gear, drive train and wheel problems also were mentioned in SDRs and owners' letters, so make sure these items receive a thorough going over on a pre-purchase inspection.

After receiving two reports of partial outboard elevator separations in Dukes, Beech issued "mandatory" service bulletins in 1989 to check the airplanes' horizontal stabilizers and elevator hinge attachment areas. The bulletin affects certain Duke 60, A60 and B60 series models. Beech said an inspection should take two men 12 hours to perform. Inspections were to be performed as soon as possible, but no later than the next 50 hours.

Modifications

Intercoolers are the mod that a lot of Duke owners are talking about right now. The talk revolves around one issue: Do the intercoolers significantly improve performance? Some Duke owners say they do, while others have mixed feelings about the investment they made for intercooling systems provided by American Aviation of Spokane, Wash. Merlyn Products has STCs and PMAs for intercooling systems for the Beech Duke.

The Duke Flyers Assn., while withholding judgment on intercoolers, listed these advantages and disadvantages: They provide more power on hot days (but increase drag, too); increase climb rate on a hot day (and decrease useful load by 50 pounds); make the engine run cooler (but enable you to overboost it); and they may increase TBO (but make it possible to overboost your engines on cold days).

Which Model?

Be careful when buying any Duke that was produced through 1975. Their reliability record wasn't the greatest, and maintenance bills were high. But starting with its 1976 models, Beech seems to have gotten its act together; Dukes from then on are no more expensive to maintain than other high-horsepower piston twins.

Keeping this in mind, use extreme caution when buying an early- model Duke—a straight 60 or A60—in the $70,000 to $86,000 range. You may think you're getting a great deal, but the possibility of an avalanche of maintenance bills is a real possibility.

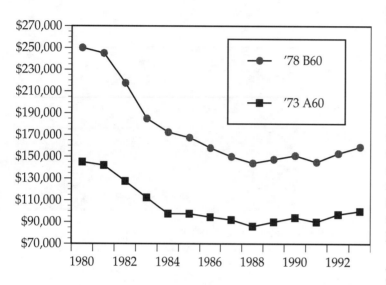

So if you can't afford a late model Duke, you probably can't afford an early model, either. We don't, though, want to suggest all older models should be avoided, because there may be some good buys.

Before opening your checkbook, though, just make sure your prospective Duke has the following: a thorough pre-purchase inspection (by a reputable mechanic); compliance with all service bulletins; updates to the latest standards; and operation by a competent pilot.

And don't be fooled by engines that may have recently been overhauled, even though they are nowhere near TBO. "If they've been overhauled under 1,000 hours, it's likely that they were not operated properly,'" says Jim Gorman of the Duke Flyers Assn. "If I had my choice, I would choose one at TBO or that had just been overhauled. Either way, you would be starting out with engines you know have not been mistreated."

Training

Although the Duke is no longer being manufactured, it won't be hard finding training or support for the airplane. FlightSafety International offers Duke proficiency training at its Beech Learning Center in Wichita, Kans. Training is available on an initial or recurrent basis. The program consists of ground school and training in a Baron 58 cockpit systems simulator.

Owners' Association

As mentioned earlier, the Duke Flyers Assn. was formed several years ago by James C. Gorman, who has owned a Duke for 17 years. Gorman said the association has been successful in providing Duke pilots and owners with information on how to reduce operating and maintenance costs and providing tips on flying the airplane.

The group publishes a newsletter and a five-page brochure with information for prospective owners. Duke Flyers Assn., Box 2599, Mansfield, Ohio 44906; (419) 755-1223 or 529-3822.

Owner Comments

Having an experienced shop and/or an experienced aircraft manager/pilot is a must to keep costs down. There are many ways to cut costs, but most shops are not motivated to tell you how. But at least if they're experienced on Dukes, you won't be training them at your expense. Don't assume a Beech dealer is experienced on Dukes. Chuck's Aircraft, San Carlos, Calif. purports to be a Duke expert. Figure $5,000 for an annual inspection if the plane's in good shape.

We bought several parts, used, through parts houses like Chuck's. Use shops, locally and out of state, to overhaul intercoolers, generators, air conditioning door actuators, etc. instead of buying replacements from Beech.

David Dick
Addison, Tex.

With its high landing speeds and gross weight of nearly 7,000 pounds, the Duke puts heavy demands on brakes, landing gear and tires.

I have flown other aircraft with far less equipment and had a much more fatiguing time doing so, while the Duke, perhaps because of the lower noise level and conveniently placed switches and other gizmos is really a pleasure to fly. Maybe part of that facility is the fact that I attended Duke school and do my best to keep proficient. I think the key to owning and flying a Duke safely is attending some structured school before one takes off to fly the aircraft unsupervised.

I usually expect that my Duke will cost from $5,000 to $10,000 in scheduled maintenance, using it about 100 to 125 hours a year, and another $10,000 to $15,000 in unscheduled maintenance, or about $25,000 in maintenance cost per year for a perfectly maintained airplane. When I owned a Bonanza and unscheduled maintenance popped up, I used to say that I was in for a $1,000 expense—with a Duke it's $5,000 or more.

Parts prices for the Duke, like all Beechcraft models, is often short of scandalous. Generators that usually last from 300 to 500 hours cost $6,500 new, and now over $2,000 to overhaul. Deicing window volt meters, which fail frequently, cost more than $1,000, as do fuel circuit board kits and lots of other little things.

Engine overhaul prices are astronomical. A new replacement engine is $65,000, and an overhaul is $35,000. I just had a top overhaul on the right side at 920 hours for $10,000. While the powerplants have been relatively trouble-free, one of the most serious problems is deterioration of the camshaft lobes as a result of lack of lubrication, and abrasion of the lobes by the lifters.

Cost/Performance/Specifications

Model	Year	Average Retail Price	75% Cruise Speed (kt)	Useful Load (lb)	Std/Opt Fuel (gal)	Engines	TBO (hr)	Overhaul Cost @
60	1968-69	$64,000	236	2,625	142/204	380-hp Lyc. TIO-541	1,600	$29,500
A60	1970-71	$79,500	237	2,625	142/204	380-hp Lyc. TIO-541	1,600	$29,500
A60	1972-73	$90,500	237	2,625	142/204	380-hp Lyc. TIO-541	1,600	$29,500
B60	1974-75	$113,500	233	2,436	142/232	380-hp Lyc. TIO-541	1,600	$29,500
B60	1976-77	$137,000	233	2,436	142/232	380-hp Lyc. TIO-541	1,600	$29,500
B60	1978-79	$158,000	233	2,436	142/232	380-hp Lyc. TIO-541	1,600	$29,500
B60	1980-81	$203,500	233	2,394	142/232	380-hp Lyc. TIO-541	1,600	$29,500
B60	1982	$243,000	233	2,394	142/232	380-hp Lyc. TIO-541	1,600	$29,500

At Duke school, when there was a Duke school, students were instructed to use two bottles of the Lycoming additive (the one that's used on the troublesome Skyhawk engine) at each oil change and one bottle midway between the recommended 50-hour oil changes.

This brings me to the biggest problem in owning a Duke, and that is obtaining qualified people to maintain it. There are a number of systems in the Duke that are common to the King Air, but very few systems common to other Beechcraft products. Your best bet, therefore, is to bite the bullet for expensive maintenance, and go to qualified and experienced Beechcraft service centers.

I have found Ronson Aviation of Trenton, N.J. and Lancaster Aviation of Lancaster, Pa. to be competent in the diagnosis of most Duke problems. Unfortunately, perhaps due to the paucity of Dukes and the number of systems, nobody has been perfect so far, and often you just have to chase the problems until you find somebody who has seen them before and can fix them. That, unfortunately, is extremely expensive and frustrating.

There are some additional caveats with regards to owning a Duke. In a humid climate, the aircraft must be aired out periodically; otherwise, it will mildew inside. In addition, if the aircraft cabin is exposed to dampness, rainy clothing, rainy passengers and the like, it should be thoroughly dried out before being sealed up again or mildew will occur.

Arthur Alan Wolk
Philadelphia, Pa.

Optional long-range tanks boost fuel supply to over 200 gallons, but figure taking along only one or two people. The Duke is fast, for sure, but the big Lycomings gobble fuel with gusto. Up high, the airplane can turn in 220 knots on 40 gph.

I have owned a Duke for three years. I have found it an outstanding aircraft to own and fly. It is a very stable IFR platform and is a real pilot's airplane. The main shortcomings of the airplane, however, are the fact that cabin and baggage space are limited, it burns a lot of fuel, and it requires a long runway. In addition, maintenance costs are relatively high.

Six months ago, I installed the American Aviation intercoolers and have a very mixed feeling about their benefits. In terms of performance, I feel that the increased rate of climb and cruise speed are offset by the fact that one is burning more fuel and putting more stress on the engines. The main purpose of installing the intercoolers was to increase the single-engine rate of climb. And, should I lose an engine at a low altitude and have to go to full power on the other engine, it would provide additional power that could save my life.

Bernard J. Belkin
Greenwich, Conn.

Beech
King Air 90

The Beech King Air 90s are often called "entry-level" aircraft. Whether they are suitable for entry by piston-twin pilots who wish to step up a notch or simply represent entry into a quagmire of cash outlays is a topic we'll explore here.

A number of subscribers asked us to check out the turbine aircraft situation as prices on older turbine birds drop to tantalizing levels. Are the benefits in performance and prestige that go with the upgrade worth the presumably higher cost of fuel and maintenance, even if the starting price is less than devastating?

One reader who purchased a King Air C90 may have put his finger on the perfect rationale for a switch as he told us: "We moved up from a 58P Beech Baron that was plagued with high maintenance costs and high downtime. Our expenses are still high, but the reliability has increased tenfold."

The entry-level label for the King Air 90 series is appropriate in other ways, too. The aircraft have a fairly golden reputation for safety and ease of handling, unlike the Mitsubishi MU-2, for example. For the pilot who can handle a piston twin, the King Air will be a baby carriage, a delight to fly. The transition comes like a breeze. There's power to spare, but not overwhelming speed or altitude performance to be daunting.

Controls are light and pleasant, and the pilot is guaranteed a big smile the first time he honks back on those props after touchdown for an awesome "pneumatic" stop with reverse pitch and finds out what he's been missing all those years.

On top of all this, there are maybe 4,000 King Airs of all types out there (about 2,500 in the U.S., according to the FAA census), so there are plenty of places for service and support. And finally, mother Beech, bless 'er, is still in business and cranking out late model King Airs and providing parts.

The classic C90. Find one with -21 engines for what many consider the best balance of performance, cost and value in a used King Air.

History of the Line

The first Model 90 King Air was essentially a Queen Air upgraded with turbo-props. Probably one of the smartest moves Beech made was to start the line with what would be a classic turboprop engine: United Technologies of Canada's Pratt & Whitney PT6, which would evolve through many upgrades during the years to come. As the airframe grew and evolved, so did the powerplant; or maybe it was the other way around. Though the internal airflow was all "backwards," the free-turbine PT6 engine was bushels of decibels quieter than

the geared Garretts. (Hold your ears when those MU-2s taxi by.)

The first-born Model 90s still out there are dirt cheap by turbine standards—i.e., $190,000 or so, according to the *Aircraft Bluebook Price Digest*—but that doesn't mean they're a good buy. They lack the reverse-pitch prop feature of later models, for one thing. And they have the old PT6A-6 engines that all too often are "over the hill." The same applies to the next few 90 series models (A90, B90 and some C90s) that have PT6A-20 engines. Overhaul costs can be astronomical, and the parts situation is disaster city.

The top of the line in the 90 series are the F90s with their big 750-shp engines, modified cowl inlets and sleek T-tails. This one is an F90-1.

According to Aviall Director of Marketing Paul Jones (Aviall is a big turbine engine overhauler), overhauls on these older engines can go as high as $150,000 to $160,000 apiece, and that's likely to be more than the entire aircraft is worth. The problem is two-fold: getting parts and getting the engine to meet specs.

Overhaul Rejects

People in the industry describe the parts situation for the -6 and -20 engines as bad. "There are an awful lot of junk dealers who buy and sell scrap parts through the black market or wherever," said Jones, "and they end up getting serviceable tags on these engines, and there's a hell of a liability problem."

Aviall, for one, won't even take in a -6 engine for overhaul. Part of the reason is the elevated cost of replacing items like turbine blades and temperature indicating systems. With it and the -20 engine, says Jones, work on the hot section too often causes the powerplant to run in a way that is not to the customer's satisfaction, requiring several trips back to make adjustments. "It's become a very labor-intensive engine."

Heading down the model progression trail, we find the A90 in 1966 came with reverse pitch props and cabin pressure boosted from a miniscule 3.1 psi to a nothing-to-write-home-about 4.6 psi, and the -20 engines with 50 more shp each. Also, the gross went up by 300 pounds.

In 1968 the B90 received a five-foot increase in wingspan along with a recontoured rear fuselage for better performance, balanced controls for lighter control pressures and a 350-pound jump in gross.

Bleed Air

With the C90 in 1971 the old supercharger cabin pressurization system was dropped in favor of bleed air from the engines. This is described as a much less fussy system to maintain, but one of our readers said he didn't like it because it added to cabin noise and sapped power from the engine. Asked about this, one King Air maven acknowledged the tradeoff with the golden quote: "There's no free lunch."

In 1976 the C90 was outfitted with the -21 engines, which won plaudits from Jones: "It's a good engine, real good."

In 1982 the C90-1 delivered yet another boost in cabin pressure to 5 psi, allowing a sea-level cabin up to 11,065 feet and an 8,000-foot cabin to FL230. (Let it be noted here that King Airs in general are not renowned for their pressurization levels, since among competitors cabin psi's commonly range from 5.5 to 6 or better.) In addition, cruise went up by 15 knots or so, thanks to raising the the interstage turbine temperature (ITT). Also, the horizontal stabilizer was strengthened and the cabin door borrowed from the King Air 200 to handle the higher pressurization.

Next came the C90A in 1984, bringing another 12 knots in cruise thanks to new engine cowlings that reduced drag but boosted ram air flow to the engines. Also, the electrical landing gear system was replaced with a hydraulic one designed to be quieter, lighter and simpler to maintain. On top of that, a rudder boost system was added to ease the piolt's workload in single-engine operations. It's activated automatically when a diminution of bleed air pressure is sensed.

Following a big hullabaloo about wing strength and cracking wing bolt concerns, Beech equipped this model aircraft with a three-element bonded spar cap that runs the length of the wing using shear fittings instead of bolts in tension as in the older King Airs. More about this later.

In 1972 the E90 came along with -28 engines, which are basically the same as the 680-shp powerplants on the Model 100s, but derated to 550 shp for extra altitude performance. And in 1979 the T-tail made its appearance on the F90, along with monster 750-shp engines that loafed along at lower prop rpms and were claimed to reduce the cabin noise level. With those big new engines, the useful load jumped up another 600 pounds or so. This aircraft was an appropriate counter to Cessna's Conquest turboprop, which has some nice performance numbers.

Cost/Performance/Specifications

Model	Year	Average Retail Price	75% Cruise Speed (kt)	Useful Load (lb)	Std/Opt Fuel (gal)	Engines	TBO (hr)	Overhaul Cost @
90	1965-66	$187,500	212	3,320	384	500 shp P&W PT6A-6	3,500	$145,000
A90	1966-67	$244,500	212	3,320	384	550 shp P&W PT6A-20	3,500	$135,000
B90	1968-70	$290,000	212	3,320	384	550 shp P&W PT6A-20	3,500	$135,000
C90	1971-73	$387,500	219	3,933	384	550 shp P&W PT6A-20	3,500	$135,000
C90	1974-75	$420,000	219	3,933	384	550 shp P&W PT6A-20	3,500	$135,000
C90	1976-78	$510,000	219	3,933	384	550 shp P&W PT6A-21	3,500	$90,000
C90	1979-81	$575,000	219	3,933	384	550 shp P&W PT6A-21	3,500	$90,000
C90-1	1982-83	$715,000	235	3,320	384	550 shp P&W PT6A-21	3,500	$90,000
C90A	1984-86	$1,020,000	247	3,878	384	550 shp P&W PT6A-21	3,500	$95,000
C90A	1987-92	$1,500,000	247	3,878	384	550 shp P&W PT6A-21	3,500	$90,000
C90B	1992-93	$2,275,000	247	3,878	384	550 shp P&W PT6A-21	3,500	$90,000
E90	1972-74	$500,000	248	4,164	474	550 shp P&W PT6A-28	3,500	$110,000
E90	1975-77	$545,000	248	4,164	474	550 shp P&W PT6A-28	3,500	$110,000
E90	1978-81	$675,000	248	4,164	474	550 shp P&W PT6A-28	3,500	$110,000
F90	1979-81	$720,000	260	4,481	470	750 shp P&W PT6A-135	3,500	$105,000
F90	1982-83	$855,000	260	4,481	470	750 shp P&W PT6A-135	3,500	$105,000
F90-1	1983-84	$1,100,000	275	4,383	470	750 shp P&W PT6A-135A	3,500	$105,000
F90-1	1985-86	$1,415,000	275	4,383	470	750 shp P&W PT6A-135A	3,500	$105,000

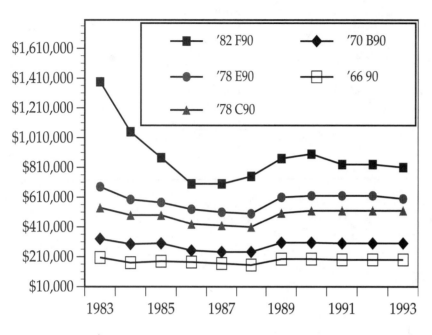

■ '82 F90	◆ '70 B90
● '78 E90	☐ '66 90
▲ '78 C90	

Then in 1983 the F90-1 placed -135A engines in redesigned cowls that once again cut drag and yielded better ram air recovery. Cruise rose some 15 knots, and climb and take-off distances were improved, as well.

Performance

When you talk about blazing-hot performance in turboprops, you don't think King Air. You think MU-2, Conquest and Cheyenne 400LS. Some of the King Air 90s, in fact, with cruise speeds not terribly far over 200 knots, can barely get out of the way of some bigger piston twins.

But beauty is in the eye of the beholder when it comes to King Airs, it seems, since in user feedback we received pilots rated performance superb quite often (especially in the F90s), and never called it "poor." But even with the F90, one respondent noted that "above 20,000 feet, performance diminishes."

Remember also, piston twin pilots, that typically with a King Air we're talking about single-engine service ceilings of over 15,000 feet and SE climb rates of better than 600 fpm—a nice safety margin over the recip crowd.

Handling

Here is where the King Airs shine. Pilots love the responsiveness and lack of quirkiness.

Said one King Air Pilot: "A very simple, forgiving aircraft. Easy to fly. Any student could take it up without any problem. On single-engine, it's as docile as a new-born babe. It lands like a bird." "Flight characteristics are unequaled in my lifetime experience," said another.

Loading and Cabin Comfort

All the King Airs have the same basic cabin width—four and a half feet—and height—about four feet 10 inches. Passenger comfort is rated fairly high. "One of Beechcraft's most noted features," said one F-90 pilot. The typical club seating allows four passengers in back, with a fifth on a side-facing seat, if necessary.

Safety

Examination of the FAA's accident/incident reports for a six-year period from 1985-91 shows only 11 fatal accidents in the U.S., with almost half of those (five) attributed to improper IFR. The only possibly aircraft-related fatal accident occurred after a C90 pilot reported losing all his instruments.

Engine failures caused by mechanical factors (14) were blamed for most of the nonfatal accidents recorded during the same period, with gear collapses coming in second (10) followed closely by inadvertent gear-ups (seven). Another half dozen landing gear malfunctions pushed gear problems, in general, into the top category, as it is with most retractable general aviation aircraft we have studied.

How bullet-proof are the PT6 engines in the King Airs? In seven of the engine-failure-related accident/incidents reported damaged turbine blades were listed. Seven more Service Difficulty Reports called out the same kind of problem on different 90-series King Airs for a total of 14 in all in the six-year period.

Though externally indistinguishable from its predecessors, the C90-1 was beneficiary of a boost in cabin pressure differential from 4.6 psi up to 5 psi, holding a sea level cabin to 11,065 feet altitude.

There's no telling (in the reports) which of these may have occurred because of improper pilot operation and overtemping, foreign object damage or some possible intrinsic weaknesses. One experienced King Air service manger, Lee Coffman of Flightcraft in Seattle, Wash., told *The Aviation Consumer* that most compressor failures he's aware of are caused by FOD (ice or other objects).

Coffman volunteered, however, that a different kind of glitch was possibly responsible for more King Air powerplant troubles, judging from his experience. This concerned the leaking of fuel from the fuel pump that is coupled to the Bendix fuel controller. The rear seal on the high-pressure fuel pump leaks fuel that in turn washes out the lubrication on the fuel controller bearings. When the bearings fail, the plastic coupling is sheared. The engine senses an underspeed and calls for more fuel, which in turn results in an overspeed.

Imagine the reaction of the normal multi-engine pilot who has been trained to yank back a *failed* engine and feather the prop when he gets an overspeed on one engine. If he were to yank the weaker, but normal, engine and feather that prop by mistake, he might be in a bind. This reportedly happened on at least one occasion. The pilot is said to have shut down the good engine, and when he realized he had an overtorque on the other engine, he shut down that one and became a glider pilot. Luckily, he managed to get the good engine restarted before contacting the ground, and made it safely to an airport.

We understand, incidentally, that FlightSafety International in Wichita, Kans. normally teaches pilots as part of its King Air training curriculum to recognize "unscheduled torque increases" and respond correctly. They do this for those particular aircraft, at least, that give this emergency procedure in their POHs.

We were able to find only two reports of this kind of problem in the accident/incident roster for the past six years, related to the fuel pump/fuel controller glitch we mentioned above. But we discovered another eight reports on the subject in the Service Difficulty Reports for the same period. These numbers would not seem to constitute a plague, but would merit attention by maintenance personnel.

In fact, a Beech spokesman told *The Aviation Consumer* that procedures for detecting a developing problem are addressed in the P&W engine maintenance manual. Since the fuel controller's lubricant is a distinctive blue color, traces normally can be seen coming out of the controller for some time before a major problem develops.

Wing Spar Concerns

In the early 1980s there was a big hubbub following wing failures in three King Airs, two of them fatal. A Canadian King Air 90 crashed in 1979 due to the fatigue failure of a spar fitting, while a King Air 200 experienced a corrosion-induced failure of a critical spar bolt in 1980, but neverthless managed to land safely. Then in 1981 a King Air E90 shed its left outboard wing panel shortly after takeoff at Mineral Wells, Tex., killing the pilot. The forward tension bolt that secures the outer wing panel had fractured because of corrosion.

The FAA issued an emergency AD grounding Model 90 and 100 King Airs until bolt inspections could be performed. Since then other ADs have been issued as the years passed, aimed at further checking the integrity of King Air wing bolts, nuts, fittings and spars. And concern about wing integrity has spurred sales of an external wing strap devised by David Saunders.

It was designed to serve as a "failsafe" structural backup by providing an alternate loadpath even in case of total failure of the main spar. The strap relieves about 30 percent of the load on the regular spar, which in turn drastically reduces its propensity to crack.

Getting on the bandwagon, even Beech, after much initial umbrage over the aftermarket Saunders strap project, offered its own "center section bridge section" designed to provide a spar backup, with a "secondary load path."

The Saunders spar strap is still offered by Western Aircraft Maintenance out of Boise, Idaho. We'll have more about this in the modifications section later on.

P3 Filters

A final safety matter worth noting here concerns the use of so-called P3 filters on PT6 engines to capture contaminants from the compressor discharge air to the automatic fuel control. Philadelphia attorney Arthur Alan Wolk some time ago obtained a settlement from Pratt & Whitney Canada for the crash of a King Air that did not have the P3 filters. Part of the settlement was that P&W would reissue a 10-year-old Service Bulletin, number 1330, warning pilots and owners of PT6-equipped aircraft that failure to use P3 filters could result in contamination and unselected rollbacks to idle.

However, Beech maintains the P3 filters are dangerous because they would cause slow engine acceleration. And the FAA has, in turn, proposed an AD requiring removal of the P3 filters on grounds that they could prevent sufficient engine acceleration for a balked landing. Attorney Wolk, incidentally, characterizes this as baloney.

Double ventral strakes for extra yaw stability and wing lockers, for extra baggage loading, are among the King Air mods offered by Raisbeck Engineering.

When asked his opinion of the P3 filter matter, Paul Jones of Aviall said he had seen neither more nor fewer problems with engines with P3 filters than those without them. If the filters are dirty, he said, they can decrease performance, but he couldn't say that people with filters had fewer fuel contamination problems.

By the same token, Lee Coffman of Flightcraft said he was flabbergasted by the hullabaloo over the P3 filter, saying he thought it was making a mountain out of a molehill.

We hope to investigate the matter more fully later.

Maintenance

Operators report good experience in maintaining their King Airs, with good support from dealers in the field and from Beech. Parts are generally in good supply, they say. "Maintenance is straightforward and easy to obtain throughout the U.S.," said one. "Beech parts aren't cheap, or even reasonable, but they are readily accessible," said another.

A very limited sampling of hourly maintenance costs showed an average on the various 90 models of $121, not counting avionics or reserve for overhaul. The range was from a low of $40 an hour to a high of $400.

In response to our request for a rating of the malfunction record of various King Air systems, most replies inclined to be quite favorable about most systems. The rating for the fuel system was the only one that received a less than wholehearted endorsement and a couple of "bad" ratings from F90 owners. Said one: "The fuel vents overboard when the auxes are full."

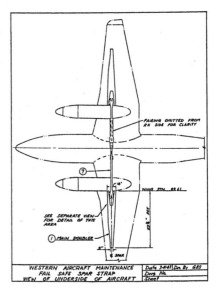

With engine TBOs rated at a generous 3,500 hours, operators should be able to look forward to a long, financially painless journey before biting the bullet to the tune of $75,000 to $95,000 *per engine* (lots more, as we mentioned earlier, for the old -6 and -20 engines, *if* you can find anyone to do the job).

Since most of our feedback responses indicated operators flew their King Airs from 200 to 500 hours each year, that means 17 to seven years to save up, or sell. But at each 1,250 hours up till then a hot section inspection is recommended. And, depending on the model, each of these can cost $6,000 to $12,000 per engine.

A diagram showing the Saunders "Failsafe" stainless steel spar strap placement underneath the wing of the aircraft. On the outer section of the wings external doublers are riveted to the lower surface.

Some King Air operators, on the other hand, prefer to use P&W's trend-monitoring system in an attempt to stretch out hot-section scheduling. (It's not supposed to have any effect on the final 3,500-hour TBO.) This is accomplished by tracking the ongoing health of the engine to detect when trends away from the norm begin. The pilot keeps track of items like torque, ITT, fuel flow and N1 state while noting OAT, IAS and altitude. And a computer program calculates how the engine should be running and whether there are deviations from the baseline.

Using this technique, according to Paul Jones at Aviall, you might get 1,500 or 1,700 hours out of it, reducing the number of hot section inspections to two instead of three.

The Service Difficulty Reports revealed the usual broad spectrum of problems, with perhaps extra numbers concerning the following categories: landing gear components with cracks and corrosion and malfunctions in gear doors and motors; cracked and corroded wheel bolt holes; cabin environment concerns like air conditioning breakdowns and pressure leaks; window and windshield cracks and delaminations; wing spar and assembly cracks and corrosion, plus a number of fuel pump failures involving worn, stripped or sheared drive splines.

AD 80-8-12, incidentally, called for inspection of fuel pump drive couplings for wear or damage, since spline wear could result in a flameout. Replacement of the coupling with a different assembly as instructed by P&W eliminates repetitive inspections.

And not only engines, but components like propellers can add up to a real piece of change when overhaul or replacement time comes around. One chief pilot told us his company had to lay out $24,000 for an overhaul involving Hartzell blade replacements. He was not happy that the replacements came at 4,700 hours, feeling they should have gone 6,000 hours with a second overhaul. The first overhaul had cost $7,274.

Modifications

The big name in King Air mods is Raisbeck Engineering in Seattle, Wash., (206) 763-2000. A raft of upgrades is available to improve performance, load and cabin noise level in the 90 series—along with the 100s, 200s and 300s, for that matter.

The most dramatic change is accomplished by installing four-blade Hartzell props in place of the standard three-blade propellers. Benefits claimed are big reductions in cockpit and cabin noise, thanks to reduced prop rpm in all flight regimes, and cooler ITT because of better prop ram air.

Also, Dual Aft Body Strakes can be substituted for the single Beech ventral fin to provide extra stability in the yaw axis, eliminating the need for yaw dampeners.

With the "Quiet Turbofan Propellers" and strakes, C90, C90A and E90 King Airs are eligible for increased gross weight (up by 400 pounds in the E90).

Raisbeck also offers main landing gear doors for the F90s to cut drag from dangling wheels. Wing lockers can be installed on all the King Airs to add 16 cubic feet of extra baggage space and permit another 600 pounds of cargo. To improve aesthetics, exhaust stack fairings are available to prevent soot deposits on engine nacelles.

Purchased separately, the new prop system for the various Model 90s costs about $39,295 installed; the strakes, $6,300; wing lockers $24,125.

Engine Upgrades

In light of the high cost of overhauling the old -6 and -20 engines, some might wonder if it wouldn't pay to simply upgrade to the -21 or -28 engines. Well, some firms have STCs to do just that, but the price of the replacement engines normally outweighs the price of the aircraft itself. So that business has pretty much gone down the drain.

Wing Straps

As we mentioned before, Western Aircraft Maintenance in Boise, (800) 333-3442 offers the Saunders spar strap. Tom Halverson there estimates they've made the mods on about 400 King Airs so far, representing about 10 percent of the fleet. He figures the strap offers not only peace of mind but an economic benefit, since with the straps installed the mandatory 1,000-hour wing spar check called for by AD 89-25-10 can be extended to 3,000 hours.

Cost of the strap installed in Boise is about $23,000, or a bit higher in the field. The stainless steel strap, which weighs 65 pounds installed, is said to cause no measurable speed loss.

After we heard from reports in the field that this program might be in jeopardy, however, because of a negative review by Morrison Knudsen, the company that owns Western Aircraft Maintenance, we queried the firm. A spokesman said they were not canceling the wing spar efforts, though Western was not the sole source of the spar mods any more.

Another upgrade program offered by Western Aircraft Maintenance replaces the electrical landing gear system in the older King Airs with hydraulic systems. Cost is $35,000 installed at Boise.

The Beech "bridge" spar strengthening kit had cost about $28,000 and was done only in Salina, Kans. Beech reports that the modification was made to 63 King Airs, but the project has faded away due to lack of interest. The last one they worked on was late in 1989.

Owner Comments

We have operated a BE C90A, since new, for six years and 1,800 hours. Performance is as advertised. Speeds have been 235 knots (actual: winter 241, summer 231) at charted torque limits of 650° ITT.

Maintenance: Access is good, but changing the filter in the hydraulic power pack causes a loss of a cup of 5606 fluid, which flows under an array of electrical circuit boards (PCBs) and settles several bays aft by the flap actuator. An external panel access to this filter would be helpful.

Engine anti-ice fail light illumination often gives a false indication.

Hot sections at 1,750 hours: $3,000 on one (no new parts) and $10,000 on the other (shroud ring, seal and two ITT probes replaced). Aircraft is on P&W trend monitoring.

Wish list (realistic): Convert the fuel system to that of the F90 series for longer range and simpler management (fewer pumps and switches). Increase pressurization to 6.0 psi.

Wish list (pure): Provide for an optional installation of PT6A-135 engines for performance enhancement.

Name withheld on request

Passengers love it, pilots love it, and my treasurer puts up with it. What more could you ask?

We purchased our 1979 King Air C90 three-and-a-half years ago and have been very pleased with the aircraft. We moved up from a 58P Baron that was plagued with high maintenance costs and high downtime. Our expenses are still high, but the reliability has increased tenfold. The plane is flown about 450 hours a year, and we have had to cancel fewer than a half dozen trips due to mechanical problems.

All maintenance and avionics work is performed by Elliott Beechcraft in Moline, Ill. Service is first rate, and they do an excellent job meeting any rush demands I may have. Beech parts aren't cheap, or even reasonable, but they are readily accessible, and parts delays have not been a problem. My all-inclusive operating costs for everything, including reserves (but not pilot salaries), have averaged $496 per hour over the last three years.

While I'm on the subject, I have to put in a plug for FlightSafety and the training they give for the King Air, specifically at the Wichita Beech King Air Center. I believe in going beyond the insurance requirements and return for recurrent training every six to eight months.

I had a gear failure (motor burned out on retraction) while flying single-pilot IFR. The real thing turned out to be easier to handle than the simulator. Since then, there have been several tough flights that I have completed with a simple "Thank you, Flight Safety." The King Air 90 is so easy to fly that it could make some pilots complacent, but it is a complex aircraft that requires recurrent training.

Guy C. Mellick
Davenport, Ia.

I am a 70-year-old ATP, 5,000-hour-plus, active pilot. I have owned 14 aircraft, including one Lear 24F for seven years and three King Airs for 12 years. I currently own a B90 built in 1968. I have previously owned two 1978 E90 models. My current plane was re-engined with PT6-28 engines in 1980 which were extensively updated by P&W in 1985.

Let me first comment generally. The King Air 90 airframe is unequaled in comfort for an owner-flown personal plane. The PT6, as is widely known, is unequaled for reliability. I cannot remember in 1,500 hours of King Air operation a flight canceled for engine problems.

Maintenance is straightforward and easy to obtain throughout the U.S. It would be hard for me to overstate my satisfaction with both the plane and the engines.

I live in the Rocky Mountains and can advise that the only 90 series plane worth having out here is the -28-powered plane. The -20 and -21-powered aircraft, even the C90A, are frequently temperature limited at altitude on hot summer days. Even the E90 (-28) is occasionally temp limited.

Oddly enough, the best of my three King Airs is the -28-powered B90. Reason: no bleed air is used for cabin heat or pressurization, resulting in a much quieter cabin and much cooler-running turbines.

I am never torque limited (compared to the E90) and rarely ever temp limited. The first and only hot section inspection was at 1,750 hours, against Beech's recommended 1,250 hours. The ITT at cruise on the B90 (-28) ranges from 600°-650°, producing a 235-knot cruise at 23,000 feet at 400 lbs/hr. The E90 departing at full gross, climbing to 25,000 at 690°, yields only 222 knots cruise at 680° in cruise. The difference is use of bleed air.

Sound level in the E90 in the left pilot seat is 92 dBA. In the B90 it is 87 dBA. Cabin in the B90 is 80-82 dBA vs. about 85-87 dBA in the 90s using bleed air.

I cannot comment on the C-90s except for a demo flight climbing out of Jeffco at 680° ITT, ROC was only about 800 fpm. I can depart Aspen (7,800 feet) at 680° at 1,500-2,000 fpm. The message is that a significant premium was paid by Beech for 90 performance to displace the supercharger and cabin heater with bleed air pressure and heat.

The old supercharger, properly installed, has a formidable life in the several-thousand-hour range. The kerosene cabin heater with an igniter cleaning every 25-50 hours provides at least the comfort of bleed air cabin heat.

As for cabin loading and cg considerations, it would be very difficult to get out of cg, except on purpose. Flight characteristics are unequaled in my lifetime experience. It is the best all-around airplane ever built.

Beech is not nearly as supportive as when Mrs. Beech owned the company. Being owned by Raytheon has sadly degraded the company's concern for Beech owners, and service provided by a "company-owned store" stinks. Too bad, but as lousy as that has gotten, it will never destroy the integrity of the 90 series planes.

In 1978 I kept track of maintenance costs for a new plane for several years. They averaged about $40 per hour then. My current estimate (budget) is about $100/hour. Fuel for normal operations is 60 gph.

Insurance is $9,000 per year. Engine reserve is $50-$60/hour for overhaul, and I haven't had an HSI since 1979, so I don't have current data. Total cash out of pocket is about $250 per hour or about $1 per statute mile.

Parts availability is first class—not necessarily from Beech, since there are many overhaul shops supplying almost anything you want for the 90s from the A/B 90 on to the current model.

We are running my machine on Part 135 and have been able to obtain almost anything we want over night.

In summary, old or new, the King Air 90 is in a class by itself, a product of sheer genius, considering it has changed relatively little in 25 years. If somebody gave me a new plane, I would immediately swap it for a King Air. There is no propeller-driven plane that can compare.

John F. Carr
Snowmass Village, Colo.

Bellanca Viking

An unusual amalgalm of materials—wood, metal tubes and Dacron—help shape the Viking persona and aesthetics. Handling is marked by very light ailerons, but heavy pitch forces.

The Bellanca Viking is one of general aviation's split personalities: a powerful four-place retractable that has great handling and superb built-in craftsmanship, but on the other hand is an antiquated design that's cramped, noisy, short-ranged and not very fast.

On top of that, the fuselage is fabric-covered and the wing is made of wood. But Viking prices are low on the used-plane market, so you can get a lot of airplane for your dollar if you're willing to put up with its idiosyncrasies—and to vigilantly guard against dry rot in the wing, which has triggered several fatal Viking wing failures and much expensive repair work.

Genealogy

The Viking's family tree (heh, heh) traces its roots back to the old Bellanca Cruisaire, a triple-tailed retractable taildragger design that looked old-fashioned three decades ago. The first model 17 Viking appeared in 1967, powered by a 300-hp Continental IO-520-D. Over the years, major changes were few, consisting mainly of various engine options. The Continental-powered Viking was called the 17-30, while the 17-31 was powered by a 290-hp (later 300-hp) Lycoming, either normally aspirated or turbocharged. Either engine was available most years.

Other changes were few, however. The original hydraulic gear and flap actuation system was notoriously balky, and was redesigned midway through the 1968 model year with electric flaps. (If you're looking at a '68 model, go for the new system.) The complex fuel system—five tanks, two fuel selectors, eight possible combinations of selector settings and several sometimes incomprehensible gauges—was simplified a bit in 1974, after a spate of fuel-mismanagement accidents. But other than that, the newest Viking is not much different from the oldest.

Production continued at a modest rate—in the peak production year, 1973, just under 200 were built—until Bellanca Aircraft Corp. went bankrupt in 1980, the year the Great General Aviation Depression began. But in 1984, Bellanca bucked the disaster trend, reorganized, and put the Viking back into production—although on a very limited custom-order basis. Only nine were built over the next two years, and none at all in 1986. Two each were sold in 1987 and 1988, but some new dealers were added in 1989: 13 were sold in '89 and '90. Orders dried up again, though, and has been was only one delivery in each of the last three years.

Resale Value

For all the praises sung by loyal owners, the Viking is held in low esteem on the used-plane market. Prices go as low as $24,000, a mere pittance for a 300-hp retractable. A 1980 IFR Viking can be had for $67,000, about the same price as a piddling four-cylinder 200-hp Mooney of the same vintage. The more common 1972-1975 models typically fetch $33,000-$39,000—less than half the price tag of an F33A Bonanza of similar vintage and horsepower.

But looked at another way—by the yardstick of original purchase price—the Viking doesn't come off so badly. New prices were quite low to begin with, so the Viking's percentage of value retained is at least decent. A 1978 Viking, for example, rolled out the factory door for only $68,000, so the current retail Aircraft Bluebook Price Digest value of $55,000 represents 81 percent of the original price. Compare that to a 1978 Cessna Skylane RG, which sold new for $64,000 and now commands $60,500, 95 percent of original value. The Viking isn't that far behind the Cessna—and it's about on a par with a 1978 Piper Turbo Arrow, which has retained about 83 percent. It should be noted that all of these values are up 15-20 percent compared to only a few years ago.

For all its power, a Viking's typical useful load is only about 1,000 pounds. Paint scheme suggests a third side window though none exists. Note big, bulbous gear doors.

Performance

By the standards of other 300-hp aircraft, the Viking is a bit of a woofer. Book cruise speeds range from a modest 163-165 knots for the normally aspirated models, and owners typically report cruise speeds in the 150-160-knot range. That's pretty pokey for a 300-hp four-placer with a tight cabin, and a good 10 knots slower than big six-seaters like the 210 and A36 Bonanza. "We feel it's about 10-15 knots too slow," concedes one owner.

The turbocharged version does better at high altitude, of course. At 20,000 feet, one owner reports 190 knots. Not bad, but still a bit slower than other turbocharged 300-hp aircraft.

It's not hard to see why the Viking falls well short of speed-demon status; the fuselage is an aerodynamicist's nightmare, with sharp edges everywhere. The main landing gear dangle beneath the wing even in the retracted position, covered by unsightly blisters. The horizontal tail has a strut. Apparently these aerodynamic atrocities are not compensated for by the wood-skinned wing, which has nary a rivet or seam lap and may be the smoothest wing on any production lightplane.

The Viking climbs strongly, however. ("Climb performance is just shy of a rocket ship," reports one hyperenthusiastic owner.) Older models, with gross weights of only 3,200 pounds, have book climb rates of up to 1,800 fpm. Although these numbers are highly suspect (the Bellanca marketing department was known for, shall we say, wild optimism about its products) owners do report excellent rate of climb, much better than Bonanzas and 210s. (Not surprising; the Beeches and Cessnas have gross weights from 50 to 800 pounds higher than the Viking, and in most cases slightly less power.)

The Viking also performs well at high altitudes. "I routinely flew over the Rockies at 16,000 west, 17,000 east, at gross weight," reports the owner of a 1972 non-turbo Viking. He also claims to have once climbed to 16,000 feet with the gear down.

Aft of the fuselage is a 15-gallon auxiliary tank that yields about an hour's flight at cruise.

Payload/Range

Again, the Viking suffers in comparison to more modern aircraft. The Viking structure is very heavy; a typical empty weight is about 2,300 pounds, which is 500-600 pounds more than a comparable-sized Mooney. (The bigger engine accounts for about 200 pounds of the difference, but the rest is apparently airframe and systems.)

For all its power, the Viking's typical useful load is only 1,000 pounds or so—less for a lavishly equipped IFR aircraft. That's not much more than 200-hp retractables like the Mooney and Arrow. And unfortunately, the Viking's bigger fuel appetite eats into available cabin load even more. Fuel capacity is either 60 or 75 gallons; with the bigger tanks full, cabin load is limited to a measly 550 pounds. "With full fuel, my 1973 Viking will carry three passengers, or two passengers and baggage," reports one owner. Comments another about his turbocharged version: "Lycoming engine, heavier than Continental, plus two turbos, equals a pathetic full-fuel legal load of two adults plus bags."

Compare that to a Cessna 210, which has a useful load pushing 1,400 pounds in some cases, and can typically haul 90 gallons and four people with bags. On the other hand, we imagine many owners take advantage of the Viking's excess climb performance by exceeding max gross weight on takeoff.

The Viking's standard 60-gallon fuel supply is woefully inadequate (three hours at fast cruise would be pushing it) and even the 75-gallon system is marginal to feed an engine that typically burns 13-15 gph at cruise and over 20 gph during climb. Count on a practical IFR range of no more than 450 nm with the 60-gallon tanks, and perhaps 600 nm with the 75-gallon tanks. And that's with tanks full. With all four seats full of FAA-standard 170-pounders and 100 pounds of baggage, the law-abiding Viking pilot will be limited to perhaps 40 gallons of fuel—enough to fly 250 nm with IFR reserves.

Handling

The Viking is almost universally praised for its light, smooth aileron control. "The best flying characteristics, bar none, of any airplane flying today," raves one owner. "It practically begs to be rolled." Gushes another, "It spoils you for riding in any other airplane." The Viking is one of the few production airplanes to have flown regular airshow aerobatic routines. (Debbie Gary, the acro ace who married the president of Bellanca, flew the Viking shows a few years ago; nowadays, a mysterious masked fellow called the Avenger does a Viking routine.)

But pay attention on landing. Power-off, with gear and flaps out, the Viking has an awesome sink rate that owners liken to Steinway pianos and elevators. "Below 100 mph, exercise caution," warns one. "The aircraft is heavy and the power curve is deep." Comments another, "Precise speed control is necessary to assure an acceptable landing." A third advises, "One has to apply aggressive back pressure after flaring to avoid a bouncy landing." Several Viking pilots told us they do not lower full flaps until landing is assured; apparently, even with 300-hp, a full-flaps go-around is quite dicey.

The steep decent angle, however, does allow a skilled Viking pilot to make very short landings—and the airplane has the power to get out of a short field as well.

IFR stability is reasonably good, according to owners. "It rides very well in turbulence, much better than an Arrow or Bonanza," says one. On takeoff, however, a heavy foot is required on the rudder to counteract the torque effect of the big engine.

Creature Comforts

The Viking's cabin dimensions are modest at best, a reflection of its 1930s design heritage. "The cabin is small for two guys my size," reports a 210-pound Viking pilot. Even a rabid pro-Viking zealot admitted that the cabin is "not roomy." He's 5-11 and 160 pounds, and says he has plenty of room for piloting tasks without bumping elbows with his front-seat passenger. Wives, kids and other small-to-medium-sized people will find the rear seats comfy enough, but big men will feel cramped.

Interior appointments draw raves, however. Many Vikings have a leather or crushed-velour upholstery that puts the chintzy interiors of Pipers and Cessnas to shame. Cabin noise, on the other hand, is awful, a fact that virtually ever Viking owner we heard from complained about. "Atrocious," said one. "Ear plugs or noise-attenuating headphones are a must."

Wings are hand crafted in the old-fashioned way, with sitka spruce spars and wooden ribs. These are sheathed in mahogany and dipped in preservative. Corrosion's no problem, but anual inspections must be made for dry rot.

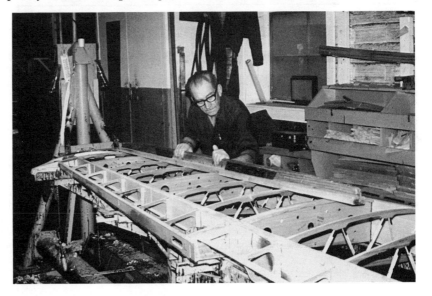

Engine Choice

Although power output is the same from the 300-hp Continental IO-520-K and Lycoming IO-540-K engines, the original buyers seemed to prefer the Continental-powered 17-30 version, which typically outsold the Lycoming 17-31 model by about two to one. This was probably due partly to the higher price tag of the 17-31 (in 1973, for example, the price difference was $1,750), and partly to the higher listed cruise speeds of the 17-30. (We doubt there's much difference in real-world speed, however; theoretically there should be no difference, and owners report no consistent pattern.) The 17-31 was also listed at about 60 pounds heavier than the 17-30. The Continental preference still holds in the used-plane marketplace. Otherwise identical 17-30s command from $500 to $1,000 more than the 17-31. Higher overhaul costs of the Lycoming (currently about $20,000, compared to $15,000 for the Continental) may play a role here, although the Lycoming's 2000-hour TBO makes the per-hour cost only a smidgin higher than the 1700-hour Continental's.

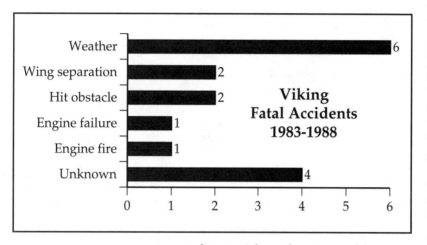

We don't think there's much to choose between the two engines; both are reasonably reliable, and we have no reports of unusual problems with either in the Viking. We imagine most pilots will simply follow their personal preference and brand loyalty, but the individual history and condition of a particular engine should be a more decisive factor than the nameplate.

The turbo is another matter. Prospective buyers should carefully consider whether the extra cost (about $6,000 in a late-model Viking), complexity, fuel and potential overheating problems are worth the benefits of turbocharging. In most cases, outside of the Rockies, at least, the answer is probably not. One reader who's owned both turbo and non-turbo Vikings advises against the turbo version.

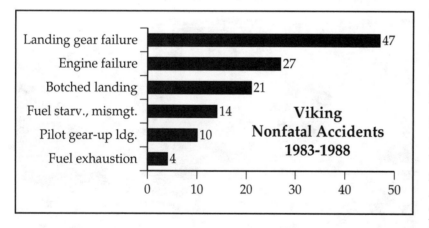

Older models have a simple manual wastegate, which, properly used, minimizes stress on the turbocharger. Later versions have an automatic wastegate that can be turned off by the pilot.

Safety

Here is perhaps another reason for the Viking's low value on the used-plane market: a relatively high accident rate. An *Aviation Consumer* study of accident rates for single-engine retractables from 1972-1981 showed the Viking ranked a mediocre 12th out of 17 in fatal accidents, and 13th in total accidents. Actual rates were 2.7 fatals per 100,000 flight hours (within a range of 0.8 to 3.3 for the 16 other aircraft tallied) and 11.0 total accidents, within a range of 4.6 to 15.0.

A detailed look at the Viking accident history shows two major design-related problems: wing spar failures and fuel mismanagement.

The Bellanca Viking's history of wing failures is a long one, and it is by no means all in the past; a 17-30 suffered a wing separation as recently as 1986. Up through 1978, the Viking experienced a total of seven fatal wing separations, which gave it a breakup rate comparable to that of the notorious Beech V-tail Bonanza. A 1975 wing failure that occurred during illegal aerobatics was discovered to have been caused by wood rot, and it triggered an AD in 1976 calling for careful inspections. Two more rot-induced failures occurred in 1978, however, and the directive has been revised periodically since then.

A 1983 failure was especially worrisome, however, because the rot occurred in a place that was not visible under the required inspection procedures. (The current document regarding wing-rot inspections is Bellanca service letter 87A, which requires a meticulous inspection of the spar with every annual.)

Six of the 11 Vikings we're aware of that suffered structural failures were 1969 or 1970 models. This may be merely a statistical anomaly—or a reflection of the fact that the older airplanes have deteriorated more—but one must also consider the possibility of a variation in wood, preservatives or glue. Bellanca insists there have been no changes in the design or manufacture of the Viking wing (except for the installation of drain holes after the 1976 AD).

The Viking's sobering record of wing failures suggests that no Viking should be considered for purchase unless it has been thoroughly inspected for wood rot in accordance with service letter 87A by an experienced Bellanca mechanic who knows what he's looking for. (Most mechanics these days think wood is a material for making wall studs and toothpicks.)

Other Viking fatal accidents show no particular pattern. An FAA print-out of accidents from 1983-88 shows 15 fatals. Beyond the two wing failures already mentioned, five were weather-related, and four were unknown. One fellow hit a mountain on a photo flight, another tried to go around and hit trees. Engine failures caused two fatal Viking crashes; one was an in-flight fire, the other a seizure after takeoff triggered by a wrongly installed oil breather that let all the oil drain out.

Cockpit is cozy but luxurious. Fuel mismanagement is one of the aircraft's bugaboos, according to accident statistics.

When it comes to non-fatal Viking accidents, one category stands out in bold relief: fuel mismanagement. In the 1970s, fully a quarter of all Viking non-fatal accidents were caused by fuel mismanagement, an extraordinarily high percentage. (One year, 1973, an astounding 50 percent of Viking accidents were the result of fuel mismanagement. It may be no coincidence that the fuel system was redesigned the next year.)

Things have improved somewhat in recent years, but the FAA accident printout covering the years 1983-88 shows nearly two dozen fuel foul-ups. A typical accident brief: "Engine quit after takeoff, forced landing in field. Fuel selector on empty tank, fuel quantity gauge showed full." Or this one: "Left main full, right main empty, right aux three gallons. Selector on right aux. Aux tanks approved for level flight only."

The problem is exacerbated by fuel system quirks that sometimes make it difficult to restart the engine after a tank has run dry in 1967-73 models. Even a former president of the Bellanca Owners' Society admitted that, if the fuel boost pump is not used, it's possible to lose up to 5,000 feet altitude before the engine will restart. On the other hand, if the fuel boost pump is turned on, there's a very good chance the engine will be flooded out and quit. "You've got to have a delicate touch on the boost pump and tickle it just right," he says. The 1974 and later Vikings have a two-position high-low boost pump and an admonition not to use the high boost position when switching tanks.

Gear collapses and gear-up landings, both inadvertent and mechanical, accounted for nearly half of all Viking non-fatal accidents from 1983-88. These rarely hurt anybody, but they are embarrassing and expensive, nevertheless. Other unusual trends: electrical failures and, in 17-30 models, muffler failures that allowed hot gases to leak and melt the magneto wires, triggering engine failure.

The evidence suggests that the later-model Vikings have better safety records. Post-1970 models have a far better record of structural integrity, and post-1973 models have a simpler fuel system, although it still leaves a lot to be desired in terms of human engineering.

Maintenance

We've gotten mixed reports on Viking maintenance. Some owners complain about high maintenance (one described a succession of $3,000 annuals and describes it as "cheap to buy, expensive to own"), while others praise it as simple and reliable and mention numbers like $500. It seems that a Viking that is hangared and well cared for is reasonably cheap to maintain, but leave it outdoors and let a few little things start to go, and it may drive you to the poorhouse, particularly if there's wing spar trouble. Overall, the typical Viking annual seemed to run about $1,500.

Owners were virtually unanimous, however, in emphasizing the need to hangar a Viking. "Absolutely imperative!" said one. "A crucial necessity," echoed another. The primary reason is to prevent the accumulation of moisture that can trigger wood rot in the wing, but it's also a good idea to protect the fuselage fabric from ultraviolet radiation and moisture.

The supposed "lifetime" Dacron covering will last a very long time in a hangar, but owners report recover jobs in as few as six years if the aircraft is left outside.

Cost/Performance/Specifications

Model	Year	Average Retail Price	75% Cruise Speed (kt)	Useful Load (lb)	Std/Opt Fuel (gal)	Engines	TBO (hr)	Overhaul Cost @
17-30	1967-70	$19,500	163	1,300	58/92	300-hp Cont. IO-520-D	1,700	$10,300
17-30A	1971-73	$24,000	163	1,125	60/75	300-hp Cont. IO-520-K	1,700	$10,300
17-30A	1973-75	$28,000	163	1,125	60/75	300-hp Cont. IO-520-K	1,700	$10,300
17-30A	1976-78	$40,000	163	1,125	60/75	300-hp Cont. IO-520-K	1,700	$10,300
17-30A	1979-80	$52,000	174	1,125	68-83	300-hp Cont. IO-520-K	1,700	$10,300
17-30A	1984-86	$95,000	163	1,125	60/75	300-hp Cont. IO-520-K	1,700	$10,300
17-30A	1987-88	$123,000	163	1,125	60/75	300-hp Cont. IO-520-K	1,700	$10,300
17-31A	1971-73	$23,000	165	1,078	68/83	300-hp Lyc. IO-540-K1E5	2,000	$12,800
17-31A	1974-76	$28,000	165	1,078	68/83	300-hp Lyc. IO-540-K1E5	2,000	$12,800
17-31A	1977-78	$38,000	165	1,078	68/83	300-hp Lyc. IO-540-K1E5	2,000	$12,800
17-31ATC	1970-72	$26,000	187	953	68/83	300-hp Lyc. IO-540-K1E5	2,000	$12,800
17-31ATC	1973-75	$30,000	187	953	68/83	300-hp Lyc. IO-540-K1E5	2,000	$12,800
17-31ATC	1976-78	$44,000	187	953	68/83	300-hp Lyc. IO-540-K1E5	2,000	$12,800
17-31ATC	1979	$57,000	187	953	68/83	300-hp Lyc. IO-540-K1E5	2,000	$12,800

We have to agree: Don't even consider buying a Viking unless you have hangar space available, and be sure to factor in hangar cost as part of the normal operating expenses. A wing spar problem can be hideously expensive. "It's real easy to go through $5,000," says Peter Connor of Yankee Aviation Services in Plymouth, Mass., who's repaired a number of Viking wings.

The other potential Viking bank-account buster is a fuselage fabric job. Typical cost is about $15,000.

Note doors covering the main gear, but not the nose wheel. The beautiful Dacron skin surface and underlying wooden wing beg to be hangared for longevity.

The Viking's landing gear is a touchy area. Comments one owner, "The nose gear linkages do not have adequate provision for lubrication." He has his mechanic completely disassemble and lube the gear at every annual.

Reports another, "The one maintenance weakness that needs to be mentioned is the landing gear. It is extremely critical to adjustment, and parts of it wear out regularly. I have very carefully rebushed the whole system, repaired cracks in the main struts, replaced countless O-rings and in general worried over the gear a great deal. I have had to replace the power pack twice. Despite all this care, it has failed to come up on several occasions, and I have had a couple of emergency gear extensions as well. I love the airplane, but I wish it had a better landing gear."

Other repeated problems include fuel tank leaks, especially in the 1967-73 models, and hydraulic leaks.

On the plus side, the Viking's fine workmanship and structural strength draw raves. The planes were essentially hand-built by old-time woodworking experts, some of whom still build and repair Vikings in the Alexandria factory. And the wings are tough. One owner describes a bird strike that splattered blood and feathers over the leading edge, but didn't even scratch the surface. (A metal wing, of course, would have been badly dented.)

The Viking is one of those airplanes that should be maintained by a specialist in the breed. The pre-eminent Viking service center is Miller Flying Service in Plainview, Tex. Owners describe their work as expert and friendly, but expensive. "They treat you like part of the family" was a phrase used by more than one Viking owner. Other good Viking shops are Alexandria Aviation in Alexandria, Minn., Air Repair in Santa Paula, Calif., and Cap Aviation in Reading, Pa. For a list of other knowledgeable Viking mechanics, call the factory at (612) 762-1501.

Service Difficulty Reports

A five-year printout of Service Difficulty Reports from the FAA confirm that landing gear glitches are the Viking's Achilles' heel. We counted nearly 50 cases of landing gear malfunctions of all kinds—nearly a third of the total reports. Primary landing gear villains were cracked drag strut brackets and worn bolt holes in the nose drag braces.

Other chronic problems on the FAA sheet: dry rot in the spar and ribs, broken mufflers (AD 76-23-3 requires 100-hour inspections), and bad engine mounts (AD 77-22-2 requires 100-hour inspections or installation of a beefup kit).

Owner's Organization

The Bellanca Champion Club offers support for both Vikings and Champions. Larry D'Attilio in Brookfield, Wisc. publishes the Bellanca Contact newsletter for owners. Phone (414) 784-0318.

Owner Comments

Peter Connor is a Viking owner. He's also president of Yankee Aviation Services in Plymouth, Mass., a former Bellanca Service Center. He describes himself as "intimately familiar" with the Viking series, and offers the following tips about dry rot and other troublesome areas that should be closely monitored during pre-purchase inspections:

A large percentage of Vikings look beautiful, and many times one will have been recently painted. Unfortunately, the prospective buyer (and uninformed mechanics as well) look only at the shiny paint, not what's underneath. The water and dry-rot problems very often occur from tears and chips in the dope finish under the enamel or polyurethane top coat. These cracks and holes must be patched before repainting. Very often, I've found that they're not. Close inspection of the wing walk is a must.

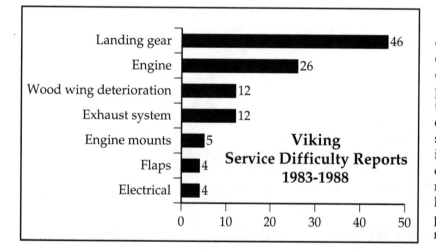

Viking
Service Difficulty Reports
1983-1988

It's a piece of mahogany plywood secured with wood screws. If there's any evidence of cracking along the seams or loosening of the screws, remove the panel and inspect the spar. In fact, on the early Super Vikings, this wing panel was screwed directly into the rear spar. The dry-rot AD, 76-08-04, requires inspection in accordance with Bellanca service letter 87A. This requires removal of wing root fairings, landing light openings, fuel transmitter cover plates and air vent covers at each annual inspection.

Check very closely to make sure they aren't painted over and have been resealed with the correct material. People say that you can detect bad wood by tapping on it. No way! It takes a very detailed inspection of the spars. In our shop, we perform a spar moisture test using a Delmhorst moisture meter, as recommended by SL 87A, on all annual inspections, and we strongly recommend it on a pre-purchase inspection. We charge $195 for this test. I believe we are the only facility in New England that has this tester. Carefully inspect the area where the flap and aileron hinges attach to the wing structure. Over-inflating the air-oil struts on a Viking will prevent the main gear from retracting completely. Mechanics not familiar with the airplane, or who don't have the service manual, sometimes do this. We find a number of Vikings with bent or broken firewall/nosegear mount brackets. This is due to the connection between the rudder and nosewheel, which, if the pilot isn't careful, cause the nosewheel to touch down in a cocked position, especially in a crosswind. Cost of a thorough annual inspection, including a proper spar inspection, should be around $875. With repair of normal discrepancies, we find the total cost usually runs $1,400 to $2,000.

I owned two Bellanca Vikings, consecutively a 1973 normally aspirated Continental, and a 1974 Turbo Lycoming for nine years, total about 700 hours for the two. There were very few troubles with either plane, but a shop that understands Bellancas is important. My recommendations: Air Repair, Santa Paula, Calif., and Miller Flying Service, Plainview, Tex.

I must emphasize the importance of keeping the wings in good shape, inspected by someone who has Bellanca experience. Dry rot is both dangerous and expensive. Spares can be iffy, but Air Repair maintains a warehouse of parts, and we never failed to find what was required, either new or used. Soon after buying the first one, I realized that a hangar was essential to protecting and preserving the wood and fabric.

Positives: outstanding aileron response, which put some fun into flying, eye appeal on the ramp, reasonable maintenance and inspection costs, modest price on the used market. Negatives: noisy, small cabin, limited payload (especially the turbo version), not as fast as people think (or the book claims), not as fuel-efficient as other retractables with same-size engines.

Wayne Thoms
N. Hollywood, Calif.

I have owned a 1974 Bellanca 17-31ATC for the last eight years. The plane's strong suit is performance: strength and speed, but not payload. We burn 15 gph and get an honest 200 mph at 10,000-12,000 feet. We outrun most Bonanzas and Cessna 210s. Other good points are fit and finish and interior lighting. It is comforting to sit inside a steel roll cage. Stalls are gentle.

The slender horizontal tail is made of wood and supported by an old-fashioned strut.

Weaknesses are the small cabin, limited payload, and only 75 gallons of fuel. Useful load is what you'd expect of a plane with two-thirds the power, but it is overbuilt and hell for stout. It is heavy, so we avoid rough fields even though ground clearance is adequate. The glide ratio is reasonable, but power off at low speed, it has the sink rate of a Steinway piano.

John Trudel
Scappoose, Ore.

We have owned a 1972 Super Viking for four years. We have the Continental engine, which gives us initial rates of climb in the 1,500-fpm range. This tapers off to 700-900 fpm at our normal cruise altitudes of 7,000-8,000 feet. Takeoff runs, even with full loads, average less than 1,000 feet. Cruise speed is 150 knots on approximately 14 gph at a setting of 22/2400. (We do not have the wheel blister option.) The cruise speeds are satisfactory, but for this engine output and fuel burn, it is about 10-15 knots slow. We have the 60-gallon fuel system, which I

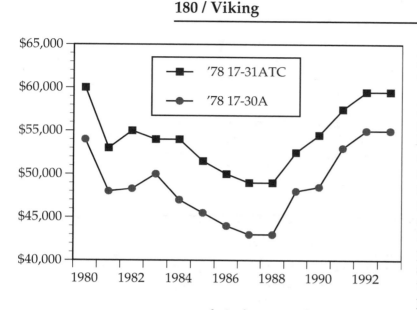

Legend:
- ■ '78 17-31ATC
- ● '78 17-30A

(Price chart, vertical axis $40,000 to $65,000, horizontal axis 1980 to 1992)

think makes the airplane a bit short-legged for serious long-distance travel, especially IFR.

I have about 1,100 hours in a large spread of airplanes, and the Viking is beyond compare in the balance of its controls. This sweetness gets a little sloppy at low speeds, however, and I feel this is why many Bellanca pilots fly fast approaches. It is also very much a trim airplane, especially on landing. Pitch control gets quite heavy with power reductions and slower airspeeds. Sink rates can initially be a little unnerving to the novice Bellanca pilot who may apply too much flap too early in the approach.

Overall comfort is good. Shoulder room is not bad if you have the front seats staggered a couple of inches. The baggage area is limited. We now have two small children, and have had to cut back our long-distance traveling because we don't have the volume to carry all the associated baby paraphernalia. Cabin sound levels are atrocious.

The fuel system betrays the ancient origins of this aircraft. We have two 15-gallon main tanks and two 17-gallon aux tanks. Unfortunately, there is only a main and aux fuel gauge. When using the mains, you can monitor fuel in the active main tank and one of the aux tanks. The situation is worse when using the aux tanks. The main gauge goes inactive, and only the selected aux tank registers on the aux gauge. Proper fuel management takes quite a bit of practice. (I can only imagine what it's like with the optional third aux tank.)

Vikings have an automatic gear-extension system with no frills. Gear drops when the airspeed falls below 83 knots, except at full throttle.

The overhead trim crank seems archaic, but once I adjusted to it, I preferred it to the trim wheels of more modern designs. The landing gear is a good but slow design. Loss of hydraulic pressure causes the gear to lower, but damage can occur because the pump continues to cycle in an attempt to get the gear up again. This can quickly burn up the motor.

Maintenance is one category that is not pleasant to talk about. We purchased the airplane in a fairly rough state with a high-time engine, and in the ensuing four years we have practically rebuilt this airplane. First we had a leaky fuel tank, then a hydraulic leak caused by an exhaust system failure that cooked the hydraulic hose. A crack in the left landing gear required a complete replacement. Then came the propeller and motor mount ADs. A mechanic well-versed in the nuances of the Bellanca is necessary.

Frank Motycka
Midland, Tex.

Boeing Stearman

For pilots who consider the modern lightplane yawn-provoking, there is a robust, swaggering alternative guaranteed to blast away boredom and represent a spanking-good investment in fun, sport and aeronautical assets. Searchers who reach beyond the more humdrum realm of the Luscombes, Navions and J-3 Cubs will stumble upon a treasure lode of classics known as the Boeing Stearman Model 75s.

The great charm of these lusty biplane warriors is that they were built like the classic brick biffy and cranked out in vast armadas. And the parts that aren't still legion can be made by a competent mechanic with a small outlay in fuss and bother.

Even the old radial engines have been guaranteed a kind of immortality since the same basic type (220-hp Continental) used in many Stearmans was built in great numbers as powerplants for military tanks. And this has left a serendipitous legacy of still-unused engine cylinders. Combine these practical considerations with the aircraft's intrinsic panache and machismo, and the appeal is obvious.

History

About 8,500 Boeing Stearman Model 75s were built over a nine-year span from 1936 to 1945 as military trainers. A couple of thousand are still left. For the Army, the airplanes were designated PT (primary trainer) -13s, -17s and 18s. The Navy designated them N2S. The nickname for both services was the Kaydet. The Royal Canadian Air Force received 300 winterized PT-17s labeled PT-27s. The PT-17s, and the Navy counterpart, the N2S-1, -3 and -4, all with the 220-hp Continental engine, were built in the greatest numbers—about 6,000 during the 1940s. About half as many PT-13s (and Navy N2S-5s) were built with the 225-hp Lycoming radial for which parts now seem to be in very short supply. The third powerplant supplied for the aircraft was the 225-hp Jacobs, with about 150 PT-18s built carrying this engine.

Presaging the future role for some Stearmans in civilian life, a batch of PT-17Bs was actually built for the military as mosquito

Sunday afternoon amid the daisies at Kobelt Field. Ancient, but ageless, this airframe had over 3,000 hours on it.

control dusters. After the war, hundreds of Stearmans were dumped on the market as surplus, available for a song—$200 to $500, some say, in crates. Many of these were snapped up and converted to cropdusting, often with 300-hp or 450-hp engines and a hopper installed in place of the front cockpit.

Buying Tips

For a big, classic, radial-engined airplane, the Stearman can be quite reasonable to buy. *Aircraft Bluebook* records are not kept on them, but typical *Trade-A-Plane* prices run anywhere from about $35,000 to well over $100,000 In fact, this category of aircraft has turned into valuable property, and people have seen their investment turn royally golden.

For the *creme de la creme* in custom conversions, Mid Continent Aircraft Corp. in Hayti, Mo., (314) 359-0500, will totally reconstruct one to like-new condition.

Complete fastidious restorations are also being made by Pete Jones, (601) 846-0228. He rebuilds about 10 Stearmans a year, stripping them down to the basic welded tubing and Sitka spruce. The fuselage frame is jig repaired, sandblasted, epoxy primed and reoiled internally. The wings and center section are given new wood, two coats of polyurethane varnish and new leading and trailing edges.

As for ex-cropdusters, some Stearman aficionados say they've found examples in good condition with extra corrosion protection, but most Stearman critics believe a lot of extra travail and money will probably be needed to bring a tired, old workhorse duster around to top condition because of the hard use and chemical corrosion. Also, the wings may have been clipped.

Word is also that front cockpit hardware is in short supply as restorers seek to convert dusters to the standard tandem cockpit configuration. Furthermore, extra fuselage structural work has to be done to finish the conversion.

Before the needle, there was the ball. . .and precious little else. No vacuum pump worries, however.

The 220-hp Continental powerplant is a popular one, mainly because parts are more readily available than for the Lycoming engines. The nine-cylinder Lycoming may be a bit smoother in operation than the seven-cylinder Continental, but some pilots feel the Continental has "more guts" and a better throttle response. Also, they characterize the Lycoming as a bit greasier and oilier, and the "shaky Jake" Jacobs as the worst in this respect. One nice thing about the Jacobs engines is that they are well supported by Jacobs Service, Inc. at Payson, Ariz., (602) 474-2014.

The McCauley propeller might deter some buyers, since there is an Airworthiness Directive that requires removal for inspection and magnafluxing every 100 hours. A Hamilton-Standard metal prop does not have this limitation. Then again, some of the birds have wooden props. Potential buyers might also keep an eye out for the tailwheel configuration. Originally, the Navy Stearmans had a tailwheel that (1) would swivel freely or (2) lock for takeoff and landing, while the Army models were steerable with the rudder pedals. Obviously, the Army system is more manageable, and lots of Navy models have been converted.

The brake system is a source of constant debate among Stearman owners. Most have long since converted to automotive master cylinders for better durability, though other diehards maintain that the original ones were just fine if you knew how to maintain them. One expert, Larry Kampel, says Cleveland brakes are the best of all, with new-type linings. At any rate, Stearman pilots say you want good brakes since you'll need all the help you can get for proper ground handling with the tailwheel configuration, especially with a nonsteerable tailwheel.

Handling and Performance

Pilots label the Boeing Stearman as a pretty honest, straightforward aircraft that was, after all, designed as a trainer. It will do all the basic aerobatic maneuvers—loops, spins, hammerheads, snap rolls. The engine is not designed for continuous inverted operation, however, and it will quit if you hold it upside down for long.

Also, aerobatic devotees should be aware that it's no Pitts Special—the controls are heavy—heavier than a T-6's, and a protracted spate of aerobatics will leave you arm-weary. The original models had only one set of ailerons, on the lower wings. Some fancy aerobatic mods add another pair of ailerons on the top wings for more maneuverability.

Stearman cognoscenti say you shouldn't worry too much about the wings or tail coming off if the aircraft is in proper condition, since it is supposed to be able to take about 12 Gs positive and seven to nine negative. "Built like a truck" is the favorite description by owners. No speed demon, though, the 220-hp Stearman will climb out at about 70 mph, cruise at about 95 mph behind a nice slow-ticking 1900 rpm max, burning about 12 gph, and come down final at about 70 mph.

A newcomer will be struck by the airplane's general docility. It's like a big kite. It doesn't have or need flaps. "It glides like a brick," said one owner in the time-honored expression. Pull the power off on final, and she'll come down sharply. In a stall, she'll buffet nicely and drop off on a wing. The toughest maneuver in the Stearman's repertoire is probably a gusty crosswind landing. Cockpit visibility of the runway on the flare is nearly nonexistent, and the pilot has to use a sixth sense and great powers of peripheral vision. And he's got to have dancing feet. The landing gear stick out like a pair of giant tree trunks, and they're about as un-yielding when you hit the ground if you haven't eased it on—there's very little give to the oleos; the monster tires probably provide as much cushion as a hard landing will allow. But the tailwheel has the luxury of its own oleo, for what that's worth.

Instrumentation will range from crude original to elaborate custom fittings. Most of the original aircraft came without electrical systems—that meant starting by the old-fashioned inertial crank, or by propping. The high prop intimidates some for hand propping, however. But some models have been updated with batteries and electric starters and navigation lights.

Systems on the airplane are rock-bottom basic. The fuel gauge consists of a graduated plastic tube with a float marker about six inches long dangling from the bottom surface of the upper wing, in the breeze, right in front of the pilot's nose. The fuel tank is located in the center section right above the fuselage. You can switch it on or off—period.

Other system controls are a throttle, mixture and mag switch. The pitch trim control is a simple swiveling knob on the left side of the cockpit—a joy to use, and an object lesson to modern aircraft designers. Naturally, this airplane has a control stick, not a wheel.

Get Parts and Maintenance

Dusters & Sprayers Supply in Chickasha, Okla., (405) 224-1201, is the big name in Stearman parts. President Bob Chambers says they can supply just about any Stearman part needed, and those they don't have they can make under PMA authority in their machine shop.

Chambers claims to have about 3,000 customers in this country as well as in Mexico and Argentina, where they apparently still use the aircraft as trainers.

Dusters & Sprayers even has parts for the Lycoming, Continental and Jacobs engines, and makes all the hardware for the front cockpits except the seats, according to Chambers. Scroungers can also get help locating parts from members of the Stearman Restorers Assn. (more about that later) and from *Trade-A-Plane*.

Although there are quite a few capable mechanics around the country who can work on the aircraft with no great problem due to its straightforward design and construction, the older hands with experience in wood and fabric are preferred, naturally. And a few are known as Stearman specialists. Among them are Larry Kampel of Kampel Enterprises in Wellsville, Pa.; and Tom Cawley of Cawley's Aviation Service at Kobelt Airport in Wallkill, N.Y. For engine overhaul, Gulf Coast Dusting in Houston, Tex., is one of the better known shops (713) 991-3520. Owners say the Stearmans are quite reasonable to maintain. Big front fuselage panels open on hinges and are held up by metal hooks for beautiful access to accessories and the master brake cylinder.

Cork-in-a-tube fuel gauge dangles below the single wing tank. Round mirror aids in inter-cockpit communications.

Construction is straightforward and simple, consisting of a massive, welded tube fuselage with longerons, covered by fabric. The tail is metal with fabric covering; the wings have wooden spars and ribs, and fabric covering, once again.

Originally, the fuel tank in the top wing had no fabric covering, but unless it now does, the tank must be pulled every year to allow an inspection of the center section, to meet the requirements of an AD.

And talk about nice touches, the flying wires that fasten to the horizontal stabilizer go through little plastic viewports, allowing easy walk-around inspection for security—another object lesson for modern designers.

Since the wing ribs are wooden, great care must be taken to ensure against rotting from moisture, especially along the aileron bay. An AD calls for drilling drain holes to prevent moisture accumulation.

A Boeing service bulletin (available from the Stearman Restorers Assn.) outlines the modifications necessary for conversion from the original military to civilian status.

By now, most of these have presumably been complied with, but buyers should confirm. The service bulletin requires items like: no spin strips on the upper wing only, replace the aluminum firewall with a stainless steel one, installation of a battery cutoff switch and CAA-approved position lights on ships with electrical systems.

Books and Manuals

A nice history of the entire Stearman line comes in the *Stearman Guidebook,* by Mitch Mayborn and Peter M. Bowers, published by Flying Enterprise Publications in Dallas, Tex. Air Service Caravan Co. in New Bedford, Mass., (508) 992-1500, can provide Stearman pilot manuals along with maintenance and parts handbooks.

Organizations to Join

As we've already mentioned, the Stearman Restorers Assn. is the one. They publish a nice-looking newsletter and can provide everything from moral support to a clearing house for parts and services. President of the Association is Thomas E. Lowe, 823 Kingston Lane, Crystal Lake, Ill. 60014, (815) 459-6873. They hold an annual fly-in at Galesburg, Ill., the week after Labor Day.

Owner Comments

I first soloed a Stearman in 1948 as a new private pilot. The checkout consisted of three or four landings and seemed easy at the time, but I had flown nothing but tailwheel planes prior to this. I flew the Stearman only a few hours but concluded that if I could ever afford one I would buy one.

The airplane has been very serviceable. It is a fine trainer both for landings and takeoffs and for aerobatics. These skills, well developed and practiced in a Stearman, transfer to adept handling of much more modern and sophisticated airplanes.

Much has been written and said about Stearmans being hard to land. They are not, but need to be kept straight, and even a strong crosswind on a paved runway can be handled with the control available. The aircraft is heavy on the controls, and one needs considerable muscle to do aerobatics. Maneuvers develop relatively slowly and must be properly flown through for good execution. This doesn't make it easy but is a training virtue.

I have flown some indifferently maintained stock Stearmans and also some highly modified working dusters, and they have all flown and handled fine, which says a lot for the underlying strength and design, which are superior to most planes of that vintage.

Fuel consumption on the 300 is about 11.5 gph cross-country and 14 for aerobatics, and roughly one quart of oil per hour. Stearmans seem to be almost universally greeted with affection, but in the last year or so more than one line boy has said, "Gee mister, what kind of airplane is that?"

I've got a pristine PT-27, which was the only Boeing Stearman produced with an electrical system and starter as standard. No other biplane has such delightfully smooth control feel. The input is through torque tubes and bell cranks, so the slack and binding of the ordinary cable setup is absent.

The Stearman is very roomy and solid. Its cowlings are like armor plate and look as if they belong on a DC-4. The tubular framework is truly massive. All this gives you a secure feeling, but with its standard engines, the 225 Lycoming and the 220 Continental, it is unimpressive in climb rate and cruise speed. I'm never in a hurry when I fly my Stearman, so it doesn't bother me. If you want speed or sustained performance in vertical maneuvers, get the P&W 450 model.

Certainly this is the safest biplane around. Besides being overbuilt, it has the most predictable low-speed handling characteristics. The stall is a long time in coming, with all kinds of signals; and with its huge wings you generally can fly out of any problems by releasing back pressure.

Once you get used to the limited forward visibility, the landings are a cinch, though you've got to stay tuned to the rudder on the rollout, particularly in a crosswind since the gear legs are so close together. It is crucially important to keep airflow over that rudder as long as possible.

For this reason newcomers to the Stearman should probably avoid days when the wind is shifting around rapidly. A nice steady 10 knots within 30 degrees of the nose is fine. Always use grass runways when available.

Parts for some old airplanes are impossible to find. You need a tool and die maker for a close friend. The Stearman is a notable exception. Apparently during the war spares were produced in amazing quantities. Any part you want is available right away from outfits like Dusters & Sprayers.

All these old airplanes have wooden wings. A lot of supposedly "rebuilt" Stearmans have 40-year-old wood behind compression members and other out-of-the-way spots. The only way to be sure is to insist on brand-new wings built up from scratch. We dismantled an airplane completely a few years ago after a crack-up. It had a beautiful cover and finish. The wood you could see with the cover off was excellent, but in the inaccessible spots behind permanent fittings dry rot and corrosion were severe.

I've got close to $40,000 in my Stearman. If a man didn't have at least thirty to spend on a completely remanufactured airplane, he'd be better off with a good clip-wing Cub or T-craft.

Cost/Performance/Specifications

Model	Year	Gross Weight (lbs)	Fuel (gals)	Engine	TBO (hrs)	Overhaul Cost
PT-13 N2S-5	1936-41 1943-45	2,950	46-	225-hp Lyc. R-680-B4B, -E	650	
PT-17 PT-27 N2S-1, 3, 4	1940-45	2,950	46-	220-hp Cont. W-670-6A, N	1,000	
PT-18	1940-41	2,950	46-	225-hp Jacobs TC6 R-755-7	1,000	$22,000
Modifications		3,200-3,520		300-hp Lyc. R680-E3, -A, -B	1,500	
				450-hp P&W R-985-AN-1, 3	1,400	$12,500

Cessna 120/140

Cessna's Model 120 and 140 were part of the crowd of post-war two-seat taildraggers. More than 7,000 120s and 140s were built during their six-year production run, and thousands are still flying today. Although perhaps lacking the classic appeal of the J-3 Cub or the funky uniqueness of the Ercoupe, the 120 and 140, with side-by-side seating, all-metal fuselage (and in some cases metal wings), and relatively good ground handling, may be the best choice among the post-war two-seaters from a purely practical point of view.

History

The 120/140 genealogy is short and fairly simple. Both airplanes were introduced in early 1946. The 140 was the "luxury" airplane and had flaps, a standard electrical system, fancy upholstery and a rear side window. The 120, aimed primarily at the flight school market, had no flaps, no rear window, plain upholstery and no standard electrical system. (An electrical system was optional, however, and many were sold that way.)

In 1949, Cessna dropped the 120 and spruced up the 140, creating the 140A. Changes included a new all-metal tapered wing with a single strut (the precursor of Cessna wings for the next 30 years), and the option of a 90-hp Continental engine in place of the 85-hp powerplant in the 120 and 140 models. Only about 500 of the 140As were built, however, before the line was discontinued in 1951. Nearly a decade was to pass before Cessna resurrected the basic 140A design, put a nosewheel and a 100-hp Continental on it and called it the 150.

Resale Market

A recent issue of *Trade-A-Plane* listed 140s for sale at prices ranging from $10,000 to $22,500, with most airplanes in the mid-teens (there was also a listing for a 140, claiming "completely rebuilt, unbelievable. Expensive."). The *Aircraft Bluebook* has average retail pegged at $9,000 to $12,000, depending on quality of restoration work. As with most older aircraft, the year of manufacture has virtually no effect on the asking price. Condition and equipment are what count. A well-maintained 1946 model with a low-time engine would command a better price than a neglected 1948.

Because the 120/140 is mostly metal and fairly common, and very similar in basic design to the ubiquitous Cessna 150 and 152, it has less "antique appeal" than aircraft like the Cub, Champ or Luscombe. For this

The 120 shown here is similar to the 140, but has no flaps or back windows.

reason, the value of the airplane is pretty well determined by its capabilities: a 100-mph two-place airplane that's real noisy and kind of hard to land. Nevertheless, the 120/140 does have antique value. The Cessna 150, for example, is basically a nosewheel 140, offering virtually identical performance, accomodation and operating costs. Yet a typical 1959 150 is worth $1,500 *less* than a comparable 140 some nine years older.

On the other hand, if you are shopping purely for cheap aerial transportation and have no interest in antique appeal or taildragger chauvanism, it makes little sense to spend the extra thousand or two on a 140. The 150 is the equal of the 140 in nearly all practical matters, and has the advantage of a nosewheel and those big flaps. But, as one loyal 140 owner put it, "Who can swagger away from a 150?"

Performance

The 120 and 140 move along at a pretty good clip. Owners report true airspeeds of between 95 and 105 mph on a fuel burn of about five gallons per hour. This is quite comparable to the Cessna 150, which flies a little bit faster on about six gph.

Climb rate is nothing spectacular, of course. One owner reports, "When I'm fully loaded, I know we'll get to altitude eventually; it's just a matter of when." The same owner reports a maximum altitude of about 11,500 feet with two people and half fuel. (Lighter, altitudes of 14,000 feet are reportedly attainable.) Some 140 pilots cheerfully fly over 9,500-foot mountain ranges, though we're not sure we'd be so bold.

The 120/140 has excellent range for this class of aircraft. The 25-gallon tank gives a no-reserve endurance of about five hours. Thus, 400-mile legs are quite practical with a reasonable reserve. Other post-war two-seaters have fuel capacities inthe 10-15 gallon range, making them impractical for cross-country travel.

Accomodation

The 120/140 cockpit is cramped, at best. The seats are the fixed-bench type, so very tall pilots will find their knees tangling i the control wheel and short ones may need a pillow to reach the pedals. The cabin is also very narrow, a trait which the 150 unfortunately inherited.

The feeling of confinement is heightened by the poor visibility through the small rear windows. (The 120, remember, has no rear windows at all.) By contrast, modern trainers like the Tomahawk and Skipper, with their wide cabins and superb visibility, are a quantum leap ahead of the 120/140 (and most other two-seaters of that era).

One trait that is especially oppressive in the 120/140: cabin noise. Virtually every owner who wrote to us mentioned the unbearable cabin din, which is apparently even worse than that in its post-war contemporaries. The only solution is a good headset or earplugs.

Handling

Most 120/140 pilots praise the airplane's handling qualities, particularly the light, crisp aileron control. "Compared to the competing fat-wing airplanes of the period (T-Craft, Cub, Champ), the roll control is a dream," gushes one owner. Adverse yaw is also reportedly less than in those similar aircraft. "The flaps are a joke," says one 140 owner, "but it's pleasant arm exercise."

On the ground, the 120/140 has the typical tailwheel instability problems: a strong tendency to get sideways and spin out during the takeoff and landing rolls, and a propensity for huge ballooning bounces if the airplane touches down too firmly or at too high a speed. These traits are, of course, considered "normal" by taildragger pilots, and can usually be adjusted to, in some degree at least. "You never make a good landing by accident," reports one owner.

Among the small taildraggers, the 120/140 is considered about average in ground handling: not as forgiving as the Cub, but easier to keep straight than the Luscombe. Ground controlability is aided greatly by the toe brakes, a vast improvement over the heel brakes to be found in some old taildraggers.

A relatively well-equipped 140 instrument panel, sporting loran, transponder and gyros. Many 120s/140s have less equipment.

One bad habit of the 120/140 breed is a tendency to nose over; it's pretty likely that any 140 on the market has had at least one noseover at some time. The problem is so common that many 140s have "wheel extenders," which are spacer blocks on the landing gear legs that move the wheels a few inches forward. This, of course, reduces the noseover tendency. If you buy one that is not so equipped, you should consider adding them.

Safety

Our most recent look at the 120/140 accident record, covering a four-year period, shows that the aircraft has an excellent overall safety record. The fatal rate was very good, and close to that of the Cessna 150, reflecting the low speeds and tame operations these airplanes tend to experience.

The overall rate, however, was very high—nearly triple that of the 150, and comparable to other two-seat taildraggers. The most prevalent type of accident is (no surprises here) the minor takeoff and landing "fender bender" that results in no injuries.

In stall/spin accidents, the 120/140 fared badly, though somewhat better than its contemporaries. Two-thirds of the fatal accidents in the airplane were stall/spins. The 120/140 had a rate five times that of a more docile airplane (the Cessna 182). Even so, comparable aircraft like the Cub, Champ and Luscombe have fatal stall/spin rates more than four times that of the 140. Note that none of these small taildraggers were equipped with stall-warning devices like those found on more modern airplanes.

Maintenance

The cost of maintaining these old, small aircraft is usually quite low. The 85-and 90-hp Continentals are reliable, and the airframes are so simple that there's little to go wrong, as long as the owner pays attention and doesn't let things go to seed. The one major expense could be the fabric covering on the wing, which will need replacing at intervals ranging from five to 20 years, depending on the type of fabric and whether or not the airplane is hangared. Even this can be avoided by replacing the fabric with metal, or by buying a 140 already so equipped. Metal wings are 30 to 40 pounds heavier than the fabric ones, but most consider the weight penalty to be worth it.

Like all aircraft, the 120 and 140 have their weak spots in terms of maintenance. Here are some items to check before purchasing any 120 or 140:

• Look for damage in the lower door posts, near the wing strut attach point. This critical structural member may be damaged by rough-field operation, ground-loops or corrosion.

• Corrosion in the carry-through spar. The top skylight window is notoriously leaky, and water often drips down onto the wing spar carry-through structure in the top of the cabin. The water collects in the channeling and can cause corrosion.

• Cracks in the tail structure and rear fuselage. A 120/140 expert tells us, "The tail is the weakest part of the airplane," and is subject to cracks, particularly around the tailwheel attach point.

• Broken or bent gear boxes. The gear box—the support structure for the attachment of the landing gear to the fuselage—may have taken a real beating from student pilots 35 years ago and neophyte taildragger pilots since then. The box can be inspected from the outside by removing the landing gear fairing and from the inside by removing an inspection plate in the cabin floor.

• Broken tailsprings. Check to ensure that the steel leaf-type tailwheel spring is still springy, but not saggy. A broken spring will cause complete loss of control on landing and could do major damage to the airplane, particularly the elevators.

Modifications

Like most vintage aircraft, 120s and 140s are highly modified by doting owners. Most of the 120/140 mods are of the minor cosmetic variety, however, and there is nothing like the mod mania that afflicts owners of Mooneys and old Bonanzas, for example. Here is a list of some of the more popular mods:

• Continental O-200 engine. As the supply of C-85 and C-90 engines shrinks, some 120/140 owners have turned to the 100-hp Continental, the same engine used in the C-150. It's literally a bolt-on conversion, with no modifications required to the engine mount or cowling. Both speed and fuel consumption are slightly higher. Since the O-200 is now also out of production, some pilots have installed the Lycoming O-235 (108-115 hp). This does require some major rework under the cowl. Performance should be better, although one proud owner of a standard 140A swears he can keep up with a friend's Lycoming-powered 140 in cruise and and nearly so in climb.

Cost/Performance/Specifications

Model	Year	Average Retail Price	Cruise Speed (kts)	Useful Load (lbs)	Fuel Std (gals)	Engine	TBO (hrs)	Overhaul Cost ea.
120	1946-49	$10,000	100	632	25	Cont. C-85-12	1,800	$7,500
140	1946-48	$10,500	88	650	21	Cont. C-85-12	1,800	$7,500
140A	1949-50	$11,250	90	650	21	Cont. C-90-12F	1,800	$7,500

Prices from *Aircraft Bluebook Price Digest*

• Metal wings. A popular mod, with good reason. Aluminum wing skins turn the 120 and 140 into an all-metal airplane, with no worries about fabric replacement.

• Wheel extensions. As previously mentioned, these move the wheels forward slightly on the landing gear legs, reducing the noseover tendency.

• Cleveland brakes. The original Goodyear brakes were rather touchy and demanded constant attention; otherwise they could lock up. Cleveland brakes are more powerful and reliable. Parts for the Clevelands are also cheaper and more available.

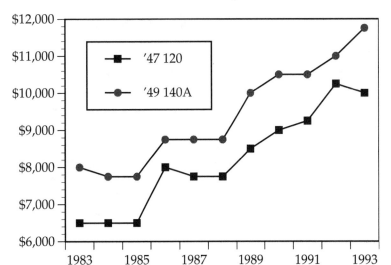

• Mixture control. There is much confusion about mixture control in the C-85 and C-90 engines. Many 120s and 140s have none; it was either removed at some point in the airplane's history, or never installed in the first place. Many believe the old Stromberg carburetors used on these engines cannot be leaned safely in flight, but veteran 140 owners assure us it can be done. However, they point to two factors: The carb must be in absolutely perfect shape, or leaning may kill the engine; and the control travel is very short, only about an inch. This makes it very sensitive, and pilots accustomed to longer control travel in other aircraft may kill the engine by pulling too far, too fast. Leaning reportedly lowers fuel consumption by about half a gallon per hour at high altitudes.

Owner Comments

Performance is consistent with its 85 horsepower—slow but thrifty. Cruise speed runs from a little over 90 mph at economy settings to just about 100 mph max cruise. Fuel consumption tends to be about 5 gph; more like 4 gph for pattern work. Although the airplane doesn't need a lot of runway, operation at high density altitude does require planning because of low climb rates: about 500 fpm at sea level, dropping off to 100 fpm at 7,000 or 8,000 feet. A mixture control might help—mine doesn't have one.

Handling is very nice. On the ground, I can just see over the nose, so S-turns aren't necessary. The toe brakes are effective, and easy to hit. I think that they help make the airplane so difficult to groundloop. More than once I've gotten into a fine swerve and thought that a groundloop was inevitable, but regained control with full rudder and some braking.

In flight, the ailerons and rudder have a lot of authority. This is particularly useful in the flapless 120, as the plane can be put into quite a slip. Makes it come right down. Stalls are not particularly exciting, although there is little warning.

The original Goodyear brakes are a chronic maintenance item. They do a fine job of stopping the airplane, but their bad reputation seems deserved. In the first year of ownership, I spent more fixing the Goodyears than it would have cost to convert to Clevelands.

Cessna 150/152

Cessna 150

Cessna 150s abound like lemmings to provide a truly mass market in fairly "modern" configuration aircraft at prices that range from modest to dirt cheap. Although most began life as trainers, they can provide fairly inexpensive personal transportation and good sport flying for any whose financial and performance aspirations are not too high.

The 150 line is an all-metal, tricycle-gear derivation of the venerable Cessna 120 and 140 tailwheel models. It first showed up in 1959, and in the years to follow it established itself as the world's premier trainer, multiplied in staggering numbers and continued right up to today (as the 152) in what has become a dynasty of no small proportions. The line has undergone a bewildering number of modifications and "improvements" over the years, but the basic qualities have remained immutable:

Durability

The aircraft are built to take it. Otherwise they never could survive the incessant pounding and manhandling of bumbling students, the rigor of bone-rattling beginners' landings, the buffeting of stalls, the wrenching of practice spins and the dynamic and thermal wear and tear on the engine of simulated emergency landings, slow flight and touch-and-goes. The Cessna 150 has few secrets. It has few elements and components that haven't been tested and tried to a fare-thee-well.

Capacity

The classic 150 trainer: old-fashioned but tough and really never eclipsed on the market. Later models like this one (1973) had tubular landing gear struts to smooth ground operations.

The 150s, especially the post-1965 models, have a baggage space of monumental proportions, but all have a cockpit of straight jacket dimensions. Cessna engineers through the years have bowed the doors out, lowered the floor pans, pared away the center pedestal and even lowered the seats in an attempt to provide more millimeters of cabin room. But they still haven't made the cabin structure basically any wider. Hence, any two adults of more than medieval stature who fly together in a Cessna 150 are destined to develop a close relationship for the duration of the flight.

Speed

When the original, bulky-fuselage 150 showed up on the aviation scene in 1959 powered by a peanut-sized 100-hp Continental O-200, it would cruise at 121 mph at 75 percent power. The latest model, after a raft of changes like redesigned cabin, swept tail, modified wheel fairings, better streamlined cowling and bigger engine—today cruises at 123 mph at the same power setting. Visibility: Nothing to brag about.

Aerobatics

The Cessna 150 Aerobat would seem to have the makings of an ideal aerobatic trainer, since it allows students to transition right into an airplane they feel comfortable with. There's a nicely illustrated instructional manual and a well-planned curriculum to whet a student's appetite. Experienced aerobatic pilots give it good marks in such maneuvers as spins and aileron rolls. But it has serious shortcomings when it comes to anything much more sophisticated.

Big rear cabin in rare cases had an optional child's seat. The rear compartment will take up to 120 pounds of baggage or kids.

Since it has a control wheel rather than a stick, for example, while doing point rolls, the "other rider" can expect to be pummeled by the pilot's elbows as he whips the wheel back and forth in the cramped cockpit. The Aerobat also is not designed for negative maneuvers, and this not only excludes a whole repertoire, but means the engine will not operate upside down for any length of time. Instructors also report that one marginal characteristic of the airplane is its tendency to get moving too fast when coming down from an inverted position, as in a split-S or perhaps even on top of a roll. Also, the prop pitch seems set so "fine" that it's too easy to overspeed the engine in descending maneuvers.

But the airplane probably suffices at least to give students a taste of something other than straight-and- level, as an appetite-whetter to advance to better aerobatic aircraft, or to allow him to get out of awkward situations he may never have encountered before.

Handling

Forgiving and always recoverable, but sharp-edged enough to demand the precision that lots of instructors prefer. The bird has a dandy set of "para-lift" flaps which will allow awesome approach angles, but until a diminution of full flap angles from 40 to 30 degrees was made on the 152, the bird was known as an anvil in a balked-landing go-around with full flaps. In general, though, the 150 is a delightful airplane to fly.

Powerplant

The introduction of 100 LL initially gave the Continental O-200 powerplant in the Cessna 150 a dose of lead-fouling problems, but users have learned to live with low-lead fuel by increased care to leaning, changing sparkplugs and oil more often, and by use of TCP additive. Deterioration of valve seat heads has been reduced by substitution of new ones made of a different material. The Cessna 152 comes with a 110-hp Lycoming O-235 engine that copes with low-lead fuel more gracefully. Reports of unexplained reduction of static rpm or uneven operation in this engine led to a Lycoming service letter listing several possible causes. One of these was possible excessive wear or looseness on the ball end of the push rods, and shortening of the rods.

Flexibility

There is a patroller version with long-range fuel tanks and a Plexiglas door, and a seaplane version that never quite caught on because of what old salts regard as too long a takeoff run with floats.

Comparative Qualities

Stacked up alongside the newer but also out-of-production two-place trainers like the Beech Skipper and Piper Tomahawk, the Cessna 152 shows up surprisingly well in nearly every performance category. Only in styling and visibility is the basic old Cessna airframe eclipsed by the newer birds—which doesn't say much for "modern" lightplane technology.

The first Cessna 150s had poor visibility to the rear, thanks to the full- enclosed cabin, were placarded against spins and had a not unattractive, stubby, vertical tail. They had manual flaps that were a delight to operate, with a lever between the seats. Baggage space, though, was quite limited. The airplane also had a disquieting idiosyncrasy which would manifest itself at odd times, as after a flight, when the pilot had just taxied up to the fuel pump and shut down the engine. The airplane might then slowly and majestically raise its nose up to the sky and squat—*clank*—on its tail.

But in the 1961 model 150, this trait was corrected by relocating the main landing gear struts two inches aft on the cabin. Also, rearward visibility was improved a mite by the enlargement of the two little aft windows by about 15 percent. In 1964 the most dramatic change in the history of the line was instituted: the fuselage was chopped down behind the wing and a neat, little wraparound window placed in the rear. This was the birth of "omni vision." At the same time, a generous-sized baggage space was opened up under the little rear greenhouse window.

Growth Trends

Perhaps to accommodate the extra baggage, the 150 received its first jump in gross weight, 100 pounds, from 1,500 pounds up to 1,600 pounds. The C-152's gross went up another 70 pounds to 1,670. In 1966 Cessna felt impelled to cut the price of the 150 by a stunning 10 percent from $7,825 to $6,995. Adding a bit of flair (though negligible aerodynamic improvement) Cessna went to the modish swept vertical tail on the 150.

In addition, 50 percent more baggage space was added as they moved the cabin wall aft by one bay. On top of that, the electric stall warning horn was given the boot in favor of the wailing, sighing symphony of a pneumatic reed stall warning which could not be disconnected by the failure of an electrical circuit. In another rather radical change the same year, Cessna did away with the quick, sure manual flaps and introduced the very modern and very languid electric flaps.

The 1967 models marked the first attempt to give cramped 150 pilots a bit more elbow room—by bowing out the doors slightly for an alleged three-inch increase in cabin diameter. Also, the floorboard just aft of the rudder pedals was lowered slightly. Other little touches: the seven-inch nosewheel strut extension was shortened to four inches and an alternator replaced the traditional generator for better power output at lower rpms.

This was also the year the seaplane version was introduced—a delightful- handling machine that failed to make it in the big time, ostensibly because it took just too long to become unstuck and away on takeoff in the lake country where every cattail length of water run had to count. In the 1968 model, Cessna provided yet another smidgen of knee room by paring a couple of inches off the width of the center console separating the pilot and copilot knees. A revised flap system was offered to allow "hands-off" flap retraction.

More Upgrades

The 1970 model gained one aesthetic distinction: cambered wingtips. A year later in 1971 the 150 inherited the nice tubular landing gear struts of the Cardinal, for smoother touchdown and taxi, along with a 16 percent wider tack width. To quiet the drumming of the prop air against the cowling and windshield slightly, the propeller was extended out front a bit. Also, the landing light was moved from the wing (where it never seemed to illuminate the correct portion of the runway) to the nose inlet.

The 1975 models were marked by newly styled speed fairings and cowling that generated an alleged five-mph higher cruise speed. In addition, both fin and rudder area were increased to provide more rudder power in crosswind landings.

The year 1976 saw the introduction of vertically adjustable pilot seats, and 1977 was the year of a pre-select flap control (again like the Cardinal's) along with a new vernier mixture to replace the traditional push-pull plunger. The 1978 Cessna 152 introduced the new 110-hp Lycoming engine, a (troublesome) 28-volt electrical system, a one-piece cowling and redesigned fuel tanks that reduced the unusable fuel to 1.5 gallons. Flap extension was limited to 30 degrees to give better performance during a balked landing. And the new Lycoming engine gave an extra 200 hours of TBO over the Continental—for 2,000 hours.

Aerobatic models demand several hundred to several thousand dollars more than commuters on the market. Use of control wheels rather than sticks is a disadvantage.

Cessna 152

Sleek and shiny, with good manners aloft, and designed to digest 100LL with ease, the Cessna 152 was to have been Cessna's ultimate improvement on the ultimate trainer—the venerable 150. But alas, a panoply of mechanical gremlins, plus high parts prices and high acquisition cost (not to mention one of the worst recessions ever to hit the U.S. aviation industry) sent new-152 sales into a screaming spiral dive just three years after the model's 1978 introduction.

The used market, as a result, now draws from a reservoir of late-vintage Cessna 152s. Though not so many years ago many were available at fire-sale prices, things have changed. With no new production trainers coming off the line, the value of the used birds has taken a dramatic upturn. Whether a used 152 represents a true bargain is another question. For the owner willing to live with 100-knot cruise speeds, frequent bouts with lead fouling, and relatively expensive (for a trainer) annual inspections, a several-year-old Cessna 152 can provide a reasonable modicum of performance and utility in the $7,000-$17,000 "sport plane" category. But the prospective 152 purchaser who thinks he's merely getting a modernized, "improved" Cessna 150 may need to think again. A fancy 150, the 152 is not.

History

"Operators of the 150 told us they wanted a training airplane that would burn 100-octane fuel, while producing lower noise levels, better fuel consumption and more payload," Cessna's vp Bob Lair remarked at the time of the 152's debut in spring of 1977. What operators got was an airplane that was—and is—subject to severe lead fouling, while delivering performance about equal to that of the Cessna 150—at a cost that made some operators wince. The original 1978 Cessna 152 (introduced in May 1977) listed at $20,635 with Nav Pac.

In changing from the 150 to the 152, Cessna gave its trainer a 110-hp Lycoming engine (with 2,000-hr. TBO) to replace the previous 100-hp Continental (1,800-hr. TBO); a McCauley "gull wing" propeller; an oil cooler as standard equipment; a 28-volt electrical system; and flaps limited to 30 degrees (instead of the previous 40). For all these changes, the 152 owner got 40 pounds more useful load than was available in the original 1958 Cessna 150 (and about 60 pounds *less* than a 1948 Cessna 140 could carry).

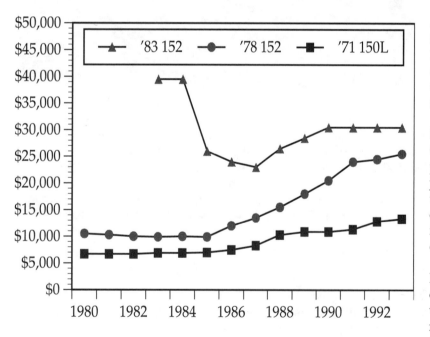

After 1978, relatively few important model changes were made to the basic 152. Those that *were* made point to the original airplane's mechanical short-comings, some of which were quite notable.

In the 1979 model year, for example, Cessna incorporated impulse couplings on both magnetos— rather than just the left one, as before—to improve the 152's conspicuously lousy starting characteristics. (Likewise, direct priming to all four cylinders was made standard.)

In addition, a split cowl nose piece was conjured up (retrofittable under a service bulletin), to enable shops to remove the whole cowling without first taking off the plane's propeller. (If you intend to buy a '78 model, be sure it has this feature.) An improved brake master cylinder, with fewer parts, first made its appearance on 1979 models.

Starter Fix

In 1980, again addressing the airplane's poor startability, Cessna went to a slower-turning starter (the applicable armature is retrofittable under Service Letter SE79-43), which allowed the impulse couplings to do their job better; and the plane's float carburetor got an accelerator pump as standard equipment. (Before, apparently, owners had been pumping the throttle to prime the engine, not realizing that without an accelerator pump, no fuel was coming from the carb.) Dual windshield defrosters were offered, and an even-more-expensive type of 24-volt battery (a "manifold" type) was made standard, eliminating the battery box.

In 1981, Cessna made the enlightened move of putting a spin-on oil filter on all 152s as standard—not optional—equipment. Larger battery contactors, with ap-propriate current capacity to eliminate contact welding, were instituted (to keep owners from having to replace so many $230 batteries after contactor fry-ups); and an avionics cooling fan became part of every avionics instal-lation. Also in 1981, the 152's list price took a 25-percent jump, the largest sin-gle jump ever, to $30,175 equipped.

For 1982, Cessna added a quick-drain to the standpipe below the fuel selec-tor (at the belly of the airplane), to allow drainage of sediment and wa-ter from the fuel system's true low point. This modification can be—and should be— retrofitted to all 150s and 152s.

Most significant change on the 152 was a more powerful Lycoming engine designed to burn 100 LL with less grief. But lead fouling continued unabated.

Finally, for 1983-model 152s, Cessna went to a 108-hp O-235-N2C engine that better tolerates the lead in 100-octane avgas; the avionics cooling fan was im-proved; a panel vacuum warning light was made standard; and the gyro panel was redesigned to allow removal of gyro instruments from the front of the panel.

Performance and Handling

In terms of cruise performance and payload, the 152 enjoys no real advantage over its Beech and Piper peers (the Skipper and Tomahawk), or the old C-150, for that matter. Top speed for the 152 is listed by Cessna as 109 knots, the same as for the Tomahawk and 150M (two knots more than the Skipper); likewise, the 152 Trainer's standard useful load of 528 pounds very nearly matches that of the Skipper (572 lbs.) and Tomahawk (542 lbs.). Some of the earlier 150s (E/F/G models) topped 600 pounds in load-carrying ability, however.

But the useful-load issue is made moot by the 152's optional fuel capacity of 39 gallons—33 percent greater than the Skipper's 29 gallons or the Tomahawk's 30. In range and payload flexibility, the 152 thus enjoys a slight edge over its compet-itors—although you may well have to sacrifice a passenger (and/or baggage) to take full benefit of the 152's longer range.

Runway performance for the 152 is good. The Cessna simply gets off quicker—and stops shorter—than Brand B or Brand P trainers (a reflection of the 152's fortunate lack of a T tail). If short- or rough-field operations are contemplated, the 152 wins hands down over its T-tail peer.

Figure on an unstick distance of 725 feet for a fully grossed 152 at sea level (versus 780 and 820 feet for the Skipper and Tomahawk); and set aside a mere 475 feet for landing roll (vs. 670 or 707 ft. for the T-trainers). The 152, incidentally, lands about 10 percent longer than the 150—apparently due to the 152's 30-degree flap-travel restriction.

So where does the 152 really shine? Its confidence-inspiring slow-flight characteristics and straightforward Cessna-like handling provide the key. The plane stalls well and with plenty of warning. (Power on, you can get zero-knots indicated before approaching the burble.) Stability in all axes is outstanding. The barn-door flaps—electric, alas—are monstrously effective (but watch out for the pitch-up on initial deployment). The 152's light wing loading makes it a bit uncomfortable in more than very light turbulence; otherwise, however, it flies very much like a miniature Skyhawk. Which is just what Cessna wanted, of course.

The 152, like the 150, also comes in an Aerobat version—which the Skipper and Tomahawk don't. (Only about one in 20 152s is an 'A' model, however.) If loops and hammerheads are your cup of pekoe, the A152 will grudgingly comply. But don't expect Pitts-like—or even Citabria-like—performance, and forget about sustained inverted flight (the engine dies).

On '76 and later models vertically adjustable pilot seats were offered. Through the years in attempts to make the cabin more comfortable, Cessna bowed out the doors and cut away floor pans for footroom.

Comfort

Although significantly better than, say, a Luscombe or Taylorcraft, the 152's cabin comfort is nothing to brag about (and in fact takes a back seat to that of either the Skipper or Tomahawk). Visibility is poor, noise level is high, and shoulder room is almost nonexistent. Thicker seat padding became standard with the 1979 models (the previous cushions taxed the endurance of even the most hardened CFIs), but even so, pillows are highly recommended for cross-country work.

Ventilation (via the wing-root pull tubes, and air leaks around the doors) has always been good in 150s and 152s, even, unfortunately, in the dead of winter. To add insult to misery, Cessna located cabin-heat and carb-heat pickoffs next to each other on the muffler shroud. (Even with carb heat turned off, the carb-heat plumbing provides a sizable plenum for the escape of desperately needed cabin BTUs.) In 1979, Cessna released a service letter, SE79-12, describing a kit to relocate the carb-heat source to the number-four exhaust riser. This allowed the muffler's total heat output to be utilized for cabin heat, resulting in a 30-percent increase in cabin heat flow. All 1980 and later 152s were delivered with this cabin-heat mod.

The first 4,100 airplanes off the line, however, did not get the deluxe heater kit, and most remain unmodified. Check for compliance with Cessna Service Letter SE79-12 before buying a '78 or '79 airplane.

Engine

In going from the 150 to the 152, Cessna switched from the venerable 80-octane Continental O-200-A to the somewhat more expensive (and powerful) Lycoming O-235-L2C. The rationale behind the engine change was threefold. First, with 80-octane avgas in increasingly short supply, more and more flight schools were reporting problems with lead buildup in their 150s' O-200 engines; Cessna wanted to give its dealers a trainer that could digest the higher-leaded 100-octane fuels. Second, the 150—which had seen empty-weight increases totaling nearly 150 pounds (or 15 percent) since 1958—was overdue for a horsepower boost. And third, Cessna— in accordance with proposed FAA and ICAO noise standards— wanted to see a reduction in the 150's internal and external sound levels. The high-compression Lycoming O-235-L2C, delivering 110 horsepower at 2,550 rpm instead of the O-200's 2,750, seemed a natural answer to all three requirements.

Many operators say that the switch to the Lycoming engine was a mistake. Although it did rid the Cessna trainer of the O-200's starter-clutch woes (the small Continental uses a $600 starter adapter that can fail frequently and without warning), the Lycoming O-235 brought its own constellation of mechanical quirks. Parts prices were, in some cases, astoundingly high: The O-235-L2C's sodium-filled exhaust valves, for instance, listed for $213.08 each—versus only $64 for the O-200's solid-stemmed valves. (Likewise, a piston for the Lycoming engine cost about twice what the corresponding Continental piston cost.)

What's more, the O-235's cylinders may not be ground oversize during a top overhaul (since it removes the nitride layer), whereas the O-200's jugs can be ground over. And if an owner elects to salvage run-out cylinders by chroming, extreme difficulty may be had in finding piston rings for final buildup. Unchromed rings must be used in chromed jugs— and no one, at present, supplies unchromed rings for O-235s.

Other service quirks that have not endeared schools or their shops to the 152's powerplant:

• As originally delivered, the Cessna 152 came with Slick 4000-series "sealed" (i.e., unrepairable in the field) magnetos. A rash of unexplained capacitor problems led to engine failures in Tomahawks using the same engine/magneto combo, but the 152 was mysteriously unaffected. Nonetheless, operators soon tired of spending hundreds of dollars on new mags every time their "throw-away Slicks" needed points or bearings. A black market in bogus 152-mag "repair kits" sprang up, and Slick finally introduced a field-repairable version of the mags.

• The O-235 is one of few recent aircraft engines that uses solid (not hydraulic) tappets. Valve lash in the O-235 thus varies with engine temperature, and O-235 valve-train clearances must be checked scrupulously every 100 hours, not unlike

Cost/Performance/Specifications

Model	Year	Average Retail Price	Cruise Speed (kts)	Useful Load (lbs)	Fuel Std/Opt (gals)	Engine	TBO (hrs)	Overhaul Cost
150, A	1959-61	$10,600	105	554	26/38	100-hp Cont.O-200-A	1,800	$10,000
150B, C, D	1962-64	$11,100	105	554	26/38	100-hp Cont.O-200-A	1,800	$10,000
150E, F, G	1965-67	$12,000	105	554	26/38	100-hp Cont.O-200-A	1,800	$10,000
150H, J, K	1968-70	$12,900	105	554	26/38	100-hp Cont.O-200-A	1,800	$10,000
150L	1971-74	$14,750	105	554	26/38	100-hp Cont.O-200-A	1,800	$10,000
150M	1975-77	$16,500	105	554	26/38	100-hp Cont.O-200-A	1,800	$10,000
152	1978-80	$27,500	107	568	26/38	110-hp Lyc .O-235-L2C	2,000	$10,000
152	1981-83	$30,000	107	568	26/38	110-hp Lyc .O-235-L2C	2,000	$10,000
152B	1984-85	$39,500	106	568	26/38	108-hp Lyc .O-235-N2C	2,000	$10,000

a motorcycle. Lycoming, in an attempt to minimize lash problems, devised hollow-aluminum pushrods with steel ball ends (the idea being that the aluminum, which expands more than twice as much as steel on heating, would tend automatically to readjust lash at higher temperatures).

Such construction calls for very critical ball-end fit tolerances, however, and—unfortunately—Lycoming's pushrod vendor failed, initially, to meet the necessary specs. As a result, pushrod "mushrooming" (pounding of the steel ball ends down into the pushrod) became common.

After a fatal accident related to pushrod shortening in November 1980, FAA issued an AD on this subject. All defective rods should by now have been taken out of circulation, but it bears mentioning that valve train clearances are critical and subject to frequent rechecking in the O-235.

• The O-235-L2C did not escape the inspection requirements of a 1981 AD (81-18-04) that called for replacement of iron oil pump impellers with late-configuration steel and aluminum ones. This caused many 2,000-hour engines to be summarily grounded.

Miscellaneous reports of low static rpm and uneven operation led Lycoming to issue a special bulletin for the O-235 (S.I. 1388C) outlining trouble-shooting procedures to restore full power. This service letter has gone through several revisions.

Lead Fouling

With the '76 models came vernier throttles in place of push-pull plungers, and pre-select flap controls. At the top of the panel is a rear-view mirror.

Lead buildup—not only in spark plugs but in nooks and crannies in the combustion chamber, and on valves—has been a persistent problem in O-235 engines. So much so, in fact, that Champion designed a special spark plug just for this engine—the extended-electrode 'Y' series (e.g., REM37BY). The long-prong plugs do not scavenge lead any better than standard plugs; they merely have electrodes that sit far enough away from lead incrustations to constantly "burn clean." Once filled with lead, the 'Y' plugs continue to fire. (But they still must be replaced often.)

Most operators find that even with judicious leaning, spark plugs must be cleaned every 25 hours in a 152. "Otherwise," remarks one A&P, "at 100 hours, you can throw the plug away—it won't even be cleanable." Lead buildup on the inside of the cylinder affects spark plug life: Lycoming found that lead can be redeposited from the combustion chamber to clean spark plugs in as little as 25 hours. Accordingly, in Service Instruction 1418, Lycoming outlines a procedure whereby O-235 cylinders can be blast-cleaned with walnut shells without removal for top overhaul. (Prior to this, some operators were finding that early top overhauls were needed to prevent lead from reaching excessive levels in O-235 jugs.)

Safety

Safety statistics for the 150 and 152 are quite good. (In this regard, at least, trainers have come a long way since Piper Cub days.) An NTSB study found the Cessna 150 series with the lowest fatal accident rate—at 1.35 per 100,000 flight hours—of any two-seater, and one of the lowest fatal crash rates of *any* single-engine aircraft, period. The total accident rate, at 10.3 per 100,000 hours, is also quite respectable, again bettering most trainers *and* four-place aircraft.

If there's one fly in the safety ointment, it's the 152's relatively weak showing against the Piper Tomahawk. A special study by *Aviation Safety* (covering the period January 1978 through April 1980) found the 152 with a 38-percent higher total accident rate than the Tomahawk. (Fatal accident rates were about equal.)

As a percentage of total accidents, the Cessna 152 is involved in disproportionately more groundloops, overshoots, undershoots, and fuel mismanagement accidents than the Tomahawk. The 152, on the other hand, fares much better than its Piper counterpart in the proportion of hard landing accidents and stall-spins.

Overall, the 152 has a sterling safety record, bolstered by the fact that there has never been an in-flight breakup of the airplane (despite a fair number of IFR-weather encounters by low-time pilots).

Maintenance

Many of the 152's early maintenance foibles (the most serious of which have been touched on above) have now been laid to rest and should not pose recurrent problems for used-trainer buyers. The 152's most serious ongoing maintenance problem involves lead fouling, which (according to some owners) can be severe even with proper leaning, the use of low-lead fuel, addition of TCP concentrate (a lead remover marketed by Alcor) to 100LL, correct adjustment of idle mixture, and switching to Champion long-prong plugs.

All of these measures are unnecessary, of course, in a Cessna 150 operating on grade-80 avgas or unleaded automotive gasoline. But unfortunately, the 152's engine is restricted to 100-octane avgas for the foreseeable future. (In all fairness, private owners should experience less lead fouling than flight schools, since much of the 152's lead fouling is due to chronic overrich operation in the pattern.)

Prospective 152 buyers should check to see whether these important service bulletins have been complied with:

• SE82-23 required a one-time inspection of 152 starter and battery contactors.

• SE81-38 outlined brake master cylinder modifications for 1979 through mid-'82 Cessna 152s (and post-1966 150s).

• SE81-24 puts a fuel quick-drain in the belly of pre-'82 Cessna 152s (and post-1966 150s).

• SE80-96 (Revision 1) calls for recurrent inspections of certain Stewart-Warner oil coolers on a variety of Cessnas, including the 152. This was also the subject of an AD.

• SE79-7 modifies the nose cap to allow removal of the cowl without first taking the prop off.

• SE79-11 and -43 concerned mods to improve the starting characteristics of pre-1980 152s.

• SE79-12 reroutes carb heat plumbing to improve cabin heat.

• SE79-16 outlines flap cable clamp mods that must be accomplished prior to 1,000 hours in service. This was also the subject of an AD (80-6-3); so make sure it has been complied with on any airplane you intend to buy.

• SE79-46 describes periodic inspection requirements for 152 carburetor airboxes. In 1982, Cessna came out with a service bulletin (SE82-12) describing an airscoop mod for the 152, compliance with which is also recommended.

• SE79-49 mandates vertical fin hardware attachment inspections every 100 hours. This now carries the force of law, under an AD (No. 80-11-04).

• SE79-57 describes a much-improved flap actuator mechanical stop for 1979 and earlier 152s.

• SE80-2: Another cabin heat mod.

• SE80-10 requires use of Loctite on certain starter screws, which have shown a tendency to back out.

We mentioned before the 152's bout with self-shortening pushrods (the subject of a late-1980 AD, and Lycoming S.B. 453). What we didn't mention is that compliance with this AD doesn't guarantee that you'll *never* see pushrod mushrooming in your 152's engine.

Early model 152 had one-piece nose caps, preventing complete cowl removal with the propeller in place. Later models have two-piece nose caps—a definite maintenance bonus.

There have been reports (not many, but a few), subsequent to the AD, of engines with the improved pushrods experiencing ball-hammering or mushrooming. Hence, along with a compression check, we'd recommend a check of valve clearances (or pushrod length) in any pre-purchase inspection of a Cessna 152.

Modifications

The Cessna 150 can be given up to half again as much horsepower and turned into a pint-sized STOL machine or a taildragger, thanks to alterations offered by several companies. Firms providing all of the above are Avcon Conversions, Inc., (316) 782-3317 and Bush Conversions, (316) 782-3851, both of Udall, Kans. Others offering STOL alterations include Horton, Inc., (800) 835-2051, at Wellington, Kans. and R/STOL, Sierra Industries, Uvalde, Tex., (512) 278-4381.

Bush sells a kit that installs 150-hp and 160-hp Lycoming engines in place of the normal 100-hp Continental. This makes for a big jump (up to about 1,100 fpm) in climb performance, a fairly healthy increase in cruise speed (up to 140 mph) and a small loss in useful load (about 30 pounds).

But some extensive juggling of weight is necessary to accommodate the bigger engine, mostly involving shifting the battery from the engine compartment to the tail section.

R/STOL provides what appears to be the most elaborate STOL treatment to Cessna 150s. This includes a sophisticated flap-aileron interconnect system with

drooping ailerons that work at different angles to match flap angles. Also part of the mod are recontoured leading edges, stall fences, conical cambered wingtips and, if needed, aileron gap seals.

For less money ($905 for the kit and another $795 for factory installation) Horton installs a leading-edge alteration, along with a new landing light lens for wing-mounted models, stall fences on top of the wing, aileron gap seals plus conical wingtips. Horton claims the job can be done in three days at the factory. The purpose of both STOL installations is to lower stall speeds and provide more controllability near and in the stall regime.

Taildraggers

For pilots who prefer taildraggers, along with Bush and Avcon, a third company, Aircraft Conversion Technologies, of Lincoln, Calif., (916) 645-3264, can supply landing gear kits. The tailwheel conversion is claimed to boost speed by eight to 10 mph, by eliminating drag and substituting prop thrust that would otherwise be blanked out by the nose gear.

There are quite a few approved mods for the 152. Brackett Aircraft offers conversion kits for installation of wet-foam air filters on the 152 (replacement elements are only a few dollars for this type of filter, whereas Cessna gets about $25 for a new paper element). Brackett filters are available through any large FBO.

Better performance and a cleaner-running engine are the highlights of a power-plant conversion for some Cessna 152s offered by a Washington mod shop called Air Mods N.W. Sprightlier takeoff, climb and cruise performance results from installation of a new prop that can be spun up to 2,800 rpm, while a higher compression ratio helps prevent lead sludge from building up in the combustion chambers and in the oil. The extra pressure does have its dark side, though, in increasing the chances of destructive detonation if the engine is worked too hard or given an improper diet.

The conversion is made up of three separate STCs that turn Cessna 152s and Aerobats built from 1978 through 1982 with 110-hp Lycoming O-235-L2C engines into 125-hp Sparrow Hawks. One of the STCs (SE792NW) covers installation of slightly taller pistons, which raise the compression ratio from 8.5:1 to 9.7:1, and an adjustment in timing from 20 to 25 degrees before top dead center. According to

Ken Blackman at Air Mods N.W., the modified engine is very similar to a version that Lycoming exported to Europe in the early 1970s.

A second STC (SA1000NW) simply allows installation of the modified engine into a 152 airframe with changes to the baffling to permit better flow of cooling air around the engine. The third certificate (SA1008NW) covers replacement of the stock McCauley "gull-wing" propeller with a more efficient Sensenich S6-series prop and spinner.

Organizations

The Cessna 150-152 Club has been around for some years. The group's monthly newsletter (The Cessna 150-152 News), edited by Skip Carden, is an excellent clearinghouse of service-related information and info on new modifications, discount parts sources, etc. Membership is $20/yr. domestic and Canada, $30/yr. foreign. Contact the club at P.O. Box 15388, Durham, N.C. 27704, or phone (919) 471-9492.

As a special service to members, the club publishes a fat loose-leaf volume called *Hints 'n' Tips* with a wealth of information on operating 150s and 152s. Included are modifications, ADs, Airworthiness Alerts, along with a host of information on servicing the aircraft. Don't miss this volume, which is updated annually.

The other big organization providing excellent service to all Cessna owners is the Cessna Pilots Assn. located in Wichita, Kans., (316) 946-4777.

Owner Comments

It's been an amazing airplane. I'd parallel that with the J-3, almost. Problems? You have the usual matter of guys pulling out the starter cable. As for reports that the nosewheel shimmies, if you land really fast on it, it'll shimmy, as it might on any airplane. But that's par for the course with a trainer. I wouldn't say the maintenance is high.

For the beating they take, they're excellent. The only problem with the Cessna 150 as a cross-country machine is the way it reacts to turbulence. You really feel the bumps. You get jolted around, compared with larger four-place airplanes. Nevertheless, it's a lot of fun, and maneuverable.

Aside from a cracked crankcase, the only maintenance problem I've had is with the nose strut, which I had to have overhauled. I bought the aircraft from an FBO who used it as a training plane, but it really held up to the wear and tear pretty well. Aside from the time in the logbooks, you couldn't tell how much it had been flown, and how hard. It had 2,850 hours on it when I bought it.

• • •

One problem with the airplane is the way the fuel system feeds unevenly with the tank selector on both. One wing gets heavy, so you have to compensate with aileron. And with my airplane it's usually the right tank that feeds first, so if you're flying from the left seat, you have to compensate for your weight and the fuel in the left tank.

• • •

It spins okay, but winds up pretty fast; it really whips around compared with other planes I've spun in training.

• • •

Cabin size is very limited for two full-sized people. You're elbow to elbow. Visibility is all right, but if they'd put a C-172-type windshield in, it would be much better. And, of course, top visibility isn't that good. In all, it's fun to fly, and it's not that expensive in fuel consumption.

• • •

We had the Horton STOL conversion on our 150, and it worked out beautifully. It just makes a good, complete all-around plane, though my husband and I probably will go to a larger four-placer next time. We really don't need the STOL for short fields; we just feel it makes the airplane safer.

The birth of "omni vision" occurred with the 1964 model 150. The fuselage was chopped down behind the wing and a wraparound window placed there.

• • •

What I like about it is that the maintenance is relatively inexpensive. This is the fourth airplane I've owned, and the newest one. The one thing I don't like about it is that to me it is a very boring airplane. Also, I don't like the fact that every time you pull up to a gas pump people ask you if you are a student on a cross-country. When you're paying money for an airplane, you like to have people say it looks nice when you pull into the pump. It's an ego thing.

I think the handling is fairly good, but I'd prefer lighter ailerons. My old Swift had lighter ones, for example. I like the way it spins for training. It's very predictable; it goes into a spin the same way every time.

To avoid problems on a balked landing, I teach my students to use just 20 degrees of flaps, and about the only time I teach them to use 40 degrees is when they get real high on the approach. My instructor taught me that, looking on 40 degrees as just an extra drag device. Electric flaps, especially on a balked landing, are a real problem since you don't have any climb capability with full flaps. I didn't feel I had too much problem with it, but the new students might.

• • •

The noise level, as in most light airplanes, is unbearable, and I think that's an area where improvement could be made. I use it quite a bit for cross-country in addition to training, and it works out pretty well. It's got pretty good range. You can figure it is a three-hour airplane, and then you have 45 minutes' reserve.

I would like to have a little more top speed on the airplane for cross-country cruising. The nosewheel is a constant problem. That's one of the weak links in the airplane. I've had nosewheel shimmy ever since I bought the airplane, and though the shimmy damper was rebuilt and rebushed, it never helped. I've had no real problem with the strut, except that it deflates about every two months, but that seems to be normal.

• • •

We have been operating Cessna 152s since 1978 and have had more than our fair share of troubles with them. Because they have required much more cranking to start, they tend to wear out batteries and starters quicker than the 150 (and they're more expensive than those of a 150 because they are 24-volt).

Plugs. Until we received the flyer from Lycoming, we kept the plug cleaning machines and mechanics busy. Suffice as to say, I'm sure that a lot of us have leaned the 152 a little too early and a little too much in order to prevent lead build-up. This, of course, eventually leads to internal (and expensive) cylinder problems.

Now some of the good points. 1) From a safety standpoint, we feel that the elimination of the last 10 degrees of flaps was a good move. 2) We have seen an upward trend in the reliability of ARC radios and nose wheel shimmy dampeners. 3) The newer seats are more comfortable which is a nice plus for those CFIs sitting in them all day. 4) The schemes, quality and colors of paint are markedly improved.

The question is . . . would I consider buying another one? Only if Cessna had equipped it with a 12-volt electrical system and a good old reliable Continental O-200A. Despite all my grievances, Cessna by far made the world's most desirable training aircraft.

Reed D. Novisoff
Long Beach Flyers, Inc.
Long Beach, Calif.

My 1978 Cessna 152 has been leased to a flying club, so perhaps all of my comments and data may not be comparable to aircraft operated by private owners. In addition, I am an A&P mechanic and do almost all of the maintenance myself, so labor cost is not included in maintenance cost, except for the annual inspection. But I am a pilot, so general comments are relevant.

Handling and performance are good, and the aircraft is certainly satisfactory for training purposes. However, on cross-country flights comfort is average to poor because of lack of leg room for the taller pilot and skimpy seat padding. Seating width is poor for large people when both seats are in use. Power is adequate under all conditions (home field elevation is only 469 feet though).

Most complaints center around the rapid lead-fouling of the lower spark plugs which causes many flights to be cancelled after ground runup with a 200-300 rpm mag drop. Even using TCP and the newer Champion REM37BY plugs, the lower ones must be cleaned every 20-25 hours. Fuel availability is limited to 100 octane at the home field—no 100LL is available—so perhaps the plugs would stay clean longer with 100LL Nose wheel shimmy is a problem from time to time due to linkage wear and the pounding the nose gear takes from students and operation primarily from an unpaved runway.

I am not too happy with the 24-volt electrical system when it comes time to replace the battery. Last year the starter shorted internally and the parts cost for starter (rebuilt) and a Gill battery was $500. Parts availability has not been a problem.

The way the aircraft is used in flight training makes it difficult to accurately check fuel consumption (takeoffs and landings, forgetting to lean the mixture, etc.) but it appears to be close to the numbers published in Cessna's Pilot's Operating Handbook.

I hope your other readers will benefit from this information, and perhaps someone has a solution for the plug-fouling problem.

Norman J. Makowski
Fairport, N.Y.

We have operated four Cessna 152s for the past three and one-half years here in our flight school. Our most popular one (a 1980 model) is doing about 700 hours per year. Hourly maintenance cost is about five dollars per hour.

They burn six gallons per hour if properly leaned, lots more if run hard or full rich. All have had lousy compression since new, and even after tops or overhauls; 65/80 is typical throughout the 2,000-hour TBO span. Valve clearances must be checked each 100 hours.

We go 100 hours without cleaning the plugs or changing the oil providing they are religiously leaned and run up to 1800 rpm for a minute before shut down. The 24-volt electrical system is a pain in the neck requiring $239 batteries at least once a year. The RT-385A radios are also expensive to repair when the lights (digits) burn out or they quit cold.

Not a bad little cross-country cruiser, the 150 can carry as much as 35 gallons of usable fuel as an option. Speed is 106 knots with everything to the wall at altitude.

All in all it is a good trainer and rental aircraft, but a few pet gripes of mine are: 1) Who needs a cruise prop (and therefore a 104-knot cruise speed) on a primary trainer used to build hours of training and proficiency? 2) It's a gas hog. 3) Cabin is four inches too narrow. 4) I miss the 40 degrees flap setting. 5) Too noisy (I *always* wear ear plugs). 6) Cessna Aircraft Co. overprices CPC supplies, parts, etc. 7) It's too damned expensive. In 1979 I bought two for $30,000.

Despite the shortcomings, it is the best airplane around for my purpose but honestly, I'd rather have a C-150 if I could find lots of clean low-time late models.

David B. O'Brien, Pres.
FBO Lakewood Airport
Bay Head, N.J.

Cessna 170

It's a good-performing, honest four-seater and also a lot of fun to fly. Like any other taildragger, though, it can bite. Though 170s still are quite affordable, prices continue to climb. Cessna built 5,136 of the airplanes in a nine-year production run that ended nearly 40 years ago. But time has taken a toll. Today, less than half of the airplanes are still flying; and accident records show that ground loops and hard landings are continuing to thin out the 170 fleet at quite a clip.

Prices for 170s, like this 1955 B model (which has modified, fiberglass wingtips), are rising fast. There's no need to rob Fort Knox to buy one, yet; but you're still likely to come out ahead, budget-wise, getting an early-model 172 and converting it to a taildragger.

Still, there are many who turn a veiled eye on the taildragger's safety record and dismiss the tricycle-gear 172—the 170's successor—as a giant step backward in airplane design. Attesting their viewpoint are the growing popularity of tailwheel conversions for 172s and the rapidly increasing prices for Cessna's original light four-seater. Cessna 170s typically are fetching substantially higher prices than other comparable four-seaters of the same vintage, including the much faster Piper Tri-Pacer. Also, the price tags on many 170s outstrip those on vastly better-equipped and newer 172s.

Though they cannot be classified as bargains, 170s still are affordable family-movers. The top average retail from the *Aircraft Bluebook* is listed at $24,000 (with a note that the price varies with the quality of restoration work). Owners characterize operating and maintenance costs as relative pittances, and they like to compare the performance and load-carrying capabilities with new four-seaters that cost far more. However, it is inevitable that the airplanes can show signs of their age, in the form of corrosion and fatigue. Though some parts are hard to find, help in the care and feeding of Cessna 170s is available from a supportive owners' group.

History

When Cessna started building 170s in 1948, it had only four other airplanes on its assembly lines. They were the svelte, two-seat, 85-hp 120 and 140 models, and the big, four-seat, radial-engine 190 and 195. The 170 actually is a stretched, four-seat version of the 140, powered by a six-cylinder, 145-hp Continental C145-2 engine (later to be redesignated the O-300A) and a two-blade McCauley propeller.

The original 170, built only in 1948, can be distinguished from its descendants by its fabric-covered, constant-chord, round-tip, V-strutted wings and by the absence of a dorsal fin. Inside the wings are three 12.5-gallon tanks (one in the left wing, two interconnected in the right), providing a usable supply of 33.5 gallons.

In 1949, the Model 170A made its debut with a dorsal fin and all-metal wings supported by a single strut on each side of the fuselage. Outboard of the struts, the wings taper out to their squared-off tips. The A-model's flaps and ailerons are a bit larger than the 170's, and the hinged flaps can be extended to 50 degrees (whereas the 170's flaps are limited to 30 degrees). The dorsal fin is identical to the one on the Model 195 and was added, supposedly, to improve directional stability. There's only one fuel tank in each of the 170A's wings, and maximum usable fuel capacity is 37 gallons.

While the original 170 is affectionately referred to, for obvious reasons, as the "ragwing," the A model sometimes is called the "straight wing." That's because unlike the 170, which has about one degree of dihedral, and the 170B, which has nearly three degrees, the 170A has no dihedral.

Para-lifter

In 1952 Cessna introduced the 170B. This model has what Cessna called "Para-lift" flaps—relatively large, slotted, semi-Fowler designs originally used on the Model 305 military observation plane, which blue-suiters dubbed the L-19 Bird Dog. Early B models have only four flap settings (zero, 20, 30 and 40 degrees). Those built after 1954 have an extra notch for 10 degrees of flap, which many pilots favor for takeoff.

In addition to being cranked up to nearly three degrees of dihedral, the 170B's wings have more twist than their predecessors'. The B model also has control balance weights that make its elevators a bit lighter to the touch.

Upper engine cowls on 170-series airplanes built before 1953 are hinged; those on later models are full pressure types with fairly large hatches that open onto the battery and oil dipstick. Airplanes built before mid-1953 also have straight, interchangeable main gear legs; later 170Bs have bowed and more acutely tapered legs, which cannot be swapped from side to side. Other changes in 1953 included addition of extra heating outlets for passenger seats and a windshield defroster, and replacement of piano-key type panel switches with push-pull knobs.

Airplanes built after 1954 can be distinguished by a cosmetic touch to their windows and by a different tailwheel-steering setup. The aft portions of their rear windows are flat, rather than round, and the airplanes have cables, rather than a rudder horn/spring system, for their tailwheels.

Tri-ing Times

Influenced, no doubt, by Piper's success with the Tri-Pacer (originally introduced in 1951 as a tricycle-gear option for the Pacer), Cessna introduced the Model 172 in 1956.

The last B models off the line differ from earlier 170s in having molded-plastic interiors, rather than cloth; an un-openable right-door window; and only one engine-cowl hatch, which opens onto both the oil dipstick and the battery. (The battery had been moved from the right to the left side of the engine compartment in 1954.)

Performance

A properly rigged 170 will cruise at 104 knots true at around 2,400 rpm (65 to 70 percent power) while burning between seven and eight gallons of fuel an hour at altitudes below 8,000 feet. Fuel can be drawn from either wing tank or from both of them at the same time (the latter is required for takeoff and landing). Direct-reading fuel gauges are located in the wing-root areas of the cabin.

Lead Problems

The Continental engine was designed to operate on 80/87-octane aviation fuel, which is increasingly becoming hard to find in many areas of the country, and many 170 owners have experienced problems on 100LL. Some have invested in exhaust-gas temperature (EGT) gauges for their airplanes and alleviate the problems by leaning aggressively. Others have sought relief from lead-fouling problems and the higher prices of avgas by operating their airplanes on premium unleaded automobile gasoline with STCs available either from the EAA Aviation Foundation in Oshkosh, Wis., or from Petersen Aviation in Minden, Neb.

Though its cabin generally is noisy and drafty, a 170 can carry four adults and full fuel. Extra heating outlets were added in 1953 to make the cabin tolerable in frosty air.

Generally, book performance numbers are achievable, according to owners. But some claim the takeoff figures in 170 POHs are conservative, at best. The book indicates that, under standard conditions, a 170 will require 1,820 feet for takeoff, 2,190 feet to clear a 50-foot obstacle. Subtract about 200 feet from those numbers if 20 degrees of flaps are used for departure. However, some owners say they regularly use up about half that amount of real estate getting aloft. The POH also shows that 1,145 feet are required for a normal landing, 1,210 feet to get in over an obstacle.

Best rate-of-climb speed is 77 knots, and climb rate diminishes from a sprightly 690 fpm at sea level to a leisurely 370 fpm at 7,000 feet. The airplane stalls at about 50 knots, clean, and 45 knots with full flaps.

Comfort and Loading

Visibility is excellent on the ground and in the air, due to the low panel and sloped engine cowl. Two wide doors and relatively big assist steps make it easy to board the airplane. Inside, there's plenty of room for four people, but 170 cabins tend to be rather noisy, and even the improved heating systems in late-model 170Bs are hard-pressed to deal with northern climes.

Unlike many other single-engine airplanes with four seats, most 170s can carry full fuel, four adults and their baggage. Maximum useful load of 170s and 170As with standard (that is, Spartan) equipment is 1,015 pounds; 995 pounds for the B model. Up to 120 pounds of baggage can be carried behind the rear seat but must be loaded through the front doors, since none of the airplanes was built with an external baggage hatch. External hatches have, however, been STC'd for the airplanes.

Handling

It would seem that, with the various changes made during the course of 170 production, there would be marked handling differences among the models. But pilots who have flown all three models say there is little difference.

Some idiosyncrasies arise from the different flap designs. The 170's are relatively small and limited to 30 degrees extension (at 90 mph, max). Though its flaps are not as effective as those on its successors (which can be extended at 100 mph), the original 170 can be slipped quite effectively. Slips with full flaps are prohibited in the A and B models, because their barn doors can block the air flowing over the tail, causing the nose to pitch down suddenly and severely. Another difference, mentioned earlier, is the lighter elevator control forces experienced in the 170B, due to its mass balance weights.

Owners seem to be split on whether three-pointers or wheelies are better for takeoff and landing. On one hand, they say, wheelies require longer ground runs and rolls, and higher airspeeds. On the other hand, the main gear legs are rather stiff, and three-pointers tend to give the tailwheel a good beating (and the occupants a good bouncing) if technique isn't perfect or the field is rough.

Swapping Ends

One long-time 170 pilot summed it up this way, "The 170 is one of the easier taildraggers to land, but any taildragger will bite you." Indeed, in a comparative study of 33 single-engine airplanes a few years ago, NTSB found 170s to be involved in a relatively high rate of ground-loop accidents. With 10 such accidents per 100,000 hours of flying time, the 170 came in fourth place. At the head of the list of ground-loopers was the Cessna 195, with a whopping 22 end-swaps per 100,000 hours. Then came the Stinson 108 and the Luscombe, each with a rate of about 13.

Close behind the 170 were its two-seat stablemates, the 120 and 140, with about nine ground-loop accidents per 100,000 hours. As might be expected, tricycle-gear airplanes fell to the bottom of the ground-loop list. The PA-22 Tri-Pacer placed in mid-range (15th, actually) with a rate of nearly three; the 172 was 29th with a rate of one ground-loop per 100,000 hours.

Studying more recent records, we found loss of control during takeoff or landing accounted for more than half of nonfatal accidents (40 out of 70) involving Cessna 170s during a recent six-year period. Though many occurred with low-timers at the controls, quite a few involved pilots with hundreds of hours in type. Also, several of the accidents involving loss of control and those involving collision with objects during takeoff or landing (there were nine of these) occurred in such formidable operating areas as country roads, rough fields and sand bars. A number of accidents were precipitated by broken main landing gear axles and wheels.

Of the 12 accidents involving either fatalities or serious injuries, four involved stalls and spins; four occurred during buzz-jobs or low-level aerobatics; and two involved continued VFR flight into instrument weather conditions (one pilot wasn't instrument-rated, the other was but the airplane wasn't suitably equipped). Two other pilots lost control of their 170s: one after the prop separated; one after a rusted rudder cable broke inflight.

Maintenance

Corrosion and fatigue cracks are the most frequent subjects of service difficulty reports filed with the FAA during recent years. Affected components include flight control cables, main landing gear support brackets, vertical stabilizer attachments, bulkheads and engine attach brackets. There was one report of severely corroded wing spars in a 170A that had been parked outside and not flown for three years.

Due to similarities between the 170 and the 172, parts are not a big problem. The International Cessna 170 Association frequently arranges to secure quantities of critical parts from Cessna Aircraft Corp. and other suppliers. A few years ago the group pooled its resources to have Cessna produce a supply of solid ("ski") axles. Two other types of axles used in production of 170s were hollow designs; and service difficulty and accident reports show that they are prone to break under excessive side loading. The association also was able to bring the price of seat tracks down substantially by placing a quantity order with Cessna.

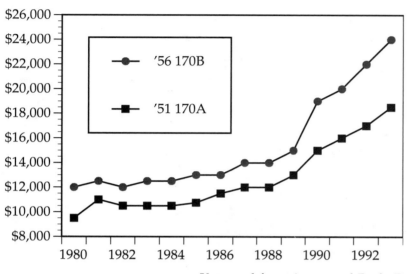

Modifications

Nearly 100 STCs have been approved, including dozens for installation of skis and floats. Many floatplane operators have opted for larger engines. Avcon and Bush, both in Udall, Kan., offer 180-hp Lycomings and constant-speed propellers for A and B models. Turbotech in Vancouver, Wash., has a 220-hp Franklin conversion for the 170B. Flap and aileron gap seals, and complete STOL modification kits are available from Horton STOL in Wellington, Kan., and from Avcon and Bush. Davids Aviation Services in San Andreas, Calif., also offers gap seals, as well as a thorough aerodynamic cleanup, complete with wheel pants, landing gear cuffs and fairings. Ponk Aviation in Camano Island, Wash., recently obtained an STC for beefed-up landing gear brackets.

Owners' Group

Efforts by the International Cessna 170 Assn. to secure needed parts for the airplanes already have been mentioned. In addition, the group publishes a monthly newsletter and four quarterly magazines containing tips on maintenance and safety, and conducts regional fly-ins and an annual convention. Velvet Fackeldey is the association's executive secretary: P.O. Box 1667, Lebanon, Mo. 65536, (417) 532-4847.

In addition, 170 owners are represented by the two big Cessna owners' groups: the Cessna Pilots Assn. in Wichita, Kans.; and the Cessna Owner Organization in Birmingham, Ala.

Conclusions

Tailwheel airplanes are great for nostalgia, but they do require some special skills that largely have been lost among today's pilots. Those who want a four-seat taildragger, and are willing to develop and hone the necessary skills, might want to consider buying an early-model 172 and having it converted to tailwheel configuration (see the Nov. 1, 1987 issue). This could actually cost less than buying a 170.

But the 170 is in a class by itself, and those who want the real McCoy aren't going to be bridled by a few extra dollars here or there. Since prices are going up, purchase can be seen as a good investment. And, as mentioned earlier, a 170 is a true four-seater with performance (if not mission flexibility) rivaling that of current production singles and acquisition and operating costs putting the brand-new airplanes to shame. Too, there's one very obvious fact: the 170 is a very handsome airplane.

Owner Comments

When I purchased my 1954 Cessna 170B in June 1987, I was looking for a taildragger that could carry my family, 100 pounds of baggage and fuel for 350 miles with reserves. The Stinson 108 and the Piper Tri-Pacer/Pacer meet the requirements about as well as the Cessna 170B, and I fully expected to end up with a PA-22 and convert it to tailwheel configuration. My 170B just happened to become available locally, and even though it cost $3,000 more than a good Tri-Pacer, I am pleased with my choice.

The plane is a nice blend of classic looks and practical utility. It runs fine on auto fuel, burning eight gph at a cruise speed of 115 mph. At altitude, it will produce true airspeeds in the 135-mph range.

Though my pre-purchase inspection showed three cylinders with compression in the 60/80 range, after putting 75 hours on the plane in three months, compression was 74/80 or better in all cylinders. The plane was in need of some TLC. It was out of rig and needed a wheel alignment. Working with my mechanic, I did most of the annual inspection myself. The only serious problems discovered were worn rudder cables, which were replaced, and a bent rod on the elevator trim actuator, which was straightened. The inspection revealed that the right wing is from a 1959 C-172, but the log has no comment as to why it was changed.

In an attempt to escape lead-fouling problems, many owners have switched to autogas with STCs from EAA or Petersen. Others have found that EGTs and aggressive leaning help their 80-octane engines cope with 100LL.

The 170B will land much shorter than it will take off. With two on board and full fuel, it is no problem to land and stop in 300 feet. Takeoff is not so impressive but noticeably better than a 172 with the same engine.

Visibility is very good for a taildragger. Taxiing can be done without S-turns, and the nose is very low in level flight. In fact, the low nose attitude in climb was my greatest problem in transitioning to the plane. Unlike most taildraggers, the runway ahead is in full view during climbout. This would fool me into raising the nose too much.

The only operational problem I have had is a stuck exhaust valve. After the second occurrence, the valve guides and stems were cleaned and I changed to Mobil AV1 synthetic oil. I had been running AeroShell 15W-50. A Continental engineer I spoke with was very high on AV1. He felt the extremely long oil change intervals Mobil has experimented with (500 hours, plus) were risky, due to lead build-up in the oil, but he cited very good experience with 100-hour oil changes in his Cessna 150 club airplane. A nice side benefit of the AV1 oil is the way minor leaks dry up, leaving the engine dry and oil-free.

The International Cessna 170 Assn. is an excellent club. It provides advice on maintenance, places to fly, etc. Members even pool their resources and get Cessna to make up a supply of parts, such as solid axles and seat rails. For $15 a year, membership is a bargain.

I compared the specifications in the recent article on the Archer and Tobago (May 1, 1988 issue). They are really in a different class, but the lack of major performance differences is notable. With the exception of range, the 170B compares very well with these new, higher-powered airplanes. Besides, the value of the 170B is going up at a very nice rate.

Gary B. Collins
Cincinnati, Ohio

I have owned a 1949 Cessna 170A for just under two years and have found it to be reliable, great fun and cheap to operate; there have been no surprises or unexpected expenses. Total time is 2,300 hours on the airframe and 860 on the engine. Last year's annual, with me helping, cost $117.

Operated according to the EAA's autogas STC, the airplane burns 7.5 gallons of unleaded regular an hour. I have not had some of the problems that other owners seem to have encountered using autogas (soot in the exhaust, etc.). I do lean aggressively, though, and keep away from higher octane autogas to avoid the toluene additives. When I have to use 100LL avgas, I always add TCP.

The airplane is noisy, but addition of a voice-activated intercom solved that. It cruises around 115 to 120 mph at 2,450 rpm.

Figure maintenance to be the same as a 172. Parts are still available, though some, such as some body parts, are no longer available. I had an entire front cowl remade locally for about $1,100.

As with buying any used airplane, a pre-purchase inspection could avoid later problems. Be especially wary for corrosion and cracked axles on some of the earlier aircraft. The International Cessna 170 Association is a great place to start if you are interested in buying one of these classics.

The airplane is just plain fun. It attracts attention wherever it goes. I use it mainly for grass-roots type fly-ins and for cross-country trips up to 500 miles. It doesn't go fast, but it's a fantastic way to rediscover the countryside; and at under $10 an hour for direct operating costs, you get to see lots of country.

Ron Adams
Germantown, Tenn.

My 170, a 1950 A model, has been in my family for the past 20 years. I feel the 170 is an excellent airplane that has extremely docile handling qualities, excellent load-carrying capabilities and reasonable speed at very reasonable operating costs. The airplane is a sought-after classic that keeps increasing in value.

I feel that Cessna took a giant step backwards when they phased out the 170 in favor of the 172. I normally cruise at 118 mph, true, on 7.2 gph. Even the 172 taildragger conversion can't match these numbers.

The airplane is great for flight training and as an all-around family airplane. The 170 is a logical move up for owners of smaller 140 Cessnas who don't want to lay out the large investment required to purchase and operate a 180.

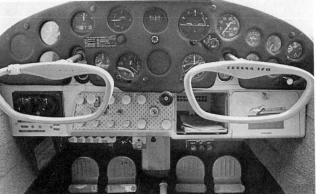

The 170 has an unusually good field of view for a taildragger. Visibility from the cockpit, both on the ground and in flight, is excellent (better than the 172). This is due, primarily, to the low-cut panel, down-sloped cowling and the close proximity of the front seats to the leading edge of the wing.

It also is an easy airplane to maintain, due to the absence of complex systems and its commonality with the 172. The O-300 Continental is an extremely dependable and very smooth-running engine and gives the 170 adequate power under most conditions. There are several STCs available to convert to 180 and higher horsepower, but I personally prefer the 145 Continental.

A low panel eyebrow and sloped engine cowl afford excellent visibility. Owners say S-turns aren't necessary while taxiing.

As Parts and Maintenance Coordinator for the International Cessna 170 Association, I find the majority of parts for the airplane still pretty easy to obtain. Cessna has been very helpful in supporting us when they were able to. The 170 association is one of the finest type-clubs, offering lower insurance rates, an inside track on maintenance and parts tips, and the comradeship of some of the friendliest and most helpful people I know.

All models of the 170 have excellent characteristics, but I feel the older ragwings and A models, in many cases, have been unfairly overshadowed by the later B models. A potential 170 owner who is shy on conventional gear time would be well advised to seek several hours of dual from an experienced taildragger-qualified instructor to acquaint himself with the peculiarities of conventional-gear aircraft.

Although there are other four-place airplanes on the market that are faster or may

Cost/Performance/Specifications

Model	Year Built	Average Retail Price	Cruise Speed (kts)	Useful Load (lbs)	Fuel Std/Opt (gals)	Engine	TBO (hrs)	Overhaul Cost
170	1948	$17,500	106	1,015	33.5	145-hp Cont. C-145-2	1,800	$8,500
170A	1949	$18,000	106	1,015	37	145-hp Cont. C-145-2	1,800	$8,500
170A	1950	$18,250	106	1,015	37	145-hp Cont. C-145-2	1,800	$8,500
170A	1951	$18,500	106	1,015	37	145-hp Cont. C-145-2	1,800	$8,500
170B	1952	$22,000	106	995	37	145-hp Cont. C-145-2	1,800	$8,500
170B	1953-55	$22,000	106	995	37	145-hp Cont. O-300A	1,800	$8,500
170B	1956	$24,000	106	995	37	145-hp Cont. O-300A	1,800	$8,500

carry more, I don't feel any offer the all-around "mission mix" that is found in the 170. When this is combined with the airplane's classic good looks, I truly feel that it makes the Cessna 170 certainly one of the finest, if not *the* finest four-place airplane ever built.

Tom Hull
Hollywood, Md.

We've operated a 1954 C-170B in our business for general utility purposes and as a backup for a P210 photo ship since 1968. The aircraft was originally outfitted as a floatplane, with interior corrosion-proofing and lift rings installed above the fuselage, but it never actually has been on floats.

Fuselage-mounted venturis keep the gyros spooled up. Lacking accessory pads and dampened crankshafts, most 170 engines cannot accommodate vacuum pumps.

We converted the 170 over to a Lycoming O-360 with a constant-speed prop in 1981. It made the plane a terrific performer compared to the standard Continental 145-hp version. A couple years after the engine conversion, we relocated the battery to the rear fuselage, which markedly improved the balance of the plane, particularly on solo flights. We also installed a camera hole in the floor.

The aircraft has proven to be reliable, with no vicissitudes in either flight operations or maintenance. Cross-country, we plan on 105 knots at 55 percent power, with fuel consumption about 7.8 gph.

The O-360 can rapidly deplete the plane's modest 37-gallon fuel capacity at high power settings, so we tend to go high and throttle back, and hope for a tailwind. Another negative is the high noise level and drafty cabin. Our plane's hands-off stability is poor.

Annuals have been running about $900 to $1,000. The plane is a bargain compared to the P210.

In conclusion, the Lycoming power greatly increased the utility and productivity of the classic old 170 airframe. It's hard to imagine a better combination for the price.

Stephen J. Power
Vacaville, Calif.

I have owned a 1952 Cessna 170B since July 1978 and have found it a very inexpensive and virtually vice-free aircraft. I do my own maintenance and very seldom have to do more than routine servicing during annuals. I also did some modifications, including an Avcon 180-hp engine conversion 750 hours ago, and changed the interior using Airtex carpets and side walls. The kits were outstanding and fit with no reworking or modification.

There are two drawbacks, however. First, the 37-gallon fuel supply is not enough for the Lycoming conversion. I wish someone would make a retrofit kit that would add another 15 gallons. Second, the instrument panel becomes a mess when you have a couple of modern radios and a set of gyros.

The airplane will carry just about anything you can close the doors on and still get out short and fly high.

Tom Schad
Del Rio, Tex.

I bought a Cessna 170B in 1964. Originally, three doctors owned the plane, but I am now the sole owner. All of us learned to fly in Cessna 120s, so this plane was absolutely no problem. A 1955 model, the plane now has almost 6,000 hours TT.

Like most Continental O-300s, my plane's engine has been overhauled "a few times." Quite a few hours have passed since the last one, but the jugs have been overhauled on an as-needed basis. As a result, I have two spare cylinders ready to go to save down-time.

In 1953, hinged cowls gave way to full-pressure types with large hatches opening on to the battery and oil dipstick.

Many years ago, the Goodyear brakes were replaced with Clevelands off a wrecked 172. This was probably the first significant update ever done on any old Cessna. The plane is flown at least once a week, unless I'm out of town or the weather is bad. In the past few years, I rarely have taken trips of more than a hundred miles each way. At one time, though, I had two kids in college in Santa Barbara and ran a weekly commuting service for myself and other parents of students who were neighbors and friends. There was minimal LAX hassle in those days.

It is difficult to establish the exact cost of maintenance, since the plane is a hobby and much of the maintenance is done when the mechanical or aesthetic problem is first noticed or the AD is first published. I would say the annual inspections have run about $200 in the past few years, though the last annual included a lot of cowling repairs and repainting of gear legs and this cost $500.

Oliver R. Nees, Jr.
Long Beach, Calif.

I've owned a 1948 Cessna 170 since 1976. The aircraft has 3,986 TT, 970 hours since a Feb. 1973 overhaul and 303 hours since a 1982 top overhaul. Other than the top overhaul, which cost $2,500 initially and about $1,000 more over the next year to correct the rebuilder's mistakes and defects, the aircraft has been inexpensive to own. Maintenance costs about $600 a year, including an average of $300 for an annual.

A Ceconite fabric job in 1975 was poorly done, and I'll have to have it redone this year. Quotes, including paint, have run from $4,000 to $5,000. Shop rates for most car or aircraft repairs in the bay area are $40 to $50 an hour (higher for cars than aircraft).

The generator has been replaced twice, the voltage regulator once. I had to have a fuel tank repaired because water had collected and corroded the bottom of the tank. The rudder bellcrank broke when the plane was hit by heavy wind while parked four years ago; flap hinges also have been damaged by wind about every three years.

I've used autogas legally since 1983. The airplane burns eight gph on short flights, 7.5 gph on cross-countries. The Cessna 170 has no bad habits. It's easy to slip, three-point and wheel-land. It slow flies at 57 mph at 1,950 rpm, cruises at 117 mph at 2,450 rpm.

The 170 is a very forgiving aircraft, though the flaps are essentially useless (unlike the Fowler flaps on the C-170B). The heater also is useless (again, unlike the 170B), but it isn't needed much in the bay area. The aircraft is easy to handle in crosswinds, though I did have one 45-degree crosswind at 30 knots where I had to use wing-walkers to park the aircraft.

A cable tailwheel system, rather than a rudder horn and spring, distinguish airplanes built during the last two years of production.

In summary, the ragwing C-170 is an attractive aircraft. It is inexpensive to own and maintain, easy to fly, gentle in a stall and hard to spin. The current market value of, maybe, $10,000 versus $8,500 purchase cost 12 years ago reflects the fact that most buyers seem to prefer the metal-wing C-170B with Fowler flaps.

Joseph J. Neff
Newark, Calif.

I owned a Cessna 170A (1951 model) for six years. In 700 hours of flying, I found performance to be adequate, even with four people aboard; cruise was about 100 knots on nine gph.

The airplane had excellent inflight handling qualities, but the small flaps on the A model left something to be desired. Ground handling was fair, with steering accomplished more by differential braking than with the tailwheel. I never did like the "soft" landing gear legs on the 170 and 170A, which would cause a teeter-totter effect when taxiing, especially in a crosswind. Later B models had stiffer gear legs, like those on the Cessna 180.

For a taildragger, over-the-nose visibility on the ground was excellent—much better than either the 120/140 or the 180. Because of inadequate heat and poor door sealing, cabin comfort was poor in New England winter weather. The back seat stayed close to OAT in flight.

My overall opinion of the airplane is favorable. However, for what some of these 170s are selling for, I would be more inclined to get a more recent vintage airplane and experience less nickel-and-dime breakdowns, as was the case with my 30-year-old airplane.

Robert S. Andrews
Claremont, Calif.

Cessna Skyhawk 172

The Cessna 172 probably ties with the Piper Cub as everyman's vision of the little airplane. Probably more people recognize the Cub name; but more recognize the shape of the Skyhawk.

A grand total of 35,773 were built during its 31-year production run, and there are close to 24,000 flying in the United States plus thousands more flying around the world. (And don't forget: it was a C-172 that was the first private airplane to visit Red Square in Moscow.

Still struttin' its stuff, the Skyhawk offers a stone-simple design that may not break any speed records, but won't break the bank, either. This particular model is two decades old.

Even for the less adventurous, the 172 continues to appeal for its simple virtues, undemanding flying characteristics, good value and availability. A lot of readers have shared their 172 experiences and expenses with *The Aviation Consumer*. Despite the wide variety of comments, enthusiasm for the aircraft is universally high. Two readers sum up its qualities quite well:

"The Skyhawk is the benchmark for a docile, easy-to-fly airplane with no rude surprises. It won't eat your lunch at the gas pumps, the maintenance hangar, or on short final. But if you're looking for speed or style, look somewhere else."

"It is the perfect all-around airplane—economical, easy to fly, easy to maintain, stable in all flight modes, roomy enough for all the stuff you'd want to haul with the back seat out or comfortable enough for four less-than-FAA-sized folks, full tanks and a couple of small daypacks with the seat in."

History

The 1949 170A taildragger was the progenitor of the C-172—and practically every other Cessna single.

Incidentally, tales about the 170 and 172 and other fascinating episodes in the development of all Cessna singles, including the Skyhook helicopter, are related in *Cessna: Wings for the World; The Single-Engine Development Story*, by William D. Thompson. He spent nearly 30 years at Cessna as an engineering test pilot; at retirement, he was Manager of Flight Test and Aerodynamics. He continues flight test and related activities as a consultant and FAA Engineering Representative.)

The original 170 was not a very good tail dragger, especially because of poor roll response (the ailerons were lifted directly from the smaller and lighter—and shorter wing span—140).

The cabin is comfortable even for four—as it should be, because time won't fly. Be sure to check those front seat tracks for slippage.

Autopilot Handicap

The 170A/B cured the problem of aileron power, but introduced new ones. The design update also included a dorsal fin. A modified Frise-type aileron was used to minimize adverse yaw, which was accomplished at the cost of poor aileron centering in cruise. According to Thompson, this hampered the performance of low-cost autopilots (a characteristic well-known by many 172 pilots.) It also exhibited less desirable characteristics in the stall, so the outer portion of the wing was twisted, or washed-out. Other forms of aerodynamic tweaking took place, all of which showed up in the 172.

The 172 really is a tricycle gear 170, but one that nearly did not make it.

Met-Co-Aire of Fullerton, Calif. had already developed a tri-gear modification for the 170. Piper's Tri-Pacer was selling well. One reason why the hoped-for scenario of getting everyone into the sky did not occur was that flying did not come easily to most people. It took considerable work to achieve even the lowest level of skill. The tricycle gear promised to simplify things considerably.

Destroy It

Thompson says in his book: "Unfortunately, Frank Martin, Sales Manager, was aware of our 'experimental freedom' and frequently made weekend visits through the shop." The result of one such visit, during which he saw the tricycle gear mockup, was a formal order to destroy it. "Fortunately for Cessna, it was disassembled and stowed away," Thompson noted. Reportedly, the concern of Cessna management was that a tri-gear airplane would not be able to handle unpaved strips and would be prone to upset during taxi. Meanwhile, the competition and the after-market were stealing sales. The upshot of competitive pressures and evaluation of the after-market mod was authorization of a secret development program to develop a tricycle gear version of the 170C, which had been certified but not put into production. The R&D effort that became the 172 was conducted at an isolated farm strip.

First flight occurred on June 12, 1955. Among the development issues and problems were controllability versus stability, the above-mentioned ground handling concerns plus fear of propeller strikes, yaw or directional stability and the need to ensure enough elevator power to overcome the high thrust line, which tended to press-down the nose gear (and encourage prop strikes).

Other issues were developing a sufficiently strong firewall structure to handle the nose gear stresses, proper alignment of the main gear, nose wheel centering in flight (and in-flight disconnect from rudder inputs) and nosewheel shimmy problems.

Obviously, many of those identified problems have yet to be satisfactorily re-solved.

The 172 main and nose gear that resulted were fairly short, achieving the lowest possible center of gravity to improve ground handling and to avoid upset. A total of 2,318 landings were made during the service test program by a number of pilots with widely varied experience to "prove" the 172s characteristics.

Land-O-Matic

Thus was born what was called the "Land-O-Matic" gear, and advertisements that basically related driving and flying: drive it into the sky, drive it into the ground (the last phrase came to have a double meaning, however). It was not quite that simple, however, and a number of modifications were made over time to improve the ground handling and cross-wind runway qualities of the Sky-hawk.

There was a performance penalty to pay for putting the third gear element in front, too. Speeds and service ceiling were degraded compared to the 170.

Models and Development

The 172 was introduced in 1956 powered by a Continental O-300-D, six cylinder engine rated at 145 hp turning a fixed-pitch propeller. Gross weight was 2,200 pounds.

The 172A, with the vertical tail swept, was introduced in 1960. The new "modern" empennage was heavier; rudder power was reduced, and directional stability was degraded somewhat.

The 172B was developed for the 1961 model year. Landing gear was shortened by three inches to improve crosswind and taxi handling while the motor mounts were increased by the same amount to retain propeller ground clearance.

A baggage door was incorporated for the first time. The upscale (it even included a starter button!), Skyhawk, version was introduced.

The first float plane version was introduced in 1961. In 1962, the C Model featured a 50-pound increase in gross weight, to 2,250 pounds.

In 1963, the "Omni-Vision" rear-window 172D version was introduced. To help overcome the further degradation in handling, the span of the horizontal tail was increased by eight inches. The center strip in the windshield was gone, replaced by a one-piece windshield. An optional child's seat for the baggage bay was introduced. Gross weight was increased another 50 pounds, to 2,300.

Models 172 E through H (1964 - 1967) featured such tweaks as a shorter nose gear stroke (three inches shorter). Electrically-operated flaps were introduced on the 172F. Many people lamented the passing of the manually-operated versions be-cause these were more precise, less distracting and easier to maintain. Also in-cluded were such improvements as better laid-out instrument panels and im-proved panel lighting.

Engine Switch

A significant change occurred with the 172I of 1968: the switch to Lycoming power, the 150-hp 0-320-E2D. In addition to new cowling and motor mounts, the

new propulsion package included an oil cooler.

In his book, Thompson notes that the force for change was an earlier corporate conviction that the 177 Cardinal—the airplane of the future—would kill the 172. So Cessna ordered 4,000 engines from Lycoming. When management admitted that the 150-hp Cardinal was woefully underpowered, the Skyhawk inherited the engine. It included the troublesome "dual" Bendix magneto (really, an almost two-in-one with a single drive).

The 172K of 1971 featured a switch from the famed Wittman spring steel main gear to tapered steel tubes that provided more fore and aft flexing to supposedly improve ground handling on rough surfaces.

This '75 Skyhawk was the 100,000 single produced by Cessna's Pawnee division. The airplane is probably still flying. The factory has long since shut its doors. The high wing shields against sun and rain, and sightings of low-wing aircraft in the pattern.

Lights Off

The landing light was moved from the leading edge of the left wing to the nose bowl of the cowl. This improved airflow over the wing (poorly-installed lenses and frames cause air flow separation and wing drop in the stall) but complicated cowl removal and greatly reduced bulb life.

The 172L of 1972 incorporated an extended dorsal fin. This improved longitudinal stability. It reduced the full-flap pitch-down tendency in slips and made it more difficult to enter a spin. The latter was a negative for training applications, however.

Bonding, which Cessna developed extensively, especially in its multi-engine and turbine models, was first tested in the fabrication of 172 baggage doors and then cabin doors.

Camber Lift

The popularity of after-market slow-flight modifications, such as the Robertson STOL kits, led Cessna to use a recontoured leading edge with the 1973 172M. The

Cost/Performance/Specifications

Model	Year	Average Retail Price	Cruise Speed (kts)	Useful Load (lbs)	Fuel Std/Opt (gals)	Engine	TBO (hrs)	Overhaul Cost
172	1956-59	$15,400	108	940	37	145-hp Cont.O-300-A	1,800	$13,500
172A,B,C	1960-62	$16,500	114	940	42	145-hp Cont.O-300-C,D	1,800	$13,500
172D,E,F	1963-65	$18,300	114	970	42	145-hp Cont.O-300-D	1,800	$13,500
172G,H	1966-67	$19,300	114	985	42	145-hp Cont.O-300-D,E2D	1,800	$13,500
172I, K	1968-70	$20,500	115	985	42/52	150-hp Lyc.O-320-E2D	2,000	$9,500
172L,M	1971-73	$23,300	115	965	42/52	150-hp Lyc.O-200-E2D	2,000	$9,500
172M	1974-76	$29,500	120	965	42/52	150-hp Lyc.O-200-E2D	2,000	$9,500
172N	1977-78	$30,600	122	770	43/54	160-hp Lyc.O-320-H2AD	2,000	$10,500
172N	1979-80	$35,500	122	770	43/54	160-hp Lyc.O-320-H2AD	2,000	$10,500
172P	1981-82	$45,000	122	770	43/54	160-hp Lyc.O-320-D2J	2,000	$9,500
172P	1983-84	$54,500	120	680	43/54	160-hp Lyc.O-320-D2J	2,000	$9,500
172P	1985-86	$65,700	120	680	54/68	160-hp Lyc.O-320-D2J	2,000	$9,500

Prices from Aircraft Bluebook Price Digest

"Camber Lift" droop, or increased radius, leading edge made it possible to operate at a higher angle of attack at low speed. However, aileron effectiveness in the stall and spin recovery were degraded. Spin entry also was made more complicated.

According to Thompson (and other factory pilots at the time), there was no measurable improvement in performance, and—tellingly —the performance data in the operating manual did not change. As Thompson notes, "Our customers typically approached and landed too fast." Not incidentally, the accident record continues to bear out that observation.

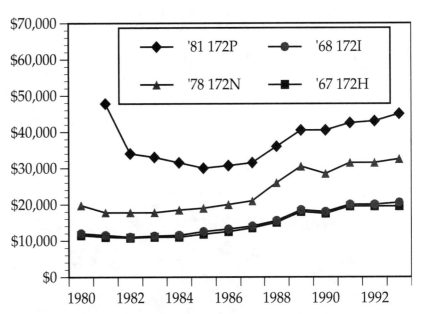

In 1974, cruise performance was improved through an effort to reduce drag and improve air flow through the cowling. This turned out to be a greater improvement than many of the other changes. At 8,000 feet, according to the factory, 75 percent cruise increased from 113 to 120 knots. This notable improvement suggests that if Cessna had paid more attention to aerodynamics than to perceived market movements, the 172 and other airplanes would have performed far, far better.

With the mandated change to low-lead (a misnomer in itself), theoretically less-polluting fuels for political as opposed to technical reasons, engines designed to operate with 80 octane fuel (the bulk of the general aviation fleet) showed various signs of distress. Lead fouling of plugs and valves rose to epidemic proportions. Deposits caused hot spots that, in turn, caused premature failure of engine components. Fuel system elements deteriorated because of new and incompatible aromatics and other additives.

Low-Lead "Solution"

The Cessna and Lycoming solution to a 100LL compatible powerplant was a disaster. In 1977 the 172N, fitted with the now-infamous O-320-H2AD, was introduced. (AD stands for airworthiness directive or anguished driver.)

The good things were 10 additional horsepower, an increase in service ceiling (and high density altitude performance) and a slight increase in speed. This was overwhelmed by the bad news, which reduced to its simplest form is poor lubrication of the valve train. This is particularly noticeable in cold weather. It was found that cold starts could cause terminal damage very quickly, with large metal contaminants introduced to bearings, oil pump and other critical components in short order.

To their credit, Cessna and Lycoming supported owners to a generous degree, as aviation goes, but it took a long time to understand the nature and cause of the problem and to devise ways to alleviate (note: not fix) it. More than 5,000 were built, and 4,784 remain on the U.S. register.

The engine was replaced in the 1981 172P with another model, the O-320-D2J. This is the last of the "real" Skyhawks. Production ceased in 1985.

Gross weight increased to 2,400 pounds. The landing light (actually, dual lights) was relocated once again: back to the left wing leading edge, but this time just outboard of the strut (less flexing and therefore less airflow disturbance there). Maximum flap travel was reduced from the usual 40 to 30 degrees to meet requirements to demonstrate a full-flap go-around at gross weight.

Radius of the horizontal stabilizer leading edge was increased. This reduced forces and improved handling qualities.

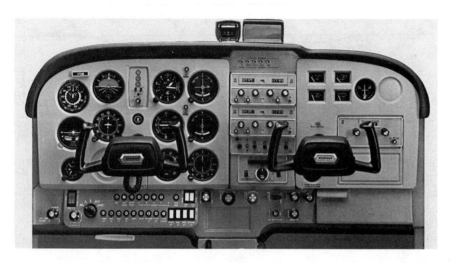

Home to an entire generation of fledgling pilots, the stable Mabel will take a lot of punishment, and its Royalite panel will crack a grin after all these years. The ARC radios are not held in such low esteem as before, it seems.

The Best, the Worst

Until fairly recently, it was easy to pick the worst 172: the notorious O-320-H2AD engined 172N. However—at least for those willing to get the information and take the extra care in terms of correct oil, proper additives and thorough pre-heating as well as commitment to regular flying, the problems of the H engine are manageable.

It is now a foot race as to whether the 172N is less desirable than the 172 through 172H —Continental O-300-D powered—models. Overhauls on the six-cylinder engine are more expensive—the *Aircraft Blue Book Price Digest* says $13,500—than on the four-cylinder Lycoming engines, which run $9,500 for the E2D and D2J (first and last) and $10,500 for the H2AD. If price is not the major concern, the last version 172P—all things being equal—is the most desirable for the average pilot looking for IFR-capable transportation.

All things being equal includes at the minimum no flight school history, no power or pipe line patrol history; good maintenance and average time; complete records; no wrecks, no corrosion and fair equipment. Infrequent use and poor maintenance probably are the biggest negatives for any 172.

Wichita's variation on the "don't buy a car that was built on Monday or Friday" largely is a reflection of degraded quality when production was being increased. As one reader claims: "The decline in Cessna quality control from about 1975 through 1979 is evident in the airframe. The 50s models have much less dimpling and oil canning skin." However, much of the factory-induced trouble—such as the widespread corrosion problem introduced by poor pre-paint preparation in the late 1970s—should have been corrected in most 172s by now.

For basic day VFR flying, an earlier 172 might be best. The original Skyhawk with the straight tail and "fastback" fuselage is the best handling. "Best" translates into the one with the most straightforward, verifiable history and usage at a price you can handle.

Generally speaking, a lot of the modifications developed by Cessna for the 172 are not improvements. Empty weight tended to go up. Handling characteristics sometimes were degraded. And most, except for the aerodynamic cleanup introduced on the 1974 172M, resulted in performance reduction. Don't be fooled by the higher-powered models. Aside from hot and high capability, the additional operating, maintenance and overhaul costs are not worth the marginal performance increases.

The 172 is the best basic transportation airplane for a price and for the average pilot ever devised. Stick to the basics.

Some readers are delighted with their Continental-powered Skyhawks, some with their H2AD (modified or unmodified) 172Ns.

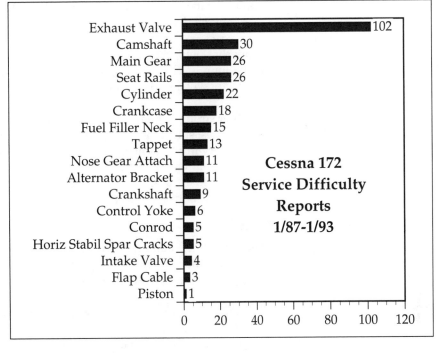

Cessna 172
Service Difficulty
Reports
1/87-1/93

Exhaust Valve	102
Camshaft	30
Main Gear	26
Seat Rails	26
Cylinder	22
Crankcase	18
Fuel Filler Neck	15
Tappet	13
Nose Gear Attach	11
Alternator Bracket	11
Crankshaft	9
Control Yoke	6
Conrod	5
Horiz Stabil Spar Cracks	5
Intake Valve	4
Flap Cable	3
Piston	1

The O-300D is unquestionably one of the most successful and comparatively trouble-free engines ever to come from Continental. But it is old, and it has two extra cylinders to maintain and repair.

And neither the pre-H E2D nor the post-H D2J Lycomings are free from valve train and other problems. The D2J is not completely happy with 100LL, either.
All the high-versus-low wing arguments included, it gets down to a matter of preference. But on sheer numbers, the 172 is the winner.

Performance

Reader letters on the 172 are interesting in their realism. Most refer it as a two-to-three place airplane with poor performance at high altitude or high density altitude. It is variously described as honest and forgiving in handling.

Most owners settle on eight gallons per hour, more or less, as the average fuel burn. Allowing for leaning errors and other variations, most owners figure their Skyhawks to be three-and-a-half to four-hour airplanes, and most who operate them IFR use 100 knots as the flight plan speed.

The 172 can easily be operated out of 2,000-foot strips. Well flown, it can handle even shorter ones. But it takes less room to land over the traditional general aviation 50-foot barrier than it does to take off, which traps many pilots. And, it is very sensitive to density altitude.

The aircraft also is sensitive to loading. Cg range is quite generous, to be sure, but tolerance to overloading is slim. The relative interior spaciousness, including the baggage bay, belies its payload limitations (and, to beat the dead horse, the performance variations with temperature and altitude).

There are few complaints about the handling qualities. And for the average—

non-aerobatic—pilot, there shouldn't be. Pitch forces are the highest of the three axes, but good speed control minimizes this.

Properly flown, the 172 can handle stiff crosswinds. Improperly handled, it suffers a high level of landing accidents. Unfortunately, too many pilots (and their instructors) believe those old drive-it-into-the-sky-and-back ads.

Another strong tendency of the 172 family is pilot-induced oscillation. In stressful approaches, such as poorly-planned ones, or those made in gusty conditions, and in recovery from bounced landings, there is an almost universal tendency among pilots unfamiliar with the 172 to "chase" pitch control with out-of-sync inputs that can cause alarming pitch excursions. The end result frequently is a loss of directional control, prop strike, nose gear failure—or all three.

Few Vices

The truth of the matter, however, is that the 172 has few vices. It has proven itself as an incredibly forgiving airplane. And it probably has enabled a great many people to be pilots who otherwise would not have survived the cut.

The 172 is well-mannered. However, low-time pilots and those unfamiliar with the type can be brought to grief with the pitch changes that occur with configuration (flap) and power changes, especially in a poorly-planned approach or during a panicky go-around or balked landing. Just a little bit of practice and experience go a long way.

One of the great strengths of the 172 is its comfort. While its dimensions are not generous, for all but the longest or widest of pilots and passengers, it is comfortable. For sightseers, the back seat of a Skyhawk is one of the best places to be.

Seats in earlier (and unmodified) models are somewhat skimpy and uncomfortable after a couple of hours. In later models, both the comfort and adjustability of the seats are good.

Support

Thanks to the population and varied utility of the 172, parts support is comparatively good. A number of firms specialize in cannibalizing airplanes for major components, and others continue to manufacture parts for the after market. Most readers have said that obtaining parts has not been a problem (although the quality of some replacement parts can be).

Modifications

Forty years ago, the general aviation industry was busy putting the tail wheel in front. Now, there are modifiers that have developed kits to put the nose wheel in the tail. You can make your 172 look like a 170! The number of modifications and suppliers for the 172 is too long to list. Everything from thicker windshields and cabin windows (reduce noise and vibration) to aileron and flap gap seals to STOL kits and engine upgrades is available.

It is worth taking the time to evaluate possible effects. For instance, additional fuel capacity is good to have, even necessary for some operators. But the reduction in payload has to be considered and the tradeoff weighed. Perhaps a combination of auxiliary tanks and a gross weight increase—which has its own limitations—is advisable.

There are owners who swear by an auto gas STC and others who have it but don't use it; those who like the extra performance of a more powerful engine (180-hp conversions are the most popular) and others who feel it is better to put the money into good overhauls of the original engine type. One owner wrote: "I considered a 180-hp O-360 kit estimated cost was close to $20,000, or the equivalent of two "H" engine overhauls a high cost for 13-17 knot increase at altitude."

Some owners feel flap and aileron gap seals pay off both in low-speed handling and improved cruise. Others say there isn't any difference.

Perhaps the best advice is to spend the time and money, initially at least, on careful inspection, replacement and repair of the basic airplane and its systems.

Maintenance

One fairly well-to-do pilot, who has owned a variety of airplanes, has described the 172 as the only aircraft he really could afford to own and operate. Most owners, particularly those who have had their Skyhawks for a few years, report fairly low annual costs.

Depending upon the service history of a particular 172, the first year or two can be very expensive. Heavily-used airplanes will need a lot of parts replaced. Landing gear elements such as main gear attach bolts, nose gear mount and the firewall suffer gross abuse and also are showing the cumulative effects of age.

Former *Aviation Consumer* staffer John Likakis now edits sister publication *Light-Plane Maintenance*. In the April, 1993 issue his article "Skyhawk Owner's Survival Guide" appears. In preparation for it, Likakis reviewed service difficulty reports (SDRs) for January 1987 to January 1993. There was a total of 103 on the airframe and 204 on the powerplant. While SDRs represent the tip of the iceberg with respect to maintenance problems in the field, they are useful indicators of weaknesses and suggest areas for careful scrutiny.

Baffles and Spalling

Likakis makes several useful suggestions. One that applies literally to every engine installation is that the condition of baffles requires regular inspection and replacement. Another is that cam and tappet spalling is a fact of life with Lycoming engines. About the only sign is metal in the oil.

Any 172 without a replaceable-element filter should have one installed; they should be cut open and examined for metal particles during frequent oil and filter changes. Oil analysis is a useful investment, too.

Also, there frequently is a relationship between SDRs and accident/incident reports that can highlight design and material problems as well as problems with pilot technique and decision making. That is the case with the Skyhawk. For a design as old and with so many airplanes operating, the number of SDRs and airworthiness directives (ADs) is surprisingly small. There is a total of 82 ADs on the 172: 33 on the airframe, ll on the powerplant (seven on the infamous H2AD engine), three on the propeller and 35 on various accessories (eight of these on magneto problems).

Clearly, the seat track continues to be a troublesome element of the Skyhawk and other Cessna singles.

The SDR and AD records do not cover all the potential problems that 172 owners and prospective owners should inspect for carefully. Some serious corrosion has been uncovered in the flying surfaces, in the belly of the fuselage and around the main gear fittings. This is a function of poor or no corrosion protection at the factory and the exposure of the individual airplane. Also, a lot of Skyhawks have been notorious leakers (and many have spent most if not all of their existence tied down outside).

Rigging and condition of control cables, pulleys, fairleads and fittings should also be carefully checked. Many 172s have been poorly or improperly rigged over the years. Corrosion has been found between cable strands that has not been visible to external inspection, and many elements of the primary flight control and flap actuating system are very hard to get to. Thus, they tend to be inspected infrequently if at all. Things like this tend to be disguised rather than fixed by a new paint job.

The design is notorious for poor nose-gear shimmy dampening. The problem is exacerbated by poor pilot technique: too much forward pressure (down elevator) on the yoke during takeoff and too many nose-wheel first or three-point landings. The latter is good technique in tail draggers; not in tricycle gear airplanes.

Accidents

The FAA record contains 1,618 accident/incident reports on the 172 between January 1988 and February 1993. By our count, 1,473 of these qualify as accidents (damage or injury), including 140 fatal accidents.

On face value, this seems like a whopping wrecking rate. If accurate information were available to convert the gross accident numbers to accidents per operating hour (or per 100,000 hours, as the NTSB does), the number would not seem very big. Especially if one considers the exposure, as well. For instance, relating the accidents to pilot experience and to type of operation would suggest that the 172 and similar learning airplanes such as the PA-28 are surprisingly forgiving.

While we don't hold as an absolute with the school that claims aircraft don't cause accidents, pilots do, there is a lot to support that in the 172 accident record.

If many of the accidents were thoroughly analyzed, the proximate cause would not be, for instance, botched landing or loss of directional control. It would be preflight actions or decisions, or failure to adhere to operating limitations, or failure to obtain current information.

The bulk of the accidents are of the fender-bender variety. A great many of them support that earlier-quoted observation of Thompson's that 172 pilots tend to approach and land too fast (a related phenomenon is that pilots tend to quit flying the airplane too soon, or during takeoff don't start flying the airplane soon enough). Don't blame it all on junior birdmen, however. Senior birdmen bend them, too. Part is familiarity or just gross contempt or its close neighbors, neglect or carelessness.

There are a large number (65) of fuel exhaustion accidents. This suggests improper flight planning or poor inflight decisions in many cases.

This and other accidents suggest another trap that is related to familiarity. Given the variations in 172 models and with aftermarket modifications, habit or expectation can lead to grief. As one owner notes, someone used to an airspeed indicator calibrated in knots might make a mistake in a 172 with a statute-mile ASI. Someone used to a 172 with additional fuel might be surprised by a silent engine in one with only 38 gallons usable.

The vagaries of the fuel system might mean very even fuel burns with the tank selector on "Both" in one airplane, but horribly uneven (and out-of-trim handling) in another.

There are many potential traps. As gentle a bird as the Skyhawk may be, there still is much to be gained through proper initial and proficiency training. This is as true for grizzled veterans returning to the 172 from heavier, faster machines as it is for the fledgling. Honest high-time pilots can relate very humbling experiences in getting reacquainted with the 'Hawk.

A Strong Design

In terms of the original design objectives —loosely paraphrased as a true four-place, low cost airplane with the most efficient (low power) propulsion system— the 172 is a design achievement that ranks up there with the DC-3 and P-51. An airplane without parallel.

More Information

The Cessna Pilots Assn. Wichita, Kans., (316) 946-4777, is widely considered to be the best source of information and support for most Cessna piston aircraft. The association runs a variety of type-specific maintenance and operational clinics, including sessions on owner-performed maintenance.

The Cessna Owner Organization (P.O. Box 337, Iola, Wisc. 54945, (715) 445-5000 appears to be largely a publishing enterprise (it has other model "clubs"), but 172 owners say the publications have good information and interesting ads on modifications.

Owner Comments

Parts are widely available for everything I've wanted done, with competition keeping the prices reasonable. Kinzie interior replacement parts are better than original and easy to install. Polyfix plastic repair kits take care of small cracks in the original Royalite. Texas Aeroplastics fairings were perfect fits.

Tall passengers (6'-2" or more) should be put in the front seat. A tall passenger in the back will make the trip "side-saddle" because of roofline intrusion. Two tall passengers in the back will be miserable.

The most valuable information resource has proven to be the Cessna Pilot's Association (CPA). Their focus is more technical than the Cessna Owner's Organization, which also does a good job of supporting the brand. Most supportive of the brand is John Frank, President of the CPA. His availability on CompuServe's AVSIG forum has been invaluable, giving me almost immediate high-quality answers to every question I've ever asked him.

Alan R. Walter
Rockford, Ill.

The plane had a history of blowing its cowl-mounted dual landing lights. We subscribed to the Skyhawk Assn. newsletter that had a modification (addition of a lord mount to the alternator mount that Dzused to the cowl nose) that took care of part of the problem. Getting a 250W bulb meant more light and a beefier element that so far has outlasted our memory of the last replacement. (Just don't operate both lamps at the same time; the circuit can't handle it).

The strut fairings that Cessna makes basically do nothing but crack. You can't glue them, so you stop-drill them, maybe tape them, but if you replace them (an expensive process), they merely crack again. Also, interior trim plastic is cracked from exposure to UV (most likely).

The high wing makes it great for lazing around the countryside at a thousand feet at 70 mph with the window open with all the world spread out below you. It is no speed demon, but that's a small compromise.

Doug Brazil
Portland, Ore.

I have a Petersen STC for mogas, and it's saved me tons of money. I've never had as much as a burp out of my 145-hp Cont. engine in spite of the horror stories concerning mogas in airplanes.

I do have some mods that have made some difference in performance, and I would recommend them to any Skyhawk owner. Les Leonard in Aquila, Ariz. (602) 685-2471, has a set of flap gap seals that are worth the money and add about 5 mph to the cruise speed and subtract about 5 mph from the landing speed. The other mod, Met-Co-Aire Wing tips also help performance.

David W. Dietz
Gainesville, Tex.

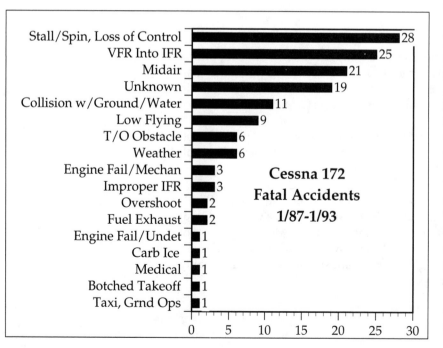

Cessna 172
Fatal Accidents
1/87-1/93

Stall/Spin, Loss of Control	28
VFR Into IFR	25
Midair	21
Unknown	19
Collision w/Ground/Water	11
Low Flying	9
T/O Obstacle	6
Weather	6
Engine Fail/Mechan	3
Improper IFR	3
Overshoot	2
Fuel Exhaust	2
Engine Fail/Undet	1
Carb Ice	1
Medical	1
Botched Takeoff	1
Taxi, Grnd Ops	1

The annual maintenance cost on the two C-172Ps in our Paramus Flying Club is $2,819. This includes engine and airframe repairs, oil and filter changes, oil analysis, static and transponder checks and exhaust valve cleaning every 400 hours. Annual avionics cost is $551, the cost of annual inspections $1,233 per airplane.

We have not had any difficulty in obtaining parts for the Skyhawks. We have experienced three stuck valves in a two-year period, and since the last incident have gone to a religious schedule of cleaning the exhaust valves every 400 hours.

William M. Shannon
Cedar Grove, N.J.

Cessna Hawk XP

Cessna's Hawk XP is a sort of muscle-bound Skyhawk—or a poor man's Skylane, if you will—that gives an edge of extra performance (XP, get it?) over the standard 172 Skyhawk for high elevations and short fields.

It shares many of the Skyhawk's good qualities—stability, forgiving flying qualities and low stall speed—but the extra complexity of the more powerful Continental IO-360 engine and constant-speed propeller exacts a price in reliability, maintenance and economics. Some people think the price is worth the benefits; others don't.

Genealogy

The Hawk XP was introduced in 1977, just as the lightplane boom of the late '70s was beginning to crest. Cessna was in the process of phasing out its ill-fated Cardinal, which had filled the marketing niche just above the Skyhawk for the previous decade. The Cardinal was never able to shake a bad early reputation (well-deserved), although the later models were fine aircraft. Cessna decided to retrench and merely upgrade the familiar old Skyhawk airframe—a proven winner in the marketplace—with a bigger engine.

In place of the four-cylinder Lycomings of 150-160 hp in the Skyhawk, Cessna put a six-cylinder Continental IO-360, an engine what was normally rated at 210 hp at 2,800 rpm, but which Cessna derated to 195 hp at 2,600 rpm for the XP. Gross weight was 2,550, or 250 pounds more than the Skyhawk.

Cardinal Stomper

In sales, the Hawk XP stomped all over its sibling rival, the Cardinal, in 1977. Despite the fact that the XP was, objectively, inferior to the Cardinal (an *Aviation Consumer* side-by-side comparison found that the Cardinal had better handling and visibility, much more cabin room, lower cabin noise, lower maintenance costs and virtually identical performance and load-carrying capability) the XP rang Cessna's cash register for 724 units that first year.

Not wishing to mess with a good thing, Cessna made only minor refinements over the XP's production run, which lasted until the general aviation crash of 1981. These included: a 28-volt electrical system; increased speed limits on the flaps; a beefed-up crankshaft with a corresponding increase in TBO; an oil filter; a removable avionics rack and cooling fan; and a recontoured elevator. Total production when the model was discontinued amounted to 1,450.

Aside from the nameplate, it's tough to tell the Hawk XP II (there was no XP I: Cessna gave all its singles a II designation at the time) from a Skyhawk. Giveaways are the constant speed prop and cowl flap.

Performance

The XP is no rocket ship. Using the same power that propels a Money at 170 knots, the XP chugs along at about 125 knots, according to owners. The XP is no faster than a 180-hp Cardinal, and only about eight knots faster than a 160-hp Skyhawk.

Gross-weight climb is 870 fpm, a tad better than the Cardinal or the Skyhawk, and about the same as the Skylane. Gross-weight takeoff performance is virtually identical to the Skyhawk. Of course the XP's numbers come at a higher gross weight, but 150 pounds of that is taken up by the heavier engine and prop. The real payload difference is only 100 pounds.

Despite the unimpressive book numbers, XP pilots rave about real-world performance. One fellow swears he gets 1,500 fpm at moderate weights, even in warm weather. In winter, he does better still. "Has near-STOL characteristics," reports another.

Useful load for a basic-IFR XP runs around 900-950 lbs. One owner of a lavishly equipped XP reports 879 pounds. With the standard 49-gallon tanks filled, the cabin load is about 600-650 pounds: three people and some luggage. Subtract 100 pounds if the optional 66-gallon tanks are filled.

At max cruise, the XP slurps 11 gph-plus, but most pilots throttle back to 10 or less. At moderate power, four hours and 450 nm is about as long as you'd want to fly one. The optional tanks stretch the range to 650 nm.

Compared to its successor, the Cutlass (same airframe, 180-hp Lycoming), the XP looks bad in terms of payload and range. The Cutlass has the same gross, but weighs 100 lbs less and burns 1.5 gph less fuel.

Handling

The XP ain't no Pitts—although we did talk to one pilot who taught himself aerobatics in a T-41B (the military version of the XP). Roll response is fairly ponderous, and pitch control is heavy, heavier than the Skyhawk. (The new elevator that appeared in 1981 reduces pitch forces.) While these traits don't do much for fighter-pilot fantasies, they do make for a stable, easy-to-fly IFR platform. The stubborn stability of the Skyhawk airframe is one of the biggest reasons it has such a good safety record.

The huge flaps cause some pitch changees, and they're so draggy in the 40-degree position that go-arounds can be a bit dicey (flap travel was reduced to 30 degrees in later models).

On the ground, the nosewheel steering is rather heavy. And the high-wing design makes the XP very susceptible to winds on the ground.

Engine

The heart of the XP's performance—and problems—is the six-cylinder Continental IO-360-K and -KB engine. It's expensive to overhaul ($14,000) and has a mediocre reliability record.

The engine's main problem seems to be that it's tough on cylinders. Low compression and/or high oil consumption are not unusual. Not everyone has cylinder problems, of course—one owner reports 1,800-plus hours of trouble-free operation—but cylinder cracks, along with piston, ring and valve troubles, seem more common thatn in similar Lycoming engines. One owner, for example, reported he had to replace two cylinders in the first 600 hours, then had a cracked piston that allowed most of the oil to leak out. Service difficulty reports for 1980-87 show 16 cracked cylinders: the largest number of reports for any single Hawk XP problem.

Undersized Rods

Connecting rods have also been a problem. A batch of undersize rods found their way into thousands of IO and TSIO-360s during the late '70s, causing dozens of failures. Though most of the failures occurred in the turbocharged engines, some failures have occurred in the normally aspirated powerplants as well. Our scan of SDRs turned up two.

There have also been crankshaft failures. Continental beefed up the crank in 1979, producing the -KB engine. It had an improved TBO of 2,000 hours. Good thing, too, given the cost of overhaul.

Maintenance

Judging from owner reports, the XP is easy to maintain; not surprising, since it has the same airframe as the old, familiar Skyhawk.

Although we found no Service Difficulty Reports on it, prospective buyers should check for damage to the firewall where the nosewheel strut attaches. The XP's nose-heaviness makes hard landing damage more likely.

Unfortunately, most XPs were made during the years for which Cessna is infamous: 1977-80. This was when the ARC avionics had their worst engineering and quality-control problems. Also, virtually all single-engine Cessnas made at this time had defective paint jobs. Trying to get airplanes out the door as fast as possible, Cessna ignored Du-Pont's specifications and used a cheap, quick primer under the paint. The result was persistent, cancerous filiform corrosion that affected hundreds (if not thousands) of aircraft, particularly those based in warm, humid climates.

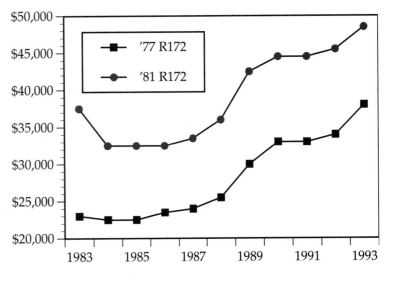

Safety

FAA does not report separate hours-flown estimates for the Hawk XP, but the similar Skyhawk has proven among the safest of four-place-fixed gear singles.

For the period 1980-87, FAA data turned up a total of 12 Hawk XP fatal accidents. Given the size of the fleet (roughly 1,400), that's not bad at all. Six of the accidents occurred in mountainous terrain, suggesting that some XP pilots may be overconfident about the airplane's performance. Only one was a stall accident.

Among the non-fatal accidents, four pilots ran out of gas, but not one crashed as a result of fuel mismanagement—tribute to the stone-simple fuel system. Landing and takeoff accidents aside, the largest single factor in non-fatal Hawk XP crashes was engine failure—11 in all for the period.

Owner Comments

For some reason, a lot of people like to knock the Hawk XP, but I'm not one of them. I've flown 15 kinds of single-engine aircraft, and none serves my needs better. Before I bought it, more than one person told me the engine was a maintenance hog, but I hope every engine I own is this good: after 1,820 hours of regular use, I've had no problems at all.

The biggest problem I have is electrical. I have a Stormscope and S-Tec autopilot, plus an electric standby vacuum pump, which is supposed to be turned on in IMC. It's very easy to overload the 35-amp alternator, and I've never been able to reset the circuit breaker in flight.

Roll rate is slow, the elevator is heavy, and slow flight requires a lot of control movement; but these traits make the airplane a dream on an ILS. It's the easiest airplane I've ever flown in this regard.

Stan Taylor
Mount Dora, Fla.

I purchased a 1980 Hawk XP new, and flew and maintained it for five years. The first problem came at 150 hours, when light corrosion set in. Cessna provided a very fair allowance for repainting. At 425 hours, I converted the derated 195-hp engine to 210-hp with the STC from Isham Aircraft. The conversion consisted of a new prop governor, tach, and fuel flow/manifold pressure gauge. The new redline is 2,800 rpm, and the full-throttle fuel flow goes from 16 to 18 gph. This high rpm can be maintained for about five minutes. This improves the climb rate considerably, and you can still throttle back for economy. With the conversion, performance is outstanding. Even the standard XP is a real performer.

The airplane was easy to fly. All told, the XP flew like a 172, performed like a 182 and would haul everything you could cram in.

Bus Blaksley
Ft. Lauderdale, Fla.

I fly a '79 XP, bought "new" in 1981. The airplane had been left out in the weather and used only for short demo flights. I have no doubt that this led to much deterioration. In the first two years the fuel drains rusted and began to leak. The mag seals, tach drive seal, prop seals and pushrod seals all had to be replaced. The pushrod seals failed again, and they still leak. A through-bolt snapped off the no. 2 cylinder at 589 hours. I find the IO-360-KB to be a very messy engine. I change the oil every 30 hours and have to add a quart every six or seven hours.

The engine has the 210-hp STC, and since the airplane is on floats most of the time the expense is worth it for the extra performance. Compared to a standard 172, it's a little heavier on the nose, but takeoff performance is outstanding.

George Watts
Canyon, Minn.

Cessna Cutlass RG

Sort of an intermediate hybrid between the venerable 172 and the inestimable 182RG Skylane, the Cutlass rode a fine line for the five years it was in production. Its ill-defined market niche, coupled with the advent of the general aviation recession, kept the production numbers fairly low. Indeed, only 1,191 were rolled out of the factory doors.

The Used Market

Cutlass prices have, for the most part, seriously lagged behind the rest of the used-aircraft market. A 1980 172RG has only now regained its original value: this has not kept up with inflation.

In fact, that same 1980 model, which cost $48,900 when new (with no equipment), lost $15,000 in its first two years. Only now has it climbed back up to $49,000 (according to *The Aircraft Bluebook* Price *Digest*).

All the same, considering the aircraft's competition, it's done reasonably well. Arrayed against it are two Cessna models (the ill-starred Cardinal RG and the beloved 182RG Skylane), as well as Piper's Arrow in its various incarnations.

While it's possible to get a cheaper 180-hp single-engine retractable, you also stand to get higher maintenance costs. By the same token, the nearest competitor for the Cutlass—Cessna's own 177RG Cardinal—offers more performance, but costs more to own.

For example, a 1971 Piper Arrow (the last year that a 180-hp model was offered) can go one knot faster, and carry almost 100 pounds more payload. However, its engine costs an extra $1,500 to overhaul. And, with only 50 gallons of fuel on board, it can't fly as far.

At the other end of the spectrum, the Cessna 177RG Cardinal will cruise eight knots faster (and carry 12 pounds more). But it uses a 200-hp engine to do it. It also has reduced range, carrying only 61 gallons of gas.

Speed, endurance, easy handling, reasonable useful load—who could possibly ask for more than the Cessna 172RG Cutlass offers?

The aircraft is no hangar queen. Owners overwhelmingly report excellent reliability and low maintenance costs.

In a sense, though, the sluggishness in price increases makes the Cutlass one of the best values to be had in the four-place retractable market. There are a number of reasons for this statement beyond pure acquisition cost.

"Bullet-Proof" Engine

While there are some Lycoming engine models that can drive an owner to tears, Cessna fortuitously chose the remarkable Lycoming 0-360-F1A6 for the Cutlass. This engine has earned a reputation for reliability far above that of most engines.

Indeed, our check of FAA service difficulty reports for the period January 1, 1984 through June, 1990 disclosed only one troubling trend for this engine—sticking valves. Even this, though, appears to be not too great a threat. Only 10 reports surfaced in our printout, with nine of them stuck exhaust valves. It's worth noting that, in the greater context of Lycoming's historic valve-sticking problems in -300-series engines, this many reports constitutes minor trouble.

Beyond this, there was nothing else of note in the records. This bodes well for an owner's peace of mind, not to mention his pocketbook.

Other Maintenance Expenses

Not to let enthusiasm carry too far, there are other items on the Cutlass that will cost an owner money. We found several matters which are almost guaranteed to become a problem for a Cutlass owner.

One is the aircraft's landing gear system. It's worth noting that Cessna never termed any of its retractable landing gear systems "Land-O-Matic" as it commonly did with fixed-gear models. Indeed, there's nothing "O-Matic" about this system at all, leading one wag to term it "Fail-O-Matic."

Like many of its Cessna single-engine retractable brethren, the Cutlass landing gear

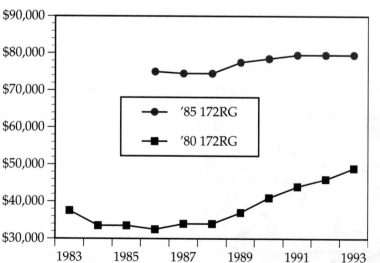

system is enough to give an owner fits. If it's not one thing (like a dead, burned-out or jammed hydraulic pump—of which we counted 13 reports), it's another (like gear leg bumper pads which prevent the gear from locking down—some 21 reports filed).

The gear leg bumper pads (also known as down-stop pads) are critical items. Most reports spoke of a pad coming loose, then jamming between the gear leg and wheel well. This prevented the leg from reaching the locked position, and it collapsed on touchdown. Fortunately, the pads are easily visible on preflight, so a pilot can check them before going.

Cracking and breaking of various gear components was another trouble spot. A prime example used to be the plastic T fitting used to help lock the nosegear down. This item was common to most of the Cessna single-engine retractables, and many a pilot and mechanic watched with bemusement and distress as the nosegear on the parked airplane simply folded up, dumping the bird on its nose.

Cessna eventually came out with a metal replacement part, and reports of this problem have since died away. However, we found three reports in our scan, so it's worth checking before buying.

Another trouble spot was highlighted by a recent Cessna service bulletin. Cracking and breaking main-gear pivots accumulated 10 reports in our survey. Wise buyers will make sure the service bulletin has been complied with before putting any money down.

Yet another problem area was main gear actuator bolts. Some 21 reports indicated loose, backed-out or broken bolts. Again, careful inspection of the landing gear is a must for any prospective buyer.

Cutlass instrument panel is fairly well laid out. However, low position of the engine gauges can be a distraction during takeoff.

And of course, like the rest of the Cessna single-engine retractables, the Cutlass is prey to a nonrecoverable landing-gear system failure. While a handpump is provided to manually extend the gear in the event of hydraulic pump failure, neither the mechanical nor the manual system will work if there's no fluid to pump. A ruptured hydraulic line or other system leak means a gear-up landing.

Compounding the problem is the hydraulic pump, which will periodically cycle on and off during flight to maintain system pressure. If there is a leak, the pump will probably be done pumping all the fluid overboard by the time the pilot realizes it's been running too long and pulls the breaker.

It's not as roomy as it looks. Although front seats offer an adequate 40 inches of shoulder room, rear seats are narrower.

Load and Performance

The Cutlass can certainly earn its keep. With a typical 1,000-pound useful load, decent cruise speeds and good range, it will get you, your passengers and some baggage to most places you want to go.

Most owners report 130- to 135-knot cruise speeds. This puts the Cutlass about even with both the Arrow and the Skylane. However, it's worth noting that the "lowly" Grumman Tiger can produce 140 knots using the same engine with a fixed-pitch prop and its landing gear hanging in the breeze. And the Skylane, of course, has a much better payload.

Interestingly, cruise speed can vary with c.g. Like the Skylane RG, the Cutlass gains speed as the c.g. moves aft (and as weight goes down). This may be due to the position of the open wheel wells (there are no gear door enclosures) on the backside of the tapered fuselage. At gross weights, goes the theory, the aircraft flies at a higher angle of attack, which causes the airflow to be disrupted as it passes over the open wells. At lighter weights and/or more aft c.g., angle of attack decreases just enough so that the wells are out of the direct slipstream. Then, the air flows smoothly by them, providing a bonus of up to 10 knots, according to one owner.

The Cutlass' other big virtue is range. With 62 gallons of usable fuel, you'll probably run out of bladder before you run out of gas. The 180-hp Lycoming sips a miserly 10 gph at max cruise, giving the Cutlass six hours of endurance. Throttled back to a more moderate power setting, fuel consumption drops to eight gph, giving the airplane a whopping eight hours or more endurance. Indeed, book figures show a range of 720 nm at 75 percent power and 9,000 feet (including reserves). Throttle back to 55 percent power, and range jumps to 830 nm.

The Cutlass is no slouch when it comes to load hauling, either. Max gross is 2,650 pounds. Cessna actually published a ramp weight for the Cutlass which allowed an extra eight pounds to taxi around with—based on the idea that about 1.3 gallons of gas would be burned before takeoff.

A typical Cutlass with an IFR panel might tip the scales at about 1,650 pounds. This leaves a half ton of useful load—quite good for a mere 180-hp aircraft. Indeed, that's enough to allow two 170-pound men and their 140-pound wives to fly away with full tanks. And there's almost always the option of trading some fuel for passenger and/or baggage weight.

Unlike its stablemates, the Cutlass is rather sensitive to balance—if by sensitive one means it's possible to load it out of limits. While the Skylane and Skyhawk are nearly impossible to get too far aft, the Cutlass can be loaded that way.

For example, load your Cutlass with 44 gallons of fuel, four 150-pound passengers and 140 pounds of baggage and the c.g. will be right on the aft limit. But, toss 200 pounds into the rear baggage area (its weight limit) and another 50 pounds on the rear hat shelf and the back seats must remain empty. It's worth noting that air conditioning was not offered as an option on the Cutlass (as it was on the Skyhawk), and c.g. problems may have been the reason.

Handling

In keeping with its roots, the Cutlass handles much like the 172. Indeed, few pilots would notice much difference. There are differences, though. The controls are a little bit lighter, and pitch trim authority is increased.

As with later Skyhawk and 152 models, the flaps on the Cutlass are limited to only 30 degrees' deflection. Although some might argue that the decreased flap deflection robs the Cutlass of some short-field performance, the airplane can still hold its own when operating out of hot, high strips that frighten away many other retractable-gear airplanes. Then, too, many owners have opted for STOL mods which more than compensate for the "missing" 10 degrees of flaps.

Ground handling, while pretty straightforward, does require some attention. Sharp turns require very slow speeds and some differential braking. Touchdown on landing should be at or very close to the stall, since wheelbarrowing can be a problem. And crosswind correction is a must at all times. Like most high-wing airplanes, the Cutlass can be blown over if not handled properly in strong winds.

Safety

This brings us to the question: How safe is the Cutlass? In a word: Fairly.

A scan of FAA accident records from January, 1984 through June, 1990 disclosed some 57 accidents. Only 15 of these were fatal. Some trends came as no surprise to those who know the airplane.

For example, the single most-common type of accident involved groundlooping. Nine Cutlass pilots couldn't keep the airplane under control once it landed. Another couldn't keep it under control before he left the ground on takeoff. Again, high wings and relatively narrow gear can make life in a gusty crosswind real interesting, real fast.

Landing-gear troubles racked up another dozen airplanes. However, fully half of those accidents occurred when the pilots either simply forgot to put the wheels down or didn't make sure the wheels were down before landing. Real out-and-out gear malfunctions accounted for only six accidents. Typically, these involved gear collapses after touchdown due to a variety of causes.

Living up to its bullet-proof reputation, the O-360 Lycoming was at the heart of only seven accidents. Two engine failures were blamed on carb ice. We can presumably discount another in

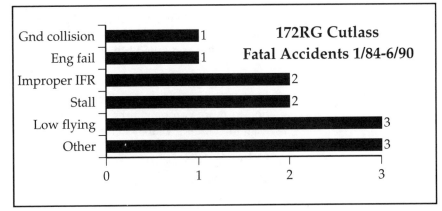

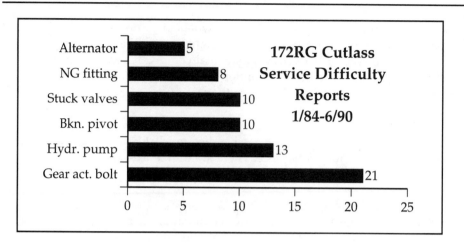

which the pilot forgot to tighten down the oil filler cap before takeoff. This leaves only four engine failures stemming from mechanical problems—an enviable record for any engine over a five-and-a-half-year period.

Fatal Accidents

When it came to fatal accidents, the Cutlass RG again proved itself a worthy aircraft. We found only 15 fatal crashes in our FAA printout.

Perhaps the most important aspect of these accidents is that none could be directly blamed on aircraft shortcomings. For example, four stemmed from that perennial pilot killer—flying VFR into IFR conditions. In the same vein, two other fatal crashes were blamed on pilots flying while intoxicated.

But the Cutlass RG is, indeed, a docile flyer. Yet one more fatal accident involved a pilot who died from a massive heart attack in flight. His passenger, who was not a pilot, was able to land the aircraft with the aid of instructions from another pilot. Certainly the Cutlass betrays its 172 roots in this incident.

Improper IFR operations (i.e., descending below DH or MDA on instrument approaches) produced two more fatal accidents. Another two were attributed to botched go-arounds that ended up with the aircraft stalling off the end of the runway.

One fatal crash resulted from an engine failure due to carb ice. Two stemmed from low-flying pilots who hit the ground (or trees) as they flat-hatted.

One final accident could only be described as weird. A Cutlass was involved in a collision on the ramp with an aircraft tug. The tug driver fell off, and the airplane ran him over and killed him.

Thus, the Cutlass RG has developed what is, in our opinion, an excellent safety record. This makes the airplane a fine choice for low-time pilots looking to transition to more complex aircraft, provided they have the financial wherewithal to keep the landing gear system in tip-top shape.

Other Safety Items

The Cutlass has other features which have a direct impact on safety. Some are minor, others not so.

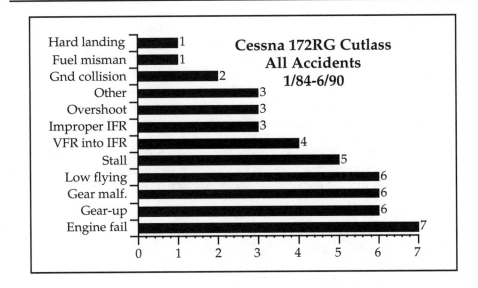

For example, one safety feature we've always touted is shoulder harnesses. The Cutlass came standard with plain-vanilla shoulder harnesses for the front seats. Inertial-reel units were available as an option, and there was even an option for the rear seats to have harnesses installed. As cheap protection against injury or death, the value of shoulder harnesses cannot be understated.

Contributing to safety also is the aircraft's low stalling speed. In the event of a forced landing, low stall speeds mean less impact energy (provided the airplane is under control at the time of impact).

Overall rugged construction is another aid during accidents. After all, the best restraints in the world won't help if the cabin crushes like an eggshell. Cessna provided the Cutlass with the same well-built fuselage that has helped make the 172 so stellar in the area of crashworthiness.

Yet one more item we like is the two-door configuration (three if you count the baggage door). This gives occupants a much better chance of escaping after a crash. Instead of having to climb over seats to get out a single door, they can egress from either side. An added bonus is the design of Cessna's door handles— they're pretty straightforward, so even non-pilot types should be able to open them easily in an emergency. (Unlike some Piper doors which have two latches and present the unfamiliar with a Chinese puzzle as they try to get out of the aircraft quickly.)

On the minus side of the safety ledger sheet are the fuel lines that run around and under the cabin. We've always felt that it's best to keep the gas as far away from the people as possible. At the very least, these lines should be of heavy-duty construction, preferably with self-sealing disconnects at the ends.

Another item we're not too fond of, safety-wise, is the historic problem of Cessna seats. As with its progenitor, reports of cracking and breaking seat rails in the Cutlass are not unknown. The seat-slip accident has already proven itself fatal on too many occasions, so prudent owners will make a careful check of the seat rails part of their preflight inspection, and making sure the seat is actually locked in place before engine start. Throw in a thorough examination by your A&P at annual inspection time just to be sure.

Comfort

When it comes to comfort, the Cutlass is no bargain. With a cabin width of only 40 inches (only for the front seats), it's cozy, to put it mildly (cramped to put it more forcefully).

Rear-seat passengers fare worse. The cabin tapers from the front seats on back, and the roof slopes down. The back seat is no place for big people.

Noise is another problem for the Cutlass. One rather informal survey found the Cutlass and the 172 among the worst of a half-dozen similar aircraft. Unfortunately, a bigger engine did not merit better soundproofing to go with it.

Admittedly related only to aesthetic comfort, some owners complain that the interior of the Cutlass is "cheap." Many of the plastic fittings, flashings and trim crack easily and wear over time. In some instances, even the most conscientious, tender loving care won't save these parts. The result is an interior more reminiscent of a $500 used VW Bug than a $50,000 aircraft.

While the high wing allows a good view of the ground going by, it also limits visibility into turns. And, of course, looking up is almost impossible without badly craning one's neck.

Mods

As previously noted, many owners have opted for STOL mods from groups like Horton, Inc. of Wellington, Kans. This is perhaps the single most popular mod for the Cutlass RG.

The secret of the Cutlass' reliability is right up front—the "bullet-proof" Lycoming O-360-F1A6 engine.

Another reasonably popular improvement involves various speed kits. Flap and aileron seals offer at least a few knots' extra cruise. These are also available from Horton.

Owner Comments

I have more than 2,000 hours in four different 1980 Cutlass RGs. Much of my flying has been from a local STOL port at 6,900 feet elevation, and I rarely operate from fields below 4,650 feet, so my comments reflect this.

The 1980 Cutlass RG is unequivocally the best airplane for the dollar that I have ever owned or flown. I fly mainly alone, or with my wife and a week's worth of baggage, or less. At 12,000 feet with half fuel, 18 in. MAP and 2300 RPM, I cruise at about 120 knots and consume eight gallons per hour of fuel.

The Cutlass is extremely reliable. All of my engines have made it to TBO plus 300 or 400 hours. I use AeroShell oil and change it every 50 hours.

Starting cold or hot is easy and reliable. The landing gear and electrical problems have been minimal, though the gear warning horn is erratic and should never be trusted. I would prefer to have it removed or deactivated, personally.

Like any four-place airplane with 180 hp, you can rarely fill the seats and the tanks at the same time. Mid-summer operations from STOL fields have to be planned for early morning departure with half tanks and light weight. Every flight with three or four adults has to be carefully planned.

Nearly all of the Cutlass RGs have had a gear-up landing. Three of my four airplanes have. The major damage is to the belly skins and antennae, so if the plane has been properly repaired, the prospective buyer has nothing to fear. The aircraft logs should show a new or overhauled prop and an engine teardown. One of my Cutlasses had a gear-up in 1982 just before I purchased it, and I have flown it more than 1,000 hours since then with no problems.

The small wheels make the Cutlass a poor airplane for anything but paved surfaces. Longer than expected grass or softer than expected soil can lead to disaster.

As a transition aircraft for training, the Cutlass is an ideal step in the 152-172-172RG-instrument-commercial sequence. It provides a good platform for instrument training and gives the student complex time at very little extra cost over that of a comparably equipped 172.

The cabin is comfortable and well organized. Noise levels are considerably higher than a 172 or a Cardinal, so conversation can be a bit awkward. The panel has room for all of the avionics that you can afford, or the Cutlass can lift. Trim is the usual tacky Cessna plastic that breaks if a shadow crosses it. The pilot's armrest is perennially broken even if given special TLC.

The Cutlass RG is not an A36 Bonanza or a Mooney 252, but it is a reliable, straightforward, fuel-efficient "speedy" plane that's fun to fly, great for trips with two adults and holds its value with the best of them.

John D. Burrington
Steamboat Springs, Colo.

We have owned our Cutlass for 18 very pleasant months. Fuel consumption is good, showing about 7.64 gallons per Hobbs hour, or 9.39 gallons per tach hour. Maintenance costs, both scheduled and unscheduled (including a prop overhaul) have averaged $13.36 per Hobbs hour ($16/tach hour). We tend to compute by Hobbs because that's how it's rented and how we're paid.

We majored the engine at 2,049 hours on the tach. It had good compression and was using one quart of oil every nine hours. The camshaft is estimated to be good for another 200 or 300 hours.

The most serious problem has been unnecessary and sometimes detrimental maintenance and repair. The airplane has had no inherent or persistent service problems, but bad rewiring of the gear warning system and other poorly done work has cost us in excess of $2,000 for burned-out squat switches, audio generators and the like. The work was all performed by an IA.

In conclusion, our Cutlass is a delight to fly. It's stable, has a useful load of about 1,001 pounds, and with 62 gallons of fuel has more range than we ever hope to use. A Horton STOL conversion was performed expertly by Larry Lujan and his crew at Gold Coast Aviation in Salinas. This has given us a flight envelope of better than 100 knots—from less than 35 knots Vso to greater than 140 knots at 75% power.

Bill and Liz Taylor
Santa Cruz, Calif.

My company purchased a new Cutlass RG in 1981. It was showing about 25 hours on the tach when delivered. As delivered, it was horribly out of rig, but my mechanics took care of that little bug in short order. I can't imagine the company test pilots and ferry pilots flying it those 25 hours being as out of rig as it was.

It now has a little more than 1,400 hours on it, and we can't praise it enough. Truly it is the best all-around airplane we have ever had.
Its flying qualities are superb. It will usually fly dirty at 43 knots, and will tolerate gentle turns at this speed. It likes to go cross country at 6,000 to 7,000 feet, and will honestly true out at a good 140 knots when flown by the book. Fuel consumption is about nine gph at this cruise. With 62 gallons useable fuel, that gives pretty long legs.

Maintenance costs are pretty routine. We replaced a magneto at around 700 hours, and the prop spinner at about 1,000 hours due to cracking. The vernier mixture control was recently replaced due to the outer housing wearing through where it goes through the firewall. We routed the new one through a rubber grommet. This has been the most expensive part we have replaced, costing about $220.

The landing gear has been virtually trouble-free. We did have to replace the operating solenoid at about 1,200 hours at a nominal cost of $35. At annual inspection, the hydraulic system never requires more than one squirt of fluid.

If any Cutlass owners have not replaced the nosegear actuator spring guide with a metallic one, I highly recommend they do so. This is a little T-shaped affair with plastic ears. It holds the nosegear downlock in place. We replaced ours at about 500 hours and found the plastic ears badly deformed. A few more landings, and no doubt the airplane would have been on its nose. I am surprised an AD was never issued on this. At the time, it was a small job, requiring about an hour and a half of labor, and the new part cost about $7.

The airplane is very comfortable on long trips. It is quiet inside. Normal conversation is possible. The factory-installed autopilot with tracker has performed flawlessly and required no work.

Cessna certainly had their ducks in a row when they built the Cutlass RG. It is a great airplane in every respect. Don't bother to call—it's not for sale.

William Polley
Enterprise, Ala.

Cessna 175 Skylark

Once upon a time when Cessna was building aircraft to fill every conceivable market niche, it concocted the Skylark. As the number designation suggests, it was supposed to fit in between the world-renown C-172 Skyhawk, on the one hand, and the world-famous C-182 Skylane on the other. It now occupies the same space, which some describe as limbo, others as bargain city.

There's no doubt that, ostensibly as a souped-up Skyhawk, with exactly the same airframe and interior dimensions, it comes with some enticing prices. But buyers must decide how much credibility to give to the awful reputation of the Skylark's geared engine.

In the aircraft's favor are greater fuel capacity than the Skyhawk, a bigger useful load, a better rate of climb and higher cruise. Weighing against it is its age—30-35 years old—the engine's reputation and its positively anemic 1,200-hour TBO.

History

The Cessna 175 fluttered like a moth onto the scene in 1958 and passed into oblivion after only five years of production, during which slightly over 2,100 Skylarks were built. There were no dramatic changes in the life of the line.

The biggest visible alterations occurred in 1960 as the aircraft was given a swept vertical tail, and engine cowling was made to look less chunky by tapering it, leaving a modest central hump on top for the prop reduction drive.

The following year the pull-type starter was replaced by a pushbutton arrangement. And in 1962 the C-175C was outfitted with a constant-speed prop and a

The Cessna 175 looks very much like a Cessna 172, except for the telltale gearbox hump behind the spinner. This was a 1961 model with a fixed-pitch prop.

cowl flap to help cool the engine. Also, the final models received a hundred-pound boost in gross weight.

Performance

One owner described Skylark performance as similar to a Skyhawk on mild steroids. He talked about getting 123 knots true on the C-175, or about 10 knots faster than a C-172. With the extra 30 hp over the contemporary Skyhawk, the C-175 naturally should climb better, and owners applaud the aircraft's ability to get out of short fields.

At a gross weight of 2,350 pounds, the Skylark is only 50 pounds heavier than the 145-hp C-172 fully loaded, so the climb margin should be readily apparent.

Since the bird has a tendency to run hot, pilots are advised to climb out at a relatively shallow angle, keeping the airspeed up for better cooling. Babying the engine at low rpms also is definitely not recommended. But since we're talking an rpm redline of 3,200, that mill is really humming, and presents a different feeling and timbre to the pilot accustomed to a non-geared engine.

The airplane is approved for autogas, which can provide a nice bit of economy, and 80 octane avgas (what's that? you ask).

Out of the 52-gallon fuel capacity, only 43 gallons are deemed usable—a surprising limitation.

Handling

The Skylark handles just like a Skyhawk: stable and benign in both calm and turbulent air with what one owner called "incredibly good short-field takeoff and landing characteristics." And the flaps are actuated with an old-fashioned bar handle rather than an electric toggle.

Cabin Load and Comfort

Once again, it's standard Skyhawk; i.e., cozy but utilitarian. Baggage capacity is 120 pounds. Doors on each side of the aircraft make access convenient, once passengers figure how to clamber up the gear struts.

With an equipped useful load of maybe 900 pounds, that means you can carry three 170-pounders and have weight left over for a lighter adult or a mess of baggage.

Maintenance

Owners reporting to us told of fairly routine maintenance, though one called out problems with nosewheel shimmy, which he said were no different from other Cessnas.
By far the preponderance of significant Service Difficulty Reports concerned the powerplant. Problem areas appeared to be broken pistons and engine mounts, along with sticking valves. To be fair, though, there were no more than four call-outs of each. Of course, there are only a couple thousand or fewer C-175s out there, and it appears that quite a few of those have had their engines replaced.

There have been very few Airworthiness Directives on the C-175 over the years, though the aircraft naturally shared the seat track grief of other Cessnas. And in 1982 there was an AD calling for a check of the engine crankcase breather.

Powerplant Blues

One experienced engine overhauler told us, "If you don't own one, don't buy one. I think I've spoiled 20 sales." Other overhaulers repeated this theme in spades. The story we got was that the engines are crummy, they're likely to go only about 800 hours before needing a top overhaul. And then at 1,200 hours they'll need the full works.

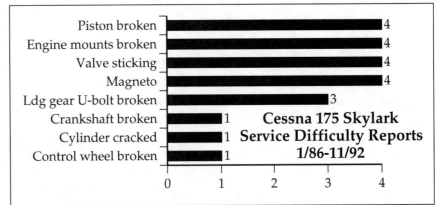

And good luck on that, because a bunch of GO-300 parts are hard to come by, and if you *do* find them they're expensive, and not of terribly high quality, anyway. One overhauler told us that the GO-300 was the latest of a raft of Continental evolutions that go back first to the O-200 (145 hp), then to the C-85 (85 hp) and then even the ancient A-65 (65 hp, naturally). And the technology is antique.

Some overhaul shops we talked with refuse to handle the GO-300, because they said they want to do a good job, and they figure no matter how well they do with that engine, the owner is not going to leave and be happy with the result. But we understand T.S. Smith is offering a bargain overhaul price of $12,500 with new cylinders. *The Aircraft Bluebook Price Digest* gives an average overhaul price installed of $14,000.

Modifications

This leads us into ways to simply abandon the original GO-300 engine in favor of something more reliable. Such as the 180-hp Lycoming O-360-A1A provided in an STC conversion kit by Avcon Conversions at Udall, Kans., (316) 782-3317.

But this can be a horribly expensive proposition. First, you have to buy your own engine, and maybe you can find a decent overhauled one for a reasonable price. Or you can buy a brand-new Lycoming from Avcon for $18,600. Then you'll need the constant-speed kit that is part of the STC, for $2,595, and the optional hardware kit for $995. And don't forget the constant-speed Hartzell, for something over $5,500.

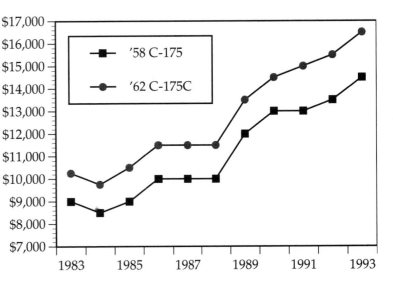

On top of that Avcon estimates your local mechanic will devote 70 to 80 man-hours on assembly work. At, say, $45/hr, that adds up to another $3,375. The grand total is a staggering $31,065, which is quite likely a whole lot more than you spent for the airplane in the first place.

Many of the old STC holders on the aircraft seem to have gotten out of the business, judging from our calls to track them down. In the old days, you could

Early model Skylarks had straight tails. The line didn't last long enough to get the rear windows.

get a cowl flap kit, for instance, and even a complete swept tail to replace the straight one.

However, Horton STOL-Craft, in Wellington, Kans., (800) 835-2051, (316) 326-2241 still offers a $799 STOL kit with wing leading edge cuffs, drooped tips, stall fences and aileron gap seals. Installed at Horton the total price is $1,594, with a coat of paint.

Safety Record

The Cessna 175 certainly does not have a reputation for wreaking mayhem on pilots, and in the last seven years we tallied only five fatal accidents in the fleet. Three of those were for unknown reasons, one from blundering into bad weather, and another from a structural failure in turbulence.

The nonfatal accident record once again focuses overwhelming attention on engine problems. By far the greatest proportion of accidents/incidents in C-175s over the past seven years involved some kind of mechanical engine failure or a power loss for some undetermined reason.

The greatest number of problems concerned broken, cracked cylinders; followed by conrods and pistons.

A few accidents were blamed on carb ice, and a handful on fuel exhaustion. The Skylark shares the C-172 tank system, permitting both wing tanks to feed at once, or either one separately.

Organization

Try the Cessna Pilots Assn. in Wichita, Kans. at (316) 946-4777.

Owner Comments

I've now owned my Cessna 175 for four years. It's a 1958 model, and still has the GO-300A. I almost typed "original engine," but remembered that it had a heart transplant at 500 hours, so the engine is not the one that it started life with.

Going over the logs before purchasing it ($10,000 in October 1988), I noted the airplane has a history of needing either jug 2 or 5 pulled at 200-hour intervals for

Cost/Performance/Specifications

Model	Year Built	Average Retail Price	Cruise Speed (kts)	Useful Load (lbs)	Fuel Std/Opt (gals)	Engine	TBO (hrs)	Overhaul Cost
Cessna 175	1958	$14,500	122	1,038	43	175-hp Cont. GO-300A	1,200	$14,000
Cessna 175	1959	$14,500	122	1,038	43	175-hp Cont. GO-300A	1,200	$14,000
Cessna 175A	1960	$15,500	122	1,038	43	175-hp Cont. GO-300C	1,200	$14,000
Cessna 175B	1961	$15,800	122	1,038	43	175-hp Cont. GO-300D	1,200	$14,000
Cessna 175C	1962	$16,500	122	1,038	43	175-hp Cont. GO-300E	1,200	$14,000

valve work. I'm just now approaching 180 since major (triggered at 550 SMOH by a prop strike), with good compressions. However, the just-installed GEM gives a clue to the jug problems—2 and 5 both run significantly hotter than the others. Where was the CHT probe? On cylinder 1, which runs slightly cooler than average!

My operating costs are running about $22/hour for consumables (fuel, oil). It's hard to judge maintenance costs, though, because I do a lot of it under supervision, and none of my annuals have been "just" an annual, so far. I've pumped $16,000 into the airplane in avionics and equipment upgrades, plus my share of the engine overhaul (all the cylinder work, including fixing three cracked rocker bosses) in my 200 hours or so of ownership, which biases the figures significantly. But I'd estimate the cost of just keeping it up is about $10 to $15 per hour. With luck, the operating costs will stay under $45/hour total, after I have a few hundred more hours on the new toys.

How does it fly? Like a 172 on mild steroids. Nothing surprising, other than the facts that the tachometer runs in a different range, and the gear is *much* taller than any airplane I'd trained in. The power differential is noticeable, but not like, say, the difference between a 172 and a 182. The extra horsepower is good for up to 123 KTAS—about 10 knots faster than a same-year 172.

It handles short-field work quite well, like most Cessnas. I bought it at a local private field, which boasted a longest runway of 1,300 feet. Even a relatively low-time pilot such as myself found the length to be more than enough for near-gross operations.

The airplane and engine are STC'd for auto fuel, and it spent many years running 87 octane autogas before I bought it. I switched it back to 80 octane, available at my home field, and developed a leak in the fuel selector almost immediately. Seems the O-rings shrank, and needed replacement. I am thinking about going back to auto fuel, at least partially, when/if I get a safe way to transport and transfer it, to reduce my costs slightly.

I bought N7039M knowing full well the reputation, and the truth about the GO-300 engine. I knew it took what some people consider non-intuitive care; i.e., running it hard, to keep it going to TBO.

Shelby Bowles cruises at 117 knots at 7,000 feet with his '61 C-175B.

It has changed some of my habits, to be sure, with more speed in climbs than I was accustomed to from training days, to keep temperatures well below danger points. But, my plugs stay clean, and the valves seem to be getting along with me just fine.

I have been debating some avionics upgrades, beyond what I've already put into it, but find myself in a bit of a quandary. Do you put a $4,500 HSI into an airplane worth $20,000? Do you put a $4,500 navigation system into an airplane that can't do more than three hours IFR, with reserves? Do you put $3,000 worth of auxiliary tanks into a plane that only does 123 knots? So far, the answers have been "maybe" to all three. The only one that couldn't be taken to the mythical "next airplane" is the auxiliary tanks, but that's the one that really justifies the other two.

Bottom line is that the plane is adequate for my purposes. It has enough speed and range to be fun, load carrying to get myself and two friends to the destination, and versatility to use just about anything that looks like an airport. But, it's far from being my dream plane. Maybe someday, but, for now, I'll have to concede that '39M is here to stay.

Jeff Brenton,
Woodstock, Ill.

I have owned a 1961 Cessna l75B Skylark Model for approximately a year.

I purchased the aircraft primarily because I felt it was one of the best buys on the market for a four-place high-wing airplane. I instituted my search by considering what type of aircraft I wanted and decided that I needed a fixed-gear full-place airplane that had good short-field capabilities and good long-term fuel reserve.

After surveying the market, I decided upon the Cessna 172. The price range on the Cessna 172 seemed to run from $20,000 and upward. Since I felt these prices were out of my range, I then began looking elsewhere, and I considered the Cessna 175. I investigated it and obtained information and literature on the aircraft and decided it might be the hidden jewel of the Cessna market. I have flown the aircraft for approximately 50 hours since purchase and have had no problems, only routine maintenance.

The area that I feel most small Cessna's have trouble with is front-wheel shimmy dampeners; these do require maintenance. I have looked over the engine log for my aircraft since manufactured in August 1960, and there has been no unusual maintenance, other than an overhaul completed at 996 hours. This was done by Piedmont Aviation. The only other unusual maintenance done on this aircraft since that time would be the replacement of the mags. This was done primarily because of the new radios that I installed upon purchase due to considerable radio interference.

I utilize 100 low-lead fuel in this aircraft and have had no problems. The oil consumption on the plane is reasonable. I have noticed, however, when I peak out at top rpm, I do tend to use a little additional oil. However, if I cut back the rpm by 100 or 150, I have no unusual oil consumption. I'm not sure whether that is due to some design consideration. I find that even at about 3,000 rpm the airplane will hit about 125-127 mph.

This is quite comfortable for the type of flying in my area which is pretty close to the sea level. On a trip south recently, I had it at about 7,000 feet, and I noticed I was able to pretty much reach the Cessna handbook speeds of 135-136 mph for my altitude. I noticed no problems (even though there is an' increased horsepower here) with a little additional weight due to the geared engine and larger fuel tanks. The actual carrying capacity of this aircraft is no better than a Cessna 172.

I consider the Cessna 175 the perfect buy for someone who is comfortable with the Cessna 172 and looking for a bargain. Though it is a little heavier on the nose, it performs to standard Cessna flying techniques. I have flown most Cessna models and find I prefer the bar

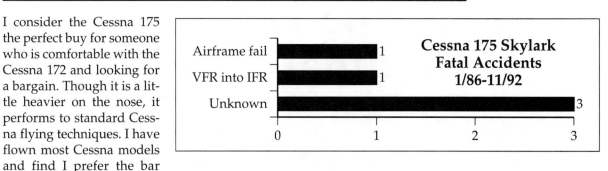

flaps. The plane has incredibly good short-field takeoff and landing characteristics and handles quite stably in rough turbulence, which is one of Cessna's trademarks.

I purchased the plane at $11,000 and with the upgrades I have made am up to an investment of $16,000-$17,000. This airplane lists anywhere from $10,000 - $18,000, depending upon the condition. A comparable Cessna 172 generally runs about $5,000-$6,000 more. I feel the Cessna 175 is a better buy than the Cessna 172.

The model I have has the reduced cowling. I am not particularly fond of the older models which have the large cowling holes since they tend to attract birds. As with any airplane, if the maintenance is done properly, you will have a fine-running aircraft. I have spoken with several other owners of Cessna 175s and I am not aware of any major problems. I would recommend the airplane to anyone who is looking for a nice plane. I would not recommend it as a trainer primarily due to the high rpms. The plane is for travel, not extended low-speed flight.

As a final note, the plane currently has 1,456 hours total time on it as of the last annual. I fully anticipate that this airplane will go another 500-600 hours.

Shelby Bowles
Waldorf, Md.

We have owned a 1959 Cessna 175 for 12 years. We flew it for nine years with the original engine and had good luck. The GO-300 needed to be run at the high end, around 3000 rpm, and it would run good. We did have a stuck valve once and replaced piston and rings twice.

We hold an STC now for a conversion to a Continental IO-360 with constant-speed prop, and it is hard to wipe the smile off my face. With the light airframe and 210-hp engine our plane outperforms Cessna 182s.

Fuel consumption is 10 to 12 gph at 150/155 mph. The old engine burned the same at 135 mph. The flight handling of the 175 is great, and the maintenance is low. I am an A&P, so that helps, but the airframe was built well. Even with the old engine the 175 was nice to fly with the speed that was available. The 172/175 fuselage was meant to have more horsepower. It gives the plane a good solid feeling. The 172 with 150/160 hp just mushes along. When the extra horsepower is added, it brings the tail up into the position where it was meant to be. Overall, we have enjoyed our 175 and would recommend a converted one highly.

Richard Barclay
Littleton, Colo.

Cessna 177 Cardinal

Clean good looks with a full cantilever wing in an airplane that has finally won the market respect it deserves.

Cessna's 177 Cardinal is one of the few cult airplanes that lives up to its followers' hosannas. It's an airplane with an intriguing history: launched with great expectations but not much engineering, an early flop in the marketplace, its problems quickly fixed, but an initial bad rep that never went away. After a troubled 10-year career, it was finally replaced in Cessna's lineup by the Hawk XP, an airplane inferior to the Cardinal in virtually every way.

Genealogy

The Cardinal was first introduced in 1968. It was designed to be the Skyhawk of the future, building on the Skyhawk's classic traits as a reliable easy-to-fly 150-hp basic four-seater, but with snazzy good looks, more cabin room, better visibility and the latest in aerodynamic trendiness, a one-piece stabilator. Cessna was so confident that the Cardinal would be a winner that it shut down the Skyhawk production line in anticipation.

Unfortunately, the hardware didn't meet the expectations. That first 150-hp 1968 Cardinal, although good-looking and roomy, was a odd-handling, underpowered dog. Cessna had sold the Cardinal as a Skyhawk replacement, but it lacked the forgiving, safe, easy flying qualities that had been the Skyhawk hallmark. Such flying qualities may have been acceptable in a bigger aircraft, but Cardinal buyers expected the Cardinal to fly like a Skyhawk. But it didn't, and the plane's poor reputation was born.

In its optimism, Cessna cranked out 1,164 Cardinals in 1968 (nearly double Skyhawk production for the year), and the dealer organization managed to sell most of them before the word got out.

Reputation Justified

Most of the 1968 Cardinal's bad reputation was justified. The wing was a "high-performance" NACA 6400 series airfoil, the same one used in the Aerostar and Learjet. But that airfoil tends to build up drag quickly at high angles of attack and low speeds, which is not a good trait in a plane flown by low-time step-up pilots. Stall speed was higher than the Skyhawk's, too. Although the book numbers for stall and rate of climb didn't look too bad, they turned out to be wildly optimistic.

The 1968 Cardinal climbed very poorly under the best of conditions, and if the pilot got the nose up a little too high, drag built up quickly, and climb rate sagged even more.

To make matters worse, the Cardinal had 50 pounds less useful load and bigger fuel tanks, so it was very easy to overload.

The 1968 Cardinal was quite sensitive on the controls, particularly in the pitch mode. The stabilator could stall in the landing flare, resulting in a sudden loss of tailpower and a sudden whomp of the nosewheel onto the runway. Porpoising and bounced landings were commonplace. Overall, its tricky landing traits, overloading tendency and doggy rate of climb made it a real handful for the Skyhawk-type pilot for which it had been designed and marketed.

Correcting the Problem

Cessna quickly realized it had made a major gaffe with the Cardinal. It restarted the Skyhawk production line and set to work fixing the Cardinal's problems. Under the so-called "Cardinal Rule" program, it retrofitted stabilator slots to Cardinals already in the field. This reduced the stabilator-stalling problem. Cessna also revamped the 1969 model calling it the 177A. Major change was the move to a 180-hp engine and a 150-pound increase in gross weight. The stabilator slots were incorporated, and the stabilator-to-wheel control linkage was changed to improve the pitch characteristics.

Despite the improvements, 1969 sales nose-dived to about 200, while Skyhawk sales rebounded to their former league-leading levels.

A New Airfoil

In 1970, Cessna made more major improvements and called the Cardinal the 177B. The 6400 series airfoil was changed to a more conventional 2400 series similar to the Skyhawk's, and a constant-speed propeller was added for better takeoff and climb performance. More stabilator changes were made as well. At last, the Cardinal had all the makings of a good airplane.

From 1971 on, the Cardinal got only minor changes. In 1973, a 61-gallon fuel tank became optional, and cowling improvements boosted cruise speed from 139 to 143 mph. In 1974, a 28-volt electrical system was added. In 1975, speed went up again, but this was merely a bit of paperwork legerdemain by Cessna. Cruise rpm limit was increased so that 75 percent power could be obtained at 10,000 feet instead of 8,000 as before. At most altitudes, side by side under the same conditions, a 1975 Cardinal is no faster than a 1974 model. In 1976, the Cardinal got a new instrument panel.

Despite Cessna's successful efforts to fix the original Cardinal's quirks, the plane continued to be a slow seller. It was the only Cessna single that didn't lead its category in sales (Piper's Cherokee 180 beat it handily, as did the upstart Grumman Tiger).

In 1977, Cessna finally gave up on the Cardinal. While jacking up the Cardinal's price dramatically, it introduced at the Cardinal's old price the Hawk XP (same performance, uglier, worse handling, noisier, more cramped, much higher fuel consumption and engine maintenance, lower engine reliability and TBO). Customers preferred the Hawk XP by a four-to-one margin.

In 1978 Cessna made one last-ditch effort to save the Cardinal. It spruced it up with some fancy interior appointments and radio packages (along with an absurdly high price tag) and called it the Cardinal Classic. Buyers weren't fooled, however, and the Cardinal Classic went over about as well as New Coke.

Used Plane Marketplace

Cardinal owners prize their craft, and the general public apparently concurs, except in comparison with the astonishing Archer. Cardinal prices generally run several thousand dollars less than a comparable 180-hp Archer. This gap closed a few years ago, but has widened again recently. For example, a '77 Archer in '91 was going for $43,500, the Cardinal for $38,000. The Cardinal however commands more than the '77 American General Tiger ($36,750) and Beech Sundowner ($26,000). (Remember that "bluebook" retail prices are like automobile sticker prices; the actual selling price is usually somewhat lower.)

Many 1968 Cardinals have been converted to 180-hp engines and constant-speed propellers. This mod essentially turns the 177 into a 177B (except for the airfoil and different stabilator linkage), and commands a premium of several thousand dollars over a straight 177. In effect, a modified 1968 177 should be priced like a 1970 177B.

Performance

The Cardinal's performance is middle-of-the-road for 180-hp airplanes. Book cruise speeds range from 139 to 150 mph, while the 150-hp 177 is listed at 134 mph. Those numbers are nowhere near as good as the Grumman Tiger (160 mph), about comparable with the Cherokee 180/Archer, and better than the pathetic Beech Sundowner.

Owners report real-world performance reasonably close to book figures, except for the 1968 model. Typical figures: 140-145 mph on 9-10 gph. The 1968 model, judging from owner reports, is fortunate to cruise 120 mph.

Climb rate is about average for this class of aircraft—again, with the exception of the 1968 airplane, whose owners universally complain about its lethargic climb performance.

Payload-Range

Owners typically report useful loads in the 850-950-pound range, depending on installed equipment. That's slightly less than the Cherokee 180 or Grumman Tiger, and not enough to excuse the owner from careful consideration of weight and balance.

Assuming a fairly typical 900-pound useful load and 49-gallon tanks, the Cardinal has about 600 pounds for people and bags once the tanks are filled. That's three FAA-standard people and 90 pounds of luggage. If you want to carry four full-size people and 100 pounds of luggage, you'll be limited to perhaps 20 gallons of fuel—barely enough to fly anywhere safely. Weight limitations make the Cardinal essentially a three-passenger airplane, or at best a two-plus-two (adults and kids).

With full tanks, the Cardinal has good range. The 49 gallons usable and typical 10-gph fuel flow allow the Cardinal to fly four hours with reserve, and cover more than 500 miles. The 60-gallon tanks available on post-1973 models boost endurance by an hour and range by 150 miles—but at the expense of 66 pounds payload. A typical 60-gallon Cardinal with tanks full can carry just 540 pounds of cabin load. The 1968 150-hp Cardinal (2,350 pounds) has a gross weight 150 pounds lower than the 177A and 177B (2,500 pounds). Empty weight is only a bit less, so the 177's equipped useful load may be as low as 750 pounds. Put in four 170-pounders and 70 pounds of luggage, and there's zero—that's right, *zero*—left for fuel. (You could ride around behind a towtug, though. Wouldn't that be fun?)

Legally speaking, the 177s converted to the 180-hp/constant-speed setup are even worse, since useful load may not be legally increased while the new engine/prop are about 50 pounds heavier. But most pilots of the 180-hp 177s fly as if they have 177As or Bs. From the performance point of view, they're perfectly safe doing that. (As far as the landing gear and wing spar go, we're not so sure.)

Creature Comforts

A major design goal of the Cardinal was interior comfort, and the goal was achieved. The cabin is fully six inches wider than a Cherokee's, and puts its sibling Skyhawk to shame. The baggage compartment is huge. From the pilot's point of view, the Cardinal feels very spacious as well, since the wing sits higher and farther back, allowing excellent visibility out of the panoramic windshield. Unlike the Skyhawk and the high-wing Cessnas, the pilot's vision up and to the side is not blocked by the wing.

One Cardinal owner reports, "It's enormous in there...I often take the rear seats out and stand up a couple of ten-speed bicycles...the legroom in back is worth boasting about...the general spaciousness makes you feel like you're riding in the back of a limousine." Overall, the Cardinal is probably the roomiest four-place airplane made (not counting semi-six-seaters like the Bonanza).

A wide welcoming door—on both sides of the cabin—is one of the hallmarks of the Cardinal line. It's probably the easiest plane ever built to get in and out of.

It's also probably the easiest plane ever built to get in and out of. The doors are as wide as a soccer pitch, and there's no wing strut to get in the way. The floor sits lower to the ground than other high-wing Cessnas, so the step up is a small one. Tall people, however, will have to duck a bit to get under the low-slung wing.

Handling Qualities

The Cardinal generally wins praise from owners for its handling qualities. Even the odd pitch characteristics of the early models are typically excused by owners in a macho sort of way. ("It may porpoise in the hands of the typical wimpy pilot, but hey, a superstud like me has no problem at all. Just a matter of technique, babe.")

In truth, the pitch sensitivity and porpoising tendencies of the Cardinal have never really been completely tamed. Pitch control forces are light (particularly compared to the notoriously nose-heavy Skyhawk and Skylane), and Skyhawk pilots are sometimes surprised by the responsiveness and pitch authority.

As one forthright Cardinal owner put it, "My own flying techniques and the Cardinal's characteristics on landing don't coincide very well. I feel like I run out of elevator effectiveness at recommended approach speeds, and thus land faster than I would like to. The very compliant landing gear saves my face a lot of times." Another owner writes, "It will porpoise for the inexperienced pilot. No problem for the owner-operator, but for this reason it is not a good aircraft for rental."

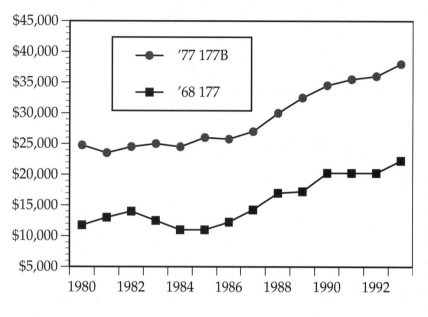

In flight tests by *Aviation Consumer* pilots, however, we've never had any problems, and frankly prefer the Cardinal's handling qualities overall to those of the Skyhawk. (Technique, babe.)

On takeoff, the Cardinal must be rotated with firm wheel pressure, at least with two people in front and flaps up. (The pilot sits well ahead of the wing.) Dropping 15 degrees of flap for takeoff, however, will fly the Cardinal right off the runway without major yanks on the wheel.

In cruise flight, the Cardinal is a good steady IFR airplane—if you can get it trimmed out laterally and keep the fuel balanced. Several owners reported gross fuel-flow discrepancies when the fuel selector is on "both," with all fuel flowing from the left wing. Left-right switching every half hour may be necessary to maintain lateral trim.

Maintenance

Owner reports and service difficulty files suggest the Cardinal is a fairly simple, low-maintenance airplane. (Ironically, the retractable-gear 200-hp Cardinal RG is a real maintenance bear, with almost four times the rate of service difficulty reports on file as the fixed-gear airplane.) Annual inspections typically run $350-500 for the basic once-over. The engine and airframe have no major flaws that we're aware of. (The 180-hp Lycoming engine, in fact, is one of the most reliable of all.)

But there are some things to watch out for:

• McCauley prop inspection. It must be overhauled every five years or 1,500 hours. Check compliance on any airplane considered for purchase.

• Oil pump gears. Pre-1976 Cardinals should be checked for compliance with AD 75-08-09 on the oil pump gears. The Cardinal's engine model was not specifically called out in the vaguely-worded AD, and some mechanics may not be aware that the AD applies. Semantic hair-splitting aside, make sure this AD has been done.

• Other generic ADs that apply to many aircraft. Stewart oil coolers, Cessna fuel caps, vacuum pumps, ELT batteries, etc., etc.

• Water leaks through the windshield and door. Many owners reported being plagued with leaks. Check the sealant and any water damage.

• "That #@%*&# Bendix mag", as one owner put it. The 1975-78 Cardinal unfortunately came with the notorious Bendix dual magneto.

• Some Cardinals, particularly those in humid coastal areas, have been afflicted with corrosion. See service bulletin SE 80-02 for details. Also, Cardinals built in 1977 and 1978 have slick polyurethane paint jobs. A nice idea, but unfortunately Cessna failed to alodyne and prime the metal properly, and there's been a rash of filiform corrosion on painted surfaces.

• Engine and fuel gauges. These are proving troublesome, and unfortunately the instrument manufacturer has gone out of business. Cessna's replacement gauges (hideously expensive, of course) are not internally lighted and therefore almost useless for night flying.

• Clunking nosewheels. These can be cured with shims and/or new O-rings. Find a mechanic who knows Cardinals to do the job. The nosewheel is like no other Cessna nosewheel.

• High engine temperatures. Owners sometimes report their CHTs run near redline in warm weather. (One says the number three cylinder runs especially hot.) This can be cured with an aftermarket exhaust pipe fairing that improves cooling air flow and reportedly drops temps by 75 degrees. (See the Mods section.)

• Cracking stabilator balance arm brackets. New stainless steel ones replace the old aluminum ones. Cessna has issued a service bulletin calling for checks at 2,000 hours.

Owners gripe that the cowling is hard to take off and needlessly runs up their annual and repair labor bills.

One other major maintenance factor: ARC radios. Virtually all Cardinals have avionics manufactured by Cessna's onetime captive ARC company. Starting in the mid-1970s, quality of ARC radios began to fall, reaching a nadir about 1977 or 1978, the last two years of Cardinal production. ARC gear, virtually across the board, rated dead last in our avionics owner surveys during that period, and there were big shake-ups at the ARC factory at the time. An ARC panel is a major liability in any 1974-78 Cardinal, in our opinion. Check reliability and repair records carefully in any aircraft considered for purchase.

In 1975, the Cardinal got aerodynamic refinements (like this wheel pant fairing) that helped boost cruise speed to 130 knots.

Safety

The Cardinal has an average accident rate—not great, not terrible. We have no recent statistics, but an NTSB study for the years 1972-76 shows the Cardinal to have a fatal accident rate of 2.4 per 100,000 flight hours. This is about average for four-place fixed-gear aircraft. (By comparison, the Skyhawk had a superb 1.5 fatal rate over the same period.) In the various categories of accidents studied by the NTSB, the Cardinal showed only two unusual traits. It ranked very poorly (29th out of the 33 aircraft tabulated) in landing accidents, and very high (best of the 33 airplanes, in fact) in landing undershoot accidents. The hard landing rate is almost certainly related to the Cardinal's pitch sensitivity and unusual control feel in the flare.

According to the NTSB, the Cardinal ranked slightly worse than average in stall

accidents. An *Aviation Consumer* study also ranked the Cardinal a bit below average, and well below the leaders in the four-place class, the Skyhawk and Cherokee.

Checking more recent accidents, we confirmed the patterns of the NTSB study. In 1979 alone, for example, there were seven Cardinal hard landing crashes, five involving 1968 models. There were also a bunch of takeoff accidents involving stall/mushes or impact with rising terrain—both a reflection of the aircraft's poor climbing ability. Again, most involved the 150-hp airplane with the 6400-series airfoil.

One of the Cardinal's best features is its spacious interior. The cabin is six inches wider than a Cherokee's.

The lessons to be learned from the accident files: be very careful about overloaded takeoffs on short runways, at high density altitudes or with rising terrain (or heaven forbid, all three). And practice those landings. (Both warnings go double for the 1968 model.)

Modifications

The most important modification for Cardinal fans is the 180-hp constant-speed engine conversion for the 1968 model, which essentially converts it to the 177B configuration. Hundreds of 177s have been converted this way.

The conversion is quick and easy, basically a bolt-on job. Two different STCs are available from Avcon Conversions (316) 782-3317 and Bush (316) 782-3851. The two are very similar. Both sell STC paperwork and kit parts if you want to buy an engine and prop elsewhere and do the labor yourself. Avcon also has an STC to convert the fixed-pitch 177A to a constant-speed prop.

Horton Industries in Wellington, Kans. (316) 326-2241 offers a STOL kit for the Cardinal consisting of a leading-edge cuff, conical wing tips and vortex generators on the vertical fin. The above-mentioned Bush also offers an STOL mod for the Cardinal.

There's a burgeoning business in Cardinal speed mods. A Canadian named Roy Sobchuck came up with most of them, but they are now marketed in this country by C² Enterprises, 3707 Pinehill Rd., Omaha, Neb. 68123 (402) 292-9327 and Aircraft Speed Mods, Ltd., 6310 Old Cove Dr., Emerald Isle, N.C. 28549, (919) 354-6630. The mods include a nose strut fairing (and a claimed speed gain of 8 mph), tailcone fairing (177B only, 7 mph) exhaust stack fairing (2 mph, 75 degree drop in engine temperature). The company also sells landing light covers, cowl cheek fairings, fuel drain fairings, ADF loop covers and mainwheel pants for which minor speed increases are claimed. The C² mods are not STC'd, but may usually be signed off on a Form 337. (Check with your AI and FAA man before installation.) The company quotes no installation times due to wide variations in skill and experience in working with fiberglass.

Owner Clubs

Cardinal owners have a choice of two clubs. The Cessna Pilots Assn., Wichita Mid-Continent Airport, 2120 Airport Rd., P.O. Box 12948, Wichita, Kans. 67277, (316) 946-4777, is the biggest, and publishes much useful technical info. However, most of it applies to other single-engine Cessnas, so the Cardinal owner may feel lost in the crowd of Skyhawk and Skylane buffs. For the true Cardinal fan, there is the Cardinal Club, 1701 St. Andrew's Dr., Lawrence, Kans. 66047, (913) 842-7016. Since Newsletter secretary Phil Harrison travels a lot, he suggests using the fax to contact the club at (913) 842-1777. It tends to be more of a rah-rah social club, with newsletters focused more on fly-ins than technical problems and solutions. We'd consider both worthwhile for any Cardinal owner.

Owner Comments

We have generally found the Cardinal to be a very reliable airplane. This is particularly true since Cessna made modifications to the early Cardinals under the Cardinal Rule program. In many respects, the original 1968 177 Cardinal is a different airplane, in both handling characteristics and performance, from the later 177A and 177B. This is primarily due to the different engine horsepower and airfoils.

We are beginning to see some parts difficulties. They can take many, many months to arrive from Cessna, and will certainly cost many, many dollars. Because fewer than 3,000 fixed-gear Cardinals were built, salvage yards generally don't have a ready supply of Cardinal parts. One thing that has really been a thorn in the side of Cardinal owners is the instrument cluster. These gauges, which include fuel quantity, oil pressure, oil temperature, cylinder head temperature, etc., were manufactured by Leigh Corp. Leigh went out of business, however, and Cessna's solution to the gauge problem was to recommend replacement with individual Stewart-Warner gauges. This is very expensive. Also, the S-W gauges are not internally lighted and require post lighting. (The Leigh gauges were internally lighted.) However, we have been able to find a shop that can repair the Leigh gauges. The Cardinal was built differently than other Cessnas,

Cost/Performance/Specifications

Model	Year	Average Retail Price	Cruise Speed (kts)	Useful Load (lbs)	Fuel Std/Opt (gals)	Engine	TBO (hrs)	Overhaul Cost
177	1968	$22,250	113	935	49	150-hp Lyc. O-320-E2D	2,000	$9,500
177A	1969	$24,500	118	1,060	49	180-hp Lyc. O-360-A2F	2,000	$10,500
177B	1970	$26,000	119	1,025	49	180-hp Lyc. O-360-A1F6	2,000	$11,000
177B	1971	$27,500	119	1,020	49	180-hp Lyc. O-360-A1F6	2,000	$11,000
177B	1972	$29,000	119	1,015	49	180-hp Lyc. O-360-A1F6	2,000	$11,000
177B	1973	$30,500	124	1,005	49/60	180-hp Lyc. O-360-A1F6	2,000	$11,000
177B	1974	$32,000	130	995	49/60	180-hp Lyc. O-360-A1F6	2,000	$11,000
177B	1975	$34,500	130	995	49/60	180-hp Lyc. O-360-A1F6	2,000	$11,000
177B	1976	$35,500	130	967	49/60	180-hp Lyc. O-360-A1F6D	2,000	$11,000
177B	1977	$38,000	130	967	49/60	180-hp Lyc. O-360-A1F6D	2,000	$11,000
177B Classic	1978	$40,500	130	857	49/60	180-hp Lyc. O-360-A1F6D	2,000	$11,000

and for this reason it's important to find a mechanic who understands the airplane. For example, Cardinal nose gears are known to develop a clunking sound. This can be cured by the use of an O-ring or by installing a shim at a certain location. This is not generally known by Cessna mechanics because the Cardinal's nose gear is not like other Cessna nosegears.

One of the more popular subjects among Cardinal owners these days concerns speed-up kits. The most popular one is marketed by C^2 Enterprises, 3707 Pine Hill Rd., Omaha, Neb. 68123, (402) 292-9327. This modification, which includes a nosewheel pant, and various fairings, is claimed to give a 15-20-mph speed increase, and some users back up this claim. C^2 also sells an exhaust pipe fairing, and we have received many positive comments about its ability to reduce engine and oil temperatures. Most people are able to install these mods under a Form 337 approval, although other FAA offices refuse to allow this.

The Cardinal was not overwhelmingly popular during its production run, despite having reasonable performance numbers, good interior space and very attractive appearance. However, since production has ceased, it seems to be gaining in popularity. In fact, Cardinal owners seem to be so fanatical about their aircraft that they could almost be considered a cult. Due to lower horsepower, the 1968 177 sells for less than the later models. Owning a Cardinal can be a real pleasure if one is willing to put up with the minor inconveniences of an aircraft built in small numbers and out of production for eight years.

John Frank
Executive Director
Cessna Pilots Assn.
Wichita, Kan.

I own a 1974 C-177B with 1,300 hours on it. It's IFR-equipped and has speed mods. Fuel burn is 37 liters/hr (that's 9.8 gph. —Ed.). Average speed with mods is 155 mph. I fly 100-150 hours per year and do my own maintenance. Average maintenance cost (not counting my own labor) comes to about $450 Canadian per year.

Very stable airplane, lots of room. Excellent cross-country machine. Up here in Canada, it gets cold in the back seat during the winter. I have fixed that with a heating modification—now people complain that it's too hot. Lots of water leaks around the doors and windshield. They have been repaired with new sealant under the wing root fairings, and new door seals. It's now quieter, and no more leaks.

The plane is very roomy. With a child seat, we carry the whole family. It looks funny as all the people unload with their baggage. People ask us, "Where did they all come from?"

Roy Sobchuck
Brandon, Manitoba

Having been trained in a Cessna 152 and wanting an inexpensive, simple and comfortable plane of my own, I figured a third-hand 1969 Cardinal with 1,400 hours time was a perfect solution. In the last four years I have averaged about 60 hours per year. It is a very easy plane to fly, but it doesn't fly itself: you must pay about as much attention as when driving on a freeway. Too much attention to the sectional can result in some unusual attitudes.

My Cardinal cruises 130 mph on 10 gallons an hour, and I can count on a 500-plus mile range with ample reserves. My only problem has arisen from inexperience with landing peculiarities. Failure to crank the trim down sufficiently can lead to porpoising or crow-hopping that makes a carnival ride seems tame. Landing too fast can cause endless floating in ground effect.

To take advantage of the 1,200-foot grass strip I built on my farm, I had a Bush STOL kit installed in Udall, Kan. (Excellent craftsmanship and fast work.) The results are well worth the price. Power off, the airplane will not stall if the wings are kept level; it just mushes down. With full flaps, one can land very slowly and steeply, with no fear of dropping in. For short-field takeoffs, put down 10 degrees of flaps, rotate at 45 mph and leap off the ground.

This is a perfect plane for family flying, but one must not be tempted to overload, which can happen because of the cabin size and luggage space. Mine has IFR equipment and some extras. With full fuel it can carry 700 additional pounds, which means four substantial males and their toothbrushes, or two average couples and goodly luggage.

Cardinal (background) was replaced by the Hawk XP, an aircraft inferior to the Cardinal in virtually every way.

Maintenance items have included tires, battery, brake discs and pads. Unanticipated expenses have included replacement of carb heat and flap control cables, new gaskets in the nose strut, corrosion in the tail cone, new starter Bendix, new compass, and new directional gyro. Annual inspection is $450 plus parts and extra fixes required. Overall, mine has been remarkably trouble-free.

I am very satisfied and do not want any other airplane.

John Merserau
Dexter, Mich.

We purchased a new 1968 Cardinal 177 to move up from a 172 Skyhawk. We were disappointed with the 150-hp engine's rather anemic takeoff and climb. We opted for the Doyn 180-hp conversion a year later. Performance was good, as long as the pilot took reasonable care and attention to density altitude. The Cardinal is a good IFR platform, stable and solid. We file 115 knots, and it handles turbulence well. The Cardinal Rule mod program by Cessna corrected tendency for stabilator to stall and drop nose on landing.

No major repairs until 2,578 hours, when we did a major overhaul on the engine at a cost of $2,700 (some years ago). Only other major cost was inspection and maintenance of Hartzell prop. Plane was repainted in 1983 and looks sharp. Now has 3,100-plus hours. My biggest complaint is Cessna's obsolete cowling, which takes too much time for removal during inspections and maintenance.

William Tyson
Kingsville, Md.

Early Cardinal instrument panels were stylish, but lopped off the right corner, sacrificing avionics space.

I bought my 1973 C-177B in 1984 for $15,000. It had not been well maintained, and my initial maintenance figures are misleading. The McCauley prop had not been overhauled in seven years (five years or 1,500 hours is the TBO time), and I had to replace the hub as well as pay for the overhaul, for a total cost of $1,500. The carb heat box fell off into the bottom of the cowling. New muffler was $220. One of the fuel filler necks was badly rusted and had to be replaced for $325. The interior Royalite is doing what old Royalite does—falling apart after drying out and getting brittle. The plastic wingtips, stabilator tips and rudder tips are also cracking.

My biggest problem is the weird C-177 fuel-feed system. I have a real problem with drainage out the overflow vents on the wingtips. I have lost as much as 12 gallons of gas in a week due to siphoning overboard. The plane sits level, and this occurs regardless of the fuel selector position. It is absolutely imperative to check fuel level before every flight if the plane has been sitting—even overnight.

I also do not get any fuel feed from the right tank when the selector is on both. I have landed after a two-hour flight with the selector on "both" and found the right tank still completely full. No wonder it flew right-wing-heavy. When the selector is on "right," however, the tank feeds fine. Lest one think from the foregoing that the Cardinal is a dog, nothing would be further from the truth. The wide doors and spacious cabin will allow a lady to enter while wearing a dress and still be a lady. The cabin has more room than most twins.

Cruise speed at 5,500 feet is usually about 122 knots, according to the DME (in still air). Fuel consumption varies from about 8.5 to 11 gph depending on throttle and mixture. I normally set it up for about 10.2 gph, which allows the engine to run cool at about 72 percent power. I normally operate at 23 inches and 2300 rpm at about 5,000 feet. The Cardinal has a yellow band on the tachometer between 1,700 and 1,900 rpm. This caution range must be adhered to religiously. My plane's logbooks show that it once threw 10 inches of one prop blade off in flight.

According to my mechanic, it had been operated in the yellow arc range, and apparently there is a harmonic vibration with a node about 10 inches from the tip.

Cardinal handling is solid. The big stabilator is powerful and likes to stay right where you trim it. Cardinals have a bad reputation for nasty landing traits, but this has not been my experience. It sits lower on the ground, and because of the low landing position there is a tendency to flare high. The Cardinal's nastiest landing bugaboo is the porpoising you'll get into if you land too fast and don't flare enough. Parked by a Skyhawk or a Cherokee, it looks like a Corvette next to a sedan. My wife likes that!

C.S. Stanley
Jackson, Miss.

We've owned a 1968 Cardinal for the last 12 years. It has been modified with the Avcon 180-hp conversion and cuffed leading edge STOL kit.

Comfort is excellent. With 45 inches of shoulder room, it is significantly more comfortable than almost anything else. Two adults can sit in a Cardinal without rubbing elbows with each other or the vibrating airframe. You can slam the door without hitting yourself. The large doors open fully, unimpeded by a wing strut. Because the Cardinal sits low enough to back into (and then swing your feet up into the plane), I sawed off the entry step. The doors have to be the largest in the industry, with the back seat more accessible than any other single-engine plane.

With the '76 model the panel was enlarged. But ARC avionics remained to plague owners.

As for visibility, unlike most other single-engine designs, the wing is located rearward so that a pilot can lean forward for complete visibility. The ability to see the leading edge is a great comfort when the plane starts icing up. We've found maintenance to be stone simple. Annuals run $150 for the AI fee and $30-$60 for consumables like oil, filters, gaskets, etc. We open and close up the plane for inspection and do all the cleaning, lubrication and other maintenance that the owner is allowed to do. The Hartzell AD cost $605 in 1983. Brake pad wear from rusting discs and rain leaks past the fuel caps ended when I got into a T-hangar seven years ago. We do some of the avionics trouble-shooting ourselves, with my partner's oscilloscope and $40 worth of manuals and test harnesses. In one case, we found a failed potentiometer. Cessna wanted $125 for the part, but we replaced it with a superior part with a more stringent mil-spec from a local electronics supply house for $3. Autopilot removal from the wing is a fine example of perverse service engineering—a difficult and frustrating task for a contortionist in a good mood.

Performance is right on book for a 1974 177B, which is essentially what you get with the Avcon 180-hp conversion. I have flown the same plane hundreds of hours with both the 150-hp and 180-hp engines, and frankly I didn't notice anything different in the way it handles other than rate of climb and a modest improvement in speed. The ability to get quickly to the smoother, cooler air at altitude is an important factor in passenger comfort. Overgrossing is easily accomplished because the Avcon 180-hp STC did not increase the gross weight as the factory did when they put in the larger engine. Our useful load is 815 pounds with all the avionics.

I believe that the Cardinal is one of the great undiscovered treasures in the used aircraft fleet. It is under-priced relative to more recently built planes of older design.

Timothy J. Kramer
West Bloomfield, Mich.

Cessna Cardinal 177RG

Unusual for a high-winger, the Cardinal RG allows good visibility inside a turn, thanks to the rear placement of the wing. This is a '72 model, with landing lights tucked under the spinner.

By many accounts, Cessna's 177 RG Cardinal has survived the ravages of time and a defunct production line quite well. It perhaps now can even be considered the queen of the used economy retractables, at least in terms of near tag sale prices.

It is less doggy in performance than similar aircraft like the Piper Arrow and the Beech Sierra, and though still 10 knots or more slower than the Mooney 201, the Cessna costs a small fortune less. For example, where a 1978 Mooney 201 recently was going for a handsome price of around $59,500, a '78 Cardinal RG could be fetched for a relatively paltry $42,500 or so, according to *Aircraft Bluebook Price Digest* figures.

Cardinal RG owners don't seem to complain too much about parts availability, though the line was closed down in 1978 after only eight years of production. And they rave about its looks and novel design features. They even seem rather inured to the aircraft's Achilles heel—its trouble-plagued landing gear system. Owners who reported to us this time sounded off a lot less bitterly on the gear problem than they did for our initial call for user feedback on the 177 Cardinal RG in 1980.

Peer Pressure

In comparison with the Piper Arrows, Mooneys and Beech Sierras that have the same 200-hp powerplant, the Cardinal RG is fastest, except for the Mooney, of course. It is roomiest, except for the Sierra. And it can carry the best useful load of all of them, by a small margin. In terms of price, it recently was $4,500 less expensive on the average than the Arrow on the used market (for a '78 model), and it surpassed the Sierra by about $7,500, at last look. Incidentally, in the last few years, the Cardinal RG has been losing value relative to the Piper and Mooney, down $9,000 compared to the Arrow and $5,500 relative to the Mooney. It's been holding its own against the Sierra.

Although the 75-percent book cruise speed for the Cardinal RG is supposed to be a sizzling 148 knots/170 mph, in the real world most owners talk about speeds closer to 140-145 knots/161-167 mph. But on the other hand, they boast of economy gas burns of eight to nine and a half gph. And with a generous 60-gallon fuel capacity on all but the '71 RGs, range is superb.

Owners report the Cardinal RGs ride well in turbulence, have nice-handling controls, provide a "stable instrument platform" and behave well in slow flight. "It is like driving a sports car compared to the cumbersome Skylane," said one owner. "Handling is superb."

Cabin Load and Comfort

As a safety-enhancing corollary to the spacious cabin, owners say the aircraft is almost impossible to load out of the cg envelope. But the baggage compartment is a strange one, since it is bisected by the hump that accommodates the retracted landing gear. This means suitcases that fit through the horizontally mounted baggage door then must be finessed into one of the two vertical slots on either side of the wheel well hump.

Said one owner, however, "The much maligned baggage compartment swallows an enormous amount of luggage, despite the hump. A useful load of 1,025 pounds works out to four adults, 120 pounds of baggage and enough fuel to fly four hours with IFR reserves. It is a true four-place single."

Whistling in the Wind

The four-foot wide cabin doors are everybody's pride and joy for ease of access, and they can catch the wind like sails to open a full 90 degrees to the fuselage. (Watch out.) Along with the benefits come some drawbacks, however, since owners still complain about door sealing problems. One said he solved the problem by simply removing the "hardened original seals" and replacing them with new ones.

But we remain skeptical in the light of comments by Bob Fields (of Bob Fields Aerocessories in Santa Paula, Calif.). Instead of providing inflatable seals for what we figured would be the ultimate solution to the problem, Fields told us he threw up his hands in frustration at getting any seals to work on the Cardinal RG, even though numerous owners came to him for help. "The variation in space between the doors and the fuselage is terrible," he said. Some portions of the doors fit too tightly, others too loosely, so when you get one part of the seal to inflate properly, another is pinched off. Fields attributed the awful fit to poor quality control.

Wet and Wild

If the doors can leak air, it stands to reason they can leak water. And so owners testify. The windshields tend to leak as well. But then Cessnas as a class seem prey to leakage problems. One Cardinal RG owner said he solved his leaky windshield problem simply by applying a bead of clear RTV around the outside of the windshield. As a final line of defense for the pilot, however, he suggested covering the pilot's left leg with a plastic chart.

Many aircraft also are noted for poor heating of rear seats in winter. The Cardinal RG tackled that problem by running heating ducts in back through the big doors. Alas, owners report little hot air makes it as far as the rear seats.

History of Model Changes

The aircraft has experienced a few modest changes through its eight-year production life. Though none is terribly significant alone, perhaps the collective improvements through the years to the landing gear system and its many idiosyncrasies amount to something. The 1972 model gained a few knots in cruise and a slightly better climb rate thanks to a new prop. Also, the fixed cabin steps were dropped. They tended to expose the bottom of the fuselage to even more grief when the aircraft landed gear-up (as they did with some regularity). Instead, small foot pads were placed on the main gear struts. In addition, landing and taxi lights were mounted in the nose instead of the wing.

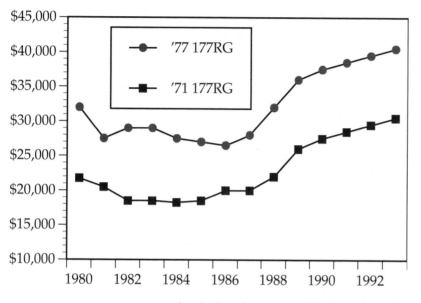

The '73 model received a slightly redesigned nose cowl and an extra 10 gallons in usable fuel—up to 60 gallons. The fuel selector system was changed from one limited to "off" and "both," to one that also provided "left" and "right" positions. The problem on the earlier model was that one tank could be depleted more rapidly than the other, since the pilot could not select either a right or a left wing tank. This often meant unbalancing the aircraft.

In 1976 the instrument panel was redesigned and enlarged, and a simplified landing gear hydraulic system was offered, along with a stronger nose gear trunion. For the '77 model, the aircraft received a fuel selector that gave it commonality with other Cessna singles, had a more positive detent and was supposed to be more easily maintainable.

And finally in 1978 the aircraft received a 28-volt electrical system and an improved gear retraction power pack that cut retraction time in half to six seconds.

Resale Value

Despite inflation, the Cardinal RGs on the whole has exhibited rather mundane resale curves, never soaring up as highly valued aircraft do. Instead, they merely sagged to a certain level in the standard four years after new, then remained pretty much on a plateau through the years, until recently, when the shortage of aircraft tugged nearly all prices upward. Thus, the original '71 model dropped from about $31,000 to around $20,000 and remained within a couple thousand dollars of that until 1988. It's now worth a little over $30,000. The last model, the '78 ship, dropped from about $54,000 to $29,000 in the classic four-year span, and has now come back to $42,500.

Safety Record

A study of accident rates in the decade 1972 to 1981 by *The Aviation Consumer* gave the Cardinal RG an excellent ranking in terms of fatal accidents and a slightly better-than-average rate in total accidents. In fatal accidents, the Cardinal RG came out third best after the Cessna Skylane RG and the Beech 33 Bonanza/

Debonair and tied with the Beech 36 Bonanza with 1.5 fatal accidents per 100,000 hours. In total accidents it was seventh out of 17 with 7.8 accidents per 100,000 hours.

What kind of accidents predominate among Cardinal RGs? A study of NTSB accident records for the years 1979-1980 by our sister magazine *Aviation Safety* showed the most—slightly over 37 percent—involved engine failures. But there seemed to be no particular pattern. Of those in which the problem could be determined, the most—three—occurred after breaks in oil hoses, but all different hoses going to different parts of the aircraft. One engine failure occurred when the oil pump impeller gear broke. This was later the subject of an Airworthiness Directive, but we noted in a three-year runout of the FAA's Service Difficulty Reports (up through September 1981) at least a dozen problems involving broken oil pump gear teeth.

Giant double doors open a full 90 degrees. But pilots report tricky problems getting doors to seal well. Squarely in the middle of the luggage compartment is a big hump that houses the retractable main gear. But load carrying remains topnotch.

Landing accidents accounted for the next highest category, with nearly 12 percent, with hard landings and groundloops leading the way in unpleasantness.

Gear Nemesis

As for the traditional nemesis of the Cardinal RG—landing gear problems—the two-year study showed it only third in the rankings along with a host of other problems like fuel management, takeoff accidents and weather-related problems. Nevertheless, failure of the gear to extend or actuator failure brought three RGs to grief.

Our earlier detailed study of 78 Cardinal RG accidents covering the five-year period from 1973 to 1977 showed once again that engine failures predominated, with about 34 percent of the accidents. These were seldom fatal. That time, though, gearup landings and gear collapses and retractions accounted for second place or about 20 percent—or a total of 16 accidents. Some of these were pilot error, however.

Stall/spin/mush accidents in the Cardinal RG were fairly infrequent. In the five-year period there were two inflight airframe failures. One occurred in bad weather and was fatal. In the second the pilot overstressed the aircraft and bent the wings, but actually managed to land safely. In general, despite the lack of wing-strengthening struts, the aircraft has a good record of in-flight airframe failures.

Maintenance

Powerplant accessories and brakes were the main problem areas reported on our most recent feedback from Cardinal RG owners. But most seemed to feel that maintenance required for the aircraft was reasonable, in general. A maintenance survey yielded average hourly maintenance costs for the Cardinal RG of around

$17 an hour and annual inspection costs averaging a bit under $800. Unscheduled yearly airframe and engine costs together averaged about $600.

We received nowhere near the litany of complaints we did on our last survey several years earlier, when owners railed about chronic maintenance problems. Biggest problem areas then were alternator failures, Bendix magneto breakdowns, cracking exhaust pipes, malfunctioning fuel quantity gauges, breaking alternate air induction doors, leaking fuel caps, hot-running engines, landing gear horn malfunctions and malfunctioning landing gear mechanisms, especially hung-up nosegear.

A check of Service Difficulty Reports from 1979 through most of 1981, however, suggested some troublesome areas. A few were: stabilator problems such as loose bolts, worn bushings and cracked brackets; cracked and broken prop spinners; cracked crankcases; broken engine oil pump gear teeth (mentioned before); Bendix magneto failures; and throttle cable malfunctions.

The 1976 models, like this one, received a simplified landing gear hydraulic system. Early years of the model's history saw it plagued with gear problems. The main gear retracts into a notch in the rear fuselage without doors.

Focus on Landing Gear

Though some owners this time around reported problems with the notoriously quirky landing gear system, the complaints were by no means legion as before. It would appear that the constant focus of attention on the problem by pilots and maintenance shops, and by Cessna's own progressive series of fixes, have diminished its impact significantly. And this comes in the face of the '81 SDR breakdown showing page after page of gear problems. (One must temper this finding, however, with appreciation for the fact that so many of Cessna's *other* retractable-gear aircraft through the years have experienced more than their share of gear problems.)

Through the eight years of its production, the Cardinal had four different landing gear systems, as Cessna strived to correct all its quirks. The first, most problem-plagued one on the '71 and '72 Cardinal RGs, was a Rube Goldberg combination of electrical and hydraulic components whose weakest link was its electrically actuated main gear downlocks. The '73 Cardinals got hydraulic downlock actuators that improved reliability. Then on the '74 aircraft the gear selector handle itself was turned into a hydraulic valve and hydraulic pressure was routed not directly but through a panel-mounted valve controlled by the handle. This system also eliminated the remote electrical control unit.

Finally, with the '78 models the 12-volt Prestolite hydraulic power packs were eliminated in favor of a 24-volt power pack of Cessna's design. This has proved to be the most satisfactory of all the systems and, of course, would be the one to choose if cost considerations permit. At any rate, potential buyers should check to see which, if any, of Cessna's recommended service instructions have been applied to which ever model they are looking at. There are at least eight of them, including numbers 71-41, 72-26, 73-28, 74-26, 75-25, 76-4, 76-7 and 77-20.

Modifications

Among the STCs published for the Cardinal RG are the following: Wing leading edge cuffs and vortex generators on the vertical stabilizer, by Horton STOL Craft, Wellington, Kans.; chrome-plated brake disc installation, by Engineering Plating & Processing, Kansas City, Kans.; installation of an air/oil separator, by Walker Engineering Co., Los Angeles, Calif.; and recognition lights on the horizontal stabilizer, by DeVore Aviation, Albuquerque, N.M.

What to Join

Cardinal owners have a choice of two clubs: The Cardinal Club, 1701 St. Andrew's Dr., Lawrence, Kans. 66047, (913) 842-7016, or fax (913) 842-1777 all hours; and the Cessna Pilots Assn., P.O. Box 12948, Wichita, Kans. 67277, (316) 946-4777

Owner Comments

The average cost over the life of my '74 Cardinal RG (purchased when it was one year old) is about $40 to $45 an hour. (That includes direct operating and fixed costs, flying about 175 hours a year.) This may be higher than average, but I spare no expense on maintenance. The aircraft is maintained by Howard Aircraft Service, at Craig Field in Jacksonville, Fla., and Bob Howard is a real nitpicker. My annuals run from $1,500 to $2,000. My hourly maintenance cost for 1984, the highest ever, worked out to $28.06.

Mechanically, the aircraft has presented only one major problem. Following a fast, no-flap landing, the nose gear collapsed as the aircraft turned off the runway. An improperly adjusted nose gear linkage was found to be at fault. Apparently the aircraft left the factory in that condition and flew for two years before the accident. At normal landing speeds, the hydraulic system apparently could overcome the air pressure on the nose gear. At high speeds this was not the case. Result: a new prop. Brake pads also were a constant problem. I should have installed chrome disks years ago. Parts, however, are no problem.

I flight plan for 140 knots at about eight to nine gph. It is a fine cross-country machine for my purposes. I usually fly the aircraft with an average of two people aboard. The handling characteristics are outstanding. The controls are firm, crisp and effective. The aircraft has the feel of a much heavier machine, more like a 182 than a 172. The stalls are mild with prompt recovery. The placement of the wing is one of the characteristics of the aircraft that I dearly love, since you are forward of the leading edge, which gives you outstanding visibility.

Cost/Performance/Specifications

Model	Year	Average Retail Price	Cruise Speed (kts)	Useful Load (lbs)	Fuel Std/Opt (gals)	Engine	TBO (hrs)	Overhaul Cost
177RG	1971	$30,500	125	1,170	50	200-hp Lyc. IO-360-A1B6	2,000	$13,500
177RG	1972	$31,500	129	1,155	50	200-hp Lyc. IO-360-A1B6	2,000	$13,500
177RG	1973	$33,000	129	1,140	60	200-hp Lyc. IO-360-A1B6	2,000	$13,500
177RG	1974	$34,500	129	1,140	60	200-hp Lyc. IO-360-A1B6D	2,000	$13,500
177RG	1975	$36,500	129	1,120	60	200-hp Lyc. IO-360-A1B6D	2,000	$13,500
177RG	1976	$38,500	129	1,093	60	200-hp Lyc. IO-360-A1B6D	2,000	$13,500
177RG	1977	$40,500	129	1,093	60	200-hp Lyc. IO-360-A1B6D	2,000	$13,500
177RG	1978	$42,500	129	1,106	60	200-hp Lyc. IO-360-A1B6D	2,000	$13,500

The avionics are ARC. What more can I say! One of the avionics people that worked on the radios said, "You really have to be wealthy to fly with ARC equipment," and I believe her. I had two problems: finding someone who would work on them, then finding someone whose repairs would hold up until I got back to my home base. I am going to install new avionics following completion of the new paint job.

All in all, I am very fond of the aircraft. Frankly, I don't find any of the aircraft of the same class being marketed today comparable to a Cardinal RG.

John D. Shea, Jr.
St. Augustine, Fla.

Early in 1980 I read *The Aviation Consumer's* Used Aircraft Guide on the Cardinal RG, and decided the aircraft had the performance and range I was looking for. Later that year I bought a 1973 model which had been operated by a flying club in Wisconsin. I selected this particular craft, which had about 2,300 hours on the airframe, because someone had the good sense to install a complete Collins Microline avionics package. This has proven to be a reliable set of equipment during many hours of IFR cross-country flying.

After purchasing the airplane, I gave it new paint, new interior and a zero-time engine and prop. Also, I replaced the horrible plastic instrument panel cover and glove box door with a hardwood panel. The cheap plastic panel does make a good template for laying out its replacement.

The airplane pretty much meets book speeds and delivers 165 mph cruise at 70 percent power. I always plan nine gph from takeoff to touchdown. Sixty gallons works out to six and a half hours of fuel on board. I was surprised that with two on board, it is relatively easy to get to 14,000 feet if you just increase the rpm to 2700 during the climb after leaving 8,000 feet. The book permits this power setting from sea level. There seems to be a lot of additional power in the last 200 rpm, which is also nice when the bird starts to collect a little ice. It sees a lot of IFR and is a good IFR aircraft. I installed a Cessna 300A autopilot a couple of years ago, and it works very well.

On two occasions, the gear down-and-locked indicator would not illuminate without a few cycles of the landing gear. After spending hundreds of dollars at repair stations where they found nothing, I was looking at the connections to the microswitches in the end of the main gear struts during an annual, and found the inline connectors to be loose on the wires. After five minutes with a soldering iron, there have been no more gear indicator problems. I suggest examining these little connectors whenever you have a chance.

I was a little concerned about the retractable gear after reading your 1980 article, but it goes up and down every time I move the switch. I've spent some time trying to reduce the noise level in the airplane even though it is fairly quiet for a single-engine machine. I found that some thin cork with adhesive backing made by Sound Coat of Santa Ana, Calif. applied on top of the glareshield running to the windshield was more effective than other sound-absorbent material on the floor or in the ceiling panels, etc. The airplane is pretty quiet now.

The door noise problem was solved by removing the hardened original door seals and replacing them with new seals. The doors will stay a lot tighter if you keep the door latch screws tight. Most of the water problem from the windshield can be solved by applying a bead of clear RTV around the outside of the windshield. The residue can be controlled with a plastic chart on the pilot's left leg. I had a Walker Engineering Air/Oil Separator added to the engine breather, and this has helped tremendously in keeping the bottom of the airplane clean.

Maintenance on the airplane is not too far out of line. The aircraft has settled into about an $800 annual, with no big surprises during the year except maybe an alternator—due, I feel, to the vibration of the IO-360. Small inspections throughout the year and a hangar have done a lot to keep maintenance costs down.

I was considering moving to a T210 for more speed and the ability to climb up through the clouds here in western Oregon, but the Cardinal RG is much more economical, very comfortable, and has been pretty darn reliable—in five years only two delayed trips—so I plan to keep it for some time.

John Desmond
Vice-president Engineering
Flight Dynamics, Inc.
Hillsboro, Ore.

In my opinion, performance of the Cardinal RG is outstanding: 140 knots at just under 10 gph. Although the book says 148 knots, I have never been able to duplicate those numbers. Handling is superb. It is like driving a sportscar compared to the cumbersome Skylane. It is a total departure from the other Cessna singles, rides fairly well in turbulence and is rock solid even at 80 knots—a good IFR machine.

As for maintenance, I purchased my '74 model in 1984 with 1,125 hours since new. Low time on a 10-year-old airplane doesn't mean much, so I bargained for a low price and expected the worst. And that's exactly what I got—chunks of metal in the oil within the next 40 hours. The engine was overhauled at one of the leading shops in central Florida. I replaced the ARC radios (just awful) with Narco and installed an Arnav loran. I also replaced the rusted and badly pitted brake discs with Cleveland chrome. In 150 hours of flying I have replaced the vacuum pump, an alternator belt, one EGT probe and a squat switch. No other gear problems to date, although a gear-up landing is noted in the logs back in '76.

The 1973 RGs benefited from an extra 10 gallons of fuel and a new fuel selector system that allowed the pilot to select left or right tanks. Also, the nose cowl was redesigned.

The cost of operation, including fuel, maintenance and reserve for engine and prop overhaul is about $29 per hour. Maintenance costs thus far have been $4 to $5 an hour, based on 120 hours a year. My last annual was just under $500. Some of the nagging problems have been grossly inaccurate fuel gauges, a damp cabin when flying in rain and a gear horn sounding off at cruise. (You play with the throttle position to make it stop.)

Cessna solved the problem of where to anchor the shoulder harness by locating it in the ceiling ahead of the wing spar. Geometry is not ideal for crashworthiness, however.

As for comfort, it is a very roomy single, even for rear-seat passengers. It's a pleasure boarding and exiting with two huge doors and no struts or wings to step over. The much maligned baggage compartment swallows an enormous amount of luggage, despite the hump. A useful load of 1,025 pounds works out to four adults, 120 pounds of baggage and enough fuel to fly four hours with IFR reserves. It is a true four-place single. Cabin noise level at cruise is less than most other singles I have flown. I really love my Cardinal. The good points far outweigh the problems. I am a CFII and have owned four other airplanes in 11 years. Considering the outrageous costs of today's new singles and the performance this airplane affords, the Cardinal RG can be the steal of a lifetime for a careful shopper. Truly this airplane could be the best single Cessna ever produced.

Vince Veltri
Sarasota, Fla.

I have owned and operated a '75 177RG for about four years. The cost of flying and maintaining it has been very low. I have flown it for about 600 hours with only one unscheduled maintenance problem, and that was for a voltage regulator. Annuals average about $250 to $350, and only routine procedures have been necessary this far. The airplane averages 145 knots on about 67 percent power, at about 9.5 gph. I have flown it on long cross-countries and find it very comfortable and quiet. In short, I think it's the best retractable that Cessna ever built. (I also have owned and flown T210s, P210s and 182RGs.)

Milton Killebrew
Victoria, Tex.

We bought our '74 Cardinal RG in '75, so now have nearly 10 years of experience to report on. The aircraft may have suffered a certain amount of abuse during its first year with a commercial charter operator. The total time at purchase was just over 400 hours, and during our first two years of ownership we ran into a number of irritating snags and repairs—none major. Since that time the RG has operated reliably, with very little unscheduled downtime. During nine and a half years, we've flown about 1,600 hours and installed a factory reman engine at the TBO of

1,800 hours. The original engine ran perfectly till the last day—and the only major repair was one piston and valve at about 1,200 hours. At 1,800 hours the engine was still giving us two hours to a quart of oil, with good compression. We also lost one alternator and one vacuum pump, fortunately not during IFR.

Much has been written about gear problems with the Cardinal RG. In almost 10 years, we've encountered two incidents, both fairly minor. On one occasion the gear refused to lower, but was pumped down manually without difficulty. The problem turned out to be worn brushes on the pump motor. Recently, one of the hinge brackets on the forward nose gear door sheared off, causing the door to twist about 45 degrees. I discovered this during the ground check, but it could have resulted in a jammed nosewheel.

The aircraft is stable and easy to fly, with low landing speed for an aircraft of its type, yet it provides reasonable cruise speeds (nothing like a Mooney, of course) and excellent range. You can fill the tanks and still take four average adults, or three and baggage without going over gross. There is no such thing as a cg problem under any normal loading situation. Endurance is up to nine hours at lower power settings, which can give tremendous range with a good tailwind. I normally flight plan for a cruise of 135 knots. We use the RG for a combination of personal family travel and business. It's ideally suited for trips up to about 500 miles, with plenty of reserves and reasonable block time. Cessna's book figures for cruise performance are quite realistic. Since installing the factory reman engine, I find speeds within one or two knots of published value.

I don't know how Canadian operating costs equate to U.S. costs, but our overall cost per hour, including fuel, hangar, insurance and maintenance, based on 175 hours per year, runs about $68 per hour, equivalent to about $50 U.S. The Canadian equivalent of a U.S. annual is a C.C.I plus a 100-hour on the engine, and runs $1,000 to $1,200 ($730 to $880 U.S.). Hourly cost of maintenance, not including engine reserve or avionics runs $17.50 an hour ($12.80 U.S.). Among the few negative comments I could mention are the cabin heater, which is very marginal. In winter with temperatures below zero F, the front seats are barely comfortable. Anyone sitting in back would freeze in short order. The ducts in the doors, which are supposed to carry heat to the rear, are next to useless.

The cabin is moderately noisy, and conversation is not easy. Seals are not too good. This contributes to the noise level, and in heavy rain there are leaks. The fuel gauges are unreliable. When the tanks are about half empty, the gauge indications wander all over. The gear warning horn is Mickey Mouse. For a year it either wouldn't work at all, or would blast away when the throttle was set for 18 inches in descent. After years of trying to adjust it, our FBO finally came up with some minor mods that appear to have cured the problem. The original paint stood up well, but eventually some cracking and fading occurred. The plastic interior and upholstery, while certainly not deluxe, is durable. It still looks good. We paid C. $36,000 in 1975, and it's worth about the same now, with a low-time engine.

Too bad Cessna stopped production. I think this is the best and smartest-looking single (except for the much costlier Centurion) Cessna has ever produced.

R.G. Shelley
Toronto, Ont. Canada

Cessna
180 Skywagon

One of the most popular and practical taildraggers ever made, the 180 enjoyed a tremendously long production run.

Although usually thought of as a bushplane, the Cessna 180 has the kind of versatility that makes it anything but an anachronism, despite its tail-gear configuration.

It might be classified as a Skylane without a tricycle gear, since the Cessna 180 Skywagon has the same engine and nearly equal weight and performance. Most buyers select this airplane, which enjoyed a production run that lasted from 1953 through 1981, because they have a specialized use in mind, such as skydiving or flying from floats or skis or wheels out of short, rough fields.

Vast numbers of these airplanes were built: Over 6,000 in all. The earliest years were the heyday, with 600 to 800 180s a year rolling out the factory doors.

Value

The first 180s listed with average equipment for $15,928 and are now worth about $34,000. The last ones, the 180 KII, cost $66,000 equipped when new and now go for $73,000.

In fact, the 180 traditionally is worth more than its sibling 182 for same-year models. Example: although you can probably find a used 1965 model Skylane for about $31,500, a comparable 180 would most likely go for $39,500, even though they have the same powerplant.

Although the taildragger does not handle quite as well as the Skylane from paved runways, it is, in general, considered a fairly benign example of the species, not given to great treachery or unusual groundlooping tendencies. However, it can be a bit of a handful in a strong gusty crosswind. An optional crosswind landing gear was offered in 1967.

The strut-braced four-placer is powered either by a 225-hp Continental O470-A in its earliest configuration, or a 230-hp O470-K, -L, -R or -U engine in later models. All but the -U version are supposed to use 80 octane, incidentally, consuming this at a rate of about 11 gph when the throttle is set to 65 percent power.

History

There were no dramatic changes in the Cessna 180 model since its introduction in 1953. The gross weight went up twice, however; it went up 100 pounds with the 180A in 1957 and went up mother 150 pounds in the 1964 G model as an optional six-seat configuration was offered along with an extra side window. Then with the

The interior is spacious enough, but could benefit from a cargo door for some uses. Notice the rear "seat."

1973 J model a cambered leading edge was added to the wing, which improved low-speed handling characteristics. The '74 model introduced optional skylights and lower door windows.

Standard fuel capacity for the 180 was 55 gallons to begin with: then this was raised to 65 in 1964 along with the upped gross weight. At the same time, optional fuel of 84 gallons was offered. The 180 models have simple, easy-to-manage fuel systems with "left," "right" and "both" tank selection positions.

Bush Operations

The main justification for the 180 naturally centers around its ability to operate from rough or unfinished fields. Like most Cessna singles it has a sturdy set of "spring" gear struts that can take a lot of abuse. The tailwheel configuration also creates less drag in high grass or sand or snow for takeoff, and in the three-point attitude the prop arc is given a bit more ground clearance.

Just about the only competitors to the 180 of a fairly contemporary design are the Helio Courier and the Maule. The Helio is the most "exotic" STOL aircraft of the bunch, with its special low-speed control devices. The Maule, of course, is fabric covered.

While the Cessna 180 is no slouch at getting in and out of rough fields, it offers "STOL" performance only a mite better than its sister ship, the tricycle-gear Skylane Though it would appear the taildragger would have a bit of an edge in other performance categories since it has one less drag-producing gear strut hanging out in the breeze, the Skylane enjoys a small margin in cruise speed and in useful load.

Cabin Capacity

Since loading flexibility is supposed to be the Cessna 180's forte, it has easily removable seats and yard-wide doors on either side of the cabin, though it lacks the extra convenience of a double rear-door arrangement like the Cessna Stationair. There is also an extended rear compartment, added in 1967. It is big enough to hold the center passenger seats when folded up, along with the rear passenger seats—or 50 pounds of cargo, provided the weight and balance limits haven't been exceeded.

Like its stablemate, the Skylane, the Model 180, later called the Skywagon, is a good load carrier. With full standard fuel, it can be counted on to haul four 170-pounders and still have enough useful load left over to take on 100 pounds or more of baggage, depending on the amount of accessory equipment on board.

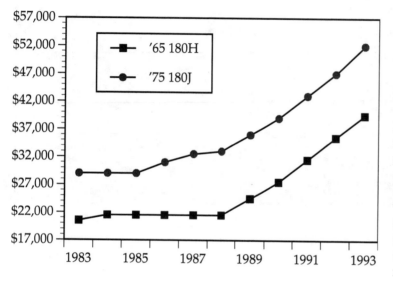

It will then offer a range of about 470 nm, including taxi, takeoff and a 45-minute reserve.

Airworthiness Directives

The Model 180 has had a fairly peaceful AD career through the years. Relatively few were issued, and none of these was too painful. Probably the most energetic one was issued in 1973 and affected several braced-wing Cessna models. It required replacement of defective wing-spar attachment fittings, and the full cost was borne by the company.

The 180 is, unfortunately, also subject to the infamous AD 84-10-1 of 182 fame, which involves inspection for wrinkles in the fuel tank bladders.

Safety

Despite the presumably higher exposure to mischief that any taildragger used for bush operations might have, the Cessna 180 has an excellent safety record. In fact, it was credited with the best (lowest) fatal accident rate of 33 different makes and models of aircraft in a special accident study conducted by the NTSB. It ranked about in the middle in terms of its overall accident rate.

When compared with the other 32 aircraft in the one area where it might be expected to have a problem—ground loops—the Cessna 180 was ranked eighth worst. It also showed up better than half the other aircraft in the hard-landing category. And despite the natural tendency of pilots to try to get 180s in and out of short fields, the aircraft was rated among the two least likely to be involved in an undershoot accident, and among a handful least likely to crack up in an overshoot.

Modifications

The most extensive upgrading mod available for the Cessna 180 is probably the Robertson STOL package. There are three main alterations involved: installation of a cambered leading edge to the wing, placing a stall fence on top of the wing between the flaps and ailerons and incorporation of a "drooping" aileron system that works in conjunction with the flaps.

These changes drop the takeoff distance over a 50-foot obstacle from 1,205 feet to 710 feet and the landing distance over 50 feet from 1,355 feet to 688 feet. They also lower the approach speed from 70 to 47 mph and cut the stall to about 37 mph.

Owner Comments

Some of the early ones had solid tailwheels, which were just wretched. They were real vibrating horrors. When I flew them down in Mexico we had a wonderful brake modification. Our mechanic would cut pucks out of old truck brake shoes, and believe me, GMC made a far better brake puck than Goodyear did.

On short-field landings, the best technique is to come in real tail-low, touch it down, dump the flaps and stand on the brakes and shove the yoke full forward. You sort of hop, skip and jump for about 200 feet, the tail comes down with a resounding bang, and there you are. You couldn't possibly take off in the same distance, even with a JATO bottle.

We regularly flew way over gross. Forty-eight gallons of fuel, 200 pounds for me, plus five passengers at 150 each, plus 100 kilos of other stuff. The tires looked underinflated and the gear was bowed, but it always got off all right, even at our field elevation of 6,000 feet. But the takeoff was definitely a prolonged and dream-like affair.

You want to check them closely for ground-loop damage. All the old ones have been around once or twice. Look for loose rivets where the gear goes into the fuselage. You may have a gear that's been improperly replaced and is out of line. That's quite common.

Panel layout is standard Cessna. Like the 182, the panel is so deep that shorter pilots may have trouble seeing over the glareshield.

Anybody who consistently tries to three-point a 180 is either a fool or a genius. People who try that usually end up riding bucking horses. It skips and hops and bounces all over the place.

A 180 spins beautifully, loops nicely and rolls reasonably well.

Never had any fuel cell trouble, never had any engine trouble or prop problems, either Hartzell or McCauley

• • •

Mine was a 1953 model. The A models, '53 through '55, had big problems with the oil coolers. The temperature gauges went right up to the red line after takeoff and just sat there. A mechanic told me that Continental's fix was a blast tube out of the temperature bulb. In the old ones

with the oil cooler that lies on its side, you had to be darned careful about long hot climbouts because you got severe oil temperature problems, which could lead to shortened overhaul life and catastrophic failures, although nothing ever happened to me.

I have quite a few hours with the 225, and it's a good engine. It's definitely more economical than the 230. In normal cruise you can run it at 11 or 11.5 gallons per hour. I could have run it even leaner, but there was that cooling problem.

When we got 'em really clean, with normal loads—say two or three people and full tanks—I flight-planned at 145 mph. Anybody who claims they cruise around at 160 is full of it. The 230S don't go any faster, and they burn 121/2 to 13.

• • •

The 180 has cowl flaps and they were forever breaking, coming off, and cracking. There's no such thing as a Cessna cowl flap that works reliably for a long period of time. They just vibrate too much, and then the linkage tears out. Overall, though, they were very low maintenance airplanes. I had no complaints at all.

The old 225 engine had a different timing than the 230, and sometimes we'd get one timed wrong at an annual, and it would run rough as hell. It's a fairly common mistake that mechanics make in the older models.

It's very demanding to land. I consider it harder to land than my Staggerwing. For one thing, it has lousy ailerons, especially at low speeds. With the 180 in a gusty crosswind, I get the feeling I'm about three twists of the wheel behind the airplane. I don't like that at all in a tailwheel airplane.

They are definitely rugged. A friend of mine hit a tree on takeoff once, bent one gear back and broke the main spar on the right side. He was 100 miles from the nearest mechanic, so he spliced the spar with a coconut log, lashed a piece of corrugated tin roofing over the broken leading edge, tied the gear on with baling wire and flew home.

• • •

The 180 is often found equipped with unusual accessories like this set of wheel-through skis.

I had a '64 model, and a lot of those airplanes were pretty doggy around the engine compartment. Things were very tight in there, and the exhaust system, being very complicated, gave us a lot of headaches. The single exhaust systems were apparently a lot better. My mechanic charges me a flat rate of 16 hours labor for an annual, plus discrepancies.

Watch out you don't get one that's been used for hauling parachute jumpers. So many are used that way, and they tend to break a lot of cylinders because of the constant full-power climbing followed by power-off glides. Those jump pilots really beat hell out of the airplanes.

• • •

The original Goodyear brakes were terrible. Anybody who had any brains put Clevelands on them.

• • •

If you're looking to buy one, you have to watch out for the worm gear arrangement in the horizontal stabilizer trim. It was always working loose. One of the first things to do on any used 180 is give the stabilizer a hefty shake. It was a pretty expensive job to tighten it up.

• • •

One thing to look for is corrosion or damage to the floats. If they need bottoms on them, it's real easy to spend $5,000 to $7,000. That's normal for rebuilding a set of floats. Corroded fuselage skins are another big problem. Look around the rivets and the seams.

One thing you should be very careful about buying a used 180 floatplane: when it comes out of the factory, it has a special factory corrosion-proofing package, but some people will take a standard 180 and put it on floats, and they're not corrosion-proofed. They don't have the stainless steel cables, zinc-chromated interiors and so forth. You should be very sure it's a factory seaplane. There's really no satisfactory way of corrosion-proofing except to do it at the factory.

• • •

Be careful about previous submersion. If it's been submerged and restored correctly, then you're okay, but not more than one out of ten is done right. And very often there's no record of submersion. A guy will flip it over, hose it off and try to sell it real quick. We've run into that problem a lot down in Louisiana. Inspect for silt up inside the headliner, behind the panel and places like that, since those places are hard to wash out quickly.

There will sometimes be wrinkles in the skin up around the firewall if the airplane has been landed hard.

You can count on a float-equipped 180 for about 120 miles per hour. The newer ones are a little faster, and some people will pull more power, but for a normal 65 percent cruise, 120 is the best you'll get with a float-equipped airplane. Fuel flow at that speed runs right around 12 gallons per hour."

Cessna Skylane 182

This 1972 Skylane was touted as Cessna's 100,000th airplane. With room for four and plenty of fuel and baggage, the Skylane dominated the "high-performance" fixed-gear scene for decades.

Even if the Cessna 182 hasn't been around as long as the Old Testament, it sometimes seems like it has. The third most popular lightplane in history, the Cessna 182 has long been the keystone of Cessna's step-up marketing philosophy, bridging the gulf between Cessna's low-profit 150/172 entry-level airplanes and the higher-profit, higher-performance 210 and light twin aircraft.

A decade earlier, this '62 Skylane marked addition of a rear window, though blunter than later models. Swept-back tails came a couple of years earlier.

Today, almost 40 years after the 182's introduction in 1956, the aircraft is still *the* basic enhanced-performance aircraft, an economical flying machine capable of hauling four people, bag and baggage, a reasonable distance, in comfort, and at a reasonable speed.

The first Skylanes rolled off the production line the same year as the first 172s. Together, the duo marked the beginning of Cessna's 20-year dominance of the single-engine market. The basic 182 design was cut in stone in those days and both airframe and powerplant have remained fundamentally unchanged ever since. The overall effect is generous, with a fuselage of ample size, topped by a big slab of a wing.

In 1958, Cessna introduced the "Skylane," a 182 fitted with enough amenities and creature comforts to raise the gross weight approximately 100 pounds, and therefore decrease useful load by roughly the same amount. Those 1958 Skylanes included rudder trim and a ratchet click elevator trim device, along with optional autopilot. Later Cessna bestowed the Skylane name on the 182, and made the marginally upscale version of the same plane the "Skylane II."

Dependable Engine

The 230-hp Continental O-470 has proved a dependable performer through the years, despite some break-in problems reported in the later O-470-S model. Those first 182s used the O-470-L engine, which featured larger cast shell cylinder heads, thinner and more numerous cooling fins, and an engine mount improved over the early O-470-K installation in the Cessna 180 design.

Cars with enormous swept tail "fins" were all the rage in the late 1950s. Eventually this vogue found its way into airplane styling, with Cessna sweeping back the tail on the 180 in 1960. Basic fuel capacity was increased in 1960, from 55 gallons to 65, with long-range 84-gallon tanks introduced as an option. Later Skylanes would boast a 92-gallon capacity.

Two years later the airplane got a rear window and electric flaps. The year 1971 witnessed an alteration to the 182 in the form of its so-called camber lift wing. The wing was given a constant radius droop—a downward curl. The aim of the droop was to provide better low speed handling and stall reaction. Combined with the aircraft's washout, the result is good lateral control even while deep in the stall zone.

Gross weight has grown steadily over the years, from the original 2,550 pounds to 2,650 in 1957 to 3,100 for the last ones built. Empty weight has also increased, although not quite as fast as gross, so that useful load numbers for the 182 have not increased dramatically, starting at 1,010 pounds in '57, and topping off at 1,377. Overall, however, the 182 design has gone through remarkably few changes over the years.

Built for Comfort, Not for Speed

Book speeds have remained in the 139 to 143 knot range through the years with evolutionary aerodynamic refinements making up for the speed penalty of higher gross weights. Most owners report such speeds are possible in the 182, but prefer to drone along at lower power settings to save fuel, with 130 knots a commonly mentioned figure. One owner reported burning 12.5 gph to get 140 knots at 75 percent power. Another said his 182, burdened with a "full load" cruised at 135 knots at 75 percent between 6,500 and 8,500 feet, while consuming a quart of oil every four hours.

The first-edition 182, a 1956 model with squared-off tail and no wheel pants. It was destined to become the third-best-selling lightplane in history.

Performance like this may seem pokey for an airplane driven by a 230-hp engine, and it is. The Mooney 201, albeit a retractable, slips through the air 30 knots faster than a 182, while using less horsepower.

While no one ever said the 182 was a racer, the airplane does climb, with 1,000 fpm easily obtainable at heavy weights, and 1,500 fpm at lighter weights (both from sea level, of course). If the 182 doesn't get you there particularly fast, it treats you kindly along the way, thanks to a spacious interior. It's a real four-seater, the kind that allows the back seat mob to abandon the fetal position and stretch out.

Two wide doors ease entry and exit. On the negative side, cabin noise levels approach brain-damage thresholds, and can make long flights fatiguing without a good pair of earplugs or headsets.

Handling

In a word, the 182 is stable. Most pilots praise it both as an IFR platform and as a reasonably comfortable aircraft in turbulence. Nonetheless, in the air, as on the ground, there ain't no free lunch, and this stability is paid for with rather heavy control surfaces.

To use another word, the 182 is ponderous, especially in pitch. With full flaps and two people aboard, flaring to land takes maximum muscle and maximum back trim. This heaviness of control is the price paid for the 182's vast cg envelope. Trying to stall the 182 with power on is probably the nearest anyone will come to aerobatic maneuvering in this staid aircraft. It will buck and shake like a bronco until the pilot either relaxes back pressure to lower the nose or settles for a pronounced wing drop.

Such performance will never come as a surprise, however, because the 182's humongous elevator forces make the airplane virtually impossible to stall by accident. Slow-speed maneuvering in a Skylane builds confidence; there's no feeling of flying right on the edge. On the other hand, aileron control at low speeds is relatively clumsy, and gusty crosswinds can prove challenging.

Loading

Unless you're transporting ingots of solid neutronium, the 182's load limits are pretty tough to bust. It's acknowledged as one of the few airplanes in which you can almost always fill all the seats, all the tanks, stuff the baggage compartment to capacity, and still be legal (and safe). Admittedly a well-equipped 182 with long-range tanks might require a degree of fuel/passenger tradeoff, but on the whole, Skylane pilots don't fuss much with weight and balance. If it fits, it's probably legal. Cg balance is also generous. One Skylane owner reports he can put himself up front, load a pair of 200-pounders in the back, fill the baggage compartment to the max, and still be within CG limits.

Safety

The Skylane has a good safety record—well above average as measured against the GA fleet overall. Both accident and fatality rates come in below the norm. FAA records from 1980-81 list 41 fatal accidents for the 182 fleet, with over three million hours flown during that period. The Skylane has among the best stall/spin accident rates of any aircraft. In both a 1972 stall/spin study from the NTSB, and a 1984 study conducted by our sister publication *Aviation Safety*, the 182 scored among the lowest in both accidents and fatalities attributed to stalls or spins.

Thanks in part to the airplane's megalithic pitch performance, in-flight structural failures are virtually unheard of. It's nearly impossible to pull hard enough on a 182 to overstress the airplane. That high-drag fuselage and fixed gear also limit speed buildup in an unintentional dive. This is in keeping with the fact that when measured overall, Cessna designs featuring wing strut braces have an excellent record of holding together when the going gets tough.

The Skylane also excels in the area of fuel management. Its no-frills fuel system consists of a high-wing, gravity-feed system, and an idiot-proof left-right-both fuel selector.

Deadly Fuel Cells

By far the most disturbing AD to emerge from the FAA's regulatory woods, AD 84-10-1 has caused thousands of Cessna owners to delve deep into the innards of their fuel-bladder equipped wings for potentially deadly water-trapping wrinkles.

For years the problem eluded detection during the traditional sump-draining preflight because the water trapped by wrinkles could also be kept isolated from the quick-drain openings. Such a tank could be sumped, and no water would show in the sample.

A simple attitude change, such as that encountered in takeoff, would spill the water out of its wrinkle containment area, through the intake, and into the engine. Too often, this water was more than the three ounces that can be stopped by the gascolator. Result: engine stoppage at the worst possible time, just seconds after takeoff. AD 84-10-1 affected all 182 models built between 1956 to 1978, at which point Cessna changed over to a wet-wing design.

Buyers should check for damage to the firewall, the result of hard or nose-low landings.

A worthwhile discussion of this AD requires some background. In an *Aviation Safety* examination of accidents from 1975 through 1981, 396 accidents in various types of aircraft were found in which water-contaminated fuel was cited as a cause or factor. A total of 155 (about 39 percent) of these accidents involved Cessna aircraft, and 39 of those mishaps involved Cessna 182s. What's more, 25 of the 39 C-182 accidents involved the P-model, the 182 model in production from 1972 through 1974.

In those days, the rubber fuel bladders installed at the plant were made of Goodyear BTC-39. The passage of time revealed that BTC-39 bladders deteriorated rapidly, becoming brittle, "cheesy," and eventually leaking copiously. An AD mandated their replacement with bladders made of stiffer BTC-67, a urethane material.

The extra stiffness of BTC-67 seems to be the contributing factor to the wrinkle problems that were to be discovered later. As Bob Stevens, then FAA manager of Standards and Evaluations, put it, "There's two ways to install a tank like this. If the tank is put in on the assembly line as the airplane is built, that's fairly easy. The tank just fits in before the butt rib. It's installing the tank in the field as a replacement where the trouble starts. As delivered in the field, these tanks aren't too wrinkled. The procedure to install is to soften the BTC-67 tanks in warm water, and then wad them up and stuff them into the wing. That's where I think the wrinkles come from."

Smoothing and Blending

The AD required an inspection of the bladders, "smoothing and blending" of any wrinkles found, and installation of new quick drains on aircraft in which the "smoothing and blending" process requirement involved movement of the drains. The chief target of the inspection is a water-trapping wrinkle that commonly extended at a 45-degree angle across the inboard rear corner of the fuel tank floor. Such a large wrinkle can trap quite a bit of water. More than a few 182 owners reported discovering their tanks harbored as much as a quart, sometimes more.

The 1972 through 1974 models in particular seemed to be afflicted by mishaps stemming from water in the fuel. Fuel caps and wrinkled bladder tanks bear much of the blame. This as a '73 model.

The entire "smoothing and blending" process is something akin to eliminating the wrinkles in a carpet. Stomping on one wrinkle can make it vanish, only to reappear somewhere else on the carpet. Often what's needed is to take up the whole carpet and lay it again. In the fuel bladder case, this move required relocation of the drains. Cessna has provided a quick-drain kit for $89 (part number SK-206-24 and 25).

Rock n' Roll!

Another move mandated by AD 84-10-1 is the famed "rock n' roll preflight." The aircraft is sumped normally, on level ground. Then the tail is lowered to within five inches of the ground while rocking the wings 10 inches up and down at least 12 times. Then the sumps are drained again, checking for any water that may have been shaken out.

After the main wrinkle has been eliminated, the AD specifies that the amount of fluid trapped by any other wrinkles must be determined. If this trapped fluid measures more than three ounces, the aircraft is placarded with the "rock n' roll preflight" procedure, making those moves mandatory before flight. The wording of AD 84-10-1 has been criticized as vague. For example, it's unclear whether these "rocking and rolling" moves have to be done simultaneously, something clearly beyond the ability of just one person. Plus, pilots of petite stature would probably find the tail-lowering maneuver impossible. And it's unclear as to just how owners of float-equipped aircraft are supposed to perform these moves.

As more and more 182s come into compliance with this AD, some evidence is emerging that it has been effective. Life-threatening wrinkles have been detected and corrected. However, there have also been reports of heavy labor costs for airplanes with particularly convoluted wrinkles.

What Else Can You Do About Water?

People often tend to overlook the matter of where the water comes from that puddles in the wrinkled fuel tanks. Answer: from leaking fuel caps. Stop water from coming in there, and you eliminate most of the problem. Unfortunately, the flush caps that were in use from mid-1959 until 1984 had great potential for leakage. The solution to the problem is use of so-called umbrella fuel caps similar to those used on Skyhawks. Cessna has kits for these. They can be one of the best investments a Skylane pilot can make.

Some other devices intended to prevent undrainable water from reaching the engine seem to us worthwhile. One consists of two small reservoir tanks located near the fuel system low point in the aircraft's belly. They fit under the 182's cabin floorboards. Designed by Skylane pilot Rodney Gross, who experienced a water-contaminated engine failure on takeoff in a 182, these tanks allow water that was not drained during pre-flight sumping to settle, and are equipped with quick drains of their own, so that water can be eliminated from the system.

Gross's system has received a revised STC, and cannot be installed until the rest of the fuel tank AD has been complied with. "These tanks are just an insurance policy," Gross said. "They don't solve the problem."

The system is available from Saturn Components Corp., 15268 Earlham Street, Pacific Palisades, Calif. 90272, (213) 454-6714.

Plastic Tanks

Another way of eliminating wrinkled fuel tanks is to install more rigid plastic ones offered by Monarch Air and Development. The tanks are made of fiberglass impregnated with a vinylester resin developed by Dow Chemical. According to Monarch head William Barton, the material is the most corrosion resistant in the plastics market today. Tanks made of the resin have been used in refineries for years to process aromatic compounds and are now being used, in fact, for underground storage of aircraft fuel.

Walls of the tanks are about 0.0075 inches thick. Replacing fuel bladders with Monarch's plastic tanks requires the wings to be taken off and rivets removed from the inboard ribs of both wings. Then a section of each fuel bay must be removed to make way for a new sump (which, unlike Cessna's, Barton says, "really is at the lowest point of the tank..."). Finally, the ribs are re-riveted and the wings re-mated.

One knowledgeable observer said he believed the plastic tanks should last as long

Cost/Performance/Specifications

Model	Year	Average Retail Price	Cruise Speed (kts)	Useful Load (lbs)	Fuel Std/Opt (gals)	Engine	TBO (hrs)	Overhaul Cost
182A	1956-57	$23,500	117	1,010	55	230-hp Cont. O-470-L	1,500	$12,000
182A,B	1958-59	$26,500	120	1,090	55	230-hp Cont. O-470-L	1,500	$12,000
182C,D	1960-61	$28,125	123	1,090	65-84	230-hp Cont. O-470-L	1,500	$12,000
182E,F	1962-63	$30,250	123	1,190	65-84	230-hp Cont. O-470-R	1,500	$12,000
182G,H	1964-65	$31,250	123	1,190	65-84	230-hp Cont. O-470-R	1,500	$12,000
182J,K	1966-67	$32,750	123	1,175	65-84	230-hp Cont. O-470-R	1,500	$12,000
182L,M	1968-69	$34,250	123	1,175	65-84	230-hp Cont. O-470-R	1,500	$12,000
182N	1970-71	$36,500	121	1,310	65-84	230-hp Cont. O-470-R	1,500	$12,000
182P	1972-74	$40,000	125	1,169	61-80	230-hp Cont. O-470-R	1,500	$12,000
182P II	1975-76	$49,750	125	1,169	61-80	230-hp Cont. O-470-S	1,500	$12,000
182Q II	1977-78	$56,750	121	1,169	61-80	230-hp Cont. O-470-U	1,500	$13,000
182Q II	1979-80	$65,750	121	1,390	61-80	230-hp Cont. O-470-U	1,500	$13,000
182R II	1981-82	$77,000	124	1,373	92	230-hp Cont. O-470-U	1,500	$13,000
T-182R II	1981-82	$84,000	157	1,319	92	235-hp Lyc. O-540-L3C5D	2,000	$16,000
182R II	1983-84	$89,250	124	1,373	92	230-hp Cont. O-470-U	1,500	$13,000
T-182R II	1983-84	$101,750	157	1,319	92	235-hp Lyc. O-540-L3C5D	2,000	$16,000
182R II	1985-86	$111,000	124	1,373	92	230-hp Cont. O-470-U	1,500	$13,000

as the airplanes in which they are installed. Bladder tanks typically begin deteriorating after five to nine years. Fuel stains underneath the wings betray the deterioration. Brand-new bladders cost about $1,200 apiece, though some can be reconditioned for from $250 to $450. Monarch Air and Development, Inc., P.O. Box 416, Oakland, Ore. 97462, (503) 459-2056.

Water Separator

Another product that emerged a few years ago appeared to be a sensible one to help eliminate engine water ingestion, assuming it got that far. This was the Silver-Wells water separator, which was basically an enlarged gascolator, so commodious that it increases the maximum permissible amount of water trapped by wrinkles from three ounces to a full quart under provisions of the AD.

The Silver-Wells separator cost $500 and had been marketed by TurboPlus, Inc. at Gig Harbor, Wash. But sales have been discontinued.

Seat Tracks

The Skylane was snared in the big AD (87-20-03) roundup of Cessnas needing seat track inspections. Aircraft with more than 1,000 hours must get them at every annual inspection, or every 100 hours if in commercial service. The purpose is to prevent the type of seat slippage that might lead to loss of control, especially in nose-high attitudes as on takeoff, when a pilot seat careening backward might be disastrous. An extra provision for preventing unwanted seat slippage is made in the form of a SAF-T-STOP that attaches to the seat rail behind the pilots' seats and is locked in place by the clamping action of a thumb screw. It sells for $29.95, or a few dollars less by the Cessna Pilots Assn.

Carb Ice

In figures released by the NTSB in 1977, an alarming number of accidents involving carb ice and 182s emerged. While the 182 isn't as prone to carb ice problems as some other designs (notably the C-150), anyone who regularly flies a Skylane in heavy weather should consider investing in a carb ice detector.

Crunch

When shopping for a used 182, examine the firewall carefully. The nose-heaviness of the 182, coupled with the airplane's heavy elevator forces, makes for frequent hard landings with a potential for gear-bending nose-low landings. The firewall is usually the first to suffer. Another casualty of the 182's nose-heavy handling is the nosewheel assembly, with buckling and shimmies the usual result.

In 1987 the Cessna Pilots Assn. reported it was investigating a number of landing gear strut failures that had occurred on 1963 C-182F models. The NTSB also was checking out the matter. Inspection of some failed struts indicated the failures occurred where there was fretting at the points where the strut comes in contact with the saddle and clamp. The association recommended the landing gear be checked for proper installation involving the 80 percent contact with the saddle, along with proper torque on the bolts, and if at all possible, magnaflux inspection. Any landing gear strut showing significant wear from contact with the saddle clamp in the forward portion, said the association, "would seem to be suspect."

Overall

Plenty of power, a big wing, heavy pitch forces, solid handling and a simple, safe fuel system (providing AD 84-10-1 has been complied with) make the Skylane one of the safest buys around.

Maintenance

The 182 is a simple, robust aircraft, with a healthy, but normal appetite for maintenance as the fleet ages. When we evaluated this airplane in 1979, readers reported annuals in the $250-$300 range. Today's readers have cited annuals in the $1,000 to $2,000 neighborhood. Looking at those numbers, it seems to us that the 182 line hasn't become any less reliable mechanically, but that maintenance and parts costs have gone through the roof.

The Skylane shares the same McCauley/Hartzell prop AD that encumbers many aircraft designs, Cessna and otherwise, equipped with constant-speed propellers. With the exception of this and the fuel bladder problem, the AD scene for the 182 is relatively clear.

Powerplant

The Continental O-470 engine has a good record, although it doesn't seem to be as reliable as the four-cylinder carbureted Lycomings. TBO for the O-470 was 1,500 hours until 1983, when it was boosted to 2,000 for the O-470-U model. A well-maintained engine should meet or exceed the TBO. The key to longevity on this engine appears to be a rigorous break-in period. "Firewall that sucker," is how one O-470 operator put it. The theory is that the heat of heavy initial operation seats the piston rings and valve seats firmly in place, cutting oil consumption and smoothing operation.

Chief virtue of all Skylanes: a big, roomy cabin tough to load out of the weight and balance envelope. It was one of many Cessnas affected by the seat track inspection AD, however.

Some 1975 and 1976 Skylanes had special engine problems that used airplane buyers should be aware of. Aircraft built in those years bore the 182 P II designation, and featured the O-470-S engine, which had a new ring design. Some of these engines had break-in problems, in some cases using as much as a quart of oil per hour. Despite its efforts, Continental apparently never really figured out what was wrong, and instead switched to the higher-compression O-470-U in 1977. The most plausible theory offered to date is that the S-series engines were babied in break-in by well-meaning owners. Check for tell-tale high oil consumption on these engines.

Valve Problems

A few years ago, Continental issued a mandatory service bulletin covering some 75 new and rebuilt O-470 engines evidently shipped with the wrong exhaust valves. It seems that soft, stainless steel valves were installed in the engines by mistake. This engine has hardened Nitralloy valve guides, which promptly chewed up the soft valves, a process resulting in stuck valves and metal particles wreaking havoc throughout the oil system. Proper valves for the O-470 engine carry part number 637781.

At roughly the same time, Continental sent out about 40 O-470 cylinder assemblies (P/N 646680) fitted with the wrong valves. By the time the problem was discovered, Continental had been sending these faulty assemblies out for almost a full year.

As of April, 1985, about 15 engines had been replaced due to extensive metal contamination of the oil. The rest were being reworked with the correct valves. During the valve replacement, valve guides must be reamed out to remove any metal build-ups.

Getting the Lead Out

The Skylane seems to have suffered less from 100LL problems than other 80-octane airplanes. Nevertheless, the proven process of careful leaning, plug rotation, and 50-hour oil changes is the best policy, along with use of TCP should lead fouling be suspected. Skylanes have paper induction air filter elements that can swell up in the presence of moisture and restrict airflow. Even worse, old paper filters can decompose to the point where they can be ingested by the engine. Such an ingestion was blamed as cause of a fatal Skylane crash leading to AD 84-26-02, which put a life limit of 500 hours on paper filters. The filter on the downed Skylane reportedly was more than 10 years old, and had accumulated 1,100 hours at the time of the crash.

This AD did not include foam induction air filters such as those made by Brackett Aircraft Co., which recommends their filters be replaced every 12 months or 100 hours if one inch thick, and every 200 hours if two inches thick. Since paper filters range in price from about $20 to over $100, the Bracketts might actually be cheaper to use. They are priced from $10 to a little under $60, and replacement filters cost even less. Brackett claims its filters stop potentially damaging particles down to 15 microns for a longer period than paper filters.

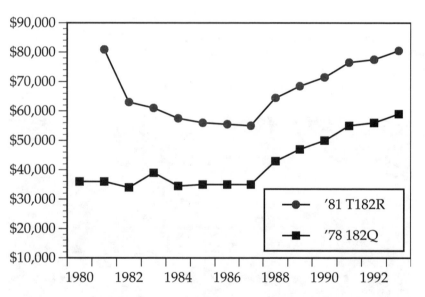

Aside from water and dirt, another factor that can cause great distress to paper, and maybe even foam filters is a "backfire" in the manifold system that belches flame out into the filter. This flame can burn portions of the filter into ashes and cinders that do no good for the engine. Suggestion: next time a backfire is encountered on startup, shut down, get out, and check the condition of the induction air filter.

In 1980 Cessna introduced a turbocharged Skylane with a carbureted, not fuel injected, Lycoming O-540-L3C5D putting out 235 hp. Judging from service difficulty reports, it seems to be operating okay.

Modifications

Although the marriage between airframe and powerplant has been a happy one in the case of the 182, there are dozens of STC'd mods for the aircraft. EAA and Petersen Aviation both hold the autogas STCs for the 182 series, with Petersen's usable for both leaded and unleaded fuels (see Owner Comments for more on the difference in fuels).

Horton STOL-craft, Inc., Wellington Municipal Airport, Wellington, Kans., (800) 835-2051, can provide both STOL and drag-reduction kits. In fact, one of the major slick-up mods offered for the 182 line originated with Charlie Siebel's Flight Bonus, Inc., the rights of which were sold in 1988 to Horton, Inc. Kit parts formerly made from thermoformed ABS plastic are now made of fiberglass-polyester. Depending on the year of manufacture, Siebel's slick-ups claim to boost a 182's cruise speed from 12 to 20 mph. Full kit prices range from $2,955 to $4,915, depending on the Model Skylane, with installation labor (at Horton, if desired) adding another $1,176 to $1,716, again depending on the model.

In 1981 the Turbo Skylane came on the scene with a carbureted Lycoming engine.

For extra security for instrument flight, Aero Safe Corp. of Fort Worth, Tex., (817) 246-7748, offers a $1,495 electrically driven backup vacuum pump.

Hughes Aviation of Amarillo, Tex. can bolt on a Ray-Jay (Roto-Master) turbo. The kits cost around $13,000 and take about 120 hours to install on an O-470-L or -R engine. The result is a turbo-normalized engine.

Owners' Group
Check out the Cessna Pilot's Assn., located at Wichita's Mid-Continent Airport at 2120 Airport Road, Box 12948, Wichita, Kan. 67277, (316) 946-4777.

Owner Comments

I own a 1981 Cessna Skylane 182R, and have put over 800 hours on it since new. There is a lot of good news about the plane, and a little bad.

First the good news: Performance. The Skylane is a terrific instrument platform, both stable and forgiving yet able to fly fast approaches when mixing it up with the big planes at major airports. Its outstanding range adds flexibility for hard IFR. Its short-field performance is exemplary, as are its load-carrying capability and, more important, its wide center-of-gravity tolerance. I can truly haul four people, full fuel, a panel full of avionics, and a little luggage, and be within both payload and cg limits.

Its controls, while not light, are balanced and authoritative, so that it handles crosswinds and turbulence very well. In fact, its smooth ride, coupled with generous inside space, make it a comfortable cross-country machine. The Skylane's speed is consistently better than book, flying at over 140 knots at most altitudes and weights. Fuel burn is as advertised—12.5 gph at 75 percent.

There's plenty of room on the panel and in the payload for a full complement of avionics (King, Stormscope) and other options (standby vacuum pumps, carb ice detector). It's noisy; headphones and intercom are a must.

Now the bad news: Cost. While parts availability and backup have presented no problems, I've had too many opportunities to find out. Annuals have cost from $500 to $1,800, even though painstaking maintenance is performed at every 50-hour oil change. Operating cost, exclusive of hangaring, insurance, and allowance for overhaul, exceeds $40 per hour. All three left-side cylinders needed rings and valves at 600 hours, although the subsequent reduction in oil use (from 4.5 hours per quart to nine) indicates there may have been a problem right from the beginning.

Now the worst news: Reliability. I'm on my seventh alternator control unit. It's no fun while IFR suddenly to be reduced to battery power, but it has happened so often that I carry a spare ACU so that at least when (and if) I land, I can get an immediate repair. Neither Cessna nor my repair shop has found a solution.

In summary, the Skylane offers balanced performance, with a cost penalty. Buy a clean used one, but if the alternator control unit is over 10 months old, replace it immediately before venturing into a cloud.

Dr. Stephen J. Browne
Cambridge, Mass.

I bought my 1981 C-182 new for $58,500 complete with the Skylane II package and Narco DME. I wanted a full four-passenger fixed- gear that I could move into immediately after getting my license, as well as one that would be a stable IFR trainer. I got my instrument ticket in the plane, and my wife (she's also a pilot) and I have owned it for four years.

Total time is 450 hours and we have perceived no engine problems. I knew that huge oil consumption was a possibility, and true to form I use a quart every four hours—always have. I change the oil and filter every 50 hours and have an oil analysis done at every change. It shows normal.

Fuel economy has not been outstanding at 12-13 gph but it is outweighed by the 1,300 pound payload and 92-gallon tanks. My bladder is out well before the six-hour range. The comfort level is quite good, and coupled with headsets for all four seats, a four-hour trip to Mexico is quite pleasant at 142 knots true.

Besides the usual ARC radio glitches, squawks have included a broken carb heat control cable (my wife's heavy hand!) at 400 hours, a turn coordinator out at 410 hours, a new battery at 375 hours, three new tires at 390 hours, as well as new landing lights every 30 hours. Other than these items, we have been trouble free. An annual inspection without any major problems runs a very healthy $1,500+. I've been told that late-model 182s normally run half this amount, but I've never seen it. As a result, my hourly maintenance costs clock in at $25 per hour.

My wife and I are happy with our airplane and have no plans for upgrading. We have a neighbor who has owned his 1962 Skylane since new and loves it still. We fly to our mountain home, where the airport elevation is 6,000 feet, a dozen times each summer, and have never had a problem taking off from the 3,000-foot strip even at gross. For us, the Skylane has lived up to our expectations beautifully. I'd buy another one!

Dr. Tom Bales
Novato, Calif.

With Charlie Seibel's full-speed equipment I cruise 160-165 mph at 10,000 feet on 2,250 rpm and 18.5 inches at about 12 or 11.5 gph and use a quart of 50-weight Shell every three to four hours. With RSTOL strips, 1,500-foot takeoffs are easily manageable.

Granted, it is a little ponderous compared to my Bonanza, but it's a wheels down grandpappy airplane and rock solid for IFR—very predictable when flying the numbers for climb, descent, approaches, etc. Baggage compartment gets wet in medium rain or more, otherwise it's tight, warm in winter and, being a high wing, cooler than a low wing in summer.

Instrument panel is big and imposing, though ARC radios are not. This is from a '72 model. Extra little complexities for a fixed-gear aircraft are cowl flaps and variable pitch prop.

Maintenance has been very predictable—no surprises, but then I'm meticulous. Nothing's too small for attention; therefore my $2,000 annuals are high. The 25-hour checkup and oil change is around $250 with no problems with either parts availability or backup.

My wife and I spent three weeks plus in the airplane last summer going to British Columbia, Alaska and the west, having plenty of room throughout—though packed stem to stern with camping, living and survival gear.

Henry G. Wischmeyer
Dallas, Tex.

We have owned a 1979 Skylane since 1981. This aircraft was purchased with 700 hours on it. It has an all ARC panel with the exception of a King 62A DME and a Sigtronics four-station intercom. In four years we have had minor navcom trouble four times—trouble that takes about $100 and three days to be corrected each time. No trouble at all with the 300 A/P or KN62A.

We average 100+ hours of pleasure flying per year. Annuals average about $350. One went to $600 because a jug had to be reworked at 1,000 hours. Seems Continental used a hammer to seat an exhaust valve guide. Other than that, the cylinders always hang in there at 72 to 76.

Our useful load is 1,146 as equipped. With a full load and 75 percent power at 6,500 to 8,500 feet we true at 135 knots. At light weights we reach 145 knots. It burns 12 gph and a quart of oil every four hours. For local flying we can get the burn down to nine gph.

Generally speaking, we like the overall performance and big plane feel it has over, say, a 172 or Cherokee. On the downside, we might wish for a little better fit and finish All of the door-to-airframe fits are atrocious, with very bad air leaks. We had a bad spell of water leaks which we finally stopped on our own through judicious use of silicon sealant. I can say that after four years the paint and interior have held up real good. We keep it hangared.

There is one mod we were really interested in: the Seibel speed mod. But another Skylane owner at our airport did it, and the only good thing he had to say about it was that it didn't slow his plane down, which was kind of disappointing because we just know that the ol' 182 could be Mooney-ized a la 201.

Bob Billa, Jr.
San Antonio, Tex.

I purchased my 1979 Skylane II in the summer of 1983. The airplane has reportedly been hangared since new. The two navcoms, ADF, and encoding transponder are ARC equipment. The ARC radios have naturally given me some difficulty, but a nearby shop knows them well and repairs them at what I think is a reasonable cost. I have also replaced a fuel gauge and sender unit. I have replaced the EGT gauge and have had the clock/timer rebuilt. I've also noticed that the static eliminators "spontaneously" break, and naturally I wonder. I've also noticed areas where the paint is peeling along with areas where filiform corrosion is appearing under the paint.

The six-cylinder Continentals have a pretty good record, in general, and seem to suffer less from 100LL than other 80-octane engines. They also are approved for autogas. But watch out for carb ice. Another disadvantage: a relatively low 1,500-hour TBO.

There was a problem with the control-mounted microphone switch wire, and I've replaced some panel lights which are outrageously priced by Cessna. Watch out for the Gill battery. I replaced mine. Gill has changed designators, and although Aircraft Components, Inc.'s catalog says the Gill 242 replaced the previous battery, in fact it's the Gill G243.

My annuals cost from $375 to $450. The first one uncovered some problems while last year's found nothing significant. I also have 100-hour inspections done, and I have oil analysis done when the mechanic remembers to submit the sample. I change the oil every 50 hours.

I love my 182. My wife, at all of five feet tall and 83 pounds, finds it too big an aircraft to handle. My flight instructor suggested electric trim might help a small person like her.

Although the 182 leaks like a sieve, I don't plan on leaving it outdoors or flying it in the rain anyway. I burn about a quart of oil every two hours. I get a lot of oil under the fuselage. I was told not to fill it to the nine-quart level unless I am going on a long trip. I do this and I have never seen the oil level go below eight quarts. I've wondered if the engine would quit using oil altogether if there were only eight quarts in the crank case; however, I'm not going to try that out.

It may seem strange that there appear to be so many faults with this aircraft; I've not named them all, yet I like it so much. I'm very picky.

John S. Ford, M.D.
Texarkana, Tex.

In 1977, I bought a 1974 Skylane with an O-470-R Continental engine. There was only one previous owner. The tach indicated slightly more than 400 hours at that time.

I have kept the airplane hangared and provide meticulous maintenance. It has been a delight to fly, and is particularly stable for IFR conditions. Annuals have generally been $600 to $1,000, although one annual was $200 when I worked with the mechanic.

After initially flying the Skylane for about 100 hours from time of purchase, I encountered a significant engine problem. The oil was found to be contaminated with metal particles during a routine oil change.

This resulted in an expensive early major overhaul. It was discovered during the overhaul that a normally floating wrist pin had frozen and was rubbing on a cylinder wall, creating metal flaking. The wrist pin had apparently frozen due to overheating.

It is my understanding that Cessna tightened the cowling in 1972. This resulted in slightly higher speeds, but apparently insufficient air was provided to cool the engine.

The problem was improved in 1975 when the O-470-R engine was replaced by the -S model. The -S engine has additional oil passages that squirt oil on the back sides of the pistons. Heat is then relieved through the oil cooler.

The overhaul was performed by Lynn Quackenbush, located in Boeing Field, Seattle, phone: (206) 763-1912. In addition to the overhaul, he converted the -R engine to an -S engine at that time. Lynn is a fine craftsman and has the special equipment for the -S conversion. He has the reputation as one of the best mechanics in the Northwest.

The engine has performed flawlessly for several hundred hours since Lynn did his magic. I highly recommend that anyone with an -R engine have Lynn Quackenbush perform an -S conversion when the engine is disassembled for overhaul.

I encountered a more recent problem with the use of automobile fuel. About a year ago, I purchased the EAA auto fuel STC.

Unleaded autogas ate the foam carburetor float and dislodged black particles from the bladder tanks. The EAA felt that the problem was due to alcohol in the fuel, but testing did not indicate the presence of alcohol.

I believe the problem is due to aromatics in unleaded fuel. I have subsequently switched to the Petersen Aviation autofuel STC that allows both leaded and unleaded auto gas. Regular leaded automobile fuel has been used for the last year with no difficulty, though this is now becoming almost impossible to find.

Ben Prince
Richland, Wash.

Cessna Skylane RG

The Skylane RG has won favor in the used-plane market as an economy retractable that is strong on room, load and comfort, and quite a bit less expensive than the bellwether Mooney 201. It is, however, nagged by mechanical and airframe shortcomings that warrant close inspection.

Most prominent of these is the landing gear system, which, judging from the FAA's Service Difficulty Reports, carries on a long Cessna tradition of retractable-gear bedevilment manifested in both its singles and twins. Prospective buyers should also be on the lookout for airframe quality control shortcomings like leaking windshields and doors.

Despite a sizable proportion of prangs due to gear problems, the airplane has an excellent safety record compared to other aircraft in its class when it comes to fatal accidents.

History

The aircraft has undergone no major changes over the years since it was introduced in 1978. But there have been lots of little ones that are significant in correcting a myriad of glitches. Buyers should make a close check of service bulletins that were complied with, or ignored, on this airplane—especially those concerning the various components of the landing gear system.

The biggest changes to the line occurred in 1979 when the bladder tanks (and all their well-known problems) were dropped in favor of integral fuel tanks of larger capacity. Also, that year the turbo model was brought out. Among the smaller changes made through the years were—in 1980—a new door latch and pin system designed to help seal the doors better, an electric fan for the avionics, to help cool the radios while taxiing, and redesigned wing root ventilators. (Some owners of '79 models complained that these would simply pop open during high-speed flight.)

In 1981 the Skylane RGs got improved battery access along with a new muffler for better heating (rear-seat passengers complain about cold feet in '79 models) and an improved fuel selector valve with more positive detents. (At least one fatal crash was reported where the pilot had the selector positioned between tanks.)

In 1983 the extension speed for the first 20-degrees of flaps was raised from 95 knots to 120 knots, as an aid to slowing down the aircraft. A low-vacuum warning light was offered, as was an electric six-cylinder primer system, replacing the manual one, for easier starting. Also, the landing gear "up" indicator light was replaced with a red "gear unsafe" light. This goes on whenever power goes to the gear pump motor, or when the gear is in transit.

In addition, the nose gear doors were redesigned so the door skins overlapped the lower cowl skin, eliminating butt joints. Service Difficulty Reports show three instances where the nose gear doors interfered with proper operation of the gear.

Thankfully, the main gear has been spared door problems—because it has no doors.

In 1984 the Skylane RGs received new "improved" composite fuel caps, and rear-seat shoulder harnesses were made standard equipment instead of options. (The SDRs suggest that leaking fuel caps have been a problem with the R182s.) Also, the copilot got a standard control wheel and rudder pedals, so these would not have to be purchased as extra-cost options.

Performance

Since the Skylane RG is most often compared with the Mooney 201, it should be noted up front that although the Mooney can be expected to beat the Cessna in a flat-out, full-power heat at altitude, it won't do so by an embarrassing margin. In fact, when the Cessna 182RG is lightly loaded, it will give away only maybe three to four knots to the low-winger. Big loads, on the other hand, seem to have a more significant retardant effect on the Cessna than with other aircraft. One owner plotted the phenomenon as giving the Skylane RG a boost of two knots for every 100 pounds it was below gross weight.

The Cessna by no means is completely overshadowed by the Mooney 201. In a side-by side flyoff by *The Aviation Consumer* between the two aircraft (when both had two aboard and about three-quarters fuel), the Cessna showed itself to have the better climb rate and to be much more adept at getting into and out of airports than the Mooney. On top of that, the aircraft showed off much more agile ground handling.

Owners of the nonturboed R182s talk about getting a healthy 150 to 160 knots at top cruise (75 percent power), burning 12 to 14 gph. Turbo owners report getting 160 to 165 knots at 9,000 to 13,000 feet with about the same fuel burn. One turbo owner reported getting 178 knots on 66 percent power at 19,000 feet with light weights.

With its 235 hp, the RG also climbs well. Full power is available on the turbo all the way to 20,000 feet. One turbo pilot said he got a 1,000-fpm climb all the way to 20 grand with full power and could pull 750 fpm nicely on a cruise climb. Said another, "I have climbed through 14,000 feet with an inch of ice at 900 fpm, and I'm here to tell you this is the true value of a strong turbocharged engine."

Range of the Cessna is nothing to sneeze at, either. With 81 gallons usable on '79 and later models, that's enough fuel for six hours of flying at high cruise speeds.

Handling

The aircraft is typical Cessna—i.e., heavy on the pitch controls, especially in the landing flare, but stable as a rock in cruise. Said one owner: "Once trimmed, it will stay put. I don't feel a real need for altitude hold on autopilot, even in hard IFR." Said another, "I lift weights for a hobby, but still had trouble holding full aft control wheel in a full stall." But he added that as an aerobatic pilot he felt he had completely explored all its flight characteristics and found them to be "fault-free." Nevertheless, the big, effective flaps do create pitch changes that require retrimming.

One flier summed it up: "It makes no unusual demands on pilot ability. It is a very safe, forgiving and rugged aircraft."

Cabin Load and Comfort

Skylane RG pilots rave about the ability of the aircraft to haul people and baggage—in spades. And they love the roominess. One six-foot-four pilot whose wife is six-two said, "We are able to stretch out and be comfortable even with four people in the plane. Even the A36 Bonanza cannot match the Skylane in interior comfort on a long trip, in my opinion." They talk about a loading envelope that would be hard to exceed and mention useful loads with IFR-equipment of over 1,100 pounds. On top of that, the double doors allow easy entry for front and rear seats, and headroom is good both front and rear.

Struts and all, the RG clips along at 155 knots or better. Light weights give a disproportionate speed boost.

The handicaps on the RG, on the other hand, are a loud cabin din, occasional leaky doors and windows, cold rear seats and, as we mentioned before, wing root air vents that sometimes pop out at higher speeds and provide unwanted air conditioning. Some RG pilots also complained of uncomfortable engine vibration at cruise.

Safety Record

During the first five years of production, the Skylane RG logged a marvelous safety profile compared with other single-engine retractables in its class—when it comes to fatal accidents. When stacked up with 17 other aircraft, the RG came out best by far, eclipsing even that longtime safety star, the Beech 33.

We tallied 23 fatal accidents from 1978 through 1985. But most of these resulted from factors that couldn't be blamed on aircraft shortcomings. Nine were weather related and three stemmed from medical problems—heart attack, stroke, alcohol. Another two were blamed on buzzing, and details from three others were still missing. Equipment failure apparently caused another fatal crash after the pilot departed IFR with a defective gyro horizon and later lost control on a missed approach. And we mentioned above the accident involving the fuel selector.

The total accident record of the Skylane RG is not, however, so golden. The Beech 33 comes out better in this category. Our survey of accident causes shows that landing gear problems were major factors in the greatest proportion of nonfatal RG accidents. We counted 21 of these from 1978 through 1985.

The greatest number involved the failure of the gear to extend, or a collapse on landing or takeoff. On only a small portion of these was the pilot blamed for inadvertently retracting it during touch-and-goes. And, interestingly enough, we noted no instances where the pilot simply forgot to extend the gear on landing.

Next largest nonfatal accident category for the RGs involved hard landings. We tallied 15 of these. The typical scenario involved a bounce, damaging the prop and possibly running off the side of the runway. On almost half of these the nosegear eventually collapsed.

Third biggest category was engine problems—we counted a dozen. Over half the stoppages occurred after takeoff. Three were blamed on magneto problems—the cam screw coming loose—and an Airworthiness Directive was issued to address the matter. Three others were related to internal malfunctions, one to water ingestion, and another quit after changing tanks on letdown. It's worth noting that none of the engine failures resulted in a fatal accident in the RG.

The next largest accident category involved fuel exhaustion—eight cases were noted. In a couple of cases fuel had siphoned out because of "unsecured" fuel caps.

Maintenance Considerations

The Skylane RGs are plagued with a sizable number of problems that merit buyer attention. Here's a list gathered from owner reports and FAA Service Difficulty Reports:

• Landing gear malfunctions. The litany of problems with the gear chronicled by the SDRs almost defies description. It's actually difficult to isolate any one or several main causes. Whereas most SDR problems usually can be tallied in singles or maybe tens, we counted over nine pages full of gear-related problems—with about a dozen cases on each page. Consider that maybe only a tenth of the cases in the field even get reported to the FAA, and you have some idea of the apparent magnitude of the Skylane RG gear problem over the years.

Some examples: main landing gear actuator bolts loose, broken or sheared; chafed hydraulic line completely failed, pilot unable to lower gear and lock; rudder cable rubbed hole thru emergency hand pump gear down line; control cable to carb heat rubbed through hydraulic line to power pac; nose landing gear actuator hose ruptured in flight; downlock actuator leaking, found piston rod assy. scored; relay became intermittent, causing landing gear to fail to operate either up or down; landing gear failed to extend due to screw missing from gear motor circuit breaker; hydraulic hose on nose landing gear actuator has a tendency to kink in the crease and stop the flow of fluid; solenoid stuck closed, causing hydraulic pump to run continuously until circuit breaker popped; nose landing gear door grabbing on fuselage skin when it tried to open, etc. etc., *ad nauseam.*

• Shimmy dampeners. Problems were legion, involving broken clamp pins, broken attach bolts, worn bellcrank bolts, cracked barrels, etc. At least one Cessna

Service Bulletin (80-67) was aimed at correcting the problem with a modification kit. Two pilots, however, said they found a cure to nosewheel vibration by increasing tire inflation to 55 psi.

• Balky throttles. At least five different service bulletins and mod kits were put out to cure the problem, and any used RG should have them installed.

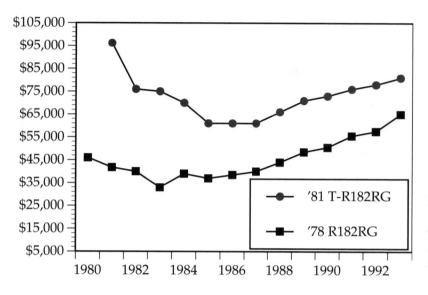

• Instrument panel "eyebrow" lights that flicker out quickly. Multiple replacements seem to be the rule. Said one owner, "I buy them by the dozen. If anyone can figure out a fix, I'll happily buy the STC."

• Cabin air and water leaks. Service bulletins address the chronic Cessna problem of leaks around the windshield and wing roots. "Repeated applications of silicone only retuned the sound of the air leak," said one owner. "Finally, they removed the windshield to discover about a six-inch gap in the sealing gasket."

• Other problems noted included turbos leaking oil, vacuum pump drive shafts shearing, aileron hinge cotter key holes badly aligned, Bendix starters failing, exhaust stacks cracked and alternator mounting bolts worn.

AD History

Despite the arduous roster of problems tabulated above, the Skylane RG has managed to get by with relatively few Airworthiness Directives, so far. And most of those that were issued affected engine accessories like the Bendix magnetos (six ADs called for inspections and mods) and the Slick magneto (one Airworthiness Directive). An inspection was also required of the Stewart-Warner oil cooler for leakage.

Much-publicized ADs called for inspection of fuel tank caps for leakage, and for inspection of bladder fuel tanks on '78 RGs for wrinkles and installation of quick drains. Others required inspection of aileron hinges for the correct location of cotter pins. Replacement of certain Marvel-Schebler carburetors and Airborne vacuum pumps was called for—as it was on many other aircraft.

Modifications

R/STOL Systems, of Sierra Industries has taken over the full list of Robertson mods. They are at P.O. Box 5184, Uvalde, Tex. 78802, (512) 278-4381.

Resale Value

After an encouraging rise in equity for RG owners in 1981, the aircraft disclosed a desultory curve in resale value to 1985, but then began to rebound. Interestingly, they overtook and exceeded the cost of the Mooney 201 in recent years. Hence, a 1980 RG goes for about $70,000 according to the *Aircraft Bluebook Price Digest* vs.

about $65,500 for the Mooney 201. Just a few years ago the Mooney cost several thousand dollars more on the used-plane market.

Owner Organization

Check with the Cessna Pilots Assn. at Wichita Mid-Continent Airport, P.O. Box 12948, Wichita, Kans. 67277, (316) 946-4777.

Owner Comments

We have owned and operated three 182RGs—one normally aspirated and two turbos. We have found them to be among the best aircraft to put on our rental line of all those Cessna has built.

But magnetos tend to cause ignition noise on radios. The engines vibrate a fair amount and cause general loosening of parts, including beacons, landing light bulbs, alternator filters and avionics. The starter Bendix is weak engaging, particularly in cold weather. The windshields leak around the base during flight in rain, and the black instrument deck covers warp. Despite the above, we recommend the aircraft highly.

Field Morey, President
Morey Airplane Co.
Middleton, Wisc.

The only problems I have had so far on my one-year-old Skylane RG are the electric flap switch and the No. 2 comm radio—both repaired under warranty. I have been very well pleased with this aircraft. The strong points are the roomy, comfortable cabin, excellent stability in rough air and smooth, six-hour cruising range, easy cold-weather starting, good load-carrying ability, a great-performing Lycoming O-540 engine and excellent short-field performance.

Also, it makes no unusual demands on pilot ability. It is a very safe, forgiving and rugged aircraft.

On a low pass for the camera, the R182RG looks like this with the gear retracted. It also looks like this sometimes when the gear won't extend for landing.

On the down side is the rather poor visibility, a too noisy cockpit that requires either ear plugs or a headset, mediocre Sperry avionics and heavy pitch forces—especially in the landing flare. It must be properly trimmed in all flight attitudes.

It cruises at 140 knots true at 65 percent power, burns 11-12 gph and uses one quart of Aeroshell 15-50 each 10 hours. Insurance is $2,000 per year and includes liability, property damage and hull. I felt the $930 cost of a recent annual was rather excessive for a new aircraft with no serious glitches.

T. Gorman
Yarmouth, Me.

My '79 Skylane RG has been highly reliable and quite comfortable, especially on long trips. I am 6'4" and my wife is 6'2", and we are able to stretch out and be comfortable even with four people in the plane. Even the A36 Bonanza cannot match the Skylane in interior comfort on a long trip, in my opinion.

Maintenance has run about $1,000 to $1,300 a year, including parts. I do my own oil changes and have assisted on annuals several times. In five years I've got

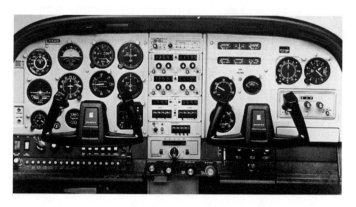

about 1,100 hours on the plane. I've had to replace a flap motor, the brake drums with chrome discs, the turn-and-bank indicator and the vacuum pump. I am now on the third battery; they seem to die at about 18 to 24 months, despite my best efforts. I've also had the DG go out in the first 500 hours. And the Bendix starter broke this past month and cost about $250 to get fixed.

The plane has Cessna radios. Both nav-coms have been reliable. The ADF has

Fail-prone instrument panel eyebrow lights are a constant source of frustration for some RG owners. ARC avionics in later years receive more passable ratings from users.

had an intermittent problem that's been worked on four times over the years. It worked reliably for the last two years, but is now back in the shop for a fifth time. The transponder has required three trips to the shop.

Kenneth B. Carpenter, M.D.
Knoxville, Tenn. 37939

Dealer warranty support on my 1979 Turbo Skylane RG was good, as far as the factory would allow. Cessna's support was fair for some things, but poor on others. Parts availability has been poor some of the time, and the prices often seem unrealistic.

We normally like to cruise between 9,000 and 13,000 feet and use 2300/23", which is 65 to 73 percent, depending on temp. Fuel consumption will be 12.5 to 14 gph and TAS from 155 to 165 knots at near gross. Performance has been good right up to maximum operating altitude of 20,000 feet.

As equipped (with a full panel of King digital avionics and a Century IIB autopilot), the useful load is 1,160 pounds. With full 88 gallons of fuel, that leaves 630 pounds payload. As with all Skylanes, the loading envelope is good, and it would be hard to exceed with normal people and cargo loads. Range with full fuel and comfortable reserves is more than 700 nm.

I'm a big person (6'3" and 200 pounds) and enjoy the large roomy cabin with plenty of headroom. The doors allow easy entry for both front and rear seats. The full articulating front seats adjust to tall and short as well as giving comfortable positions for long flights. Rear-seat headroom and legroom is good. Noise level is fairly high. Cessna's doors and windows are not fitted and sealed very well. The ventilation system is good; however, the front wing root vents tend to come open unexpectedly at high speeds. (It was a good system for 120-knot Skyhawks.) Heating is okay for front seats, marginal in back, especially with the air leaks and high, cold altitudes. Carry a blanket.

Handling is typical Skylane—very stable with moderately balanced controls. Once trimmed, it will stay put. I don't feel a real need for altitude hold on autopilot, even in hard IFR. It has very effective flaps both for extra lift and high drag. They do produce pitch changes which necessitate retrimming. Rudder control is adequate for pretty heavy crosswind landings.

The Lycoming engine requires very different procedures than the Continental O-470 in the fixed-gear Skylane. Throttle linkage and adjustment is very critical for the turbo model, to operate both carburetor and wastegate properly and smoothly. The modification kit available from Cessna took three or four times as long to install and adjust as Cessna estimated. The air intake flange on the carburetor air box broke off at about 300 hours while in flight, resulting in loss of turbocharging and drop in mp. The replacement box has a riveted flange rather than a crimped one and should hold up better.

Be really careful about using carb heat on the ground. The box with the flapper valve has big holes that can allow solid matter to enter, then go into the turbo when carb heat is applied. Cessna disputes this and wouldn't pay for a new turbocharger.

Incidentally, as long as I operate at high enough power settings to keep turbocharger activated, I have not had any carb ice problems. Engine temperatures normally run on the cool side of the green. Even at 18,000-20,000 feet and high cruise powers, the temperatures stay low even with cowl flaps closed. I have had no vacuum pump problems yet, but will likely install the cooling kit available from the Cessna Pilots Assn.

We have had no gear problems, and so far no evidence of corrosion under paint. (The aircraft is hangared in Sacramento, Calif. with hot, dry summers and cool, damp winters.) The fuel caps are still sealing fine, but I will replace with vendor-produced new metal caps this winter as a precautionary measure.

Cost/Performance/Specifications

Model	Year	Average Retail Price	Cruise Speed (kts)	Useful Load (lbs)	Fuel Std/Opt (gals)	Engine	TBO (hrs)	Overhaul Cost
R182	1978	$60,500	157	1,200	56/75	235-hp Lyc. O-540-J3C5D	2,000	$13,500
R182	1979	$65,000	157	1,200	88	235-hp Lyc. O-540-J3C5D	2,000	$13,500
TR182	1979	$69,000	173	1,150	88	235-hp Lyc. O-540-L3C5D	2,000	$16,000
R182	1980	$70,000	157	1,200	88	235-hp Lyc. O-540-J3C5D	2,000	$13,500
TR182	1980	$75,000	173	1,150	88	235-hp Lyc. O-540-L3C5D	2,000	$16,000
R182	1981	$75,000	157	1,200	88	235-hp Lyc. O-540-J3C5D	2,000	$13,500
TR182	1981	$81,000	173	1,150	88	235-hp Lyc. O-540-L3C5D	2,000	$16,000
R182	1982	$86,000	157	1,200	88	235-hp Lyc. O-540-J3C5D	2,000	$13,500
TR182	1982	$91,000	173	1,150	88	235-hp Lyc. O-540-L3C5D	2,000	$16,000
R182	1983	$97,500	157	1,200	88	235-hp Lyc. O-540-J3C5D	2,000	$13,500
TR182	1983	$103,000	173	1,150	88	235-hp Lyc. O-540-L3C5D	2,000	$16,000
R182	1984	$107,000	157	1,200	88	235-hp Lyc. O-540-J3C5D	2,000	$13,500
TR182	1984	$117,500	173	1,150	88	235-hp Lyc. O-540-L3C5D	2,000	$16,000
R182	1985	$117,000	157	1,200	88	235-hp Lyc. O-540-J3C5D	2,000	$13,500
TR182	1985	$127,000	173	1,150	88	235-hp Lyc. O-540-L3C5D	2,000	$16,000
R182	1986	$129,500	157	1,200	88	235-hp Lyc. O-540-J3C5D	2,000	$13,500
TR182	1986	$144,000	173	1,150	88	235-hp Lyc. O-540-L3C5D	2,000	$16,000

We're on the third alternator control unit. This one, however, has been operating for about 350 hours. The windshield had a bad air and water leak when delivered. Repeated applications of silicone only retuned the sound of the air leak. Finally they removed the windshield to discover about a six-inch gap in the sealing gasket. Annuals and other engine/airframe maintenance runs about $1,200 to $2,000 per year.

In summary—the Turbo Skylane RG is like all Skylanes—a big, comfortable four-seat airplane. It loads easy and flies easy. It handles dirt and sod strips almost as well as the fixed gear, but has the additional speed and altitude capabilities. I like the airplane and basically have been pleased with performance and reliability of most systems.

James W. Elliot, D.D.S.
Sacramento, Calif.

In the 15 months that I have owned my '78 Skylane RG, the average price for a similar airplane has appreciated about $4,000—not bad for an investment, although the last new equipped price (when they were making them) was about $120,000, which makes used planes very attractive. Cost per hour in the last year, including engine, hangar, insurance, replacements, repairs and maintenance comes to $22.65 per hour.

The Lycoming O-540 engine is simply great. It has 1,620 hours on it and I haven't put a dime into it, and the lowest compression reading taken recently was 75 over 80. It burns a quart in about 10 hours.

Stacked up against the Mooney 201, the RG falls short by a few knots in a race at altitude despite its extra 35 horses. But in airport performance it outshines the low-winger. In recent years, the Cessna has also caught up in resale value.

The high performance and low stall speeds make it a safe airplane for people who don't fly professionally. The minuses are the usual Cessna leaky windows and doors and the average interior and appointments. The nosewheel gave me a periodic chatter problem on landings and takeoffs, with constant bushing replacements required, until I realized that we mistakenly kept the air pressure in the tire too low. Increasing tire pressure to 55 psi seems to have solved that problem. The other problem is the constant need to change nav and red panel lights.

Donald S. Prusinski
Hales Corners, Wisc.

My 1982 Skylane RG is every bit as good as your publication—maybe better on a cool, clear day. It is the roomiest four-seater in the sky, with kidney-busting range. Loaded to maximum gross weight, it regularly makes the trip from Miami to Beech Mountain, N.C. in four hours and 20 minutes (plus or minus wind) with well over an hour of fuel remaining. I cruise between 7,000 and 12,000 feet with the throttle wide open at 2350 rpm, regularly see 155-160 knots true (depending on weight), and average 12.5 gph.

Because the airplane has integral wing tanks, no reservoir tanks, and a fuel drain at the fuel selector valve, the fuel system does not hide water that will drown you after takeoff, as many Cessna high-wings do. (The fuel selector valve should be placed on "both," however, before preflight draining.) I consider it the safest single-engine retractable around.

Just to make sure, however, I added an Aero Safe standby vacuum system (which I heartily endorse); a low-vacuum warning light (which is now available from Cessna as an inexpensive retrofit); a carb ice detector (which, now that I am able to monitor the venturi, seems to have proved itself largely unnecessary); a graphic engine monitor (which provides an enormous amount of information and much peace of mind); new old-style fuel caps, with restrictors (also available in an inexpensive kit which took three man hours to install, and which appears to have eliminated all traces of water from my tanks); and a Terra TRA-2500 radar altimeter.

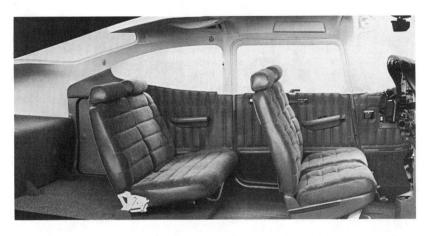

The RG cabin is roomy and comfortable, but doors and windows may leak. Gear door hump impinges on the baggage compartment.

Its Imron paint job is holding up nicely, and even though it is tied down outside in southern Florida, filiform corrosion is not a significant problem.

Every silver lining has its cloud, of course. There are times when I feel like I am supporting a small army of A&Ps and ETs in the southeastern U.S. The normally aspirated Lycoming O-540 has so far purred like a big cat—but it is a cat which eats all manner and kinds of exhaust gaskets. I've tried them all, and none of them work very well.

I left the cowling in place for a while once, and a blown gasket went undetected long enough to cause erosion requiring removal of a jug and resurfacing of the mating surfaces. That was an expensive lesson. Frequent inspections of the exhaust gaskets are highly recommended. When the jug was off, we also found that the stem of the exhaust valve had a chunk missing from it.

Lead fouling ceased to be a problem when I began using TCP. On balance, I am pleased with the engine.

Although I do a lot of night flying, every light bulb in the airplane is original issue, except the four glareshield eyebrow lights. I buy them by the dozen. If anyone can figure out a fix, I'll happily buy the STC. The main gear legs are also a problem; they attract rust. I've had them stripped and repainted twice so far, and they require constant attention. The rubber step-pads on the gear legs were poorly glued, and trapped a lot of moisture. I did not discover the damage until one of the pads came off. I recommend that the pads be removed, the damage corrected and a rectangle of wingwalk compound be painted on as a substitute.

I also had to replace all four door hinges at 500 hours because of virulent dissimilar-metals corrosion where the hinge fingers grasp the pins. The job was labor intensive, and the new hinges were not cheap. I now keep the hinges bathed with LPS-3.

The nose gear shimmy damper and the strut collar to which it attaches are weak links. Any leaks should be corrected at once. After some initial problems and failures, I have had good success at removing the vibration it is designed to damp simply by keeping the nose gear tire fully inflated at all times.

Like most Cessnas, the 182RG exhibits good short-field and low-speed handling performance.

The wing fuel tank access plate sealant deteriorated to uselessness at 350 hours, and a complete resealing of all eight covers was required. Stainless steel screws should be substituted when this inevitable project is encountered. The steel hardware securing the rotating beacon lens clamp should also be replaced with stainless, or a loss of the entire assembly is predictable.

Surprisingly, my factory-issue ARC avionics have been much more reliable than I had any right to expect.

Annuals run around $800. My operating cost per hour (which includes fuel, scheduled and unscheduled maintenance, tiedown, lots of insurance, etc.) is approximately $60 to $65 per hour, depending on flight hours. Parts are readily available, and Cessna support has been exemplary. Maintenance costs notwithstanding, I would not trade the airplane for your cramped (but sexy) Mooney, even if you threw in a 10-year subscription to *The Aviation Consumer*.

Joel D. Eaton
Miami, Fla.

Prior to my Skylane RG ownership I bought a 1979 Cessna 180 Skywagon. The most noticeable difference between the 180 and the 182RG was in engine roughness. The O-540 Lycoming was rougher and louder than the Continental O-470. It had a "beat" at cruise that caused the visors, compass and panel to vibrate. I flew another RG of the same vintage (1978), and it did the same.

In spite of careful leaning, I was never able to get the fuel consumption below 14 gph except at high altitudes (10,000 to 12,000 feet), when it would pull only 18" mp and 13 gph. After the contamination scare, I went to Shell semi-synthetic "W" oil and the consumption decreased dramatically. As an engineer, I am doubtful of miracle cures, as well as an engine that doesn't use oil, but I didn't add more than one quart between 50-hour changes afterward.

My main recollection of the engine, however, was its hard starting characteristics. I heard the same from other owners. (I moved up to a light twin after 500 hours and two years with the RG.) We blamed the sidedraft HA-6 carburetor—too many cubic inches for the carburetion, etc. Lots of throttle pumping usually did the trick, but after the easy-starting O-470U engine, I had my doubts about the big Lycoming. Cessna and Lycoming people were no help.

According to them, the problem didn't exist. I left it at country airports on two occasions because of this. I had the carburetor overhauled to comply with the metal float AD, the primer lines and nozzles checked repeatedly, and careful spark plug gapping and maintenance. All to no avail. Upon selling the plane, the mechanic doing the pre-purchase examination noted that the impulse coupling was worn. It was replaced, and the engine started easily. So much for my local mechanics' diagnostic abilities.

Despite the starting stubbornness, however, the engine ran strongly, and gave a measure of reassurance in those heavy-weather and dark-night excursions that it would keep running as long as it got its share of 100LL.

I never have had problems with carb ice as I did with the O-470 Continental. Overall the Skylane RG is hard to beat. I'm going on to a Baron, but know if I have to come back in the future, it will be like welcoming an old friend once again.

Charles D. Haynes, P.E.
Tuscaloosa, Ala.

My '79 Skylane RG had some filiform corrosion when I got it; so I invested in a new paint job, complete with the epoxy primer it should have had all along. I also put on chrome brake discs. I specifically shopped for a '79 or later to avoid the fuel bladders.

The maintenance has been entirely reasonable. The most recent annual, with my assistance, was $650. This included a starter drive gear and a seat rail. I budget $10 an hour for maintenance, and put in lots of my own time on preventative items.

I have already purchased the new-style fuel cap kit ($73 for both sides). Your article on that subject was correct; it will be a lot of labor to install them, involving draining the tanks and removing access panels, since the new adaptors install from inside the tank. However, in a six-year-old airplane like this the adaptor necks for the flush-style caps are getting rusty, and would need replacement soon, regardless.

Keyhole slots on the underbelly enclose the retracted landing gear without doors, which presumably reduces the malfunction burden somewhat. Smaller-than-usual tires fitting into those slots, however, make the RG less suitable for rough strips than the standard Skylane.

The turbocharged Lycoming O-540 engine shakes at idle; it runs so rough at runup that one wants to taxi to the nearest mechanic, but it is remarkably smooth and quiet at the top of the green (2400 rpm). It would appear that the turbo is a very effective muffler. I always cruise at 2400 rpm, and any attempt to reduce the cruise rpm below that results in a noticeable increase in vibration. My point of reference is the Continental O-470 in my '74 Skylane that idled very smoothly but was an ear bruiser at cruise.

It appears that the turbo throws a small amount of oil into the induction air stream. This shows up as an oil leak at the junction of the induction duct and the carburetor air box.

When I first got the plane, I had the turbo rebuilt to eliminate this, but it did not help. So I sealed the joint with silicone, and now the oil passes into the carburetor instead of onto the belly.

Later this week my wife and I are leaving on our fourth trip to the Bahamas in this plane. I can imagine no other plane that I would rather have for this trip.

Peter F. Hebb
Peterborough, N.H.

I purchased a 1979 Turbo 182RG with 1,050 hours on it. Although redline is 31 inches mp, I normally take off with about 28 inches. This allows the turbo to spool up, which may increase manifold pressure. Only knowledgeable pilots can fly this plane because it can be *easily* overboosted. However, I have had no problems learning how to fly it. In adverse weather (possible ice) I have been able to do a full-power climb (31"mp, 2400 rpm) up to 17,000 feet with two passengers and baggage and maintain a constant 1,000 fpm climb the whole way up. Normally, a cruise climb setting will give a very respectable 750 fpm.

I flight plan with 70 percent power for 150 knots true. The big cowl flaps, coupled with the engine's low turning speeds, keep the engine within all temperature limits in climb. Only once, when I was in south Georgia at 10,000 feet with the OAT at 70 degrees, did I have to open the cowl flaps to keep the engine cool in cruise. In descent, this plane is fast and can go to the top of the green if not careful. Since the gear can be extended up to 140 knots indicated, I have never had a problem getting down to pattern altitude (when cleared to descend by ATC).

My only complaint is getting the plane slowed down enough (to 95 knots IAS) to lower 20 degrees of flaps. The nose will pitch up with flaps. You must be prepared for this and push on the yoke even if you make a power reduction. If Cessna had any sense, they would have cleaned up this plane (as they did the 210) and taken Mooney on head-to-head. With the full fuel payload, range, altitude capabilities and terrific accident record, this plane is a sleeper.

Ronald Z. Mason
Columbus, Ohio

Good lines, good balance, good speed and load carrying. The Skylane RG has it all, except for good attention to details. Appropriately parked beneath a water tower, bladder-tank-equipped models suffered from water in the fuel.

Cessna 195

From out of the past rumbles one of aviation's all-time classic beauties. A vision in metal modeling with living room comfort and a reputation as a groundlooping-Lena, the Cessna 190-195 sets up great internal stresses among potential buyers seeking a satisfying balance between practicality and a touch of class and mystique.

History

Cessna cranked out some 1,200 of the 190s, 195s and military LC-126s between 1946 and 1954. The main distinction between the four different models built is the engine configuration. The C-190 came with a Continental radial putting out 240 hp. The C-195 had a 300-hp Jacobs, while the A and B models had a 245-hp and 275-hp Jacobs respectively. There was plenty to choose from that first year since all but the 275 were offered concurrently.

Elegant and trim, with a cantilever wing, the aircraft was one of the last radial-engine models.

The C-195B came out rather late in the production cycle, but its R755-B2 engine is generally considered to be the most reliable of the group, even though all three of the Jacobses have the same displacement. The 300 received a deeper intake manifold to get its extra 25 horses, but this seems to make it more susceptible to case cracking. The other significant changes were slightly larger flaps along with a modified horizontal tail at serial number 16084. And in 1953 the Goodyear crosswind gear was offered as standard, along with a lighter, springier set of main gear struts.

Performance and Handling

Owners report they get from 117 to 140 knots on the various models with a fuel burn of 12 to 19 gph. With 76 gallons of usable fuel on board, that means a range of from 500 to 800 nm. With the 275-hp Jacobs, count on a cruise of a bit over 130 mph, burning about 13.5 gph, with a comfortable no-reserve range of about 600 nm.

The aircraft is described as having "authoritative" pitch and rudder control, but ailerons are a bit on the heavy side. One owner characterized handling as similar to a Cessna 210, except for the "more ponderous" aileron control. Stalls are gentlemanly. Although the aircraft is commonly described as an excellent, stable instrument platform and cruise ship, it possesses an annoying tendency to wander in pitch in a mild never-ending phugoid. One pilot bemoaned the lack of a more capable autopilot to counter this characteristic than the "old, heavy Lear L2," which he said was the only one approved.

Another comment shed some doubt on the "stable instrument platform" characterization. Said one flier, "Since it has no dihedral, it is impossible to trim the airplane to fly hands off."

Suggested ways to land the C-195 without groundlooping it are, naturally, legion. The Cessna owner's manual suggests doing it three-point, and many owners subscribe to this philosophy. Others swear by the wheel landing technique, if only in crosswinds or gusty wind conditions.

But everybody agrees that the pilot must keep highly alert throughout the entire landing process. Said one reader: "Airspeed control on final is the key to good three-point landings (70 knots or less), and the pilot *must* remember to look straight down the runway until the airplane has slowed to a walking speed.

The Shaky Jake with the cowling off. The entire engine swings out on its mount. The oil filler aft of the engine takes a whopping five gallons. The right type of spinner makes for better cylinder cooling.

"Taking your eye off the runway to glance in the cockpit is inviting a groundloop. It must be remembered that this is a relatively heavy taildragger with the c.g. located well behind the main gear. Allow a swerve of more than 10 or 15 degrees to develop, and you don't have enough brake to stop it. A groundloop in this airplane will usually cause major damage to the gearbox, fuselage and wing."

Cabin Load and Comfort

Roominess is the aircraft's strong suit, with space for four comfortably, or five cozily. The useful load on an IFR-equipped 195 goes around 1,200 pounds, which allows full fuel and four 170-pound adults plus about 29 pounds of baggage.

The view out the cabin is really nothing to brag about, since the windows are long, but not terribly deep, except for a monster skylight right above the pilots' heads. Many 195 pilots say visibility is quite good in cruise (though abominable in taxi and on the landing flare), while others say they live constantly in fear of a midair because the pilot's head is lodged just about in the wing root.

In cold weather the 195 offers instant cabin heat thanks to a Southwind gas heater located right under the rear seat. One pilot had an interesting adventure thanks to this configuration when a spare can (a cardboard can, actually) of oil he'd tossed in the back rolled around and made contact with the heater, generating a bit of cockpit IFR.

Investment Value

With the passage of years, inflation, and perhaps their reputation as classics have slowly brought the resale value of the 195s up beyond their equipped price when new. Tracking a 1952 B model, we noted a big trough in the 1960s and early 1970s when the aircraft was selling for only about $6,000. Then in 1973 the price took a jog upward to about $9,000, and in 1976 commenced a steady climb until in 1979 it peaked out at $20,000. Since then it has risen steadily to about $45,000 according to the *Aircraft Bluebook Price Digest*, following the general trend of most aircraft to climb in the last couple of years. The various models range in average *Bluebook* price from about $42,000 to $45,000.

Safety Record

According to the National Transportation Safety Board's special study of single-engine aircraft accidents between 1972 and 1976, the Cessna 195 enjoys the unhappy distinction of being the worst groundlooper of all 33 aircraft compared. It was worse than even the Luscombe 8. The aircraft also came away in that report with the stigma of having the second highest overall accident rate—just behind the Luscombe 8, incidentally. Things improved somewhat in the fatal accident rate, with the C-195 coming out 11th worst.

And although the aircraft experienced only two in-flight airframe failures during the period studied, that brought the rate up to fourth worst among the 33, based on flying hours.

We understand that during the period 1964-1977 there were five fatal in-flight airframe failures. One of these seemed to involve pilot incapacitation due to carbon monoxide, another was a spin in the clouds, one a wingtip failure, another an empennage separation.

Cessna 195 owners are justifiably proud of the fact that so few Airworthiness Directives have been issued against the aircraft through the years since it was introduced. But one of them requires an inspection of the wing spar and addition of a steel reinforcement kit. It was issued following a fatal accident involving what was believed to be fatigue failure of the front wing spar fuselage carry-through lower cap. According to Dwight Ewing of the the Intl. 195 Assn., however,the rear wing spar had not been bolted in the wing root, so the problem wasn't fatigue failure at all. But the AD was never revoked.

Misdirectional Control

As we mentioned earlier, by far the greatest number of accidents and incidents tallied by the NTSB and the FAA on the Cessna 190-195s concern groundlooping this taildragger. We counted 43 of these in the six years on printouts made for us. Damage was to pride, airframe and pocketbook in each case; no injuries were reported.

Fatal accidents in this period were caused by engine failures in three cases. In one, the aircraft had lost oil from a fractured rubber hose from the oil sump to the main screen, with the pilot making an emergency descent in bad weather. In the second, water was found in the fuel after the crash. Two other nonfatal accidents were also caused by water in the fuel. The third fatal accident occurred after the number one piston disintegrated. The aircraft was reported to have an oil leak from the vicinity of the oil cooler prior to departure.

Another nonfatal engine failure and forced landing was blamed on carburetor ice, and quite a few C-195 pilots report great care has to be taken to avoid this problem, because the engine is quite prone to build carb ice. Yet another engine failure, this one in the traffic pattern, resulted from fuel starvation because engine vibration caused the fuel selector valve to move to the off position.

Another pair of fatal accidents stemmed from problems on climbout or go-around. One took place in high density altitude conditions in the Grand Canyon when the pilot made a steep turn and stalled. In the other, the pilot attempted a go-around late but neglected to move the prop pitch to the takeoff range.

A final fatal accident involved a float-equipped C-195 which the pilot attempted to take off in wind gusting to 35 knots with an unbalanced fuel load. The wingtip dug into the water, and a passenger drowned.

Many of the groundlooping accidents were caused simply by pilot inability to keep the aircraft going straight down the runway during the landing, sometimes in gusty crosswind conditions. However, a fair number were blamed on faulty brakes. Even though some pilots said it was impossible to nose over the big bird by hard braking on the landing roll, even after a wheel landing, in several instances pilots did just that, and even flipped the aircraft over on its back. The Goodyear brakes the aircraft came with are often described as inadequate, with Cleveland brake conversions making a big difference.

At least one pilot claims that groundlooping problems can be corrected by the use of the proper tailwheel tire: i.e., a channel tread.

For some help in managing the aircraft, Larry Bartlett of Pagosa Springs, Colo., makes videos on how to fly and land C-195s.

Landing Gear Struts

In some groundloops involving Cessna 190 and 195 aircraft, more than embarrassment results because one of the landing gear struts is torn off. Reader Larry Bartlett has some information on that topic:

"Two types of spring steel gear legs were installed. The later type, on the '53 and '54 models, was thinner and weighed about 20 pounds less. It is often referred to as the 'Wasp' or 'Spider' gear, or sometimes as the 'light' gear. The earlier 'heavy' gear is much stiffer, and I think causes more damage in a ground loop since it generally tears out of the fuselage, whereas the 'light' gear will spring or spread out and remain intact. I have no empirical data to support this, but all totaled 195s that I've seen that were groundlooped (and I've seen a few) had the 'heavy' gear."

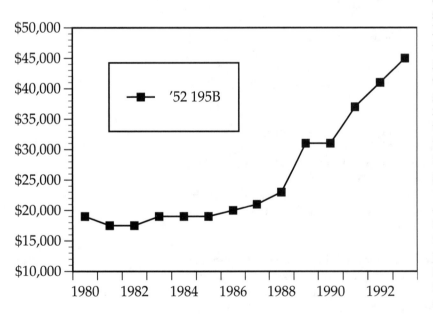

A never-ending debate rages on the use of cross-wind wheels for the taildragging Cessnas. Some old, experienced pilots maintain that only fools fly without them; others maintain that with a little care and experience, a pilot will have no problems.

The Goodyear castering gear was installed as standard equipment in 1953, and about 75 percent of the aircraft currently flying have them. Bartlett, for one, dislikes them. "I guess they do reduce the possibility of a groundloop and cover up for sloppy pilot technique, but I hate the looks of them," he says. "Aesthetically, the airplane needs wheel fairings, and they will not fit over the crosswind gear."

Another C-195 pilot said the narrow nine-foot track of the main gear adds to the problem of landing the 28-foot-long aircraft. "Once you let the tail wheel swing outside the track of the mainwheels on rollout, even with full differential braking, you will probably groundloop," he reported.

Short-field Performance

In the accident listing for a recent six-year period only four patently obvious cases were reported of C-195s getting into trouble with short fields. In one instance already mentioned, the pilot attempted to land on a short private field, overshot, then attempted a go-around too late and stalled (with coarse prop pitch). In the other, the pilot stalled on takeoff in a high-density altitude situation. In two other cases the pilots landed long while attempting to cope with strong crosswinds.

For a Cessna the aircraft has uncharacteristically modest flap "power." The aircraft has a strange-looking set of split flaps that project down from the bottom of the wing, not from the trailing edge, but several inches forward. Naturally, they provide no lift, just drag.

This was the last 195 to roll off the Cessna line, in August 1954. It belongs to Dwight M. Ewing, president of the International 195 Club.

Said one pilot, "Slow flight is a dream, and as a result you can make very short landings. Unfortunately, the lack of a Fowler-type flap keeps it from being a true short-field airplane. The split flaps are good speedbrakes, but provide no lift."

Judging from the NTSB's big study of single-engine accidents, however, the C-195 has a comparatively rotten record in overshoots. Its accident rate in this category was second only to the Grumman Traveler. Note that because of the low number of hours flown by C-195s, only five overshoot accidents were needed to achieve that rate.

A set of slightly larger flaps was added with the B model along with a shorter-chord horizontal stabilizer and modified trim tabs. But some pilots say the bigger flaps don't really affect performance in a beneficial sense that much. In fact, they seem to make it more difficult for a solo pilot to land three-point, according to Dwight Ewing, president of the International 195 Club.

Maintenance

Naturally, maintenance on these old birds is something of a chore because they're rather rare, and not too many mechanics nowadays are familiar with the old radial engines. Owners say, however, that the parts situation is really not too bad these days. But a glance at the 195 Club's newsletters shows that scrounging, upgrading and trading of parts is a matter of continuing concern.

The engines go about 1,000 to 1,200 hours on the TBO, with frequent oil changes recommended (at around 25 to 30 hours). An overhaul or an exchange will cost $13,500 from the Jacobs Service Co., depending on the engine and number of accessories. Working on the old radials is made easier by an engine mount design that allows the powerplant to be swung out from one side, as on a hinge.

One common problem with the 195s is leaking tail struts. Owners through the years have resorted to various cures, including installing Chevy valve springs. But some believe Granville Strut Seal might be the answer.

Old heads advise potential buyers to feel the fuselage skin in front of the main landing gear struts for smoothness, because it's hard to disguise rupturing of the gearbox, as it's called, by groundlooping. Owners are wont to extoll the grand old birds by claiming that only one solitary Airworthiness Directive has been issued during the entire history of the bird. And of course that was the big one concerning the wing truss. But the records show three others on the 190 and two others on the 195.

One required inspection of the rudder cables to detect premature fraying at the forward pulley. Another called for inspection for cracking and failures of the cowl mounting ring channels, until new channels and stiffening angles were installed. A third required inspection for fatigue cracks in the elevator spar webs at the outboard hinges until reinforcing doublers were installed. A final one, shared with many other Cessnas, involved checking the electrical system to prevent in-flight fires.

Electrically operated split flaps generate drag, but no appreciable lift. They at least tend to point the nose of the aircraft down on approach.

Parts and Service

Despite the fact that these days Cessna provides little more than moral support to the some 720 Cessna 190s and 195s still registered, owners report the parts situation is not too bad. In fact, it should even improve, thanks to a whole new enterprise devoted to building and overhauling the Jacobs engines.

The Jacobs Service Co. in Payson, Ariz. acquired the type certificates, tooling, drawings and parts inventory from Page Industries. It also received PMA approval, and does overhauls as well as provide exchange engines. Check with shop foreman Jim McCracken at (602) 474-2014.

A west-coast maintenance and repair facility that is characterized as "excellent" by the International 195 Club is Ray's Aircraft (run by Ray Woodmansee) at Porterville, Calif. Ray's bought out Andy Brennan of Brennan Formed Sheet Metal Parts, which manufactures sheet metal parts for the C-195. And they shipped the whole facility from Torrance, Calif. to Porterville.

Out in the East, Air Ads of Dayton at the Moraine Air Park is well known for its repair and service work on 195s. Down south in the Florida panhandle, John Hambleton of Gulf Coast Air Service in Fort Walton Beach does the same. And in the Illinois area, Phillip Van Reeth and his son, of Lombard, Ill. have developed an FBO serving the aircraft.

Operating Characteristics

Along with the panache of the big radial-engine Cessna comes a healthy dose of fussing—even before you can start the grand old bird. Since oil collects in the bottom cylinders if the aircraft has been sitting more than a few hours, the pilot must pull it through five to 12 blades, depending on whom you talk to. This will allow the start to generate less of a smokescreen. The pilot is not home free once he gets taxiing, either, since many of the old radials begin to heat up with prolonged ground operation. This is one reason C-195 pilots like to avoid big, busy airports with long rides to and from the active, and much sitting in line waiting for takeoff. Some owners even install double oil coolers to diminish the problem.

And the type of spinner installed has an effect on the cooling efficiency of the aircraft—though presumably only after the aircraft is airborne. The so- called Cessna "floating" bullet spinner is generally regarded as the most efficient. But some owners have used BT-13 spinners because they were more easily available.Though the engines are designed for 80 octane avgas, quite a few C-195 owners report they have used autogas with success.

Modifications

Although owners say only one autopilot, the Lear L2, is approved for the 190-195s, we note that Brittain had an STC for its B2C system.

Judging from the comments of owners, one of the most useful conversions is from the troublesome old Goodyear brakes to Cleveland brakes, which are many times more effective. Some say they're almost too effective and take a cautious touch or they can get the pilot into trouble. Also, of course, the airplane can be equipped with floats and is regarded as a marvelous seaplane whose squirrelly ground-looping tendencies have been purged.

We understand also that a number of 195s have 330-hp Jacobs L6MB engines that came from surplus World War II stocks in Canada and were installed with a modified cowl to accept the larger engine. Some 195s also received 450-hp Pratt & Whitney powerplants. And a 350-hp turbocharged version of the Jacobs was developed by Page,using an AiResearch turbo. Also, the Jacobs Service Co. is developing a 325-hp fuel injection mod for the 275-hp engine that not only should reduce fuel consumption and even out fuel flow to the cylinders but eliminate the specter of carb ice.

Organization to Join

The International 195 Club takes good care of members and publishes a slick-looking bulletin. Contact Dwight Ewing at the club address of P.O. Box 737, Merced, Calif. 95340, (209) 722-6284.

Rationale

The airplane obviously oozes aesthetic appeal. It has to be one of the all-time sculptured beauties. And at less than $50,000 or so, can it really be matched in a broad-shouldered contemporary ship of similar performance? As one owner comments: "In summary, the Cessna 195 is a five-place all-metal airplane which will produce an honest 139 knots on 15 gph. No AD hassle, easy maintenance, easy to fly. Have we really made any progress in 30 years?"

Cost/Performance/Specifications

Model	Year	Average Retail Price	Cruise Speed (kts)	Useful Load (lbs)	Fuel Std/Opt (gals)	Engine	TBO (hrs)	Overhaul Cost
C-190	1947-53	$42,000	139	1,335	80	240-hp Cont. W-670-23	1,000	$11,000
C-195	1947-53	$45,000	148	1,300	80	300-hp Jacobs R-755-A2	800	$22,000
C-195A	1947-53	$43,000	139	1,320	80	245-hp Jacobs R-755-9	800	$20,000
C-195B	1952-54	$45,000	143	1,300	80	275-hp Jacobs R-755-B2	800	$21,000

Answer: maybe not in looks and classic aura, but in safer, easier ground handling, certainly anything with tricycle gear excels. And for a similar investment, something on the order of the 1964 to 1974 Skylane will offer fairly similar cruise speeds and load- carrying ability with better parts availability, and a pretty decent cabin size. But as they say, love is blind.

Owner Comments

The Jacobs engine is a very reliable unit and does not have any unusual maintenance problems, but it does have some quirks. Smokey starts are common, more so than most radials, and it must be pulled through 10 or 12 blades to clear oil from the bottom cylinders if it has been sitting more than several hours. The engine will produce carburetor ice faster than an ice maker, and in cool, moist air it should be flown with partial carb heat, using the installed carburetor air temperature gauge.

Many times in flight in clear air the engine will cough or sputter momentarily, leading many to believe the mixture is too lean. But the "Shakey Jake" is merely swallowing some ice. A major difference between the Jake and other engines is that instead of two magnetos, it has one mag and a battery distributor just like a car. You might say it has a one-and-a-half ignition system instead of a dual system because the loss of the generator will soon have you operating on one mag.

The airframe is solid; you might say it was built like a tank. Parts can usually be found for most anything. The hardest parts to find have been cowling sections and the gearbox.

Good brakes are essential on this airplane. A Cleveland conversion is available and it does a great job. It is expensive, but well worth it. The only problem with the Clevelands is that they provide more braking action than the gearbox was designed to handle. I've seen two cases of popped rivets in the gearbox due to hard braking with the Clevelands installed. You have to really bear down on the Goodyears, but a light touch will do the job with the Clevelands.

Larry Bartlett
El Paso, Tex.

The best feature is the large internal volume. In the front you sit up in chairs off the floor, as at your kitchen table, and in the back you can stretch your legs out as in a Cadillac Limo.

The worst feature to me is the visibility to the sides in level flight. The pilot's head is located in the wing root; hence, to scan, one must duck down in an uncomfortable position, or lean forward.

Paul Taipale
Bellevue, Wash.

The biggest problem with the plane is the air-filled tail shock unit, and I found few who flew the plane who had not had a large spring installed inside the shock and used that to reduce the vibration. I tried for a long time to keep the darn shock filled, and most of those you see are sitting down low on the wheel, indicative of the fact that their tail shock doesn't work either.

Flying machine and art object, this was John W. Duff's aircraft. When the cabin door is opened, a retractable entrance step lowers automatically. Under the aft seat was a gas-fired heater.

It is a smooth-flying machine—easy to fly, wonderful and stable platform, big and comfortable. I can't remember having difficult landings, and always made wheel landings to keep pressure off the tail and its poor shock.

The flaps don't do anything for all practical purposes as far as slowing you down; but they do pitch you forward so you can see to land.

Art Brothers
Salt Lake City, Utah

It has been a most satisfying aircraft. It is as steady in all types of weather as you can expect a single-engine civilian craft to be. In the air, it feels much like a Cessna 210, except it is more ponderous in aileron control.

Its one big drawback initially is its ground handling. Visibility over the nose in three-point attitude is nil, the slow-turning prop (2200 rpm at takeoff while delivering 300 hp) provides plenty of torque to contend with. All of this adds up to what is probably one of the most difficult civilian aircraft to handle on the runway. On landing, it is worse. For the first few months of ownership, the local airport wags will sell tickets to your landings. However, once you master the aircraft, the feeling of accomplishment is tremendous, and more of a thrill than you will ever get with any modern tricycle-gear plane.

The only real annoyance is the tendency to overheat on the ground. Despite twin oil coolers, the tightly cowled Jake will run near the top of the green arc at cruise in the summer, and takeoffs and landings are out.

If you buy a 195, buy it in the winter, when you can get your 100 takeoffs and landings for your checkout at a rate of more than one per day. On normal operations, the handbook even suggests you do part of the runup while taxiing as "fast as safely possible" to the runway. You can live with it, but crowded airports need careful planning.

You can find modern aircraft that go faster on less fuel, but if you are willing to pay for your enjoyment, for sheer classic elegance, panache, *joie de vivre*, return to the challenge and romance of flying, you can't beat the 195.

Carlos R. Diaz
Clinton, Md.

My 195 receives more attention from lookers, gawkers, askers, admirers than any aircraft I have seen. And the roomy, solid comfort will impress you. The best 195 combination is a 275-hp Jacobs engine, Cleveland wheels (no crosswind gear), IFR radios and nice paint and interior. You'll love it. It is the Cadillac of all Cessna singles.

Thomas J. Schmid
Roseburg, Ore.

Tail strut leakage is a chronic problem, but Granville Strut Seal seems an effective antidote.

The engine was susceptible to carburetor ice, the fuel system had a tendency to collect water, and flight in icing conditions was hazardous because the fuel tank vents had a tendency to ice up.

Twice during flight in turbulence my rear door opened in flight. This unnerved my rear-seat passengers, but didn't seem to affect the flight characteristics adversely. I was able to close the door after I cranked down the left front window. I found that wheel landings were consistently better than three-point landings. You can brake a 195 as soon as the main gear is planted on the ground, so wheel landings require no more distance than three-pointers.

David M. Baker
Huntington, W. Va.

The horror stories about groundloops can be corrected by the simple use of the proper tailwheel tire—a channel tread.

Reports of engine oil overheating can in all cases be traced to improper type of spinner and elimination of cowling cooling rings. Many owners use a blunt bullet spinner, then wonder why they have to add oil coolers. The bullet spinner deflects the airstream outside the cowling while the original Cessna spinner directs the airflow to the cylinders.

Several propeller seal modifications are STC'd and are available at a reasonable price to eliminate prop oil leakage permanently. Cylinder head bolts should be tightened ever 250-300 hours. And exhaust valve clearance should be checked at that time. If the engine is equipped with valve rotators, no adjustment of valves will normally be necessary.

I could not get the comfort, speed and safety at double the price of my aircraft.

Harry E. Reed
Baldwinsville, N.Y.

Cessna 206/207 Stationair

The Stationairs are among the few aircraft that allow the pilot to fill the seats and the tanks, carry a bit of baggage and still be legal (and safe) to fly. Coupled with the designs' relative simplicity, these big singles are coveted by bush operators and light air taxi groups.

Dubbed by some as "a 172 with a gland problem," the Stationairs are the penultimate evolution of the sturdy Skyhawk lineage. (The Caravan might be considered the ultimate "super Skyhawk.")

Growing Up

Changes have been few and far between for the Stationairs. And even those changes that have been made through the years haven't been tremendous. In 24 years of production dating back to 1964, probably the most substantial changes have been engine-related. In 1967, the normally aspirated model got a horsepower boost from 285 hp to 300 hp. In 1977, the turbo models got a jump in power, going from 285 hp up to 310 hp.

Other changes along the way included name changes. Evidently, like most of the country at the time, Cessna was a bit confused in the mid-1960s. Having introduced the 205 (a stretched version of the Skylane) in 1963, the next outgrowth of this design appeared a year later in the form of the 206. Dubbed "Super Skywagon," it was intended from the outset as a cargo/utility aircraft (seats were optional equipment).

By 1965, the 205 was dropped from Cessna's production line, and the P206 Super Skylane was introduced. Essentially, the P206 was just the 205 reincarnated, though. However, there was now a conflict of terminology. Obviously, Cessna couldn't continue selling two aircraft called "206," so they added a "U" to the original Super Skywagon, which then became the U206 Super Skywagon.

In 1970, a year after Cessna introduced the Skywagon 207, the P206 was dropped from production. The name of the U206 was then changed to "Stationair" in 1970. The Skywagon 207 followed suit in 1978, becoming the Stationair 7.

Camber-lift wings, which feature a slightly cuffed leading edge, were added in 1972. These improved low-speed handling at almost no cost to cruise speeds. At the same time, the baggage compartment got a seven-inch stretch (more on this later). An aerodynamic cleanup in 1975 boosted cruise speed by about six mph. The cleanup included more-

At home on the range or at an urban airfield, the Stationair can get heavy loads in and out of places most aircraft fear to tread.

Spacious interior can hold four people quite comfortably. Back row passengers might get a little cramped, though.

streamlined wheel pants and improved cowl flaps.

A stretch of the fuselage brought what would eventually be called the Stationair 207 into being in 1969. One more seat was added, bringing the number available to seven. Useful load went up by about 30 pounds. An additional bonus was the inclusion of a nose baggage compartment, easing the task of getting the CG in the proper place during loading.

In 1980 the seventh seat of the 207 was widened to hold up to eight passengers. This created the Stationair 8, but the designator remained 207. The world would have to wait for the Caravan to see the 208 and the ultimate evolution of the high-wing, strut-braced single.

Cubic Questions

When it comes to carrying a load, the Stationairs were designed for it from the wheels up. The simple steel-spring main gear can absorb astounding amounts of punishment, and while the nosegear isn't nearly as strong, it does seem to be very durable.

The big rear cargo doors—which create an opening more than 44 inches wide—make getting bulky cargos inside less of a chore than in other aircraft. Indeed, in the "U" (for Utility) models there are no seats, leaving a mostly flat floor for cargo. Another nice touch is the lack of a lip at the doors, so cargos don't have to be maneuvered up and over to get them inside. Specialty kits were made available so the Stationair could take on such jobs as glider towing, parachute jumping and even aerial hearse service.

But despite the Stationair's large cargo area, operators often find themselves confronting the problem of "cubing out." Essentially, this means that the load fills the cargo space available before the aircraft reaches its gross weight limitation. For example, imagine having to haul a couple of tons of toilet paper. A few hundred pounds would fill the cabin, leaving many hundreds of pounds of useful load that can't be used.

Aiming at a solution to this problem, Cessna (and some aftermarket STC houses) came up with an optional under-the-fuselage cargo pod. It may not look pretty, but it does increase the volume available for cargo.

With or without the cargo pod, the Stationairs offer ample loading flexibility. The allowable CG range is fairly wide, making cargo/passenger positioning less of a juggling act than with many aircraft. However, despite some pilots' assertions that, "If you can get it in, you can take off," weight and balance computations are not optional. Several accidents over the years show it is possible to load a Stationair outside its envelope.

Comfort

While the Stationairs have large cabins, they're not long on comfort with a full load of passengers. Noise levels, particularly during takeoff and climb, can be fairly high as piston-engined singles go. And the rear-most seats—row three in the 206, rows three and four in the 207—leave little in the way of leg room.

Indeed, the puny bench that constitutes the seventh and eighth seats in the 207 would best serve small children. Since the seat is low-slung and the cabin tapers on all sides at this point, the average adult may emerge from a long flight looking like Quasimodo (and ready to ring the pilot's bells for making him sit back there).

Another comfort consideration is the baggage compartment. In spite of Cessna's best efforts, it doesn't quite match the capabilities of the passenger compartment. As a result, passengers may find themselves sharing space with their bags. However, the underslung cargo pod can really help here, freeing up elbow room by moving the bags below.

Performance

Obviously, the Stationairs are not speed demons. Like their Skyhawk antecedents, they are draggy and rather lumbering. Top cruise speeds will run in the 145-knot area while burning 15 gallons per hour or more. Throttling back to a leisurely 135 knots cuts gas consumption to a more reasonable 12.5 gph.

Handling matches the aircraft's size. Pilots who enter the Stationair after climbing the Cessna model ladder may find the the aircraft is just more of the same (only heavier). One owner has described the Stationair as handling like a heavy 172.

This is not without its benefits, though. It makes the Stationair an excellent IFR platform—stable and rock-solid. It also makes for a relatively smooth ride in turbulence that brings out the barf bags in other aircraft.

Despite a large cabin and big useful load, lack of volume is sometimes more of the problem than any lifting deficiency.

Another benefit is that the Stationair is reluctant to stall. Pitch forces are fairly heavy to begin with. Compounding this is the generally nose-heavy loading of the airplane. Since the CG envelope is so long, and most everyone wants to sit up front, the CG is often at or near its forward limit. Also, with power on, the deck angle required for a wings-level stall is alarming. Put it all together and the Stationair is not generally a willing participant in stalls.

A drawback of this nose heaviness is a tendency to arrive nose first during landing, especially at light weights. It takes a hefty pull on the yoke to flare properly. Thus, the Stationairs are no strangers to hard, nose-first landings that

sometimes damage the aircraft. In the 207 version, the nose baggage compartment can simply add to the nose heaviness. However, using less than full flaps for landing (say only 20 degrees) can ease the control forces required to flare.

Maintenance Matters

The Stationairs may be simple in design and construction, but they're not cheap to keep. Perhaps because of their often rough-and-ready lifestyle, or because they do tend to be flown a lot, the Stationairs managed to rack up an impressive 802 Service Difficulty Reports (SDRs) during the last five years, according to FAA.

A number of trends involving the airframe emerged during our SDR survey. Problems with the tailfeathers were the most numerous. For example, water retention in the elevator and trim tab was cited in 24 reports. Both the elevator and trim tab are filled with a type of foam to provide stiffness, and the foam can soak up water. This leads to a number of problems, not the least of which is corrosion. It also can unbalance the elevator, leading to possible flutter problems (although no reports of this have been received). Painstaking examination of the elevator and trim tab are in order at each annual or 100-hour inspection (although some method of drainage wouldn't hurt either).

Cracking of the horizontal stabilizer attach fittings, along with pulling of the rivets, screws and nuts in this area, accounted for 20 reports. Although this is a fairly well known problem with the Stationairs, it's still something to look out for.

The fuel selector was the target of AD 85-02-07. The AD mandated inspections for the presence of the selector roll pin and for excessive freeplay of the selector shaft. There were 16 reports in which mechanics found the problems specified in the AD during compliance. A check of the logbooks before purchase should quickly show if this AD has been complied with. If it hasn't, get it done as soon as possible.

Cracking Bulkheads

Maybe it's not pretty, but for pure utility it's hard to beat a Stationair.

A newly emerging trend for the Stationairs involves cracking of the forward bulkhead which also serves as the doorpost. We found 23 reports of forward bulkhead cracking. Also, we have learned of another three aircraft on which this problem was discovered in early December of 1990 (the SDRs on these aircraft were filed too late to make our printout). At this time, FAA is preparing to release an Airworthiness Alert about this problem, and is contemplating an AD as well.

Of perhaps lesser import, we noted some problems with the landing gear. Cracking brake discs garnered six reports. Interestingly, the original-equipment McCauley brakes accounted for only two of these, with Clevelands making up the rest. In a similar vein, cracking wheel halves received eight reports, only this time the McCauley wheels were cited in seven of these, Clevelands only once.

An item to check during annuals and 100-hour inspections is the nosegear drag link. Broken bolts, pulled bolts and broken linkages were reported seven times.

Powerplant Problem

The engine accounted for many reports, covering many problems.

Big cargo doors make loading bulky items easy. It's worth noting that the flaps must be up to get the doors open, though.

The one most commonly reported was cylinder cracking. For the most part, these reports were confined to the IO-520-F. Out of 69 reports of cylinder cracking or breaking in our survey, the IO-520-F accounted for 49 of them. No other -520-series engine installed on a Stationair was affected to such an extent by this problem. Only one other model—the TSIO-520-M—made it into double digits with 10 reports.

Crankcase cracking was also a problem, again primarily for IO-520-F engines. Of 33 reports of case cracking, the -F engine accounted for 27. Fortunately, case cracks can now be welded, saving plenty of money.

Likewise, the -F engine racked up the most reports on crankshaft failure (eight out of 11 filed) and connecting rod failure (also eight out of 11).

Safety

Accidents will happen, and the Stationairs are not excepted from this rule. We examined NTSB data for the years 1983 through 1986 and found 204 accidents involving the 206/207. However, aside from engine failures, the Stationair's accident picture speaks more of the foibles of the pilots and the rigors of the aircraft's lifestyle than to any inherent flaws in the design.

Cost/Performance/Specifications

Model	Year	Average Retail Price	Cruise Speed (kt)	Useful Load (lb)	Std/Opt Fuel (gal)	Engines	TBO (hr)	Overhaul Cost
U206, A	1964-66	$41,500	142	1,800	65/84	285-hp Cont. IO-520-A	1,700	$15,000
U206B-D	1967-69	$46,500	142	1,800	65/84	300-hp Cont. IO-520-F	1,700	$15,000
TU206A-C	1966-68	$48,500	147	1,650	65/84	285-hp Cont. TSIO-520-C	1,400	$18,000
U206E/F	1970-72	$49,750	142	1,700	65/84	300-hp Cont. IO-520-F	1,700	$15,000
TU206E/F	1970-72	$55,000	147	1,650	65/84	285-hp Cont. TSIO-520-C	1,400	$18,000
U206F	1973-75	$58,000	142	1,760	65/84	300-hp Cont. IO-520-F	1,700	$15,000
TU206F	1973-75	$64,000	147	1,660	65/84	285-hp Cont. TSIO-520-C	1,400	$18,000
U206G	1976-78	$71,000	147	1,690	65/84	300-hp Cont. IO-520-F	1,700	$15,000
TU206G	1976-78	$77,000	152	1,610	61/80	310-hp Cont. TSIO-520-M	1,400	$18,500
U206G	1979-81	$89,500	147	1,690	61/80	300-hp Cont. IO-520-F	1,700	$15,000
TU206G	1979-81	$97,500	152	1,610	61/80	310-hp Cont. TSIO-520-M	1,400	$18,500
U206G	1982-84	$115,500	147	1,690	61/80	300-hp Cont. IO-520-F	1,700	$15,000
TU206G	1982-84	$129,000	152	1,610	61/80	310-hp Cont. TSIO-520-M	1,400	$18,500
U206G	1985-86	$146,500	147	1,690	61/80	300-hp Cont. IO-520-F	1,700	$15,000
TU206G	1985-86	$162,500	152	1,610	61/80	310-hp Cont. TSIO-520-M	1,400	$18,500

Source: *Aircraft Bluebook Price Digest*

Cruise speeds aren't spectacular, but the Stationair wasn't intended as a speed demon.

When the topic is engine stoppages, two main types predominate: crankshaft failures and fuel system failures. Indeed, in terms of actual mechanical breakdown, crankshaft failure was almost the only problem we found during our survey of Stationair accidents. Five accidents stemmed from this problem.

Fuel system problems accounted for the bulk of the remaining engine failures. Troubles ranging from fuel pump failure to broken hoses and lines to disconnected throttles to trash clogging the system brought down 11 Stationairs. Interestingly, wrinkled fuel bladders played a role in one of these accidents. The wrinkles trapped eight gallons of fluid—but not water, as AD 84-10-01 pointed out. In this case it was the last eight gallons of fuel in the tank. The engine then quit from fuel starvation.

Fuel contamination did, however, cause six accidents. As might be expected, it was water in the fuel in all six cases. Wrinkled bladders were specifically mentioned in only one case.

Wind Upsets

Belying the Stationair's 172 heritage, four of the big birds were blown over while taxiing. However, it takes fairly strong winds to get this airplane turned over. Three of the four instances of this occurred in winds of more than 25 knots. (Respectively, 35-knot gusty winds, winds of 29 knots with higher gusts, and winds of 27 knots with gusts to 35.) Jet blast was also a factor in one case, while it caused another when the pilot taxied directly behind a taxiing Boeing 737.

There were a few accident trends worth noting. Groundloops during landing and takeoff (both on land and on water) accounted for 34 accidents. Flying VFR into IFR—a perennial killer—was behind 20 accidents. Low flying led to another 12 accidents. Finally, the relatively high number of mid-air collisions is disturbing. We found six collisions during our four-year survey, which is more than most other aircraft accumulate during a similar interval.

When it came to fatal accidents, there were no really unexpected trends. Of 36 fatal crashes during our survey, 15 stemmed from pilots pushing the weather and either flying into a mountain (or trees on takeoff in one case) or attempting to scud run and hitting poles, etc.

Notably absent from the accident picture were in-flight airframe failures. Like other strut-braced Cessnas, a draggy airframe and rather high control forces combine with good stability and great structural strength to make in-flight break-ups extremely rare.

The Competition

About the only other choices available for those looking for a good load-hauling single are the Piper Cherokee Six and Saratoga. At first glance they might seem to be neck-and-neck. For example, they are nearly identical in load hauling and power.

The Pipers also have some distinct advantages. One of these is TBO. While the best one can hope for from any Stationair model is a 1,700-hour TBO, the -540-series Lycomings bolted on the Pipers have a TBO of 1,800 hours (for the TIO-540-S1AD), and as much as 2,000 hours in the case of the IO-540-K1G5 on the Saratoga and Cherokee Six.

On the other hand, the Pipers are not known for their ruggedness. And they are no strangers to in-flight breakups. Besides, they cost more to buy and they're not as easy to load (Piper PR shots of a piano being loaded notwithstanding). As an added bonus, the high wings offer some shelter from sun and rain while the loading is underway.

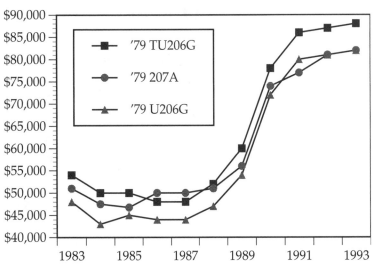

Mods

There's probably a modification available for the 206/207 to allow it to do most anything someone might want to do.

Those who fancy flying to some remote lake for fishing can install either Whipline or Edo floats. Heading for the snow-bound areas? Skis are available, too.

You may need more fuel to get there, so maybe a set of Flint Aero long range tanks is in order. Order them from Flint Aero in Sangee, Calif.

Perhaps the premier performer on floats, the Stationairs can be make a living off (and on) the water.

And don't count on finding big long flat places to land and take off from once you get there, either. If you're really planning on getting out in the toolies, a STOL mod might be just the ticket for those tight fields. Horton, Inc of Wellington, Kans. can provide all those nifty STOL things like drooping ailerons, stall fences, leading edge cuffs and so on.

Support Group

If you like the feeling of belonging, then the Cessna Pilot's Assn. is for you. They're in Wichita, Kans. at (316) 946-4777. If you don't get that warm and fuzzy feeling from belonging to a special group, you should still join, since the CPA newsletter contains enough tips and information that membership pays for itself.

Owner Comments

I bought my Turbo Stationair from a friend about nine years ago. It's a 1976 model with long-range tanks. It had been on lease-back to a flying club before I bought it. As with most rentals, the majority of people just didn't respect the equipment as if it was their own.

As a result, the engine required a complete overhaul at 1,200 hours. Fortunately, this was all done about 200 hours before I bought the airplane Since then, I have flown about 500 hours on the rebuilt engine, prop and turbo.

The engine has run flawlessly so far. At cruise I run at 23" MP and 2300 rpm, setting the mixture for about 12 gph using my fuel computer.

I do all my flight planning at 150 mph, and it seems to run true to within a few minutes on any trip of less than a few hours. I have not made any effort to clean up the rigging or aerodynamics, which I'm sure would help appreciably.

The Cessna radios, gauges, etc. are a joke. I had the entire (plastic) instrument panel removed and remade using 0.090 aluminum and painted dark grey. Almost all of the avionics were changed to King.

The new panel is beautiful, albeit expensive. But I just got tired of having the panel literally fall in my lap and never knowing if the Cessna instruments were going to work. I could watch the fuel gauge on the right tank drop to empty in 15 minutes, then stay there for the duration. Conversely, the left gauge wouldn't move at all for two hours, then it would drop to zero. That's not much of a confidence builder.

Everything else in the ship that's plastic and subject to wear is either broken or has been replaced. I was appalled when the notice came out for the seat rails and stops, and I examined how the seats are attached to the airframe through those tiny little rails and keepers. God help anyone that's counting on the seat to stay in place in any significant high-G loading without the aid of the seatbelt to hold you in place.

Stationair panel is big enough to hold most modern avionics. Note the rear-view mirror on top.

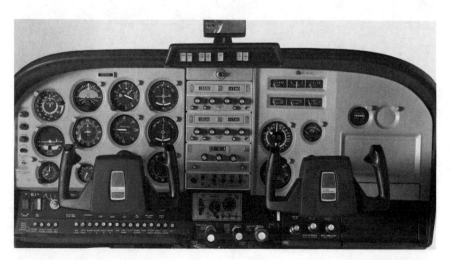

I recently moved from California to Nevada, and made excellent use of the plane as a station wagon. I opened the two large rear doors, removed the seats and was amazed as to the amount of "junk" I could stuff in the thing and still remain legal.

Then, with the tanks full, I could leave the San Joaquin Valley with 90 degree temperatures and easily climb over the Sierras—only 50 miles distant—at 13,500 feet.

The airplane is extremely noisy inside, and by necessity I must use headsets to communicate either with the passengers or with ATC.

I understand the noise level can be reduced considerably with proper insulation, and I intend to do so when the interior is updated.

I have not dealt with the factory, so I cannot comment on their support. Any parts have been purchased through after-market dealers.

Annuals have run from $400 to $1,800, depending on how much effort I put forward to help and how many items needed repair or replacement. One continuing maintenance problem has been nosegear shimmy. I just can't seem to keep the nosewheel fairing in place more than a year without cracking. I've been able to use fiberglass and make some repairs, but soon it's so bad it has to be replaced.

I've always experienced severe buffeting if the nose is allowed to settle too soon after landing. Taxiing too quickly will cause it to start shaking, and there's no stopping it once started without pulling the wheel into your lap and reducing speed.

Hot starts were a problem if the airplane was flown, then sat for less than an hour and a restart attempted.

Finally, another pilot saw my plight one day as I was grinding away and suggested that I reverse the mixture and throttle (that is, mixture full lean and throttle full forward). This works like a charm and I have never had another problem on a hot start.

The ship has seen limited use (500 hours in nine years), but I can truly say it has been near bulletproof, has never failed to fly and perform to my expectations. I've always had the luxury of having the ship hangared, so I may not experience some of the weathering problems encountered by an airplane that is tied down and exposed to the elements.

I fly VFR only and appreciate the rock-steady performance once everything is trimmed. It's a safe, solid ship that handles the mountain turbulence well over the Sierras. It's also an appreciating investment that will last the rest of my flying days.

Dean Watts
Carson City, Nev.

After 11 years and 4,000 hours as a Skylane owner, my family grew to five in number. So it was either a 210 or a 206 for us. In 1979 I bought a 1977 TU206 with 50 hours on it for $51,000.

I use my plane mostly for the daily commute from Concord, Calif. to a 4,000-foot dirt strip on my ranch in northern Napa County. It is really an airborne pickup truck as I haul sheep, goats, baby buffalo, bees, poultry, seed, fertilizer, gas engines, etc.

After the plane is loaded, I sit on the horizontal stabilizer, and as long as the nosewheel doesn't lift off the ground, I know I'm "in the envelope."

As for maintenance, I replaced the engine at 1,200 hours due to crankcase cracking. I installed a factory-new engine and have had no major trouble other than one failed magneto in the last 1400 hours. I generally fly at 28" MP and 2350 rpm, using 20 gph and leaving the cowl flaps open (my reasoning being that cool engines give a long life).

I'd love to buy a new 206, but they don't make them anymore. So my plane will go to the detail shop pretty soon to reseal the doors (very noisy) and to fix the cracks in the interior plastic. Yes, I fly a bit slower than my 210 friends, but I don't have to worry too much when I fly into those short rocky strips in Idaho's back country or Utah's slickrock canyon area.

Norman Pease
Orinda, Calif.

We have had a 1972 Turbo 206 for 12 years and have logged more than 2,000 hours in it between my son and myself.

The original 285-hp engine was replaced with a factory-new 310-hp TSIO-520-M which has gone through TBO and been overhauled to new specs. The airplane is equipped with large main tires, tip tanks, intercooler, factory oxygen and full IFR panel. We fly it IFR and find it an excellent instrument platform and very stable.

A 206 is not a speed demon, but we file for 130 knots at 65% power, and we eventually get where we're going. The high-altitude capability of the turbo allows greater speeds when long trips warrant climbing to take advantage of winds and thinner air.

Fuel consumption is high (more than 17 gph at 65%), but load-hauling capability is excellent. With the two back seats removed, four people can go on long trips and not have to be too careful about baggage, and still have room for souvenirs on the return flight.

My wife and I have flown the airplane to Mexico on five different occasions, covering the length and breadth of that country. Most of the trips have been with four on board.

We have also flown it to Alaska (Prudhoe Bay, Point Barrow, Kotzebue, Nome and most of the larger and some smaller towns in that state). For flying in such places as Alaska and Mexico, a 206 would be hard to beat because of its short-strip and load-carrying capabilities.

It is a joy to fly because of its stability compared with a 150, 172 or 182. With the tip tanks, we have enough gas for 5:45 plus a 45-minute reserve. This works out to about a 750-nm range.

Maintenance costs seem high, but when you compare them with other airplanes they are not out of line. Parts availability has not been a problem.

If our airplane were destroyed for some reason, we would replace it with another Turbo 206.

James Scott
Pomeroy, Wash.

Cessna 210, T-210 Centurion

To use a sports analogy, the Centurion is like the brawny fullback who can outrun everybody. But he's had knee surgery and maybe even a bypass operation. You've got to respect his speed and heft, but naturally have a few reservations about his durability.

The C-210 in many ways is a truly remarkable airplane, one that evokes expressions of awe and respect from owners. Even with the normally aspirated models you're talking about cruise speeds around 170 knots/195 mph, coupled with useful loads of about three-quarters of a ton, equipped.

Add to that cruising ranges of 1,000 nm and better with full tanks, and you have an airplane to be reckoned with when shopping for a fast aerial U-Haul.

Historical Perspective

The aircraft is the classic case of the "grandfather clause" carried to extremes. Certified way back in 1959 as a 2,900-pound airplane with a strut-braced wing and a redline speed of 174 knots, it's evolved into a 4,100-pound 325-hp pressurized behemoth with a 200-knot redline, designed to fly above 20,000 feet in icing conditions.

And all this has been accomplished under the certification standards of the old CAR Part 3 rather than the more stringent current FAR 23. Cessna reports that with later models it has conformed to newer criteria, but of course it is under no obligation to prove this. The matter has been a debating point in connection with the C-210's in-flight airframe breakup rate. (More about that later.)

Truly a super plane, the Centurion carries a tremendous load at marvelous speed. The downside is a Pandora's box of mechanical problems.

Landing Gear Gripe List

The aircraft owes its origin to even earlier sources, since it sprang, like Adam's rib, from a Cessna 180 airframe. One of the interesting challenges posed to Cessna engineers way back then was to figure a way to retract the gear into the fuselage, since the wing, perched on top of the fuselage, did not lend itself to housing the retraction mechanism. Their efforts were not crowned with glory. The results, through a series of attempted upgrades, have bedeviled 210 owners ever since. Even to this day Service Difficulty Reports show landing gear problems remain at the top of the gripe list among owners and mechanics—by far.

As the years went by, a series of changes were also made to cabin, wings and powerplants. In 1962 the cabin was enlarged a bit and outfitted with rear win-

Big roomy cabin makes the 210 an ideal four-placer, with plenty of space for baggage. The rear two seats are underkill in comfort. Note the gear-well hump behind the rear seat.

dows. Then, in 1964 engine power rose from 260 hp to 285 hp, and in 1965 a turbocharged model was introduced that went on to outsell the normally aspirated model by nearly two to one. In 1967, presumably to counter the scoffing of competitors, Cessna replaced the strut-braced wing with a cantilevered one, at the same time boosting the fuel capacity from 65 gallons to a whopping 90. However, since the airframe breakup rate of cantilever models way exceeds that of strutted ones, some critics question the wisdom of that change. (The retractable Skylane RG retained its struts, by comparison.)

In 1970 Cessna made a big change in the cabin, boosting the seating from four places to six—to accommodate four adults and two kids, and adding extra baggage space, all the while raising the gross weight by a significant 400 pounds to 3,800 pounds. Then, in 1971 takeoff horsepower was boosted once again, to 300.

Gear Improvements

In 1972 Cessna made an important effort to improve the landing gear mechanism, by replacing the old engine-driven hydraulic system with an electro-hydraulic one. Taking the process one step further, in a dramatic stroke Cessna in 1979 simply did away with gear doors and all the extra mechanical bother they represented. (Mod shops today will do the same for owners of older aircraft, for a price.) There seems to be negligible if any speed sacrifice. Also in 1979 Cessna raised the gross weight to 4,000 pounds with the 210N model, and in 1985 raised it once again to 4,100 pounds for the 210R.

Since the Centurions were highly desired as instrument-flying ships, the specter of instrument loss from simple accessories like alternators and vacuum pumps led Cessna in 1982 to offer optional dual alternators and vacuum pumps. The dual pumps became standard with 1983 models as turbo ships were certified for flight in icing conditions. Pneumatic boots naturally imposed an extra burden on the vacuum pump system.

Also on the 1983 models, Cessna began installing new Slick pressurized magnetos to prevent misfiring at high altitudes. And in 1984 engine TBO went up from 1,400 to 1,600 hours, and shoulder harnesses were made standard equipment on all seats.

Performance and Handling

As we mentioned before, the C-210 series aircraft go like bats. Pilots note cruise speed is easily 160-170 knots, climbout around 750 fpm at 120 knots indicated, though one owner boasted he could do an "easy 1,500 fpm" with two people on board. With an IFR-equipped payload of about 970 pounds after full fuel, a late-model Cessna 210 can haul the astonishing load of five adults and about 22 pounds of baggage for each rider. No other single comes close except the Piper Saratoga, which is still about 30 pounds shy. Furthermore, the Centurions have an unusually broad center of gravity envelope that tolerates loading extremes that would cause aerodynamic chaos in other airplanes—like the Bonanza for instance.

The airplane does not have well-harmonized controls. Though ailerons are delightfully quick for such a big airplane, pitch pressures are heavy, as in the Skylane. The other side of the coin, as one owner noted: "Although somewhat built like a truck, with controls to match, nevertheless it is a most dependable IFR platform in adverse weather."

Thanks to limited elevator travel, the big Centurion is tough to wrangle into a full-stall break, so there's nothing nasty about stalls. Since it's the heaviest airplane in its class, it must naturally be handled with respect, especially on landing. Judging from the number of hard landings, swerves and runway overruns and gear collapses in the accident reports, this is a matter to be reckoned with.

Although most Cessnas have an excellent reputation for short-field operation, the C-210, on paper anyway, does not shine in this category in comparison with its peers. Minimum runway over a 50-foot obstacle tallies out at a little over 2,000 feet, which is close to the figures given for the Beech A36 Bonanza, but longer by several hundred feet than for the other Bonanzas and the Piper Lance/Saratoga in the big-single class. Nevertheless, one pilot who had stepped up from a Skyhawk to a '78 T210 told us: "The biggest surprise has been the superb handling qualities in the pattern. When there are a half dozen jetliners lined up on final to Phoenix Sky Harbor, the 210 can slip in between them on a tight, short approach just like the C-172 could. True, the stick forces are high at slow speed, but judicious use of the electric elevator trim alleviates that problem."

Cabin Comfort, Finish

With a cabin width of 44 inches in the middle and a height of 47 inches, the aircraft has a roomy interior for four adults and perhaps two kids. Wrote one happy owner: "It's been a family machine, comfortably carrying, for example, four skiers averaging about 165 pounds, skis, boots, poles, banjo, guitar and clothes for a week."

Another summed up his attitude toward the fifth- and sixth-seat arrangement: "The back seats are really only for short trips or small people."

Although in the past we received quite a few complaints about the "cheap" Royalite instrument panels, our latest call for reader feedback did not turn up any derogatory comments along this vein. Neither did we receive any complaints of leaking windshields this time around, though one pilot said his baggage compartment leaks "with all precipitation."

He also complained that the rear cabin has a serious heating deficiency. "The difference between the N and R models (he's owned both), is that the '86 model is a flying freezer for anyone behind the pilot. The pilot roasts; the midseat passengers require full winter gear, and water freezes behind them." He noted he'd complied with service bulletins on the matter. "But my family remains reluctant to fly again this winter," he added. In this context, we noticed Cessna has issued Service Bulletin SEB87-5, designed to improve the cabin heating system. It includes a heat exchanger seal to prevent outside ram air from entering the exchanger, and the simple artifice of a removable insulated cabin curtain to separate the cabin passenger area from the baggage compartment. Cessna claims these provide a "significant increase in cabin temperature."

Maintenance

Most of the owners offering feedback on 210s reported an average maintenance burden and what we figured were rather low prices for the annual inspection for an aircraft of this size and complexity; i.e., from $800 to $1,500. (We've been averaging a lot more for our Mooney 201, incidentally.)

Though production of 210s has ceased, owners reported decent parts availability, but high prices. One owner said he was exasperated, however, with Cessna's policy of selling parts only through dealers, with no drop shipping, even if purchased through a dealer. This, he said, meant that in his part of the country (the Greater Philadelphia area), parts had to come from one of several dealers 50 to 100 miles away, meaning the aircraft was AOG at least once a year for an extra week "with bureaucratic supply delays, often for trivial parts (e.g., landing gear relay, etc.) being purchased through a third party who is not working on the plane and may not order what is requested."

Landing gear glitches have plagued 210s for years—a true Achilles heel. High wing, low cabin floor makes for ideal cargo loading, however. Later models did away with gear doors for simplicity's sake.

Landing Gear Malaise

A number of owners reported problems with gear doors on their 210s, and a survey by *The Aviation Consumer* of FAA Service Difficulty Reports from the years 1985 through October 1988 showed that, indeed, landing gear problems dominated the list, by far—with 131 reports. (Traditionally, of course, the FAA estimates SDRs represent a 10% tip of the iceberg.)

Sample comments: "Unable to lower gear, landed gear up." "Gear failed to extend. Hand pump did not help. Landed gear up." "A forced gear-up landing was accomplished due to lack of hydraulic pressure . . ." "Aircraft made a wheels-up landing when landing gear failed to lower."

Among the various components blamed for gear problems: Thermal relief valve in power pack unseated; landing gear door valve failure; hydraulic reservoir depleted from chafing by control cable; filter housing ruptured in flight; power pack pump failed, causing continuous running and overheating; power pack motor burned, etc.

We tallied quite a few more gear-up landings on the SDRs than were reported in the accident briefs for the same period.

Blazing Saddles

The historic nemesis of the older Centurions, fatigue cracks in landing gear saddles, has apparently not abated completely. We counted 25 reports of cracked saddles in the latest run of SDRs. All 210s built from 1960 to 1969 live under the shadow of this problem. With luck, the cracks are found during annual inspections. If not, the saddles eventually break, and the pilot discovers his problem when one landing gear leg hangs up in the half-way position.

AD 76-14-07 issued in 1976 to deal with the problem calls for dye penetrant inspections at 1,300 hours and at annual inspections afterwards. But mechanics have found cracks sooner in the life span. Saddle replacement was required for 1960 and 1961 models, but even they must be replaced every 1,000 hours at a cost of $1,000 to $1,500. Buyers should check the saddles and replacement times on these aircraft.

The 1962-67 models had the same original defective saddles, but differences in the retraction system allowed an improved saddle to be retrofitted. But even they have not eliminated the cracking problem.

Later, 1968 and 1969 model 210s came with the "improved" saddles as original equipment, but they must be inspected at 1,200 hours and annually thereafter, and still run the risk of eventual cracking.

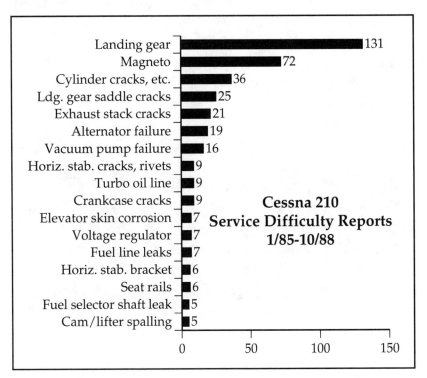

Cessna 210
Service Difficulty Reports
1/85-10/88

Finally, the landing gear system was redesigned in 1970, thus apparently ridding the 210 line of the cracking saddle scourge.

Magneto Problems

Mag failures came in second worst in our tally of Service Difficulty Reports, with 72. These involved Slick magnetos on not only pressurized and turbocharged 210s, but normally aspirated ones as well.

The FAA issued an AD late in 1988 (88-25-04) calling for inspection of pressurized mags for moisture contamination within the next 50 flight hours, and at each annual thereafter for Part 91 operators. But the SDRs suggested that contamination represented only part of the problem with the Slick mags. Others called out failures from a variety of causes such as bearing failure, worn brushes, partially disintegrated distributor blocks, worn gear teeth, broken impulse coupling and broken mounting flanges, to name some.

We talked with Slick Aircraft Products to see if they could explain the problem, and they said they believed it occurred when pilots flew through visible moisture, and was a function of the "plumbing" design on the C-210, taking air from the induction manifold. They suggested the problem was not as great in other aircraft like the turbo Mooneys and the Piper Malibu, which also use pressurized Slick mags.

As for other types of magneto problems, a Slick representative suggested some might be related to improper maintenance in the field. In particular, extensive improvement and changes in Slick magneto components since 1980 mean that some critical parts must be mated, and this means a mix-and-match use of cannibalized parts by some mechanics can pose a real problem.

The average pilot must jack up his seat to see over the gargantuan panel, but then must duck to see out of the side window. Fuel gauges, on the right side of the panel in some models, deserve attention in view of the aircraft's high rate of fuel mismanangement accidents.

Buyers might make it part of their pre-purchase exam to try to ascertain whether the magnetos have been inspected with a case opening at 500-hour intervals, so major problems may be forestalled.

Cylinder Cracks

Third highest on the list of Service Difficulty Reports was cylinder cracks, with 36 of these called out. Pressurized and turbocharged 210s dominated the roster with this problem, but it occurred on normally aspirated 210s as well. One mechanic ventured as the probable cause overheating due to over leaning and improper cooling procedures with turbocharged powerplants.

In 1986 Cessna brought out a service bulletin (SEB86-3) tagging, in turn, a Continental SB (M86-7) calling attention to "unexplained" cylinder barrel cracking that had caused instances of head to barrel separation. Inspections were required, to be repeated every 100 hours, on certain serial number IO-520 and TSIO-520 engines.

The Continental engines on C-210s were also prey to a number of crankcase cracks (we counted nine reports), though we usually think of this as the main province of Beech Bonanzas and Barons.

In addition, those old bugaboos of any aircraft—vacuum pump and alternator failures—took their toll on C-210s as well, with 35 of these reported. In this context, AD 82-6-10 requires certain Cessna 210s to have two operable vacuum pumps before flying into instrument weather conditions.

Potential buyers should also take care to check the horizontal tail for a variety of problems, including stabilizers and brackets for cracking. Cessna brought out several service bulletins (SEB88-3, SNL87-18 and SEB87-2) aimed at strengthening various tail components. And make sure the elevator skin itself has not become corroded thanks to water absorption by the foam filler. Especially scrutinize horizontal stabilizers on older model 210s.

The FAA has received numerous reports of damage (loose or broken rivets, cracking and other problems) near the forward fittings, bulkhead and doublers. The problem is confined to fuselage station 209, and Cessna has kits to repair the problems or prevent them from happening. Single-engine Service Letter SE72-29 describes the kits available to owners.

Filiform Paint Problem

Check used 210s built between 1977 and 1982 and based in hot, humid seaside areas for possible filiform corrosion.

Safety Record

In our last major survey of accident rates among single-engine retractables in 1984, the Cessna 210 came out with a very poor rating in total accidents and a slightly worse than average rating in fatal accidents. To be specific, it was the third worst out of 17 aircraft compared in total accident rates between 1972 and 1981 and eighth worst in fatal accidents. (These figures do not include the P210, which came out with a better score in both categories.)

Only the old Piper Comanche and Beech 24 Sierra had worse total accident records for that period. Our close-up inspection of accident data for 1975 and 1976, along with 1985 through 1987, highlights two areas of biggest concern through the years: engine failures for mechanical and other reasons and fuel mismanagement.

During the latter period ('85 through '87) fuel mismanagement claimed by far the greatest number of nonfatal accidents (see the nearby chart), with engine stoppage in second place. Time and again the National Transportation Safety Board Briefs report C-210 pilots for some reason simply running out of fuel—exhausting every drop of usable gas in the tanks. But some also "flame out" because they fail to switch to a tank with fuel remaining.

It's worth noting that not until 1982 did the line receive a "both" tanks fuel

Cost/Performance/Specifications

Model	Year	Average Retail Price	Cruise Speed (kt)	Useful Load (lb)	Std/Opt Fuel (gal)	Engines	TBO (hr)	Overhaul Cost @
210, A	1960-61	$24,000	165	1,600	65, 68	260-hp Cont. IO-470-E	1,500	$10,500
210B, C	1962-63	$27,500	160	1,220	65/84	260-hp Cont. IO-470-S	1,500	$10,500
210D, E	1964-65	$29,000	166	1,260	65/68	260-hp Cont. IO-470-E	1,500	$10,500
210F, G	1966-67	$32,000	166	1,435	65/84, 90	285-hp Cont. IO-520-A	1,700	$11,500
T210F, G	1966-67	$34,500	194	1,350	89	285-hp Cont. TSIO-520-C	1,400	$13,000
210H, J	1968-69	$37,000	167	1,440	90	285-hp Cont. IO-520-A, J	1,700	$11,500
T210H, J	1968-69	$40,000	194	1,350	89	285-hp Cont. TSIO-520-C, H	1,400	$13,000
210K	1970-71	$40,500	167	1,552	90	300-hp Cont. IO-520-L	1,700	$11,500
T210K	1970-71	$44,500	190	1,620	90	285-hp Cont. TSIO-520-H	1,400	$13,000
210L	1972-73	$46,000	164	1,552	90	300-hp Cont. IO-520-L	1,700	$11,500
T210L	1972-73	$50,000	190	1,620	90	285-hp Cont. TSIO-520-H	1,400	$13,000
210L	1974-75	$53,500	164	1,552	90	300-hp Cont. IO-520-L	1,700	$11,500
T210L	1974-75	$58,000	190	1,476	90	285-hp Cont. TSIO-520-H	1,400	$13,000
210L, M	1976-77	$61,500	171	1,552	90	300-hp Cont. IO-520-L	1,700	$11,500
T210L	1976	$65,000	197	1,476	90	285-hp Cont. TSIO-520-H	1,400	$13,000
210M, N	1978-79	$72,000	171	1,552	90	300-hp Cont. IO-520-L	1,700	$11,500
T210M	1977-78	$74,500	197	1,476	90	310-hp Cont. TSIO-520-R	1,400	$14,000
210N	1980-81	$85,000	170	1,580	90	300-hp Cont. IO-520-L	1,700	$11,500
T210N	1979-80	$87,000	197	1,476	90	310-hp Cont. TSIO-520-R	1,400	$14,000
210N	1982-83	$114,000	170	1,580	90	300-hp Cont. IO-520-L	1,700	$11,500
T210N	1981-82	$110,500	221	1,700	90	310-hp Cont. TSIO-520-R	1,600	$14,000
210N, R	1984-85	$156,500	170	1,580	90	300-hp Cont. IO-520-L	1,700	$11,500
T210N	1983-84	$154,500	221	1,700	90	310-hp Cont. TSIO-520-R	1,600	$14,000
210R	1986	$185,000	170	1,580	90	300-hp Cont. IO-520-L	1,700	$11,500
T210R	1985-86	$190,000	221	1,780	87/115	325-hp Cont. TSIO-520-CE	1,600	$14,000

selector position along with the left and right tank choices. This has turned out to be nearly infallible in Cessna Skyhawks. Since there is a generous 89 gallons of usable fuel available—enough for five to six hours at high cruise speeds—it's astonishing that so many pilots flame out. A possible factor on older 210s might be location of the fuel gauge on the right side of the instrument panel. But in 1978 Cessna relocated the gauges on the lower throttle pedestal directly above the fuel tank selector switch.

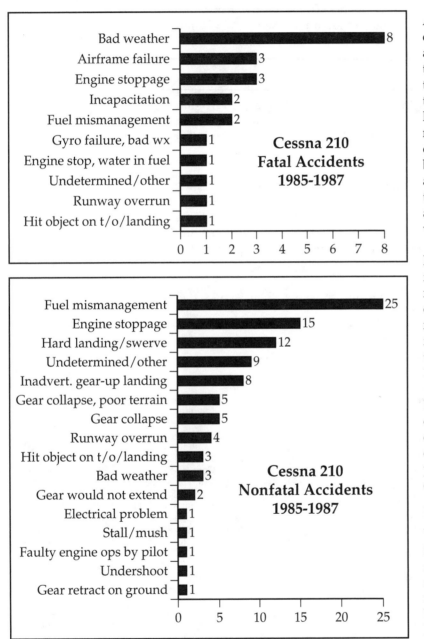

Cessna 210 Fatal Accidents 1985-1987

Cessna 210 Nonfatal Accidents 1985-1987

Another factor that has come in for considerable attention recently centers around the need to make sure during topping-off that the fuel tanks are actually full. This is not always a simple task unless the aircraft is completely level during the refueling process. A number of Centurion pilots have run out of fuel after calculating their range based on full tanks that weren't actually full. The moral is: Don't simply trust the line personnel to fill the tanks, and doublecheck how many gallons were pumped onboard.

It never ceases to amaze how many fliers with complete engine stoppage manage to get the aircraft down without killing themselves. But C-210 fuel mismanagement resulted in only two fatal crashes compared with 25 nonfatal prangs in the three-year period from 1985 to 1987.

By the same token, only three fatal crashes resulted from engine failure, compared to 15 nonfatals. The biggest cause of fatal accidents in the three years: bad weather, accounting for eight crashes.

Engine Failure

What causes C-210 engines to give up in flight? The accident briefs identified a broad mix of problems, such as: oil lube block to connecting rod bearing, with resulting rod failure; main bearing moved; bad overhaul; fuel lines loose; connecting rod bolt failure; crankshaft failures; P210 mag arcing; piston separation; fatigue failure of an exhaust valve; bearing journal failure, starving oil to the conrod; carburetor ice; oil starvation after overhaul, on a test flight. The threat of engine stoppage from vapor lock seems to have receded, if we interpret the latest data correctly. At the end of 1981 Cessna introduced kits designed to eliminate vapor lock by installing vapor return lines. Service Bulletin

SE81-33 applyied to 1976-1979 T-210s and P210s, which Cessna believed had the worst of the vapor problems. The kits are similar to the fuel system in the 1962-1963 aircraft, which have experienced few vapor lock problems.

Then in 1988 the FAA rescinded AD 80-04-09 that had required installation of insulated fuel lines ahead of the firewall (per Cessna Service Letter SE79-60) on some 3,000 T-210s and P210s, to combat the fuel vapor problem. Why after all these years would the agency take such action? A spokesman told us that apparently one aircraft had fallen through the regulatory cracks, so to speak, but in view of the fact that the vapor lock problem—so prominent in the early 1980s—had apparently "gone away," they felt there was no need to enforce installation of the mod on that aircraft.

POHs now advise pilots encountering fuel fluctuations to switch on their aux fuel pumps, taking care, of course, to adjust the mixture at the same time to avoid flooding the engine. But we should note that a number of engine stoppage accidents were unexplained, and the engines worked after the accidents, so the possibility of vapor lock should not be excluded.

One pilot reported he had experienced a catastrophic engine failure in a 1960 C-210 and crashed into the surf off California after part of the engine and prop separated from the airplane, chopping off part of the right wing in the process. He blamed the failure on hydrostatic lock during starting. A bent connecting rod, he said, caused failure of the wrist pin and connecting rod and crank shaft, in that order. The fuel injectors on the IO-470, he noted, were located over the valve stems, and while the plane was parked, a leak in the fuel distribution valve allowed fuel from the overhead tanks to drip onto the stem. It flowed down the valve into the cylinder causing the lock. We had no other reports of this phenomenon on the 210s.

In-flight Airframe Failures

In recent years considerable attention has been focused on the rising rate of in-flight breakups of Centurions. However, our last check of statistics on breakups between the years 1977 and 1983 showed the 210 to be only third worst among the four big retractable singles in this category. The Piper Lance had the poorest record with 6.5 breakups per million hours, with the Beech 35 models second with 4.8 and the C-210 third with 3.3. The Beech 33/36, incidentally, logged the best record in this area, with a rate of only 0.5.

We tallied three fatal airframe failures in C-210s in the three years 1985-1987, all involving apparent encounters with dangerous weather such as thunderstorms. There was some concern that aileron flutter might have contributed to several 210 breakups. Cessna beefed up and rebalanced ailerons starting with the 1985 models, and mod shops now provide retrofits for older aircraft.

Wrinkled Bladders

Watch out for Cessna 210s with fuel bladders. These aircraft were manufactured until the late 1970s. The bladders are expensive to replace, and may have water-trapping wrinkles.

Modifications

Quite a few Centurion owners have good things to say about intercooler mods as a means of cooling off engines and giving extra performance. Three companies specialize in retrofitting this STC'd equipment, or selling kits so it can be done by local mechanics. One is Aircraftsman, 2870 E. Wardlow Rd., Long Beach, Calif. 90807, (714) 393-0884. Their kit is priced at $3,995, and they'll do the installation for $500. Others are Riley International Corp. at 2206 Palomar Airport Rd., Carlsbad, Calif. 92008, (800) 841-1115 with a kit price of $3,200 and Turboplus in Gig Harbor, Wash., (800) 742-4202. Their kit price is $4,995.

We noted one comment on the Turboplus installation in the Cessna Pilots Assn. newsletter that changing the oil filter takes extra effort because a portion of the intercooler system has to be removed to get at it. Aircraftsman's and Riley's intercoolers are less complicated in this context, the C-T210 owner reported.

Speedbrakes

Turboplus used to sell speedbrake kits, but hasn't for some time. Precise Flight has received an STC for electric speedbrakes, which replace hydraulic ones offered in 1984. Price is $2,895, with 32-hour installation time ($1,120, approximately). Precise Flight, 63120 Powell Butte Rd., Bend, Ore. 97701, (800) 547-2558.

Autogas

Petersen Aviation, Route 1, Box 18, Minden, Neb. 68959, (308) 237-9338 has an STC allowing 91 octane autogas to be used in IO-520 engines when modified with their alcohol-water injection system. It's also available for 80/87 octane engines.

Elaborate Robertson STOL mods include drooped ailerons, recontoured wing leading edges, stall fences and gap seals. They are now marketed by R/STOL of Sierra Industries.

Petersen's so-called ADI (anti-detonation injection) system costs $6,000 for the C-210 (plus $1,000 for installation) and comes with a mod to prevent vapor lock, which is more of a problem with autogas. Petersen Aviation also has a fuel system mod for 210s to correct fuel vaporization problems.

Flint Aero in El Cajon, Calif., (619) 448-1551, can provide wingtip tanks for the cantilever wing 210s, adding an extra 33 gallons. The price is $5,775.

R/STOL by Sierra Industries, Inc., in Uvalde, Tex., (512) 278-4381, has taken over the Robertson mods and can install them. One of the most elaborate STOL kits available, for D, E, F models, it includes drooped ailerons when flaps are down, recontoured wing leading edge, stall fences and gap seals. Cost is $5,115 for the kit. Installation should take another 40 to 50 man-hours.

If you fly your 210 in hot climates, Keith Products in Dallas, Tex., (214) 407-1234, will sell you an air-conditioning kit for $7,971. If you are concerned about oil spilling out all over the belly of your Centurion, consider contacting the Cessna Pilots Assn. for a free (for members) set of so-called Baylock drawings (named after the fellow who devised them) that reposition the crankcase breather line. And if you don't mind spending $895 and another 30 hours of installation time, you can get rid of the gear doors and associated hydraulic paraphernalia on your 1970-78 210 with a Uvalde gear door removal kit from the Uvalde Flight Center of Sierra Industries.

Vacuum Loss

To prepare for the unpleasant possibility of loss of vacuum pressure, a number of companies have STCs providing auxiliary vacuum pump systems. Parker Hannifin Corp. has one; Allison-Coffer, Azle, Tex. has an STC for an electrically driven pump as a standby. Also, Precise Flight offers a standby vacuum system that works without any external pump.

To ease fears of aileron flutter, a place with the interesting name Airplane Help, in Carlsbad, Calif. (619) 931-8788, makes updates to meet 1986 210R factory specs. They are 100 percent mass balanced and contain new ribs for stiffening.

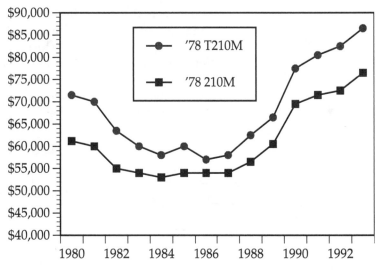

O&N Aircraft Modifications in Factoryville, Pa., (717) 945-3769, does work not only on the 210 ailerons, but on the rudder and elevator as well. The O&N kits insert new rib assemblies in the rudder and aileron and add balance weights to 100 percent mass balance elevator, rudder and ailerons. The kit price is $1,850, or $3,250 installed. The company also provides baggage compartment fuel tanks (29.4 gals. usable) for L, M and N model Centurions at a price of $3,100 for the kit or $3,900 installed.

To squeeze a little better low-speed handling out of the Centurions, aileron gap seals, conical fiberglass wing tips, stall fences and leading edge airfoil mods are available from Horton STOL-Craft, Wellington, Kans., (800) 835-2051.

Societies

Get in touch with the Cessna Pilots Assn., Wichita Mid-Continent Airport, 2120 Airport Rd., P.O. Box 12948, Wichita, Kans. 67277. John M. Frank, (316) 946-4777, is editor of the association's four-color monthly newsletter. The National 210 Owners Assn. headed up by John M. Stratton from La Canada, Calif., (818) 952-6212, publishes a newsletter periodically.

Owner Comments

I own a 1973 Cessna 210L with one partner. In our opinion, the aircraft is, without a doubt, the best six-place single on the market for the money. We have had relatively low maintenance except for the gear doors, which we recently brought up to new standards. The 210 really does fly with six passengers and a small amount of luggage. We can cruise at 160 knots and burn 13 gph at 9,000 feet.

Handling qualities of the 210 are heavy compared to a plane like the Mooney or Bonanza, but the other qualities of speed, payload, fuel, etc. make up for this one factor. The aircraft handles well in weather and is very stable in flight. We are presently insulating our plane like the Riley models and upgrading the windshield to one-quarter inch thickness. We intend to keep our 210 for a long time.

Alex Lancaster
Sarasota, Fla.

I own a 1981 210N, fully IFR equipped and with Rnav, S-tec two-axis autopilot and Horton STOL conversion. Last year the annual was $800, with no problems. This year it was $2,200 due to a $1,200 propeller charge caused by acid eating the prop under the boots from a previous prop cleaning.

The plane is a pleasure, comfortable, indicates 150 knots at 23/23 and will climb at any speed you wish. It handles four people and all the baggage you can stuff in. Range will outlast any bladder. Holds 90 gallons usable, and the overall average is 13-15 gph on fuel. I cannot imagine anything better in a single-engine.

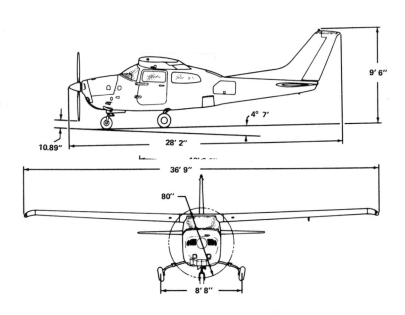

Sidney F. Shapiro
Memphis, Tenn.

The 210's "heavy-on-the-controls" reputation is well deserved. When learning the 210 transition, the increased P-factor during max. performance take-offs made me reconsider the purchase. In cruise (consider that is 98 percent of the flight) the heavy control feel becomes a virtue.

The only handling downsides are: smaller pilots must use the trim to fly

Pilots should note that if the aircraft is not level when being topped off, it may not have a full load of fuel.

the elevator, and during the approach-to-landing phase it is possible to develop a quite-pronounced sink, leading to a hard landing. This is particularly irksome, considering that when loaded in the front seats only, the elevator does not seem to be very effective. The cure, of course, is not to remove the last two inches of power until over the runway.

Maintenance: We will dispense with the usual comments about ARC avionics. We fly serious IFR and removed them all before attempting it. Engine: No engine work has ever been done to this plane although it is at 1,640 hours. I am using Phillips multigrade. The usual batch of vacuum pumps, prop overhauls and starters, and every solenoid has been replaced. Brakes: It is likely that during maintenance a brake line can be positioned so that during gear cycling it will "pop" back into contact with the drum. Care must be used. We have removed the gear doors since fatigue cracks dictated door replacement. We lost two to four knots, and acquired a hollow, "air-over-Coke bottle" sound. It's safer, though.

Problems: Not many really; just a lesson learned. I had complained of the throttle cable being very hard to push when I was low time in the aircraft. So 10 to 12 mechanics tried it, and none seemed to think anything was unusual. I went flying at zero degrees F, with ground wind at 30 mph and found myself high on short final, reduced power to zero. And when it came time to add two to three inches on short final, I could not move the throttle cable and landed in the snow about 500 feet ahead of the runway.

Fortunately, the grass and snow were nearly as well packed and level as the runway (very short) and so no damage, other than to the throttle cable, was caused. I consider this a serious problem, especially in 210s—enough so that I check other 210s on the ramp even at the risk of offending the other pilot. Feedback indicates that when checked out, about half the aircraft had problems in this area. Apparently grease buildup is one problem, and grooving of the core when in the full off position is the other culprit. Before purchase, I had considered many aircraft, but decided on the 210 because of cost, speed, loading and method of loading. We carry a lot of heavy equipment, and I don't want to carry it over the wing.

Louis Bornwasser
Louisville, Ky.

I purchased a used 1976 T210 in 10/86 for $40,000. Since then I have invested another 40 more in paint, interior, King Silver Crown, Northstar loran, Riley intercooler, S-Tec A/P, Shadin fuel flo, odds and ends—1200TTSN, 50 SPOH. Performance: After adding the intercooler a year ago, I saw a 10-knot increase, run at 27 inches MP, true airspeed of 180 knots at 11,500, and a loran GS of 175 knots. This is with four adults (720 lbs), full gear/luggage, two miniature Schnauzers and 65 gallons of fuel. Engine is the TSIO-520, 285 hp. I am very happy with these numbers for my needs.

Handling: The T210 has the reputation of being "yoke-heavy," but this never was a bother to me. I transitioned from a 172 to a 182 to the 210. However, since adding the electric trim and the S-Tec (w/alt. hod, climb and descend functions) with the 300 Navomatic, handling is a dream.

Conclusion: Weighing all the pros and cons of owning a 210, I feel for my needs—a big family and big loads, with a need for decent speed—I know of no single-engine airplane for $40,000 to $80,000 that can do all that.

Ken Lloyd
La Crescenta, Calif.

Early 210s had lots of smaller windows, and the wings had struts, and are less likely to be ranked in breakup statistics.

Cessna Pressurized P210

Porthole-size windows identify the pressurized 210. It's big, fast and able to carry half a ton of payload. Early models carried as many troubles.

Pressurization doesn't come cheap. The penalty in cost and complexity makes the pilot pay extra for comfortable flight above the weather without sucking on oxygen through masks and cannula. In the case of the Cessna P210, pilots paid even more dearly in mechanical grief through the first years of production as the manufacturer struggled to make corrections for a series of design blunders.

The P210s nevertheless (or maybe, therefore) offer the lowest price of entry into the world of pressurized flight—except perhaps for the old Mooney Mustang. And it's heartening to note that P210 owners with upgraded models who responded to our latest call for feedback more often heaped compliments than scorn on the beefy singles.

They waxed euphoric about its ability to lug a humungous load in considerable comfort and quiet at a fraction of the purchase cost (and maintenance misery) of a Piper Malibu. But rarely did they claim the cost of ownership was cheap.

Painful Evolution

The P210 was hardly a fresh, innovative design exercise. Instead, it was a derivative of nearly two decades of C-210 Centurions. But its introduction in 1978 was greeted with accolades and filled order books. Almost 400 rolled off production lines in the first two years, and buyers basked in the glow of Cessna's pronouncements that the aircraft represented a daring leap in technology.

This claim was somewhat wide of the mark, since the airframe, as we've already noted, was vintage '60s, the basic Continental TSIO-520 powerplant had been around for years, and the pressurization system was borrowed from the pressurized Cessna Skymaster (which, incidentally, had its own share of troubles!).

Then, in 1980, the image of the glamorous pressurized single began to crumble. A pair of P210s crashed after engine failures caused by detonation. The FAA issued emergency ADs calling for extra-rich mixtures to cool the engines, along with other anti-detonation measures that reduced performance and, of course, boosted fuel burn significantly. The detonation apparently was caused by a poorly matched engine-turbocharger combination. High back pressure on the exhaust system and very hot induction air temperatures caused the engines to run hot and, sometimes, experience destructive detonation from the excessive heat.

In May 1981 Cessna announced a major program (optimistically called "Performance Plus") to retrofit all P210s at Cessna's cost with a new turbocharger. This was supposed to eliminate the need for ultra-rich mixtures and provide improved range, performance and fuel economy. The FAA even made the new turbo mandatory with an Airworthiness Directive. What the retrofit did, instead, was to lower performance, with P210 pilots finding they couldn't hold manifold pressure or cabin pressure above 16,000 to 18,000 feet. Said one owner: "The new turbo has turned the airplane into a sick dog at altitude."

Another Fix

Late in 1981 Cessna came up with another solution to the problem: a new air induction system that would be retrofitted free by the company, to restore the lost performance. Consisting of a larger intake scoop and redesigned air plenum, it increased manifold pressure by up to seven inches at high altitude. "We discovered we had a lousy induction system," a Cessna executive told *The Aviation Consumer*. Service Letter SE81-45 provided the details. We can't imagine that any P210s escaped this upgrade, but buyers should check it out, to be sure.

More Improvements

Next, with the 1982 models the P210 received a bunch of significant improvements that couldn't be retrofitted to older models, and that make these aircraft more desirable buys, of course. Among these were a new "slope" turbo controller that maintains deck pressure at a steady two inches above manifold pressure, in the process eliminating a lot of unnecessary load on the turbo. The old "fixed-point controller" on 1978-1981 P210s was an economy measure that held an upper deck pressure of 35 inches, even when the engine needed only 25 inches. This caused the turbo to work a lot harder than it had to, resulting in more exhaust back pressure and hotter induction air. (Upper deck pressure is the pressure between the turbo compressor and the throttle butterfly.)

The 1982 models also received a new fuel system with two significant features: proper vapor-return lines and a "left-right-both" fuel tank selector system that reduces chances of fuel mismanagement. Other upgrades included: valve, ring and valve guide improvements and a TBO hiked 200 hours to 1,600 hours; dual vacuum pumps and alternators available as options; improved cowl flaps to reduce chances of overcooling on descent; a TIT (turbine inlet temp.) gauge, along with a restriction of 1,650° TIT to limit leaning and keep exhaust temps down.

Perfection At Last?

In 1985 Cessna brought out the P210R model, with major redesign work that finally turned the aircraft into a real winner. There was a more powerful 325-hp engine. After having often pooh-poohed the need for an intercooler (long used on pressurized Cessna twins), one was finally added to the big single.

Along with engine compartment improvements came significant airframe upgrades like longer wings and a three-foot-longer horizontal stabilizer. The extra wing span (over two feet longer with some 10 feet of new wing area) allowed an extra 30 gallons of fuel in the tips and helped climb performance. Fuel capacity rose to a generous 120 gallons, eliminating the complaint by many P210 pilots that earlier models were a bit short-legged on range. Since the tips feed by gravity into the mains, there is no pumping or switching required, so from the pilot's standpoint the aircraft seems to have one big tank.

The new tail allowed elimination of the downsprings and bobweights required in the control systems to achieve proper stability in the old 210s. This made pitch forces much lighter, so takeoff rotation, steep turns and the landing flare could finally be managed with one hand.

On top of all that, the new P210R flies much faster than older P210s. Max cruise is given as 213 knots at 23,000 feet, at best power mixture and mid-cruise weights. That is more than 20 knots faster than the earlier model. Under more typical conditions—65% power at 20,000 feet with best economy mixture—book cruise is still a healthy 190 knots.

Choosing a Model

From these model transitions, it's obvious that the most stellar of all the pressurized 210s is the P210R model, though it commands a hefty price commensurate with its value. And here we're talking about $235,000 or so retail for an average-equipped '85 model, according to the *Aircraft Bluebook Price Digest.* Next in rank is the "Mark II" model built in 1982 and 1983 (none were delivered in 1984). The '82 model was going for about $145,000 at last glance at the *Digest.* And finally, the last choice would be the "Mark I" models built between 1978 and 1981. The former lists at around $96,000.

Used-Plane Market

Although not many years ago the P210 was held in such low esteem that one could be bought for about the same price as a comparable T210, time has seen its value climb and the margin between the two increase. So today where a 1983 T210 goes for about $156,500, according to the *Bluebook,* the '83 P210 could fetch around $168,000.

Looking over the high-performance single field, however, we see that the Beech B36TC remains in a class by itself, on a price ledge far above the lower-grade pressurized Cessna. Check the average cost of an unpressurized '83 B36TC, for example: it's $181,500. Obviously, a more equitable match-up would be an '85 P210R, with all its improvements, and the '85 B36TC. Now the balance swings in the other direction, with the figures coming out to $235,000 for the Cessna vs. $220,000 for the Beech.

Performance

Owners report fairly potent cruise speeds for the big single, ranging from 175 to 195 knots, depending on power setting and altitude, with the P210R breaking the 200-knot barrier quite easily. Fuel burns are substantial, however: 15-20 gph for

Cost/Performance/Specifications

Model	Year	Average Retail Price	Cruise Speed (kts)	Useful Load (lbs)	Fuel Std/Opt (gals)	Engine	TBO (hrs)	Overhaul Cost
P210N	1978	$96,000	187	1,600	90	310-hp Cont. TSIO-520-P	1,400	$18,000
P210N	1979	$104,000	187	1,600	90	310-hp Cont. TSIO-520-P	1,400	$18,000
P210N	1980	$114,000	187	1,600	90	310-hp Cont. TSIO-520-P	1,400	$18,000
P210N	1981	$129,000	187	1,600	90	310-hp Cont. TSIO-520-P	1,400	$18,000
P210N	1982	$145,000	187	1,600	90	310-hp Cont. TSIO-520-AF	1,600	$18,500
P210N	1983	$168,000	187	1,600	90	310-hp Cont. TSIO-520-AF	1,600	$18,500
P210R	1985	$235,000	212	1,629	85/115	325-hp Cont. TSIO-520-CF	1,600	$19,000
P210R	1986	$275,000	212	1,629	85/115	325-hp Cont. TSIO-520-CF	1,600	$19,000

early models and up to 23 gph at 75% on the P210R. Because of time-to-climb limitations and cabin pressurization levels, most P210 pilots told us they prefer cruising below 20,000 feet—at 14,000 to 19,000 feet on average. One owner of a '79 P210N claimed, however, that he could get climb rates of 700-800 fpm with a cruise climb of 120 knots low and 110 knots above 10,000 feet. One P210R owner said, on the other hand, that he could "easily achieve" 1,000 fpm to altitude.

As we noted earlier, range on the 90-gallon fuel capacity of early models is considered limiting by many owners. "Currently, our range is about 750 nm with a 30-minute reserve," said one, noting that in his next P210 he hoped to get the wingtip fuel tanks to increase range. "Because of its high carrying capability," he said, "we frequently are nowhere near gross weight when I take off with my wife and two children and baggage."

The six-place cabin is snug and cozy and quiet and, if pressurization is on in the summer—boiling hot. Even with full fuel, expect to carry up to five adults and baggage. Rear seats are kid-sized.

And another pilot complained that he found it impossible to actually load a "full" 89 gallons in his '79 P210N. The NTSB, incidentally, is investigating complaints that Centurions in general cannot always be loaded to book figures, especially if the aircraft are not on a perfectly level surface during fueling. "I now flight plan to use no more than 70 gallons," the pilot above warned.

Typically, pilots also told us they preferred not to lean too aggressively, in order to prolong engine life. "Gas is relatively cheap when overhauls and reliability are considered," said one. A conservative rule of thumb is to plan for 20 gph, block to block, at high cruise speeds. With IFR reserves, that's only about three hours' cruising time.

Handling

The P210 is a heavy hunk of machinery, on the ground and in the air. As one owner observed, don't expect to shove one around on the ramp without help, or a hand-operated power tug. The routing of control cables through tight-fitting air seals where they pass through the pressure vessel naturally increases control forces. But as with most Centurions, aileron forces are lighter than pitch forces by a large degree, though elevator response is much improved in the P210R model.

Part of the reason for the heavy pitch forces is the typically monster loading envelope permitted by the aircraft. Load more in the rear, and bicep power required is reduced on the landing flare. Owners universally commend the Rock of Gibraltar stability of the aircraft in IFR flight and turbulence.

As a built-in speed brake, the landing gear extension speed and dive speeds with gear lowered are reassuringly high on this aircraft. On the '78 P210, gear lowering speed is 140 knots/161 mph indicated, but with the '79 models it was raised to 165 knots/195 mph, thanks to elimination of the gear doors. With both aircraft, however, the pilot can dive right to redline Vne speed of 200 knots/230 mph with the gear already extended. Needless to say, this might come in handy on a speedy descent if pressurization were lost.

Flight checks in the P210R showed a moderate pitch-up with 20 or 30 degrees of flap were suddenly extended, and a pitch down with flap retraction after takeoff. The stall was preceded by a good horn warning and light buffet, with excellent aileron control down through stall recovery.

Loading

All the Centurions are renowned for their load-hauling, and the P210 is no exception. Owners typically report payloads after full fuel of a whopping 900 to 1,000 pounds. That translates to five (170-pound) guys and a bit of baggage.

On top of that, the loading envelope is so broad and forgiving that it's extremely difficult to louse up c.g. calculations. In fact, the P210 flier is more likely to find himself loaded out the front end of the center-of-gravity envelope rather than the rear, particularly on well-equipped airplanes. Note that there are five loading areas: three rows of seats, plus a rear baggage compartment inside the pressure vessel, and another one farther back, outside the pressure enclosure. ("Watch out for shampoo and toothpaste," warned one owner.)

Cabin Comfort

One owner summed it up: "It is exceptionally quiet and smooth. Passengers love it. They feel like they're in an airliner." As with other Centurions, things are fine for riders in the front four seats; but relegate the dinky rear seats to kids or baggage. Cabin width in front is a decent, if not lavish 42 inches.

An especially snug feeling is fostered by the smaller-than-normal windows and quiet cabin, thanks to pressure sealing and turbocharger muffling of exhaust roar. In winter, the extra heat kicked out by the pressurization system further enhances snugness. But in summer, it's a bummer unless the aircraft has air conditioning, and pilots may prefer to keep it off until climbing to cooler altitudes. Otherwise, they can roast. "Even though Cessna has designed a fairly efficient bleed air intercooler for the cabin air," one owner told us, "the air still enters the cabin piping hot."

Naturally, the great charm of the aircraft is the benefit of pressurization—namely, the elimination of oxygen masks at altitudes above 12,500 feet and reduction of ear discomfort among passengers and pilots in descents. But be aware that the P210 pressurization system is not Star Wars technology. The pressure differential is a rather anemic 3.35 pounds, the lowest of any current pressurized airplane. On top of that, the system has no rate controller. It simply starts to pressurize at the altitude selected by the pilot, maintains that cabin altitude as long as it can, and then maintains the max differential as the climb continues.

Maintenance

Owners don't characterize the P210's maintenance burden as nasty, but they concede it's no light consideration, especially to maintain a feeling of security. "We have obviously been very happy with the airplane and would recommend it highly," said one, "but only if you're prepared to shell out the maintenance dollars required to keep it in tiptop flying condition." He figured direct per-hour operating costs, excluding interest and hangar fees, ran them about $110, based on a 50-hour progressive maintenance schedule.

Naturally, the 1,400-hour TBO on the earlier engines is nothing to boast about. But even that figure's not etched in stone. "The 1,400-hour engines will make

TBO," said one owner, "but usually with one top overhaul. Mine was topped at 700 hours." Judging from Service Difficulty Reports, cylinder cracking is a matter to be reckoned with. Also, buyers should check to see if aircraft have Inconel exhaust systems. Without them, the P210 system is regarded as quite troublesome and carries a 50-hour AD inspection for cracks.

Interestingly, on the other hand, gear malfunctions show up rather infrequently on the P210's SDR roster—something of a refreshing departure among Cessna singles. But magneto failures and vacuum pump failures showed a disturbing trend. Some of the mag failures resulted in engine stoppage and forced landings. And vacuum loss in IMC can spell disaster. Dual systems can be retrofitted to all P210s, and are mandated by AD for any equipped with the known-icing option.

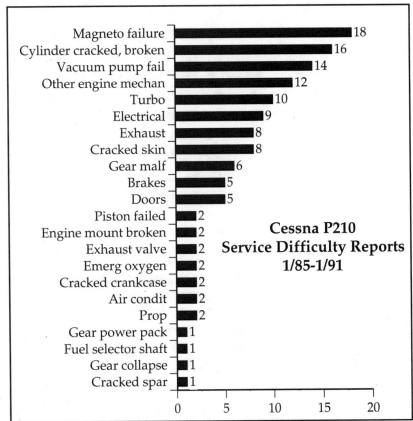

Cessna P210
Service Difficulty Reports
1/85-1/91

By the same token, dual 60-amp alternators were available on 1982 P210s, and some 1980 and 1981 models were retrofitted at the factory. Some earlier P210s have a small emergency standby generator, which is not as good, but better than nothing.

Most owners responding to our survey indicated they had experienced little trouble out of the ordinary with Cessna's ARC avionics—another refreshing development and a departure from past owner reports. But one owner complained that Cessna's avionics cooling fan was noisy and failed frequently. He preferred a King retrofit.

A Philosophy to Live By

In summary, buyers should be prepared to assume some not insignificant maintenance costs commensurate with operating a complicated aircraft. "A purchaser needs to consider the P210 as a large general aviation airplane in keeping with the traditions of 400 series Cessnas, etc.," advised one owner. "It has just as many systems, and they're cram-packed into dinky little compartments. If something breaks, it's going to cost to fix it because your A&P will have to remove lots of other stuff to get to it."

Safety Record

The greatest portion of P210 accidents in recent years can be attributed to engine mechanical problems, fuel exhaustion and fuel mismanagement. Luckily, these most often were not killers. Instead, weather accidents dominated the fatal toll—flying from VFR into IFR conditions or simply improper IFR operation or spatial disorientation.

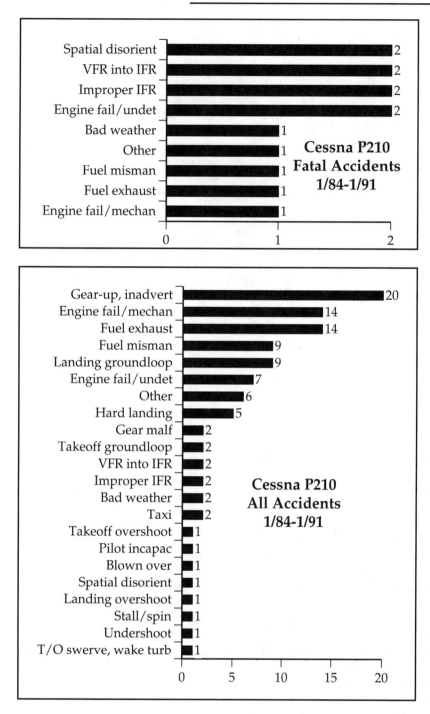

Cessna P210 Fatal Accidents 1/84-1/91

Cessna P210 All Accidents 1/84-1/91

Modifications

Intercoolers can be provided by several organizations. Among them are Riley International Corp. (kit price $3,200) in Carlsbad, Calif., (800) 841-1115; Turboplus (kit price $4,995), in Gig Harbor, Wash., (800) 742-4202; and Aircraftsman ($3,995), at Long Beach, Calif., (714) 393-0884.

Speedbrake kits are available from Precise Flight ($2,895) at Bend, Ore., (800) 547-2558. Turboplus used to offer them, but hasn't sold kits for some time.

Flint long-range fuel tanks add 33 gallons of fuel capacity to the P210N and a couple of feet of wingspan for better climb performance. Cost of the kit is $5,775 from Flint Aero, El Cajon, Calif., (619) 448-1551.

Rudder, elevator and ailerons can be stiffened and mass balanced to improve the flutter margin, by O&N Aircraft Modifications at Factoryville, Pa., (717) 945-3769. This company also can provide baggage compartment fuel tanks, priced at $3,900 installed, with 219.4 gals. usable. Myron Olson also was working on an STC for a 450-shp Allison-powered turboprop version that would cost $330,000 on an exchange basis.

The R/STOL Hi-Lift Systems kit is offered by Sierra Industries at Uvalde, Tex., (512-278-4381). This firm also can eliminate gear doors on early P210s.

Organizations

The Cessna Pilots Assn. headed up by John Frank out of Wichita, Kans., (316) 946-4777, supports the P210 and all other Cessnas. They publish a slick monthly color magazine. (The National 210 Owners Assn. headed up by John M. Stratton out of La Canada, Calif., (818) 952-6212, publishes a newsletter periodically.)

Owner Comments

I am part owner of a 1979 Cessna P210, and a wonderful airplane it is. Let me give you some of the good news first, and then I'll close with some of the bad news: cost! My two partners and I fly the airplane approximately 350 to 400 hours per year. Many of our trips are 700 miles or more. It's a wonderful cross-country airplane in which we frequently carry four grown men, four sets of golf clubs and baggage and full fuel. I know of no other single-engine airplane anywhere near this price that can accomplish such a mission.

We flight plan for 175 knots TAS; however, at 19,000 feet we are frequently approaching 200 knots. We burn approximately 20 gph, including climb and descent. Our aircraft is intercooled, and we can climb out at a very high rate without any significant cooling problems. However, we must be careful during descent not to supercool the engine.

The aircraft is extremely smooth to fly, and control forces are not excessive if the aircraft is properly trimmed. Fail to trim properly, and you've got a real horse on your hands. It's a stable instrument platform, and we feel most confident flying the aircraft in all types of weather. In my judgment, de-icing equipment is a must for this type of airplane, and you can be assured that in the next P210 we get that we will have known-icing certification.

Because of its high carrying capability, we frequently are nowhere near max gross weight when I take off with my wife and two children and baggage. Accordingly, I hope that in our next P210 we will get the wingtip fuel tanks to increase our range. Currently, our range is about 750 nm with a 30-minute reserve. The tip tanks would get us to 1,000 nm with IFR reserve or 4.5 hours of IFR flying with 1.5 hrs of reserve.

Enlarged airscoop is one of the features of the final, finest P210R, with a bigger engine and intercooling. Open slot on the underbelly is the doorless gear well. Later P210s without gear doors have high gear lowering speeds of 165 knots, acting as speedbrakes for quick descents if pressurization should be lost.

We have Cessna 400 avionics, which have not caused any significant problems for us, although when they overheat we periodically have a problem where the avionics will recycle, and all of the frequencies will be lost.

The direct per-hour operating costs excluding interest and hangar fees runs us about $110 based upon a periodic 50-hour progressive maintenance schedule. In addition, we periodically replace parts such as the vacuum pump and the gear motor, even though they're still operating properly.

We do not baby the engine and normally fly it with 70-75% power, but we do not lean very aggressively, and in the past 500 hours have had only minor problems, with the exception of having to replace two cylinders that had cracked. Mattituck Air Base indicated that they had similar problems in other engines, and as a result paid for part of the cylinder replacements, even though the engine was out of warranty. (By the way, Mattituck is a great place with which to do business.)

As a result, we don't feel the manner in which we fly the airplane contributed to the cylinder problems. All in all, this has been a great airplane. Because of our maintenance schedule, we have had only one no-go situation in 2.5 years, and that was when a brake lining separated during taxi.

There is no question that this is an all-weather aircraft. Accordingly, it should have some things that it doesn't, such as boots, a stand-by alternator and copilot instruments. We have been very happy with the airplane and would recommend it highly, but only if you're prepared to shell out the maintenance dollars required to keep it in tiptop flying condition.

Roger J. Tuttle
Bedford, N.H.

My partners and I own a 1978 Cessna P210 which was modified in 1985 (Javelin Conversion). This modification substantially improved performance, allowing cruise climb to FL230 at 1,000 fpm or better and level cruise at 200 knots TAS.

The most desirable aspect of the P210, however, is its pressurization (to FL230 without O_2). This one feature makes the aircraft worthwhile for anyone who flies much of the time above 12,500 msl. Add exceptional stability, and you have an instrument platform unequaled in a reasonably priced single. The comfort, performance and range (with optional baggage fuel tank) make 1,000-nm trips an easy one-day affair. The annual averages around $1,100 here in Colorado. We have not had any difficulty with parts availability.

One caution: The P210 is a high-performance aircraft that demands a continuing high level of proficiency from its pilot.

David B. McDaniel
Grand Junction, Colo.

My company owns a 1979 P210N equipped with a Turboplus intercooler and a full panel of Cessna ARC 400 series avionics. I fly the airplane on company business coast-to-coast, border-to-border approximately 250 hours a year. I normally fly between 13,000 ft. MSL and FL200 at 21 in. and 2450 rpm. Fuel flow is 15-16 gph at 50-75° rich of peak EGT. This power setting delivers a TAS of 175-180 knots, depending on temperature and altitude. With full fuel (534 lbs.) my payload is close to 1,000 pounds.

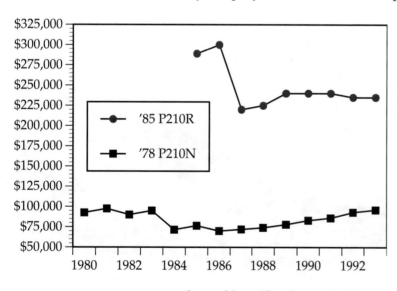

The airplane is comfortable, fast and carries a respectable load. The pressurization is very nice, although the original factory door seals were a constant problem (they leaked). I recently replaced them with electric inflatable door seals, and this solved the problem. The Cessna/ARC radios have performed adequately with no more than normal problems and repair costs. (I've been flying with Cessna radios for 10 years and have never had any unusual or overly expensive problems.)

One definite problem area is the fuel tanks. Maximum fuel is 89 gallons, but I've found it impossible to get that much actual fuel in the tanks. On one occasion after *topping* both tanks, I had to make an emergency landing when the engine quit after burning only 79.2 gallons on the totalizer, and no matter what we tried we couldn't get more than 81 gallons in the airplane. I now flight plan to use no more than 70 gallons. I've read all the articles and heard Cessna's arguments about the 210's fuel system, but the bottom line is *it's a bad system*.

I have the oil changed every 25-30 hours with inspections at 50 and 100 hours, plus the annual. My expenses for the last 12 months, with 248 flying hours include $1,560 for the annual, $2,939 for miscellaneous repairs, $2,884 for avionics and $1,234 for oil changes. This (plus other items like insurance, fuel, hangar, mortgage, etc.) works out to $143.40 per hour. I bet this is a lot cheaper than flying a Piper Malibu.

Conclusion: Dollar for dollar this is the best single-engine airplane available. I wouldn't want anything else unless it were a pressurized twin.

Lengthened wingtips on the P210R yield more fuel capacity and better climb. Lengthened horizontal tail greatly improves handling and lowers pitch forces, plus eliminating cumbersome downsprings and bobweights.

Ray Yillik
Ontario, Calif.

We added Precise Flight speed brakes (to our 1985 P210R), which we highly recommend. They provide an excellent way of managing descent from the flight levels without shock cooling. This is especially helpful descending into Denver from the west, where you may be held very high very late.

The Continental TSIO-540-CE engine presented the only difficulty when compression dipped to 28 at 507 hours and required a top overhaul. Continental through Arapahoe Aero and Westar Aviation stepped up to take care of the problem and added a choke as well as cermichrome. In the 200 hours since then, there have been no problems. Engine temperature is running about 50 degrees cooler than before.

Marc R. Rumack
Littleton, Colo.

I own a 1982 P210. The '82 models are debugged versions of the earlier vintage. The changes are many and varied, but the redesigned fuel system, turbo and induction system and factory dual systems are most important. The leather, fabrics and other interior appointments were also greatly improved in '82 to create a vastly different and more reliable P210. Pressurization spoils. I don't always need it, but the strong, quiet, extremely comfortable cabin is full time—high or low. The system is simple. Maybe too simple. I would occasionally appreciate a variable rate control.

I've loaded five men and gear with good results and no complaints. I have yet to haul six, however. I occasionally remove the center seat closest to the door. Doing so provides easy entry/exit, room to wallow, and leaves a spot for my Golden Retriever.

The P210 doesn't fly like a Pitts, but it is responsive and unbeatable in the bumps. It doesn't wiggle around like an A36 or a Malibu, so I save money on sic-sacs. The notorious "heavy elevator" goes away with people and/or gear in back. Proper trim management covers the pressure when lightly loaded.

I installed a Riley intercooler, which is a nice addition. I bought it for engine longevity and reliability, but the performance is there if you want it—as advertised. I run at 70-75% (I/C corrected) on no less than 17.5 gph and 50° to 100° rich of peak TIT. Gas is relatively cheap when overhauls and reliability are considered. My mechanic, Irv Swieter, Swieter Aircraft, Inc., does a lot of 210 work, so parts and support have never been a problem. I chose the P210 over an A36. I admire Beech quality, but I'd need a booted 58P to match the capabilities and mission profile of the Cessna P210.

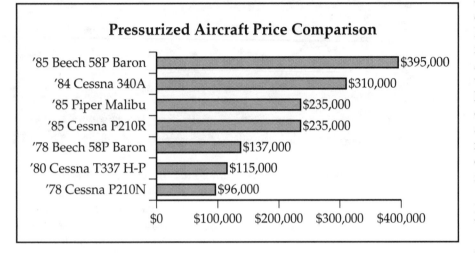

Pressurized Aircraft Price Comparison

'85 Beech 58P Baron	$395,000
'84 Cessna 340A	$310,000
'85 Piper Malibu	$235,000
'85 Cessna P210R	$235,000
'78 Beech 58P Baron	$137,000
'80 Cessna T337 H-P	$115,000
'78 Cessna P210N	$96,000

Robert W. Petersen
Waterloo, IA

I enclose copies of my file on problems I have had with my Cessna P210 with reference to maintenance, company backup and the airplane's strengths and weaknesses. It seems to me that one could sum it up by stating that Cessna took a good engineering concept, cut corners on component quality, assembled the aircraft with an American automobile quality control mentality that has allowed the Japanese to clobber us, and then whined and stonewalled their way out of financial responsibility for the situation. If an owner has the perseverance and the funds to buy his way out of the situation, the result is a fine-performing aircraft.

Norman E. Gaar
Overland Park, Kans.

I moved to pressure from a Bellanca Turbo Viking because my wife suffered painful ear block problems on descent. The P210 has ended the problem. And we've eliminated the oxygen masks. The seller of this 1978 P210 claimed that I could true 180 knots at 68% power at altitudes I favor: 14,500 to 17,500. It comes very close, and the higher the better. We full fuel plan on just over 900 pounds legal in cabin and baggage compartment; CG is rarely a problem.

Maintenance costs are low. The first engine went to full 1,400 hours TBO; we are working on the second. Annual costs are modest because we've had few squawks of consequence. No parts problems because we haven't needed many parts. We still have the gear doors, which were eliminated on later models, and can be removed via an STC on this one. They work fine, and the P210 is quieter and faster with the doors. Am I happy with the P210? Yes! One final point: Its value has increased significantly since I bought it. It has been a good investment.

Wayne Thoms
No. Hollywood, Calif.

Cessna
Skymaster 337

Cessna's push-pull twin, the 337 Skymaster, is a tantalizingly risky used-plane bargain. Suffering from a poor reputation among pilots, it can be bought at fire-sale prices well below the cost of other twins of similar performance.

But the potential downside is huge maintenance bills—particularly in the turbo-charged and pressurized models—because of poor engineering and quality control at Cessna's Pawnee Division. On the other hand, for a pilot who knows the fine points, shops around carefully, and who doesn't object to some of the Skymaster's unique features, a used 337 can provide a lot of performance for a little bit of money.

Sleek and slow, the aircraft offers superb visibility all around since the leading edge of the wing is set far back on the fuselage. Centerline thrust is supposed to add a safety factor with an engine out. The small windows identify the pressurized model.

Genealogy

The Skymaster first appeared in 1964 as the fixed-gear Model 336. With its front-rear engine layout, high strut-braced wing, and down-and-welded gear, the 336 was a radical departure indeed from the light twins of the day. But Cessna sold almost 200 336s that first year, and revamped it into the retractable-gear 337 Skymaster in 1965. The design evolved only a little over the years, progressing from the A model in 1966 through the 1978-80 H model, with minor refinements. The engines remained the same throughout the Skymaster's career: the 210-hp six-cylinder Continental IO-360.

A turbocharged version, the T-337B, appeared in 1967, but was dropped in 1972 with the addition to the Skymaster line of the pressurized P-337 version, with uprated 225-hp engines. The turbo was revived in 1978, but Skymaster sales had begun slipping by then, despite the great general aviation sales boom of the late 1970s. After selling between 80 and 115 Skymasters a year throughout the early and mid-1970s, Cessna saw sales drop to only 61 in the boom year of 1979 and less than 50 in 1980. Cessna pulled the plug following the 1980 model year, after a total Skymaster production run of 2,058, plus 332 pressurized versions.

Major model changes were few. Gross weight crept up over the years, starting at 4,200 with the 337A and increasing to 4,300 (B model), 4,400 (C model) and 4,440 (E model). With the 1971 F model, Cessna increased takeoff weight to 4,630 pounds, but max landing weight remained 4,400. (The P-337, with its 30 extra hp, had a takeoff weight of 4,700 pounds, and max landing weight of 4,465.)

Empty weight crept up as well over the years, however, and the useful load of the later versions wasn't all that much greater than the early models, although the 1971 model claimed to have 150 pounds more useful than the 1970 version.

In addition, the 1971 model had padding of the panel, door posts and seats for improved crashworthiness, plus an extra engine access door. In 1972 the electrical system—a long-time Skymaster trouble-spot—was improved. The 1973 model saw the replacement of the straight hydraulic landing gear system with the electro-hydraulic "power pack" gear, a change that turned out to be of dubious value. In 1974, the prop syncrophasers were improved. The 1975 model had more fuel capacity in the long-range tank option—148 gallons, up from 124. Radar was introduced as an option in 1977.

Cessna's last-gasp refinement efforts were, unfortunately, more cosmetic than real. The final 1980 version sported a "new instrument panel treatment including a burled elm wood grain panel cover that adds rich, attractive styling." Despite the irresistible lure of such features, almost nobody bought any Skymasters that year, the airplane's last.

Used Plane Market

To be blunt, the Skymaster is one of the worst dogs on the used-plane market. The oldest models go for only $26,000 in reasonable shape—a little more than half the price of a Twin Comanche of similar vintage. If the engines are due for overhaul, you could probably buy an old Skymaster for four figures if you really wanted to.

(Like many old, low-value twins with expensive engines, the value of an early-vintage Skymaster depends almost entirely on the engine condition. A double overhaul will run close to $29,000, not much less than the value of the plane with the new engines.)

Later models do better. A 1980 cream-puff IFR Turbo Skymaster might go for around $79-80,000—about $8,000 less than a comparable Piper Seneca II, which uses the same engines. But the Skymaster still pales by comparison to a B55 Baron, for example, a 1980 version of which is worth over $125,000. Even a 1980 pressurized Skymaster would command only about $115,000.

In terms of percentage resale value retained, the Skymaster looks pretty dismal. Assuming "bluebook" retail prices for a 1978 model, the Skymaster has retained just 50 percent of its original value. That situation is improving, though: three years ago it was only 45 percent.

The Skymaster resale picture is improving, like that for many airplanes Several people we talked to say that 337 prices have been continuing to rise. Like many aircraft that got bad reputations early (Yankee, Cardinal, etc.), the Skymaster may be starting to achieve a sort of cult status, with most of the planes eventually falling into the hands of people who like their peculiarities, which tends to keep the supply down and prices up.

Performance

The Skymaster lacks the sizzling performance of a B55 Baron, or the frugal efficiency of a Twin Comanche. But it doesn't look bad next to the generation of "light-light" twins (the Piper Seminole and Beech Duchess) that followed it. And the turbocharged models can put up some pretty decent cruise numbers if you take them high enough.

Book cruise speed for the normally aspirated Skymaster is about 165-169 knots. But, as one owner put it, "The manufacturer doesn't cheat any more than normal on owner's manual performance figures, and it comes pretty close to delivering the claimed performance when it is 800 pounds under gross." In the real world, typical Skymaster cruise speeds are around 150-155 knots, with the occasional optimist reporting 160 knots. One owner who also owns an A36 Bonanza reports that the two aircraft have almost identical cruise and climb performance.

The turbo and pressurized models will push 190 knots at 20,000 feet, their maximum certified altitude. At the non-oxygen middle altitudes, 170-180 knots is a typical speed for the turbo models.

Reported fuel burns ranged from 16 gph to 22 gph, with 19-20 gph typical for a 150-155-knot cruise. For comparison, a Twin Comanche will do about the same speed on 100 less horsepower and a lot less gas. Efficiency is not a Skymaster hallmark.

Landing gear malfunctioning has been a chronic trouble point with Skymasters, and the biggest cause of accidents.

Rate of climb ranges from a modest 1,300 fpm in the old 336 to a pathetically lethargic 940 fpm in the last 337H models. (Climb goes down as gross weight goes up.) We're unaware of any other twin-engine airplane with a book rate of climb below 1,000 fpm—even the old 150-hp Apache had a book climb of 1,250 fpm with both engines running.

Runway performance, on the other hand, is pretty good. Some owners even go so far as to claim STOL qualities at moderate weights. The Skymaster uses the good old Cessna formula—long, tapered wing and big flaps—to achieve stall speeds (and therefore takeoff and landing speeds) well below those of most twins. Stall speeds with flaps range from 63-70 mph, depending on the gross weight of the particular model—10 to 20 mph below conventional twins like the 310 and Baron.

As a result, a Skymaster will get off the ground in less than 1,000 feet at gross weight—a feat very few other twins can manage. Barrier performance is not quite so good, however; the lethargic climb rate brings the Skymaster's 50-foot takeoff figures down to the middle of the light-twin pack. Landing ground rolls are around 700 feet, also among the best of the twins.

Single-engine Performance

The single-engine climb rates of all the light twins tend to be very similar—200 to 300 fpm—because engine-out climb rate is a certification point around which the airplane is designed. FAA requires a certain minimum climb, figured by a formula relating to stall speed, and the manufacturers typically bump up the gross weight to the point at which the airplane just barely meets the FAA minimum. (Any excess engine-out climb capability is, in effect, wasted payload. And payload numbers sell airplanes.)

So it's no surprise that the Skymaster's engine-out rate of climb is right in there at

200-300 fpm on most models. What is surprising is the difference between the front and rear engines. Using the 1974 model as an example, rear engine climb is 320 fpm, but the front engine can manage only 270 fpm. The reason is apparently that when the rear propeller is turning, the airflow over the rear fuselage remains attached. But it separates when the rear prop stops, increasing drag.

Engine-out service ceiling is also typical for light twins—7,100 on the front engine, 6,100 on the rear (again, we're using the 1974 model as an example.) The turbo models naturally do a lot better; engine-out ceilings range from 15,000 to 20,000 feet.

Payload-Range

A Cessna press release from the 1970s describes the Skymaster as "a full six-place airplane with nearly a ton of useful load." This is utter bullpuckie. One owner accurately describes the two rear seats as "a joke, to say the least." And the press release conveniently forgets to mention that with the fifth and sixth seats installed, there is no baggage space whatsoever. (If you must carry six people and bags, an optional belly cargo pod was an option on later models.) Consider the Skymaster a nice four-placer.

Actual real-world useful loads run around 1,500 pounds—not bad at all, and several hundred pounds more than a Twin Comanche, for example. Standard fuel is 88 gallons, and that still leaves better than 900 pounds available for payload, more than enough for those four passengers and lots of baggage. Standard fuel is just barely adequate, however, unless you throttle way back—a little more than three hours with IFR reserves at fast cruise.

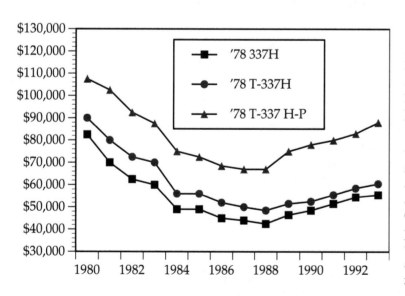

The long-range tanks—148 gallons in 1975-80 models, 123 in earlier models—solve the range limitations nicely, at the expense of payload, of course. One owner reports that with long-range tanks full, he has seven-plus hours at 150 knots with 650 pounds of payload (three people and bags). Not a bad compromise.

Accommodation

As we said before, consider the Skymaster a four-seater, with two more available in an emergency if nobody has any baggage. Oddly, the P-337 may carry only five people; it was certified under different rules that require an emergency exit in a six-seat airplane. Rather than put in the exit, Cessna simply limited the seating to five.

The air-stair door is an attempt to give the Skymaster a "big-airplane feel," but it gets mixed reviews. "Cumbersome" is how one owner puts it.

The Skymaster is a roomy airplane. "Lots of creature comforts," reports one owner. "Good cockpit space," says another. "I am comfortable with my 6'4", 200 pounds and very long legs. In other planes, like the Mooney, Cardinal and Trinidad, the yoke pins my left leg against the side bulkhead. Not the Skymaster."

Visibility is excellent, about as good as it gets in any light airplane, single or twin. The view down is unlimited, of course, and the wing is set far back enough that it doesn't block upward vision, as it does in most Cessna singles. The good visibility is not only a safety feature, but it adds to the feeling of roominess in the cockpit as well.

The Skymaster may be roomy, but it's noisy. Both engines are attached directly to the passenger compartment, and sympathetic vibration can be a problem, particularly without the prop synchronizers.

Handling Qualities

In normal flight, the Skymaster has typical Cessna handling: heavy in pitch, reasonably responsive ailerons. (The P-model has especially light ailerons.) Pilots praise its IFR stability. "It makes a stable instrument platform and handles turbulence well, without excess yaw," is a typical comment.

Windows became smaller through the years, as unpressurized models took on the tiny-window format of their pressurized stablemates, presumably for conformity of construction.

The noteworthy aspect of the Skymaster's handling—indeed, the whole reason for the airplane's existence—shows up when an engine fails. Instead of the normal yaw-roll-stall-spin scenario that too often follows engine failure in a normal twin, the Skymaster continues to fly straight ahead. An unprepared or rusty pilot can take his time and concentrate on the task of identifying and feathering the prop on the failed engine, without worrying about losing control.

The Skymaster has no minimum control speed in the usual sense. The FAA considers the Skymaster so easy to handle with a failed engine that it doesn't even require a normal multi-engine rating to fly it. Instead, there's a special center-line-thrust rating.

One owner sums up the Skymaster design philosophy succinctly: "Much of my operation is mountain, IFR and/or night. I wouldn't feel safe in a single-engine plane, but since I only fly 100-125 hours a year, I don't feel I could stay as current and competent as I should be in a standard-configured twin."

Another owner, however, cautions Skymaster pilots against overconfidence. "I do think the plane has been oversold to low-time pilots. I was at or perhaps beyond my level of competence in the plane at 500 hours with 18 months of IFR experience. I am still not as smooth in controlling this plane as I would like to be. I believe that some of the blame for the Skymaster's high accident rate must be placed on the seductiveness of thinking that centerline thrust makes a twin just like a single. This is just not true."

We heard from one Skymaster pilot who credits the airplane's engine-out handling qualities with saving his life. He had skipped the preflight before takeoff, failing to notice that (for reasons too complex to explain here) the left fuel tank was full but the right one empty.

Shortly after takeoff, he found he needed nearly full right aileron just to stay level. Then the rear engine, feeding from the right tank, quit. "In any other twin, the flight would have terminated right then," he says.

But he was able to keep the Skymaster under control, restart the engine, climb to altitude, and burn off enough fuel to eventually make a normal landing. "No other airplane would have forgiven my oversight, singles included," he reports.

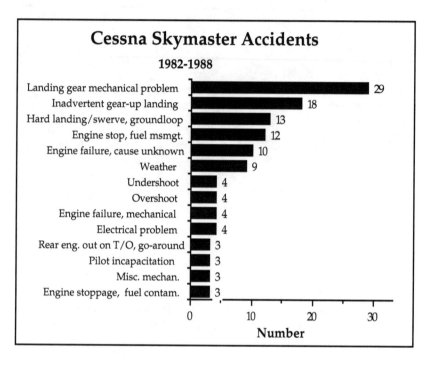

Cessna Skymaster Accidents

1982-1988

Cause	Number
Landing gear mechanical problem	29
Inadvertent gear-up landing	18
Hard landing/swerve, groundloop	13
Engine stop, fuel msmgt.	12
Engine failure, cause unknown	10
Weather	9
Undershoot	4
Overshoot	4
Engine failure, mechanical	4
Electrical problem	4
Rear eng. out on T/O, go-around	3
Pilot incapacitation	3
Misc. mechan.	3
Engine stoppage, fuel contam.	3

When Skymaster pilots aren't having mechanical problems with the landing gear, they initiate the trouble on their own by forgetting to lower it on landing. Accident causes with only one occurrence were not listed in this graph.

Another owner describes losing an engine in a P-337 shortly after reaching 19,000 feet on a long flight to do some quail-hunting. Not wanting to miss the fun, he simply descended to 15,000 feet and kept flying, arriving only a little behind schedule. He bagged his quail.

Safety

Despite the theoretical promise of the Skymaster's "safety twin" centerline-thrust design, and the occasional "I was saved by the Skymaster" anecdote, the sad fact is that the Skymaster has a lousy overall accident record. Even more ironically, its rate of engine-failure accidents is actually higher than most standard twins.

A 1984 *Aviation Consumer* study found that during the period 1972-1982, the 337 had 2.5 fatal accidents per 100,000 flight hours—16th worst fatal accident rate of the 18 twin-engine aircraft we studied. Only the Aerostar and Cessna 411 ranked lower. Median fatal rate for the group was 1.3 (nearly twice as good as the Skymaster) and the best of the lot, the Cessna 414, rated 0.8, which is three times better than the Skymaster.

For total accidents, the picture was similar. The Skymaster ranked 15th out of 18 with a rate of 9.5 per 100,000 hours. Median was 5.8; the lowest rate was 3.2.

Focussing on engine-failure accidents, the picture is even more puzzling. Despite its docile engine-out handling qualities and lack of minimum-control speed, the Skymaster ranked a dismal 16th out of 20 in a 1980 NTSB study of fatal engine-failure accidents in twin-engine aircraft.

Several of the Skymaster's fatal engine-failure crashes occurred when the rear engine quit on takeoff, and the pilot apparently failed to notice the failure and continued the takeoff. Such accidents have plagued the Skymaster for years; Cessna eventually added a warning light and revised the takeoff checklist to require advancing the rear throttle first for takeoff.

A look at two dozen Skymaster fatal accidents shows no other obvious pattern; the crashes are a fairly random assortment of weather, fuel exhaustion, stalls and ground impacts of various sorts—the usual mix.

Non-fatal accidents do show one pattern: fuel exhaustion. Cessna bragged about the reliability of the capacitance-type gauges in the Skymaster, but they were unreliable, and their location on the right side of the panel made them hard to read. Furthermore, a Skymaster with the long-range fuel system has only two gauges for four tanks; the pilot turn a switch to read either the main or aux tank for each engine.

In our judgment, this is a bad piece of human engineering that has caused fuel-mismanagement problems in other aircraft like the Bellanca Viking.

Several fuel-starvation crashes may have occurred because of poor design of the check valves in the vapor return line of certain model Skymasters. On 1975-80 model 337s with long-range tanks, the check valves are mounted horizontally, which makes them more likely to stick in the open position. Because the vapor return line runs to the manifold instead of the fuel tanks, a stuck valve allows some fuel to reach the engine even when the selector valve is turned off.

The problem is, if the pilot inadvertently turns the fuel selector off, the engine will continue to run at moderate power. That's fine, until the pilot goes to high power—for takeoff or go-around, for example. Then the engine quits, and the pilot has no idea why. (At least when the engine quits immediately after a fuel selector change, the pilot may think to check the selector.) One attorney investigating the problem believes at least eight Skymaster fuel mismanagement crashes may be related to this phenomenon.

Maintenance

Here's the potential Skymaster nightmare: runaway maintenance costs, particularly in the turbo and pressurized models. The Skymaster was the most complex aircraft ever engineered and manufactured by Cessna's Pawnee Division, which otherwise built only the Cessna single-engine line. The evidence suggests the Pawnee Division simply wasn't up to the task, particularly in the 1975-80 period when production was growing rapidly and Cessna was plagued with an epidemic of design, engineering and production problems.

Pressurized models like this one will push 190 knots at 20,000 feet, their top certified altitude.

For example, the pressurized Skymaster was initially such a disaster that the first year's production was recalled to the factory for complete remanufacture and modification.

And listen to the plaintive cries of one owner who traded in his 1973 model for a brand-new 1978 337H in the hope that it might reduce the frequency of visits to the service department of his local Cessna dealer: "In the nine months and 130 hours since then, I seem to have experienced nearly all the standard joys of 337 ownership, including but not limited to: (1) inoperative synchro-phaser (two times); (2) rear alternator shaft oil seal leaking (three times); (3) defective cabin door lock and problems with the door latching mechanism; (4) shaft twisted off rear vacuum pump; (5) cracking of rubber grooves of all three tires; (6) erroneous indication by left-hand fuel gauge; (7) rear EGT inoperative; (8) gas leak in right wing tank; (9) water leak around

Cruise speeds are a modest 150-155 knots. On an engine-out situation, the rear engine yields a better climb rate because of greater efficiency.

cowling cover at base of windshield.... There have been 35 other minor squawks .. . but I have my Skymaster blinders securely on, and am hoping that after this initial period of de-bugging I will be able to give up the more or less permanent spot which I have been occupying in my dealer's shop."

Most of the Skymaster's problems seem to be in the systems. The basic airframe is a stout one, with the rugged strut-braced wing. And remember that the military version of the Skymaster, the O-2 observation aircraft, did plenty of rough duty in Vietnam, often flying home with bullet holes and worse. "It took a hell of a beating," recalls one civilian Skymaster owner who had previously flown O-2s in Vietnam. (As a point of interest, he also mentioned that it was "a very stable rocket and gun platform.")

At least the used-Skymaster buyer has the chance to get a debugged airplane. Closely examine the logbooks and service records of any Skymaster considered for purchase. And be sure to keep a sharp lookout for these chronic Skymaster problems:

• Oil leaks in the rear engine. Loose rocker box covers, a chronically leaky quick-drain and a sloppy breather tube seem to be the main culprits (although one Skymaster buff claims the problem is entirely psychological, due to the fact that the bottom of the rear cowling is more easily visible than the front). Skymaster aficionados tell us it is possible to run a dry-belly Skymaster, but you'll have to keep the rocker-box covers tight, eliminate the quick drain and modify the breather tube to post-1975 configuration.

• Defective landing gear switches. Cheap plastic switches plagued the Skymaster during the mid-1970s (as they did other Cessna models). Actually, the entire landing gear system is a mechanic's nightmare; eleven—count 'em, eleven—hydraulic actuators in all.

• Aluminum wiring. Certain model Skymasters had aluminum wiring and cheap connectors, a certain recipe for electrical gremlins.

• Crack-prone engine crankcases in pre-1973 models. Engines remanufactured since then should have been retrofitted with heavier cases. Look for the "H" logo on the heavy cases.

• Water leaks around the windshield were a chronic problem in older models. Check for possible rain damage, and check the condition of the windshield sealant.

• Hot-running rear engine. Carefully check the cooling baffle seals in the rear cowling. Also check the rear temperature gauge. One Skymaster buff we talked to swears that the "hot rear engine problem" is a red herring due to defective gauge installations. He says he's installed precisely accurate digital six-probe CHT gauges in two Skymasters in which the standard Cessna gauges indicated a hot-running rear engine. In both cases, the better gauge showed that the rear engine actually ran cooler than the front. The owner says he now climbs with the rear cowl flaps partially closed and temps well in the green.

• ARC 300 radios. These were notoriously shoddy and unreliable during the mid- and late 1970s. Avoid them if at all possible. If not possible, be prepared to spend a bundle keeping them going.

• Defective paint jobs. When Cessna switched to DuPont Imron on the Skymaster

Cost/Performance/Specifications

Model	Year	Average Retail Price	Cruise Speed (kts)	Useful Load (lbs)	S.E. Service Ceiling (ft)	Fuel Std/Opt (gals)	Engine	TBO (hrs)	Overhaul Cost @
337	1965	$26,000	167	1,565	8,300	93/131	210-hp Cont. IO-360-C/D	1,500	$14,000
337A	1966	$28,000	167	1,585	8,200	93/131	210-hp Cont. IO-360-C/D	1,500	$14,000
337B	1967	$30,000	167	1,685	7,500	93/131	210-hp Cont. IO-360-C/D	1,500	$14,000
T-337B	1967	$31,500	196	1,515	20,000	93/131	210-hp Cont. TSIO-360-A/B	1,400	$15,500
337C	1968	$31,500	166	1,750	6,800	93/131	210-hp Cont. IO-360-C/D	1,500	$14,000
T-337C	1968	$32,000	195	1,705	18,600	93/131	210-hp Cont. TSIO-360-A/B	1,400	$15,500
337D	1969	$32,000	166	1,745	6,800	93/131	210-hp Cont. IO-360-C/D	1,500	$14,000
T-337D	1969	$32,500	195	1,485	16,200	93/131	210-hp Cont. TSIO-360-A/B	1,400	$15,500
337E	1970	$32,800	166	1,820	6,500	93/131	210-hp Cont. IO-360-C	1,500	$14,000
T-337E	1970	$34,500	223	1,780	14,400	93/131	210-hp Cont. TSIO-360-A	1,400	$15,500
337F	1971-72	$36,750	166	1,935	5,100	93/131	210-hp Cont. IO-360-C	1,400	$14,000
T-337F	1971	$38,000	194	1,780	14,400	93/131	210-hp Cont. TSIO-360-A	1,500	$15,500
337G	1973-74	$40,000	169	1,517	6,900	90/150	210-hp Cont. IO-360-G	1,500	$14,000
T-337G-P	1973-74	$56,000	204	1,533	18,700	150	225-hp Cont. TSIO-360-C	1,400	$15,500
337G II	1975	$45,000	169	1,517	6,900	90/150	210-hp Cont. IO-360-G	1,500	$14,000
T-337G-P	1975	$65,000	204	1,533	18,700	150	225-hp Cont. TSIO-360-C	1,400	$15,500
337G II	1976	$47,000	169	1,517	6,900	93/131	210-hp Cont. IO-360-G	1,500	$14,000
T-337G-P	1976	$72,000	204	1,533	18,700	150	225-hp Cont. TSIO-360-C	1,400	$15,500
337G II	1977	$50,500	169	1,517	6,900	90/150	210-hp Cont. IO-360-G	1,500	$14,000
T-337G-P	1977	$79,000	204	1,533	16,500	90/150	210-hp Cont. TSIO-360-C	1,400	$15,500
337H II	1978	$55,500	169	1,687	6,900	90/150	210-hp Cont. IO-360-G	1,500	$14,000
T-337H II	1978	$60,500	200	1,608	16,500	90/150	210-hp Cont. TSIO-360-H	1,400	$18,000
337H II	1979	$61,500	169	1,687	6,900	90/150	210-hp Cont. IO-360-GB	1,500	$14,000
T-337H II	1979	$68,000	200	1,608	16,500	150	210-hp Cont. TSIO-360-H	1,400	$18,000
T-337H-P	1978	$88,000	204	1,533	18,700	150	225-hp Cont. TSIO-360-C	1,400	$15,500
T-337H-P	1979	$99,000	204	1,533	18,700	150	225-hp Cont. TSIO-360-CB	1,400	$15,500
337H II	1980	$70,500	169	1,687	6,900	150	210-hp Cont. IO-360-GB	1,500	$14,000
T-337H II	1980	$79,500	200	1,608	6,500	150	210-hp Cont. TSIO-360-HG	1,400	$18,000
T-337H-P	1980	$115,000	204	1,533	18,700	150	225-hp Cont. TSIO-360-CB	1,400	$15,500

(as well as the other Pawnee models) in 1977, it ignored DuPont requirements for metal preparation and priming, using a cheap, quick wash primer instead of the required alodyne and epoxy primer. The result was an epidemic of filiform corrosion, particularly in warm, humid coastal areas. Check the geographical history of any 1977-80 Skymaster; if it's spent much time in Florida, the Gulf Coast or California, look scrupulously for filiform corrosion, And be suspicious of a recent paint job; in many cases, the corrosion comes right back after a year or two.

• Landing gear solenoids. Post-1974 models have improved solenoids, part number 9881201-1.

Service Difficulty Reports

The SDRs reveal some familiar patterns. Leading the Skymaster breakdown parade are the landing gear system (36 reports over six years) and electrical system, especially the alternators (24 reports). The Continental IO-360 and TSIO-360 also came in for their share of black marks, most of them in well-known trouble areas: cracking crankcases, broken crankshafts (the 1979 and 1980 models have -CB engines with beefier cranks), bad connecting rods, and broken oil pump/tach drives. Cylinder problems were also widespread, with numerous reports of head-to-barrel separations.

Incidentally, the turbo and pressurized models accounted for more than half of all the Service Difficulty Reports. Moral: complexity equals maintenance bills. (For example, the P-337's TSIO-360-C engine has more than 80 service bulletins issued against it. And its unique engine installation geometry can make even routine maintenance work a real chore.)

Modifications

STOL mods are popular on Skymasters, and you may find three different types on used Skymasters: the full-blown Robertson system, with drooped ailerons and flap-actuated elevator trim (now sold by Sierra Industries Inc., P.O. Box 5184, Uvalde, Tex. 78802, (512) 278-4381; and simpler systems involving only vortex generators and recontoured leading edges and wingtips from Horton STOLcraft, Wellington Municipal Airport, Wellington, Kans. 67152, (316) 326-2241 or (800) 835-2051

American Aviation at S. 3608 Davison Blvd., Spokane, Wash., 99204, (800) 423-0476 is now offering an intercooler installation for the pressurized Skymaster and the turbo models. By reducing induction air temperatures, the intercooler increases critical altitude, reduces manifold pressure required for maintaining power, and generally lets the engine run cooler and with less strain.

To get the Skymaster down more quickly, spoilers are an option available from Spoilers, Inc. of Gig Harb or, Wash., (800) 544-0169. The hinged spoilers are electrically controlled and hydraulically actuated.

Owner Group

Dick Whitaker published an informative Skymaster newsletter filled with tips, complaints and hosannahs from various Skymaster owners for years up until his sudden death in May 1991. At presstime Whitaker Enterprises was looking for someone to continue the newsletter and was asking any who were interested to contact them at Box 1950, Liberal, Kans. 67901.

Owner Comments

My partner and I purchased our 1973 337G Skymaster in 1986. It had a total time of 1,050 hours, and we paid slightly under $20,000. The "bluebook" retail price at the time was $29,000. The 1973 model was the first year with the electric Power-Pac for the gear system, as opposed to the more troublesome hydraulic system on pre-1973 models. The clamshell door is cumbersome and the rear two seats are a joke, to say the least. They literally sit on the floor, and an adult has a great deal of difficulty sitting in these seats comfortably for any length of time.

From a pure numbers viewpoint, the Skymaster is an impressive plane. Single-engine performance is extremely docile, and on either the front or the rear engine, it will cruise about as fast as a Cessna Skyhawk. On both engines, its performance is very similar to my 1980 A36 Bonanza, which my partner and I routinely fly side by side. At 70 percent power, both aircraft stay right with each other. As most people already know by now, the Cessna avionics are for the most part are wanting.

Skymaster placement of fuel gauges way over on the right side of the panel is less than ideal in thwarting fuel mismanagement.

Alden Buerge
Joplin, Mo.

I owned a 1967 337B Skymaster from 1972 until 1985. It gave us faithful service and we reluctantly traded it for a B55 Baron when we were faced with two engine overhauls. I still look back at the Skymaster as a special aircraft that deserves far more respect and popularity than it received over the years.

First of all, it did what it was conceived to do: add a margin of safety to twin-engine flying by eliminating Vmc. The airplane remains controllable on either engine right up to the moment of stall.

There are a number of other special features that I miss. The Skymaster is roomy and has more creature comforts for the pilot and passengers.The high wing lets you get in and out in the rain without getting wet. I greatly miss the superb visibility.

The performance was extremely close to the figures published in the handbook. We always flew at conservative power settings in the hopes of trading speed for engine life. With the tanks filled we cruised at 150 knots with 7.5 hours endurance and 650 pounds payload. Leaving the aux tanks empty gave 5.5 hours endurance and a payload of 885 pounds. Fuel burn was less than 19 gallons per hour. The Skymaster is a bit heavy in pitch on liftoff and flare, but otherwise there are no unusual flight characteristics.

The Skymaster flies quite nicely with gear down. The recommended procedure is to leave the gear down on takeoff until at least 500 feet, since the plane will still climb with gear down and either prop feathered. The gear retraction process is rather slow (about 14 seconds) and increases the drag quite significantly during that time.

Many aviation buffs think the Skymaster is ugly, and names such as Mixmaster and Skythrasher are familiar to all of us. But beauty is in the eyes of the beholder, and the Skymaster has a functional beauty that is most appreciated after owning one.

Since the Skymaster has no nose bay in which to place a large radar dish, a smaller one must be hung on a wing.

John Blalock
Winter Park, Fla.

I own a normally aspirated 1966 Skymaster with 2,400 hours total time. The front engine is 350 SMOH, the rear 750 since new. I've now owned the plane for 30 months, through two annuals. The main problem I encountered was a persistent low-grade hydraulic leak, which required refilling the system every 25 hours or so. It has now been resolved, on the fifth try. My annuals cost in the $1,000 range. On one, we had to replace a cylinder on the rear engine because of low compression. No other major engine work has been required. One cowl flap motor had to be rebuilt, and I have replaced an alternator, vacuum pump, manifold pressure line, and oil temperature gauge.

My fuel burn is usually between 15 and 16 gallons per hour at a cruise speed of 150-155 knots. I generally fly between 8,000 and 12,000 feet. My operating cost of $100 per hour includes a reserve of $15 for engine overhaul. The operating cost is higher than a single, but I like the duplication of systems and the ability to maintain altitude in the mountains on one engine. I have experienced two engine failures in single-engine airplanes, a pair of experiences I might not have survived so well had I not been VFR and within gliding distance of an airport.

The Skymaster's handling on one engine is gentle. It is a stable airplane, and makes an excellent instrument platform. I love the airplane.

Roger Howe
Mt. Shasta, Calif.

I'm on my third Skymaster. The first two were turbo models, and I now have a P337. I have about 1,000 hours in cross-country and in the Sierra Mountains and no downtime on any trip due to maintenance problems. I do not feel my maintenance problems have been excessive or unusual for a twin, except the cost of a good reman engine (TSIO-360C) can be high ($16,500-plus Victor used "cert." case and crank).

I added intercoolers three months ago and increased speed by 9-10% and climb performance by 20%. Also, the cabin is much cooler. Ventilation without the intercoolers is is very poor in the P models. Since adding the intercoolers, I'm very pleased with the result both in performance and comfort.

Name withheld on request

Cessna 310

The 310 has earned the appellation "versatile," with good reason. There are few other models with so many variations, and few light twins offer as much all-around performance.

Individual owners and commercial operators responded in one voice: enthusiastic. Usually, there is some equivocation and even regret. Not a hint of it from the 310 owners who took the time to write in some detail (including a couple who shared their cost spreadsheets).

"No aircraft has given me more overall pleasure"; I would not trade for any light twin on the market"; "As an overall package, size, useful load, comfort, speed, economy the 310 cannot be beat." "For the money, there is no better light twin available"; "A wonderful airplane." Larry A. Ball, who runs The Twin Cessna Flyer, an association that he says includes more than 1,200 C-310 owners, told us: "There is no bigger bang for the buck."

What It Can Do

Even the later, heavier 310s can take off and land over a 50-foot barrier in less than 1,800 feet with a well-trained pilot at the controls of a well-maintained airplane. Single-engine performance is better than most light twins.

The airplane can be flown in high- density airspace without causing heartburn for ATC and other airplanes. It can be fit into a low-performance traffic mix at smaller fields, as well.

The early 240-hp 310s can crank along at 170 KTAS at max cruise. From the 310C on, 185 knots is easily on tap (although most pilots accept a less dinful cruise at 60 to 65% power and are very happy with the 170 to 180 KTAS that results). All the models can haul a decent load, too.

One great strength of the 310 is that Cessna still supports the airplane with parts and information. While a lot of owners don't like the prices, most are grateful for the support. It is an advantage, especially considering that the 310 has been out of production for a dozen years.

Out of production, but not necessarily outdated, the 310s are handsome-looking, fast-flying haulers that come in a myriad of versions. This is a long-nosed '78 model.

Tracing the Line

The first production Cessna 310 was built in 1954; the last in 1981. Ball says 5,447 were built. Also, the U.S. Air Force purchased 196 310s in two versions (designated U-3A and U-3B). All were built under the same type certificate: 3A10. For the first 16 model years (1955-1970) there was a "new"

No matter what model year, the 310s have good, though expensive (some say outrageous), support from the factory, and a topnotch owners' organization, the Twin Cessna Flyer, and its TAS Aviation Technical Center. This is a short-nose '72 model, the first for which the rear cabin window was added.

model annually, covering the 310 through the 310Q. In the trivia category, there were no models designated E, M or O. The 310Q and T310Q had five-year production runs and were superseded by the final 310, the R, in 1975. The R was built for seven years. The model was abandoned in 1981.

Grouping

Cessna puts the various versions into five broad groups: the 310 to 310D (about 1,294 aircraft), 310F to 310K (1,105 units), 310 L and N (roughly 405 airplanes), 310 P and Q (approximately 1,108) and 310R (1,432).

Anthony R. Saxton is director of maintenance at TAS Aviation, of Defiance, Ohio, and serves as technical adviser to the Twin Cessna Flyer. He separates the 310 series into three groups: 1954-1961 310 to 310F "which had the straight or 'tuna' style tip tanks"; 1962 -1974 310G to 310Q "which had the canted to 'Stabilla' [sic] tanks and short nose"; and the 310R of 1975-1981.

With the major variations and the many detail changes and refinements, there is a lot of sorting-out to do to select a 310 that best fits your budget and operating profile. One pilot who has owned three 310s, says, "It took over six months of diligent effort to find an aircraft that was in sufficient shape to warrant the investment."

Picking the Best

In addition to checking the configuration and equipment of a given model, there are a few other factors that should be on every evaluation form. These include age, use history and maintenance history, as with any airplane.

Disuse is just as bad as misuse; it is a form of neglect. One owner says the early (310 - 310B) carburetted models seem to develop a variety of problems if they aren't regularly flown. In reality, this can be said about any airplane.

With the long production run and the many variations of 310s, a prospective purchaser can choose from cheap (Blue Book on a 310 starts at $23,000, and Saxton of TAS says as low as $20,000) to latest with known-icing, good avionics, radar and writing desks.

Inside that new-looking 1981 310R could lurk a several-thousand-hour check-running, student-suffering nightmare with brittle engines. As one owner writes, "Cosmetics can cover a lot of ills and poor maintenance."

Problems to Look For

All models through the 310H of 1963 had overwing exhaust, which is one of the

major causes of corrosion in 310s. However, introduction of under-wing exhaust on the 310I did not fully correct the problem. Several maintenance shops say that careful maintenance, including regular cleaning of surfaces subject to exhaust and other corrosive elements is a first line of defense.

Almost all owners with experience mention the landing gear as a problem area. Preventive maintenance and proper rigging—along with good operating technique—are the best forms of insurance. While later versions, especially the 310R, had improved structure, attach fittings, bearings and other elements, failures still occur.

Though the 310s are six-seaters with delightfully beamy cabins, great for cross-country cruising, the rear two seats are too cozy for comfort except for children. A wide baggage door is a valuable option. This is a '76 model.

To quote Saxton again: "The gear requires recurrent proper repair and adjustment. Service Bulletin ME76-2 addresses cracks in the main landing gear side braces with installation of Service Kit SK-414-8E. We have found numerous aircraft in need of this costly repair. The cost for 1954 through 1966 models will be somewhere around $7,000. Other models run slightly over $3,000.

"Nose gear is tender right through the 310R. Ball of the Twin Cessna Flyer says: "The bellcrank under the pilot's feet, part number 08421022, has caused many 310 models to be landed without the nose gear down and locked."

Preferable Models

All things being equal, for pilots who plan to operate IFR regularly, the 1967 310L and later models (or earlier models with electrical system and other upgrades) are the most desirable. The generators and mechanical voltage regulators—and the electrical system monitoring aids—are troublesome and tend to fail in sneaky ways. A number of pilots have found out the electrical system was out of juice only when they realized too late that the gear was not extended.

The 260-hp IO-470 engine, especially the -V version used in the 310K through 310Q, has been one of the most successful Continental engines.

Unmodified earlier models will have panels that reflect the random (or put it where it fits) school of instrument arrangement. Upgrading the avionics on earlier models frequently results in a plus beyond better performance and reliability: weight saving that increases payload and may make weight and balance simpler.

Because of variations among models, vague maintenance history, age and abuse, Ball recommends that pilots determine the maximum purchase price their wallets can handle, spend no more than 75 percent of that on acquisition and bank the other quarter to handle "surprises."

The Competition

During much of its production life cycle, the 310 lived with a variety of competition. The Piper PA-23 series made its production debut a year ahead of the 310 and they both were ended in 1981. A variety of Barons, especially the E-55 and 58,

Sturdy-looking, but with underpinnings frequently described as spindly and quirky, 310 landing gear systems need lots of expert attention. The bellcrank under the pilot's feet has caused many expensive landings with the nose gear not properly down and locked. Shown is a '79 model.

and the Piper PA-31 Navajo series, especially the 310-hp "original" are somewhat competitive.

Competitive until you get to price, that is. All were still being produced in 1981. A 310R is 64 percent of the price of a Beech 58. A T310R is 77 percent the price of a 310-hp Navajo. Only the Aztec is lower in the resale market, averaging nearly $30,000 less than a 310. The 310 indeed offers a lot of performance for the dollar.

Performance

In addition to the good cruise and runway numbers mentioned above, the 310 provides better than average single-engine performance in the hands of a well-trained and very sharp pilot.

Up through the 310G, the series is about average for baggage space (about average means frequently having to carry some in the cabin). With the stretched cabin of the 1963 310H, more baggage space was opened up.

Along with that, weight and balance has to be watched more closely. The nose was extended starting with the 310K, which helps spread the load. The nacelle lockers introduced on the 310I makes loading options even better.

An optional large baggage door was introduced on the 310P. It greatly eases the task of loading and arranging aft baggage.

By the 310I, cubic feet available certainly began to exceed the lifting and weight-and-balance capacity of the airplane. C-310s with lots of avionics and other options compound the loading exercise. Even without radar, some 310s with full fuel push the forward cg limit with just a pilot in front, so there are times when seating has to be assigned.

Basic (that means unequipped—stripped, really) empty weight started at 2,840 pounds for the original. It exceeds 3,000 pounds by the 310C, nears 3,200 in the 310P and exceeds 3,600 in the 310R (turbo models are heavier still).

Payload with full fuel varies all over the lot, depending upon the model, equipment and fuel tank arrangement. Usable fuel capacity can be 100, 132, 142, 182 or 203

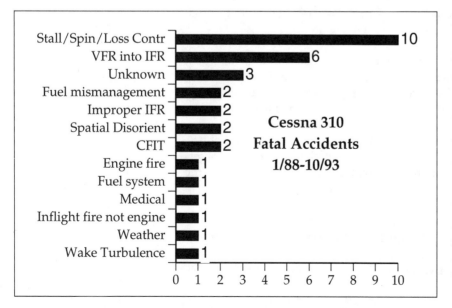

Cessna 310 Fatal Accidents 1/88-10/93

Stall/Spin/Loss Contr	10
VFR into IFR	6
Unknown	3
Fuel mismanagement	2
Improper IFR	2
Spatial Disorient	2
CFIT	2
Engine fire	1
Fuel system	1
Medical	1
Inflight fire not engine	1
Weather	1
Wake Turbulence	1

gallons—from 600 to 1,218 pounds of fuel. Payload in a lightly equipped 310C with auxiliary tanks might exceed 700 pounds, while it could be as low as 400 pounds in a 310R.

Other loading and operating considerations were introduced in the later models. As maximum operating weight increased, limits such as maximum landing weight and zero fuel weight became factors.

Zero fuel weight is a payload limitation that confuses some pilots. A T310R, for example, has a zero fuel weight of 5,015 pounds. Anything between that and maximum ramp weight has to be fuel. In one aircraft, maximum payload is 1,059 pounds, which can handle six FAA adults (170 pounds) and 39 pounds of baggage. Figuring a maximum ramp weight of 5,534 pounds, 519 pounds of fuel can be put in the main tanks.

Calculating climb to cruise altitude of 12,000 feet, this allows just under three hours of flight plus reserve at 65% power. The airplane can cover roughly 500 nm in still air with max payload. With all tanks installed and full, on the other hand, it can haul a couple of people and some baggage more than 1,200 nm, again at 65% power.

Flight Handling

The 310 quickly gained a reputation as a pilot's airplane (in the not-easy-to-fly category). Ground handling was a bit awkward. There was a Dutch roll tendency in flight, particularly at low speeds and in landing configuration.

Pitch changes with configuration changes are pronounced, especially in the earlier models. Pilots experienced in 310s quickly learn to anticipate pitch force changes with healthy inputs of elevator trim.

Dutch roll tendency was never totally eliminated, and a bit of Dutch roll can be severely aggravated if a transitioning pilot starts fighting back. (One technique, similar to that used in Lear and other airplanes with the characteristic is to apply just a touch—nearly imperceptible—of cross-control input, and just sit with it while the airplane settles down.)

Dutch roll tendency in particular and low speed wallowing in general is aggravated by the leverage of fuel out there in the main—wing tip—tanks.

The 310 is a solid, heavy-feeling airplane. Almost all pilots who have flown it call it an excellent IFR airplane. While control inputs take a bit of muscle, especially at higher speeds, the airplane is less likely to be displaced than airplanes with lighter control response.

It tends to wallow a bit at lower approach speeds with the gear and flaps hanging out. It is an easy airplane to fly "by the numbers," which is one of the characteristics that makes it a good instrument airplane. Visibility is good. By the 310Q, with its extended windshield, it is superb, even with the tip tanks and nacelles to create some blind spots.

The 310 does not tolerate abusive or careless flying. While the number of loss-of-control accidents has been greatly reduced—largely through good training—they still occur and usually are terminal mistakes.

Cessna 310 Service Difficulty Reports 1/88-10/93

ENGINE
Cylinder	107
Valve train	19
Oil seals	9
Mags/ignition sys	7
Connecting rod	6
Crankshaft	6
Eng controls	5
Misc	5
Exhaust sys	4
Filter	3
Cooler	3
Breather	3
Dipstick	3

LANDING GEAR
Main	104
Nose	56
Switches	21
Misc	7

AIRFRAME
Spar/spar cap corrosion	11
Bulkhead/doubler crack	10
Engine mounts	10
Skin crack/corrosion	4
Emergency exit	3
Cabin step	1

MISCELLANEOUS
Instruments/panel	14
Deice (inc prop deice)	9
Seat back	5

AFTERMARKET
Door Seal	2

FUEL SYS
Lines, corrosion	14
Misc	10
Lines, abrasion	8
Elec pumps	8
Hoses	6
Eng. driven pumps	5

PROPELLER 62

ELECTRICAL
Alternator/gen	20
Starter	8
Voltage reg	4

BRAKE SYSTEM 5

WHEELS/TIRES 3

FLIGHT CONTROLS
Attach/actuators	15
Cables	8
Skin	2
Heater	7
Oxygen	2
Vacuum	2
ELT	2

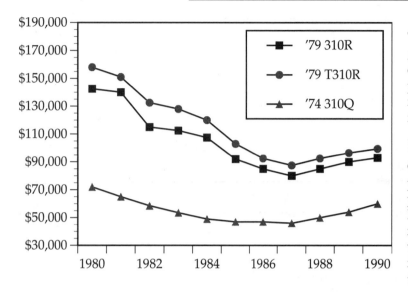

The 310 is easy to slow down, with good gear and flap speeds. Consistent approaches or patterns can be flown by managing power setting and configuration. Just remember that when it runs out of airspeed it quits flying fast.

Engine Loss Precautions

Consistency in technique and in speed and power management is important in any airplane, but it is very noticeable in airplanes like the 310. During takeoff the period of maximum exposure—initial climb attitude with gear down or in transit—is pretty long in a 310, since the gear takes it own sweet time. And pilots are pretty busy.

While some pilots choose to accelerate to cruise climb speed shortly after takeoff, experiments with some 310 models suggest that climbing at Vxse, or best single-engine angle of climb, is preferable while the gear is retracting. Altitude is more important than airspeed in the event of an engine failure shortly after takeoff.

Training Centers

Train, train, train. And then get recurrent training. To a man, the owners who wrote emphasize the value. One owner had praise for Simcom Training Centers of Orlando, Fla., (800) 272-0211. Flight Safety International offers 310-specific training, including simulator training, at its Wichita, Kan. facility for prop-driven Cessnas, (800) 227-5656.

The Twin Cessna Flyer also provides operational procedures and maintenance training. According to Larry Ball, these are offered in several locations each year.

Cost/Performance/Specifications

Model	Year	Average Retail Price	Cruise Speed (kt)	Useful Load (lb)	Std/Opt Fuel (gal)	Engines	SE Ceiling (ft)	TBO (hr)	Overhaul Cost @
310, A	1955-56	$25,000	178	1,750	100	240-hp Cont. O-470-B,M	8,000	1,500	$14,000
310B	1958	$27,000	178	1,850	100/132	240-hp Cont. O-470-D	8,000	1,500	$13,000
310C-F	1959-61	$31,500	191	1,751	100/132	260-hp Cont. IO-470-D	7,450	1,500	$14,500
310G-H	1962-63	$37,000	191	2,037	100/132	260-hp Cont. IO-470-D	7,450	1,500	$14,500
310I-J	1964-65	$40,000	194	2,037	100/132	260-hp Cont. IO-470-U	6,850	1,500	$14,500
310K-L	1966-67	$44,500	193	1,975	100/142	260-hp Cont. IO-470-V	6,850	1,500	$14,500
310N	1968	$46,000	193	2,075	100/182	260-hp Cont. IO-470-V	6,850	1,500	$14,500
310P	1969	$53,000	193	2,030	100/182	260-hp Cont. IO-470-VO	6,850	1,500	$14,500
310Q	1970-71	$56,000	192	2,086	100/203	260-hp Cont. IO-470-VO	6,680	1,500	$14,500
310Q	1972-74	$64,500	192	2,086	100/203	260-hp Cont. IO-470-VO	6,680	1,500	$14,500
310R	1975-77	$85,500	194	2,047	100/203	285-hp Cont. IO-520-M	7,400	1,700	$15,000
310R	1978-79	$100,500	194	2,047	100/203	285-hp Cont. IO-520-M	7,400	1,700	$15,000
310R	1980-81	$121,000	194	2,047	100/203	285-hp Cont. IO-520-M	7,400	1,700	$15,000
T310P	1969	$58,000	226	2,108	100/182	285-hp Cont. TSIO-520-B	18,100	1,400	$18,000
T310Q	1970-74	$68,000	225	2,086	100/203	285-hp Cont. TSIO-520-B	18,100	1,400	$18,000
T310R	1975-78	$94,000	223	1,777	100/203	285-hp Cont. TSIO-520-BB	18,000	1,400	$16,500
T310R	1979-81	$124,000	223	1,777	100/203	285-hp Cont. TSIO-520-BB	18,000	1,400	$16,500

Prices from *Aircraft Bluebook Price Digest*

Pilots who are not well trained have walked away from the 310 with unpleasant memories. Pilots who learn the airplane find it very satisfying to fly.

Management Demands

The later the model (or the more the mods), the more the 310 is a management airplane. A good autopilot (preferably with a yaw damper) is a very useful tool, especially if you do much real IFR flying.

Fuel management is demanding until you become thoroughly familiar with it (and unless you keep to the clock in your in-flight systems management). And fuel management begins at the gas pump. Untrained line people mistake the auxiliary tanks for the mains and the mains for auxes, despite placards and color coding.

The plumbing is important, too. The fuel transfer pumps are in the mains (which you should be able to hear when you engage the master switch. If not, walk out to the tanks and listen) since these are no-go items. If your 310 has the nacelle tanks, the transfer pumps are lubricated by fuel. Forget to monitor the (gaugeless) transfer, and you could have an expensive remove and replace job.

The turbo models will yield a ground-lapping cruise speed of 205 knots, though burning a hefty 35 gph. The incidence of cylinder failures is higher in these models.

Time and timing are very big in 310 fuel management. Anything but level cruise flight is supposed to be done using the main tanks (and think of what you need for descent, approach and possible missed as your main tank bingo fuel).

The 310 induction system is such that excess fuel is generated. The excess is returned to the mains. If a pilot selects auxiliary tanks or starts to transfer fuel from the nacelle tanks too soon, a lot of expensive and necessary fuel can be sent into the atmosphere through the vents.

One rule of thumb is to burn from the mains until the two quantity needles point at each other—half full, or 150 pounds—then start transferring wing locker fuel (if only one nacelle tank is installed, it is necessary to select crossfeed to balance the fuel load—fuel imbalance provides enough leverage to disconnect the autopilot and create some weird handling sensations in IMC). When nacelle fuel is all transferred, it is time to use the auxiliary tanks.

Icing Gear

A lot of 310s are equipped with anti- and deice equipment. Some pilots mistakenly assume this means they are approved for flight in icing conditions. This misconception is exacerbated by some Cessna sales literature that talks about all-weather flying and deicing equipment.

Known-icing certification was not obtained until late in the life cycle of the 310R. C-310s exhibit a characteristic common to many Cessna singles and twins: just a trace, say one-eighth inch, of ice on the horizontal stabilizer greatly degrades performance. It causes a higher cruise angle of attack (pitch attitude). Airspeed degrades noticeably. The increased angle exposes more of the airframe to ice.

Owners give good marks to the big 310 instrument panel and controls for human engineering, but not always to the Cessna radios. And the fuel system on later models can be easily mismanaged.

More power is required (and icing around the air inlet can disturb flow and cause CHT and oil temperatures to rise. Perhaps cowl flaps are required. Drag increases. All in all, it is not a happy circumstance.

There is a lot to learn about safely operating a 310. Good training is a critical investment.

Comfort

Passengers who are not enthusiastic airplane riders can get pretty claustrophobic in the rear seats of early 310s. Even with the substantial changes made to the roof line and addition of the rear window in the 1972 310Q, some people feel confined.

The cabin is wide, especially in later models in the cockpit and mid seats. Even in later models, the fifth and sixth seats are marginally comfortable, especially since there is little leg room and the seats essentially sit on the floor.

Noise level approaches the painful in some models at high power settings. Good, working synchrophasers help, as does dynamic propeller balancing.

The 310R, despite the purported advantages of the three-bladed props, is among the noisiest because of the extended nose. The sides are flat, helping to amplify and drum the blade slap throughout the fuselage. Noise and vibration are high. Power reductions are greeted like blessings to unprotected ears. Good ear protection is a must.

Maintenance

One owner writes: "It is a sad state of affairs that our airplanes could be worth more in parts someday than they are as flying machines." Some owners report that qualified maintenance technicians are becoming scarce, so that more money is spent on education—trouble shooting—than should be. Other owners travel far afield to get qualified service.

While this was not confirmed at press time, there was a period when the worst thing that could happen to a 310 (or other tip-tank Cessna twins) was to have a main tank damaged. They are hard to come by. One owner of a 310R whose airplane was run into by a fuel truck lost the use of his airplane for nearly five months while a replacement was located and fitted.

Most owners say the parts situation is okay considering the state of the business, although quite a few are getting replacement parts from the breaker's yard rather than new from the factory.

Everyone mentions care of the landing gear as a very important element of preventive maintenance. However, both Ball and Sexton mention that compliance with a Cessna service bulletin and kit (ME76-2 and SK414-8E) to modify main landing gear side brace attach points has not been good. Saxton said, too, that early 310Rs have a service kit for nose gear bay cracks that many airplanes (through serial no. 310R0816) have not had installed.

An auxiliary fuel pump wiring change and switch replacement for all fuel-injected versions is important and inexpensive, according to Ball. Saxton says the mod runs from $600 to $1,000.

The 310 has a very good AD history, but given the recurrent problems with the landing gear, corrosion, propeller problems and the need to poke and prod in hard to reach spots to verify condition, this is not the time for on the job training. As one technician mentioned in an SDR covering a split flap condition, the airframe had several thousand hours on it, and the broken element in the actuating mechanism was as old and apparently never inspected.

Many recurring problems, including landing gear and corrosion, can be managed through preventive maintenance, including proper cleaning and lubrication.

Saxton points out that servicing 310s is "reasonably simple and requires a minimum of [special] equipment and tooling."

He calls the O- and IO-470 engines "moderately reliable" and the IO-470V, "aside from occasional valve guide wear, have proven to be a paragon in longevity and serviceability." Early 310Rs have IO-520M engines with light crankcases that are prone to cracking, and all 520s have a lot of cylinder failure.

Much of the latter probably is due to thermal shock (multiplied on turbocharged versions). Most owners say their engines will get to TBO so long as they aren't pressed to the maximum all the time.

Modifications

There are lots of modifications for 310s (we count 154 STCs issued on various models). Some of these help upgrade earlier models with improved instrument panels, windshields and windows.

Some of the most popular mentioned by owners are conversion to Cleveland wheels and brakes, addition of vortex generators (available for 310G through R from Micro Aerodynamics, (800) 667-2370—and from VG Systems for the 310R (check for other models), (800) 992-3435.

Sierra Industries, (512) 278-4381, offers a number of aerodynamic kits, including the old Robertson kits.

There is a large number of engine modifications, additional fuel systems and autopilot and yaw damper STCs. BF Goodrich has a number of STCs for various deice systems. Both Colemill and RAM offer engine modifications for certain models, and Riley Aircraft Corp. has a number of STCs on engine and airframe mods. An inflatable door seal modification is widely recommended (Bob Fields Aerocessories of San Paula, Calif. is the STC listed).

There is also a number of exhaust system modifications to help alleviate one corrosion problem and a battery box mod to help with another.

One owner said the mod he would most like now would be spoilers. Precise Flight, (503) 382-8684, developed a nacelle-mounted speed brake that, according to a company spokesman, has been fitted to a number of 310s. A revised version is currently in development.

Operating Costs

The 310 offers a lot of performance for the price. Owners say direct costs range from about $125 to over $200 per hour, depending upon equipment, age and so on. Owners who have taken the time to fully cost operation, including the cost of money, figure hourly costs at from more than $300 per hour for low utilization to approximately $200 an hour for 150 hours per year.

That is pretty hard to beat for a truly high-performance twin that offers enough capability to compete with typical airline service.

For More Help

Nearly all the owners mentioned the Twin Cessna Flyer, (800) 825-5310, and TAS Aviation, (800) 843-9927. Somewhat surprisingly, no owners suggested the highly regarded Cessna Pilots Assn. (800-852-2272).

There also is a 310/320 Newsletter published quarterly by David and Mary Neumeister, (517) 882-8433). It covers SDRs and occasional owner feedback and some sources.

For factory information, call Cessna Multiengine Technical Support, (316) 941-7550.

Owner Comments

I chose the Q model for its IO-470-VO engines over the R model with its IO-520s because of the lower incidence of cylinder cracks and engine ADs. Parts availability is no problem, though costs are high. Total hourly costs run $175 to $250. The Navomatic autopilot is not very reliable.

Flap rod corrosion from exhaust gases is a constant concern, though it has not been a problem. Recurring ADs are few.

This is an expensive but reliable twin that can deliver superior all-weather performance. Cabin comfort and loading are worth the small cost in speed and interior finish. Acquisition and resale costs are overshadowed by maintenance and operational costs for this class of aircraft.

Charles R. Burnett, M.D.
Memphis, Tenn.

The 310R was quite easy to transition into, except for its inclination to go belly-up inverted if you even come close to Vmc. For this reason, I immediately went out and put Low Thrust Detectors on my aircraft.

In 1990, after attending a demonstration flight, my plane was one of the first 310Rs to get Micro Aerodynamics VGs installed. This modification is the only aircraft product I have ever seen or purchased whose performance matched or exceeded the manufacturer's claims.

At this time, I have no hesitation about slow flying in the pattern behind a Cessna 150 with gear and flaps down and my left engine windmilling. Most often the 150s will prove faster.

Insurance though the Twin Cessna Flyer has proved 20 to 30 percent cheaper than equivalent aircraft and, interestingly enough, the rates are actually cheaper than I paid for my large singles.

Last June I attended the Twin Cessna Return to Wichita Fly-In, and was impressed by the support Cessna is offering and continues to give for aircraft they have not produced in almost 12 years. The only negative factor about Cessna relates to their charges for some parts which, although available, are artificially expensive.

A Cessna double-pole, double-throw switch (for the electric trim) lists for over $240. This switch is made by Mason Electronics to mil. specs and can be bought for $38 if you know the proper part number from your local electronics supplier. This type of price gouging, I think, should not be allowed.

Jack L. Aronowitz
Fort Lauderdale, Fla.

I feel somewhat qualified to write about the 310, as I have owned probably 30 or more over the last 30 years. As a hobby business, I deal in twin-engine Cessnas. I buy them, refurbish them and put them back on the market.

As an airplane that was in production from 1954 to 1981, Cessna had the opportunity to work out an awful lot of bugs. I find the O-470 in the early 310s are very fine engines with serious carburetion problems if the airplane is not used regularly. With the advent of the IOs in 1959, right through the last Q models in 1974, the Continental O-470 variations seem to be excellent engines.

I have instructed in the 310 since the early 60s, and the major point that I try to make for each and every pilot is that the nose gear (on the pre-R models) is quite spindly and very sensitive to side loads.

As the fleet ages, the linkage becomes a bit weak and deserves special attention on maintenance checks. If the linkage breaks, there is no way to lock the nose gear down in flight. I would have to say that the nose gear is the weak link in the entire 310 system.

As an overall package, size, useful load, comfort, speed, economy, the 310 cannot be beat. The control layout, location of the throttles, props, gear, flaps, trim wheel, all lend themselves to a pilot's airplane.

Nice to fly, easy to fly, a good instrument platform. The old "Dutch roll" tendency was, I believe, generally a function of mild over control and getting slightly behind the airplane.

Paul S. Soulé
Miami, Fla.

Cessna
Crusader T303

Cessna's last piston twin design, the Crusader, has many appealing qualities. All around, it is the most thoughtfully designed light twin and one of the most interesting modern general aviation concepts. Unfortunately, its production life was brief: Only 297 were built during four years. Also unfortunately, more than one definition of the word "light" applies to it.

In the last heady days of the traditional light-aircraft industry (that's the late 70s to you youngsters), Cessna designed and built a prototype of the Model 303 Clipper, a light twin to compete with the Beech Duchess, Grumman American Cougar and Piper Seminole.

To its credit, the company stopped to assess the market and decided it wasn't big enough. Cessna design engineers, led by the highly regarded David R. Ellis, went back to the drawing boards and returned with a totally different concept.

The mid-mounted horizontal tail: a thing of beauty designed to reduce propwash vibration and improve elevator effectiveness. But watch out for over-rotation on takeoff. Also, several fixes were needed to prevent rudder oscillation in icing.

History and Development

Cessna's perception of the market niche had changed greatly. The new airplane was now a cabin-class twin, air stair door and all, aimed at the business and air taxi markets to fit above the Seneca and to mix it up with Navajos and Model 58 Barons and its own 400 series aircraft.

Redesignated the Model T303, the new design was closer in concept to the 400 series twins, such as the 402, 414 and 421. But it didn't look like anything else in the Cessna product line, in much the same way that the 177 Cardinal was a radical departure from any other Cessna single.

The Crusader definitely is not a parts-bin, bolt-on assemblage that typified the development of 100 and 200 series Cessnas. It displays much of the trickle-down application of human factors and more sophisticated aerodynamic, structures and manufacturing techniques that was first applied to the Citation and then to the 400 series.

Cruciform Advantages

Unlike any other Cessna, it features a cruciform tail. The horizontal stabilizer is mounted approximately one-third of the way up the prominent vertical stabilizer. Among the advantages claimed for this arrangement are less disturbed airflow from prop wash and better pitch qualities with configuration changes. (One former high-ranking Cessna official suggests that using a cruciform tail design on the 340, 425 and 441 would not only have improved the flying qualities of these airplanes and reduced interior noise and vibration, but would also have eliminated the disastrous empennage failures and troublesome fixes in the 340 and 441.) Like the 400 and 500 series designs, the smooth wing is bonded. Each wing has a single integral fuel tank.

When Pan American World Airways objected to anyone else calling an airplane "Clipper," the trade name was changed to Crusader (neither LTV nor the Navy seemed to mind). Including the radical redesign from the 303 to the T303, the development took six years, which included a lot of wind tunnel evaluation and testing—unusual for a light airplane—and more than 1,000 hours of flight tests using two prototypes. At its official introduction late in 1979, a Cessna official claimed that more research and testing had gone into the T303 than any light twin or single the company had built.

Less Than Optimal

As a design, it is quite refined. A number of interesting aerodynamic devices have been incorporated. The wing was originally designed with a leading edge cuff to provide lower stall speeds and better low-speed handling. Flight tests disclosed some elevator buffeting in approach and landing configurations and at high angles of attack. With flaps extended, disturbed airflow was created by interference with the extended nacelle wing lockers, too. Longitudinal stability was less than optimum (meaning not quite good or terrible).

Through wind tunnel testing, the cuff was scrapped and replaced with a variety of airflow control and energizing devices. These are mounted in the wing root/ fuselage junction area, on both the inboard and outboard engine nacelles just above the wing leading edge, on the vertical fin above the horizontal stabilizer (to improve rudder effectiveness) and on the upper surfaces of the semi-Fowler flaps.

The trick to all of this was to improve control effectiveness and handling qualities in all flight regimes without performance penalties. More work was required later to deal with problems during flight in icing conditions (more about this later).

Nothing Artificial

The extensive attention to configuration and to keeping the air flowing properly resulted in another feature: Unlike many Cessnas, there are no downsprings, bob weights, control interconnects or other artificial devices in the Crusader.

The main landing gear is trailing link, which makes less-than-perfect arrivals seem quite smooth. The gear operating system is the troublesome electrically actuated hydraulic operating system that has plagued so many owners and operators of Cessna retractable singles. However, emergency extension is free-fall. The system has been comparatively troublefree in the Crusader.

The powerplants are lightweight versions of Continental's 520 series rated at 250 hp. The TSIO 520-BE is 65 pounds lighter than other turbosupercharged, injected variants. That immediately elicited concern from a lot of operators who considered most Continental engines to be too lightweight already. Garrett turbos with hydraulic wastegate actuator/controllers were bolted to the engines by Cessna. A fire detection system with both visual (a light) and aural alerting is standard (fire suppression is not). Initial recommended TBO was 2,000 hours, compared to 1,400 hours on the 285-hp TSIO-520Bs on the turbo 310. The standard alternators provide a paltry 60 amps—too little for the electrical demands of an aircraft in this category. But 95-amp alternators were offered as an option (provided as part of the optional deice equipment).

Counter-Rotating Props

The Crusader installation also marked the first use of counter-rotating power-plants by Cessna. Another distinction is that the engines use a comparatively high 8.5/1 compression ratio. This, together with the desire for increased fuel efficiency through more aggressive leaning, results in a maximum power setting of 72 percent in cruise in standard or higher atmospheric conditions. Pressurized mags were included from the beginning.

There are no cowl flaps. In a variation of updraft cooling, engine compartment air exhausts through louvers in the top of the nacelle. Rate of flow/temperatures are controlled by shutters beneath the louvers that are actuated by, well, cowl flap controls in the cockpit.

Cockpit Design

The well-designed cockpit is backed up by big-airplane features like three-axis trim and a dual main bus electrical system with dual avionics bus. The electrical system, including all switches, is clearly organized.

There are no chintzy reset-only circuit breakers; all are push/pull. Power-related instruments are well located with reference to power controls. The fuel system is a simple on-off-crossfeed and the fuel gauges are mounted directly above the selectors on the aft end of the power quadrant console. While the cockpit is well laid-out for single-pilot operation, there is enough room on the panel for copilot flight instruments, particularly if something more modern than ARC avionics are installed. Many T303s have been equipped with weather radar.

Cabin Load & Comfort

The four-seat main cabin carries its nearly four-foot (47.75 in.) width all the way back to the door. While it is cozy with all seats filled, it is pleasant and well lighted by three generous windows on each side. Certainly in terms of the spacious appearance and access it is a big improvement over the tapered-cabin C-310 it was designed to replace.

The only emergency escape other than the door is a copilot's side door or hatch, which is hinged at the top.

There is a lot of room for baggage, too. In addition to the aft end cabin compartment, there is a nose bay and a set of wing lockers. There are more cubes than weight allowances. The cabin baggage bay is limited to 200 pounds, the nose bay to 150 pounds of avionics and luggage, and 120 pounds in each of the wing lockers.

Model Changes

Few changes were made during the T303's short production life (1982 to 1984 model years). Aside from incremental improvements to structures and systems as a result of service difficulties, only two major changes were made. Known-icing approval was obtained in 1982. In 1983, an optional cargo door was offered. It extends the main cabin door opening from 24 to 56 inches. The aft bulkhead was relocated also, increasing cabin length another 6.5 inches and cubic volume by four feet. The weight penalty is 19.5 pounds.

Other options were added, including fuel pressure limiters, fuel totalizers, low-fuel warning lights, heavy-duty battery, air conditioning and the already-mentioned copilot flight instruments with dedicated pitot/static system. Two other options are desirable. One is the yaw damper. Despite all the attention to aerodynamics and handling, in turbulence the airplane gets very uncomfortable, particularly for passengers.

The other is a heavy-duty wheel and brake option. In standard form, the Crusader's maximum landing weight is 5,000 pounds. With optional heavy duty wheels and brakes, it is approved for a max landing weight equal to the 5,150 pound maximum takeoff weight. Zero fuel weight for all configurations is 4,850 pounds.

While T303 serial numbers run from T30300001 to -315, a total of 297 were built. Part of the discrepancy is accounted for by a block of serial numbers assigned to aircraft that were not built (247 to 258). Sales extended from 1981 (31 were delivered) to 1986, when two were sold. The peak year was 1982, when 131 deliveries were made (interim years: '83—57; '84—65; and '85—1).

Fore and aft baggage loading makes for flexibility. Crusader was the first Cessna with counter-rotating props. Nosegear shimmy has been a problem.

Pricing

The initial base price was $229,500 in 1982. In 1983 it went up to $260,250 and in 1984 to $278,450. The last list price for the higher-performing T310R, in 1981, was $188,000. Even allowing for avionics and other equipment included in the base Crusader cost, it was priced considerably higher than its predecessor.

Its price new also was at least $50,000 higher than a comparably equipped Seneca III. Other competition to the T303 depends upon what you are looking for. For personal use, anything from the B55 Baron (which in similar model years also cost less than the Crusader) and B58 at about the same price, to the higher-priced turbocharged B58, Cessna 402C and Navajo are in the range.

All of the others carry higher payloads with full fuel and all outperform it at altitudes where turbocharging doesn't come into play. Above 10,000 feet, where turbocharged airplanes begin to outperform their normally aspirated cousins, the T303, with its lower power output, is the slowest.

At typically equipped weights, however, the Crusader has a higher payload than the 310, the pressurized 340 or the 414. And in terms of systems, pilot workload, handling qualities and passenger appeal, only the latest model 414 offers more—of course, at higher initial, operating and used prices.

An Edge

The T303 is fuel efficient for its performance. Its most direct competitor is the Seneca III. At typical operating altitudes, their performance is close enough that in the hands of the average multiengine pilot there really is no difference. But the Crusader will save a few bucks per hour due to its lower fuel burn. And in more subjective areas, such as appearance and impression, the Crusader has an edge. It also has the edge in handling qualities and in related operational areas. For instance, both approach flaps and gear can be extended up to 175 KIAS. With gear extended, the airplane can be dived right to redline (210 KIAS). At the other end of the speed range, Vmc is 65. Vsse (minimum safe [intentional] single engine— the fudge factor the manufacturers added to most twins) is 80 KIAS. Stall speed dirty is 58 KIAS.

Handling qualities are very good when all is working. The blend of systems, cockpit organization and handling make the Crusader a very manageable airplane to fly on instruments (especially with the yaw damper option installed and properly rigged). With all the speed and descent management options available, it can operate in any mix of traffic without putting undue stress—including shock cooling of the powerplants.

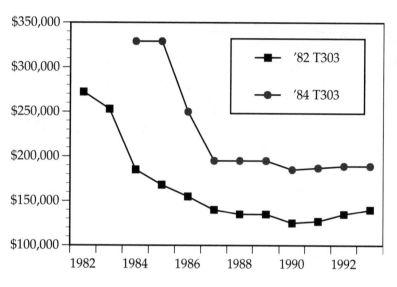

The only characteristic pilots should watch out for is the tendency to over rotate during takeoff.

Insufficient Rudder Trim

During single-engine operations, pilots will discover that rudder trim is not enough to neutralize the forces required. The leg on the working engine side will get a lot of isometric exercise that quickly becomes tiring to just about anyone but an Arnold Schwarzenneger. This was obvious during single-engine work during the writer's first Crusader flight; it became an annoyance and ultimately a distraction during a night IFR flight when an engine was shut down because of flagging oil pressure. (The fault was later traced to a broken oil line. The cause most likely was vibration.)

Although maximum power is obtained at a relatively low 2,400 rpm, noise and vibration levels are high. Because the horizontal tail is up out of the propellor wash, rpms can be set as low as 2,100 in cruise. Most operators seem to have settled on 2,200 as the best compromise. Reduced rpm has a noticeable effect on occupant comfort.

Performance

The Crusader will clear a 50-foot obstacle (standard day, sea level, of course) on takeoff in 1,750 feet and will land over the obstacle in 1,450 feet. However, accelerate/stop distance is 3,185 feet. In other words, there is no surplus power in the going or stopping department if anything goes wrong.

Single-engine rate of climb when the airplane is cleaned up is 220 fpm in ideal circumstances. That performance margin (remember, it was achieved by a better than average factory pilot) is reversed with poor coordination or with anything hanging out. Gear down, it changes to a 130 fpm rate of descent. Full flaps make it 230 fpm down. Even a windmilling propellor results in a 30 fpm descent. Go to Denver—even go to Bridgeport on a summer day—and the safety margin disappears. This is not peculiar to the Crusader; it is shared with most piston twins.

If for no other reason, the temptation to fill the tanks, all the seats and baggage areas, too, should be scrupulously avoided. As with any other light twin, to do so is a game of Russian roulette.

The other caveat is that the more sophisticated the systems in a given airplane, the more knowledge and proficiency is required of the pilot. The Crusader definitely fits into the sophisticated-systems category. The more options there are to troubleshoot or correct a fault, the more decisions there are to be made.

Light, as in Flimsy

Practically from the start of service, the less flattering aspects of "light" twin became apparent. It also became apparent that good design work was undercut by poor manufacturing. Many parts of the airplane, and many systems, accessories and components were not up to real-world stresses and strains. In addition to design and supplier weaknesses, there was poor quality control on the factory floor. To its credit, the factory has not orphaned the airplane. Attempts to improve its shortcomings continue.

The basic appeal of the design (and the pressures of carrying expensive airplanes in dealer inventory) resulted in many Crusaders being put in commercial service, from the originally intended air taxi applications to multiengine and instrument training. This is indicated in accident/incident reports, airworthiness alerts and service difficulty reports (SDRs) in which the purpose of flight or total time are reported.

The roomy cabin and rear-entry airstair door get high votes from users.

While the information is too inconsistent to do a statistical analysis, more than half the fleet has well over 1,000 hours. About seven percent of the fleet has over 3,000 hours. Several airframes have flown in excess of 5,000 hours (the highest we found recorded, in an SDR filed in April 1990, was 5,757 hours). Since the average personal-use airplane logs less than 100 hours per year and the average professionally flown piston aircraft in corporate use flies just over 300, the Crusader is being put to work.

Service Difficulties

Somewhat surprisingly, the engine has stood up fairly well. Of the 402 SDRs filed between 1985 and 1991, 46 were engine related. A number of the engine-related SDRs referred to high-time engines where embrittlement, "cheap" overhauls and similar problems were encountered. But there have been a lot of problems under the "hood," many related to the turbochargers or turbocharger-caused heat-related problems.

The most troublesome accessory has been the ignition system. There were 60 SDRs on the magneto system, most referring to Slick 4200 and 6200 series. A number of the reports referred to repeated problems. A number of problems have been caused by moisture in the pressurized magnetos. Several technicians recommended more frequent inspection of the filters for contamination. This is consistent with the experience of many aircraft equipped (or retrofitted) with pressurized magnetos to correct arcing and other ignition problems associated with turbocharged engines.

Alternators have continued to be another troublesome accessory. Almost from the start, there have been drive problems involving alignment, pulleys and thrown belts. There were 16 alternator SDRs filed in the period reviewed.

Trailing beam landing gear smooths landings, but the gear has had its share of mechanical problems.

The fuel pressure system and auxiliary pumps have also seen fairly large-scale problems, with 22 SDRs filed. The comments are indicative of more extensive problems: "Nine pumps in seven months/602 hours." "The high side lasts six months at most." "This fleet of five aircraft usually has at least one pump replaced in each aircraft per week."

Gear Problems

The landing gear continues to be a problem, despite a number of fixes. This is another system for which comments in the SDRs suggest the problems are greater than the number of reports filed. With respect to the nose gear fixes, one report said, "the improved part is still failing." In a 1989 SDR, a technician noted "out of a fleet of six, all (actuating brackets) have been changed at least twice." Several recommended that the gear actuating brackets be inspected every 50 hours.

Twelve SDRs dealt with brake system master and wheel cylinders. One report stated that they had experienced ". . . constant problems with brakes. The hydraulic reservoir is too small for the demand or to handle small leaks (its capacity is four ounces)." There were six SDRs relating to vertical stabilizer attach fittings. This problem, which appears to be a combination of improper manufacture and the effects of vibration, also was the subject of an airworthiness alert. One shop recommended inspecting the area every 100 hours.

Another area worthy of close inspection is in the outer wing. There were three reports of strobe light wires chafing through fuel vent lines. Most of the other SDRs covered a wide range of problems with no discernable pattern. Surprisingly, there was only one SDR dealing with the avionics.

Another area with few reports that nevertheless bear watching or periodic inspection is the circuit breaker panel. It can be affected by water leaks through the pilot-side ice window. It occurred four times on one aircraft, affecting the gear operating circuit. In several instances, the circuits failed internally and could not be isolated or reset by the pilot.

Service Bulletins

Cessna has issued more than 30 service bulletins on the Crusader. Of the 27 *The Aviation Consumer* has seen, eleven were mandatory and eight recommended. Also, 53 service letters have been issued. A number of these relate to troubleshooting and other maintenance procedures.

Many of the service bulletins relate to both SDRs and ADs. For instance, four deal with the turbocharger and exhaust systems; one with engine mounts. Four apply to the landing gear. One corrects a problem with the wing/engine nacelle attach system, another the nose baggage door latching system. Another optional bulletin deals with replacing Slick with Continental magnetos.

There are four dealing with the deicing system and the aerodynamic affects of ice accumulation at the junction of the vertical and horizontal stabilizers. Twice, FAA rescinded known icing approval. In 1986 Cessna devised what appears to be the final fix. The modification includes a revised fairing and additional vortex generators. The latter are mounted on the vertical stabilizer below the horizontal tail surface. Given the service history of the Crusader, it is somewhat noteworthy that only one other AD has been issued that concerns it alone (and not systems common to other aircraft). This applies to the nose gear actuator attach fitting and requires repetitive 50-hour inspections or the installation of an improved fitting.

To its credit, Cessna has provided free parts plus a labor allowance on these ADs, as well as on several of the service bulletins.

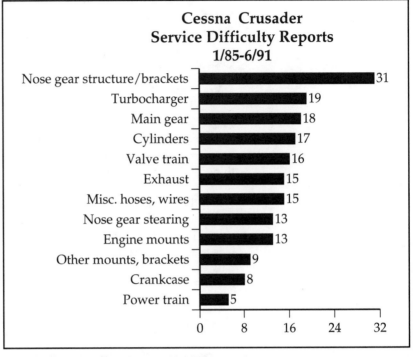

Safety

Given the apparently high utilization of the small Crusader fleet, the accident record is fairly good. Between June 1983 and June 1991, a total of 32 accidents was reported.

There were three fatals, in which a total of eight people were killed. One of the fatal accidents occurred when an experienced pilot on an IFR flight plan apparently stalled at night in snow showers while on downwind for a visual approach. In the second, a non-instrument-rated pilot lost control at night in IMC and snow showers. And in the third a pilot encountered icing and lost control.

It is also noteworthy that a comparatively high percentage is clearly mechanically related (15 of 19), and four others are suspect. Eight are engine related, three stem from gear failures and one each airframe, electrical system and brakes. Only two were caused by fuel exhaustion, one by gear retraction and one by running off a slush-covered runway.

Cost/Performance/Specifications

Model	Year	Average Retail Price	Cruise Speed (kt)	Useful Load (lb)	Std/Opt Fuel (gal)	Engines	SE Ceiling (ft)	TBO (hr)	Overhaul Cost @
T303	1982	$140,000	180	1,870	155	TSIO-520-AE	13,000	2,000	$19,000
T303	1983	$157,000	180	1,870	155	TSIO-520-AE	13,000	2,000	$19,000
T303	1984	$189,000	180	1,870	155	TSIO-520-AE	13,000	2,000	$19,000

Though, as we said earlier the Crusader is an interesting combination of appealing attributes, it still is plagued by design and manufacturing shortcomings. Some of the higher time airframes are beginning to show the effects of age. It wouldn't be wise to buy one without a careful study of the records to ensure that all modifications and improvements have been made. Also, have a complete white-glove inspection of the airplane, engines and accessories made by a qualified technician experienced with the Crusader. In retrospect, if Cessna had stuck with the piston-aircraft business, there undoubtedly would have been a beefier version of the Crusader, as well as higher-powered and pressurized models. On balance, Cessna was going in the right direction with the T303.

Owner Comments

I have owned and operated my Crusader since January 1985. I purchased it as a factory demonstrator directly from Cessna with 214 hours on the plane. Terms of the purchase also included an annual inspection, which turned out to be the best thing that ever happened to me.

When the annual was completed, significant corrosion was found on all cylinders on the left engine, and the compression rating on the No. five cylinder was just below 13 psi. The right engine also had light to severe corrosion on five cylinders. One was pulled from the left engine for a more detailed inspection, and a casting flaw on the engine block was also discovered, which necessitated a complete new left engine.

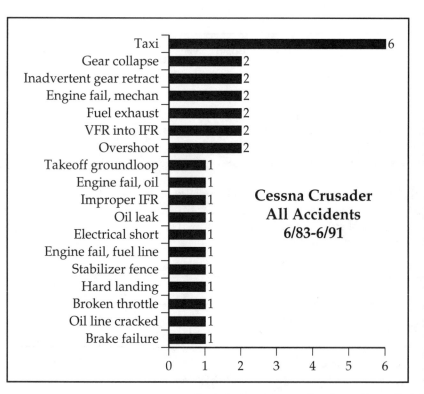

**Cessna Crusader
All Accidents
6/83-6/91**

By the time everything was completed and the plane was back in flying order, I ended up with a completely new left engine and entire new "top" on the right engine. Total cost came to $50,272, of which Cessna and/or Continental paid $48,264. This covered all parts, engines, pro-rated labor, etc. I now have about 940 hours on the plane. Other problems I have experienced were as follows:

1) Replacement parts are extremely expensive. For instance, I had to replace a tachometer at 618 hours, at a cost of $1,560. This seems outrageous to me.

2) At 762 hours I discovered something which at the time caused me great concern, and still worries me. On an annual inspection it was determined that the left flap was unairworthy due to extreme heat damage. In trying to determine the cause of the problem, it became evident that the fuel tank drain valve is located immediately outboard of the exhaust pipe. When the system was installed at the factory, apparently a washer was missing, which caused a "minute" gas leak. At some time in landing configuration with full flaps extended, the heat given off from the exhaust system was sufficient to ignite a small amount of fuel

from the drip, causing a blowtorch effect on the flap. As far as I am concerned, location of the fuel tank drain valve directly behind the exhaust pipe is an extremely poor one, and incredibly dangerous. Total cost to replace the flap also amounted to approximately $3,000. In addition, the plane was grounded for almost one month.

3) At 775 hours during work on an exhaust system AD which necessitated pulling both turbochargers, it was determined that one of them had casting flaws, and cracks had developed. This required replacement of both turbochargers at a cost of $3,500. In addition to the above items, I have had a continual recurring problem with the Slick pressurized magnetos on the plane. To date I have suffered four magneto failures, including one almost simultaneous failure of both mags on the right engine just after rotation with the plane at max gross takeoff weight and IAS + 10 conditions. Fortunately, I was on a 15,000-foot runway and was able to land straight ahead. Aside from the above problems, I thoroughly enjoy the Crusader. The airplane is an absolute delight to fly and is extremely stable in all weather conditions.

Being located in the Pacific Northwest, I log a significant number of IFR and night operations and have found that the plane flies well in all conditions. It has an extremely high gear and flap speed, which allows a lot of flexibility when getting slowed to landing configuration, and overall I am extremely pleased with the plane's comfort and reliability.

At the time I purchased the plane, the factory estimated that direct operating costs would be about $78.92 an hour. To date my figures have averaged $113.24 per hour. Fuel and oil have averaged $54.40 per hour, and maintenance costs $58.84 per hour. Maintenance costs are almost twice the cost of the factory estimate, but I believe this is due to the dramatic increase in the price of airplane parts since 1984. After factoring in replacement reserves of approximately $25 per hour, I end up with a cost per flight hour of $138. This compares to Cessna's estimate of $103 per hour based on 1984 figures.

I maintain my plane to FAR 135 conditions, and normal 50-hour inspections run about $285 plus parts, while 100-hour inspections (annuals) have averaged $1,380 plus squawks. I have found the original factory performance estimates to vary in accuracy somewhat. I normally preflight based on a 170-knot cruise speed, while Cessna estimated 180 knots. I fly at 72% power with the mp and rpm at 24/24, and average 26 gph of fuel. I found the range slightly better than book.

Overall, I have been extremely pleased with the airplane and its performance. Its short-field characteristics are excellent, and the trailing link landing gear system makes it almost impossible to botch a landing. In addition, compared to other light twins in its class, the stairway door, large cabin area and emergency exit located by the copilot's seat are to be considered real plusses.

The plane can also carry a tremendous amount of luggage, people, etc. and still remain safely within all CG and gross weight requirements. Overall, I would rate the plane a solid eight on a scale of one to 10, and other than having to pay the extremely high cost of replacement parts, I have thoroughly enjoyed the plane over the last 700 hours.

William J. Allred
Portland, Ore.

Cessna 340

As a relatively easy step up to the high-flying comfort of pressurization, the 340 has proved itself a popular personal transport and corporate runabout.

If sheer numbers are any indication, the 340 actually is the second most popular pressurized twin. There are nearly 1,000 registered in this country (out of about 1,200 built), placing the 340 a close second to its big brother, the 421 (with well over 1,000 registered). In third place is another one of Cessna's medium twins, the 414, with just shy of 800 on the registry.

Though the service ceiling reaches nearly 30,000 feet, most owners operate between 16,000 and 24,000 feet.

The 340 and 414 are very similar, sharing the same wing, flaps, ailerons, landing gear and engines. (The 421 has geared engines.) Because it's lighter and has a smaller cabin, the 340 cruises about seven to 12 knots faster than the 414 on the same fuel. But for the speed, the 340 sacrifices payload; and even the most ardent aficionado (and most 340 owners seem to really like their airplanes) will admit that if you fill all the seats, you won't be able to carry enough fuel to go very far at all. One owner quipped that the six seats in his airplane are little more than an illusion.

However, most 340 owners seem to have little use for all six seats; they typically fly with only two or three people aboard and enough fuel for a good three or four hours, with reserves. Owners say their airplanes are pleasurable and easy to fly, though they do give rightful nods to the airplane's labyrinthine fuel system and its tendency to sink readily when dirty and slow.

If the prospect of flying above most weather and traffic snarls, free of the constraints of nosebags, appeals to you, the price for admission varies from about $90,000 for an early model to over $310,000 for one of the last off the line. After that, to stay in the game, figure on shelling out anywhere from $160 to $260 for each hour you fly the airplane.

Smaller Step

Cessna Aircraft Co. introduced the 340 in 1972 as "the step-up airplane for light twin owners." The company had said pretty much the same thing two years earlier when it unveiled the 414, but that airplane really was a lower-cost option for those considering purchase of a pressurized medium twin, such as a Beech Duke, Piper P-Navajo or 421. The 340 was intended to be a step up from unpressurized light twins, such as the 310, Aztec and Baron. Though a 300-series twin, the 340 has the aura of a heavier airplane. It sits tall on its 400-series gear and has an air-stair door behind the left wing.

Engines installed on 340s from 1972 through 1975 were Continental TSIO-520Ks, which produce 285 horsepower at 33 inches manifold pressure from sea level to 16,000 feet. However, most of the K engines in early 340s have been converted to Js (by Riley and Western Skyways) or Ns (by RAM). The TSIO-520J engine, used on early 414s, produces 310 hp at 36 inches manifold pressure. The N engine, installed on later 414s and 340s, produces 310 hp at 38 inches. The major difference between the K engine and the J and N variants is that the latter are equipped with intercoolers (which reduce temperature of induction air as it moves from turbocharger compressors into induction manifolds).

Changes

Although the airplane incurred a host of minor tweaks during its production run, there were very few significant changes. The most significant of these occurred in 1976, when Cessna began installing TSIO-520N engines on the airplane. This change was accompanied by an expansion of the model designation to 340A.

The N engines produce their rated 310 hp up to 20,000 feet and provide higher cruise speeds and better climb and single-engine performance. Three-blade McCauley propellers, formerly an option, also became standard equipment in 1976; earlier 340s came with two-blade McCauleys.

Certification for flight into known icing conditions, when properly equipped, came in 1977. The next year, a maximum ramp weight of 6,025 pounds was approved, and max weight for takeoff and landing was set at 5,990 pounds for the 340A (compared with 5,975 pounds for the 340).

The last notable change occurred in 1979, with the switch to TSIO-520NB engines (the B denotes use of a heavier crankshaft). Subsequent modification of cylinders, valve lifters and piston pins by Continental increased TBO of the NB engines from 1,400 to 1,600 hours in 1983. But Cessna didn't build any 340As (or much of anything else) that year; and after putting together a scant 17 of the airplanes in 1984, production was terminated.

Performance

Though service ceiling touches nearly 30,000 feet, most owners operate between 16,000 and 24,000 feet, where they get 190 to 205 knots on about 30 gallons per hour at 65 percent power and 200 to 217 knots on 32 to 34 gph using 75 percent power.

Rate of climb at sea level is a rather sprightly 1,650 fpm, but climb performance tapers rapidly above 20,000 feet to a dawdling 300 to 400 fpm in the mid-20s. The 340's single-engine ROC is 315 fpm, better than the 414 (290 fpm), Beech P58 Baron (270) and the Piper 601P (240) and 602P (302) Aerostars. In its class, the 340 is outshined only by its much lighter, centerline-thrust stablemate, the Pressurized Skymaster, which climbs 375 fpm on one engine. Single-engine minimum control speed is 82 knots. Stall speeds are 79 knots, clean, and 71 knots in landing configuration.

To its credit, Cessna provided information on accelerate-stop and accelerate-go performance in 340 POHs. The book indicates that, under standard conditions, a 340 that loses an engine at lift-off speed (91 knots) can be brought to a full stop within 3,000 feet of brake release. The book also indicates that should a pilot decide to go after losing one on lift-off, the airplane will clear a 50-foot obstacle after traveling less than 4,000 feet over the ground after brake release.

The performance figures above are for 340s with 310-hp engines. Those that still have 285-hp K engines (if any) are nearly 20 knots slower in cruise, use roughly 200 feet more runway for takeoff and climb 1,500 fpm on both engines, 250 fpm on one.

Handling and Comfort

"No bad habits" is how most owners characterize the handling characteristics of their 340s, and most claim to have had very little difficulty transitioning to the heavier twin from lighter and less complicated aircraft.

The airplane does present a double whammy of sorts, being rather clean and therefore difficult to slow down on one hand, and having relatively low gear and flap operating speeds on the other. For example, flaps can be extended 15 degrees at 160 knots (the limit is 156 knots in the first 300 airplanes built) to help slow the airplane down to max gear-extension speed, a pitiable 140 knots. But slowing the airplane to 160 knots without shock-cooling the engines can be a problem (especially in the keep-em-high and drop-em-like-anchors ATC environment). Owners say descents and approaches require careful planning.

Once the airplane is slowed down with gear and flaps deployed, however, it tends to sink like a rock, according to owners, and some power must be maintained right into the flare.

The heavy-iron ambience of the air-stair door wears off quite quickly when occupants must squeeze through a very narrow (seven-inch) aisle to their seats. Once seated, though, the cabin is quite comfortable. The 340's cabin is 46.5 inches wide and 49 inches high, about the same size as an Aerostar's and 4.5 inches wider than a P-Baron's.

Systems

The pressurization system is the same as those found in Cessna's 400-series twins. Maximum differential is 4.2 psi, providing an 8,000-foot cabin up to 20,000 feet; above that, the cabin "climbs" with the airplane. Most buyers passed on the standard automatic-control set-up, which activates and deactivates while climbing or descending through 8,000 feet, and equipped their 340s with the optional variable-control system, which allows the pilot to program cabin altitude and rate of climb. The variable system maintains a sea level cabin up to 9,000 feet, then maintains the pilot-selected cabin altitude until a 4.2-psi differential is reached.

Managing the pressurization system actually is a piece of cake, requiring only a few seconds each flight. The pilot merely dials in field elevation plus 500 feet before takeoff and landing, and cruise cabin altitude on initial climb. (Of course, saying that you don't have to fuss much with the system doesn't mean you don't have to monitor it carefully during flight.)

Fuel Fun

It's the fuel system that keeps a 340 pilot on his toes. Start with the tip tanks, the mains, which hold 100 usable gallons. Add up to four auxiliary wing tanks, two holding 40 gallons, the other two holding 23 gallons. Throw in locker tanks, which add another 40 gallons. That's up to 203 gallons in containers strewn throughout the length of the wings. Remember to use the mains, alone, for takeoff and landing. The engines will feed directly from the auxiliary tanks, but fuel in the lockers has to be transferred to the mains. Of course, you have to make room in the mains, first. And if you have only one locker tank (which many 340s do have), remember to use crossfeed; dump all 120 pounds from a locker into one tip tank, and the imbalance will be enough to upset even your autopilot.

Unfortunately, Cessna never got around to simplifying the fuel systems in its 300-series twins (Crusader excepted) as it did in most of the 400s.

Empty Seats

Probably the biggest drawback to the 340 is its load-carrying ability. Most are very well equipped and can accommodate only around 1,600 to 1,700 pounds of fuel and payload. (The useful loads shown in the accompanying specifications table are maximums and valid only for unequipped airplanes.) Load enough gas for a 4.5-hour flight with reserves, and you can take along only two passengers and their bags. Fill the seats with 170-pound FAA clones and pack away their regulation 30 pounds of baggage each, and you can carry enough fuel for a 1.5-hour jaunt.

Considering the severe payload limitations, the baggage space in the 340 seems a cruel joke. Among the cabin, nose and locker compartments, there's a cavernous 53 cubic feet of space in which a maximum of 930 pounds can be crammed. That is, however, the maximum. Most 340s have at least one fuel tank occupying a locker, and nose baggage compartment space typically is compromised by avionics gear.

Clamshell airstair door spells cabin class. C-340 was appropriately promoted as a "step-up" airplane for light twin owners.

Modifications

Much the 340 fleet has had engine modifications performed by RAM Aircraft Corp. in Waco, Tex., (817) 752-8381. RAM, which enjoys an excellent reputation among owners of 300- and 400-series Cessnas, has offered a variety of mods under different names. Currently on deck are the Series II and Series IV packages, which feature new camshafts manufactured by Crane, brand-new steel cylinders, and Hartzell Q-tip props, among other things. Both packages include a seventh stud on crankcase cylinder pads, which reduces the stresses in these areas that often cause cracks.

According to RAM's specs, the Series II mod improves climb performance by 500 fpm, single-engine climb by 30 fpm and cruise speeds by five knots. Also, it provides a 150-pound boost in useful load for the 340A, 165 pounds for the 340. Series II engines are rated at 310 hp, but the Series IV mod increases the rating to 325 hp (at 41 inches manifold pressure and 2,700 rpm). RAM's figures include 600 fpm and 60 fpm improvements, respectively, in two-engine and single-engine climb performance, and 10 knots more cruise speed. Useful load is increased 300 pounds in the 340A, 315 pounds in the 340.

Improved intercooling systems now are available from American Aviation of Spokane, Wash., (509) 838-5354. The installation includes ram-air inlet ducts below the engine nacelles and more efficient (American says 28 to 70 percent more efficient) heat exchanger cores. The company says its system cuts the temperature of air entering the engine from about 170 degrees to 80 degrees, improving rate of climb by up to 300 fpm and adding up to 15 knots in cruise.

A STOL mod for 340s is offered by Sierra Industries in Uvalde, Tex., (512) 278-4381. It includes installation of Robertson-designed Fowler flaps and a trim spring that precludes the need to retrim the elevators when the flaps are raised or lowered. Sierra says the mod decreases accelerate-stop distances by 40 percent and improves short-field performance about 15 percent.

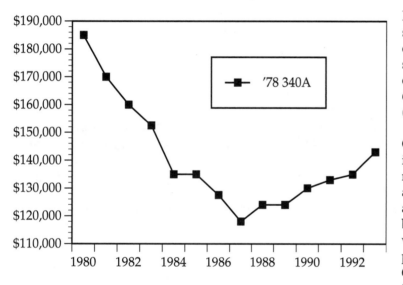

Precise Flight, Inc. in Bend, Ore. makes speed brakes for the C-340. They're of novel design, and come projecting in the airstream from a snug enclosure at the aft end of the engine nacelles. Their address is 63120 Powell Butte Rd., Bend, Ore. 97701, (800) 547-2558.

One of the most intriguing safety-enhancing mods for the C-340 is Micro AeroDynamics' vortex generator STC, which for all intents and purposes eliminates Vmc and gives great control at low airspeed. A bonus is a 300-pound boost in the gross weight. The company is located at 4000 Airport Rd., Suite D, Anacortes, Wash., (800) 677-2370. RAM Aircraft has also gotten into the vortex-generator business and can offer an STC kit on the C-340 for less than Micro's. Their kit lowers the stall eight knots clean and four knots dirty. Thanks to improved control effectiveness, the Vmc drops by 11 knots, which also pulls it below the stall speed, just like Micro's.

Maintenance

Like any other high-performance airplane, a 340 is not one to tolerate skimpy maintenance. If overhaul prices in the $20,000 range (times two), annual inspections at several thousand dollars and operating expenses above $200 an hour are enough to curl your toes (as they do ours), don't expect to have a good time owning a 340.

Those with the wherewithal to have a good time, though, should be aware of a few items gleaned from recent service difficulty reports that might conspire to ruin their day. First, there are the TSIO-520 crankcases, which have a history of cracking. In mid-1976, Continental switched to heavier cases, which helped a bit but certainly provided no panacea. A couple of knowledgeable sources estimated that about two-thirds of the engines flying in 340s right now probably are cracked in one place or another. But not all cracks are critical, and the same sources said they've been seeing far fewer catastrophic engine failures caused by crankcase cracks. The reports also showed cracked cylinders and cylinder heads to be a rather frequent problem. Cracked and blown-out cockpit windows were the subject of several reports, as were cracked Bendix mag housings and distributor blocks, loose horizontal and vertical stabilizer attach bolts and cracked waste gate couplings.

Also among the reports was a smattering of leaking and chafed fuel system fittings, cracks and loose bearings in wheels, broken and frayed airstair door support cables, broken turbocharger oil scavenger pump gears and cracked and corroded exhaust system components.

Of course, any prepurchase inspection will include a check for compliance with all ADs, and there have been quite a few. One requires removal of certain oil filters, which were found prone to leak. Another AD (88-03-07) requires inspection of fuel crossfeed lines for chafing and modification of firewall stiffener flanges and fuel lines. AD 87-23-08 calls for ultrasonic inspection of the crankshafts in TSIO-520J, K and N engines for cracks during the next overhaul or teardown.

AD 87-21-02 requires installation of restrictors in fuel filler ports to prevent misfueling (several 340s have been mistaken for turboprops by line personnel). AD 86-13-04 requires cylinder pressure checks for leaks. One very important directive to check for is 82-26-05, which requires visual checks for cracks in the rudder balance weight rib every 100 hours until a new rib is installed. Such cracks have been the subject of numerous service difficulty reports.

The cabin holds six in pressurized comfort, but don't expect more than minimal range with full seats. The 4.2 psi pressurization (in a '78 model) gives a cabin altitude of 10,000 feet when the aircraft is at 23,500 feet.

Safety Record

Several owners told us their 340s are easy to fly. Stout fellows, these; but truth be told, we'd be hard-pressed to think of any other type of civilian airplane that extracts higher premiums on a pilot's discipline and good headwork than a pressurized (ergo, turbocharged) piston twin. We're talking high work load in an airplane with enough systems and assorted gizmos to trick any pilot into illusions of all-weather capability.

Among the accidents we looked at (1984-1986) are several involving 340 pilots who tangled unsuccessfully with Mother Nature on an off day. Three airplanes bearing loads of ice stalled when their pilots attempted to land them. One pilot lost control after radioing that he had flown into "a cell"; another hit a mountain while trying to pick his way VFR through a line of thunderstorms. Three airplanes were damaged when they slid off icy runways during landing attempts. One 340 pilot hit trees after spotting the runway environment during a localizer approach on a dark, foggy night; another collapsed his landing gear after completing an ILS approach to minimums. One 340 settled back onto the runway, gear-up, after losing an engine during takeoff; another, with its fuel selectors improperly positioned, was damaged in a forced landing after losing an engine while on initial climb.

Both engines in yet another 340, with fuel selectors positioned on empty tanks, lost power at the start of a VOR approach. Two airplanes crashed when their pilots unsuccessfully attempted to transition from single-engine approaches to two-engine go-arounds during training flights. One pilot lost control after losing both vacuum pumps during an IFR flight. Another pilot aborted takeoff when the left nose baggage door popped open and locked upright, and the 340 rolled off the runway and down an embankment.

Wing lockers are great for extra loading, but some nacelles may have aux. fuel tanks, adding to the complexity of a by no means stone simple system.

It was determined that a support channel for the baggage door was bent and would allow the door to be closed and apparently locked without actually being locked.

In another case, a pilot radioed that he was returning to the airport shortly after takeoff because of a "serious problem." The 340 crashed in a heavily wooded area, killing all four people aboard. Investigators found it had been refueled with Jet-A.

Back in 1980 the fatal crash of a C-340A into the sea near Ketchikan, Alaska triggered an AD that grounded the fleet briefly, and beefed-up tails were eventually fitted to all 340s. That crash was apparently caused by structural failure of the aircraft's horizontal stabilizer. The pilot had reported a tail vibration, and then radioed that the tail had fallen off and the plane was going down.

Summing Up

If it's a light pressurized twin you're looking for, there aren't that many choices. Besides the 340, there are the Aerostar 601P and 602P, and the Pressurized Baron. The Aerostars are the "pilots' airplanes" of the group; they're fast (about 20 knots faster) and demand no less than sharp, heads-up flying. However, payload capacity is even worse than the 340's, and though the cabin is the same size, the Cessna twin's feels more roomy and comfortable. The Baron is slightly faster than the 340 and has a greater useful load; but it is a bit more expensive.

More than the Aerostar and even the Baron, the 340 exudes cabin class, thanks to its airstair door and tall stance. And it can outclimb the other airplanes. (If you really want a cabin-class twin, check out a 414. It isn't that much more expensive, and the 414A has a much simpler fuel system.)

Of course, we can't overlook (or can we?) the 340's little half-brother, the Pressurized Skymaster, which is much lighter (4,700 pounds gross) and push-pull powered by a pair of 225-hp Continental TSIO-360s. As detailed elsewhere in this volume, the Skymaster has fallen woefully short of living up to its intended role as a "safe" twin. And, though one of the airplanes can be picked up for a fraction of what the other pressurized twins cost, it won't be an inexpensive airplane to own, thanks to design and production flaws.

Owner Comments

We operate our 1975 Cessna 340 an average of 150 to 175 hours per year. All operations are Part 91, and we file IFR on all trips. It is our first pressurized aircraft, and it has been a good choice for our normal trip length. Typically, we carry two to four people 500 to 600 nm. It is a very comfortable airplane and, except for the extremely narrow aisle, provides plenty of room for the passengers.

Performance and handling also are good. Our 340 usually is flown between 16,000 and 24,000 feet, where 205 knots at 65 percent power and just over 30 gph are normal; with 75 percent power giving 215 knots at closer to 35 gph. Traffic is rarely a problem at these altitudes, and the 4.2 psi cabin pressure differential allows us to get over most weather and take advantage of winds.

Care must be taken in balancing cabin payload and fuel. We carry 163 gallons of fuel, but some 340s can hold as much as 203 gallons. This, coupled with a full avionics package, deicing equipment, radar and air conditioning, will drastically cut available cabin payload. However, I appreciate the loading flexibility; if I need to fill the cabin, I can still make most trips with one fuel stop.

At first, maintenance was horrible. The aircraft had been flown only 50 hours in the three years before we bought it, and the inactivity and lack of care took a toll. Once the problems were solved, the upkeep became reasonable. Annual inspections run $1,600 to $2,000, if there are no major surprises. Among our surprises were cracked crankcases at 900 hours and ensuing overhauls that ran about $12,000, each. Total operating cost, including insurance, reserve for overhaul and avionics, ranges from $160 to $165 per hour. Parts seem to be readily available, but they don't come cheap. Two or three days is an average wait for parts.

Overall, we have found the Cessna 340 to be an excellent step into the owner-flown, pressurized twin market. The average owner/pilot will find that, despite sometimes high cabin workloads and a complex fuel system, the 340 is a comfortable and easy plane to fly.

Eric E. Maurer
Cleveland, Tenn.

I own a 1982 Cessna 340 with approximately 700 hours total time. The aircraft had been stored for about two and a half years before being put into operation in the fall of 1985. It now is on a lease-back for charter operations.

Cost/Performance/Specifications

Model	Year Built	Average Retail Price	Cruise Speed (kts)	Useful Load (lbs)	Fuel Std/Opt (gals)	Engine	TBO (hrs)	Overhaul Cost @
340	1972	$91,000	226	2,278	100/180	310-hp Cont. TSIO-520-N	1,400	$20,000
340	1973	$95,500	226	2,252	100/203	310-hp Cont. TSIO-520-N	1,400	$20,000
340	1974	$100,000	226	2,219	100/203	310-hp Cont. TSIO-520-N	1,400	$20,000
340	1975	$110,000	226	2,219	100/203	310-hp Cont. TSIO-520-N	1,400	$20,000
340A	1976	$124,000	244	2,122	102/203	310-hp Cont. TSIO-520-N	1,400	$20,000
340A	1977	$134,000	244	2,112	102/203	310hp Cont. TSIO-520-N	1,400	$20,000
340A	1978	$143,000	244	2,126	102/203	310-hp Cont. TSIO-520-N	1,400	$20,000
340A	1979	$155,000	244	2,116	102/203	310-hp Cont. TSIO-520-NB	1,400	$20,000
340A	1980	$175,000	244	2,114	102/203	310-hp Cont. TSIO-520-NB	1,400	$20,000
340A	1981	$182,000	244	2,104	102/203	310-hp Cont. TSIO-520-NB	1,400	$20,000
340A	1982	$192,000	244	2,077	102/203	310-hp Cont. TSIO-520-NB	1,400	$20,000
340A	1984	$310,000	244	2,077	102/203	310-hp Cont. TSIO-520-NB	1,400	$20,000

A 100-hour check runs about $1,800. Expense for other routine maintenance averages about $10 per hour. Thus far, major maintenance items have included: prop overhaul for $2,200; repair of corrosion in numerous wing areas, $2,000; cylinder work because of low compression, $1,500; and repair of cracks in the supercharger turbine for about $2,000. I suspect some of the wing corrosion began during the storage period. The engine and turbosupercharger work probably was necessitated by a number of different pilots flying the aircraft in charter work and giving less than the tender loving care these engines require.

One other significant, but not terribly expensive structural repair was required on the aft mount of the left tip tank. The doubler was cracked and the fasteners were loose.

As an owner, I would be happier with less exposure to major maintenance costs. As a pilot, I am delighted with the aircraft. It is fast, comfortable and a joy to fly. Below 10,000 feet, it is much like many other light twins; but, with the comfort of an excellent pressurization system at 15,000 to 18,000 feet, the airplane really comes alive with both speed and fuel efficiency. TAS of 220 knots is realistic.

Stop-start distance with an engine loss at liftoff is a fairly tidy 3,000 feet.

There is one characteristic a pilot should be aware of. Limiting speeds for 15 degrees of flap and gear-down are 160 and 140 knots, respectively. So, some planning for an ILS or even a VFR landing is required to avoid significant power excursions and concomitant pain to the superchargers. When clean, the airplane wants to fly and doesn't want to slow down. Once dirty, however, without substantial power, the 340 is a rock.

Flap extension does require trim change; and, whether by accident or design (Cessna, take a bow) electric trim switch activation during the full period of flap movement results in a perfect and smooth transition.

With a careful check on current condition and previous maintenance, a well-priced C-340 is the best pressurized twin in its class on the market.

Frederick J. Lind
La Mesa, Calif.

Our cloud-seeding company owns five Cessna 340s, four of them RAM or Riley 310-hp conversions, the other a 340A. We also maintain a couple more for outside customers. Our 340s mostly are flown at altitudes between 17,000 and 26,000 feet, and are loaded near gross. At 65 percent power (without external seeding equipment), they cruise around 190 knots true and burn 16 to 17 gph per engine. We lean conservatively, on the theory that gas is cheaper than cylinders. Though the airplanes are flown by several different pilots, cylinders have not been a major problem.

Most operational flights are conducted in icing conditions. The 340 handles ice fairly well, though you can count on losing airspeed. The inboard boots are a help, and a yaw damper is nice in turbulence.

Engine-out characteristics are good at lighter weights, but the tail loses authority at higher loads. It is an easy airplane to land smoothly, even in bad crosswinds; the airplane stays put once on the runway. The fuel system keeps you on your toes, but it isn't unmanageable.

The worst feature is that, if you lose an engine-driven fuel pump, you are restricted to using only the main tank on that side, because neither the aux tank nor crossfeed is available. A recent AD (87-23-11) requires inspection of the crossfeed lines behind the firewall, which is time-consuming and expensive if new lines are needed.

Most parts are readily available, though overpriced. But, for some reason, fuel selectors and their parts are hard to come by. Watch out for the ARC radios, of course; the 400 series avionics are junk. Make sure the main gear side brace links aren't loose; they serve as downlocks and are easily rebushed.

A leading cause of early engine overhauls is cracking cases, even the latest "heavy" cases. Look out for exhaust cracks in the "Y" and elbow beneath the turbos (even the newer Inconel "AD-proof" ones) and in the older turbo housings. The new AD requiring ultrasonic inspections of crankshafts needs to be done only when an engine is apart; it should be done during overhauls, anyway, since the original service bulletin came out in 1981. To avoid this, however, you can change to -B engines from TCM.

An excellent source of advice, parts and modifications is RAM in Waco, Tex. They know these aircraft and their engines inside and out.

Hans Ahlness
Weather Modification, Inc.
Bismarck, N.D.

My love affair with my Cessna 340A began in November 1977, when I found her in a Cessna dealer's hangar in Atlanta. She was one of those very rare and very desirable Cessnas without any factory-installed avionics. I was, therefore, able to outfit her with a complete complement of King avionics, including a KFC 200 autopilot/flight director, and two loran receivers, an Arnav 40 and a Northstar.

The airplane has been a true joy to own and fly, although, as in any relationship, there have been a few testy moments. The worst occurred several years ago, when an AD note required an inspection of the horizontal tail after every 10 hours of flight. Ultimately, Cessna solved the problem by replacing all of them, at no expense to the owners.

The 340A is a good performer but not a true "scorcher." This is the small price paid for more room and comfort. One can plan on 195 knots, true, at 10,000 feet and 215 to 220 knots at FL 230 while burning 50 gph in climb and 32 gph in cruise. Speeds 10 knots or so faster are possible, but the expenditure for fuel is not worthwhile.

Climbing to FL 230 in 20 minutes at maximum gross weight while indicating 120 knots is about average. Range is excellent (with 182 gallons of fuel). I routinely return to Georgia from the West Coast IFR with only one stop enroute.

Handling is excellent and the airplane has no bad habits. It is a good instrument platform. Though comfortable, it is not designed for really tall or large people. It is, I believe, a little small for cabin-class charter work.

Maintenance is routine for any turbocharged piston twin, and pressurization has added virtually nothing to the cost of maintenance. Parts availability and backup are excellent, especially when dealing with RAM Aircraft, Inc. in Waco, Tex., or Yingling Aircraft, Inc. in Wichita.

No pressurized twin is really economical to operate, but the 340 is probably one of the least expensive. I average about $300 per hour, including fuel, annuals (which usually run about $7,000), routine maintenance and insurance, while flying about 125 hours per year. Being able to fly at the higher altitudes in complete comfort is well worth the price.

Anyone owning a Cessna 340 should early-on become acquainted with the people at RAM Aircraft. They are the

Since the gear lowering speed is rather low, a useful mod is Precise Flight's speedbrake system. The brakes are stowed in the aft engine nacelle, and deploy in the airstream laterally, then dropping additional blades underneath for drag.

finest source of useful modifications and expertise.

My airplane has their brake, Q-tip prop and electronic synchrophaser mods. It soon will have their Series IV engines installed, and I look forward to the attendant increases in climb performance, single-engine performance and speed, as well as the 300-pound increase in useful load.

These will no doubt make a fine airplane even finer. For me, the Cessna 340A is the ultimate personal airplane. The love affair goes on, and the relationship grows even stronger with each flight.

William D. Lowery, Jr.
Albany, Ga.

We've owned our 1981 340A about a year. We had a Seneca but wanted pressurization and the capability of flying a little higher. I love to fly the airplane.

It's a pretty nice, comfortable small twin. Transitioning was no problem. The airplane is pretty straightforward, but you really do have to take care in fuel management.

The 340's big downfall is payload; if you fill it up with fuel, you don't have much left. One of the reasons I bought the plane with high-time engines is that I hope next year to get the RAM conversion, which adds 300 pounds to the gross weight.

Elwood Scaggs
Ellicott City, Md.

Cessna 401/402

The 402C boasted a longer wing and simplified fuel system lacking the trademark "Stabila-tip" tanks

Among twins, the Cessna 402 wins prizes neither for speed nor aesthetics. The 402, above all else, is simply a workhorse. A a commuter, the rotund Cessna can carry 10 passengers and 100 gallons of gas, and still be under gross weight. As a cargo hauler, the 402 can heft more than 2,500 pounds of petrol and freight with ease. In its Businessliner configuration, the wide-oval Cessna can whisk six execs coast-to-coast with but a single fuel stop.

Such versatility helped Cessna sell more than 1,900 402s (and close to another 600 401s) during its production run, which lasted from 1967 to 1985.

Like all complex twins, however, the 402 comes with a formidable repertiore of mechanical and operational quirks. The airplane's landing gear, fuel and exhaust systems are notoriously complex and require TLC (Tending Lotso Cash) to keep in tip-top condition; the 402's turbocharged Continental TSIO-520 engines (TBO: 1,400 hours) are prone to crankcase cracks; and the wing structure on pre-'79 models must be eddy-current inspected at 6,500 hours, and every 1,000 hours thereafter, to detect cracks.

Add to this the fact that the airplane has been subject to a couple of hundred service bulletins since its introduction and you can appreciate why average-equipped early models (with ARC radios) sell for less than $60.000, while later models, with many improvements incorporated (i.e., service bulletins oboleted), can go for as much as $365,000

History

The 402 began life as the second of Cessna's 400 series twins (the first was the 411) in 1967. Basically a re-engined 411 with an enlarged rudder, the 402 was intended from the start to serve a dual role: the interior (featuring a reinforced bonded-honeycomb floor) was designed to accommodate up to ten seats, all quickly removable for conversion to cargo operations. A non-cargo version of the 402, called the 401, was offered concurrently, with six-passenger seating standard. Except for interior appointments and an optional cargo door onthe 402, the two airplanes were the same.

In 1969, the 402 got a stretched nose for added baggage space, and was redesignated the 402A; the 401, however, retained its shorter beak. The advent of the 402B the following year saw optional fuel go to 184 gallons (nearly all are so equipped). Also, various systems changes were made; for example, fuel pumps were put in the "Stabila-tip" tanks in response to an AD.

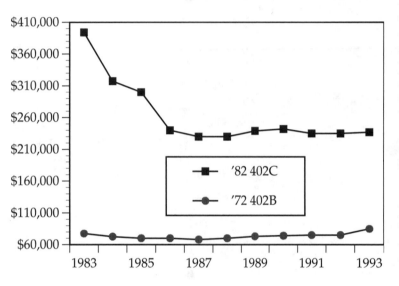

As acceptance of the workhorse 402 increased, sales of the 401 lagged. Consequently, in 1971 Cessna resorted to the somewhat unusual tactic of lowering its price by $1,450, to $108,500. The tactic flopped, however. Only 21 airplanes were sold at the lower price, and Cessna axed the 401 the following year.

Meanwhile, numerous improvements were made to the 402B:

• 1971: Padded window posts, instrument panel trim, and control yokes became standard safety features, and an engine nacelle fire extinguishing system was offered as an option.

• 1972: Heat-resistant silicone engine shock mounts were introduced, along with stainless steel turbocharger heat shields. Also, a simpler exhaust system was made standard; access was improved to the landing gear and flap motors; and a new landing gear system, featuring an aural annunciator coupled to the throttles and the flap preselect switch, was incorporated.

• 1973: The familiar Cessna "portholes" were replaced on the 402B with rectangular windows, for an increase of 711 square inches in window area; the cabin interior was lengthened by 16 inches; a fold-down instrument panel (for easier access) was made standard; optional fuel went to 207 gallons; an avionics master was added; and improved turbo controllers were made standard.

• 1975: A "known icing option" equipment package was offered.

• 1977: Polyurethane paint became standard, and an optional flushing toilet was offerd.

• 1978: A Halon cabin fire extinguishing system was offered, to put out avionics and nose baggage compartment fires.

Far and away the most significant year in the 402's history was 1979, when Cessna introduced the 402C. With the C model, the 402 got 325 hp engines to replace the 300 hp mills in use until then. The new engines also boasted a TBO increase of 200 hours, up to 1,600. The familiar tip tanks were dropped in lieu of rivetless, bonded wet wings with a five-foot greater span. The ground track increased by four feet, and the complex mechanical landing gear was supplanted by a simpler, faster hydraulic system borrowed from the 414A. Useful load went up by 348 pounds. Along with all these improvements the price went up by $27,400, to $231,740.

Performance and Handling

Cessna's 400-series twins are not noted for their zippy handling. Nonetheless, the series is generally given the nod for honest flight characteristics, albeit the mass of the fuel in the tip tanks tends to make the early models a bit less responsive in roll than the 402C. As you might expect in an airplane that can haul ten people, pitch stability and stick force varies with cg: the further aft the center of gravity, the lighter the elevator control and the less stable the aircraft. At far-aft cgs, according to one 402C pilot, the airplane can feel "squirrely longitudinally."

Yaw stability in most twins is not something you write home about, and this seems to be the case for the 402. One might suppose that the late-model 402Cs, lacking the tip tanks, would dampen out yaw excursions better than the earlier models; but according to one pilot, even the 402C "wiggles vigorously" in turbulence without the optional yaw damper.

Load-carrying capacity, not handling, is what people buy 402s for, and this is where the airplane truly excels. The 150-cubic-foot cabin—wider than a 90-series King Air—will carry up to a ton of people or freight; with the optional cargo door, a 47- by 40-inch hole can be opened up in the side of the fuselage for loading bulky objects. In addition, 55.5 cubic feet of storage is available *outside* the cabin, in two wing lockers (120 lb. each), a standard 26 cu ft. nose baggage area (350 lbs) and an optional 11 cu ft. nose compartment (250 lbs). In some models the nose compartment can hold objects up to 6' 5" long. Non-cabin baggage areas can thus take on an amazing 840 lbs of freight. No wonder drug smugglers like the 402.

Of course, all of this capacity makes overloading the 402 relatively easy, particularly if optional fuel tanks are installed. With full aux fuel, the 402 can carry 1,242 pounds of fuel alone; thus the full-fuel payload for a moderately-equipped 402C is on the order of 1,000 pounds. Early 401s and 402s were limited to a maximum of 1,200 pounds aft of the front spar (i.e., in wing lockers and/or aft cabin). We know of at least one 402 that banged its tail on the ramp when all of its passengers stepped to the rear to deplane.

Perhaps it is worth noting that the wing lockers are not really suited to carrying anything but the lightest of light-duty baggage; the bottoms of the locker bays are wing skin structure. Even if padded carpeting is in place, it is easy to dent the underwing skins—a point that prospective buyers should bear in mind.

Properly loaded, the 402 turns in creditable takeoff and climb performance, even at gross weight. A fully loaded 402B lifts off after 1,695 feet of ground roll at sea level (no wind), assuming an unstick speed of 105 mph. To clear a 50-ft. obstacle under the same conditions requires 2,220 feet. (Flaps are left retracted on takeoff, since Cessna's split flaps—a holdover from the 310—produce vastly more drag than lift.) Once airborne, the 402 climbs initially at 1,610 fpm (1450 fpm for the 402C) at its all-engine Vy of 126 mph. After initial power reduction, a cruise-climb of 140 mph produces a 1,000-fpm rate of ascent, each engine burning 17 gallons per hour.

In cruise flight, an early 401/402 will deliver an honest 200 mph at 10,000 feet on 66-percent power (27" and 2,450 rpm). Book fuel flow under those conditions is listed as 28.9 gph. (At 20,000 feet, the same power setting yields 223 mph TAS, according to the book—but most 402s are flown at non-oxygen altitudes.) The higher horsepower, tip-tankless 402C is slightly faster, delivering 221 mph at 10,000 feet with 72 percent power.

Range—in the older models—varies from 675 miles with standard fuel (100 gallons usable) at 72 percent power at 10,000 feet, to just over 1,400 miles at 55 percent power and 20,000 feet with full optional fuel (180 gallons usable), with no reserves. The 402C comes with a standard fuel capacity of 213 gallons, which gives the aircraft long legs indeed—up to 1,400 miles with reserves. Some cabin payload must be sacrificed to fly with full fuel, naturally, but even with all tanks topped, you can count on carrying five people and baggage.

On landing, the 401/402 requires 1,765 feet past a 50-ft. obstacle (777 ft. of ground roll) at its maximum touchdown weight of 6,200 pounds (100 below gross). The heavier 402C requires 2,485 ft. over the 50-ft. obstacle and 1,055 feet of pavement. A Robertson STOL kit is available for the 402 which cuts these distances by approximately 20 percent.

Single-Engine Characteristics

One might think that a twin that can scream skyward at some 1,610 fpm after liftoff—and maintain 11,700 feet on one engine—might have a superb (or at least decent) single-engine rate of climb. 'Tain't so. As with its chief competitors in this class (the Piper Navajos), the 401/402 suffers from very marginal single-engine rates-of-climb. At sea level, a 402B loaded to gross can only manage 225 fpm on one engine, which—at the plane's Vxse (engine-out best angle of climb speed) of 114 mph—gives a climb gradient of just 138 feet per nautical mile. Needless to say, the slightest defect in piloting technique will quickly knock such numbers into the ditch. (One wonders how many commuter airline customers would willingly board a 402, if they knew the plane's engine-out performance capabilities—or lack of same.)

The 402's single-engine climb rate improves somewhat with the offloading of fuel or cargo, but not dramatically. According to Cessna's charts, one can expect a 150-fpm gain (at sea level) for every 500 pounds below gross.

The 402's Vmc (minimum single-engine control speed) isn't particularly good, either: at 95 mph, the 402's Vmc is 10 mph higher than the Navajo's. (The Robert-

Cost/Performance/Specifications

Model	Year	Average Retail Price	Cruise Speed* (kts)	Useful Load (lbs)	Fuel Std/Opt (gals)	Engine	TBO (hrs)	Overhaul Cost ea.
401, -A	1967-69	$58,000	205	2,660	102/184	Cont. TSIO-520-E	1,400	$18,000
402, -A	1967-69	$63,000	205	2,660	102/184	Cont. TSIO-520-E	1,400	$18,000
402B	1970-75	$89,000	205	2,560	102/207	Cont. TSIO-520-E	1,400	$18,000
402B	1976-78	$110,000	205	2,560	102/207	Cont. TSIO-520-E	1,400	$18,000
402C	1979-81	$185,000	210	2,800	213	Cont. TSIO-520-VB	1,600	$18,500
402C	1982-85	$315,000	210	2,800	213	Cont. TSIO-520-VB	1,600	$18,500

Prices from *Aircraft Bluebook Price Digest*

son conversion lowers the 402's Vmc to 83 mph.) Cessna lists a "safe single engine speed" of 105 mph for the 401/402 and suggests this be used as the "decision speed" below which a takeoff, in the event of engine failure, should not be continued.

It's worth noting, however, that the 402's 225 fpm single-engine climb rate is predicated on a Vyse (engine-out bestROC speed) of 118 mph, *plus* gear and flaps retracted, *cowl flap on the bad engine retracted,* the faulty engine feathered, and five degrees of bank maintained in the direction of the good engine. If all of these conditions are not met, then the 225 fpm figure is no longer valid, even at 118 mph. On balance, Cessna's 105-mph Vsse seems more than a trifle optimistic.

Happily, Cessna's redesign of the 402 in 1979 resulted in improved engine-out performance for the 'C' model: The 402C, while 300 pounds heavier than its predecessor, nonetheless manages a 3,100-foot higher SE service ceiling (14,800 feet) and can climb at 301 fpm (for a gradient of 173 feet per nautical mile)—by no means rocket-like, but considerably better than the previous models.

Interestingly, the heavier 402C requires a longer distance to accelerate and then stop (3,740 feet for the 'C' versus 3,055 feet for early model 402s), but the distance needed to lose an engine and then continue takeoff is less for the 402C: 2,870 feet versus the tiptanked 402's 3,990 to 4,370 feet (the exact distance depends on the year model). Obviously, in any aircraft of this class, it pays to study single-engine performance charts carefully before shoving the throttle levers forward.

Safety

Notwithstanding the 402's lackluster engine-out performance numbers, the airplane gets relatively high marks for safety. A 1980 NTSB study of light-twin engine failure accidents showed the "401-411" group to be better than average in engine-out safety, in terms of total accident rate per 100,000 night hours as well as fatal accident rate per 100,000 hours following engine failure.

But when the data for the 401 series is separated from other data, the 401 comes out looking spectacular, with a total engine-failure accident rate of 0.5 per 100,000 hours—better, in fact, than any other piston twin examined by the study. (The next-best score was turned in by the Navajo series. The worst scores were provided by the Aero Commander 500s, at 3.46; the Beech 18, 2.78; and the Cessna Skymaster, 2.39.)

Subsequent statistics are not quite as good. An examination of FAA Accident and Incident Report data for the 401/402 series reveals a total of 20 fatal accidents occurring between 1977 and 1982. One of these was a midair collision. The rest fell into the following categories: At least ten accidents occurred in IFR weather, with pilots of four aircraft descending below minimums or landing short. Four planes hit the ground during climb or cruise, at least one of them apparently involved in a buzzing episode. Two aircraft crashed after inflight engine fires developed. Two more planes—one of them a 401 flown by a pilot with medical problems—rolled inverted on final approach with one engine out. One aircraft overran the end of the runway on a high density altitude takeoff.

Among the nonfatal accidents, several patterns are noticeable. An astounding 82 instances of landing gear failure or collapse (11 on takeoff, 71 on landing) were recorded in the past five years, 35 of them involving late-model 'C' aircraft.

Broken bellcranks, brackets, torque tubes, rod ends, and scissors bolts were among the items mentioned in the write-ups. Poor maintenance was cited in a handful of instances; but in most cases, simple fatigue seemed to be the chief contributing cause.

Against this dismal backdrop, we have an additional 21 reported instances of accidental wheels-up landings. Cessna, over the years, made minor changes in the design of its gear condition warning system in the 401/402; but to this day, the gear lever and lights remain small and inconspicuous on the panel, located low and virtually out of sight. One wonders whether a larger gear selector (a la Aztec), placed higher on the panel (a la Mooney 201), would not reduce the number of gear-up incidents.

Some 42 accidents and incidents were ascribed to engine malfunctions of various sorts: Tutbocharger and exhaust-system failures accounted for 14 incidents (eight of them resulting in fires); cylinder failure was noted in five instances; at least three crankshaft failures occurred; and there were 18 miscellaneous power-loss incidents (various causes, some undetermined).

Eleven cases of nose baggage doors popping open in flight were recorded from 1977 to 1982, none fatal. On top of this, three crew doors came open unexpectedly (a pilot's door is optional on the 402), and two emergency exits departed the scene. At least seven incidents involved the unsuccessful termination of flights in stolen aircraft, unexplained abandonment of aircraft, and/or the seizing of controlled substances.

Maintenance Considerations

Some 1,824 Service Difficulty Reports were recorded by FAA between 1977 and 1982—a large number, to be sure, although one must bear in mind that Part 135 operators, which account for a sizable portion of the fleet, are required by law to submit reports on many mechanical problems that would normally go unreported by Part 91 operators.

Several noteworthy patterns appear in the 402's SDR history. The principal mechanical problems include failure (due to defective bearings, shorted connections,

Panel space is generous and equipment lavish, as is typical in this class of aircraft.

There's lots of space, but loading requires careful attention to weight and balance considerations.

and bad diodes) of Prestolite and Crittenden alternators; elevator trim actuator threads stripped (lube problems, etc.); failure of flap extension cables (with some reports of misrigging) and flap actuator rods; loose screws and rivets in fore and aft main landing gear forgings; dozens of cases of cracked MLG trunnions, brackets, bearings, and torque tubes; a dozen instances of cracked Cleveland discs; defects in wheels and wheel bearings; baggage door latch problems; cracks in elevator hinges and horizontal stabilizer skins, and movement of stabilizer attach hardware; more than 100 cracked crankcases (some of them "heavy duty" cases); 19 con rod or con rod bolt failures; Il spoiled tappets; more than six dozen cases of upper cylinder distress (including 29 instances of headlbarrel detachment); numerous leaking fuel-pump through-bolts (the subject of an AD requiring onetime inspection and retorquing of these bolts); a handful of tach-generator shaft failures; and several dozen instances of cracked or blown exhaust stacks, clamps, etc. But overall, the plane is said to be reliable.

Modifications

Robertson Aircraft Corporation offers a comprehensive STOL (short takeoff or landing) conversion for the 402 in which the airplane gets Fowler flaps, flaperons, double-hinged rudder, and interconnected trim. Takeoff roll is said to be reduced by 42 percent, landing roll by 23 percent, Vmc by 12 mph, and accelerate-stop distance by 39 percent.

RAM Aircraft Modifications, offers powerplant conversion packages for the 402A and B in which the early models' TSIO-520-E engines (300-hp, 1400-hr. TBO) are replaced by intercooled TSIO-520-N engines with pressurized magnetos (310 hp, leOO-hr. TBO), for a slight improvement in top speed and up to 35 percent improvement in rate of climb.

Owner Comments

The 402B is a benignly conventional airplane—an ordinary, viceless airplane in most ways (if you can call anything with that kind of single-engine performance "viceless"). It's a big airplane, which is one of the things that makes it nice for smuggling—you can't see in the windows while it's parked on the ramp.

We didn't have particularly good range; three and a half hours was about as far as we could go. We just had wing aux tanks and tips, no locker tanks. We would stop in Albuquerque, then Wichita or St. Louis. We'd often have to stop in Ohio, We could have made it to the East Coast in three hops if we had used small fields, but we wanted to use major airports as much as possible.

We flight-planned for 170 knots, flying mostly at 10,000 to 12,000 feet.

It's a pretty uncomfortable airplane on long trips. It makes you want pressurization, if only because the airplane would be quieter, more comfortable. You're sitting there droning away, and the noise level is high. It's not a true transcontinental airplane.

The airplane does have tremendous cubic capacity, It's unbeatable. We looked at a number of other airplanes, but there was no way to get that kind of space. Our problem was not weight, but cubes—cubic feet. (We were never in any danger of going over gross; our cargo was low-density,) We wanted to avoid having to stack the stuff up against the windows

The nose baggage compartment was great. You can hide a lot of stuff up there.

Other comments about the plane: Single-engine performance was not great. The aircraft would just about hold altitude on a typical California day. That's about it. The panel was nice, logical—well laid out. We had King radios. Not a hell of a lot of the avionics worked much of the time.

It was a nice airplane to land, tremendous crosswind capabilities. It handled like a big, heavy aircraft—which, of course, it was.

The plane handled well overall. You never got the violent pitch-down on initial deployment of flaps, for instance, that you got with the Cessna 310. The book figures were pretty much accurate, for our plane.

The only problem we had with the airplane was that the shrouding of the engines was pretty cheaply done; you had to be very careful to keep the baffles tight.

Also, we had a lot of problems with the left engine, which turned out, eventually, to have zero compression on one cylinder. It ran pretty hot. As a result, the engine gauges were always askew, and you were never quite sure which gauges were right or wrong. (The throttle quadrant was a forest of staggered levers—we never could get anything to line up.) One thing you *were* sure of was that the paint was discoloring aft of the cooling louvres on the left cowl. So we always ran full rich on that side.

The other slight problem with the 402 is that it's too tacky an airplane, in its interior, to be used as the quick-change airplane that it was intended to be. The interior parts are cheap and will not stand up to constant removal and reinstallation. The plastic cracks, the rugs come up, etc. The decals and placards are forever peeling off, too. It's really a tacky airplane,

The general feeling the airplane gives you, looking back on it, is one of shoddiness; there's no quality anywhere. We eventually sold our 402, but you can see why a lot of people in the drug business have no hesitation in simply torching the thing when they're done with it,

Cessna 414 Chancellor

Parts-bin hybrids with spacious cabins and relatively small, efficient engines, 414-series airplanes can carry lots of fuel or a small crowd with their belongings—but not both. Also, the big Cessna have safety records that are unmatched by any other light twin.

All told, Cessna Aircraft Corp. built nearly 1,000 of the airplanes—roughly a 50/50 split between early tip-tanked 414s and wet-wing 414A "Chancellors"—during 15 years of production. The original intent was for the 414 to be an easy step up to pressurization, and over the years the airplanes have become popular as workhorses for small charter and corporate flight departments, as well as comfortable transports for private owners.

An early 414 is distinguished by four cabin windows, tip tanks and beak-like nose. Another window was added in 1973, when cabin length was stretched 16 inches.

Today, prices range from around $92,000 to over $435,000 for well-equipped 414s with mid-time engines. Operating and maintenance costs are attractive when compared with those of competing airplanes, such as the big-brother 421 and Beech Aircraft's Duke. Yet, they are not inconsiderable.

In a study of accident records some years ago, the 414 stood out as the safest light twin. Of course, any airplane's safety depends a great deal on the proficiency of its pilots; and there are several good training programs available to help keep 414 pilots in top form. Indeed, many insurance companies insist on such training.

Stepping Stone

Cessna borrowed components from existing 400-series airplanes to come out in 1970 with a model to bridge the price gap between unpressurized and pressurized twins. It had basically the same tail and "wide-oval" fuselage as the 421B, and the 401's wing. The engines were adapted from those used on the 401 and 402 models—the differences were intercoolers and provisions for bleed-air cabin pressurization. List price was $138,000—$35,000 less than the Duke and some $50,000 less than both the 421 and Piper's P-Navajo.

Engines were 310-hp Continental TSIO-520-Js, and propellers were three-blade McCauleys. According to Cessna, 4.2-psi cabin pressure differential could be maintained by either engine operating at 60 percent power. Six seats were standard; a seventh was available as an option. Maximum takeoff weight was 6,350 pounds; max landing, 6,200 pounds.

In the years following its introduction, the airplane saw few major changes. One of the most important came in 1973, when cabin length was increased 16 inches, and a fifth side window was installed. Electronic prop synchrophasers became standard equipment in 1976, when two versions of the airplane were put on the market: a bare-bones 414 and a 414II, which came with an assortment of ARC 400-series avionics equipment.

That year, too, most limiting and recommended airspeeds were boosted a few knots (except Vmc, which was lowered from 84 to 82 knots), and the -J engines were replaced with TSIO-520-Ns. The difference is that an -N engine uses 38 inches of manifold pressure, rather than 36 inches, and 2,700 rpm to produce its rated 310 horsepower from sea level to 20,000 feet. (Actually, the engines can maintain rated power much higher, but manifold pressure limitations are imposed above 20,000 feet to preclude excessive internal temperatures.)

Plumber's Nightmare

Cessna called them "Stabila-Tips"; everyone else called them tuna tanks. At any rate, the tip tanks were supposed to contribute stability while keeping the fuel supply well away from the cabin. Standard usable fuel capacity of early 414s was 100 gallons (50 in each tip tank). Optional auxiliary and locker tanks were available to boost usable fuel capacity to 180 gallons at first, then to 203 gallons in 1973.

The fuel system in early 414s is complex, especially with extra tanks installed, and proper fuel management keeps the pilot quite busy. The drill is to run the engines off the mains (tip tanks) for 90 minutes before switching to the auxiliary tanks. This makes room in the mains for fuel and vapor returned by the engines. Though the aux tanks feed directly to the engines, fuel from locker tanks can only be transferred to the mains. Before doing so, however, the pilot has to ensure there are fewer than 20 gallons in each tip tank. Fuel transferred too early is merely pumped overboard. And there are only two fuel-quantity indicators, both with three-position switches, to help the pilot keep track. The system left plenty of room for error.

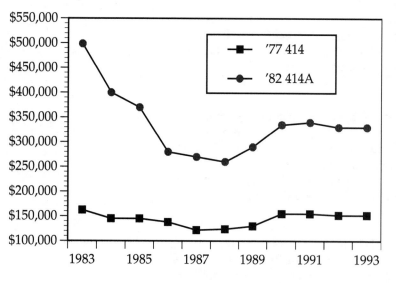

Enter the Chancellor

A simpler fuel system was among a host of improvements unveiled in 1978 with introduction of the Model 414A Chancellor. Tuna, aux and locker tanks were obviated by a 4.5-foot longer, bonded wing holding 206 gallons of usable fuel in internal bays. Controls consisted of on/off/crossfeed valves, and a fuel flow computer/indicator was added to the options list.

A 30-square-foot increase in wing area accommodated a 400-pound increase in maximum takeoff weight and a 550-pound increase in landing weight. A ramp weight of 6,785 pounds was approved to allow for the consumption of about six gallons of fuel during start, taxi and runup. Also, a zero-fuel weight of 6,515 pounds was published (above that limit, only fuel can be added) to preclude excessive bending loads on wing-attach structures.

The 421's longer nose also was grafted onto the 414A, making space for an extra

410 pounds of baggage and avionics. All told, maximum useful load was boosted about 200 pounds, and an eighth seat was added to the options list. Pressurization differential was increased to 5.0 psi to enable the airplane to maintain cabin altitudes of 10,000 and 11,950 feet at cruising altitudes of 26,500 and 30,000 feet, respectively. Limiting speed for the extension of 15 degrees of flap was raised from 164 to 177 knots; landing gear operating and extension speeds also were increased to 177 knots, from 143.

Beginning in 1978, Cessna offered three basic equipment packages. In addition to the bare-bones model and the ARC 400-equipped 414AII, there was a III version with ARC 800- and 1000-series avionics, a Bendix RDR 160 weather radar and 100-amp alternators.

TBO Boost

After the Chancellor debuted, there were few further refinements. One of the most important, though, was the switch in 1979 to TSIO-520-NB engines, which have improved crankshafts. Four years later, Teledyne Continental Motors incorporated some changes to the -NB's cylinders, valve lifters and piston pins, and increased the engine's recommended TBO from 1,400 to 1,600 hours. Continental also published overhaul procedures to enable -NB engines to get the TBO boost.

Despite that, cylinder head cracking has been a persistent problem for the -N and -NB engines (as well as for other IO-, TSIO- and GTSIO-520s). An AD issued in 1986 requires cylinders to be pressure-checked for leaks every 50 hours until the engine has amassed 500 hours.

End of the Line

Other noteworthy refinements to the Chancellor included modification of fuel pickup valves, which raised usable fuel capacity from 206 to 208 gallons, and optional lightweight 100-amp alternators in 1980; and installation of both a fuel manifold valve heater to prevent icing and "threadless" prop blades, which cut empty weight by 12 pounds, in 1984. The last Chancellors were built in 1985.

Performance

Service ceilings are above 30,000 feet, but few 414 owners fly nearly that high. Most prefer the upper teens and lower 20s, where they get about 190 knots on 32 to 34 gph at 65 percent power. A pilot in a hurry will see about 205 knots on 38 gph at 75 percent power.

With relatively high power loadings (10.2 pounds per horsepower for the 414 and 10.8 pph for the 414A, compared with 9.9 pph for the 421C and 8.9 for the Duke), the airplanes require a lot of runway. A 414A, for example, needs more than 4,000 feet of asphalt to accelerate to rotation speed and, then, screech to a halt at gross weight under standard conditions and at gross weight.

Single-engine performance at sea level is average; about 240 fpm for the 414 and 290 fpm for the A model. This compares with 350 fpm for the 421, 315 fpm for the 340A and 307 fpm for the Duke. At 11,350 feet, the 414's single-engine service ceiling was a bit below average; but, at 19,850, the 414A is tops in its class.

Creature Features

Owner-pilots give high marks to cockpit room and layout of systems controls. Though early ARC radios have earned a poor reputation, one owner indicated his vintage King Gold Crown's aren't much better. Owners like the twin's handling characteristics, too; only slight trim changes are needed when flaps or landing gear are reconfigured.

The big cabin and copious baggage space are the 414's fortes. The cabin is the same size as the 421's and accommodates up to eight seats. There is enough room in the aft cabin, the nose and wing lockers of a 414 to hold 930 pounds of baggage. With its bigger nose and lockers, the 414A can carry 1,500 pounds.

Loading Flexibility

Fuel, baggage and seating capacities provide considerable mission flexibility. You can't fill the tanks, stuff the nooks and crannies, and help seven people aboard, though. With full tanks—enough fuel for nearly 4.5 hours with IFR reserves—a well-equipped Chancellor will have room left in its weight-and-balance envelope to accommodate six FAA-standard people with their toothbrushes. Load a six-person marketing staff with 800 pounds of equipment, and there will be room left for only about 1.5 hours of fuel.

Narrow aisle and relatively low ceiling prevent graceful entrance; but once seated in the "wide-oval" cabin, pilots and passengers will find plenty of elbow room.

Maximum useful load of a 414A is 2,430 pounds. That's 380 pound less than a 421 can hold, but 60 pounds better than the Duke and 315 pounds better than its small-cabin stablemate, the 340A.

Safety Record

Statistics compiled by NTSB several years ago showed the 414/414A to have the best records among piston twins both in total and fatal accident rates. Between 1972 and 1982, the airplanes were involved in 0.8 fatal accidents per 100,000 hours flown. This compares with 0.9 for the 340, 1.2 for the 421 and 1.3 for the Duke. (The 411's record of 7.6 fatal accidents per 100,000 hours was the worst of the lot.) Overall accident rate was 3.2 per 100,000 hours, compared with the Duke's 5.6. (Again, the 411, with 16.7 accidents per 100,000 hours, was the pits.)

One reason for the 414's relatively good safety record is that most are flown by professional pilots; but there are several good training programs available for private pilots, as well as pros.

Maintenance Matters

Ensuring that all ADs have been complied with before buying a 414 will take a lot of work, because there have been several dozen of them (not counting a flurry of service bulletins). AD 86-13-4, which requires periodic inspections for cylinder cracks. Other notable directives requiring periodic work include: AD 75-23-8, which requires inspections and service of the exhaust system; 76-13-7, replacement of main landing gear fork bolts; 77-13-22, inspections for crankcase cracks; 82-13-1, inspections of Bendix magneto blocks until they are replaced; and 85-13-3, which requires radiographic inspections of engine mount beams for cracks.

Another AD, 86-1-6, required replacement of a group of Airborne vacuum pumps that had not been manufactured properly. 87-21-2 requires installation of fuel port restrictors to make it a bit harder for improperly trained or apathetic line personnel to fill a 414 with jet fuel.

Review of 570 service difficulty reports submitted to the FAA between 1981 and 1988 revealed other problem areas, including fuel pumps that didn't work, worn bearings that caused main landing gear to jam in their wells, cracked torque tubes and bellcranks that precipitated gear collapses, circuit breakers that refused to be pulled by anything but a pliers, broken engine rocker arm shafts and bosses, broken alternator bearings and drive couplings, exhaust-corroded flap track hinges and deteriorated dipstick components found in the oil.

Additional problem areas were brought to our attention by Gordon Cragg, a Texan who makes his living buying and selling 340s, 414s and 421s. Main landing gear webbing in early 414s apparently is susceptible to cracks and is expensive (100 hours of labor, per side) to fix. "Wye" components, which direct the flow from both exhaust manifolds into the turbocharger, are particularly prone to cracking. Pressurization controller diaphragms are good for only about five years. The cabin pressure dump switch on the right gear should be checked regularly. Another area to check, says Cragg, is the firewall, which is subject to corrosion. He also has found cracks in heated windshields to be another recurring problem.

Summing Up

A 414 appears to be a good choice for anyone who wants a pressurized airplane with a big cabin and lots of baggage space. Compared to its biggest competitors— the 421 and Duke, a 414 provides a lot of room for people and baggage. Although it's slower than the other two, a 414 can carry a modest load relatively economically.

Cost/Performance/Specifications

Model	Year	Average Retail Price	Max Cruise (kt)	Rate of Climb (fpm)	Useful Load (lb)	Std/Opt Fuel (gal)	Engines	TBO (hrs)	Overhaul Cost
414	1970	$92,000	218	1,580	2,224	102/184	Cont. TSIO-520-J	1,400	$20,000
414	1971	$96,000	218	1,580	2,224	102/184	Cont. TSIO-52-J	1,400	$20,000
414	1972	$103,000	218	1,580	2,224	102/184	Cont. TSIO-520-J	1,400	$20,000
414	1973	$113,000	218	1,580	2,224	102/207	Cont. TSIO-520-J	1,400	$15,000
414	1974	$123,000	218	1,580	2,224	102/207	Cont. TSIO-520-J	1,400	$20,000
414	1975	$133,000	221	1,580	2,224	102/207	Cont. TSIO-520-J	1,400	$20,000
414	1976	$145,000	221	1,580	2,224	102/207	Cont. TSIO-520-N	1,400	$20,000
414	1977	$152,000	221	1,580	2,224	102/207	Cont. TSIO-520-N	1,400	$20,000
414A	1978	$255,000	224	1,520	2,428	213/—	Cont. TSIO-520-N	1,400	$20,000
414A	1979	$260,000	224	1,520	2,428	213/—	Cont. TSIO-520-NB	1,400	$20,000
414A	1980	$275,000	224	1,520	2,428	213/—	Cont. TSIO-520-NB	1,400	$20,000
414A	1981	$290,000	224	1,520	2,428	213/—	Cont. TSIO-520-NB	1,400	$20,000
414A	1982	$330,000	224	1,520	2,428	213/—	Cont. TSIO-520-NB	1,400	$20,000
414A	1984	$350,000	224	1,520	2,428	213/—	Cont. TSIO-520-NB	1,600	$20,000
414A	1985	$435,000	224	1,520	2,428	213/—	Cont. TSIO-520-NB	1,600	$20,000

It is important to note that a 414 also is seven knots slower than its little brother, the 340, which has the same engines and many of the same systems. And, if it's just pressurization you're looking for, and you're going to be flying with only another person or two aboard, you might want to give the 300-series Cessna a close look, first.

Owner Comments

Our company has owned a 1974 Model 414 for four years. We traded up from a 340 for the bigger cabin and better range. We looked at a 421 but were concerned about the engines. We also considered a Duke but found the 414's cabin more spacious and the parts situation in our area better for that airplane. It has been reasonably inexpensive to operate, very flexible in terms of mission capability and weather capability, and relatively easy to fly.

I fly the airplane an average of 250 to 275 hours a year on business, and it also averages 25 to 75 hours on charter. We operate it on a Part 135 certificate, using a professional pilot. Our typical profile is two to three passengers over a trip length of 700 to 800 nautical miles. We usually operate from 17,000 to 21,000 feet, where, at 68 percent power, we get about 205 knots on roughly 32.4 gallons per hour.

The 414's weight-carrying capability is rather limited, compared to a 402 or a Navajo, which are both cabin-class, also, but unpressurized. Our useful load is about 1,620 pounds; a comparably equipped 402 probably carries 2,000 pounds. With pressurization, you do lose a little with all that weight of the heavy airframe.

We have had no major problems and very few minor problems. It's been a dependable airplane. We haven't had a canceled trip yet. Both engines are RAM - NB conversions from the original TSIO-520-Js. They have been very dependable; I really can't say enough nice about the people from RAM.

ARC avionics, surrounding a Sperry weather radar in this 1982-vintage 414's panel, are a weak point common to all of Cessna's piston airplanes. Autopilots in 414s were hit with three ADs. Airborne vacuum pumps, too, have been troublesome.

The only problem we've had with parts was waiting six months to get a fuel-selector valve. Otherwise, a lot of the parts are still pretty readily available. Except for the selector valve, I've never had to wait more than two or three days for a part. Of course, the biggest complaint I have about parts is their cost.

We had ARC radios in our 340, and they were awful. We were spending $3,000 to $4,000 a year on avionics maintenance. So, when we got the 414, we ripped the ARCs out and replaced them with King Silver Crown equipment.

One thing I would recommend for anyone considering a 414 is replacement of the regular brakes with Cleveland heavy-duty units. That made a huge difference in our airplane's stopping performance and in maintenance. And I'd say, if you're going to buy any cabin-class twin, you should

plan on including training at FlightSafety as part of the operational expense. I go through the training two or three times annually.

Gregory Novak
Minneapolis, Minn.

We have operated a 1970 Cessna 414 an average of 100 hours a year for five years. During that time I have been the only pilot, and our maintenance has been done by the same shop. We average two hours per trip and always file IFR; 190 knots (65 percent power, 35 gallons per hour average) works very accurately for flight plans. Most of the time, we file for 12,000 to 15,000 feet and rarely have any traffic. We go higher only if weather, winds aloft or a longer trip make it practical.

My total flying time over the last 42 years is nearly 6,000 hours, with over 4,000 hours in multiengine aircraft. Most of my time was logged in the following aircraft: Bonanza, Doyne-converted Apache, 310, 320, 414, Aerostar 600 and 800 Turbo Aero Commander.

The 414 is more comfortable for pilot and passengers than any of our previous aircraft. It's more spacious, quieter and has tremendous baggage capacity without cg problems. As a pilot, I appreciate its smoothness, IFR stability and how wonderfully it can be trimmed out. Of all the aircraft I have flown, I prefer the 414 for instrument flying, because you can let go and it hangs in there beautifully. During turbulence it's not bad, but it's not as good as the Aerostar.

We don't have air-conditioning but do have the high-speed blower system, which keeps us quite comfortable, even in southern California. The heater system works well; passenger comfort is never a problem.

Maintenance summary (five years of operation): routine maintenance, $22.60 per hour; annuals, $4,580.52 average; avionics/instruments, $25.16 per hour. Insurance has averaged $2,837.50 a year. Originally, we had $2 million limits, but we have reduced that to $1 million for the last three years to offset increased rates.

We have not had any problems getting parts. The engines run beautifully; after 1,100 hours since remanufacture, compression and oil consumption compare favorably with new engines. They run smoothly with no skipping or carbon-tracking at altitude.

Our biggest problem has been maintaining the early vintage King Gold Crown avionics. With hindsight, we should have upgraded when we bought the airplane five years ago. In all fairness, much of the high avionics cost was caused by constant personnel turnover in the avionics shop.

We climb at 30 inches and 2,450 rpm, indicating 130 knots with a rate of 600 feet per minute. The engines never even come close to their red-line temperatures.

This year, we probably will trade up to the best Super RAM 414 we can afford. We know of no other aircraft that offers so much, including pressurization, for under $100,000. In our opinion, we would have to get a propjet for any meaningful improvement, and that's not practical with an average load factor of two.

William W. Klaus
Granada Hills, Calif.

The mainstay of my business is buying and selling 340s, 414s and 421s, which I've been doing since 1975. I guess I've probably owned about 50 414s. The biggest difference between the 414 and 340 is, of course, cabin size. In the owner-flown market, where the owner also is flying the airplane with maybe one or two passengers aboard, the 340 is a little faster, and useful loads, believe it or not, are similar.

A 414 doesn't have a tremendous amount of useful load, but RAM Aircraft, up in Waco, has come up with some modifications that help a little. A problem is that people see eight seats in the airplane and think they can fill all of them. When I sell an airplane, I try to get the guy to go to FlightSafety for training. Once he gets in the simulator, he'll understand that a fully loaded 414 is not the place to be with an engine failure.

One of the biggest problems I've run into is that many shops around the country just don't know how to maintain the airplane. I've gone into several purchase situations where a 414 had just had an annual done by a "Cessna engine dealer" and I found 50, 60 squawks on the airplane. So, it's almost imperative that, for a person looking to buy a 414, the airplane be prepurchased by an extremely knowledgeable shop. And, just don't say, "Hey, do you guys know about 414s?" Go in there and say, "How many 414s do you currently maintain? Have your guys been to school?" I tell people that if they've spent $2,500 for a pre-buy inspection, they've gotten by cheap.

The TSIO-520 is a decent little engine, but it has some problems that I don't think are ever going to be solved. One, of course, is case cracks. I can just about guarantee that if you look hard enough at the engines, you'd find cracks in certain areas of 70 percent of them. But you have to know where to look; I've seen them occur under the magnetos. A case crack is going to cost $5,000 to repair.

The radios have a stigma that's only partially deserved, I think. ARC had absolutely crappy radios until 1978, when they came out with a better package. I have found the mean time between failures of 1978 and newer radios is a lot better. However, the big problem is that nobody works on the radios. Even in Houston, there is only one shop qualified to work on 400-series radios. There are probably only 30 or 40 shops in the country that do good work on ARC equipment.

Despite the negatives, the 414 really is a spiffy airplane—a good unit all the way around the board. It's very easy to fly, as long as you get proper training. It's got really good roll characteristics, and stall problems are practically nonexistent.

It's important to find a shop that knows the airplane, though. When you're looking at a shop, see if they've got service manuals and service bulletins in stock. Ask them how they'd accomplish a leak check on a 414's exhaust system. Ask how many 414s they're currently maintaining, and then call those owners.

If you get a good 414—one with a good set of engines and a good exhaust system—it's going to cost you $200 to $250 to operate, including insurance, and maintain properly. My advice is that, if a person isn't willing to spend that much on the airplane, he shouldn't even mess with it.

Gordon Cragg
Houston, Tex.

Cessna 421 Golden Eagle

With the 421, Cessna managed to assemble a host of features that buyers of high-performance piston-engine twins relish. It has a wide, spacious cabin that is both quiet and able to carry up to 10 people in shirt-sleeve comfort at oxygen altitudes.

Unfortunately, a high price comes attached to these comforts. The systems complexity needed for an airplane like the 421 translates into high maintenance requirements (and high operating costs).

Darkening the picture even further are the Continental GTSIO-520 engines that power the 421. Early models had TBOs as low as 1,200 hours. Later models, with beefed-up crankcases and other refinements, can supposedly go as long as 1,600 hours. Low TBO might not be considered a major drawback, if the engines would actually make it to TBO, but they often don't.

Taken together, the maintenance costs for airframe and engines can be enough to drain even the healthiest bank accounts. Perhaps this is the reason used 421s can be bought for as little as $55,000.

History

First rolled out in 1968, Cessna's 421 was an immediate hit. Some 200 of the big birds were sold that year, beating the Beech Duke—the only competitor to debut that same year—by 184 airplanes. (The 421s only other competitor—the pressurized Navajo—didn't come out until two years later.)

The 421 was indeed a big bird. By comparison with the Duke, its cabin was huge. The GTSIO-520 engines, producing 375 hp, allowed a maximum gross weight of 6,800 pounds. However, TBO was a pathetic 1,200 hours.

The original 421 came with a 170-gallon fuel capacity. This was carried in the distinctive "Stabila-tip" fuel tanks, and gave the aircraft a range of nearly 800 miles. Optional fuel tanks raised capacity to 255 gallons, boosting range to almost 1,200 miles.

The next year—1969—found Cessna refining the design slightly. The result was the 421A. This model got an extra three inches of length, and an extra five gallons of standard fuel. Gross weight increased by 40 pounds, but empty weight rose by 15 pounds.

The 421B came out in 1970. There were no discernable differences

The 421 is capable of hauling a relatively large number of people in comfort. It has remained one of the more popular pressurized twins, commanding premium prices on the used market.

between it and the 1969 421A model.

Worthwhile Refinements

In 1971 Cessna began producing the 421B Golden Eagle. Now the refinements started to count. Gross weight went up by 410 pounds to 7,450 (empty weight went up by 174 pounds).

Late in 1971, a nose job added more than two feet to the airframe's length, permitting a larger baggage locker in the nose. This baggage area could accommodate an object up to six feet long and weighing 600 pounds—provided none of the space and weight were traded off for more avionics (which would have to go in the same area). In all, the 421 could now carry a total of 1,340 pounds of baggage (600 in the nose, 340 in the aft cabin area, and 200 in each wing locker).

Extended nose, extra side window and "Stabila-tip" wingtips mark this specimen as a 421B. Note the landing light in the tiptank.

Of course, carrying this much baggage leaves only 1,640 pounds left over. With full fuel (standard 175-gallon tanks), there would be only enough weight margin for three 192-pound people. Attempting to carry five 170-pound people with the same baggage load would cut the allowable fuel down to 131 gallons.

An extra foot was added to each wing in 1971, resulting in a 5,000-foot increase in service ceiling, and slight increases in all-engine rate of climb (up to 1,850 fpm) and single-engine rate of climb (up by five fpm to 305 fpm). Single-engine service ceiling fell a bit to 13,000 feet even.

In 1972, cabin pressure differential was increased from 4.2 inches to 4.4 inches. It was increased again, to five inches, in 1973. The cabin was enlarged, as were the windows. The 1975 model year brought a known-icing package as an option.

Radical Changes

The 421 underwent some radical changes in 1976, resulting in the 421C model. Gone were the "Stabila-tip" fuel tanks, along with their bladders. These were replaced by a wet-wing design, and standard fuel capacity shot up to 213 gallons (270 optional). The hydraulic gear system was replaced with a mechanical one in a different configuration (the mains were turned outboard instead of in). This increased reliability, somewhat.

While max gross weight remained the same (7,450 pounds), empty weight went up to 5,048 pounds. Single-engine service ceiling also went up to 14,900 feet. Single-engine rate of climb was boosted to 1,940 fpm.

Getting rid of the tip tanks increased the stability of the

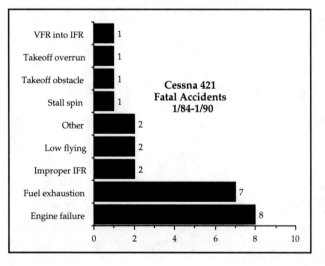

Cessna 421
Fatal Accidents
1/84-1/90

VFR into IFR	1
Takeoff overrun	1
Takeoff obstacle	1
Stall spin	1
Other	2
Low flying	2
Improper IFR	2
Fuel exhaustion	7
Engine failure	8

421 somewhat. Cessna also increased the size of the fin and rudder. This produced better handling under both normal conditions and with an engine out.

The 421 was produced in this form until 1985. Sales had been steadily sagging, and only seven were built that year. Cessna then dropped the line, having sold only 77 of the big twins between 1982 and 1985.

Performance

Book performance of the 421 looks great, with cruise speeds listed as 230 knots for the 421 and 421A models. Later models boasted even higher cruise speeds, with the 421C listed as capable of 240 knots at 20,000 feet.

In the real world, though, cruise speeds are a bit less. The 421 and 421A might actually turn 210 knots, burning 40 to 45 gallons per hour. The 421B could manage 220 knots at that fuel flow. The 421C

Cessna 421 Engines: Handle with Care

With so many myths and misconceptions flying around concerning the GTSIO-520 engines of the 421, The Aviation Consumer decided to take an in-depth look at them. We obtained two separated printouts of FAA service difficulty reports (SDRs)—one detailing only engines; another, much broader search under the 421.

What we found in some ways reinforces a few of the myths about the GTSIO-520—cracking of the cylinder and crankcase, for example. In our engines-only printout, we found a welter of reports concerning case cracking. The same held true for the broader search for 421-only records. The problem seems predominate in the 1976 through 1980 models with the -L engines. For example, in the 421-only printout, of 29 reports of case cracking, 19 were -L engines. The -N engine ran a distant second with six reports, followed by the -H (two reports) and the D (one report).

Cylinder cracking and breaking also turned up with disturbing frequency. The engines-only printout revealed some 35 instances, while the 421-only search turned up 33. Again, the -L engine led the pack with 18 of the 33 reports. The -H engine took second place with 13.

Other trouble spots of note included valve rotator springs, with 12 reports spread almost evenly across the -H, -L, and -N engines.

Piston troubles garnered 20 total reports. Broken piston pins (eight reports, five of which were for the -L engine), unseated or broken piston pin plugs (six reports, five on the -L), and pistons which simply failed (seven reports, three each for the -L and -H engines) accounted for the majority of these reports.

---

models are about the same. (These "reduced" cruise speeds might reflect the need to baby those Continental engines.) As one owner related, "It's as fast as the earlier King Airs, but a hell of a lot cheaper to operate."

But even the reduced cruise speeds depend on flying high. At 10,000 feet the

Fuel selectors are mounted on the floor between the pilots' seats. Emergency crossfeed shutoff is an excellent safety feature.

421C, for example, can barely manage 200 knots at 75 percent power. For short hops, the 421 is no speed demon.

It is, however, a fairly good load hauler, though not spectacular. With full fuel and full baggage, a 421C would be 216 pounds overweight. Trying to carry four 170-pound people with the full 1,340 pounds of baggage means carrying only 63 gallons of fuel—enough for about an hour with VFR reserves.

A more realistic loading example would probably be four 170-pound people, with 60 pounds of bags each. This allows full fuel and

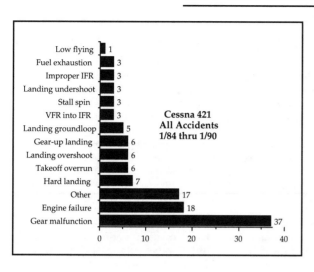

Cessna 421
All Accidents
1/84 thru 1/90

Low flying	1
Fuel exhaustion	3
Improper IFR	3
Landing undershoot	3
Stall spin	3
VFR into IFR	3
Landing groundloop	5
Gear-up landing	6
Landing overshoot	6
Takeoff overrun	6
Hard landing	7
Other	17
Engine failure	18
Gear malfunction	37

keeps the weight under gross. With the optional 270-gallon system, this loading would allow some 247 gallons of gas.

Handling

The 421 is certainly no fighter aircraft. On the other hand, it's not a truck, either. Owners report the aircraft is well-mannered and straightforward, although the early models with the Stabila-tip tanks tended to have slightly ponderous roll control.

But owners speak with one voice when the topic of handling comes up: They love this airplane. The comment most often heard, whether from the owner of a 1969 421A or a 1981 421C, runs along the lines of, "excellent instrument platform, easy to fly, very stable and quiet."

It's worth noting, though, that the enlarged fin and rudder on the later models make engine-out handling a bit easier. Also, models which don't have the tip tanks tend to be a little more stable in turbulence.

Comfort

Owners rave about the degree of comfort the 421 affords. This is especially true for those making their first foray into the world of cabin-class twins.

The 421C is the ultimate refinement of the Golden Eagle line. Although popular with charter outfits, the 421C doesn't carry as much as earlier models.

For example, one owner of a 1978 421C Golden Eagle had previously been flying a Mooney 231, "but tired of sucking on oxygen and the discomfort of a non-pressurized speedster with not much room and no engine redundancy." Another owner comments, "Cruising in a quiet, pressurized, roomy cabin simply cannot be beaten." He owns a 421A. Yet another owner, who bought a 421B after owning a Beech Duke and several Cessna 340s, said the 421 offers, "small airline comfort and speed."

Room is certainly the name of the game when it comes to 421s. A 55-inch-wide cabin is hard to surpass (that's wider than some King Air models). With a "normal" seating arrangement, the 421 provides plenty of room for the passengers. The slow-turning geared engines act to reduce noise levels. On the whole, both pilot and passengers can exit at the end of a flight without feeling cramped and without needing hearing aids—something that can be said of few piston twins.

Engines

If there's a dark side to the 421, it's the engines. Those GTSIO (standing for Geared, Turbocharged, Injected, Opposed) Continentals are finicky and temperamental. They do not take kindly to ham-fisted pilots.

The original 421 had GTSIO-520-D engines. While these engines didn't invent crankcase cracking, they went a long way towards making it widely known. The high horsepower per cylinder that these engines produce (60 hp per jug) made low TBO almost inevitable. Making these engines even more popular is the hefty overhaul price—$28,500 each. (By comparison, the TIO-541 engines of the Beech Duke cost $32,000 to overhaul, but have a TBO of 1,600 hours.) The 421B got a slightly improved GTSIO-520-H engine. However, TBO remained at 1,200 hours and overhaul price is $29,500. Finally, in 1976 with the 421C, the heavier-case GTSIO-520-L engine appeared. TBO remained at 1,200 hours for the 1976 and '77 birds and rose to 1,600 hours for the 1978, '79 and '80 model years. Overhaul cost rose to $29,500 for the -L engine.

A wide, spacious cockpit makes for a wide, spacious panel. Side consoles for circuit breakers and switches leave more room for instruments. Location of engine gauges along top center of panel is an

The case beef-up helped reduce case cracking complaints somewhat, but the problem still hasn't been licked. A five-year printout of service difficulty reports for this engine revealed some 26 reports of crankcase cracking. On average, the cracks appeared at about 1,097 hours total time. Also, cracks appeared an average of 635 hours after overhaul.

The latest 421 models—those built from 1981 through 1985—got the GTSIO-520-N engines. Even this engine has suffered from the case-cracking problem. Six reports surfaced of case cracks for the -N, with average times of 749 hours—far below the rated TBO of 1,600 hours. But case cracking is not the only problem facing the 421's engines. Two other problems appear common to all models:

• Broken connecting rods: 14 reports, distributed among all engine types. Average time in service: 980 hours.

Cost/Performance/Specifications

Model	Year	Average Retail Price	Cruise Speed (kt)	Useful Load (lb)	Std/Opt Fuel (gal)	Engines	TBO (hr)	Overhaul Cost @
421	1968	$55,000	255	2,563	170/255	375-hp Cont. GTSIO-520-D	1,200	$28,500
421A	1969	$57,000	261	2,588	175/255	375-hp Cont. GTSIO-520-D	1,200	$28,500
421B	1970	$92,000	270	3,024	175/255	375-hp Cont. GTSIO-520-H	1,200	$29,000
421B	1971	$96,000	270	3,024	175/255	375-hp Cont. GTSIO-520-H	1,200	$29,000
421B	1972	$100,000	270	3,024	175/255	375-hp Cont. GTSIO-520-H	1,200	$29,000
421C	1976	$200,000	277	2,402	213/270	375-hp Cont. GTSIO-520-L	1,200	$29,500
421C	1978	$237,000	277	2,402	213/270	375-hp Cont. GTSIO-520-L	1,600	$29,500
421C	1981	$350,000	277	2,402	213/270	375-hp Cont. GTSIO-520-N	1,600	$29,000

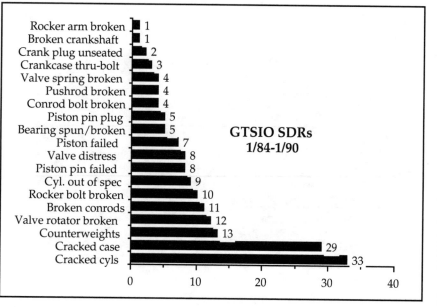

GTSIO SDRs
1/84-1/90

Rocker arm broken	1
Broken crankshaft	1
Crank plug unseated	2
Crankcase thru-bolt	3
Valve spring broken	4
Pushrod broken	4
Conrod bolt broken	4
Piston pin plug	5
Bearing spun/broken	5
Piston failed	7
Valve distress	8
Piston pin failed	8
Cyl. out of spec	9
Rocker bolt broken	10
Broken conrods	11
Valve rotator broken	12
Counterweights	13
Cracked case	29
Cracked cyls	33

•Crankshaft counterweights: 13 reports, distributed among all engine models. Counterweights become loose, detach, or wear heavily. Typically, the first indication of this was discovery of metal chips in the engine oil.

In all, those GTSIO-520 engines need to be carefully managed. Overboosting on takeoff is one of the big reasons behind the troubles. The throttles must be handled slowly and carefully, with the pilot constantly checking manifold pressure during the groundroll, watching for upward deviations.

In flight, engine temperatures demand attention. Cylinder-head temperatures that go too high or too low lead to cylinder problems. Letting down calls for precise planning to prevent shock cooling. Steady climbs demand equally good management. Indeed, FAA service difficulty reports turned up some 35 instances of cracked or broken cylinder heads between 1985 and 1990, pointing to the need to treat the engines carefully.

Interestingly, every owner we spoke with, and every owner who wrote in, made it a point to explain how carefully they operated the engines. This is a marked change from a decade ago, when many owners were apparently painfully ignorant of the potential for harm if the GTSIO engines were mistreated.

Other Problems

The FAA service difficulty reports also turned up some other important trouble areas. Each deserves careful examination both before buying a used aircraft and as part of routine maintenance.

Alternators are one of the biggest trouble sources. A total of 74 reports turned up pointing to alternator failures for various reason. Some of the most common included failure of the alternator drives, failure of the bearings, and high brush wear. Also, there was a significant number of reports which simply stated, "alternator inop."

Tied with the alternators for first place was the landing gear system, which also turned up 74 reports. Problems were concentrated mainly in the later 421B and 421C models. Other items to keep an eye on: nosegear trunnions (eight reports), breaking bellcranks and bellcrank bolts (11 reports), broken up- or downlock hooks (seven reports), broken nosewheel steering bellcranks (three reports).

Safety

True to form for the GTSIO engines, the leading killer of 421 pilots is engine failure. Eight fatal accidents in six years were attributed to engine failures, while in terms of all accidents, engine failures came in second with 18 over the period. Those big engines demand careful attention both in flight and on the ground.

Running a close second in the fatal accidents (seven) was the broad category we call "Other." This catch-all bin includes accidents like one involving a brand-new 421 pilot who mistakenly pulled back the prop controls instead of the throttles just after takeoff. He had just obtained his multiengine rating in a Baron which has those controls reversed. Or the 18,000-hour commercial pilot of another 421 who suffered an apparent heart attack immediately after takeoff.

But perhaps the single most common cause of 421 accidents is a landing gear system problem. While landing-gear related accidents are rarely fatal, they can be dangerous and are generally pretty expensive. The pattern of the service difficulty reports reflects this accident trend. Landing gear problems accounted for 37 accidents. Each of these was an out-and-out malfunction of the gear system which led to a reportable accident.

However, this is only a small part of the picture. Gear malfunctions racked up literally dozens of incidents with too little damage to qualify as accidents. Painstaking maintenance of the landing gear system is the only hope to avoid joining the hundreds of 421 pilots who've slid into home over the years.

Mods

There are literally dozens of modifications available under STC for the 421. Some—like installing a seatbelt for the toilet—are minor, but others can make a real difference. A few of the more important ones, in our opinion:

•Shoulder harnesses for older models that don't have them. Available from Ryan International Airways, 1640 Airport Road, Mid-Continent Airport, Wichita, Kans. 67209

•Yaw dampers are a popular add-on item for early models. Two companies—S-Tec (Route 4, Building 946, Wolters Industrial Complex, Mineral Wells, Tex. 76067) and Century Flight Systems (F.M. 1195, P.O. Box 610, Mineral Wells, Tex. 76067)—offer them.

•RAM Conversions of Waco, Tex. has several offerings for the 421. One mod which boosts performance and adds some style puts winglets on 1976 through 1979 models. Claimed performance boosts include 12- to 15-knot higher cruise speeds and much faster climb rate. RAM plans on having certification testing completed by the end of this year for 421s built from 1980 through 1985.

When overhaul time rolls around, RAM offers its own factory-reman overhaul package. Among many other things, their overhaul includes pressurized mags, steel cylinders, improved baffling, seal-less slip-joint exhaust, a new camshaft, flow matching and balancing, new props and governor overhauls, and a one-year, 480-hour warranty. If that's not enough, they even throw in a 110 pound gross weight increase.

•For those who have lots of money and

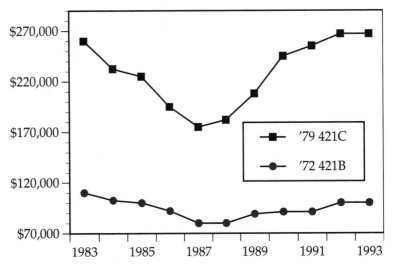

want lots of performance, Riley International offers turbine conversions. Interested owners can opt for STC SA1361SO, which mounts the perennial Pratt & Whitney PT6A-135 engines. Riley International, 2206 Palomar Airport Road, Carlsbad, Calif. 92008, (800) 841-1115.

Owner Comments

I purchased a 1978 421C Golden Eagle in October of 1988. I had been operating a Mooney 231, but tired of sucking on oxygen and the discomfort of a nonpressurized speedster with not much room and no engine redundancy.

The search for an appropriate twin involved a lot of research and soul searching. We wanted enough power to operate safely off of 3,000- and 4,000-foot strips and still be able to haul a decent load. We looked at the performance charts of Cessna 340s, 414s and finally the 421. There was no question about it—the 421 was the easy choice with a 2,160-pound useful load. However, now the fun began as all the "expert" twin gurus began to unfold horror stories about the nature of the 375 hp GTSIO-520N Continental engines.

I called the Cessna Pilots' Association to discuss the 421 with their experts. I discussed it at length with a former Air Force buddy who owns part of a commuter service which operates 421s. I also talked to the folks that maintain his 421s.

All of these people had the same story to tell—if you treat those engines right, they'll go to TBO. What they told me was perfectly applicable to any high-flying, turbocharged engine. The first time you spend three hours at 25,000 feet and chop the throttles for a poorly planned descent, the resulting shock cooling will cause cracked cylinder heads or worse. Based on this, we made the purchase.

For just over a year now, and 140 comfortable, pressurized hours, we couldn't be happier. We get a 230-knot cruise at 25,000 feet. The Cessna-provided charts state the cruise at 73.5 percent power at 25,000 feet should be 241 knots at recommended lean power, but you won't get this speed until you've burned off some fuel. True, I bug the heck out of controllers to assure we can start our descent at least 90 miles out. And we are very gentle with the engines, but isn't that the way to treat any airplane, not just the 421?

During the past year we have repaired a NAV unit, had the fuel flow computer overhauled, replaced the battery under warranty, and replaced nine digital display units. Our first annual inspection had me wondering what skeletons would be found behind the inspection plates, but much to my surprise we heard only praise from the mechanics about the great shape of the 2,700-hour bird. Except for elective items I wanted changed out, this annual cost me less than the last annual on my Mooney!

This airplane is a great performer. The cabin is quiet with good crew visibility, it's a stable instrument platform, and it has positive control in crosswind landings.

No man-made machine is perfect, and I don't wish to seem overly enthusiastic, but if our flight experience for 1990 is as good as it was in 1989, I'll be hard to convince that there is any better pressurized, high-flying, fast, safe piston twin.

Robert Cass
Apopka, Fla.

I own a 421A, and I believe it to be the ultimate in owner-flown piston twins. I also believe the older models have been unfairly maligned in the past, and thus offer an exceptionally good buy on the used aircraft market. Cruising in a quiet, pressurized, roomy cabin simply can't be beat.

The aircraft is very stable and predictable in all but extreme weather conditions. Load flexibility is excellent. With full fuel (222 gallons), I can fly 1,500 nm, and with 150 gallons I can go 1,000 nm. And that 150-gallon fuel load will allow my 421 to carry myself and four passengers with 180 pounds of baggage.

I believe that the 421B offers very few advantages over the 421A, other than slightly more baggage space. Useful loads are comparable. The 421C is slightly faster, flies slightly higher and farther with slightly more useful load. However, it costs substantially more to purchase.

I have not yet experienced any major maintenance or parts availability problems. It's absolutely essential, though, that you deal with a mechanic who knows the 421 inside-out.

My aircraft has been re-engined with the newer -H engines from the 421B. This is a definite advantage over the original engines, which had a poor reputation for making it to TBO.

Operating costs have averaged $500 per hour, flying 100 hours annually. This includes all expenses. Previously, I owned a Comanche 260C, and that cost $300 per hour.

In summary, I believe the older 421s, provided they have been well maintained, are an excellent buy for the owner pilot who is serious about going places comfortably and safely.

Paul Grant, M.D.
Toronto, Canada

I have owned a 421B for almost two years. I find that the aircraft gives speeds and fuel consumption very close to book. I fly using conservative power settings (28 inches/1,700 rpm—about 58 percent power). On trips with more than one hour at cruise altitude, I lean to 75 degrees rich of peak. On shorter trips, I lean to 100 rich of peak. With this power setting, airspeed becomes a function of altitude. From 4,000 to 6,000 feet, TAS is about 170 knots. From 9,000 to 12,000 feet, I get about 175 knots. Between 12,000 and 17,000 feet, it's about 185 knots. Fuel consumption runs 40 to 45 gallons block to block.

The 421 handles excellently. It is very stable for IFR. Loading is adequate, and any reasonable loading scheme will not affect cg much. However, with full passenger load and baggage, don't plan on flying more than an hour and a half, with reserves.

The instrument panel layout is very easy to manage in the single-pilot IFR environment. The seats are very comfortable, and the noise levels are low. Passengers always give very favorable comments.

Because I own a Part 135 operation (even though this aircraft is not part of it), I am able to keep very careful track of the aircraft's costs and maintenance. You should expect to spend about $1,000 for 50-hour inspections, and approximately $3,500 to $4,000 for 100-hour/annual inspections. Non-routine maintenance might include replacement of the bladder tanks ($1,500 each), replacement of transfer pumps and nacelle tanks.

The engines have not been a problem due to careful powerplant management. Power adjustments should be made slowly, and no more than two or three inches of adjustment at a time.

Owners would be wise to carefully read the recent Continental service bulletin concerning torsional vibration. This is associated with low manifold pressures at high rpm. This usually occurs during landing when the pilot attempts to reduce power below 14 inches while maintaining 1,800 or 1,900 rpm. The pilot will feel a rumbling from this. Thus, it is important that he remain well ahead of the aircraft so that he does not have to use this type of power reduction until the moment of touchdown.

Overall, I would agree that the 421 is truly the king of the piston twins.

Antranig Asianian
President, Sullivan Aircraft Service
White Lake, N.Y.

I own a 1973 421B which I purchased in July, 1989. Although my experience is limited to about 50 hours in the 421, I find it beyond my every expectation. Transitioning from a Cessna 310G was very smooth, with the biggest problem just getting used to all the room inside. The aircraft is very stable, quiet, easy to fly, and makes an excellent IFR platform.

I usually flightplan for 15,000 to 16,000 feet at 185 knots, with an average fuel consumption of 43 gallons per hour. Endurance at this rate is more than five hours, but I'm more comfortable limiting my legs to about four hours.

My typical load is two to four people. I operate from a 3,200-foot-long, 100-foot-high airport, and regularly fly into a 6,000-foot long, 7,000-foot high airport. I keep the aircraft somewhat under gross all the time.

Most remarks about the high maintenance costs of the 421's engines seem to come from those who don't own one. While all but the 421C have a low TBO, there is a lot of turbocharged engine there that will require a lot of maintenance if you run it hard. If you fly it like it belongs to you and you have to pick up the maintenance tab, you can expect excellent service with routine maintenance.

In my opinion, a 421 offers a lot of capacity and performance for the money. You do pay for the performance. (If you don't need or want that performance, the 414 has the same capacity and is more economical.) For me, the 421 will do nicely until there's a Citation with my name on it.

Robert McNutt
Fullerton, Calif.

Cessna
425 Conquest I

Called the turbine 421, Baby Conquest, the baby carriage, entry-level turboprop and other diminutives, the 425 is in our book the best all-around businessman pilot-operated jetprop. Just be prepared to pay a price that extends far beyond initial purchase.

Cessna filled out its broad range of aircraft with turboprop models very late in the game. The company leapfrogged the category by going directly to jets early in the 1970s. Beech already largely owned the turboprop market by then, which may have affected the thinking of Cessna management.

The original Conquest, the Garrett TPE-331-8-powered 441, was introduced in 1977. The 425, originally dubbed Corsair, was brought out in 1979 and certificated in July, 1980. The bloom was off the rose for general aviation by then, and Cessna had been going through several very difficult years.

Several Cessna high-performance twins were suspected of design errors that led to inflight airframe failures, particularly the 441, its piston-powered look-alike 404 ("Titan") and the 340. Expensive, utility-destroying ADs were applied while the company tried to fix the problems. For instance, the 340 empennage had to be inspected every 10 hours of operation for a period of time.

The 425, in short, was introduced in inauspicious times. Its production life was short: while the 425 was offered by Cessna as a new airplane through 1987, it is thought (not confirmed) that production actually ended in 1984. Approximately 236 airplanes were built. According to an FAA aircraft census, 181 remain U.S.-registered.

At least in terms of current engines and principal components, it is highly unlikely that Cessna will ever again build a Conquest. The company is said by dealers to have evaluated starting up 425 and 441 production but have decided that the asking price would be too high in relation to what the market might accept and what other airplanes cost. With equipped "little" King Airs (the C90B) priced at about $2.3 million and larger ones ranging from $3.5 to nearly $5 million, turboprops are competing with turbofans in price.

For instance, the new CitationJet sells for approximately $2.8 million. The Swearingen SJ-30, which is still in development, will be priced about the same if the company can raise enough money to

It may look like a Cessna 421 Golden Eagle with turboprops, but there are significant differences. The wing is bigger and the empennage much beefier, and the tail has a distinct dihedral, among other things.

put it in production. Beech, Cessna and Lear all offer a variety of jets priced competitively with King Airs.

Even the single-engine TBM-700 turboprop costs nearly $1.4 million, and the unpressurized utility Cessna Caravan is nearly one million.

Despite the comparatively small population, the market for used 425s is quite active and, for the most part, the airplane is favorably regarded. Its key strengths are relative economy with good performance, including good balanced field numbers, excellent handling characteristics (including face-saver landings), a very-well-designed cockpit for single-pilot operation, good cg range and load-

The "wide-oval" cabin is rated comfortable and the vibration level fairly low, with the synchrophaser on and judicious experimentation with prop settings. It's almost a "fill-the-seats" airplane, but watch the cg.

ing options, and a comfortable cabin.

For a properly maintained airplane, dispatch reliability is high, and operational simplicity makes it comparatively undemanding to fly.

One of the elemental strengths of the design is the nearly bulletproof Pratt & Whitney of Canada PT6 free turbine engine. The A-112 version installed in the 425 is a fairly unsophisticated one that is not highly stressed. It is flat rated at 450 shp. For pilots transitioning to turbine power and for operators at smaller airports, PT6 power is the right choice and is easy to support.

The inflight shutdown rate is impressively low, which is why so many pilots call it bulletproof.

What It Is Not

The 425 is widely referred to as the turbine 421. Quite a few aviation writers who should know better do so. Aside from the powerplants, there are a number of distinctions and very different systems, so that it makes as much sense to call a 421 a pressurized 411, or a 414 a wide-body 340.

All are products of the same basic design and design philosophy. Fortunately, the later 400 series airplanes reflect many of the lessons learned in designing, developing and building the 500 series Citations.

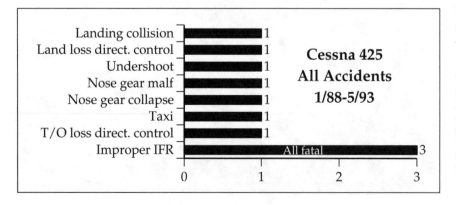

Landing collision		1
Land loss direct. control		1
Undershoot		1
Nose gear malf		1
Nose gear collapse		1
Taxi		1
T/O loss direct. control		1
Improper IFR	All fatal	3

Cessna 425
All Accidents
1/88-5/93

The wing span of the 425 is about three feet wider and wing area 10 square feet greater than the 421 wing. The 425's horizontal stabilizer has a distinct dihedral (and, as a former senior Cessna official later said, it really should have been a cruciform tail to negate the adverse affects of propeller wash [now called whirl mode vibration], but the company did not want to spend the extra bucks).

The aft fuselage structure is much beefier than that of the 421. Just count the rivets from the cabin door aft on the two airplanes.

A lot of performance numbers are fairly close. But that is at a takeoff weight of 7,450 for the 421 and 8,600 for the 425—more than half a ton heavier. Basic empty weights are about 250 pounds different, but the 425 lifts nearly double the fuel weight of the 421 (2,452 and 1,236 [1,572 with aux. fuel on the 421]). Both all-engine and single-engine rate of climb are fairly close (1,950/345 for the 421 and 1,875/380 for the 425. The 421 wins the accelerate/stop race (3,630 to 3,800 feet), but the 425 runs away in accelerate/go (4,960 for the 421 to 3,360 for the 425).

The 425 has the advantage of propeller reverse and an autofeather system—a no-go system, by the way—that greatly simplifies aircraft control in the event of an engine failure. At comparable weights, of course, the power and higher aspect ratio wing advantages of the 425 enable it to run away and hide from its piston-powered cousin. Then, compare the in-flight failure and unscheduled removal/repair rates of the two engines. No contest. The turbine is far superior.

For the properly trained pilot of a well-maintained airplane, the superior systems and performance of the 425 result in greatly reduced workload compared to the 421 or any other piston twin.

History of the Line

At its introduction as the Corsair, the 425 had a maximum takeoff weight of 8,200 pounds and basic empty weight of 4,870. Full usable fuel weight of 2,452 pounds (366 gallons) and average optional equipment weight of 375 pounds left a pretty miserly 503-pound payload.

Maximum takeoff weight was increased to 8,600 pounds in 1983; basic empty weight increased by 52 pounds, leaving most of the increase for payload. At the same time, the 425 was formally induct-ed into the "Cessna Propjet" family: it was renamed the Conquest I. No more privateering.

Earlier 425s could be modified to the new weights quite easily, and all have been. Zero fuel weight increased from 6,740 to 7,000 pounds; maximum landing weight remains 8,000 pounds. Most other chang-es to the 425 are system or operationally related, such as improved static wicks and additional avionics options.

Probably the most important of the latter is the optional Sperry (now Honeywell) SPZ-500 flight control system. Even at its

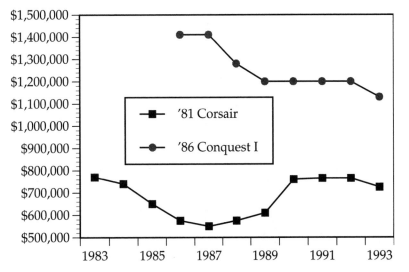

$75,000 additional cost, it is a big improvement over the ARC (Cessna) 1000 FCS, which has been one of the weak links in the 425 and other Cessna twin systems. Some 425s were equipped with the ARC 800 series autopilot, which is even less desirable than the 1000. One *Aviation Consumer* reader says the 800 in his airplane has a mind of its own despite many attempts to correct its abrupt pitch excursions.

From the beginning, Collins avionics have been an option worth the price differential over the standard ARC system. To be fair, it should be noted that a number of operators had good experience with their ARC avionics (and a Cessna technician, when asked about the early experience with the 425, said everything was great ..."except for those @#$![:~^[Collins radios"). *The Aircraft Blue Book Price Digest* has a footnote that suggests reducing the price of a used 425 by $15,000 to $20,000 if it is equipped with ARC 1000 series avionics.

As a requirement for British certification, a master caution warning system was added. This is a useful addition because the annunciator panel can be hard to see in direct sunlight, even though it is mounted at the top of the panel, under the glare-shield.

Another noticeable improvement was made in the later run of 425s: better interior design, fit and finish. Appearance, comfort and durability all were improved. Redesigned cabinetry also provided more leg room for passengers in the principal four club chairs.

Another factory option made available in 1982 was Cessna's Cescom maintenance program. A genuine programmed maintenance scheme in its later form, Cescom provided more flexible inspection options that could reduce total hours and cost for those who scrupulously followed the recording and reporting requirements. A service life recorded on Cescom would be a strong plus for any used 425. Regular readers of aircraft resale advertisements will note that such programs as Cescom, various engine maintenance programs and good service bulletin compliance history are considered sales advantages.

A number of improvements have been missed by operators who do not carefully review product information, improvement and service bulletins from Cessna and component manufacturers. These include glass replacement windshields (although some technicians claim this change has not completely solved cracking and delamination problems), replacement of troublesome torque gauges with electric ones, water drains to control circuit breaker and avionics systems contamination and shorting and a number of engine modifications.

Cost/Performance/Specifications

Model	Year Built	Average Retail Price	Cruise Speed (kts)	Useful Load (lbs)	Fuel Std/Opt (gals)	Eng Out Svc (ft)	Engine	TBO (hrs)	Overhaul Cost
CE-425	1981	$725,000	251	3,753	372	17,200	450-shp P&W PT6A-112	3,500	$85k/105,000
CE-425	1982	$740,000	251	3,753	372	17,200	450-shp P&W PT6A-112	3,500	$85k/105,000
CE-425	1983	$800,000	251	3,753	372	17,200	450-shp P&W PT6A-112	3,500	$85k/105,000
CE-425	1984	$880,000	251	3,753	372	17,200	450-shp P&W PT6A-112	3,500	$85k/105,000
CE-425	1985	$960,000	251	3,753	372	17,200	450-shp P&W PT6A-112	3,500	$85k/105,000
CE-425	1986	$1,130,000	251	3,753	372	17,200	450-shp P&W PT6A-112	3,500	$85k/105,000

Prices from Aircraft Bluebook Price Digest

The best Conquest I is one fully up-to-date on hourly, cycle and calendar maintenance, ADs, service bulletins and kits, product improvements, updated electrics—including connectors, good and current avionics. It should also pass the most meticulous, every-nook-and-cranny inspection by an experienced 425 technician. Theoretically that means one of the last off the line. Realistically, it can be one of the first.

The best-looking Conquest I, with the newest interior and latest paint job may be a beast in disguise. Cosmetics are appealing, but they are the least important part of any airplane purchase. There are many thousands of buyers who were lured by good looks, only to find they had bought turkeys.

Performance/Load Carrying

While the 425 does not have the payload lift capacity of a C90 King Air, it is very nearly a fill-the-seats airplane. With lots of lard and luggage toward the rear of the airplane, cg has to be checked very carefully, but the loading range is quite wide.

Zero fuel weight (anything between 7,000 and 8,600 pounds has to be fuel) still leaves a healthy maximum payload of crew, passengers and baggage or freight of 1,673 pounds for a typically equipped airplane.

The typical 425 can seat eight: two seats in the cockpit, four club seats, an additional full seat on the left rear side of the cabin and a belted potty seat. Even with maximum number of seats, there is a generous baggage area in the aft cabin (about 30 cubic feet and up to 500 pounds). The cavernous nose houses another 22.4 cubic feet of baggage area with a maximum load of 400 pounds.

There is a lot of cubic space in both the cabin and baggage areas that could tempt those lacking caution and experience to exceed load limits. Yield not to temptation. Aside from cg concerns, exceeding maximum loads can cause serious performance deterioration, especially in high density altitude conditions.

In sea level, standard temperature conditions, at gross weight the (well-flown) 425 can clear a 50-foot obstacle after a run of 2,420 feet and land over the same barrier in 2,120 feet. With the already mentioned accelerate/stop and accelerate/go distances of 3,800 and 3,360 feet, a properly qualified pilot can safely operate from 4,000-foot runways with room to spare. If you are used to flying a Skyhawk or a Cherokee, that may sound like a lot of runway. For a nearly 9,000 pound airplane, however, it is very good.

Rate of climb is good enough to make it practical to climb into the flight levels for even relatively short trips. The 425 operates best between FL230 and 280. While maximum speed of 260 knots comes at 18,000 feet, fuel burn is high. At FL260, max cruise power produces 251 knots and 1,240 nm still-air range. In the mid-20s, the 425 is a five-hour-plus-reserves airplane. With a maximum operating speed of

Big-city or boondocks airport, the Conquest 1 is comfortable with 4,000-foot runways (allowing for accelerate/stop/go distances) for properly qualified pilots. That big nose has utilitarian value: its cavernous baggage compartment can hold up to 400 pounds.

230 KIAS and max gear operating of 175 and approach flap of 174, the 425 can return to pattern altitude very quickly when necessary.

Systems Limits

When you move into this category aircraft, systems become major factors in defining performance. A properly equipped 425 is approved for operation in known icing conditions. Its equipment, thanks to the ability to bleed heated air from the engines for more than pressurization and vacuum systems, is more capable than most piston twins so long as everything is maintained properly (dirty, aged deice boots are as likely to leak, and ice is as likely to stick to them in strange places and shapes as any other airplane).

Better systems tend to lead pilots to accept worse conditions. It becomes a vicious cycle. For instance, heavy precipitation or the chance of icing conditions require that the engine inertial separators be extended. This device forces inlet air to make a sharp turn, separating large rain drops, ice particles and snow, which are shunted overboard. The system results in a decrease in torque and an increase in inter-turbine temperatures (ITT). In itself a power reduction, ITT must be closely monitored. If it exceeds limits, power must be further reduced to keep temperatures within allowable limits.

The operating manual, on the other hand, recommends higher power settings and higher speeds to reduce ice accumulation on unprotected parts of the airframe. In a notes section, it mentions that half an inch of ice accumulation results in a cruise speed reduction of as much as 30 knots. For too many of us, the more capability we have, the further we push conditions.

Flight Operations

As noted above, the Conquest cockpit is well organized. It also is quite comfortable for most pilots of average to large size. Visibility is very good. Control harmony in flight is fair. Pitch is the heaviest force, and this is by design. Appropriate trim input is a key to flying the 425 smoothly.

Pitch changes with configuration changes are modest. They are more obvious with power changes—particularly gross power changes as from approach to missed approach or go around.

There are not peculiar tricks, however. From both the pilot eye-level perspective and physical/reaction demands, the 425 probably is the simplest of all the turbo-props to transition too. Thus the nickname "baby carriage." Pilots transitioning from light twins will have a bit of trouble at first with control pressures, trim use, aircraft performance and weight (inertia). But good training and a bit of experience quickly leads to confidence. Engine management, from start-up to shut down, is as important as how well you can shoot an ADF approach where the flying budget is concerned. Poor power management can lead to premature failure or, at the least, much higher HSI and overhaul costs. They cost gobs of money.

Flying the airplane entails extra time and extra care during pre- and post-light operations. There are good tricks to learn. For instance, if a quick landing and turnaround is planned, shutting off the bleed air source from one engine about 15 minutes out, then starting that engine first on the turn around means lower start temperatures and lower stress on both engines.

On the ground, both before and after flight, it needs special care, and operations such as ground towing and refueling must be closely monitored.

Comfort Levels

Starting with the first 400 series twin, the abominable 411, Cessna has advertised the wide oval cabin. Sure enough, like an oval laid on its side, the Cessna cabin affords a good bit of elbow room. This, together with generous windows and reasonably comfortable seats, creates a comparatively high degree of passenger comfort.

The combination of good basic cockpit design and roominess makes the 425 pilot more comfortable than many other turboprop designs. Accommodation of tall pilots is determined largely by the type of cabinets installed between the flight deck and the cabin than by available room to adjust the seats.

A Conquest with well-balanced rotating components and a fully-functioning propeller synchrophaser can be relatively quiet and comfortable at cruise power settings, especially at propeller rpm less than 1900. Each airplane has an ideal rpm that can be figured with practice. Good propeller balancing makes it even better. For a number of 425s, the best compromise of noise and vibration occurs at propeller settings of between 1825 and 1850 rpm. Experimentation pays off, because once cruise power is established, vibration is more of a noise-generating factor. The two major sources are prop vortex hitting the nose cone and being transmitted forward through the tail (the fuselage acts like a megaphone).

Noise level is competitive. Crew and passenger space is more than competitive. The 425 is a good airplane in these respects.

Support

At least the Conquest is not an orphan. Despite the fact that no 425s have been produced in nearly 10 years, Cessna support is commendable, according to a number of operators, particularly in comparison with what is offered by most other manufacturers or former manufacturers. Cessna also can be a good source of research materials for determining what the proper maintenance status of a 425 should be. The few bucks (or hundreds of bucks for all materials) represent a worthwhile investment.

The cockpit is well organized, and piston pilots can make the transition easily and expect a greatly reduced workload, provided they have a dose of learning about the subtleties of powerplant management.

So, too, it pays to get to know someone in customer service at Pratt & Whitney. While the PT6A-112 is a fairly old and mild version, there is much to learn about modifications and recommended procedures. For instance, one reader who bought a 425 had a nearly $55,000 shock when discovering the original cobalt inlet guide vanes had been replaced by nickel vanes (that large payment included hot sections inspections).

More basic changes have occurred—which operators on Cescom or on the mailing lists at Cessna and PWC would have known about—that increase propulsion system serviceability and durability (and reduced major maintenance costs). Among these

are compressor washes. A mod was introduced that adapted a fitting much like the one on a garden hose to make compressor washes easier to perform.

Powerplant Eye-Openers

PWC has a lot of eye-opening information for operators. Among these are some of the reasons for regular compressor washes. You might accept the necessity in a high salt-content environment. Pratt specialists can show you maps of concentrations of contaminants such as sulfur that occur at cruise altitude in parts of the North American continent where you might expect the air to be pristine. Among the relatively simple modifications that can be made to the 425's engines is one that reconfigures the inlet nozzles to reduce temperatures in the combustion section of the engine during starts.

What some operators of turbine engines never learn and others learn only after very expensive inspections and overhauls is that heat is both the friend of performance and the enemy of endurance. Going for maximum performance all the time means running temperatures to the recommended limits. Given the vagaries of most gauges and the benefits of just a few degrees lower temperature, a little touch of conservatism can mean literally thousands of dollars reduced cost during a HSI or overhaul, not to mention diminishing the stress that could result in one of those rare inflight failures.

Decisions

Even during its heyday, there were not many qualified Conquest support organizations. Today, they are few and far between, and some are qualified in nameplate only. One reader writes that he wishes he could turn back the clock and swap his 425 for his old 421, which he remembers as superior in every way to the Conquest.

Another, after a long period of research, comparison and number crunching bought a 425 to replace a 414. Despite the considered approach, there were a number of surprises related largely to the condition of the airplane at purchase and to the demands for maintenance in terms of frequency, downtime and cost.

While the care and feeding of a high-performance piston-powered airplane and a turbine are not that different, proper maintenance is more important for the latter if for no other reason than the higher costs involved to fix problems. Everything related to 425 is more serious and potentially more expensive.

This is not the kind of airplane to use for on-the-job training for technicians for your local, or favorite but unqualified shop. That's a major reason for unhappiness with the 425 and similar airplanes for many operators. Selecting the wrong shop can be as expensive as neglecting proper maintenance altogether. The best approach is to talk to other Conquest I operators to get their recommended service and information sources. Keep meticulous records, too. Get involved in an information-sharing network of operators and service/support organizations. It can serve as effective early warning and help keep operational readiness up and costs down.

Modifications

Most of the mods available for the 425 are fuel management systems and conversion of the standard nickel cadmium batteries for lead acid types. Also, McCauley has an STC to covert the standard three-bladed propellers to the four-blade "Black Mac" system.

Maintenance Record

The known maintenance record of the 425 fleet, consisting mainly of service difficulty reports (SDRs) and airworthiness directives (ADs), has disclosed some shortcomings of the design. While there has been no overwhelming weak point, several problems identified in the field have resulted in ADs. There are a few that suggest careful inspection in hard to get at areas is required. These areas include control cables at pulleys, fairleads and pressure vessel seals and window retainers.

Service difficulties that resulted in ADs include wing spar cap cracks caused by landing gear loads, windshield attach point failures, nose landing gear actuators and horizontal stabilizer attach fittings.

There have been a few reports of accessory corrosion and contamination, including air conditioning tubing, oxygen system elements, engine mounts, oil lines and hydraulic system elements. When you consider the temperature and humidity variations between sea level at summer and operation for a few hours in temperatures of -20 to 30 degrees centigrade, the possibility for condensation/contamination/corrosion is evident.

Thorough pre-purchase and periodic maintenance inspections are essential. Selection of a knowledgeable maintenance site is key. Again, talk to experienced operators to solicit advice. For the most part, the low bidder for airframe or engine work should be avoided like the plague, unless there is evidence to suggest it really is a bargain.

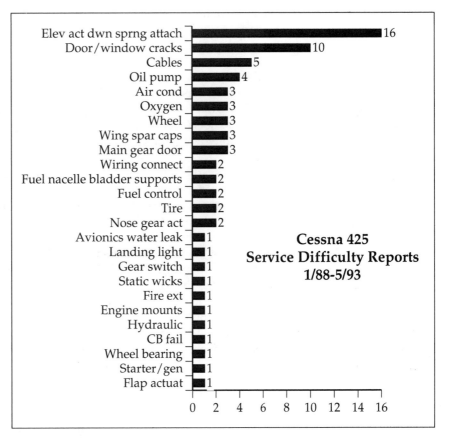

Cessna 425
Service Difficulty Reports
1/88-5/93

Owner Comments

After over 4,000 hours in 11 years in our C414 Chancellor, we replaced her (Oct. '91) with the best Cessna 425 that I could find. Now, after 522 hours and 510 landings, we couldn't be happier. This aircraft continues to amaze me with its reliability, capability and performance. At first glance, I expected a 414A with 45% more power, 25% more speed and much greater load capacity. It is certainly all of that plus a *lot* more.

As for handling, it has a much more solid and stable feel (especially above 200

KIAS) and far superior quality of control in approach and landing in the gustiest of crosswinds, than the 414A, which was very good. Performance meets or exceeds the POH in every respect. The *new* Beech C90A and slightly used Cessna 441 that we tried out were a little short of their POH predictions.

Loading: You still must watch the aft CG, but it is friendlier than the 414A in that respect. Our Conquest is loaded, but you can still carry almost 600 lbs. plus pilot with full fuel for 1500+ nm or almost 1,400 lbs. plus pilot for 900+ nm.

Comfort: We were spoiled by the 400 Cessna's wide-oval cabin. It is also much quieter than the high-powered C-441. I think that the 414A was quieter. However, it was also *much* slower and not nearly as smooth. Performance: The first owner regularly ran "top-of-the-green" power and was getting 280 knots in the low to mid twenties. For the first 400 hours I ran max-cruise-power from the POH. This resulted in TASs of 250 to 270 knots, average fuel use of 76.2 gph and a block speed of 220 knots (average trip 0:58).

For the past 108 hours I have been enjoying max-range-power or something in between (depending on the hurry, and the winds aloft). Now I am running along at TASs of 210 to 260 knots with an average fuel use of 63.6 gph and a block speed of 209 knots (average trip 1:17). I enjoy a quieter ride along with 14% less fuel and 5% more flying, plus cooler ITTs.

This aircraft has been on the Cescom program since new and the factory support has been very good, and parts availability has not been a problem. The main advantage over the old aircraft has no doubt been reliability. Less than a third the down-time for maintenance, and inspections are just inspections—no surprises.

The most obvious weakness is that the cabin pressure system is not quite equal to the performance potential of the aircraft. It has the same differential pressure capacity as the 414A with twice the climb and three times the descent rates. (It does have a much greater bleed-air supply for this, which also contributes to the noise factor.) The most troublesome maintenance factor has been the electrical system. You have to watch for loose connectors, terminals and wires as well as bad breakers and hidden fuses.

Art Johnson
Cape Coral, Fla.

I now have approximately 400 hours in a Conquest, including several long trips. The plane is a dream to fly and provides a very stable platform for IFR conditions. The PT6 engines are almost bulletproof and provide plenty of power. The fuel-burn rates for flight planning equated to about 500 pounds the first hour and 400 pounds each hour thereafter.

The Cessna 1000 Series Radios, contrary to rumor, have performed well. The only exception is the LED lighting, which has a tendency to need replacement. The only other weakness is the engine gauges (torque, fuel flow and fuel gauges), which are a constant problem. In summary, I couldn't be more pleased with my Conquest and find it a pleasure to fly.

Howard J. White, III
Palo Alto, Calif.

Cessna 441 Conquest

Severe problems with the tail early on have apparently been fixed; the 441 now represents one of the best choices in a used turboprop.

Cessna's 441 Conquest turboprop is a thundering paradox of an airplane: at once a superb performer, yet symbolic of one of Cessna Aircraft Corporation's darkest hours. The plane is fast, far-ranging and fuel-efficient, yet it will be years before the memory of The Great Tail Affair fades completely. But the specter of The Tail doesn't seem to bother used turboprop buyers much anymore; a 1978 Conquest has retained a higher percentage of its original value than any other popular turboprop.

History

The Conquest was a natural outgrowth of Cessna's piston-twin line. The company had introduced its very successful Citation in 1972, figuring that the comparatively frugal, inexpensive fanjet made turboprops obsolete. But then turbine fuel quadrupled in cost virtually overnight in 1974, and it became clear that the superior fuel economy of the turboprop (compared to jets, at least) would assure it a permanent niche in the business aviation world. Cessna had been flying a prototype of a large-cabin piston twin called the 431, and decided to resurrect it as a turboprop. The huge 425-hp Continental piston engines were replaced by Garrett TPE-331-8 turbine engines rated at 636 hp each, and the 441 was born.

It came on the market in late 1977. Cessna was a decade behind the field getting into the turboprop marketplace, but the Conquest's impressive performance numbers gave every hope that the company would catch up fast. And then, just a month or two after the grand unveiling, tragedy struck. A Conquest with seven people aboard broke up in the air over Alabama. Cessna quickly claimed to have determined the cause of the crash: flutter of the elevator triggered by a broken trim tab actuator. The plane was grounded by the FAA.

In the ensuing months, it became clear why Cessna figured out the cause of the crash so quickly. The elevator/trim system had been giving trouble for years during Conquest prototype testing. when the plane had first been designed there was internal debate at Cessna about the placement of the horizontal tail. At least one Cessna engineer (the chief aerodynamicist on the Conquest project, in fact) thought it should not be positioned low on the fuselage, where it would be buffeted by constant propwash. He was overruled by senior management. Almost from the first test flight, the Conquest prototype suffered tab actuator loosening problems. It was repeatedly redesigned and beefed up, to no avail. Finally, Cessna's flight test department sent a memo to management pointing out the continuing problem and pleading for a major redesign of the tail.

Management refused; the basic tail design would remain unchanged, and the .tab actuator was beefed up yet again.

Cessna, acting under its Delegated Option Authority (DOA), went ahead and certified the Conquest in mid-1977 with the tail problem still unresolved. The FAA, unaware of the long history of tail troubles, gave its rubber-stamp approval. Meanwhile, two different Conquests on sales demo tours had experienced constant tail trouble. One Cessna demo pilot even encountered flutter, but was able to land safely. In what we believe now must be regarded as a major breach of prudent management and corporate integrity, Cessna started selling Conquests anyway.

The tragedy occurred within two months.

After the grounding, Cessna worked feverishly to redesign the tab actuator. By March, 1978, it had come up with yet another beefup, this one claimed to be literally 50 times stronger than necessary. The Conquest fleet, then numbering only a few dozen, took to the air again, and Conquest operators and company executives breathed a sigh of relief.

But not for long. In May, l979, a Conquest with the redesigned tab actuator suffered a severe tail vibration and pitch-up, but managed to land safely in Monterey, Calif. The tab actuator was found broken. The fleet was again grounded for four months while an entirely new horizontal stabilizer was designed. The new tail had a second spar, more ribs and thicker skins.

Cessna engineers now believed the fault was not the actuator, but the tail structure itself (particularly the bonded leading edge), which vibrated excessively and eventually caused the tab actuator to work loose and/or break.

The redesign took four months, and retrofitting the 106 airplanes in the field another two months. Finally, in December, l979, the Conquest fleet was back in the air again. This time, the fix seems to have worked. However, other problems have cropped up in the tail in recent years. AD 91-16-7 calls for repetitive inspections of the horizontal stabilizer forward attach bulkhead for cracks. If any are found, a reinforcement must be installed.

Cessna Trying Harder

Conquest buyers actually benefited from the whole unfortunate affair. To protect the reputation of the Conquest, Cessna went to great lengths to support the plane. The company provided loaner airplanes to Conquest customers during the second grounding, and refurbished the airplanes to the latest configuration before returning them to service. One Conquest owner reports the company paid for a new paint job, all new windows, five changes of the HSI and "dozens of other minor changes." Virtually every service bulletin we checked provided for full parts and labor credit. A used Conquest buyer can count himself lucky for missing the 1979 nightmare, yet reaping the benefits of Cessna's efforts to rebuild the airplane's reputation.

Production

There are very few differences between Conquests in the field. All aircraft below serial number 110 (78-79 models) are essentially identical, having been updated during the great tail retrofit. Serial numbers 153 and above had new engine combustion chambers to combat power-robbing carbon buildup. (This is called the 402 engine mod, more of which later.) Serial 173 and later (1981 models and up) were approved to fly up to 35,000 feet—5,000 feet above the original certificated max altitude. Both mods are retrofittable and should be part of any used Conquest under consideration.

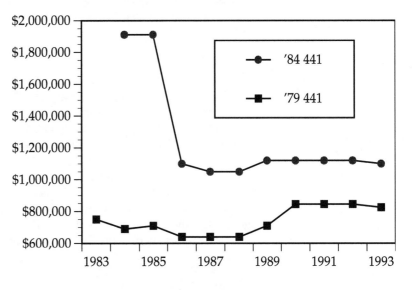

Other changes included the usual evolutionary avionics upgrades. In all, 362 Conquests were produced: the last models were sold in 1986.

Resale Value

Despite the aircraft's unfortunate history, the Conquest has retained its resale value very well. Comparing 1980 models of competing turboprops, for example, the 441 has retained more of its original base price than any other aircraft in its class—far more than some. The 441 has an 85% residual value, compared to an average of about 70%. The worst in the class is the Mitsubishi MU-2, the 1980 model of which is worth only 54% of its original cost.

Performance

There have been several turboprops introduced since the Conquest came out, notably aircraft like the Beech Starship and Piaggio Avanti. Among its contemporaries, however, the 441 boasted a newer design: at the time of its introduction, it was the only aircraft in its class with a design less than a decade old.

The Conquest has excellent speed, range and climb performance, and its fuel efficiency is better than any of its contemporaries. Max cruise speed is 293 knots, second only to the MU-2 and 20-30 knots faster than comparable King Airs. But fuel consumption is far less than the MU-2's. At normal cruise power, the Conquest turns in 278 knots at 33,000 feet while burning about 375 pph of fuel—a sparkling 5.0 mpg. This efficiency is reflected in an extraordinary 2,000-mile plus IFR range, among the best of turboprops, and considerably better than its stablemate, the Citation.

Thanks to the high-aspect-ratio wing, time to climb is also good. The Conquest will reach 30,000 feet in about 22 minutes, and its 35,000-foot ceiling in just over

30 minutes. The 35,000-foot limit is higher than most turboprops, and is a major reason for the airplane's high efficiency.

Operators report that the Conquest is routinely able to operate in the 30,000-foot range without the long, struggling climbs that limit most turboprop operators to the mid-20s in everyday use. Part of the Conquest's efficiency stems from its ability to climb quickly and fly high, where turboprop efficiency is dramatically better.

The Conquest's single-engine performance is about average for the turboprops. Vmc is 92 knots, right in the middle of the pack, and single-engine climb rate is 715 fpm. Climb gradient is also very good. Runway performance is about average; accelerate-go distance is about 4,000 feet at gross weight and standard conditions.

Loading

Useful load generally runs around 3,800 pounds in normal configuration. With a full load of fuel (475 gallons, or about 3,180 pounds), this allows a cabin payload of just over 600 pounds, or three people (including crew) and a bit of luggage. A full cabin of eight people and bags leaves room for 2,800 pounds of fuel, enough to fly about 1,500 miles with IFR reserves. That's pretty good.

As with all long-cabin variable-seating airplanes, care must be taken when loading the last few tail-end Charlie passengers aboard. Aft c.g. limits can easily be exceeded unless counterbalancing baggage is loaded into the nose cargo bay. But generally, the Conquest has decent loading and balance characteristics, in contrast to aircraft such as the Piper Cheyenne II, which is extremely sensitive to aft loading.

Creature Comforts

The Conquest has a big cabin. It's nearly 13 feet long, longer than any comparable turboprop except for the cavernous 100 and 200 series King Airs. Cabin width and height are about average, or perhaps a tad less. Seating arrangements range from eight to a rather crowded eleven. The Garrett engines make the Conquest a bit noisier than comparable PT-6-powered aircraft, particularly on the ground.

Flying Qualities

The 400 series Cessnas in general have a reputation for pleasant, well harmonized controls, and we've heard some pilots say the Conquest is the best of the lot. It also has a trailing-beam type main landing gear for soft touchdowns and a wide main-gear stance for good runway handling.

We received no owner reports about single-engine handling qualities. However, the NTS (Negative Torque Sensor) system on the Garrett engines, a type of auto-feather device that quickly sets the propeller to a near-feather position in case of power loss, should help the pilot out in the critical task of quick identification and feathering of the failed engine. And we're pleased to note that the Conquest flight manual drives home the fact that a slight bank into the good engine (which results in a skid) is necessary to achieve the listed single-engine performance.

Maintenance History

The Conquest, as one might expect from such a complex aircraft, has had its share of service problems. However, Cessna has been generous with warranty repairs, and many Conquest service bulletins have been company paid. So it's likely that any used Conquest will have had most service bulletins complied with.

Nevertheless, a potential buyer should be aware of several potential trouble spots, and carefully examine the maintenance history of the aircraft to determine compliance. Among the Conquest's maintenance checkpoints:

• Environmental system problems. Serial numbers 1-74 had lots of problems with vent fans, air cycle machines and other parts of the heating/air conditioning system.

• Starter/generator failures. Improved brushes were fitted to serial numbers 106 and later.

• Nosewheel. The first 62 airplanes had defective nosewheels, but even the "improved" model on later aircraft should be modified.

All of the above improvements were almost certainly made to the first 109 aircraft during the four-month grounding for the tail retrofit. Since the Conquest's return to service, however, the following problems have cropped up:

• Window delamination. Make sure the aircraft has the improved PPG windows. Several Conquests had to have a complete set of new windows. (Cessna footed the bill.)

• Pressurization outflow valve. Older models were subject to cracked retaining rings, while serial numbers 120-176 were pinpointed for possible cracked poppet valves. The cracked retaining ring problem may have been related to the famous "wandering Conquest" crash that killed LSU football coach Bo Hein.

• Wheel-well modifications. Problems with tire clearance led to a redesign of the wheel well. Older aircraft should have been modified.

Engine Problems

Potentially the most serious Conquest problem (now that the tail has been fixed) is power loss in the Garrett TPE-331-8 engines. During 1979 and '80 there were reports of unexplained power loss as aircraft time passed 500 hours or so. One *Aviation Consumer* reader reports his airspeed fell off from the normal 290 knots to 260. The cause was found to be carbon buildup in the combustion chambers, which caused erosion of the hot-section parts and consequent loss of power. In August, 1980, Cessna and Garrett announced the "402 mod," essentially a new combustion chamber designed to reduce carbon buildup. We would not advise buying a Conquest without this mod, unless the price is correspondingly low to account for premature hot-section overhaul and combustion-chamber replacement. By this time, most if not all 441s should have the mod installed.

Other sources of power loss in the Garretts have proven to be due to inadequate compressor clearance, leaking anti-ice valves, flow divider problems, bad secondary fuel nozzles and leaking igniters. (Only the Champions leak: look for AC igniters.)

There was an Airworthiness Directive issued this year: AD 93-2-1 calls for replacement of certain fuel manifold assemblies.

Service Difficulty Reports

A scan of the SDRs on file for the Conquest reflect most of the problems mentioned above. We noticed an extremely large number mentioning control cable problems (either frayed, worn or misrouted). There were also some reports that reflect poorly on Cessna's quality control, such as multiple rivet holes for the aft attachment of the horizontal stabilizer (this was reported on eight aircraft), oxygen regulators installed backwards and four-ply tires installed at the factory instead of the minimum required six-ply.

However, most of these difficulties occurred in the early years. For example, of the 512 reports for the years 1978-1982, only about 12 percent were received in 1982. And of course the population of airplanes in the field was much higher during 1982.

Owner Comments

I bought serial 79 new at the beginning of 1979 and thus unwillingly became a member of Cessna's experimental department. When the airplane was flying again with a new tail in December of '79 (and a number of other updates and improvements), I was a fairly disgruntled customer. Cessna provided me with a 340 to use during the downtime, which was better than nothing, but not very satisfying after having laid out a million dollars for a turboprop.

I got reasonable service from that time forward. There have been many irritating problems; i.e., new paint job, new windows, five changes of the pilot's HSI (and finally installing a Collins PD-108), dozens and dozens of minor changes, all paid for by Cessna, I might add, to their everlasting credit. The airplane was down for weeks at a time with these miseries. I run the 441 on Part 135, so the downtime has been lethal. The latest major catastrophe appears to be the engines. After 200 hours, we started getting a dropping off in true airspeed. At 750 hours we were getting 260 knots instead of the original 290. Once again, we had expense and downtime fooling around with recompensation and Lebow tests. Eventually we were approved for the 402 mod. Another month of being grounded. The cabin windows were replaced at this time, too.

The airplane is a delight to fly. It literally has no bad habits. Our customers also find it comfortable and reasonably quiet. The range is sensational. If Cessna can ever get the bugs out, the 441 has no peer. I have flown all of the current turboprops and am typed in the Lear and Citation. I have 5,000 hours (ATP). The airplane is flown on 135 operations about 200 hours/year by another professional ATP, who spends most of his time looking after the maintenance and concomitant record keeping.

One flight problem does exist, however. When the airplane is flown at high altitude and then descends to ground level when the humidity is high, all of the windows fog up tight. This can happen during the approach (and has) or immediately after landing. The defrost blower is completely inadequate for the job. We have obtained a quote to fix this and you guessed it! Instead of installing a $50 blower, a $2,300 mod is required. I believe the 441 is the easiest to fly and probably among the safest of the currently available turboprops.

G.W. Balz
Kalamazoo. Mich.

Cessna Citation 500 series

The original Citation spawned a lot of jokes. But in the tradition of the ads saying, "they all laughed when I sat down to play the piano," the little Citations have had the last laugh as the most popular (read successful) bizjets in the world

In 1968, Cessna Aircraft Co. created a big stir at the annual National Business Aircraft Assn. meeting when it announced its decision to enter the business jet market. Some thought it brassy; others, not credible. Almost everyone forgot that Cessna had already built a large number of military jet training and light attack aircraft, the T/A-37 (Tweety Bird).

Single-Pilot Operation

One original objective for the Citation was to get it approved for single-pilot operation. This would support the claims of simplicity and make transition to propellerless flight less intimidating. The cockpit was designed with that in mind. While Cessna failed on its first try for single-pilot approval, it is widely agreed that Citation cockpits are the best, ergonomically speaking. About the only dispute is over the vertical-tape engine instruments that were the coming thing in the late 1960s. Most pilots still prefer round gauges. Many other cockpit layouts, greatly aided by the integration electronic instruments provide, are getting close to Citation simplicity, but Cessna continues to lead the way. And, as a bonus, the good human factors engineering trickled down to other, prop-driven Cessnas.

When people talk of the single-pilot Citation, most people talk of the original Citation—that's wrong. In truth, all the 500 series Citations can in some way be flown solo. From a practical standpoint, though, the Citation I/SP and the Citation II under a pilot exemption are the two most likely to be operated by a lone pilot except for ferry flights.

Airline Standards

Certification was to FAR Part 25 which, the promotional literature at the time trumpeted, is the same standard governing airline aircraft approval. The Citation was backed by what the company termed a total program of training, service, maintenance and centralized warranty. The latter means customers would not have to deal with a number of component vendors.

The Citation support package was and is quite thorough. The warranty includes labor and runs (this is a sample from 1977) for three years on the airframe, two years or 1,000 hours on the engines, two years on the standard avionics package and one year on everything else. It also included a free year's participation in Cessna's automated maintenance scheduling, reporting and recording system, Cescom.

Another break with tradition was the agreement signed with American Airlines to provide crew training. This served several purposes, including the cachet of airline-quality training (in business aviation's first simulator with visual display) and removing Cessna from the pressure to approve pilots who might not come up to standards.

Finally, the company provided customers with a very short options list and an airplane ready to fly away from the factory in full livery. This was and is a departure from the widespread practice of delivering "green" airplanes to completion centers for installation of avionics and interiors custom built to customer specifications.

The Near Jet

Cessna described the original Citation at the time as the first business jet to sport "second-generation," high-bypass turbofan engines. The Pratt & Whitney of Canada (PWC) JT15D-1 engines selected—rated at 2,200 pounds of thrust—fit the role of the Citation as a compromise between turboprop and jet. One large advantage was that the turbofan is fuel efficient compared to pure jet engines, especially at mid-level altitudes.

This worked to the Citation's advantage in another way: it was a struggle to operate at or near its original certified maximum operating altitude of FL350, especially with any payload in the cabin or on a warmer than standard day (i.e., frequently). The Citation can fly with reasonable fuel burns in the upper teens and into the twenties.

The turbofan also contributes to better balanced field performance. A big item in the early marketing effort was the claim that the Citation could operate to 1,200 airports other jets could not while it also touted accelerate-stop/accelerate-go performance better than many turboprops. In fact, to this day, Cessna takes aim at turboprops as well as other jets in its advertising, claiming that total operating costs per mile (not per hour, of course) equal or better those for turboprops.

The Cast of Citations

The original Citation has spawned a family of airplanes. Two families, really: the 500 series and the 600 series are quite different. (And these soon will be joined by a new 700 series. The Citation X, or Model 750, is a mach 0.90 speedster with an IFR range in excess of 3,000 nm.)

Model designations are not enough. The Model 500 encompasses two quite different airplanes in terms of configuration and performance, and a number of improvements and performance increases in between. Only the marketing names, Citation and Citation I, distinguish the major differences. The only distinction between the Citation I Model 500 and the Model 501 Citation I/SP, approved for single-pilot operation, is paperwork.

The Citation first flew in September, 1969. First deliveries were made in 1972;

The Citation first flew in September, 1969. First deliveries were made in 1972; production ended in 1977 with 349 units built. Some changes and improvements made to the original Citation include switching from electrically-heated windshields to a bleed air anti-icing system; and incremental weight increases from the initial maximum takeoff weight of 10,850 pounds to 11,500, then 11,650 (serial no. 71) and finally 11,850 pounds for serial numbers 303 and higher.

Engine performance at altitude also was improved through the addition of improved internal components, and maximum operating altitude was increased from FL350 to FL410 with an attendant increase in maximum pressure differential (originally 7.6 psi, up to 8.5 psi) to provide the FAA-required cabin altitude of 8,000 feet. Optional thrust reversers were first offered in 1975.

Two new Citations were announced in 1977: the Citation I (and I S/P) and II. The new Model 500 had a slightly reprofiled and expanded wing. Span was increased from the original's 43 ft. 11 in. to 47 ft. 1 in. An improved engine, the JT15D-1A, was still rated at 2,200 pounds but further improved high altitude performance. Production of the Citation I ended in 1985. Approximately 342 were built.

The higher aspect ratio wing improved climb performance and made higher cruising altitudes more practical at higher-than-standard temperatures and with heavier payloads. Even the last versions of the original Citation tend to run out of steam at around 30,000 feet except when very lightly loaded or on very cold days. The Citation Is get to altitude faster and can practically be flown at FL350 and higher on most days.

Citation II

First deliveries of the larger Model 550 were made in 1978. Production ended in 1984 and then was restarted in 1987. The fuselage is 42 inches longer than the Model 500 (LOA is 47 ft. 2 in. compared to 43 ft. 6 in.). The increased cabin length accommodates up to four more seats (maximum certificated passenger capacity is 10; for the Citation I it is six). More than 640 units have been delivered.

An improved wing profile plus wider span (wingspan is 51 ft. 8 in., aspect ratio is 8.3) and uprated, 2,500-pound-thrust JT15D-4 engines take the II out of the Near-Jet category completely. Standard day rate of climb is more than 3,300 fpm, maximum cruise speed is 385 knots, and maximum operating altitude is FL430. Maximum fuel capacity is 150 gallons higher (742/5,009 pounds).

The Citation II/SP, Model 551, is the least popular Citation. FAA restricts the 551 to a maximum operating weight of 12,500 pounds (the 550 is 13,300). The quirk of paperwork is that even when flown by two properly qualified pilots, the II/SP can haul 800 fewer pounds than its identical sibling. In the real world, this has turned out to be a substantial penalty.

Citation SII

The Model S550, introduced in the 1984 model year, is a departure from the 500 series. The fuselage is the same as the Citation II, but the wing is designed employing supercritical design techniques. There are other aerodynamic changes, as well, to optimize the wing for climb and high-altitude cruise performance. Production ended in 1988; 160 SII's were manufactured.

The S550 powerplants are rated at 2,500 pounds but use the JT15D-4B variant, which has a TBO of 3,000 hours compared to 3,500 on the Citation II's engines.

Maximum operating altitude is FL430 (pressure differential is 8.8 psi). Fuel capacity is 862 gallons/5,818 pounds. The SII and SII/SP can carry more, farther and faster than its stable mates. On the other hand, it does not have the good balanced field length performance of the straight-wing Citations.

The single-pilot, or SII/SP version does not have the weight restriction that limits the 551. There is an exemption covering single-pilot operation. More on this subject later.

Citation V

The Model 560 was introduced in 1988. The Citation V fuselage is 20 inches longer than the 550's. The extension, which makes LOA 48.9 feet compared to 47.2 for the II and SII, is made forward of the wing leading edge and stretches the cabin by 17.7 inches.

The 560 also has a redesigned, larger empennage. Span of the horizontal stabilizer is increased (to demonstrate the family resemblance or continuity, the proof-of-concept 560 started life as one of the original Citation Is, then saw duty as the prototype II and SII). Powerplants are 3,200-pound-thrust versions of the JT15D, the -5A, flat rated to 2,900 pounds to improve hot and high performance. Maximum operating altitude is FL450; pressure differential is 9.0 psi maximum. Despite its maximum operating weight of 15,900 pounds, the balanced field length performance of the 560 is better than a Citation II.

CitationJet

The Model 525 was a success almost as soon as it was announced during the 1989 NBAA meeting —21 years after the first Citation. Inevitably, it is being compared to the original, and by literally every measure it is better. For climb, cruise speed, performance at altitude and fuel efficiency, the 525 is an impressive airplane.

Powered by a variant of a turbofan originally designed by Williams Research for cruise missiles, the Williams/Rolls FJ44 is rated at 1,900 pounds thrust—300 lower than the JT15D-1. Approved for a recommended 3,500-hour TBO, it is smaller, lighter and burns roughly 20 percent less fuel. It also produces enough bleed air to provide anti-ice for the wing. (The horizontal stabilizer uses pneumatic boots for deice; the vertical fin does not need anti- or deice.)

A big element in the 525's impressive performance is the natural laminar flow wing, especially when coupled with better aerodynamic refinement throughout the design, which sports another distinction from others in the series: a T-tail. The 525 is slightly smaller in most dimensions than a 500. LOA is 42.6 feet; wingspan is 46.8 feet. There are seats for five passengers.

In a family with excellently designed cockpits, the CitationJet's is the best in terms of its organization for single-pilot operation.

Single-pilot Approvals

It took Cessna nearly a decade to achieve one of its original objectives for the Citation: FAA approval for single-pilot operation. Today, all the 500 series airplanes have that approval in one form or another. In Cessna's first two attempts to obtain single-pilot flight approval, the FAA looked more at the airplane and its equipment. In both cases, pilot workload was judged very high in high-density airspace, especially in weather.

Single-pilot approval generated considerable negative reaction in the industry and among pilots, too. While some reasoned that insurance companies would put more limits on single-pilot operation than FAA, others responded emotionally. In time, the flap subsided—in part because single-pilot operations were not commonplace and in part because Citations with just one flight crew member did not rain from the skies. After its approval of the 501 and 551, FAA began to rethink its approach to the issue. It began looking more at pilot qualifications than the airplane and its equipment.

Pilot Qualifications

In 1984, FAA approved exemptions for the Citation II and SII to permit single-pilot operations up to their maximum operating weights so long as "...certain experience, training and proficiency requirements..." are met. Essentially, this is a type rating, a single-pilot transition course and annual proficiency training.

The Model 560 is covered under the same type of arrangement. This reflects the excellent Citation cockpit design as well as the fact that FAA now is considering the pilot the key factor in Citation flight safety. Actually, the most stringent requirement is being placed on the model best designed and equipped for single-pilot operation. The Model 525 requires a specific single-pilot type rating, and the training is not easy.

This approach is being taken, not because the CitationJet is harder to fly, but because the FAA is concerned about the type of pilot/owner who is likely to buy a CitationJet. The "what if" profile is a businessman or sportsman pilot moving up from high-performance singles, piston twins or possibly turboprops. FAA wants the training to be thorough and difficult to make sure the pilot can get up to mental speed with respect to the airplane and the operating environment. This is in contrast to the typical Citation operation, where experienced, professional pilots do most of the flying.

Insuring the Single Pilot

One reader comments that insurance premiums, limitations and requirements rob his single-pilot Citation of its practicality. Some insurance companies will not even cover single-pilot operations. Those that will have stringent requirements.

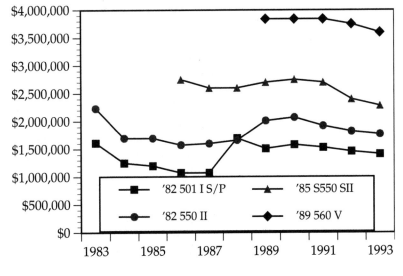

Cessna Citation Resale Value

One underwriter who did not want to be identified said that as a rule of thumb a pilot should have 5,000 hours, a lot of actual instrument and multi-engine time, at least 500 hours of turbine experience and, preferably, a type rating in a jet aircraft.

Even for the 501, which is the most likely to attract pilots who want to fly solo, an insurer probably will specify that a type rating be earned at an approved facility (to eliminate some of the quick-rating schools) and will stipulate semiannual or annual recurrent training. Recurrent training is highly recommended, and it ought to be an element in the operating budget for single-pilot or two-crew operations.

Best Choice

Practically speaking, the Citation I is the best bet for someone seriously thinking of regular single-pilot flying. The larger models, with greater passenger capacity, might have insurance priced beyond reason for anything but VFR ferry flights. And the limited utility of the Citation II/SP, even with two qualified pilots, makes it absolutely the least attractive of all. There are no other civilian, business or commercial use jets with certification that permits single-pilot operation.

There have been enough tweaks and systems revisions and engine component changes even from serial number 350 and up that it needs a knowledgeable person to properly perform an evaluation on a specific aircraft even before determining inspection, service letter and bulletin and AD status. A professionally conducted evaluation of even relatively simple jets like the Citation can cost $20,000 and more. It's good insurance.

Performance

Both the Citation I and II can operate out of 3,000 ft. fields (sea level, standard day, of course). Single-engine performance is astounding to piston twin pilots, with single -engine ceilings of 21,000 and 25,200, respectively and single-engine climb rates of 800 and 1,000 fpm.

According to Cessna figures, a Citation I can carry six passengers more than 1,300 nm with IFR reserves. The II/SP range, because of the weight restriction is 1,469 nm, while a II operated under the single-pilot exemption can exceed 1,700 nm.

Speed is not the strong point of the Citation. Heavy at FL350, the I will true just under 350 KIAS at maximum cruise thrust and approximately 300 at long-range power. The II pokes along at roughly 375 and 291 KIAS, respectively.

Of course, by piston and turboprop standards, Citation performance is pretty darn good. And, over the typical trip length of less than 500 miles, the difference in time between the Citation and faster aircraft is very small.

Flight Handling

Hands down, the 500 series Cessnas are the easiest-to-fly jets there are. Visibility is excellent. Thanks mainly to the straight wings, there is less Dutch roll tendency than in a Baron or Duke. Approach speeds are slower than some turboprops and within roughly 10 knots of most others (and some piston twins). Lightly loaded, they really can be flown slowly in the pattern.

Up at cruise altitudes, maximum speed (Mmo) is low enough that Mach overspeed, jet upset and other potential problems are not issues for the Citation. To descend quickly, there are low- and high-speed techniques, either of which will get the airplane from FL410 to sea level in under 15 minutes without using the speed brakes.

Any pilot with experience flying pressurized, multiengine aircraft to their full capabilities will find transition to the Citation very easy. The workload—systems management, scanning, fuel management, power settings—is much lower. The environment is better, too. In addition to the large windows, noise level is comparatively low, as is vibration. Fatigue is less of a factor than in many airplanes.

Pilots transitioning from simpler or lighter aircraft will find the Citation more of a challenge. To a Mooney pilot, to suggest one extreme, a Citation will be ponderous and unresponsive both on the ground and in the air. Mass and inertia take some getting used to. For all its apparent simplicity, the Citation punishes careless or untutored operation. Anything built to fly high, in weather and fair distances is complicated. The Citation is a collection of systems; knowing how to operate, isolate, correct or compensate for them takes a lot of education and practice. Some place operating restrictions on the airplane. For instance, there are brake energy and cooling considerations that can preclude a fast turnaround.

All the Citations are straightforward flying machines, but they do have their own characteristics. The I and II in particular are not flown onto the runway like most jets. They are extreme floaters. When runway length is no factor, it doesn't matter much. But when making the book numbers is important (as it is at most general aviation airports), the pilot must be precise in organizing the approach, managing configuration and power. Then comes decision time: land or miss. The power must be reduced while still flying. It takes a bit of practice.

Pilot, Passenger Comfort

Pilots get the best seats in the house. The 500 can carry four in the cabin in reasonable comfort. The fifth (or fifth and sixth, if no refreshment center is installed), are a little less comfortable. The 550/551 accommodates six quite well.

Noise levels are reasonably low, although the rear-seat passengers hear a lot more of the engines, especially if they are not synchronized. With engines properly trimmed and in synch, noise level is good, especially in comparison with propeller-driven airplanes. Heating and cooling balance can be a problem, and cooling without optional/retrofit freon air conditioning systems is inadequate in hot climates.

Support

The good news is that Cessna supports Citations very thoroughly and aggressively. It is trying to make the company-owned Citation maintenance facilities competitive with any other competent facility. Cessna keeps a roster of specialists available worldwide. There are field service reps, an 800 hotline, and Wichita-based technical reps who are plugged into a software database that approaches an expert system.

As with the airframe, the engine benefits from a large population and a number of facilities competing to maintain them. The reputable engine specialists also have field service reps to help you and your technicians of choice maintain and fix JT15Ds. Properly maintained and operated (think of the condition levers as money spigots and the engine gauges as the calculator), the JT15D, like its PT6 cousin, is about as bulletproof as an engine can get. Abused and ignored, a hot section inspection (HSI, too) could cost more than $100,000 rather than the $35,000 a prudent operator has been banking. Overhaul of a JT15D that is current and well cared-for will run between $150,000 and $200,000.

Open Your Wallet

The numbers involved stagger people approaching jet aircraft. Hourly operating costs run upwards of $450 each hour even for the Citation I. Average maintenance per flight hour runs from 1.7 to 2.5 man hours.

Among the information Cessna provides new owners are lists of suggested tools and spares, including a pro forma budget. A library of documents, from checklists to maintenance manuals and parts lists, costs nearly $1,500 and annual revision service runs close to $1,000.

The maintenance schedule is very thorough and demanding. Some periodic inspections require a lot of downtime because of detailed inspection of fuel and other systems.

Maintenance Records

Comparatively few ADs have been issued for Citations, and most have been eliminated from the repetitive list by fixes. Both the Citation I and II were affected by inspection and finally reworking of the wing spar cap for cracking and the powerplants had a fan blade problem. No ADs apply to 1990 and later IIs, although the SII has been hit with cable inspection and two engine ADs that apply only to the JT15D-4B.

Between January 1, 1989 and November 19, 1993 a total of 791 SDRs were reported to FAA. A number of the recurrent problems have been addressed with service kits (another important reason to make sure an aircraft has been kept current with all improvements). As one example, there have been a number of pressurization failures caused by bleed air duct separation. One shop mentioned installing a kit developed to resolve a recurring problem on Citation II's to Model 500's that suffered the same glitch.

Other environmental system problems have involved door seals (even on the 560, which has double door seals) and the air cycle machine (ACM) used for air conditioning. The defog blower, essential for descent into hot and humid conditions, has been a continuing problem on a number of aircraft.

Control system cable wear is a regular problem. Cessna has revised inspection and wear standards a couple of times, but many shops recommend more regular and careful inspections, anyway. Numerous occurrences of chafing or interference have been reported that are traced to QC misses at the factory.

Accident Record

The safety record of the whole Citation series is excellent. It is a tribute to the excellent cockpit layout, comparatively simple systems, modest performance and high training standards.

For those who feel the cost of attending the premier institutions—Flight Safety and Simuflite, (American no longer offers Citation training; its simulators are being operated by Simuflite)—it is worth noting that for many years there were no fatal Citation accidents in aircraft flown by pilots trained at these schools.

In Summary

For the first venture into the jet world, there can be no better introduction than the Citation and its outstanding safety and ease of operation. They are the only business jets approved for flight by just one pilot. And they have decent performance and comfort, especially compared to propeller-driven airplanes.

If you want to consider moving up to jets, and there is no experience in-house in buying, operating or maintaining one, start with one of the buttoned-down people at Cessna marketing. They will spend a lot of time educating you.